psychology

man in perspective

ARNOLD BUSS

Professor of Psychology

The University of Texas at Austin

psychology
man in perspective

JOHN WILEY & SONS, INC.,

NEW YORK

LONDON

SYDNEY

TORONTO

For Syd and Florence

*This book was set in 9 pt. Trade Gothic Light with
Baskerville italic display by Progressive Typogra-
phers, and printed by Halliday Lithographers.
The color insert was printed by Smeets of Holland.
The designer and illustrator was Jules Perlmutter.
The editor was Sally Harriman. Picture research
was done by Marjorie Graham. Stanley G.
Redfern supervised production.*

Cover: *Fluorescent Sea* by M. C. Escher. Escher
Foundation, Haags Gemeentemuseum, The Hague.

Library of Congress Cataloging in Publication Data:

Buss, Arnold Herbert, 1924-
Psychology: man in perspective.

Bibliography: p.
1. Psychology. I. Title.
BF121.B847   150   72-10595
ISBN 0-471-12641-1

Printed in the United States of America

10 9 8 7 6 5 4 3 2 1

preface

Introductory Psychology is one of the most popular elective courses in college today — probably because students are deeply curious about their own behavior and that of their friends and relatives. One goal of this book is to sustain the interest and perhaps even to enhance it by presenting material on sex, aggression, language, guilt, identity, self, and a variety of other topics that fascinate students. But these topics are presented in the context of a science of behavior — on the assumption that we can best understand these complex and intriguing matters through a rigorous, scientific approach. For example, the way to unravel the secrets of hypnotic deafness is to investigate it in the laboratory under conditions of strict control and close observation (see Chapter 2).

Many students want to know more about the origin of man's behavioral dispositions. Is man inherently aggressive? Is he dominated by instincts as are many animals? These and related questions are answered, some tentatively and some conclusively, in the context of the evolutionary approach of the book. Adaptation is emphasized in a way that leads to a better understanding of the roots of behavior. For example, perception is discussed in terms of its functions: to extract information from the light, sounds, chemicals, and mechanical forces that surround us in the environment; specifically, man's vision is geared to discover the salient shapes and patterns of moving objects and events that are important in adjusting to the environment. It is strongly rewarding for students to discover the functions of perception, instrumental learning, and so on, for such information offers a clear rationale for studying such material. Otherwise, the mastery of topics such as learning and perception can easily be degraded to a mere exercise in memorization of material with little meaning. By relating the behavior to its adaptive function, we supply the relevance that students (indeed, all of us) need to motivate learning.

The subject matter of psychology is so diverse and complex that the beginning student can easily become bewildered. There is no single solution to this problem, and this book uses two approaches. First, the material is unified by the theme of evolution, with its emphasis on man's behavioral heritage, man's uniqueness, and the adaptive aspects of behavior.

Second, the student is offered perspectives from which to view behavior. Any attempt to understand behavior requires assumptions at the outset, and often the assumptions are implicit rather than openly stated. Thus we can distinguish two assumptions underlying theories of motivation. Man can be viewed as a *passive* organism, responding to internal needs as they arise; he is seen as a *reactor,* who is *pushed* into activity. Alternatively, man can be viewed as an *active* organism, continually moving in his environment; he is seen as an active *seeker,* who is pulled in one direction or another by objects and events around him. These two perspectives provide an overview that helps a student to understand the complexities of motivation.

Man's behavior may also be examined in somewhat broader perspective. He can be viewed as an information-processer, a social animal, a thinker, and so on. Seven models of man are presented (see Chapter 1), and the book is organized around these models. Each section of the book examines a different aspect of behavior (perception, learning, cognition, socialization, and so on), and the student begins his discovery of each area with a perspective based on the appropriate model of man. This organization should minimize bewilderment and facilitate understanding.

The book contains many diagrams, for in illustrating concepts and processes, a schematic figure supplies the imagery that many students require for understanding. Also, imagery offers one of the best aids to retaining material (see Chapter 19).

Virtually every chapters contains a Research Report—an extended description of one or more experiments. The student needs to discover how facts are gathered in any given area, but the details are too extensive to be included in the text. However, once in each chapter the details of data collection are presented in the Research Report to give the student a feel for the "how" of research, as well as the products of research.

The book consists of thirty short chapters. Each chapter is brief enough to be read at one sitting. Many students complain that the chapters in their texts are so long that boredom sets in. The solution is short chapters, which have two other advantages. First, the material in each chapter tends to be more homogeneous—linked by common threads of content, research techniques, or theory. Second, there is more flexibility in the *sequence* of reading: the reader can skip an entire chapter and return later. With longer chapters, it is harder to alter the sequence of reading.

Each chapter starts with a list of topics included in the chapter. There is no summary at the end of the chapter—an omission that requires comment. When a chapter is long, the material diverse, and organization weak or absent, the student must have a summary at the end to help him to retain the material. The need for a summary is built in the way texts are traditionally written. But when the chapter is short, the material homogeneous, and the organization tight, no summary is needed. The student can more easily remember the content of the chapter because his storage and recall are aided by brevity, organization, imagery, and, above all, *understanding*. Moreover, there are summary tables in most chapters that coalesce facts or theories into a form that is easy to remember.

This book originated more than six years ago with two other psychologists who then decided to concentrate on their own research. They are Martin Manosevitz and Richard Schiffman (who supplied some of the material on perception). I also acknowledge with appreciation the assistance secured from my publisher from its advisory editors—Daniel Katz, William Kessen, Brendan Maher, and George Mandler—and from a number of outside reviewers, including the following: Jackson Beatty, U.C.L.A.; Neil A. Carrier, Southern Illinois University; G. P. Frommer, Indiana University; Gordon G. Gallup, Jr., Tulane University; Geoffrey McKee, Northern Arizona University; and Robert M. Stutz, University of Cincinnati. In addition, there were many of the author's colleagues and students whose help was essential in the writing of this book. There are so many that space would allow only a listing of their names—a paltry reward for unselfish contributions. They know who they are, and they know how much I am in their debt.

AUSTIN, TEXAS   *Arnold H. Buss*
OCTOBER, 1972

contents

psychology

man in perspective

section one
Introduction

chapter 1
theme and variations

*Evolution — models of man — reaction
systems — plan of the book — private experience
and behavior — stimulus-response approach —
cognitive approach*

The subject matter of psychology is so diverse as to bewilder the student. It would help in bringing order out of chaos if there were a single, all-embracing theme that encompassed the various topics of psychology. The only perspective that appears sufficiently grand in scope is that of *evolution.*

The impact of Charles Darwin's theory of evolution sent shock waves through the life sciences for decades after its publication in 1859. Its importance for psychology was minimized by the unfortunate emphasis the original theory gave to anatomy and physical traits such as strength and agility. But the modern theory of evolution, as it has developed during the past several decades, has correctly noted the crucial role of behavior in the evolution of species. As a result, comparative psychology has enjoyed a resurgence, with primate psychology in particular undergoing spectacular growth; social and developmental psychologists are looking more closely at man's heritage for clues to a better understanding of human behavior; and behavioral genetics (the study of the effect of heredity on behavior) has become important enough to be included as a chapter in many introductory psychology texts.

Evolution places man in true perspective: man is as animal with features shared with lower animals and as a unique species with features not seen in any other animal. Just as we seek understanding of current political events by examining our political heritage, so we seek understanding of behaviors now present in man by examining his evolutionary heritage. Consider two aspects of man's visual perception: the ability to distinguish colors and the ability to see in three dimensions (stereoscopic vision). Both evolved in primates as part of adaptation to life in the trees; color vision adds considerable information in the highly visual environment of trees, and swinging from branch to branch would be highly dangerous without precise knowledge of space in all three dimensions. When man evolved, these adaptations were retained, and human vision is essentially the same as that of monkeys and apes.

Man also possesses abilities that, though present in lower animals, have developed further in man. Monkeys and apes can handle and manipulate objects, but man's manual dexterity has evolved so far beyond this that he has reached the levels required of the concert pianist or the skilled surgeon. At first glance language would appear to be another example of a common feature that has merely developed further in man, but closer examination reveals that this is probably not so. True, most animals communicate with each other through various means (sights, sounds. touch, and odors), but only man uses the symbols, concepts, and rules that comprise language.[1] In fact, language — or the cognitive ability that underlies the use of language — may well be the psychological characteristic that most clearly separates man from other animals.

Thus an evolutionary perspective not only reveals those features shared with other animals and those developed further in man but also, by contrasting animal behavior with human behavior, casts in bold relief man's uniquely human characteristics (see Figure 1.1). But this is not all. When man's behavior is placed in a sequence that has evolved over eons of time, we can discern *trends* in behavior. Thus, during the progression from

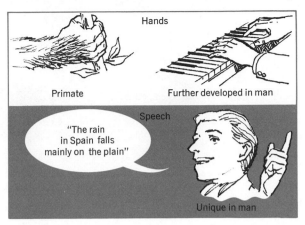

Figure 1.1 *An evolutionary perspective of man's behavior.*

reptiles to mammals to man, instinctual behavior gradually waned and the experiences of the individual animal gradually became more important (see Figure 1.2). The behavior of lizards is mainly programed in the hereditary material, and one member of a lizard species is little different from another. The behavior of humans, though in part determined by heredity, is mainly determined by the events occurring during the life cycle, and one human is very different from the next.[2]

The approach of this text is frankly anthropocentric (man-centered), a point of view that is not optimal for studying all behavior. Neither the biologist nor the comparative psychologist places man at the peak of an evolutionary ascent, and both would insist on evaluating each species' behavior in terms of its environment. But we are studying the behavior of *man,* and other animals are of interest only because they furnish information about man. Accordingly, the focus will be on the evolutionary line that led to man, especially animals that are closely related to man.

The evolutionary approach leads to a search for the *adaptive* aspects of behavior. Adaptation may be tentatively defined as the process whereby an animal fits itself to its environment. The fit can be achieved by means of anatomical and physiological adaptations, as for example, the warmth-pro-

---

[1] *This issue is still being debated, with some psychologists emphasizing the uniqueness of man's language and others its continuity with animal communication(see Chapter 28).*

[2] *This oversimplifies a complex issue: the joint influence of heredity and environment on behavior (see Chapter 4).*

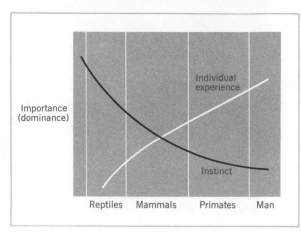

Figure 1.2 Instinct, individual experience, and phylogeny.

tecting fur of animals living in frozen climates. Or the adaptation may be largely behavioral: man's skin offers little protection against the cold, but he keeps warm by building fires, by hunting animals for their furs, and by building shelters.

Many of man's behavioral tendencies, like those of most animals, are adaptive, having survived the weeding-out process of natural selection. But the present era is a mere tick of the clock on the grand scale of evolutionary time, and tendencies that once were adaptive may no longer have a function. Some characteristics may be on the way to extinction but are still present and perhaps even harmful; the tendency to flare up in anger may belong in this category. Others may be associated with behaviors that themselves are highly adaptive. In brief, we shall be alert to the adaptive aspects of behavior but aware that some behaviors are nonadaptive or even maladaptive. Man has been radically changing his physical and social environment, a process that surely renders some of his behavioral tendencies obsolete.

The thrust of this exposition is that man's behavior is best understood when it is placed in an evolutionary context, one that leads to the right questions. What is the evolutionary history of the behavior? Is it adaptive, and if so, how? In an introductory book we cannot furnish detailed answers to these questions, if indeed detailed answers are always available, but we can render the account more meaningful by emphasizing the animal history and the adaptive aspects of behavior.

Models of Man

Man may be regarded as a biochemical entity that exchanges energy with its environment, as a cog in the machine of society, as one of God's creatures, or in any of many other ways. Biology, sociology, religion, and other disciplines all study man, but each has its own special vantage point. In taking a particular stance in the study of man, each observer inevitably emphasizes certain features and neglects others. Consider three approaches to sexual intercourse. The biologist views it in terms of the life cycle of the organisms and the means by which they propagate the species. The sociologist concentrates on the impact of culture, variations in behavioral practices within society, and the way in which the participants have been socialized. The clergyman is concerned with the moral implications of the act, especially in relation to love, marriage, and procreation. Thus each specialist views man's behavior from a different vantage point, enhancing certain aspects and diminishing others. In other words, each has his own *model of man.*

The discipline of psychology has not one but several models of man, each emphasizing a particular aspect of behavior. They may be grouped together under three headings: man behaving *alone* (or at least in a nonsocial context), man as a *social* animal, and man as an individual *self.*

Man Alone

Like most animals, man moves through successive cycles of sleep and wakefulness, rest and activity, and hunger and satiation. This is one model of man: as an *aroused organism,* with ups and downs in motivation and activity (see Figure 1.3). Recurrent tissue needs must be satisfied, muscles must be exercised to maintain proper tone, and the body must rest after strenuous activity. These basic rhythms of life, which fall under the heading of *biological motivation,* are major determinants of the ebb and flow of human activity.

But man is not a lowly form of sea life, floating on the tides of biological activity. He is a shaper and a molder, who strives to make adjustments to the world around him. This model is man as an *adapter.* Primitive animals can rely on instinct in coping with the events that befall them, both the

Table 1.1
Reaction Systems and Models of Man-Alone

REACTION SYSTEM	MODEL OF MAN	OVERTNESS	DIRECT IMPACT ON ENVIRONMENT
Instrumental	Adapter	Most	Greatest
Affective	Arousal		
Perceptual	Sensor		
Cognitive	Thinker	Least	Least

threats and opportunities. Man cannot rely on instinct and must learn virtually everything he needs to survive. How does man acquire new ways of responding? How does he modulate and change his behavior? How does he rid himself of responses no longer needed? Such questions are generated by a model of man as an adapter.

To adapt, man needs information; hence a model of man as a *sensor,* seeking and receiving stimulation from the environment. The world around us abounds with delightful and frightening sights, pleasing and harsh sounds, delectable and disgusting smells and tastes, soothing and abrasive touches, and so on. Man not only passively receives such stimulation but actively searches for it as well. He may shrink from too much stimulation (the garish sights and meaningless noise of modern urban life), but most men cannot tolerate being deprived of stimulation. An absence of stimulation may be more threatening than too much stimulation (Bexton et al., 1954).

Information provided by the senses can be stored for later use. Man can link the past with the present, the present with the future. He can plan, scheme, and imagine, and this is the model of man as a *thinker.* In anticipation of future events, we imagine possible actions and their outcomes, try out in fantasy one response or another, construct a daydream that obviously cannot come true, and in general engage in covert, mental processes. Each of us knows that such thinking occurs "inside the head," but another person can

infer it from its overt products. For example, if a man says, "The cube root of 125 is 5," we can infer prior mental processes.

The four models of man-alone correspond roughly to the four *reaction systems* (see Table 1.1). A reaction system is an aspect of behavior analogous to the digestive system as an aspect of physiology.

The *instrumental* system includes all responses, verbal and nonverbal, that have an impact on the environment. Examples are talking, walking, pushing, reaching, hammering, sawing, and so on. The behavior involves either the skeletal muscles or the vocal cords, and it is overt and easy to observe; by far the majority of behavior studied in American laboratories for the past 50 years has been instrumental.

The *affective* system involves the "emotional" aspect of behavior, in which the person usually becomes aroused. It includes such reactions as anger, fear, elation, melancholy, affection, and hatred, as well as such motivational states as hunger, thirst, and pain. These reactions vary along the dimensions of acceptance-rejection, like-dislike, pleasure-displeasure, and approach-avoidance. Traditionally, these dimensions are lumped under the single heading, *affect.* Such responses can be observed, but they are less overt than instrumental responses. Note that the affective reaction system is only one part of the larger arousal model of man.

The responses in the *perceptual* system are

Figure 1.3 Arousal model of man: asleep (low arousal), and awake and active (moderate to high arousal). (KEN HEYMAN)

more covert. We watch, listen, feel, taste, and smell, and the movements involved in these perceptual responses are so minimal that they must be labeled covert. The process of taking in information has virtually no direct consequences for the environment, and in most instances the process must be inferred from subsequent events.

The *cognitive* system includes all the responses falling under the heading of private experience: thoughts, plans, fantasies, and dreams. It is entirely covert and must be inferred from self-reports and other behaviors. Obviously, such responses have an impact on other behavior, but they have none on the environment.

These four reaction systems vary along the dimensions of overtness and consequences for the environment, with instrumental behavior at one end and cognitive at the other. Instrumental behavior, being most overt and having the greatest

impact on the environment, is the easiest to study, and it has received the most attention. Affective behavior is less salient, but it can be observed and its physiological aspects can be recorded by various means (heart rate, blood pressure, skin resistance, and so on). Perceptual and cognitive behavior, being less overt, are the most difficult to study; they are like the proverbial iceberg, showing very little above the surface.

It requires little reflection to conclude that one's focus can determine the kind of approach adopted. An interest in instrumental behavior often leads to a fairly strict behavioristic orientation, with its emphasis on observable behavior. An interest in thoughts and fantasies usually leads to a cognitive approach, with its emphasis on covert, underlying responses that must be inferred from other observations. These two approaches, among the most dominant ones in psychology today, will be discussed below.

Social Man

Man is capable of acting *alone*—thinking, feeling, and doing in the absence of others. But he is basically a social animal who lives in groups and is dependent on others for love, comfort, and security. The cruelest punishment is to banish man from others, as in the solitary confinement used even today in prisons.

Man is born as a helpless infant who will perish if not nurtured by an adult, usually the mother. This mother-infant interaction, the first and probably the most basic of man's social relationships, is a prime example of one of the social models of man: *man as attached to another person* (see Figure 1.4). Infantile attachments to parents, at first the only relationships, spread to brothers, sisters, and other members of the family. The maturing child forms bonds of warm friendship, usually boys with other boys and girls with other girls. As

the adolescent reaches adulthood, he becomes capable first of sexual love and then of parental love. Thus there is a cycle of attachment that starts with the person as an infant being cared for by a parent and ends with the person as an adult caring for an infant of the next generation.

During this developmental sequence, the child is initiated into the ways of his family, community, and larger society. He learns a particular language (spoken with a regional accent), what is right and wrong, and what is expected of him as a boy or girl, man or woman. This *socialization* model of man emphasizes the processes by which man becomes a member of society. One side of the coin is the learning of self-control (resistance to temptation), and the other is the learning of values cherished by the group and society (loyalty, ambition, masculinity, femininity, and so on).

As a social animal, man spends much of his life in groups. Whatever the context, whether at

Figure 1.4 Man as attached to another person.   (KEN HEYMAN)

school, play, or work, a significant part of each day is spent as a member of one group or another. Thus the third social model is of *man as a member of groups.* This model examines how groups are formed, how members communicate, how dominance is established, and how power is distributed.

The three social models of man cover the psychological aspects of man's relationships with others. This topic is close to the field of sociology, which examines *collectives* of men, but the perspective of sociology is that of society: organizations, collectives, and their functions as components of society. Psychology takes the perspective of *man* as he functions within groups and organizations.

Man, the Person

Whatever any individual does either alone or as a member of a group, he sees himself as acting consistently. "To thine own self be true" expresses a principle that each one of us applies to himself. At issue here is the consistency of an individual as he behaves in different contexts. This perspective requires that we step back and look at the individual as a whole—as the total of all his reaction systems and of his social interactions.

The basic model is of *man as a personality.* It focuses on those features of behavior that cluster together in an individual, allowing us to recognize each other and distinguish one from another. Some persons continually seek change and new stimulation, and they are bored by a routine and scheduled existence; others, at the opposite pole, thrive on sameness, stability, and regularity, and they are upset by novelty and deviations from routine. If these preferences are consistent across situations and over time, they are basic components of an individual's personality. This model directs our attention to the *consistencies* of behavior—those aspects that describe a person's life style, thereby distinguishing him from others.

A subsidiary model views man in terms of normality and abnormality. The perspective is the same: those consistencies that make one person different from others. But the model of man as abnormal emphasizes social and biological *norms* (the expected and socially prescribed behaviors required for adjustment). This model directs our attention to strange, unusual, and disturbed behavior—in general, the ways in which individuals deviate from social expectations.

Plan of the Book

This text is organized around the various models of man. After this introductory section and a section on the biological aspects of behavior, the remainder of the book deals with behaviors relevant to the models. Each section deals with one of the seven models (see Table 1.2), starting with the more biological aspects of behavior and ending with the more social aspects.

Private Experience and Behavior

Psychology is best defined as the science of behavior, but this definition is insufficient unless the term *behavior* is also explained. Its meaning should become clear in this section. The word *psychology* literally means "the study of the soul or mind," a definition generally used in everyday speech. It dates back to an older tradition that insisted on the primacy of inner experience and feelings in the study of behavior.[3] This view is maintained today by a small group of psycholo-

[3] *The interested reader should consult Natsoulas (1970) for a discussion of the complexities of "inner awareness and knowledge."*

Table 1.2
Plan of the Book

MODEL OF MAN	SECTION OF THE BOOK
Aroused	3. Arousal and Motivation
Sensor	4. Perception
Adapter	5. Learning
Thinker, Knower	6. Cognition
Socialized	7. Socialization
Person	8. The Person
Member of Groups	9. Social Behavior

gists, called phenomenologists or existentialists, who assert that the basic data of psychology consist of the private experiences of each person.

During the last century, many psychologists entertained similar notions, believing that they could obtain data merely by asking a subject to inspect the contents of his mind. The method of looking inward, called introspection, implicitly assumed that the mind could see or feel just as our eyes and skin can. They discovered to their sorrow that the "mind's eye" is merely a metaphor and that "inner feelings" are not sensory events comparable to vision and touch. All their subjects reported were the stimuli to which they were exposed.

Furthermore, as Mandler (1962) has shown, there is a logical problem: Private experience can remain private only if it is not expressed, but to become meaningful to anyone else (and certainly, to be dealt with by scientists), the inner experience must be made public. It must be communicated through language, and words simply cannot do justice to the full range of thoughts, perceptions, and feelings that comprise private experience. Anyone who has tried to tell another of his own feelings of exaltation or of deep love knows that this is true. Reports of private experience are necessarily second-hand, having been filtered through the medium of language. The outcome is likely to be a pale and distorted picture of what really went on inside.

In the face of these problems, one solution is to deny private experience as a legitimate concern of psychology. Early in this century Watson (1913) rebelled against mentalism and with one bold stroke discarded consciousness, feelings, thoughts, dreams — in brief, all mental processes. This position was shocking because it denied the private experience that each of us knows he has, but it did provide the basis for a scientific psychology. However, this solution — ridding the field of a sticky problem by ignoring it — is no longer acceptable to most psychologists. The term *behavior* now includes both overt and covert responses, both motor responses and fantasy. But it is recognized that private experience must be treated as an inference, not as a fact:

> . . . *we have learned in everyday life to infer what goes on in another person's mind: often wrongly, but many times correctly, especially when we can observe also what is happening to the other person at the time (what stimuli precede his responses). The inference from behavior is not a simple matter of seeing a smile and knowing the smiler is happy (he may or may not be), but a complex judgment from all the relevant data.*
> (HEBB, 1966, P. 7.)

A statement about another person's inner experience is an *inference* that requires supporting *observations* (see Figure 1.5). His self-report simply cannot be trusted as it stands. Our private experience, in addition to being strained through the medium of language when we communicate it, is also full of misperceptions. For example, some blind persons who can walk about without bumping into objects believe that they can do so because of their "facial vision." Laboratory research has established that this is wrong; they locomote by listening to echoes of sounds bouncing off objects. Though reports of inner experience contain enough mistakes to make us distrust them, the solution is not to ignore them but to demand verification from other sources. If private experience is treated as an inference and kept

Figure 1.5 Private experience can only be inferred by others.

separate from facts, which are directly observable, then it should certainly be studied.

To be wary of sources of information is part of the healthy skepticism of all scientists. The psychologist is no more skeptical than the physician investigating his patient's complaints: the physician seeks objective evidence (X rays and laboratory tests) to match against the patient's self-report, which itself is treated as merely another source of information about events occurring inside the body.

Treating private experience as an inference does not remove all sources of disagreement among psychologists. Many believe that Watson (1913) was fundamentally correct, though he went too far in discarding *all* private experience. Watson's intellectual heirs, who continue to work mainly with animals or with humans in simple learning situations, adhere to a stimulus-response approach. They assert the primacy of overt, instrumental acts, and they assume that inner experience may largely be ignored in explaining such behavior.

Their counterparts, cognitive theorists, neither deny the importance of instrumental responses nor insist on the primacy of private experience (as do phenomenologists). They focus on the products of experience and how they are stored and retrieved. The difference between these two approaches is not the only one that divides psychologists theoretically, but it is probably the most important one. A brief discussion of these positions may help the reader to understand the model of man as an adaptive organism.

The Stimulus-Response Approach

Stimulus-response psychologists assume that all behavior can be analyzed in terms of a relationship between a stimulus and a response. Any object or event is a potential stimulus, but obviously only those that can be registered by our senses are capable of affecting behavior. Actually the stimuli that psychologists study are response-defined: those objects or events that regularly and systematically precede a response. The sequence starts with isolating a response and proceeds with a search for the stimuli that precede or elicit the response. Thus the definition is initially circular (anything that regularly precedes a response), but it does not remain so. After continued observation, the psychologist knows which objects or events evoke the response, and this knowledge enables him to predict what will happen when he applies the stimuli.

Stimuli and responses, the fundamental units of analysis in this approach, are in a sense artificial. Behavior itself occurs in a continuous flow over time, and from this flow stimuli and responses are selected for study (see Figure 1.6). Thus in a conversation one person's response is the stimulus for the other's response, which in turn is the stimulus for the first person's response, and so forth. Stimuli and responses are abstracted from behavior with the stimulus marking the beginning of the period under analysis and the response marking the end. The flow of behavior continues, but it may no longer be of interest to the observing scientist.

If responses are part of a continuous flow of behavior, how are they selected? One basis is convenience; some aspects of behavior are easier to observe and measure than others. A more important criterion is that the response have an adaptive function—that is, that it is in some way related to the survival of the individual or the species.[4]

The stimulus-response approach originated in the study of animal behavior, especially instrumental behavior. It assumes that the same psychological principles underlie the behavior of men and animals; because of this assumption

[4] *In the laboratory, psychologists often study responses that rarely, if ever, occur under natural conditions. The underlying assumption is that the laws of behavior are general, applying equally to both kinds of responses.*

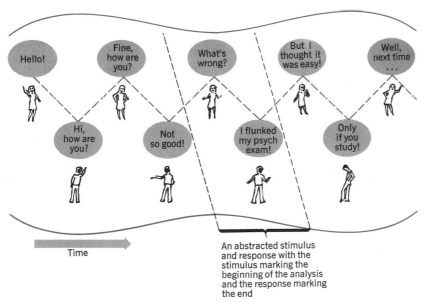

Figure 1.6 *Speech moves back and forth. The response of person A is the stimulus for person B's response which is the stimulus for person A's next response and so forth.*

animals can be used in psychological experiments and are preferred as more convenient and controllable subjects.

A hypothetical, but typical, experiment illustrates the approach. A hungry rat is placed in the start box of a T-maze and allowed to explore the maze (see Figure 1.7). Each arm of the T-maze is marked by a circle, one black and one white. The rat must learn to turn toward the arm marked by the white stimulus. When it does, there is food in the goal box; otherwise not. The positions of the stimuli are of course switched randomly so that the rat learns to respond to them rather than merely to turn in one direction. The response measure is either the number of correct responses per group of trials or the number of trials required to reach a criterion (say, 90 percent correct responses). Such an experiment yields a quantitative picture of how a rat learns a black-white discrimination.

In this example the stimuli and responses are clearly observable and easy to specify: the stimuli are black or white circles, and the responses are turning left or right. When we move from experimental findings to explanations of behavior, the meaning of the terms *stimulus* and *response* become more complex, referring to *classes* of events (or objects) and *classes* of responses. A rat

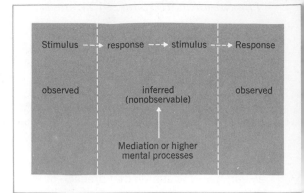

Figure 1.8 *Observed and inferred stimuli and responses.*

trained to run in the direction of the white circle would also crawl or hop if it were made to, or it would respond to an elliptical white stimulus if one were presented. Thus the particular stimuli and responses of any given experiment are regarded as samples of *classes* of stimuli and responses.

The terms have been further stretched in an attempt to deal with the more complex behaviors that are emphasized by cognitive theory. Thus stimulus-response psychologists have extended these terms to hypothetical events occurring inside the organism. Higher mental processes are explained by assuming that an ordinary stimulus elicits an *internal,* covert response, which itself serves as an internal, covert stimulus for the overt, observable response (Figure 1.8).

In brief, the concepts of stimulus and response have been extended in two directions: to include broad classes of stimuli and responses and to include internal, *inferred* stimuli and responses. Such extension has been accomplished only at the cost of precision, with stimulus and response no longer being the completely overt, objective, and specifiable notions they once were. Stimulus-response psychologists had either to maintain the precision of the concepts and restrict their use to a small range of instrumental behaviors, or to stretch the concepts in an attempt to deal with higher mental processes. Most have chosen the latter course.

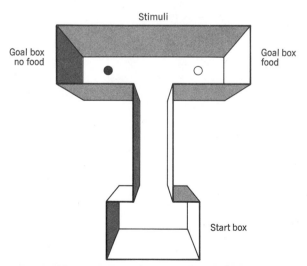

Figure 1.7 *Apparatus for typical stimulus-response experiment.*

The Cognitive Approach

Cognitive psychologists are interested in more complex and covert kinds of behavior, such as thinking, planning, and imagining. The focus is on human behavior, though the approach has been used in dealing with animal behavior (thus Tolman [1948] in attempting to explain the maze behavior of rats, used theoretical notions as *hypotheses, expectancies,* and *cognitive maps* of the environment). The organism is seen as an active seeker of information, which is then stored in memory as a representation of the world around it. In man these representations are variously called ideas, concepts, and plans. These inferred processes develop programs that lead to behavior, which in turn furnishes clues about the inferred processes.

A hypothetical experiment demonstrates the approach. A person is presented with a number of wooden blocks of varying shape and pattern and told to sort them into three groups (see Figure 1.9). The experimenter pays no attention to the manner in which the blocks are moved about, such instrumental behavior being of no importance here. Rather, he searches for the principle underlying the sorting, the concept the subject uses to classify the blocks. This he discovers by examining how the subject sorts the blocks: on the basis of either their shape or their pattern. The focus of interest is on the cognitive processes leading up to the sorting behavior, not in manipulating the blocks. And these cognitive processes, being covert, must be inferred.

As we mentioned earlier, stimulus-response and cognitive approaches have divided psychologists for several decades. In part the difference may be attributed to the area of interest: the stimulus-response approach arose from the study of in-

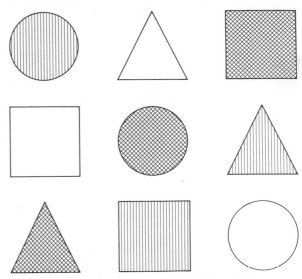

Figure 1.9 *Blocks that can be sorted for shape or pattern.*

strumental behaviors, especially those observed in animals, whereas the cognitive approach arose from the study of complex, covert behaviors, especially those observed in man. Consistent with these traditions, stimulus-response psychologists emphasize the commonality of the behavior of men and animals, whereas cognitive psychologists emphasize the uniqueness of human behavior. As psychologists explore man as a thinker and knower, they become more cognitively oriented. The issue cannot be resolved merely by ceding animal behavior to stimulus-response psychologists and human behavior to cognitive psychologists. Regardless of its intellectual tradition, each group has staked a claim on the other's territory.

chapter 2

research and theory

Attributes of science — observation — experimentation — experiment on hypnosis — functional relationships — correlations — frequency distributions — sampling — uniqueness — hypothesis and theory — determinism and free will — fact and inference — science and cognition

Man is the most curious of all the animals. In his search for knowledge he discovers information that may be important or trivial, true or false. In his search for understanding he constructs theories that are primitive or sophisticated, true or false. Presumably, the quest for knowledge and understanding is as old as man himself, with man eternally trying to comprehend earth, sky, birth, death, and—more relevant to this discussion—his own behavior.

In terms of this history, science is a late-comer, preceded (and still accompanied) by common sense, revelations, and religion. Science is clearly not the only path to truth; all any scientist would claim is that it is the best path to the truth. Errors inevitably occur in science, but they are eventually discovered and eliminated. Scientific method is used by human beings; therefore it is fallible, but it is the only method that is *self-corrective*. The basis for this strong declaration will become clear in the next few pages.

Science means different things to different people, but there would probably be general agreement on six features (Fincher, 1964). Science is

1. Rational—it employs reason and logic in working up explanations.

2. Empirical—it is based on observations.
3. Self-corrective—the ultimate appeal is to facts (observations), not to outside authority.
4. Systematic—though it proceeds by trial-and-error, the search for facts and explanations is systematic, not haphazard.
5. Objective—its findings must be public and repeatable.
6. Quantitative—it seeks to measure as well as describe events.

Underlying these features are two assumptions. One is that *events are lawful,* which, as applied to psychology, means that we should be able to discover the determinants of behavior—the historical and immediate causes of its occurrence. Stated another way, behavior is assumed to be determined, rather than to occur randomly. The second assumption is that we can lay down *a set of rules governing the accumulation of systematic knowledge.* These rules involve ways of asking questions and means of obtaining answers. The endeavor may be divided into several aspects: observing behavior, assembling and describing findings, and theorizing. This may not be the sequence any particular researcher uses when he studies behavior, but we are more interested in general features of research in psychology than in how any given psychologist proceeds. One *logical* sequence is: observing, describing, and theorizing.

Observation

Every normal human being is capable of observing the world around him, and he is strongly motivated to do so. Everyday observations provide the information needed for individual adjustment, but they tend to be casual, uncontrolled, subjective, and unverifiable. Science demands that observations be systematic, controlled, objective, and verifiable.

It requires considerable training to attain the expertness needed for scientific observations. The student looking through a microscope may think he sees something that is not really there, but miss the important features easily discerned by his experienced instructor. Training in where and how to look is crucial in any setting requiring objective observation—the scientist in the laboratory, the physician in the examining room, and the de-

tective at the scene of a crime. The untrained amateur tends to overemphasize the trivial at the expense of the important; worse still, he tends to make inferences and report them as facts.

The *conditions* of observation are usually important, and the scientist always specifies them. He states precisely how he obtained his facts, so any other trained investigator can repeat these conditions and verify the facts himself. Any scientist can err, because the observations of even a trained observer have a subjective element. But when two or more scientists independently arrive at the same facts, there is little possibility of subjective error. This is the meaning of scientific objectivity.

Consider a typical report of an unidentified flying object, made at dusk or after dark. The report might read: "I saw a round object about as big as a house, hovering above the ground about a mile away and giving off a faint glow; then it zoomed away fast—at about 2000 miles an hour." This is a fairly conservative statement, but the conditions of observation suggest that it is not factual. A trained observer would recognize that at dusk there is too little light to see clearly, and darkness plays tricks on the eyes; distant objects may appear close, and stationary objects may appear to fluctuate. Perceptual problems do not end with poor viewing conditons. Perceived size, distance, and speed of an object in the air are all related. The smaller the object, the farther away it seems and the slower it appears to move (see Figure 2.1). If the observer knew the object's size and distance, he might accurately estimate its speed. Even if he knew only its size, he might make a reasonable guess about its distance and speed, but he would be moving in the direction of inference and away from straightforward observation. If the observer knew none of the three properties in advance, his "observations" could only be unreliable guesses. An unidentified flying object is by definition unknown; an observer could not possibly know how large it is. When an object is airborne, it is extremely difficult to judge its distance because all the usual clues of distance (except apparent size) are based on ground clues (buildings, trees, and hills). When an airliner appears very small in the sky, we know it is flying high because we already know its actual size. We also recognize that its apparent slowness is explained by its great distance. The observer of an unidentified flying

Figure 2.1 *Perceived size, distance, and speed are all related. We know the nearer plane is smaller because we already know its size although here "The Spirit of St. Louis" appears larger than a commercial jet.*

(TRANS WORLD AIRLINES PHOTO)

object has no advance information, and therefore his report of size, distance, and speed is likely to be distorted by both inferences and perceptual limitations.

Behavior can be systematically studied in one of two broad contexts: under natural conditions or in the laboratory. Each has its strengths and weaknesses, and they are best regarded as complementary.

Naturalistic Observation

It is of considerable value to observe animals and humans behaving in their natural habitat, without the constraints imposed by laboratory procedures. This method if favored by ethologists, those zoologists who study animal behavior in its usual environment. It has for many years also been the preferred method of developmental psychologists who wish to study such behaviors as dependency and aggression as they occur in play situations and in nursery schools. Occasionally it is used by social psychologists studying group phenomena.

Festinger et al. (1956) surreptitiously joined a quasi-religious sect that predicted the end of the world on a particular day. As members of the group they could observe the behavior of other members when the prophecy failed, without their presence altering the behavior they were recording.

Observing the natural behavior of adult humans runs into the problem of individual privacy. Many psychologists consider it unethical to observe someone who does not wish to be observed, which means that the consent of subjects should be obtained. Such consent is relatively easy to obtain in most instances, but few adults would agree to having their sexual behavior recorded and measured. When the investigator is unable to observe the behavior he wishes to record, he can fall back on reports by the subjects. Thus Kinsey (1948) interviewed men and from their reports obtained an interesting and, at the time, shocking account of sexual practices, ranging from common heterosexual intercourse to sexual behavior with animals. Such indirect measures of behavior are subject to bias and distortion, but, used with care, they provide valuable information that is simply not otherwise available.

Laboratory Experimentation

The scientist making naturalistic observations must wait for the events to occur; in the laboratory he makes the events occur and can therefore establish *causality*. The essence of laboratory research is *control*. When an experimenter discovers an effect, he tries to insure that it is caused by his experimental manipulations and not by other conditions.

In the simplest case the researcher manipulates only one variable,[1] the *independent variable*. He then measures its effects on the *dependent variable*, which in psychology is behavior. For example, a researcher might investigate the effect of the amount of material to be learned (independent variable) on how well it is retained (dependent variable). How would he know that any changes in retention were caused *solely* by differences in the amount of material to be learned? Perhaps the changes in the dependent variable were caused by differences in the temperature of humidity of the experimental room, time of day, or season of the year. These *extraneous variables* might affect the results of the study, but it is doubtful that they would. Presumably, their effect would be very small, and therefore they are allowed to *vary randomly*. All such factors would be distributed equally among the experimental conditions on a chance basis, which means that they would not *systematically* affect the outcome. No experimenter can equate or hold constant every possible extraneous variable because there are simply too many possibilities. He controls the ones that appear to be relevant and allows the remainder to vary randomly. How does the experimenter decide which variables are important and which are trivial? There are no rules, only the talent and experience of the researcher. The following research report illustrates some of these problems and their solutions in an investigation of the effect of hypnosis on hearing.

[1] *A variable is just what the term implies: anything that can vary over a range of values.*

Research Report

It is believed that a suggestion given to a hypnotized person can cause him to be temporarily deaf. Barber and Calverley (1964) tested this notion, using both subjective reports of deafness and an objective measure based on delayed auditory feedback (see Figure 2.2). In this technique the subject's speech is recorded and played back to him as he speaks, but with a delay of 2/5 second. After a few moments his speech begins to deteriorate: loudness increases, speech slows down, and there are repetitions, errors, and stuttering. Of course, if the subject does not hear the delayed speech, it cannot interfere with his ongoing speech.

The subjects were 42 college women. First, each one read one form of a standard oral reading test with delayed auditory feedback. Then the women were randomly assigned to three groups of 14 each, treated as follows:

1. Hypnosis—the subjects were hypnotized with a standard procedure and were told that they would not hear the voice coming through the earphones.
2. Nonhypnotic Suggestion—the subjects were not hypnotized but were told to ignore, or be deaf to, the voice coming through the earphones.
3. Control—the subjects were not hypnotized or given any suggestions.

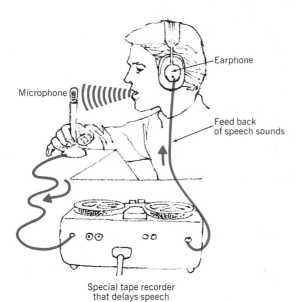

Earphone

Microphone

Feed back
of speech sounds

Special tape recorder
that delays speech

Figure 2.2 Technique for producing delayed auditory feedback.

Then all subjects read from another form of the reading test, and
their speech was recorded. Immediately afterward each rated how well
she heard her own speech through the earphones. The results are
shown in Table 2.1. As expected, virtually all the Control subjects
reported hearing normally, and most of the Hypnotized subjects reported sounds being muffled, though none reported total deafness.

Table 2.1
Number of Subjects Reporting Partial or Total Deafness (Barber & Calverley, 1964)

GROUP	HEARD NOTHING	SOUNDS MUFFLED	HEARD NORMALLY
Hypnotized	0	9	5
Nonhypnotic suggestion	2	11	1
Control	0	1	13

Unexpectedly, most of the Nonhypnotic Suggestion subjects also reported that the sounds were muffled. Thus the effects of the experimental manipulations on *subjective hearing* are clear: suggestion of deafness, whether with or without hypnosis, caused subjects to report a loss of hearing; hypnosis itself had no special effect.

The subjects' recorded speech was examined by the experimenters for words that had been mispronounced, stuttered, omitted, or repeated, as well as for rate and intensity of speech — all ordinarily affected by delayed auditory feedback. These objective indicators revealed no differences among the three groups of subjects or between subjects who reported hearing normally and those who reported partial or total hearing loss. In brief, neither hypnotic nor nonhypnotic suggestions of deafness affected hearing *as measured objectively,* though suggestions did affect subjects' *reports* of how well they heard.

This experiment was controlled for a number of features:

1. Sampling — the subjects were *randomly* assigned to groups.
2. Materials — a standard oral reading test was used.
3. Sequence — all subjects read twice, first one form and then another.
4. Hypnosis — one group of subjects was hypnotized; two groups were not.
5. Suggestion — two groups were given suggestions about deafness; one group was not.
6. Subjective report — subjects' reports were supplemented and checked against an objective measure.

Laboratory Versus Naturalistic Methods

In the laboratory the experimenter can control extraneous variables; manipulate independent variables; and isolate, quantify, and objectively measure dependent variables. In a natural setting the researcher must allow nature to take its course, without influence or manipulation by him. He must record behavior as best he can, sometimes sacrificing precision, objectivity, and reproducibility. Of course the two methods we are describing represent extremes of research activity. The laboratory researcher sometimes attempts to copy nature by setting up "natural" situations in the laboratory, even at the cost of losing control. On the other hand, the naturalistic researcher sometimes imposes laboratory-like controls on the situation he is studying, even though its naturalness may be reduced.

In terms of precision and control, the advantage seems to lie with laboratory experimentation. Why then is naturalistic observation ever used? One reason is that laboratory research on certain kinds of human behavior would be unethical. We could not allow a young child to be frightened severely to determine whether permanent psychological damage might occur; in fact, no human being should ever be placed in a situation that might lead to lasting harm. Another problem is that some kinds of research require so much time that human subjects could not be kept in the laboratory for the period required — e.g., the effects of childrearing practices on later behavior. The only answer to these ethical and practical problems is to use the method of naturalistic observation.

Another reason for observing in nature is the artificiality of most laboratory situations. The constraints that yield control and objectivity tend to make the laboratory situation irrelevant to everyday life. In many areas of study the setup does not have to be precisely analogous to everyday life, but in some it does. The natural situation is of course relevant, by definition. Actually, the two methods can be used sequentially, with naturalistic observation providing the ideas and hypotheses, and laboratory experimentation testing the hypotheses and narrowing the range of possible explanations:

The answer to this dilemma between observations that have relevance only for a given problem and observations that are rigorous and reliable is that neither laboratory experiments nor naturalistic nor field studies can stand as devices for furthering scientific inquiry. A psychological inquiry gains its relevance and significance, in large part, because of the experimenter's naturalistic and casual observations before he introduces constraints into his gathering of data on which his conclusions will depend. The inquiry gains its reliability and rigor, on the other hand, because of the constraints and controls that the experimenter can exercise on the setting and the other variables that will be used to test the validity of his initial ideas and hypotheses.

(HYMAN, 1964, P. 57.)

These points may be illustrated by research on how blind persons avoid bumping into objects around them. Many blind people believed that they had "facial vision," and casual observation of the way they avoided obstacles in everyday life seemed consistent with this explanation. There was no clear way of testing the notion in a natural setting, but a series of experiments in the laboratory provided the decisive evidence.

Supa et al. (1944) reasoned that if the face could "see," covering it up would eliminate the ability to avoid objects. It did not; blind subjects avoided obstacles as well with a hood over the head as without it. If facial vision was not responsible for obstacle avoidance, perhaps hearing was. Therefore sounds were prevented from reaching the subjects' ears by plugs or were masked with headphones that hummed. Blind subjects bumped into objects that they easily avoided when their hearing was unobstructed. Clearly, the cues used by blind persons in natural settings must consist of sound reflected from objects, and further research strengthened this explanation. Blindfolded normal subjects learned to respond to sound as they walked about and thereby devel-

oped the ability to avoid objects (see Figure 2.3), but sighted deaf subjects could not acquire this ability (Ammons et al., 1953). Not all sounds were equally good cues: high-pitched sounds led to a better obstacle-sense (Cotzin & Dallenbach, 1950).

This research demonstrates how ideas that emerge from naturalistic observation can be tested rigorously in the laboratory.[2] There was an orderly progression from observation to hypothesis to laboratory test. Furthermore, laboratory research went beyond the testing of the original hypotheses to the addition of new precise facts (the best range of sounds for avoiding obstacles). This example favors the laboratory as the ultimate testing ground, but in many instances data derived from the laboratory must be checked out in the field. Thus fear can be studied in the laboratory, but to really frighten subjects is both impractical and unethical. Any conclusion derived from the *experimentation* on mild fear should be checked out in field situations involving strong fear—for example, fear in parachute jumpers (Epstein & Fenz, 1962) or patients about to undergo major surgery (Janis, 1958).

The Results of Research

The immediate outcome of a research project is a mass of recorded observations. Not every bit of

[2] *Ideas for research may also arise in the laboratory and be tested later in the field, but this occurs less frequently.*

Figure 2.3 *Blindfolded normal subjects can learn to avoid objects, but blindfolded deaf subjects cannot avoid.*

behavior is recorded; it would be too cumbersome and time-consuming, and it would yield mostly irrelevancies. The recorded observations, which have already been selected from a much larger potential number of observations, are called *data* (singular, *datum*). Data sometimes omit a signifi-cant aspect of behavior, but it is difficult to judge in advance which aspects are significant. Like knowing which variables to control, judging which behaviors are relevant is an art. Ultimately, the only critierion of correctness for selecting the de-pendent variable is whether the measure leads to larger generalizations and explanations.

Functional Relationships

The results of laboratory experiments are usually expressed as changes in the dependent variable in relation to the independent variable. The author investigated the relationship between size of stim-uli and amplitude (intensity) of response (Buss, 1967). Subjects were instructed to either shout or whisper at will words presented one at a time. The words were names of animals varying in size from a worm to a whale. The names had previously been scaled to yield numerical estimates of size. The data are plotted in Figure 2.4. The horizontal axis represents the stimulus values (independent variable), and the vertical axis represents the number of shout responses (dependent variable).

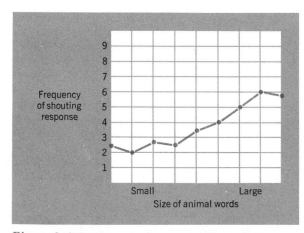

Figure 2.4 Tendency to shout as a function of the size of the animal.

(It does not matter whether shout or whisper responses were plotted because the subjects had to make one or the other response, which means that one is the inverse of the other.) This graph clearly shows that the larger the animal, the greater the subjects' tendency to shout its name. This is a *functional relationship:* a description of how the dependent variable changes in relation to the independent variable. The graph summarizes a mass of data in a form that enables the reader to grasp the results easily; some of the most basic data in psychology are presented in this way.

A functional relationship is *causal,* describing the effect of the independent variable on the de-pendent variable. It derives from the experi-menter's control and manipulation of the indepen-dent variable; as he alters its values, he causes changes to occur in the dependent variable. But in much research, especially that conducted in natu-ral settings, the psychologist does not manipulate variables. He must confine himself to observing and recording different sets of observations and then determining their relationship, which is *correlational.*

Correlations

Consider the two variables of social class and in-telligence (as measured by a test). Social class varies, say, from that of unemployed ghetto-dwellers through professionals to wealthy landed gentry. Intelligence varies from persons so stupid that they cannot learn to speak through those barely capable of learning to speak through those barely capable of learning to read through those capable of high academic achievement and finally to those few persons labeled "genius." It has been found that the higher a person's social class status is, the higher his intelligence test score tends to be (see Figure 2.5). When one variable goes up, so does the other; when one goes down, the second does also. But this does not mean that changes in one *cause* changes in the other. Perhaps social class status determines one's in-telligence in the sense that higher-status people are inherently brighter, but intelligence might equally be a determinant of social status in the sense that brighter people achieve high status. The fact that the two variables are correlated does

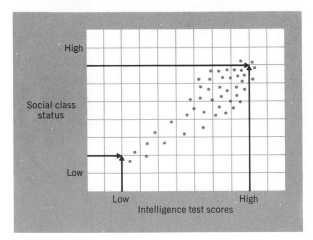

Figure 2.5 Correlation between social class status and intelligence test scores.

not tell us which one determines the other.

Another example is relevant to the control of aggression, a salient topic in this violent era. The aggressive behavior of children has been found to correlate with punishment by their mothers. One interpretation assumes that punishment angers the child, leading him to aggress; if this were true, we could diminish aggression by eliminating punishment. An alternative view is that the child first aggresses, thereby eliciting punishment from his mother; if this were true, the only recourse might be to breed less aggressive individuals. There is at present no way to decide between these two alternatives, and they might both be correct. In brief, *correlation does not imply causation.*

Science attempts not only to describe but also to quantify. It is a step forward in precision to move from a description of a correlation as high or low to a quantitative figure. The appropriate statistic is the *correlation coefficient,* the computation of which need not concern us. Actually, there are several kinds of correlation coefficients, all yielding the same basic information: the quantitative strength and the direction of the relationship between two variables.

The correlation coefficient varies between the limits of $+1.00$ and -1.00. The plus sign indicates a *positive* relationship; when one variable goes up, so does the other. The correlations between social class and intelligence test scores and between children's aggression and their mother's punish-

ment are positive. The negative sign indicates an *inverse* relationship; when one variable goes up, the other goes down. Examples may be found in the relationship between skill and speed. The more a typist practices, the less time she needs to complete a given passage: as practice goes up, typing time goes down. A *zero* correlation means that the two variables are completely unrelated: a knowledge about one tells us nothing about the other. As a rough rule of thumb in psychological research, a correlation above .70 represents a strong relationship, one below .30 represents a weak one.

Frequency Distributions

Functional relationships and correlation coefficients represent data already summarized. Data are rarely presented in raw form because they are difficult to comprehend. Suppose we assembled the grade-point averages of every member of one university's sophomore class. There might be thousands of such scores, and merely listed, they would make no sense. They would have to be organized and summarized.

College sophomore grade-point averages usually vary from a low of 0 to a high of 4.0. The first step in collating the data is to group them into intervals of 1.0 each. Then they can be plotted, as in Figure 2.6a, (*following page*) with grade-points on the horizontal axis and the number of students achieving that grade point on the vertical axis. Each grade-point interval is represented by a bar, and the higher the bar, the greater the number (frequency) of students achieving that score. This is a *bar graph.* If the tops of the bars are connected and the bars omitted, the result is a *frequency distribution* (see Figure 2.6b), (*following page*) a visual representation of all the grade-point averages of the sophomore class. This graph offers two kinds of information: the most frequent scores and the spread of scores. These are the two most important features of a frequency distribution: *central tendency* and *variability.*

Measures of central tendency are designed to summarize the entire distribution in a single score. The best measure of central tendency for most distributions is the arithmetic mean, or, more simply, the *mean.* This is the average score:

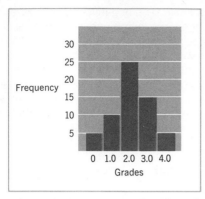
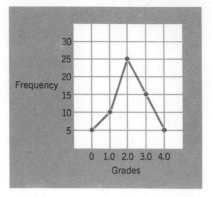

Figure 2.6 (a) *Bar graph of hypothetical sophomore grade-point averages,*
(b) *Frequency distribution of hypothetical sophomore grade-point averages.*

the sum of all the grade points divided by the total number of students. The mean is the most commonly used summary measure not only in science but also in everyday life. For example, if a New York Mets fan argued that his team were better hitters than the New York Yankees, he would surely buttress his argument by comparing the team averages of the two ball clubs.

The other basic information about a distribution is the variability (dispersion) of the scores, the spread of scores around the mean. Consider three distributions with the same mean but different variability (Figure 2.7). In *a* the spread of scores is so great that the mean is a poor representative of the distribution. In *b* the spread is less, and the mean is a better representative. In *c* scores cluster so tightly around the mean that it is a precise estimate of them. *The smaller the spread of scores, the better the mean represents the entire distribution.* When scores are dispersed over a wide range of values, it is risky to attempt to summarize them. Yet the risk must be taken; whenever data are summarized for better handling and communication, some information must be omitted. The mean represents a distribution, but it does so better or worse depending on the variability of scores in the distribution.

Generally, there is no way to summarize data, or to conduct research for that matter, without omitting *some* information:

Any procedure for processing scientific data — indeed any scientific observation — begins and ends with the
omission of many details and differences. When we report averages, numbers of people in categories, correlation coefficients, or summaries of our data, we do so only by violating a variety of distinctions that, for many purposes, may turn out to be quite important. What is important is that, depending on the question we are asking, some forms of pooling and reduction make more sense than others.

(HYMAN, 1964, P. 67.)

Sampling

The researcher does not stop when he has presented his summarized data. He then generalizes from his limited observations to a much larger class of possible observations, subjects, and events. In the research on how blind persons avoid obstacles, only a small number of subjects were used in only a few situations, but the results are assumed to apply to all blind persons who can move about in a variety of situations. This kind of inference, which is implicit in every experiment, is basic to research.

Scientists work with *samples* and then make generalizations about *populations* or *universes*. The researchers on facial vision sought facts that applied not only to their particular sample of blind people, but to all blind persons. They could not know with certainty that their facts were generalizable to the entire population of blind people, but there is evidence consistent with this assumption: there were several experiments, and each sample

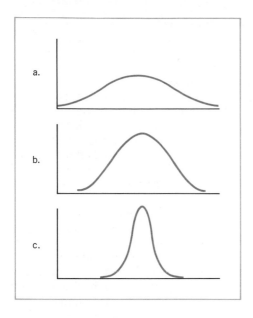

Figure 2.7 Three distributions with the same mean but different variability.

of blind subjects yielded essentially the same results.

There is always a potential error in generalizing from a sample to a universe. Random error cannot be eliminated, but it can be kept small. Whatever the size of the error, the researcher must be able to estimate how reliable his data are. Such estimates of error are based on statistical methods too advanced to be discussed here.[3]

Generalizing from a sample to a universe involves both *random error* and *systematic error*. If a sample is drawn from a population on a chance basis, there should be no systematic error. If there is no special selection of subjects, then the sample should be *representative* of the population. Stated another way, each person in the population has an equal opportunity to be included in the sample. However, if the selection of the sample is in some way biased, the unrepresentative sample will lead to a faulty generalization about the population (see Figure 2.8).

The best-known blunder involving a biased sample was the Literary Digest poll in 1936, which attempted to predict the winner of the 1936 presidential election. This magazine drew its sample by pulling names at random from telephone directories, and there was an attempt to represent various sections of the country. Their prediction of a Landon victory was far off the mark, and the magazine was buried along with the Republican party in the Roosevelt landslide. The pollsters' mistake lay in using telephone directories; during the Depression era telephones were owned mainly by wealthier and more privileged persons. This sample undoubtedly favored Landon and Republicans in general, but it was unrepresentative of the electorate.

The solution to problems like this is a procedure called *stratified* random sampling. The researcher first decides which variables must be controlled

[3] *Statistical methods yield* estimates *of what would occur if the experiment were repeated many times. As noted earlier, a scientific fact is one that can be duplicated when the observations are repeated.*

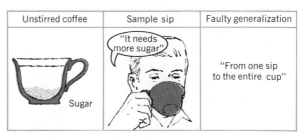

Figure 2.8 Generalizing from a sample.

in his sampling. For example, in this country there are varying proportions of blacks and whites, rural and urban dwellers, members of the various religions, and so forth. Once these proportions have been decided (after consulting the census), the researcher selects a random sample within each category. With this kind of approach, pollsters have been able to avoid fiascos such as the Literary Digest survey.

The issue of generalizing from sample to population concerns not only subjects, but stimuli, events, and situations. The particular apparatus used, the behavior studied, the stimuli used, and even the experimenter — all are samples of larger groups. Some populations are small enough to be sampled completely, although the effort is rarely worth the trouble. Occasionally the effort is deemed worthwhile, as in the U.S. census every decade. The human population has an upper limit and therefore is capable of being completely sampled, but the population of atoms is unlimited and is thus too large to be encompassed. With rare exception, scientists do not deal with an entire population; they generalize to the universe from which the sample is drawn.

Uniqueness

Samples consist of individual subjects, events, and things, and each member of the sample is different from every other one. Every event is unique, but the scientist is interested in general laws and explanations. He resolves this paradox by treating each unique event as a member of a *class* of events. Each happening and each subject are regarded as part of a sample of a larger population of subjects or events. Thus the scientist recognizes that uniqueness exists, but he does not deal with it as such.

Science does not use any special rule of logic in working this way; it is the way we all operate in everyday life. First we assign an individual event to a class of such events, and then we assume that the individual event has all the properties of the class. The properties of the class presumably are known from previous observation, and thus we can predict what will happen next. Consider the behavior of an individual person. The only way to proceed is to assign each of his responses to a

class of his *behavior over time.* Thus, if he usually sits in the same seat in the lecture hall, it can be predicted — within the limits of error — that he will sit there next time.

Consider the alternative way of treating uniqueness. If each event is regarded as having nothing in common with any other event, then knowledge of the past would be worthless in dealing with the future. That the sun rose today and a million yesterdays would offer no basis that it would rise tomorrow. Today's sunrise surely is different in certain respects from every other sunrise, but it shares certain features with all other sunrises, and these common features enable us to predict that the sun will rise tomorrow. The scientist, no less than anyone else, is interested in classes of events, and he treats the unique as merely an instance of the general. Stated another way, he treats the unique event as a sample of one and attempts to find other samples before generalizing to the universe. In this context a class equals a population or universe.

The researcher cannot record and measure everything, so he seeks characteristics involving class membership:

The exhaustive description of an individual event is not aimed for in the scientific analysis of the world nor can it be hoped for in any descriptive enterprise. All macroscopic (large scale) events are absolutely unique. It is a further mistake to exaggerate the degree to which this lack of concreteness reflects a special failing of the scientist. The abstractive or summarizing character of descriptions is shared by differential equations, maps, gossip, and novels alike. So-called scientific description, however, abstracts those things which are most relevant in terms of causal-analytic and predictive aims.

(MEEHL, 1954, P. 130.)

It may be argued that this way of looking at things completely loses the individual event. How can a small number of classes generate different combinations to yield an astronomical number of unique events? Meehl answers this by citing how human fingerprints are identified. The fingerprint of every individual is unique, but billions of fingerprints can be classified and assigned values on about six dimensions. Just a few values on each of these dimensions are sufficient to distinguish one fingerprint from every other one. Thus from a small number of classes, a unique object may be identified. This is the way science proceeds: by treating unique events as members of a class of events, sharing common properties. That members of the same class differ in some ways, perhaps even in most ways, is indisputable, but they are similar in crucial ways—that is, in ways important in leading to general laws and explanations.

Theory

In building a body of knowledge, psychologists proceed in essentially the same way as do other scientists. Occasionally they stumble over facts they were not specifically seeking. One psychologist started out to raise disease-free monkeys and inadvertently discovered the disastrous effect of the mother's absence on a primate's behavior. But most facts are sought to evaluate a formally stated theory of a vague hunch. Scientific knowledge is nothing so trivial as a Sears, Roebuck catalog of facts; it is a collection of facts systematically arranged and placed in the context of explanation. In trying to explain facts, scientists construct hypotheses and theories. In current usage, a hypothesis attempts to explain a small or limited set of facts, whereas a theory attempts to encompass a broad range of facts and may even include several hypotheses. Thus the origin of species is explained by Darwin's *theory* of evolution, and the notion that hypnotized persons would fail to hear was a *hypothesis*. However, the borderline between a hypothesis and a theory is so vague that the terms are often used interchangeably.

Theories and hypotheses are constructed to explain facts already known, such as functional relationships and correlations. The observation that blind persons can move around without bumping into objects was a fact that cried out for explanation. As we noted earlier, the hypothesis suggested by blind persons themselves was that their faces could "see"; the notion of facial vision was suggested as an explanation of certain facts of blind persons' locomotion. Why should the hypothesis be accepted? If the hypothesis is said to be a good one because it explains facts already

known, the explanation is circular. Circular explanations explain nothing. An example from everyday life concerns willpower. If a man tries to give up smoking cigarettes and fails, it may be said that he has a weak will; if he succeeds, it may be said that he has a strong will. The hypothesis of strong or weak willpower may appear to explain the behavior, but it is nothing more than a restatement of the behavior itself.

To be worthwhile, a hypothesis must be testable. It must lead to predictions that may be checked out as true or false. Thus there are three separate steps in constructing a theory or hypothesis:

1. Make an assumption that explains facts already known.
2. Derive testable predictions from the assumption ("if the hypothesis is true, such and such should happen").
3. Check the correctness of the predictions by obtaining evidence.

This sequence and how it applies to the hypothesis of "facial vision" are shown in Table 2.2. The obtained facts are clearly opposite to the predictions generated by the hypothesis, which means that the hypothesis should be discarded. As we know, it was discarded, and psychologists subsequently hypothesized and then confirmed the correct basis for locomotion by the blind: hearing.

The hypothesis of facial vision was relatively easy to test and discard. That the face could "see" was an unlikely possibility, and the fact that blind persons could still avoid objects when their faces were covered killed the notion. But this is the exception rather than the rule; though a single experiment may disprove a hypothesis, one study rarely knocks out a *theory*. Usually a single fact or experiment merely strengthens or weakens a theory. A new theory with few facts to sustain it may be destroyed by only a few contrary observations. An older, established theory tends to be hardier. When observations oppose such a theory, the facts are sometimes questioned rather than the theory. Of course, if contrary facts continue to turn up, the theory is seriously weakened. But even a weak theory accounts for some facts, and no one easily abandons an explanation, however faulty, if there is no explanation to replace it. Thus theories

Table 2.2
Three Steps in Theory Construction

STEPS	EXAMPLE
1. Account for facts already known.	1. Blind persons can "see" with their faces and thereby avoid objects.
2. Derive testable consequences from the assumption; make predictions.	2. If the face is covered, blind persons will no longer be able to avoid objects.
3. Obtain evidence concerning the predictions.	3. With the face covered, blind persons still avoid objects.

Conclusion: The hypothesis is incorrect. Seek another one.

are not so much abandoned as replaced. There are often several contending theories in any domain of knowledge, so there are candidates available to replace any theory tried and found wanting. A theory may gain ascendance over its competitors merely because it is fashionable and there is a bandwagon effect. But theories survive in the long run only if they are sufficiently buttressed by facts. DETERMINISM AND FREE WILL. Like all scientists, psychologists assume that they are capable of explaining all the events in their domain. No one claims that there is presently sufficient knowledge and adequate theory to account for all behavior, but in principle a full account should be possible. Stated another way, psychologists assume that *all behavior is determined,* and their main task is to discover the variables that determine behavior. This assumption cannot be defended with data; it is merely one of the axioms that comprise the scientific approach.

Nevertheless, this assumption runs counter to the opinion of each individual about his own behavior. Each person believes that in many everyday activities he has a choice to make and that it is up to him to decide which course of action to take. If there is free choice, the behavior

cannot be determined. Interestingly enough, most persons do not make the same assumption when observing the behavior of others. They assume that they understand how another person behaves and can predict what he will do, directly implying that the other person's behavior is determined; for if he had free will, there would be no way to predict his behavior.

This difference in orientation may provide a solution to the dilemma of free will versus determinism. From the perspective of the individual person, he has free will and is not shaped by causal variables; from the point of view of the observer, especially the scientist, the behavior of the person being observed is determined by antecedent and current variables. Consider the behavior of a college sophomore on a weekend evening (see Figure 2.9). From his point of view, he can attend a movie, study for an exam, or play cards, and *he is free to exercise his options.* This approach to behavior is not right or wrong, for there is certainly no way of testing it. Eventually, the student will make one of the three responses, presumably "because he wanted to."

The psychologist approaches this situation with an entirely different perspective. He requires infor-

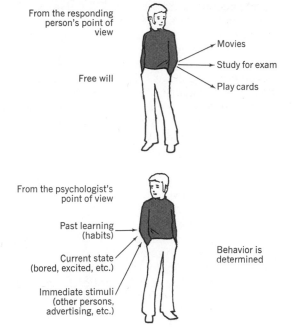

From the responding person's point of view

Free will

Movies

Study for exam

Play cards

From the psychologist's point of view

Past learning (habits)

Current state (bored, excited, etc.)

Immediate stimuli (other persons, advertising, etc.)

Behavior is determined

Figure 2.9 *Free will and determinism: a matter of perspectives.*

mation about the student's previous behavior in similar situations, his current state of arousal, and the stimuli immediately available to the student. These are the causal agents that determine the student's behavior—that is, which choice he makes. Some of this information may come from the student himself, but he will usually not know the precise basis for his choice (though he may verbalize one).

The psychologist himself has no choice in this matter; he must adopt the perspective of the observer and opt for determinism. This assumption is required by science, and to reject it is to reject the scientific approach. Some psychologists find it difficult to make this assumption, and we can certainly sympathize with them. Man is the only animal that appears to be aware of the contingencies in his environment and the only one that can communicate his awareness. Furthermore, it may be part of man's demand for individual freedom to assert that each man has the freedom to choose. All the scientist can do in the face of this assumption is assert that this perspective is incompatible with a scientific approach to behavior. Even in everyday life most of us have observed persons who believed that they could exercise a choice

when in fact they had no options at all. In brief, it appears to us as experiencing individuals that we have free will, but the scientist sees our behavior as determined by the variables acting on us. The difference in approach is due to a difference in *perspective*. It is not a matter for debate; the scientist must assume determinism.

FACT AND INFERENCE. Another basic canon of science is that facts must be kept separate from inferences. As we mentioned earlier, there are strict rules governing the collection of facts: observations should be objective, precise, and repeatable. Facts refer to events or objects that exist and that can be observed by anyone who has the requisite skill and equipment to make the observations. Inferences are made up (constructed) to account for facts already known, and these inferences (hypotheses) are evaluated by collecting new facts. If inferences are not kept separate from facts, then facts cannot be used to evaluate inferences.[4]

[4] *It may be difficult to separate fact from inference in studying such covert behaviors as thinking and fantasy. Such responses must be assessed indirectly, and different methods may yield different sets of facts. This point underlies the importance of knowing not only the facts but how they were obtained.*

Unfortunately, our language and everyday thinking tend to trap us into merging fact with inference. Thus it is *factual* that objects fall toward the center of the earth, and the notion of gravity is an *inference,* but most of us refer to gravity as if it were a *thing* that exists, rather than a hypothesis constructed to account for the behavior of falling objects. Similar problems occur in psychology. The term *anxiety* refers to the individual's *response* to a threatening stimulus: widened eyes, accelerated heartbeat, flushing, trembling, sweating, and so on. This response is an observable fact, but *anxiety* is also used in another way, to mean "a motivator of defenses." Here the psychologist *assumes* that an observed behavior (for example, compulsive handwashing) has an underlying cause, anxiety; he *infers* the anxiety from the presence of the behavior. This dual use of the term anxiety, to mean both behavior and inferred state, has caused considerable confusion: Does the psychologist mean that the individual is calm but engaging in defensive behavior? Such ambiguity can be removed if different terms are used, one for the behavior and one for the inference. One possibility is to reserve the term *fear* for the response and the term *anxiety* for the inferred state that presumably motivates defenses.

The term *intelligence* illustrates another kind of ambiguity, also involving confusion between fact and inference. The term refers to the score attained on a standard test of intelligence, and it is sometimes referred to as I.Q. (intelligence quotient). But it also refers to a generalized ability to perform well on intellectual tasks (problem-solving, manipulation of symbols, reasoning, and so forth). The generalized ability is *inferred* from the *fact* of the score attained on a particular test. to ignore this distinction is to invite confusion. We shall reserve the term *intelligence* for the broad, inferred ability and use *test performance* for I.Q. or intelligence test scores.

Science and Cognition

A parallel may be drawn between the development of science in Western culture and the development of logical thinking in each person. Early attempts to explain natural events were primitive and egocentric, as, for example, the theory that the sun and stars revolve around the earth. One ancient theory, astrology, linked movements of the planets and stars to individual personalities and events. Astrology is now enjoying a resurgence even among college students, perhaps because of a revulsion against science and the technological products of science. Scientists have been asked why they hold astrology in such low regard. The reasons are that the theory cannot be tested because it is too vague, and it offers no explanation of how the stars might influence people on earth. Some students remain unsatisfied with this answer, and they prefer to base their decisions on their horoscopes. To test their faith, one might pose this dilemma: the surgeon says that an emergency appendectomy must be performed immediately, but the patient's horoscope predicts that it is a bad day for momentous decisions. It might be guessed that few critics of science would bet their lives on the nonscience alternative.

During the past several centuries prescientific notions such as astrology, palmistry, and ghosts have yielded to more logical explanations and rigorous ways of testing explanations. There is a parallel development in children, whose early imaginative (but incorrect) beliefs about natural events give way to more rational explanations. As astronomers centuries ago exchanged an earth-centered theory of the solar system for a sun-centered theory, so each child exchanges his early self-centered view of the world for a more objective view.[5] Around the time of puberty the young adolescent acquires the ability to detach himself completely from immediate stimuli, as, for example, in mathematics and chess. These cognitive developments are the source of the objectivity and abstract reasoning that are the hallmarks of scientific method.

The child, limited by immature cognitive skills, views the world in simplistic terms. The adult is better able to see the world in all its complexity. One of the major cognitive tasks is to simplify the extremely complicated environment, first in taking in information and then in storing it for later recall. In this task, generalizations and stereotypes are

[5] *Cognitive development is discussed more fully in Chapter 17.*

helpful, though they tend to oversimplify the environment.

The scientist faces the same problem in seeking explanations, and theories tend to be simpler than the events they explain. The author of this book faced a related problem. Complex material had to be condensed and presented simply enough for an introductory course—at the risk of omitting something important. Yet complex material had to be included when it was sufficiently important—at the risk of confusing the reader. The aim here, as in the laboratory and in everyday life, was to avoid both risks, with a slight tendency to include difficult material when it was of sufficient importance.

section two
biological aspects of behavior

chapter 3
evolution

*Heredity — DNA — chromosomes — genes —
population genetics — natural
selection — adaptation — diversification — the
evolutionary model — man as a mammal —
man as a primate — bipedalism — hunting —
man's unique features*

Man evolved from lower forms. We know this not as a fact but as a theory so well established by facts and so widely accepted that there is disagreement only on details. Man's lineage can be traced back through more primitive creatures and finally to the chemical molecules believed to mark the beginning of life. The origin of life, lost in the mists of time, and the chemical processes that sustain life are matters that concern biologists. But the evolutionary process that comprises man's own history and the passage of life from one generation to the next are issues that also interest psychologists. This chapter deals specifically with the processes of evolution and man's animal heritage.

Heredity

In the chain of life that starts with man and continues back to simple organisms, each link in the chain is a generation of living creatures. Each generation reproduces itself, and the continuity from one generation to the next stretches back through the billions of years that life has existed on this planet. As individuals men die, but the part that produces offspring is immortal: the genetic material.

Information

The individual organisms in each generation begin simply with a single cell and develop into many-celled organisms of great complexity and organization.[1] The construction of each organism must start from scratch, using energy to organize raw materials into a complex biological system. The new organism is in most respects like those of the previous generation:

In its immediate aspect, heredity is the phenomenon of like begetting like in successive acts of reproduction. Like begets like because parent and offspring both develop by processes controlled by the same kind of information. Clearly there must be a sense in which it is true to say that what is reproduced and transmitted from generation to generation of living organisms is the information needed for their creation.

(SIMPSON & BECK, 1965, P. 146)

[1] *We are referring to animals in the line that led to man.*

What is the nature of the information? When a builder constructs a house, he uses blueprints; information is coded in a set of drawings made by an architect. Lumber, concrete, steel, glass, and other raw materials are assembled into a structure according to a *plan. Biological* information needed for constructing the new organism is contained in a complex molecule called *DNA.* The way this information is transmitted from one generation to the next involves *genes* and *chromosomes.*

DNA. These three letters stand for deoxyribonucleic acid, an immensely long molecule that is usually arranged as a double helix (see Figure 3.1). The rungs of the intertwined ladders consist of bonds between molecules of four substances called nucleotides. On each ladder, the chain of nucleotides on one side exactly complements the chain on the other side.

It is the *sequence* of nucleotides that contains the vital information. Though there are only four kinds of nucleotide, their sequence on the chain can differ in enough ways to provide all the messages that might be needed. It is analogous to combining only two elements, dots and dashes, to form the letters of the alphabet (Morse code) or to combining the 26 letters of our alphabet to form

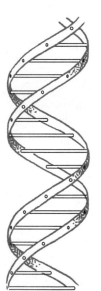

Figure 3.1 Diagram of DNA.

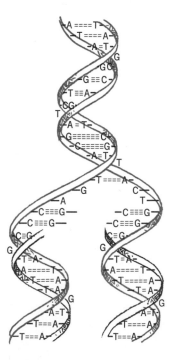

Figure 3.2 Reproducing itself.

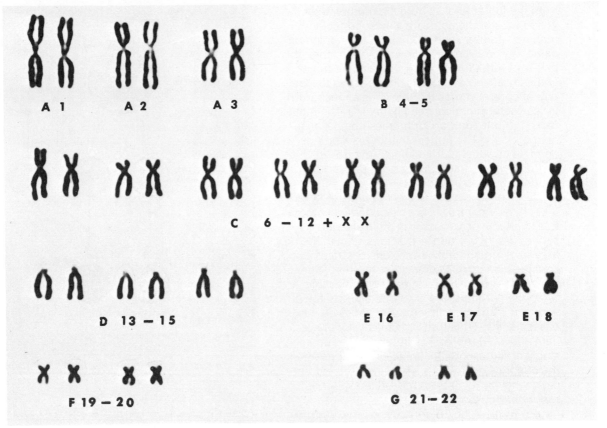

A 1   A 2   A 3   B 4-5

C 6 — 12 + X X

D 13 — 15   E 16   E 17   E 18

F 19 — 20   G 21—22

Figure 3.3 Female human chromosomes arranged in pairs. (Courtesy Arthur D. Bloom and Shozo Iida, Department of Human Genetics, University of Michigan.)

the huge number of words contained in the English language.

The information contained in DNA controls the synthesis of proteins, specifically the amino acid sequence in proteins. The details lie within the province of biology and need not concern us here. What does concern us is that DNA can reproduce itself. The two ladders first separate, and then each ladder splits (see Figure 3.2). Each half ladder uses itself as a template[2] to construct the other, complementary half of the ladder. Then the four ladders pair off and intertwine to form two

[2] *The term* template *is used analogically. Examples in everyday life include molds for casting molten metal and molds for making gelatin desserts or cookies.*

double helixes—where previously there was only one double helix. This is believed to be the basic genetic process underlying reproduction. CHROMOSOMES. The human body consists of cells, each of which consists of a nucleus and surrounding cytoplasm. Most of the hereditary material is located inside the nucleus in structures called *chromosomes* (literally, colored bodies, so named because they absorb dye and become deeply colored). Chromosomes consist of DNA plus protein and other supporting components.

There are 46 chromosomes (23 pairs) in every cell in our bodies (see Figure 3.3) with the exception of the reproductive cells, which have 23 chromosomes. When a sperm and an ovum unite, the new organism (zygote) has 46 chromosomes, 23 from the father and 23 from the mother. In both genders 22 of the pairs are almost perfectly matched. In men, one member of the remaining pair of chromosomes is larger than the other; this pair is called XY. In women, the last pair match, and it is called XX. It is this difference in the last pair of chromosomes that provides a mechanism for sex determination (see Figure 3.4). The mother can contribute only an X chromosome because her pair is XX. The father contributes X or Y depending on which particular sperm fertilizes the ovum: an X sperm produces a girl (XX), and a Y sperm produces a boy (XY).

GENES. These are the *functional* units of heredity —each gene controls a specific chemical process. It is chemical processes, run off in specific sequences, that produce the traits seen in the new organism. Presumably, each gene occupies a specific position on a specific chromosome. There are many genes aligned along each chromosome, and when the chromosome is passed along to the offspring, the entire complement of genes on it is passed along. Thus traits (such as color of eyes, hair, and skin) represented by the genes on a single chromosome are linked: if one appears in the offspring, the others are likely to appear because they have all been passed along on the same chromosome.

The simplest kind of inheritance involves major *dominant* and *recessive* genes. A given trait may show a wide range of variability. Eye color, for example, varies over a wide spectrum of colors. Alternate forms of a gene for a given trait are called *alleles;* thus if there are 20 different eye colors, there are 20 alleles of the gene for eye color. In the simplest situation, traits are determined by a pair of genes, one from the father and one from the mother. When both genes of the pair are for the same variant of the trait, the offspring is *homozygous* (same alleles) for that trait. For example, if the offspring receives a gene for blue eyes[3] from the father and another gene for blue eyes from the mother, the offspring is homozygous with respect to eye color (see Figure 3.5). When the genes in a pair are for different forms of the trait, the offspring is *heterozygous* (different alleles) for that trait. If the father passes on a

<hr>

[3] *Strictly speaking, there is no "gene for blue eyes." This is merely a simple way of describing very complex programs for the development of the new organism.*

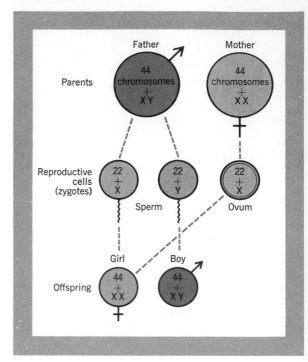

Figure 3.4 Sex determination in reproduction.

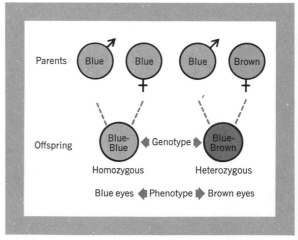

Figure 3.5 Dominant and recessive traits.

gene for blue eyes and the mother one for brown eyes, the offspring will be heterozygous and it will have brown eyes. Note that the brown-eye gene and the blue-eye gene are alleles of one another.

In this example the brown-eye allele predominates over the blue-eye allele. In other words, brown eyes are *dominant* and blue eyes are *recessive.* In this kind of inheritance, when there are competing alleles, only one trait will appear in the offspring—the dominant one. The trait determined by the recessive allele simply does not appear in the offspring. Obviously, there must be a difference between the makeup of the genetic material and the traits that actually appear in the offspring, a difference that is reflected in the phenotype-genotype dichotomy. The *phenotype* is a trait that appears in the individual; it is a product of both genetic endowment and the course of development. The *genotype* is the individual's underlying genetic makeup, which may or may not become manifest as traits. The phenotype is visible and observable; the genotype is hidden and inferred.

Traits that can be either present or absent (blue eyes, for example) are determined by single *major genes.* But most traits (and virtually all inherited behavioral traits) exist in graded amounts. Height, weight, and skin color all vary over a range of values, distributed in the population in a normal (bell-shaped) curve. These traits are determined by *multiple minor genes.* Less is known about polygenic inheritance, which is unfortunate because it underlies virtually all the behavioral characteristics that are inherited. For example, intelligence, which is in part determined by heredity, consists of a number of intellectual skills, and therefore it is not surprising that its inheritance involves many genes.

Population Genetics

An animal may develop, mature, strengthen its muscles, and sharpen its skills, but it cannot alter its hereditary material; moreover, each animal has a limited life span. But for evolution to occur, both flexibility in genetic material and enormous amounts of time are necessary. Individual organisms, having neither the flexibility nor the time, cannot be the units of evolution. In fact, in the perspective of evolution, each of us is no more than

a container of hereditary material, a transient way station mediating the flow of genetic information.

The unit of evolution is the *population:* a group of similar organisms of essentially common ancestry, living in the same area and capable of mating successfully. Several populations may comprise a *species,* which consists of all the organisms capable of mating successfully, whether or not they are likely to do so.

Man, being unable to produce offspring with any other animal, is a species. Within the species of man there are populations called *races:* populations of individuals having different frequences of genes.[4] For example, blacks tend to have darker skin than do Caucasians, though the two races grade into one another without clear boundaries.

Figure 3.6 diagrams the relationship between populations and races, using domestic animals as an example. Domestic dogs and cats each constitute a species, and they do not and cannot mate successfully with one another. Within the canine species, great danes obviously differ considerably from dachshunds; these two *breeds* (roughly equivalent to populations) *can* mate successfully but they rarely do. Similarly, Persian cats and Siamese cats, being from different populations, usually do not breed.

Within any population there may be considerable diversity of traits—as for example, among blacks or among Caucasians. The sum of all the *genotypes* in a population is called its *gene pool.* The gene pool can be increased by *mutations:* changes in the genes that result in altered traits in the next generation. Most mutations are harmful and therefore are not retained over successive generations. Nevertheless, a few lead to adaptive traits. They are ultimately the only source of new traits within a species, which means that they are a fundamental cause of the changes that underlie evolution.

Natural Selection

In most species only a small proportion of the offspring reach maturity and breed the next generation. Twentieth-century man is exceptional in this respect, owing to advances in medical knowledge

[4] *Race is a controversial concept in anthropology, but the position presented here is generally accepted.*

and technology. One hundred years ago and earlier, a high proportion of infants died at birth or soon afterward, and childhood diseases denied maturity to another large segment of the population. Thus in both animals and humans (until recently), the majority of individuals in any given generation cannot cope with their environment and fall by the wayside. The minority that reproduce have, in a sense, been selected by the environment to pass on their hereditary material to the next generation. Natural selection, the key to evolution, is based solely on this kind of success in reproduction.

Reproductive success determines which genes will predominate in future generations. The animals that breed most successfully leave behind more offspring, contributing a larger and larger share of individuals to each new generation. Traits that lead to reproductive success eventually predominate—that is, they are naturally selected.

Reproductive success is not merely a matter of producing a large quantity of new organisms. A single fish may lay millions of eggs, but only a few of these survive to adulthood and *breed the next generation.* It is not how many are born but how many survive and reproduce in their turn. In higher animals, especially mammals, there are fewer offspring, but they are better protected and nourished, and a greater proportion of them survive to adulthood.

Nor are biological variables the only ones. In the line that leads to man, males and females must seek each other and respond in a way that guarantees fertilization. These acts are *psychological,* involving perception, motivation, and often learning. Behavior is no less involved in natural selection than is anatomy or physiology.

In brief, success in reproduction is determined by a number of variables. The sequence has been summarized by Simpson:

(1) Male and female must occur in proximity or must find each other.
(2) In many, especially the more complex animals, they must be sexually acceptable to each other and must mate.
(3) Fertilization must occur.
(4) The gametes (sperm and ovum) must be genetically compatible.
(5) Normal embryological development must occur.
(6) Offspring must survive to breeding age and become successful reproducers in their turn. (1958, P. 19.)

Unfortunately, some followers of Darwin have overemphasized the last stage, suggesting the slogan "survival of the fittest." Natural selection is not based merely on two animals fighting, with one surviving. It is based on the six variables just listed, the sum of which determines success in reproduction.

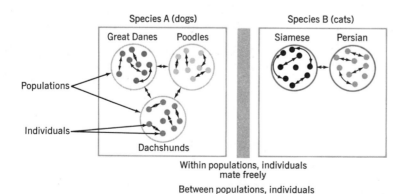

Figure 3.6 Population and space.

Adaptation

There are never enough natural resources to sustain all members of a population or species for an unlimited length of time. In a benign environment with little competition for the resources, animals thrive and proliferate at a rate that soon outstrips the food, water, and air available or attracts a suficient number of predators to thin out the overstocked area. Because animals have too many offspring for the available natural resources, there is always fierce competition for them. It is not so much a violent, open battle between individuals as a quiet, covert contest between the more efficient and the less efficient members of the population. Those most proficient in obtaining food and avoiding danger are most likely to survive through the breeding period and leave offspring behind when they die. The essence of adaptation is possessing traits or having available responses for coping with the environment, whether it is better eyes for extracting more information, better teeth for extracting more nourishment, or better means of resisting poisons.[5]

The causal sequence starts with the environment, for it is the animal that must adapt to the environment and not the other way around. Changes in the environment must elicit changes in the animal's approach to it, or the animal perishes. Species that do not evolve means to cope with changes in the environment perish too.

There are two types of adaptation in evolution—specialized and generalized. The first consists of *fixed, specialized traits* that attune the animal precisely to the particular environment in which it finds itself. This type of adaptation can occur only in stable environments, whose uniformity extends in time over hundreds or thousands of generations. The best adapted animals will be those whose traits are fixed and unchanging and specially tailored to the demands of the environment. These traits are so stable that they will develop in the individual organism no matter what the environment is. This fixity and specialization of traits

[5] *Insecticides may wipe out most of the local members of a pest species, but those that adapt are resistant to the poison. We now have to contend with pests that thrive on insecticides.*

has been successful for only a few species, but it does not and cannot take into account changes in habitat:

The road to extinction is paved with the remains of beautifully but specially adapted types. Final evolutionary victory over the malevolent environment requires progressive movement into new broad adaptive zones. Many lines never move out of old zones; others fail in the attempt; but those that succeed form the advancing army of organic diversity and increasing general adaptive efficiency. (SAVAGE, 1963, P. 103.)

Generalized adaptiveness is the second type. These adaptations do not fit precisely any particular environment, but they do fit a range of environments. Specialized adaptation can be compared to a baseball player who is a superb pitcher but plays other positions poorly; generalized adaptation is like a utility infielder who can play all the positions reasonably well. An animal with less specialized traits can cope with changes in habitat during its lifetime; a population with such traits can cope with changes occurring over generations. This kind of adaptation is most likely to occur in unstable environments; the animal never becomes too closely attuned to its surroundings because conditions are likely to change, rendering the more specialized animal inefficient and helpless. Generalized, flexible traits allow an animal to deal with a variety of adaptive zones. Man is the best example of a creature with many generalized characteristics. For example, in spite of his lack of fur, early man adjusted to cold climates because of his ingenuity in obtaining furs and hides from animals and in lighting fires for warmth.

The two types of adaptation should both be represented in the gene pool of any population. To adapt to a habitat, a population must have genetic stability and at least some specialized traits; these will attune it to the environment as it is and for as long as it continues uniformly. But the population must also be capable of change to meet the sometimes radical shifts either in the environment or when members of the population seek new adaptive zones; this requires genetic flexibility and generalized traits. Both types of adaptation are necessary, and the population itself can remain adaptive only so long as it maintains a dynamic balance between them.

Adaptation is of course related to natural selection. Other things being equal, those animals with superior strength and ability to cope with the environment will be favored by natural selection. This is what Darwin (1859) meant when he referred to survival of the fittest. But other things are not equal, and survival is only part of the story; the remainder consists of reproductive efficiency. Natural selection favors those traits, and only those traits, that lead to reproductive success. Presumably, the better-adapted animals will be those who survive to maturity and breed, and are healthy enough to produce many offspring. But this is not always true. Among men today there is no evidence that the brighter, healthier, stronger individuals are producing more offspring than those parents less favored; in fact, they may be producing fewer children.

Diversification

There is some truth in the observation that Darwin's book *The Origin of Species* explained everything about evolution except the origin of species. Adaptation to the environment is favored by natural selection because it usually leads to reproductive success. Organisms that are better adapted produce more offspring on the average, and therefore their traits come to predominate in the population. Though natural selection accounts for the presence of traits, it is not sufficient to explain the variety of species that inhabit the earth. For this we need the concept of *speciation:* the evolution of populations into different species.

Speciation

The basic mechanism of speciation is isolation, and the sequence is illustrated in Figure 3.7. Initially, as two populations emerge from one, their geographical territories overlap. There is frequent interbreeding and a free interchange of genes. Were the spatial nearness and the consequent interbreeding to continue, the population would obviously not diverge. However, as populations grow,

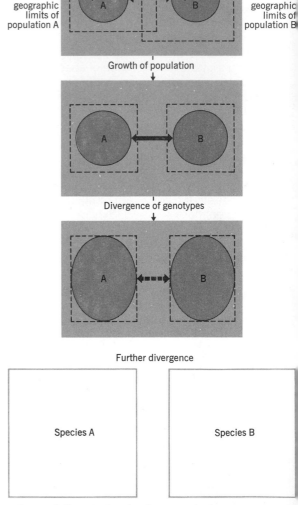

Figure 3.7 Isolation leads to speciation.

they require more territory for the larger number of individuals. As the two populations spread out, there is less contact between members of each and consequently less interbreeding. As the separation continues, the two populations become geographically isolated.[6] This occurs when the distance between them is too large for individuals to negotiate, or when natural geographical barriers intervene (cliffs, mountains, swamps, rivers, or barren land). A few hundred yards might suffice to isolate two populations of worms, but hundreds of miles might be needed to isolate two populations of birds,

While the process of isolation is going on, each population is evolving along lines laid down by natural selection. Each is adapting to its own special environment. Given enough time, the two populations will develop different sets of traits. Eventually, the traits diverge so much that interbreeding is impossible. Interbreeding might be prevented by: (1) differences in the breeding season; (2) different appearances, leading to sexual unattractiveness; (3) different patterns of behavior during courtship; or (4) incompatible genes, which prevent fertilization. Thus geographic isolation can lead to *reproductive isolation.* When two populations can no longer interbreed, they are different species, by definition.

Diversity and Adaptive Radiation

Populations and species occupy areas of land or water in which they survive and reproduce successfully. An environment to which an organism can be adapted well is called an *ecological niche.* Natural selection weeds out those members of a population that are poorer in adapting to their environment because they consequently are poorer at reproduction. Those members that predominate in the populations are therefore well adapted to the particular ecological niche, and they tend to breed successfully. The population tends to expand, reducing the natural resources

available per individual. Thus population pressure forces a move to a territory with greater available natural resources. Such an environment is available either before any species has occupied it or after a species that previously occupied that environment has moved on or become extinct. Throughout the long course of evolutionary history many species have become extinct; it is the fate of most species.

If natural selection favors organisms adapted to a particular environment, under what conditions can organisms successfully move to a new environment, one to which they are less adapted? There are two conditions. The first is *preadaptation.* A trait that is adaptive in one environment may also be of some value in another environment. For example, a hand that is adapted to grasping branches while the animal moves through the treetops is also *incidentally* adapted for grasping a stick to be used as a tool or weapon (see Figure 3.8). Preadaptation implies no goal or purpose. In this case the basic adaptation is for a tree-dwelling life; its by-product is preadaptation for dwelling on the ground and using a stick as a weapon. Such a preadaptation undoubtedly was useful to our apelike ancestors when they made the transition from trees to the ground.

Some preadaptations have little use in the original environment. In every population there is a broad range of traits represented in the gene pool, contributing to the dynamic balance between fixity and plasticity. As populations evolve and as environments gradually change, the gene pool is

---

[6] Geographical *isolation is only one way in which populations become separated. Among humans, for example, differences in skin color, religion, and nationality isolate humans from one another.*

The same hand that can grasp a tree branch (adaptation)

Can grasp a stick to be used as a tool or weapon (pre-adaptation)

Figure 3.8 Adaptation and preadaptation.

Lobe–fin fish

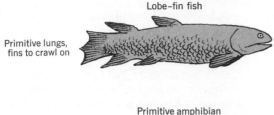

Primitive lungs,
fins to crawl on

Primitive amphibian

Better lungs,
legs to crawl on

Figure 3.9 Adaptations to water that were preadaptations to land.

in a constant but slow-moving state of flux. Some of the traits in the population may have little adaptive value in the present habitat but may have considerable value in a new habitat.

The second condition for a successful move to a new environment is a relative *absence of competition* for the natural resources. When an organism moves to a new environment, its initial adaptation necessarily is poor. Gradually, adaptation will improve under the pressure of natural selection. In the initial stages a poor adaptation succeeds only when the ecological niche is wide open.

The transition of animals from water environments to land illustrates this point. Lobe-fin fishes, thought to be the forerunners of primitive amphibians, had two pairs of fins with thick, fleshy lobes in their centers (see Figure 3.9). They also had primitive lungs, which were used whenever the oxygen content of the surrounding water became too low for gill breathing. Both the lungs and the lobe fins were adaptations to a changing environment: lakes and ponds were drying up, and the stagnating waters were becoming devoid of oxygen and food. In their search for food and better water the lobe-fin fishes crawled over brief stretches of land, using their lungs to breathe air and their fins to locomote. In theory, it is but a short step from a lobe-fin fish to a primitive amphibian, which is at home both in water and on land.

The lobe-fin fish had lungs and the forerunners of limbs, both successful adaptations to life in shallow water. These were also preadaptations to life on land. Their initial adaptation to land must have been poor, but there were no land animals to compete with them for food or to prey on them.

The move from water to land thus succeeded because of both preadaptation and the absence of competition. A similar evolution could not take place today: such a poorly adapted creature would be crowded out or devoured by the creatures already well adapted to life on land.

When a species of animals moves into a new ecological niche and encounters no opposition, it diversifies quickly (on the evolutionary scale of time). Populations grow rapidly, and there is considerable genetic variability. The pressure of a mounting population forces the animals to spread out over the terrain, and they come to occupy areas that differ in natural features. Natural selection then works to favor those best adapted to specific habitats. Each specific habitat calls for slightly different adaptive traits, which means that animals in different locales begin to diverge in their traits. Such rapid diversification in response to a new ecological niche is called *adaptive radiation.*

Adaptive radiation has occurred many times in the course of evolution. When reptiles evolved from amphibians and moved inland, they found virgin land and no competition. There occurred an extremely broad radiation which took many directions, including reptiles that flew and reptiles that returned to water. The reptiles became so well adapted to the environment that they dominated all other animals for more than 100 million years.

In brief, the modern theory of evolution explains the rich diversity of life by the following processes.

1. Natural selection favors those traits that are most adaptive to the environment so long as

adaptation is correlated with reproductive success.
2. Isolation causes a diversity of traits to arise within a group of animals because of the pressure of natural selection in the direction of traits adaptive to a *specific* habitat.
3. This adaptation leads to *reproductive* isolation, which prevents animals with different traits from interbreeding successfully and therefore insures further diversification of traits.
4. Preadaptations and new ecological niches without competition enable animals to move into radically different environments, which eventually leads to very different forms of animals.

The Evolutionary Model

The problem Darwin set for himself was to account for the enormous diversity of plant and animal life. The first step in solving this problem is to assume that each species possesses features that are adaptive in a specific environment. This assumption implies a *purposive* process, with some hand guiding evolution toward better adaptation. But, as Campbell has pointed out, "The most exciting contribution of Darwin is in his model for the achievement of purposive or end-guided processes through a mechanism involving blind, stupid, unforesightful elements" (1966, p. 26).

There are three sequential components in Darwin's model:

1. *Variability.* "Mistakes" in duplicating genetic material (mutations) lead to a variety of possible adaptations. Which features pass on to the next generation is determined by chance: the random combinations of genes that occur in mating.
2. *Section criteria.* Natural selection determines which features will survive over many generations. Ultimately, there is only one criterion: success in reproduction. But this single criterion depends on a variety of subcriteria—for example, staying alive and healthy until maturity, attracting a mate, mating successfully, and rearing the next generation. The traits that

meet such rigorous criteria will be the ones retained over successive generations.
3. *Preservation mechanism.* The method of preserving adaptations is the duplication process of the DNA molecule. Some of the genes of the parents are passed on to the offspring.

These three components comprise the essentials of the evolutionary model. It applies not only to evolution but also to a variety of psychological processes. An example is a general model of the learning process, which moves from trial-and-error to selection by means of reward and finally to retention by unknown changes in the nervous system. Table 3.1 compares evolution and learning as examples of how the general model may be applied.

Man as a Mammal

As our primary interest is man, we shall examine those characteristics in man that originated in lower animals. Man is first of all a vertebrate, with a backbone, attached muscles, a central nervous system, and a gut. More specifically, man is a mammal, and this is where our story begins. (Both mammals and birds evolved from reptiles, but the divergence between the two is so great that we shall ignore birds.) Mammals represent a giant evolutionary step in the line of animals that has culminated in man. Mammals differ from reptiles in temperature regulation, arousal, reproduction, and maturation (see Table 3.2).

Temperature Regulation

Whereas the body temperature of a reptile fluctuates with changes in the external temperature, mammals carry on their life processes relatively independently of the temperature of the surrounding air. This shift required an entire series of adaptations, most of which have been retained in man. There must be a regulating system that signals the presence of too much heat or cold and initiates the changes needed to keep the body temperature within the appropriate limits. This system, which is analo-

Table 3.1
A Model Encompassing Evolution and Learning

ESSENTIAL STEPS	EVOLUTION	LEARNING
1. Variability	Different traits, as means of adapting	Trial-and-error, different responses tried
2. Selection criteria	Natural selection (success in breeding)	Selection by means of reward (attaining goal, escaping pain or danger)
3. Preservation mechanism	Genes, chromosomes	Retention by unknown changes in the nervous system

Table 3.2
Reptilian and Mammalian Characteristics

	REPTILES	MAMMALS
Blood	Cold	Warm: temperature regulation
Variations in arousal	Small	Great: exploration, sleep
Reproduction	Eggs	Fetus: presence of mother
Maturation time	Short	Long: nurturance, much individual learning

gous to a home thermostat, will be discussed in Chapter 6.

The mechanisms for conserving and expending body heat are well developed. To conserve heat, mammals have fur or hair, a layer of fat just beneath the skin that acts as insulation, and a blood circulatory system that constricts to cut down on the surface outflow of heat. To expend body heat, hair or fur is flattened against the skin to reduce its thickness, water is evaporated in the form of sweat or saliva, and surface blood vessels dilate to increase the surface outflow of heat. In addition to these physiological mechanisms, there are behavioral mechanisms for controlling internal temperature. Mammals (and other animals) curl into a ball during cold weather, and they seek warmer spots locally or warmer localities; they also exercise to produce heat. In warm weather, they stretch out their limbs, offering more surface for cooling, seek cooler spots or water, and remain quiescent.

Maintenance of high internal temperature requires fuel to stoke the furnace. Therefore mammals must have a rich food supply. The main adaptation consists of teeth that not only can seize food but can chew, cut, and grind it more efficiently. These mechanical aids to digestion are supplemented by enzymes that start the digestive process in the mouth. Such adaptations serve not only to maintain body heat but also to provide the energy required for high-level, sustained activity. Wolves hunt by pursuing their prey until the prey is exhausted, and the long chase requires energy reserves that can be stored only by eating richer and more concentrated foods and digesting them more fully. This adaptation reaches a peak in the flesh-eating carnivores, such as lions, wolves, and bears; the concentrated protein and other nutrients of their prey are sufficient to maintain their energy reserves for several days after eating. When an animal does not need to eat all the time just to sustain its high metabolic rate, it has time for other things, and it may become curious about its environment.

Arousal

As a group, reptiles are passive and relatively inactive animals. They can be roused to high levels of activity, but only for short periods of time. They spend much of their lives sleeping or drowsing, and they tend not to explore or to be curious about their surroundings.

Mammals are relatively active and curious. Many are capable of sustained levels of high activation, and their sleep tends to be deeper. They seem to have a craving for new stimuli and spend considerable time in exploring the world around them. In brief, mammals vary considerably in level of arousal. When awake, they are extremely alert and active; when asleep, they descend to deep levels of slumber.

Reproduction and Maturation

One of the most radical shifts in the evolution of mammals from reptiles was the change from the mass production of eggs to the production of only a few offspring with good chances for survival. In virtually all mammals the fertilized egg is retained within the body of the mother, where it is protected and nourished until considerable growth has occurred. In the constant environment of the mother's womb the mammalian fetus is as well fed and secure as any creature can be in this world.

This happy condition lasts only until birth, after which nourishment and protection are no longer internal and automatic. The major biological adaptation is the mammary glands, which give this class of animals its name. All the other adaptations crucial for the infant's survival are *behavioral*. Mammalian mothers, and to some extent fathers, have strong tendencies to shelter, protect, feed, and even instruct their offspring. Without benefit of these parental behaviors the infant would surely perish, so it is not surprising that all mammals possess the nurturing tendencies needed to sustain their helpless offspring.

The instructional aspect is particularly important for future behavior. The young animal, when it is not suckling, busily explores its environment. Its play behavior may lead to dangerous situations or it may not lead to the responses needed for later independence. The parent offers a behavioral model for the young animal to imitate, as well as early supervision of exploratory behavior and punishment of incorrect or dangerous responses. Both the imitation and the trial-and-error learning offer possibilities for bypassing heredity as a means of passing on information to the next generation. Fewer behavioral tendencies need to be encoded in the hereditary material, giving the developing organisms more freedom to learn from experience and more flexibility within their own life spans.

Man is a mammal with all the characteristics we have been discussing. He is warm-blooded and maintains a high level of metabolism and body temperature. His diet is rich enough to require only periodic eating, and it sustains a very high level of energy-consuming activity. His reproductive efficiency is high, representing the extreme of the trend toward bearing fewer offspring at a time but maximizing the chances of their survival. Parental nurturance and instruction continues for a long period, allowing time for learning and social interaction.

Man as a Primate

As mammals evolved, most adapted to habitats on the ground, but some primitive, insect-eating mammals took to the trees. Eventually, these tree-dwelling insect-eaters evolved into higher forms, and it is from them that primates evolved (see Figure 3.10). The evolutionary trend that starts with tree shrews and ends with man is hypothetical but is supported by many facts. The tree shrews are primitive insect-eaters with snouts, eyes directed toward the sides, and small brains. Primate evolution then moved in the direction of an opposable thumb for grasping branches, more forward-directed eyes, three-dimensional vision, a reduced snout so that visual fields could more completely overlap, and bigger and better brains. A late adaptation placed more emphasis on the arms for locomotion, and the brachiating primates (those that

swing from branch to branch) closer to man have long powerful arms and shoulder sockets that allow more complete rotation of the arms.

Life in the trees led to profound changes in locomotion and perception, the residuals of which may be seen in man. The following lists have been modified from those of Campbell (1966). The adaptations for moving through the trees were:

1. No specialization of limbs, free mobility of joints in several directions, and five fingers or toes on each limb.
2. Nails to replace claws, the nails supporting finger pads sensitive to touch and, together

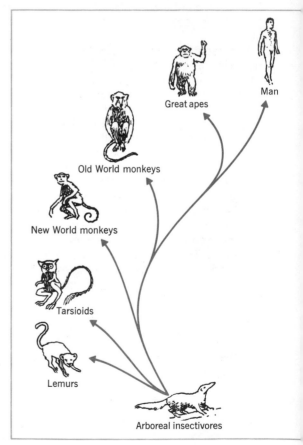

Figure 3.10 Evolution of primates.

with hairless, toughened palms, capable of maintaining a firm grip.
3. Improved motor control and balance.
4. The beginning of upright posture.
5. Maintenance of small body size, relative to ground-dwelling mammals.

The perceptual adaptations involved an increasing dominance of vision:

1. Large eyes and a better retina, combining to yield improved sensitivity, acuity, and color vision.
2. Visual fields overlap (binocular vision) to yield excellent depth perception.
3. Enlargement of the bones around the eyes for better protection.
4. A diminution of the sense of smell together with a corresponding reduction in the snout and the parts of the brain related to smell.

The logic of these adaptations is clear. Though claws help to grasp trees, a sure sense of touch and a grasping hand are more efficient. Odors linger for a long time on the ground but are lost quickly up in the trees, rendering a keen sense of smell superfluous. A ground-dweller moves in only two dimensions along the surface of the earth, but for a tree-dweller the third (vertical) dimension is equally important. A tree-dweller needs three-dimensional vision so that it will move precisely where it intends to in all three dimensions. Mistakes result in a long drop to the ground, which may cause broken bones and perhaps death.

These primate adaptations have been retained in man. Vision is his dominant sense; he has three-dimensional color vision with excellent sensitivity and acuity. The forward-looking eyes and reduced snout characteristic of the human face are essentially characteristics of a higher primate. Man's thumb is opposable, his fingers have pads backed by nails, and his grasp is powerful. His posture is upright, his sense of balance is excellent, and several of his joints can move and rotate in more than one plane. This is the basic ground plan of physical man; the auxiliary primate features that more directly affect man's behavior will be discussed later.

Evolution of Man

Man's most recent ancestor was a primate, but no one knows the precise circumstances or the specific sequence that led from an apelike primate to a manlike ape and finally to man (see Eckhardt, 1972). But there is agreement among most anthropologists on the roles of bipedalism (two-legged locomotion) and hunting.

Bipedalism

An ape can stand erect or walk on two feet only briefly; most of the time it stands or locomotes on its feet and knuckles—essentially a four-legged posture. Man stands, walks, and runs on two legs. The evolution from four-legged to two-legged locomotion involved adaptations of the feet and pelvis. The feet gradually became flatter, offering a broad enough base to balance on two feet the weight that was previously balanced on four. The pelvis tilted backward to accommodate an upright posture and to support all the weight above it. The buttocks enlarged with the addition of massive muscles needed to balance and turn an erect, two-legged animal.

There were virtually no accompanying changes in the torso and arms. In fact, the three major parts of the body evolved at entirely different rates (see Figure 3.11). The upper body and arms remained essentially the same during the shift to bipedalism. Man's torso, internal organs, and arms are little different from those of apes. The pelvis and legs changed radically to meet the demands of two-legged posture and locomotion. While these adaptations occurred, the size of the brain and the shape of the skull were more or less constant; only later, presumably as a consequence of hunting, did they change—as we shall see in the next section.

A two-legged posture freed man to use his hands for exploring and shaping his environment. A creature with hands can *use* tools and, together with a sufficiently complex brain, can *make* tools. Thus bipedalism was a giant step forward in the evolution of man in that it freed his hands to manipulate and shape the environment.

Bipedalism is so basic to man's functioning that

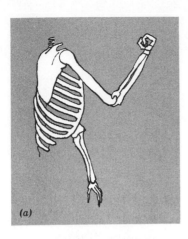

(a)

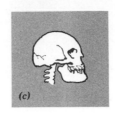

(c)

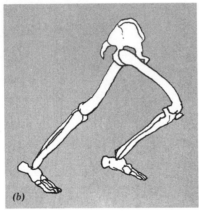

(b)

Figure 3.11 Diagrammatic representation of the human skeleton showing the three major functional divisions that evolved at different rates and that are surprisingly independent during their evolution.

it evolved in spite of several negative features. When man stood up on his hind legs, he weakened his body in four ways (see Figure 3.12):

1. A thicker, tilted pelvis offers a narrower birth canal in women, with attendant birth problems and incomplete development of the infant's brain at birth.
2. A sagging gut that rests on layers of muscles increases the possibility of hernia.
3. Poor circulation in the legs often leads to varicose veins.

4. A weakened lower vertebral column, leading to a common adult ailment—lower back pain.

These "scars of evolution" (Krogman, 1951) are maladaptive, and their presence attests to the importance of the adaptation that caused them: bipedalism, which freed man's hands.

Hunting

Upright posture freed the hands for manipulation, and man's ancestors could then use tools and weapons. It is not clear whether weapons were necessary to replace the natural weapons of teeth, agility, and brute strength, or the development of weapons brought on a decline of these natural weapons because they were no longer needed and therefore not adaptive. Whatever the origin, man's ancestors used weapons for hunting and used tools (sticks or bones) for getting under the skin of their victims to the meat beneath, man's nails being too weak to break the skin of most animals.

Hunting probably started as a means of supplementing a vegetarian diet. Once weapons could be used and carried from one place to another, man's ancestors could become more carnivorous. Hunting itself led to profound changes. It required planning and cooperation between hunters in tracking and killing the prey. Some kind of communication was essential, and early forms of speech were probably helpful. After the kill, the food had to be shared not only by the hunters but also with those who stayed behind (see Figure 3.13). This necessity led to a division of labor and cooperative behavior.

It is a small step from a tool-using, apelike animal to primitive man. Hunting, which became man's major method of obtaining food, involves the skilled use of weapons. Hunting also promotes the behaviors just mentioned: communication, planning, and cooperation. If these were adaptive traits, they would be favored by natural selection. Animals that could use tools better, plan better, communicate better, and cooperate better would be more likely to survive and leave offspring. The kind of manipulation needed for skilled use of tools and weapons requires the central neural in-

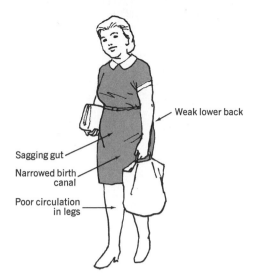

Weak lower back

Sagging gut

Narrowed birth
canal

Poor circulation
in legs

Figure 3.12 Scars of evolution.

tegration that can come only from the brain. Therefore, animals with larger and more highly specialized brains would be favored. A larger brain opens up greater possibilities for speech and for a shift from mere tool *use* to tool *making.* It requires somewhat more intelligence to make a tool, planning its eventual form and use, than it does to pick up what is around and use it as a tool. Apes use sticks as tools or weapons, but they do not make tools.

Figure 3.13 Neanderthal encampment.
(FROM J. AUGUSTA AND Z. BURIAN, PREHISTORIC MAN. COURTESY ARTIA.)

Table 3.3
Man's Heritage

FEATURES SHARED WITH PRIMATES OR MAMMALS	UNIQUE FEATURES
1. Physiological: warmblooded, variations in arousal.	1. Completely bipedal: hands free for manipulation
2. Reproduction: fetal development in uterus, mother-infant bond, long period of development	2. Tool-making: uses tools to make tools
3. Sensory: vision dominant	3. Language: encoding of experience, communication
4. Motor: manipulation by hands	4. Culture: social reality and customs, continuity and accumulation of knowledge
5. Social: group living, attachment to others, communication	5. World view: self-consciousness, "above nature"

Man's Heritage

Man combines features shared with lower forms with features that are uniquely human (see Table 3.3). Man's animal heritage is extensive. He is a mammal in body symmetry, body support, metabolism, and reproduction, and he shares with other mammals broad behavioral tendencies concerning mating, nurturing the young, and relations with other members of the species. Man is a primate in his three-dimensional color vision, clever hands, and prolonged developmental period.

Man is also distinct. His posture and means of locomotion free his hands for manipulation of tools and weapons, and he is the only animal that *makes* tools. Man is the only animal to possess true speech. Other animals can make sounds and even communicate by the tone or timbre of the sounds, but these do not constitute speech. Speech consists of communication by means of symbols that are strung together according to *rules,* and in this, man is unique (see Chapter 28).

Foresight and planning may be seen in the higher animals, especially primates, but the level is primitive in contrast to man's highly developed capacity to envision future possibilities. Man alone is self-conscious and can see himself as set apart from the rest of the natural world.

Man's motor coordination, speech, learning, and foresight are all associated with his special brain. Not only is man's brain huge compared to animals of comparable size but it is more highly specialized. The evolution of this brain occurred as man developed the motor and intellectual characteristics we have labeled unique. Good motor coordination is an obvious adaptive advantage, and it must have been favored by natural selection. Such coordination requires appropriate neural integration of messages to and from muscles, which means that individuals with better-developed sensory and motor areas of the brain would be favored by natural selection. Similarly, speech, learning, and planning all require a bigger and more specialized brain. Thus the evolution of man's brain and his advanced intellect must have occurred together in a positive feedback system: The adaptive intellectual skills required a larger and more complex brain, which in turn made possible further advances in intellectual abilities.

More than any other animal, man bypasses heredity and passes on acquired characteristics to a significant extent. He accomplishes this within the context of his social organization, especially through the knowledge and skills acquired in previous generations being taught to the new generation. Such teaching is also present in other animals—for example, lion cubs are taught to stalk their prey—but this kind of education is crude and trivial compared to the education given to a developing child. A member of the present generation of men can acquire knowledge first accumulated by men a thousand generations ago. Such transmission of acquired learning need not be restricted by time or distance, for the stored information can be retrieved in another time and at

another place. Man's knowledge is cumulative because each new generation does not have to discover for itself what was discovered by previous generations. As knowledge accumulates, more time is required for tutelage. Man has the necessary time, for he has the longest period of infancy and childhood of any animal. The development of the individual organism is thus of much greater importance in man than in any other animal.

We have discussed in general terms the ways in which man is similar to other animals and the ways in which he is distinctive. He cannot be assigned to only one place in nature because he is both an animal and something more than an animal. Some of his behavior has evolved only slightly from comparable and similar behavior seen in lower organisms, but their behavior provides only a dim background for understanding man's behavior. The relationship between man and the lower forms from which he evolved is analogous to the relationship between the adult and the child he developed from. Some aspects of the adult's behavior can easily be traced back to his childhood, but others concern situations that arise only in adulthood and cannot be explained by the events or behaviors of childhood. When we have exhausted man's evolutionary heritage as a source of understanding his behavior, we then turn to what is distinctively human.

chapter 4
development

*Evolutionary trends — neoteny — parallels
between evolution and development — growth,
differentiation, organization, and self-regulation — twins — genes and environment — critical periods — temperament-adaptation,
affective-meaning, and instrumental-meaning
periods — hierarchical model — genetic,
biological and psychological
factors — maturation — models of development*

The time scale of human evolution — millions of years — overwhelms comprehension with its enormity. It is simply too large to be understood in concrete terms and must remain an abstraction. But the time scale of a human life — roughly seven decades — possesses an everyday reality that can be immediately grasped. Virtually all cultures mark the milestones of individual life: birth, maturity, and death. In this chapter we are concerned only with the first segment of the human sequence, development; this is the period from conception to maturity.

Evolutionary Trends

In searching for evolutionary trends, our focus is on the vertebrates, the line that eventually led to man. During vertebrate evolution there was a general tendency to prolong the developmental period. Primitive vertebrates tend to mature quickly, the "childhood" being a brief moment in the time scale of individual life. Some sub-mammalian species are essentially adults almost from the time of hatching. The young animals must achieve adult status quickly or be eaten by predators. Slow maturers, if unprotected, tend to

Table 4.1
Comparative Developmental Periods in Mammals (from Needham, 1941)

KIND OF MAMMAL	PRENATAL PERIOD (WEEKS)	BIRTH TO MATURITY (YEARS)	LIFE (YEARS)
Mouse	3	1/4	4–5
Rabbit	4	1/6	8
Cat	8	1	12
Dog	9	2	15
Hog	17	3	30
Goat	22	2	12
Man	38	25	75
Horse	48	5	35
Elephant	104	20	100

be weeded out by natural selection. Fast maturers survive to breed the next generation, and they come to predominate in succeeding generations.

It is in mammals that the developmental period first becomes a significant portion of the individual animal's life. Among most mammals the offspring are carried within the mother's body for an extended period of pregnancy. After birth, mammals nourish, shelter, and protect their young until the new generation can care for itself. In many mammals there is indoctrination of the young in the ways of the species. During mammalian evolution there is a sharp increase in the length of the developmental period, and, with rare exception, the more closely related the mammal is to man, the longer is its period of development (see Table 4.1).

Animals with fewer built-in mechanisms require more time to learn the ways of their species because there is more to learn, and man represents the end point of the trend. Having fewer automatic responses, he depends more on *learning* to cope with his environment. Each human infant must learn to become a human being, and this process of attaining *social* maturity takes longer than attaining *biological* maturity does.

The difference between biological and social maturity raises an interesting issue. Reproductive maturity cannot be delayed too long without risking a decline in the number of offspring. However, other physiological and behavioral systems could mature slowly and still be retained by natural selection. One extension of the trend toward longer development is the retention of immature characteristics in animals that are otherwise mature. This persistence of infantile or juvenile features into adulthood is called *neoteny.*

Neoteny is most clearly seen when two species, one more advanced than the other, are compared. In the less advanced species, many of the features present in childhood disappear in adulthood, whereas in the advanced species many of the childish features are retained in adulthood. As a result, the *adults* of the advanced species are quite different from the *adults* of the more primitive species but similar to the *young* of the more primitive species. For example, the infant chimpanzee has several anatomical characteristics that are simply not seen in the adult chimpanzee (see Figure 4.1): (1) face at right angle to body, (2) small, flat face but large braincase, (3) comparatively large brain volume, (4) small teeth, and thin nails, and (5) sparse body hair. These features are all retained in the adult human, which accounts for the human-like appearance of the infant chimpanzee.

In addition to these *anatomical* features, there are *functional* parallels between adult man and infant ape in growth of the brain, sequence of or-

ganization of the brain, and ability to learn. Like all mammalian young, infant primates are considerably more plastic and educable than adults. Similarly man is more plastic and educable than primates and other mammals. A primate that retained its flexibility and docility throughout maturity would more closely resemble man. Such a change, presumably brought about by mutations and preserved by natural selection, would bridge the gap between primates and man:

. . . the shift from the status of ape to the status of human being was the result of neotenous mutations which produced a retention of growth trends in the juvenile brain and its potentialities for learning must also have undergone intrinsic change, for no amount of extension of the chimpanzee's capacity for learning would yield a human mind. (MONTAGU, 1962, P. 314.)

Thus man's cognitive abilities and potential for learning — basic aspects of man's psychology — may have evolved as the logical and final ex-

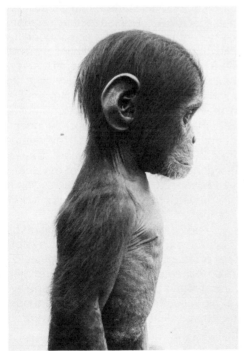

Figure 4.1 An example of neoteny: chimpanzee juvenile resembles humans, but adult chimpanzee shows little resemblance to human. (ASHLEY MONTAGU)

tension of the evolutionary tendency toward a longer period of individual development.[1] Whether or not this hypothesis proves correct, it properly emphasizes early development as basic to understanding the adult organism.

Parallels Between Evolution and Development

During the long history of animal life on earth there have been several biological trends as animals evolved from primitive, simple creatures to advanced, complex creatures. Four of these evolu-

[1] *The concept of neoteny can account for the origin of many human behavioral tendencies:*

If it can be shown that behavioral neoteny is a generalized human trait, an important conceptual advance will have been made toward understanding many of the distinctive attributes of man. The prominence of such traits as playfulness, curiosity, inventiveness in human behavior, the persistence of infantile attachments — all of these would be seen in a somewhat different light. So, too, would the loose relationship between hormonal factors and sex and maternal behavior.
(MASON, 1968, P. 96.)

tionary trends are mirrored by tendencies occurring during the development of individual animals: growth, differentiation, organization, and self-regulation.[2]

The most obvious tendency is simply an increase in the number of cells comprising the animal — that is, *growth*. Though the origins of life must remain speculative, no one seriously doubts that the most primitive creatures consisted of a single cell. Over the course of millions of years, one-celled microscopic animals evolved to many-celled animals as large as elephants and whales. Analogous to this *evolutionary* growth in size is the *developmental* growth from the one-celled fertilized egg to the many-celled adult (see Figure 4.2). The underlying processes are different, but the generalized model is the same. The model, discussed in the last chapter, contains three sequential components: variability, selection criteria, and preservation mechanisms.

As animals evolved from one-celled to many-celled organisms, their various parts *differentiated*, each specializing in a particular function. In addition, animals themselves become more specialized, as species adapted more closely to their particular environments. The typical history of a class of animals starts with a generalized animal, which, over thousands of generations, differentiates into a variety of species specialized to take advantage of highly specific local environments. The developmental history of a single animal follows a parallel path. It begins with a young organism that is generalized, and it proceeds toward specializations. At first, development can move in many possible directions, but once a direction is taken, the change is irreversible (see Figure 4.3). The animal can no more revert to a plastic, generalized form of earlier development than an advanced, specialized species can revert to a primitive, unspecialized species of earlier phylogeny.

Growth and differentiation would inevitably lead to chaos without *organization*. During evolution, as species progressed toward greater specialization, their components were more and more integrated by central regulation. For example, in the evolution of nervous systems, the head end tended to control the parts behind it. This is a *hierarchical*

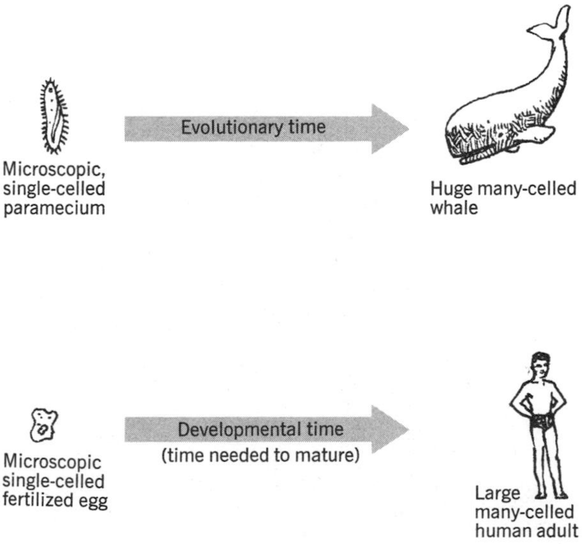

Microscopic, single-celled paramecium — Evolutionary time — Huge many-celled whale

Microscopic single-celled fertilized egg — Developmental time (time needed to mature) — Large many-celled human adult

Figure 4.2 *Evolutionary and developmental growth.*

[2] *Some of these ideas derive from Nagel's (1957) speculations about development.*

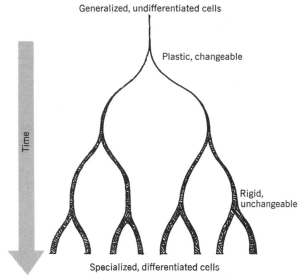

Generalized, undifferentiated cells

Plastic, changeable

Time

Rigid, unchangeable

Specialized, differentiated cells

Figure 4.3 Differentiation leads to loss of flexibility.

Growth

The most obvious aspect of biological development is growth. Each organism adds cells and expands tissues as it progresses from the diminutive size of infancy to the full stature of adulthood.

Accompanying this increase in size are increments in a variety of abilities and behaviors. For example, the growth of intelligence (test scores) parallels body growth. The growing child continually adds language, memories, perceptions, motor skills, and general knowledge to his behavioral repertoire. This *accumulation* of a behavioral repertoire fits the stimulus-response approach, which attempts to explain how each particular act is learned. If there were not more to psychological development than sheer growth, this approach would suffice as an explanation. We shall return to this issue at the end of the chapter.

Differentiation

If we had to choose a single concept as the key to development, it would be differentiation. Its manifestations are widespread and its implications di-

organization, with one component regulating others. During development, there is a parallel trend toward organizing disparate systems into a smoothly functioning whole.

Finally, species have evolved in the direction of *self-regulation,* as may be seen in the relative independence of higher animals of fluctuations in the environment. Thus warmblooded mammals are less at the mercy of variations in surrounding temperature than are coldblooded reptiles. There is an analogous developmental trend. The infant mammal is helpless and depends completely on adults for food, shelter, and protection; the mature mammal can provide for itself and is therefore relatively independent of *social* fluctuations.

In both evolution and development the four trends may be regarded as sequential (see Figure 4.4). Growth results in a larger organism and a need for differentiating among various components. Differentiation leads to complexity and a need for organization. Organization, in turn, leads to regulation of various components, which promotes self-regulation. This sequence shows how the four trends are related in evolution and development, but it is an oversimplified scheme intended for illustration, not explanation. Regardless of how the four trends are related, each is an important aspect of the development of behavior.

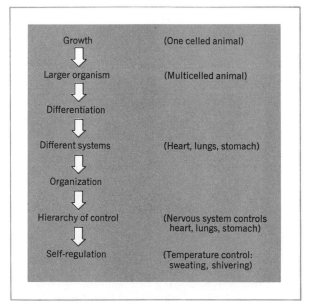

Figure 4.4 Sequence of the four trends.

verse. Though a knowledge of biological differentiation is necessary to understand psychological differentiation, we shall of course emphasize the latter.

Cleavage

The period before birth is divided into three phases:

1. Germinal, 0–2 weeks.
2. Embryonic, 2–6 weeks (attachment to the uterus).
3. Fetal, 7 weeks to birth (responds to tactile stimuli).

During these three stages the new organism develops from a simple, one-celled organism to a complex, many-celled animal. The first important differentiation—cleavage—occurs during the germinal period.

Life begins with a fertilized egg. Within this union of sperm and ovum are contained all the genetic instructions needed for the development of a full-blown adult animal. At first the new organism divides into daughter cells, each of which subsequently divides. The progression is geometric—2, 4, 8, 16, and so on. At first no growth occurs; the total mass of cells is no larger than the original fertilized egg. This process is called *cleavage,* describing the *splitting* of the original cell into many smaller cells. In man, the new organism has 16 cells by the time it arrives at the uterus on the fourth day; these 16 cells cleave rapidly to form hundreds of cells within a short time, and the organism increases in size.

All the cells are part of the same organism, and each cell contains within its nucleus all the encoded instructions needed to form an adult organism. Only rarely do the daughter cells separate to form two distinct organisms (twins); in man this occurs only in the first or second cleavage. When separate organisms do form, they are *identical twins* with the same heredity, because they derive from the same fertilized egg. Not all twins are identical. If two eggs ripen at the same time and both are fertilized, the resulting *fraternal twins* are the products of the two separate fertilizations. They are no more alike in their heredity than

brothers or sisters are (see Figure 4.5).

Comparing fraternal with identical twins offers clues about the relative contribution of heredity. Both kinds of twins, being born at the same time, tend to receive similar rearing. Therefore, if identical twins are more alike in behavior than fraternal twins are, the similarity is likely to be hereditary. (Identical twins are always of the same gender, but fraternal twins may or may not be of the same gender; the reader should be able to understand why this is so.)

Genes and Environment

Cleavage occurs during the *germinal* stage. The cells do not merely divide; they also begin the long process of differentiation, which carries over into the *embryonic* and *fetal* stages. In man, there are three layers of tissue—ectoderm, mesoderm, and endoderm. The cells in these three embryonic layers are essentially the same, all being derived from the original fertilized egg. They all have the potential for becoming any of several kinds of specialized tissue: heart, lungs, kidney, muscle, bone, nerve, and so on. The guiding factor in specialization is their location: what each cell becomes is decided by the cells around it. These surrounding cells comprise the physical and chemical environment, which means that ultimately it is the *internal environment* of the organism that provides direction for the differentiation of generalized cells into specific tissues and organs.

There appears to be a paradox here. The form and structure of the developing organism are determined by the instructions contained in the *hereditary material,* but the specific course of differentiation is directed by *local environments* within the embryo. The explanation of the paradox lies in the way heredity works. The hereditary instructions direct the manufacture of enzymes and other chemicals, but this manufacture is also affected by such conditions as temperature, pressure, and acidity. These physical conditions, which are probably the fundamental determiners of differentiation, vary considerably from one locale within the embryo to another. Presumably, one combination of temperature, acidity, and pressure is needed to derive brain tissue and another combination to derive heart tissue.

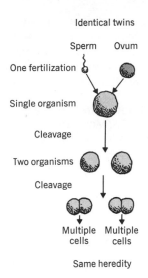

Identical twins

Sperm　Ovum

One fertilization

Single organism

Cleavage

Two organisms

Cleavage

Multiple　Multiple
cells　　cells

Same heredity

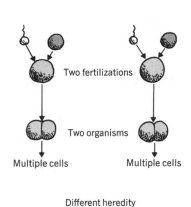

Fraternal twins

Two fertilizations

Two organisms

Multiple cells　　Multiple cells

Different heredity

Figure 4.5 *Identical and fraternal twins.*

For example, there are Siamese cats whose fur is generally light except for dark areas at the toes, the tips of the ears, and the nose; there are also rabbits with similar coloring. These rabbits and the Siamese cats carry a gene that should lead to dark fur, but most of the fur of these animals is light. The explanation lies in a temperature differential; the gene does not produce dark fur unless the body temperature is below 92°F. This was established by research on rabbits. First, a patch of white fur was shaved off, and during regrowth an ice pack was strapped to the shaved area (see Figure 4.6). The new fur that grew in under the ice pack was dark. In such rabbits and in Siamese cats the only areas with dark fur are at the extremities, which are known to be cooler than the rest of the body: the tips of the ears, the nose, and the toes. Thus body temperature acts directly on the action of the gene to produce pigment in a small portion of the body and no pigment in most of the body. This is an especially clear demonstration of the chemical basis of the actions of genes, and of course chemical reactions are influenced by the physical variables we mentioned earlier: acidity, temperature, and pressure.

If we construe environment in its broadest sense, there is an important lesson here. Assume that environment includes both the internal environment of the embryo and the external environment of the postnatal organism. Heredity establishes a *potential* that requires the environment for its *realization*. The hereditary instructions are not completely specific; they are generalized blueprints whose fine details are elaborated only when development begins. The hereditary instructions are translated and acted on in an environment that can vary considerably. The greatest effect of environment occurs during the development of the structures and systems blueprinted in the genes. Specifying the *timing* of this development is an important issue for biology and psychology.

Critical Periods

In understanding developmental timing, the concept of *critical periods* has been important in both fields. The clearest demonstrations of biological

Himalayan rabbit　　Fur plucked from back　Black fur grown out in
　　　　　　　　　and ice pack applied　　plucked region

Figure 4.6 *Heredity and environment: color of fur depends partly on temperature.*

critical periods have been *transplant* experiments, especially those in salamander embryos. The lens of the salamander's eye forms from generalized embryonic tissue. If the potential lens tissue is transplanted *early* in development to the region of the left hind limb, it develops not into a lens but into hind limb tissue. But if the potential lens tissue is transplanted *late* in development, it becomes not limb tissue but a lens. There evidently are critical periods in the developmental sequence that begins with undifferentiated tissue and ends with the specialized tissue of the lens. *Before* a specific developmental period the undifferentiated cells are uncommitted and will differentiate into whatever kind of tissue they are surrounded by, even after transplantation to different body areas. *After* this critical period the cells are committed to a specific development characteristic of their original locale. Thus after the critical period tissue transplanted from the lens area will become lens tissue regardless of where it is transplanted.

Once the differentiation occurs, it is irreversible: the direction is set and the form is determined. The early, primitive cells can develop in a number of directions, but they later differentiate into specialized cells and lose their plasticity, which cannot be regained.

There are analogous *psychological* critical periods during which experiences leave a lasting mark on behavior. The best example is a phenomenon called *imprinting*. Consider the problem of a newborn animal in identifying what kind of creature it is. All animals must be able to recognize their own kind, sorting them out from the variety of animals that are about in nature. Failure to recognize one's own kind is clearly maladaptive because only members of the same species can breed successfully. If there were no mechanism by which members of the same species could recognize each other, the species would not breed successfully and would therefore die out. Furthermore, animals that are superior in recognizing each other as breeding partners will be more successful breeders, and therefore the mechanisms responsible for such recognition will be favored by natural selection.

Each species differs from all others in at least some detail of size, color, form, odor, movement, or vocalization. The most efficient recognition mechanism would be an innate and highly specific one. Such a mechanism is present in certain insects and birds; the newly hatched animal needs no experience to follow only other members of the species. The mechanism is innate and highly specific.

This highly specific recognition mechanism occurs in very few species. Most species must rely on postnatal experiences in sorting out their own kind. Natural selection operates only with what is available. Anything that enhances successful breeding will be favored by natural selection, and a less specific mechanism might work just as well as an innate highly specific mechanism for recognition. The generalized mechanism might be that *the first moving object identifies the species.* The first moving object seen by the newly hatched gosling is almost always its mother. The gosling follows this object and none other, thereby sorting out its kind from others. When the crucial stimulus is *any* moving object, a problem arises. As time passes, the gosling will see moving objects that are not geese, and it must not follow them. Thus the critical period should be long enough to acquire the special learning but brief enough to keep it specific. What the young animal learns during this period becomes so deeply ingrained that the phenomenon has been labeled *imprinting*.

How do we know that the gosling will follow *any* moving object it first sees and not just its mother? The original research was conducted by Lorenz (1965), though there were reports of similar phenomena during the last century. Lorenz raised a gaggle of geese from birth. He was the first moving object they saw, and they imprinted on him, following him everywhere (see Figure 4.7). Later one of the goslings was placed with its parents and their accompanying brood; the gosling ignored its parents and returned to Lorenz. The early learning occurred during a period when *any* moving object would be followed. In this instance Lorenz was the one the goose followed and identified with. That these geese imprinted on a human does not mean that the imprinting mechanism is flawed; this extremely artificial situation occurs rarely in nature. The mechanism works naturally almost without error.

Imprinting has been demonstrated with insects, birds, and mammals (see Sluckin, 1965 for a re-

Figure 4.7 *Goslings following the first moving object they saw — Konrad Lorenz.* (NINA LEEN)

view). Some of the research has occurred in natural settings (Lorenz', for example), but much of it has taken place in the laboratory. It was laboratory research that revealed the underlying determinants of the critical period during which the following response is learned.

Research Report

Hess (1959) performed the classical experiments on ducks and chicks. The birds were incubated in the laboratory and hatched in the dark. They were kept in individual dark boxes and removed only for the imprinting experience and later for testing. The birds saw daylight, ate, and drank only after they had been tested, so that none of these experiments contaminated the imprinting with the test of its effects. The imprinting apparatus is shown in Figure 4.8. A male decoy suspended from a moving arm proceeded around a circular runway. It was kept warm, and a loudspeaker played the call *GOCK, gock gock gock*. The young bird was placed near the decoy, the lights were turned on, and after a brief interval the decoy started on its way. The imprinting period lasted less than an hour, after which the bird was returned to its box. The entire procedure was mechanized so that there was no contact with any animals or humans, or in fact with any moving object but the imprinting stimulus.

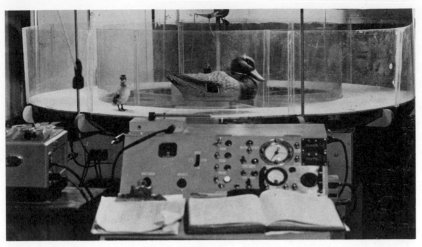

Figure 4.8 Hess's imprinting apparatus.
(ECKHARD H. HESS, THE UNIVERSITY OF CHICAGO.)

The testing procedure consisted of giving the young animal a choice between going to the male decoy to which it had been imprinted or going to a female decoy alike in shape but different in color. The male model made the gock call while the female model gave the call of the real mallard female calling her young. Four test conditions followed each other in immediate succession, and the choice of the animal in each condition was noted. If the duckling gave the positive response of walking to or staying with the object to which it had been imprinted — the male decoy — in all four of the tests, then imprinting was regarded as complete, or 100 per cent. These tests involved choices between (1) stationary and silent male and female models, (2) stationary and calling male and female models, (3) silent male model, calling female model, both stationary, and (4) stationary and silent male model, calling and moving female model.

(HESS, 1962, PP. 228-229.)

The scores derived from these four tests comprised the dependent variable. Hess varied the age (in hours) at which the ducklings were imprinted, and the findings are shown in Figure 4.9. The curve rises to a peak at 13–16 hours, and then drops to nearly zero at 26–32 hours. Thus the critical period for ducklings is less than a day; thereafter they will not follow just any object that moves.

What determines the limits of the critical period? One variable must be the ability to locomote. The following response cannot be imprinted if the bird is too immature to walk steadily and keep up with the moving stimulus. Thus the critical period starts when the bird can walk; the better it walks, the better should be the imprinting.

The critical period ends when the young animal avoids the stimulus, but why should an animal avoid a stimulus? An obvious possibility is fear, and Hess tested this notion. He exposed ducklings of various

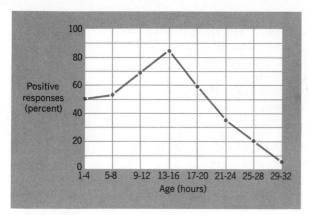

Figure 4.9 *Critical period for imprinting of duck-lings.*

ages to the decoy and counted their fear responses; fear reactions increased steadily with age. It was now clear how the critical period begins and ends: it is initiated by the ability to locomote and ended by fear reactions. It follows that the curve of increasing locomotor ability plus the curve of increasing fear reactions should yield a net curve resembling that of the critical period. Hess (1959) plotted these curves, which are shown in Figure 4.10. Locomotor ability increased rapidly from the time of hatching to its peak at 13–16

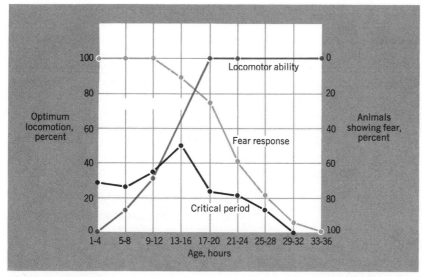

Figure 4.10 *Critical period of imprinting: a result of locomotor ability and fear interacting.*

hours, and then it levels off. Fear is absent for the first nine hours, but then it increases steadily to a peak at 33–36 hours. The third curve is a plot of the strength of imprinting, the same curve as that in Figure 4.9. Note how the imprinting curve rises as locomotor ability rises, and then drops as fear reactions increase. The fear response does not usually remain at a high level, and most animals eventually ignore the stimuli that elicited fear early in their lives.

In most species the critical period is not as sharply defined as it is for ducks, chickens, and geese. Even for these three animals the findings have not always been consistent, and it is known that imprinting can occur even in the absence of the following response. Grier et al. (1967) demonstrated this point neatly by imprinting chicks *before hatching*. They directed a beeping sound to chicken eggs for roughly one week before hatching. Shortly after hatching, the chicks were exposed to a moving toy that made the beeping sound, a novel sound, or no sound. The chicks followed the toy most when it beeped, less when it made a novel sound, and least of all when it made no sound. They clearly had been imprinted on the beeping sound, which means that the critical period for imprinting of these animals starts *before* birth.

Are there similar critical periods for mammals? Dogs will form social attachments to humans only if they are exposed to humans during the first three months after birth (Scott, 1962). If they do not interact with humans during this critical period of social attachment, they can never be completely tamed. Concerning humans, there is only speculation that there may be critical periods of development. There can be no *experimental* research for ethical reasons, and evidence bearing on critical periods in humans is indirect and inconclusive. There have been attempts to assemble some of the facts of development into a scheme that includes critical periods. One of the most comprehensive models is Thompson's (1968).

A Critical Periods Model of Development

Thompson starts by distinguishing between input and output. *Input* consists of information coming from the environment through sensory mechanisms (eyes, ears, and so on) to the brain. *Output*

consists of responses directed at the environment (walking, talking, and so on). At birth, both input and output are minimal; the newborn infant can sense little of his surroundings, nor can he do anything about them. Gradually, he begins to take in information and soon can easily distinguish a variety of sights, sounds, and smells. There is a much longer delay before he can crawl, creep, coordinate hand movements, and in general engage in integrative motor responses directed at the environment. Thompson (1968) puts it this way: "Organisms are so constructed that input must come before output, and they start gaining information about the world before they can do very much with this information" (p. 158).

Input (stimulus) differentiation is assumed to occur at a faster rate during development than does output (response) differentiation. It follows that there are three distinct age zones or critical periods of development (see Figure 4.11):

1. Both input and output are undifferentiated. The young infant can respond to his environment with only a generalized reactivity (crying, cooing, kicking, and so on) that falls under the heading of *temperament*.
2. Input becomes differentiated, but output lags behind. The older infant or young child can now clearly distinguish a variety of stimuli, especially social and emotional stimuli. He develops likes and dislikes, attachments to others and fear of others — in brief, a set of *affective meanings*.
3. Both input and output are differentiated. "During this age-zone, due to the gain in output or response differentiation, complex learning gains ascendancy. Affective cues can now come to elicit coping or instrumental response" (Thompson, 1968, p. 181).

Thus the child learns how to solve problems and how to make his way in the world, that is, he learns *instrumental-meaning*.

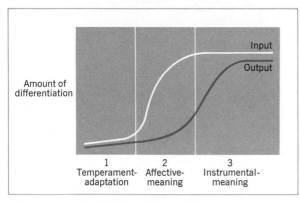

Amount of differentiation

Input

Output

| 1 | 2 | 3 |
| Temperament-adaptation | Affective-meaning | Instrumental-meaning |

Figure 4.11 Critical periods and input-output differentiations (Thompson, 1968, p. 159).

THE TEMPERAMENT-ADAPTATION PERIOD. The extremely young animal, though incapable of fine discriminations and coordinated responses, can be aroused by the sheer presence of stimulation. It can gradually become accustomed to mild stimuli, a process called *habituation*. And it can learn precisely the opposite—to become aroused or fearful when confronted with strong stimuli— a process called *sensitization*.[3]

Thus the effects of very early experience may move the young organism in one of two directions: toward being placid and relatively unemotional or toward being excitable and relatively emotional. At our present state of knowledge, it is not easy to predict which direction a given animal will take. The effects of early experience are extremely complex, permitting no simple generalizations. But most researchers agree that early experience can profoundly affect the animal's general levels of arousal and emotionality—that is, *temperament-adaptation.*

THE AFFECTIVE-MEANING PERIOD. During this age-zone input differentiates, while output remains primitive and diffuse. The young child can recognize and distinguish a variety of stimuli, both social and nonsocial, but can respond only with gross, generalized behavior. He is capable of emotional conditioning, whereby his reflexive approach or avoidance responses become attached to previously neutral stimuli. Thus a child can learn to fear many objects and events which are intrinsically harmless. The process consists of linking a harmless stimulus to a dangerous one, so that after such pairing the harmless one comes to elicit fear and avoidance. This learning, called *classical conditioning,*[4] is the source of the many fears of childhood.

This is also the critical period of socialization, when animals and (presumably) humans learn social attachments. The child learns the positive value of (affection for) the familiar persons (and locales) around him and the negative value (fear) of strangers and unfamiliar surroundings. The young animal's perceptual abilities sharpen considerably during this period, but its response output remains relatively undifferentiated—mainly approach, avoidance, and emotional responses.

THE INSTRUMENTAL-MEANING PERIOD. During this age-zone, output differentiates, and the child can gradually begin to cope with his environment. A predominantly emotional, involuntary orientation shifts to a predominantly instrumental, voluntary orientation. For example, previously the child smiled almost reflexively as a passive reaction to familiar adults; now he smiles voluntarily as an active response that elicits pleasant reactions from adults.

The child now learns to connect responses with their consequences, a process called *instrumental learning,* which may be viewed as learning the meaning of the various instrumental responses available to the child.[5] It leads to purposive, goal-directed behavior, as the child acquires more of the behavioral means that enable him to attain his goals. He can more readily inhibit immediate, impulsive responses in favor of the long-range responses that he knows will eventually lead to the reward. In brief, the child learns the capabilities that allow him to shift from a passive, emotional reactor to an active, instrumental seeker. The characteristics of this period, together with the rest of the model, are summarized in Table 4.2.

Organization

Thompson's model specifies three critical periods, each with its dominant kind of learning. At the end

---

[3] *Habituation and sensitization are discussed in Chapter 12.*

[4] *Classical conditioning is discussed in Chapter 13.*

[5] *Instrumental learning is discussed in Chapter 14.*

Table 4.2
Model of Critical Periods of Development (Thompson, 1968)

ZONE	DIFFERENTIATION		BEHAVIOR MAINLY CHANGED	DOMINANT TYPE OF LEARNING
	INPUT	OUTPUT		
Temperament-adaptation	Low	Low	Generalized arousal	Habituation
Affective-meaning	High	Low	Social and emotional reactions to specific cues	Classical (emotional) conditioning
Instrumental-meaning	High	High	Specific acts that alter the environment	Instrumental conditioning

of the development (adulthood) these three might exist side-by-side (see Figure 4.12a). This model assumes that habituation dominates early in development, with emotional conditioning and instrumental learning assuming importance in successive later stages of development. At the end of development, all three would be roughly equal in importance. This model assumes minimal organization, each component merely existing together with the other two.

An alternative model assumes a *hierarchy* of components (see Figure 4.12b).[6] At first habituation dominates, but in the second period it diminishes and yields to emotional conditioning. In the last period of development, instrumental learning becomes dominant over the other two. Thus in the adult most learning concerns solving problems; there is some emotional conditioning and very little habituation.

This hierarchical model of learning processes

[6] *A hierarchy is essentially a* vertical *organization, with higher elements dominating lower elements. In a military hierarchy, for example, a major gives orders to a captain, who gives orders to a lieutenant, and so on.*

illustrates a broad approach to development, the orthogenetic theory of Werner (1948). He assumed that there are sequential stages of phases of development. The earliest psychological processes in development are primitive, rigid, relatively undifferentiated, and low on the evolutionary scale. These are followed by more mature processes, which are flexible, relatively differentiated, and high on the evolutionary scale. Though earlier, primitive tendencies wane in importance, they do not disappear. Rather, they are organized into a hierarchy of processes in which later ones dominate and earlier ones are held under inhibitory control. This abstract sequence can be made concrete by examining one aspect of sensory-motor development.

It concerns what Bruner (1969) has called "the mysterious midline barrier." What happens when an infant, having grasped a toy in his right hand, is presented with an object on his right side? If he is 6 months old, he may bang it with his closed right hand but make no attempt to cross the midline and grasp it with his left hand (see Figure 4.13a). His sensory-motor coordination is primitive, inflexibly bound by the implicit rule, "Objects seen on

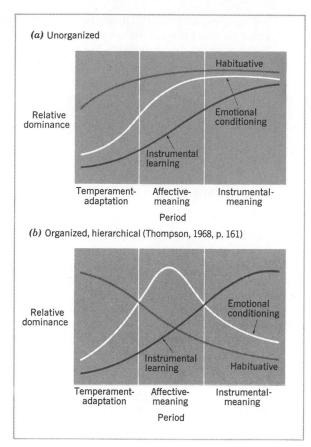

(a) Unorganized

Relative dominance

Habituative

Emotional conditioning

Instrumental learning

Temperament-adaptation | Affective-meaning | Instrumental-meaning

Period

(b) Organized, hierarchical (Thompson, 1968, p. 161)

Relative dominance

Emotional conditioning

Instrumental learning

Habituative

Temperament-adaptation | Affective-meaning | Instrumental-meaning

Period

Figure 4.12 Unorganized and organized systems in development.

one side are grasped only by the hand on that side." As he matures, the infant develops new sensory-motor processes, and by 18 months he can reach across the midline barrier to pick up an object with the opposite hand (see Figure 4.13b). Now he is following a more advanced, flexible rule, "Pick up objects with the free hand." The old rule has not been discarded, and objects on the right side will still be picked up by the right hand, if it is free. But this earlier, "same-sided" tendency is now part of a hierarchy, and it can be inhibited and superseded by a more advanced developmental tendency.

Children acquire sensory-motor coordination through play and games. When a boy first tries to

throw a football toward a moving receiver, he aims directly at the receiver (see Figure 4.14a). During the brief interval of the ball's flight, the receiver moves forward a few feet and the ball lands behind him. As the boy matures and practices, he inhibits his inclination to throw at the target. This primitive tendency is surrendered for a more advanced one: throwing ahead of the receiver (see Figure 4.14b). In this new mode, the boy aims the football so that its trajectory intersects the path of the running receiver. The earlier method is still available when the target is stationary, but the newer method overrides it when the target is running.

Other examples of this kind of organization may be found in perception, thinking, and memory. Heinz Werner and Jean Piaget, outstanding developmental theorists, assume that such sequences and organizations govern all aspects of psychological development.[7] Their theories specify the stages and the processes in considerable detail, especially in the area of cognitive behavior (see Chapter 17).

[7] *This model of development is discussed at the end of the chapter.*

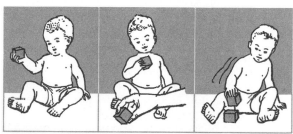

(a)

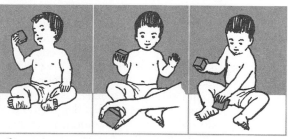

(b)

Figure 4.13 The mysterious midline barrier (Bruner, 1969).

Figure 4.14 The development of sensory-motor coordination.

(a)   (b)

Self-Regulation

When a system is organized hierarchically, it is capable of inhibitory control. Dominant components can regulate subordinate components, either allowing behavior to occur or inhibiting it. Such regulation gradually increases throughout the developmental period, reaching a peak at maturity. For example, in our culture very young boys are allowed to cry when they are hurt, frustrated, or rejected. It is too early for them to inhibit the affective response. However, they are pressured throughout childhood to suppress tears, which are considered a sign of weakness and femininity. Gradually, inhibitory control is achieved and most American men refrain from weeping except at funerals.

In a sense, the development of all mammalian young may be regarded as moving toward self-regulation. The helpless newborn depends completely on those around him for the very sustenance of life. This biological dependence is matched by psychological dependence. Parents or substitute caretakers must offer the child both social stimulation and controlling supervision if he is gradually to take his place as a member of the group. Step by step, the child begins more actively to explore his social environment and more independently to control his own behavior.

All societies demand at least minimal self-regulation by their adult members. The young child must first achieve bowel and bladder con-

trol, and assume responsibility for feeding himself. Later he must master the tensions of waiting and delay of gratification. In brief, the control of behavior passes, at least in part, from others to the individual himself. Examples range from early control over excretion to later ability to forego immediate rewards in working toward a distant goal.

In our own society, we demand that adults resist temptation and operate within a given code of morality. Young children cannot achieve such self-regulation, and one of the major aspects of socialization concerns this issue: *self*-control of forbidden impulses (see Chapter 23).

Heredity and Environment

Heredity and environment, in combination, account for all behavior—indeed, for all life. But one can be emphasized at the expense of the other in attempting to explain behavior. Thus there are hereditarians and environmentalists. This issue of nature versus nurture has been pronounced dead many times, but it is surely a lively ghost and the issues remain as controversial and important today as they were at the turn of the century.

One point must be clarified immediately. It makes no sense to compare heredity with environment *in a single individual.* Each of us is a joint product of the two influences, and there is no way of disentangling them. But there are methods of attributing behavior to heredity or environment across groups of individuals. For example, we can determine whether identical twins show more similar behavior than do fraternal twins. If they do, then we can infer that the behavior has a clear hereditary component, making the reasonable assumption that identical twins are treated no more alike than are fraternal twins. In brief, using appropriate methods of study, we can distinguish between heredity and environment so long as we refer to *groups* of persons, not to the individual. An example of behavior that is strongly determined by heredity is intelligence (see Chapter 24).

We have been using the terms heredity and environment as though their meanings were precise and consensual. That they are not is illustrated by this example:

Gravid female moths, hyponomenta padella, *lay their eggs on the leaves of the hackberry plant and die shortly thereafter. The eggs hatch, the larvae eat the leaves and eventually become mature. Females of this new generation in turn select hackberry leaves on which to deposit their eggs. Another race of moths prefer apple leaves as an oviposition site. The difference between the two races has been perpetuated, generation after generation, for many centuries. It would appear to be the example par excellence of a genetically-controlled behavior trait. But such an explanation is insufficient.*

When eggs of the apple-preferring type are transferred to hackberry leaves, the larvae thrive on the new diet. Thirty per cent of the females developing from these larvae show a preference for hackberry leaves when it comes time for them to deposit their eggs. (BEACH, 1955, P. 408.)

Thus an apparently clear instance of genetically determined behavior turns out, on closer examination, to be partly determined by the environment. Does this mean that the behavior is not innate? And where does heredity end and environment begin?

Four Factors

To answer these questions, we shall use a scheme modified from Hebb (1966). There are four factors or determinants that influence behavior: genetic, biological, psychological-constant, and psychological-variable:

1. *Genetic.* This factor is the genetic material (DNA), which contains a blueprint for the developing organism. The genes comprise the hereditary variable; the other three factors are environmental, either internal or external.
2. *Biological.* This factor includes all the internal chemical and biological variables that affect development before and after birth: nutrition and oxygen from the mother to the fetus, the elimination of waste products, and the presence of drugs, poisons, or any physical events that damage or destroy tissues. Also included are all the external variables that determine postnatal growth: sufficient and varied nutrition, absence of poisons such as polluted air or water, and negative physical influences. In brief, the biological factor consists of all the

nonpsychological variables in the environment that possibly affect behavior.
3. *Psychological-constant.* This factor includes experiences that normally occur before and after birth in the lives of *all members of the species.* Stimulation is minimal during the fetal period, but there are enough stimuli to elicit reflexes, especially toward the end of pregnancy. After birth, all infants are *normally* exposed to a mother and to a range of sensory events: sights, sounds, smells, and physical contacts.
4. *Psychological-variable.* This factor includes the experiences that vary from one member of the species to the next. They are of course postnatal events, the psychological stimuli of the fetal period being common for all members of the species. Thus one infant might be given much attention, many toys, and generally enriched environment; another might be given little attention, few or no toys, and a generally impoverished environment.

This classification may help in removing ambiguites from such widely used concepts as "constitutional," "innate," and "experiential." Table 4.3 summarizes the relationship between these concepts and the four factors. *Constitutional* refers to the genetic and biological factors—that is, all the nonpsychological determinants of behavior. *Innate* includes not only genetic and biological factors but also the early experiences we label psychological-constant. Finally, *experiential* refers to the two nonbiological factors, psychological-constant and psychological-variable; it comprises all the psychological stimulation ever received by the organism.

Unlearned Behavior

We have avoided using the term *unlearned* because it is more ambiguous than the other concepts. The ambiguity originates in two meanings of the term *learned:* (1) behavior determined mainly by the psychological-variable factor, the highly specific experiences of the individual organism; and (2) behavior determined mainly by the psychological-constant factor, the generalized experiences of all normal members of the species.

Table 4.3
Concepts and Factors in Development

CONCEPT	FACTORS
Constitutional	= Genetic, biological
Innate	= Genetic, biological + psychological-constant
Experiential	= Psychological-constant + psychological-variable

With learning so defined, it follows that, aside from a few simple reflexes, all behavior is learned. But if all behavior is learned, how can there be unlearned behavior? Hebb (1966) resolves the paradox:

This does not say that all higher behavior is "learned," in the usual sense of that word: much of it is unlearned, but dependent on previous learning. The first temper tantrum; the spontaneous avoidance of strangers at about six months of age in man, four months in the chimpanzee; the first new sentence constructed by the child, or the first imaginative response; none of these can be called learned behavior, but all require other learning that has resulted from exposure to the normal environment of the species. (P. 158.)

Hebb is pointing out the importance of the psychological-constant factor. Most of us are aware of the genetic and biological factors, and individual experiences press on us everyday. But it is easy to forget that much of the stimulation that occurs early in life is not individual but common to all members of the species. Its effects are best seen when this factor is *subtracted* from the life of the individual, as in the following two experiments with rats.

Female rats normally build nests and suckle their young immediately after birth. Birch (1956) reasoned that early licking experiences were an important determiner of such behavior. To test this reasoning, he prevented such licking. Young female rats were fitted with rubber collars large enough to prevent self-licking but not other activities (see Figure 4.15). When these females reached maturity, they bred and had normal pregnancies. Just before the birth of their offspring, the collars were removed. Birth was normal, but maternal behavior was not. These mothers generally failed to retrieve their young or suckle them properly. Worse still, when they first licked the pups, they promptly ate them. Self-licking evidently inhibits biting and eating responses. When self-licking was prevented, the inhibition failed to develop, and the mothers' licking their pups led directly to eating.

Riess (1954) took female rat puppies from their mothers after weaning and reared them in empty cages. As adults, these rats bred and subsequently gave birth to their own young. But they did not suckle the offspring—they merely carried them around like objects; and their nests were poorly constructed.

The mothering activities of female rats (building a nest, suckling young, and retrieving them) are unlearned behaviors, but they depend upon prior experiences (licking, contact with mother, presence of nest-building materials). When this early stimulation is denied them, the unlearned behavior expected of this species simply does not occur. Thus we can appreciate the importance of the psychological-constant factor by subtracting it from the organism's experience and discovering that later behavior is grossly abnormal.

Maturation

Physical maturation, determined by genetic and biological factors, proceeds along systematic lines. Certain zones of the body grow faster than others, and developmental trends of this kind affect the maturation of *motor behavior*. Two trends are of immediate interest. The first, called *cephalocaudal* development, proceeds from the head (*cephalo-*) to the bottom of the backbone or tail (*caudal*). At first the head end develops faster, and only late in development does the tail end begin to catch up. Thus an infant can control his arm movements before his leg movements,

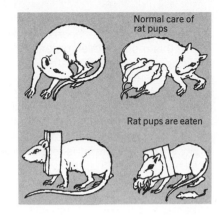

Figure 4.15 An example of a psychological-constant factor: self-licking.

and his head before his trunk.

Proximodistal development proceeds from the center of the body to the periphery, and from the trunk to the limbs. The sequence of growth and motor control moves from near to far: upper arm, lower arm, hand, fingers.

The two developmental trends, cephalocaudal and proximodistal, are diagramed in Figure 4.16. These *physical* maturation sequences are determined by the blueprints in the genes, as they are worked out during development. No psychological variables are involved, only the genes and the biological environment in which they function.

In contrast, psychological maturation involves early experience, the stimulation common to all members of the species. But how can the effects of the psychological-constant factor be distin-

guished from those of the psychological-variable factor? One way would be to select a pair of identical twins, which would control for the genetic factor and minimize any differences due to the biological factor. Then one twin would be given special training and the other twin, none. Presumably, there are no differences between twins in the psychological-constant factor, so that any differences in behavior would have to be attributed to the psychological-variable factor.

This is what McGraw (1935) did in her classical study of twins.[8] One twin, Johnny, was trained in a number of motor skills long before the other one, Jimmy. Later, Jimmy practiced activi-

[8] *The twins were later identified as fraternal, not identical, but the difference was not essential in this study.*

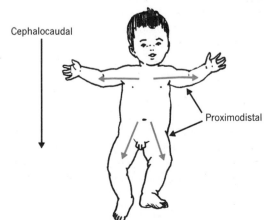

Figure 4.16 Cephalocaudal and proximodistal development.

ties that Johnny had already practiced, and thereafter the twins were tested and compared periodically.

In activities common to all of us, Jimmy caught up with Johnny very quickly: creeping, walking, and grasping objects. Practicing these motor acts conferred no special benefit, Johnny being no further advanced than Jimmy or a comparable group of normal infants.

In activities involving complex motor coordination, Jimmy never caught up to Johnny. These activities are acquired by only some members of the species: riding a tricycle, climbing, and roller skating. Practicing these complex, coordinated skills conferred special benefits, which were maintained for a long period of time. Beyond this study with twins, there is abundant evidence that early special training of children in such sports as tennis and swimming has life-long effects on the level at which these sports are performed. Concerning highly individual activities, the earlier the training, the higher the maximal level of performance.

These facts suggest that the psychological-constant and psychological-variable factors affect different kinds of behavior. Early sensory experience (psychological-constant) is required for those activities expected of all normal humans. Performance of an act like walking requires no special training and will not benefit from such training. But for complex skills, mastered by only some persons, special training (psychological-variable) is required; in general, the earlier the training is received, the better is subsequent performance.

Two Developmental Models

In studying the period from birth to maturity, one can assume that man is passive or active.[9] Each assumption generates a developmental model of man.

The Passive Model

The infant is assumed to begin life as a "blank slate" on which messages are laid down by experience. He is shaped entirely by his environment, or

in the words of a mental hospital patient, "I am a product of what has been done to me."

In this model, development consists of the accumulation of learning—the growth of knowledge, of a response repertoire, and of skill in responding. There is no universal *sequence* in development, only the sequence in which learning occurs—and this varies from one child to the next.

If this model appears familiar, it is because it closely fits the stimulus-response approach that was outlined in Chapter 1. The passive model is essentially the stimulus-response approach to development. The person is a product of what he learns, and the only "built-in" tendency is a readiness to learn. In these terms, development consists of the addition of stimulus-response connections.

The Active Model

This model assumes that the newborn infant has preprogramed tendencies to interact with the environment in certain ways. Man presumably becomes what he makes of himself; he takes the lead in dealing with the environment, rather than merely receiving stimuli passively. His experiences during the course of development shape the *content* of his behavior, but the *form* of his behavior (the *way* he perceives, learns, or reasons) is determined by an orderly, universal sequence of *stages*. Thus a prelanguage stage is followed by a language stage, which alters the way the child stores experience. The shift from prelanguage to language in dealing with the environment concerns the *form* of behavior, and it is a universal sequence. The *content* of the language—English, Spanish, or any other language—depends of course on the immediate environment in which the child develops.

If this model seems familiar, it is because it closely fits the cognitive approach outlined in Chapter 1. Cognitive theorists focus on how the child *re*-presents the environment and how he organizes experience. They assume that these *formal* aspects of behavior (the *how* rather than the what) develop in a fixed, universal sequence.

[9] *This discussion derives from one by Langer (1969).*

Contrasts and Implications

The two models take divergent positions on several issues discussed in this chapter. Concerning the heredity-environment interaction, the active model assumes a strong inherited component in development (specifically, the *form* of behavior), whereas the passive model assumes that the environment is the major determinant. Concerning development trends, the passive model embraces only growth (the steady accumulation of experiences), whereas the active model emphasizes differentiation and hierarchical organization.

As general strategies in studying behavior, the two models have implications beyond development. Thus the passive model implies that man is merely a pawn in the hands of fate, directed by the events that befall him, whereas the active model sees man as a self-actualizer who largely determines his own fate. The passive model regards a child as being socialized by parents and others; the active model regards a child as modifying the actions of those who attempt to socialize him. The passive model sees the nervous system as a reflexive organ, receiving sensory inputs and transmitting motor outputs; the active model sees the nervous system as an integrative computer that plans programs for subsequent action.

In brief, the passive model treats man more as a *physical* object with minimal organization. This model attempts to understand man in the simplest terms and with the fewest assumptions. The active model treats man as a *biological* organism with very complex organization; in attempting to understand such complexity, an insistence on simplicity and parsimony would be foolish. These two strategies will appear repeatedly throughout the book, as we proceed through various aspects of behavior.

chapter 5

the nervous system

*What the nervous system does — the neuron —
conduction — reliability and speed — transmission — the synapse — neural transmitters — parallel
and divergent transmission — evolution of
nervous systems — nerve nets — the central
nervous system — why the brain is in the head —
dominance of the forebrain — dominance of the
cerebral cortex — horizontal, vertical, and
circular organization of the brain — models
of the nervous system*

Why should we study the nervous system? We do so for essentially the same reason we look under the hood of an automobile to understand what makes it go. The driver needs no knowledge of the engine and transmission to drive his car, but without such knowledge he cannot possibily comprehend the mechanical basis of his transportation. Similarly, we could examine behavior at its own level, with no knowledge of the nervous system, but we would then fail to understand the underlying "mechanics" of behavior.

The human nervous system has four distinct functions: communication, coordination, storage, and programing (see Figure 5.1).

1. *Communication:* Receiving information from the environment and from inside the body, and sending it to and from the brain.
2. *Coordination:* Controlling the activities of various parts of the body so that behavior is integrated rather than disjointed and fragmented.
3. *Storage:* Encoding and storing experiences so that they can be used later as a basis of action.
4. *Programing:* Setting in motion plans for fu-

(1) Communication	(2) Coordination	(3) Storage	(4) Programing
Sees attractive college girl	Moves closer to her and starts a conversation	Remembers that she is in his psychology class	Plans to ask her to the demonstration that evening

Figure 5.1 Four functions of our nervous system.

ture actions; engaging in covert, implicit ("inside the head") rehearsal of behavior.

These are properties of the brains of many animals, but they are seen in the most advanced form in man. In fact, evolutionary trends in behavior are mirrored in the evolution of nervous systems, from very simple ones in lower forms to the intricate and complex one in man.

The Neuron

The basic unit of all nervous systems is the *neuron,* a cell specialized for the conduction and transmission of information. Many kinds of neurons have evolved, each adapted to a particular function. For simplicity, we need distinguish only three types:

1. *Sensory* neurons are specialized to relay information over long distances from receptors (eyes, ears, and so on) *toward* the brain.
2. *Motor* neurons relay information over long distances *from* the brain to effectors (muscles and glands).
3. *Association* neurons spread information over very short distances but among a broad network of similar neurons.

Sensory and motor neurons are essential for fast, sure conduction of messages—the *communication* function of the nervous system. Asso-

ciation neurons are needed to spread the message to the various components of the nervous system—the *integration* function.

The form of a particular neuron varies with its specialized function, which means that there are many sizes and shapes of neuron. For exposition, it suffices to present a schematic, "typical" neuron (see Figure 5.2). The *cell body* helps to nourish the neuron and keep it operating. From this cell body project *dendrites,* which branch off as do the branches of trees. There is also an *axon,* which is longer and has few branches; the axon—or each of its branches—terminates in a brushlike end branch, which lies close to the processes of other nerve cells or connects with muscles or glands. In the simplest case, the nerve impulse (message) proceeds: dendrite → cell body → axon → end branch. The *passage* of the nerve impulse down the neuron to the end of the axon is called *conduction.* The *transfer* of the impulse to the next neuron (or to a muscle or gland) is called *transmission.*

Conduction

The fastest, surest path for a message to take through the nervous system is along the axon of a large sensory or motor neuron. The axons of these neurons are specialized for reliability and speed in conducting neural impulses.

RELIABILITY. The nerve impulse is an *electrical* phenomenon, a sudden current that surges down

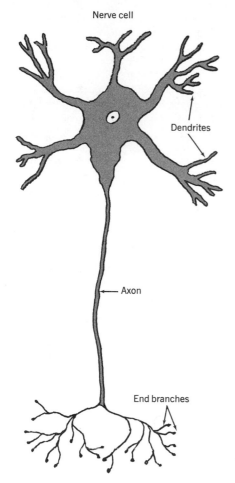

Nerve cell

Dendrites

Axon

End branches

Figure 5.2 *Idealized diagram of a neuron.*

the length of the axon.[1] A neuron will initiate a nerve impulse only when it is sufficiently stimulated. Each neuron has its own *threshold of stimulation:* below this intensity of stimulation, the neuron does not fire; at or above this intensity, it fires.

When the neuron is adequately stimulated, it fires a nerve impulse of a given specific intensity. This intensity is constant; if the neuron fires at all, the resulting nerve impulse is always at the same strength. This characteristic is described by the

all-or-none law: the neuron either fires completely or not at all. The input to the neuron merely triggers the nerve impulse; it has no effect on its intensity.

In this respect the firing of the neuron is analogous to the firing of a pistol. The velocity of the bullet depends solely on the amount of explosive, not on trigger pressure. Slight pressure on the trigger yields no response; sufficient pressure attains the threshold, and the bullet is fired; still more pressure has no effect. Like the firing of a bullet, the firing of a neuron depends on sufficient stimulation, but the intensity and duration of the nerve impulse depend solely on properties of the neuron itself.

Thus the neuron carries its own "explosive." The

[1] *This electrical occurrence is believed to be based on the exchange of sodium and potassium ions through the membrane of the axon; study of such submicroscopic events is best left to students of neurophysiology.*

nerve impulse moves rapidly down the axon, and at each point along the way the electrical impulse is renewed. This means that the impulse is *propagated without decrement:* its intensity is constant, remaining the same at the end of the axon as it was at the beginning. In brief, this means of conducting the impulse is *reliable.*

SPEED. Animals low in the evolutionary scale tend to be small and slow moving, and their nerve impulses need not travel fast or far. A worm burrowing through the earth is not often confronted with sudden stimuli; even if it were, its muscular apparatus is not (and need not be) geared for quick response. Animals that must react quickly to a variety of sudden stimuli possess neural adaptations that increase speed of conduction:

1. *Fiber diameter.* The larger the diameter of a nerve fiber (axon), the faster is neural conduction along it. Lower forms tend to have fibers of smaller diameter, and higher forms tend to have fibers of larger diameter.

2. *Myelin sheath.* So far we have described only *unmyelinated* nerve fibers—those without an insulating sheath. A *myelinated* nerve fiber is surrounded by a myelin sheath that provides insulation from the environment around the axon (see Figure 5.3). The sheath is broken at short intervals, called the *nodes of Ranvier,* at which the axon membrane is bare. In a myelinated fiber the nerve impulse hops from one node to the next, skipping over the sections between the nodes. This kind of conduction is somewhat faster than conduction in an unmyelinated fiber; for example, a myelinated frog nerve fiber can conduct at the same speed as a unmyelinated squid nerve fiber—fifty times larger—can conduct. With few exceptions, vertebrates have myelinated fibers and invertebrates do not, and there is a corresponding increase in the speed of con-

duction as we move up the evolutionary scale from invertebrates to vertebrates.

3. *Warmbloodedness.* Like most biological processes, conduction is speeded by heat. The higher the temperature, the faster is neural conduction. The body temperature of a cold-blooded animal varies with the environment. When the environment is cool, neural conduction is slow and the animal's reactions are sluggish. When the environment is warm, conduction is faster and so are the animal's reactions. Mammals, being warmblooded, maintain an even, warm body temperature; thus their neural conduction is on the average faster than that of coldblooded animals.

In brief, there are several adaptations that increase the speed of neural conduction. Increased fiber size, which has the disadvantage of requiring excessive space within the animal, is present mainly in lower forms. The myelin sheath is a vertebrate adaptation. Warm, constant temperature is a mammalian adaptation. Neural conduction is thus an example of progress in evolution: more advanced forms have faster conduction without an increase in the size of axons. The highest speed of conduction is found in myelinated, mammalian nerves—approximately 200 miles per hour.

Transmission

For a nerve impulse to jump from one neuron to the next, it must overcome a barrier. It is at this point, the junction between two neurons, that control and integration are achieved. The nervous system—especially the brain—must be protected from trivial messages. These can be stopped at the barrier, just as a secretary protects her boss from unnecessary distractions. But the brain must

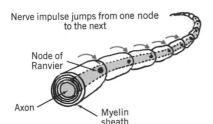

Figure 5.3 *Myelin sheath: an adaptation for speed.*

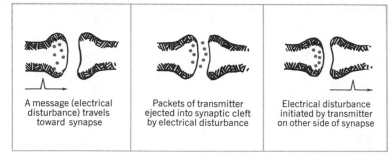

| A message (electrical disturbance) travels toward synapse | Packets of transmitter ejected into synaptic cleft by electrical disturbance | Electrical disturbance initiated by transmitter on other side of synapse |

Figure 5.4 *Details of synaptic transmission.*

also be open to important messages; these can be pushed through the barrier by means of facilitating mechanisms.

THE SYNAPSE. The barrier, or junction, between two neurons is called the *synapse:* the *functional* connection between the axon terminal of one neuron and a dendrite (or cell body) of another neuron. Transmission across a synapse is *chemical* (see Figure 5.4). The nerve impulse surges down the axon of the *sending* neuron, causing the release of a transmitter substance. This chemical diffuses to the dendrite of the *receiving* neuron, causing an electrical disturbance in the receiving neuron. If the disturbance is strong enough, the receiving neuron will fire. (This is the *threshold* notion we discussed in the previous section.)

A receiving neuron is connected synaptically with many sending neurons. The synapse just described is *excitatory:* the input from the sending neuron causes an electric disturbance on the receiving neuron, which fires if its threshold is reached.

An excitatory synapse enhances transmission; an *inhibitory* synapse diminishes it. The inhibitory neuron releases a substance that renders it more difficult for the receiving neuron to fire. These two kinds of synapses, excitatory and inhibitory, complement each other in achieving neural control. One lowers the barrier, allowing important messages to go through; the other raises the barrier, stopping trivial messages.[2]

NEUROHUMORS. The chemicals underlying transmission of the nerve impulse from one neuron to another are called *neurohumors.* These

[2] *Each sending neuron is either excitatory or inhibitory. In this respect, there are two kinds of neurons, one inhibitory and the other excitatory.*

substances act very fast in stimulating the receiving neuron, and so long as they are present in sufficient quantity at the synapse, the receiving neuron fires. To prevent such sustained transmission, inhibiting chemicals neutralize the neurohumors. Thus there are two kinds of chemicals underlying neural transmission: one to overcome the synaptic barrier and another to prevent excessive transmission.

What would happen if there were either too much or too little transmitter substance at the synapse? One answer has come from studies on the effects of many of the drugs currently being used. Lysergic acid diethylamide (LSD) is chemically similar to one brain neurohumor, and amphetamine is similar to another. It is believed that such drugs trigger excessive transmission of nerve impulses, thereby causing the abnormal states sought after by the drug user (peculiar sensations, images, and thoughts).

Drugs related to neurohumors may also be beneficial. Some of the forms of severe behavior disturbance, especially depression, may be caused by the presence of abnormal neurohumors. Drugs related to neurohumors have successfully altered mood states — either by elevating a depressed mood or tranquilizing a state of anxiety.

SUMMATION. At an excitatory synapse, the sending neuron causes a small electrical disturbance at the receiving neuron. If the input is too small to reach the threshold, the receiving neuron does not fire and the small disturbance fades away. But if a second input arrives from the sending neuron before the first has completely disappeared, the two inputs summate. Where a single input might not be intense enough to make the neuron fire, the sum of two inputs might reach the threshold and cause the receiving neuron to

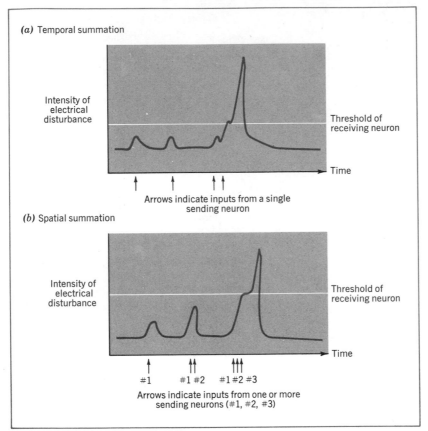

(a) Temporal summation

Intensity of electrical disturbance

Threshold of receiving neuron

Time

Arrows indicate inputs from a single sending neuron

(b) Spatial summation

Intensity of electrical disturbance

Threshold of receiving neuron

Time

#1   #1 #2   #1 #2 #3

Arrows indicate inputs from one or more sending neurons (#1, #2, #3)

Figure 5.5 *Temporal and spatial summation.*

fire. This combined effect is called *temporal* summation (see Figure 5.5a).

The receiving neuron has many excitatory synapses. An input from any one of these might not reach threshold, but if inputs from three sending neurons arrived simultaneously, they might cause the receiving neuron to fire. This is called *spatial* summation (see Figure 5.5b).

Inhibitory synapses can also summate, the inputs erecting a formidable barrier against transmission of the message. Receiving neurons have both excitatory and inhibitory synapses. When both excitatory and inhibitory sending neurons fire, the outcome depends on the *algebraic* sum of these opposing inputs, a "consensus" of the sending neurons. Thus the events occurring at the synapse of a single receiving neuron are extremely complex. With this in mind, consider

the complexity of the human brain with its 10 billion neurons.

Parallel and Divergent Transmission

Let us return to two of the basic functions of the nervous system: rapid, reliable communication and integrated control. One is carried out at the expense of the other. Fast, reliable movement of impulses requires relatively uninterrupted neural paths and impulses of sufficient intensity to overcome the barriers imposed by high thresholds at synapses; the solution is *parallel transmission*, which occurs when neurons are bunched together side by side (see Figure 5.6a). When dendrites and cell bodies are in such close proximity, they tend to receive inputs at the same time. The nerve impulses are conducted down the parallel axons and reach the synapse at the same time, at almost the same place. This convergence of impulses in space and time enhances their *summation,* which increases the intensity of the excitatory input to the receiving neuron, thereby guaranteeing transmission of the nerve impulses. Parallel transmission may be found wherever there is a need for fast, sure transmission of nerve impulses.

Parallel transmission delivers a rapid, reliable message, but it does not allow for the spread of the message to other centers, which is necessary for integration and modulation of neural impulses. For the spread of communication, divergent transmission is necessary (see Figure 5.6b). The path of the impulses diverges and splits up into a network that connects many neurons. If parallel transmission resembles a throughway that enables transportation to occur with swiftness and certainty, divergent transmission resembles a network of back roads that allow only slow, unsure transportation but cover the countryside. Divergent transmission is less reliable but needed for integration. Thus both parallel and divergent transmission are needed, parallel for speedy delivery of messages and divergent for spreading the communication to many associative neurons so that modulation and integration can occur.

Evolution of Nervous Systems

One-celled organisms neither possess nor need a nervous system. Such systems originated in primitive animals, and the evolution of nervous systems was one component of the evolutionary trends toward more complex and specialized animals. The human nervous system is the most specialized one known, and its complexity stands as a barrier to understanding how it works.

Our approach will be to start with simpler nervous systems and to outline the specializations that were added in the course of evolution. One component originated in passive, primitive sea animals; another, in lowly worms; and a third, as recently as primate evolution. The specializations may be divided into three sequential phases:

1. Neural control becomes *centralized.*
2. The *brain* evolves and comes to dominate the nervous system.

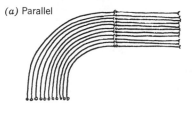

(a) Parallel

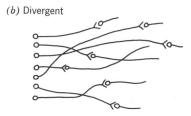

(b) Divergent

Figure 5.6 *Parallel and divergent transmisson (Hebb, 1966).*

3. A specialized brain tissue, the *cerebral cortex,* evolves and becomes the most dominant component in the brain.

The Nerve Net

The most primitive nervous system, the nerve net, is found in the *Hydra,* a lowly sea creature that moves slowly if at all (see Figure 5.7). The neurons are spread around the outer layers of the animal in an unspecialized network. Nerve impulses move slowly in all directions, as the message is distributed throughout the body. This slow, diffuse communication is all that this slow-moving animal needs. When the animal's requirements are this minimal, even a nerve net is sufficient, and this kind of nervous system has been retained as a component of more advanced systems. For example, the human digestive system contains nerve nets, which are sufficient to control the sluggish movement of food through the digestive tract. We become aware of the presence of this primitive nervous system only when confronted with indigestion: the pain is a diffuse, generalized sensation, in keeping with the diffuse, generalized character of the nerve net.

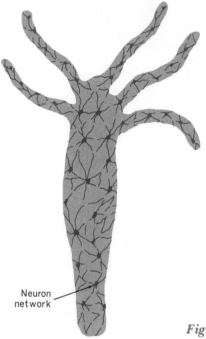

Neuron
network

Hydra

*Figure 5.7 A primitive nervous
system: the nerve net of the Hydra.*

The Central Nervous System

As higher animals evolved, their tissues specialized and became more organized. As part of the trend toward greater complexity and organization, the nervous system split into *central* and *peripheral* portions. Our line is descended from bilaterally symmetrical animals (left and right side are mirror-images), which comprise most of the higher forms of animal life. Organized for locomotion, they have a long axis, a head end, and a tail end. And they are segmented.

The roundworm, *Nereis,* illustrates a simple form of central nervous system (see Figure 5.8). The system is segmented, with clumps of cell bodies clustering to form knobs in each segment. These clusters are ganglia, agglomerates of neurons' cell bodies specialized for relaying messages. The ganglion in each segment serves as a relay station for that segment.

This system communicates messages, usually from more dominant parts of the nervous system, to effectors. It is so successful an adaptation that it has been retained, with some modification, in larger forms. Our bodies contain chains of ganglia parallel to the spinal cord. These chains of *sympathetic ganglia* relay messages from the spinal cord to a variety of visceral organs, including heart, lungs, stomach, and bladder.

Why the Brain Is in the Head

The presence of ganglia marks a significant step forward in the evolution of neural control. They are the precursors of brains, and man's brain may be regarded as a huge, overgrown ganglion (or set of ganglia).

In any bilaterally symmetrical animal the head ganglia are larger and more specialized than those in the lower segments. Such animals move *forward* into the environment, and the most important of their sense organs are located at the head end. Ganglia tend to be located near sensory organs, where they serve to relay messages from the senses to the effectors. Cephalic (head)

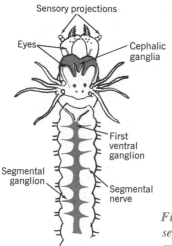

Figure 5.8 *The simple, segmented nervous system of a roundworm.*

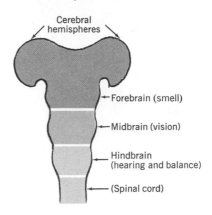

Figure 5.9 *Three parts of a simple vertebrate brain plus the spinal cord.*

ganglia receive direct impulses from the nearby eyes and sensory projections. The importance of these sensory organs of the head is reflected in the greater size and dominance of the cephalic ganglia. This is the beginning of a trend, called *encephalization,* which leads to the brain's domination of the remainder of the nervous system. It also explains why the brain is in the head.

As cephalic ganglia evolved, more neurons were added and the mass of cell bodies became more compact. Neurons became specialized for particular functions; for example, some nerve cells began to secrete chemicals that stimulate other nerve cells or effectors. The next step was for cephalic ganglia to *initiate* messages, rather than merely relay them. These messages either stimulated or inhibited ganglia located farther back in the animal, thereby exercising cephalic control over lower centers.

These adaptations comprise the transition from a head ganglion to a brain. A brain possesses the complexity and organization to carry out these functions:

1. Receive and analyze messages from sense organs and lower centers of the nervous system.
2. Control the nervous system by inhibiting or stimulating lower centers.
3. Program complex, sequential activities.

The origin of the brain as a sensory ganglion is reflected in its anatomy. The primitive vertebrate brain consists of swellings at the top of the spinal cord (see Figure 5.9). These swellings are named for their anatomical position with respect to the long axis of the animal: hindbrain, midbrain, and forebrain. Each of these parts arose in primitive vertebrates in the same way that ganglia developed in lower forms—as relay stations for sensory impulses coming from receptors in the region of the head:

hindbrain	hearing and equilibrium
midbrain	sight
forebrain	smell

This arrangement conforms to the position of sensory organs in the head. The nose or snout is at the very front of the head, the eyes are back a little and above, and the ears and balance receptors are still farther back. The three divisions of the brain are thus located in areas corresponding roughly to the locations of the sense organs from which they receive impulses.

The *hindbrain* has two major functions. It is the integrating center for a variety of visceral relexes, such as those involved in breathing, blood circulation, and digestion. It also relays sensory and motor impulses to higher brain centers. The *midbrain* is dominant over the other parts of the brain. It receives sensory inputs relayed from both the hindbrain and the forebrain and sensory messages from the eyes. In lower forms such as fishes the midbrain is the primary center of integration and control. The *forebrain* is merely a relay center for olfactory (smell) impulses, passing them on to the midbrain for correlation and control.

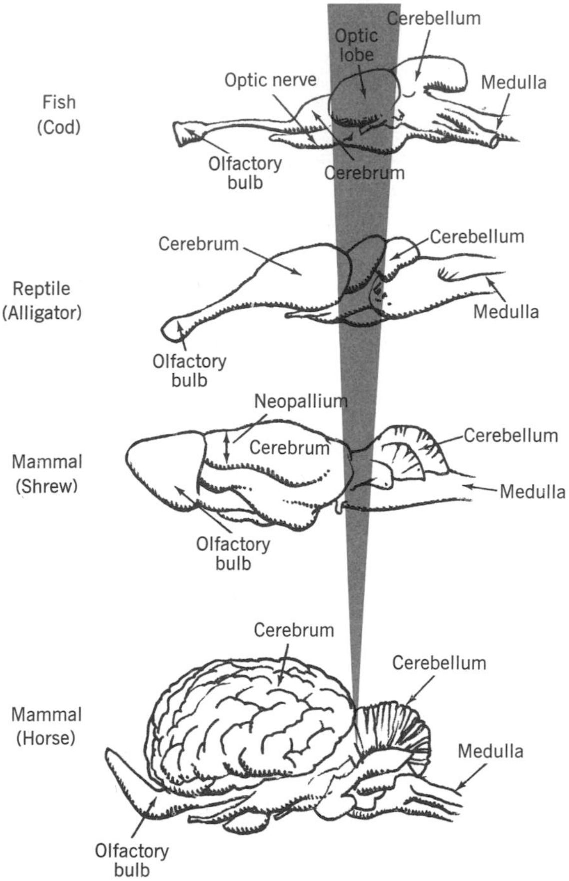

Evolution of the Brain

During the course of vertebrate evolution—from fishes to amphibians to reptiles and finally to mammals—there are two outstanding trends in the architecture of the brain. The first is the enormous growth of the cerebrum (cerebral hemispheres) and other parts of the *forebrain,* concomitant with increasing dominance by this part of the brain (encephalization). The second trend is the appearance and expansion of the cerebral cortex, which comes to dominate the other parts of the forebrain and the rest of the central nervous system. There is an accompanying reduction in size and importance of the midbrain. As Figure 5.10 shows, there is little change in the hindbrain during vertebrate evolution, but the midbrain dwindles in size. The forebrain (cerebrum) expands greatly, crowding over and overshadowing the rest of the brain, and the cerebral cortex expands so much that it must convolute (fold) to increase its surface and stay within the confines of the bony case of the brain. These twin trends of vertebrate evolution, encephalization and corticalization, comprise the final stages of the sequence that starts with nerve nets and ends with the brain of man.

In vertebrates, the cerebrum is divided into two cerebral hemispheres, connected by *commissural fibers* so that the left part of the brain is not isolated from the right part. The cerebral hemispheres consist of two kinds of material: white matter and gray matter. The white matter (so called because the myelin sheaths are white) comprises the neural pathways: axons conducting messages to and from the cerebrum. The gray matter consists of cell bodies and fairly short axons and dendrites, the neurons being very small and highly interconnected. In lower vertebrates this gray matter is located inside the cerebrum, surrounded by the white matter. During vertebrate evolution the gray

Figure 5.10 Expansion of the forebrain, reduction of the midbrain in vertebrate evolution (Simpson & Beck, 1965).

matter moves to the outside, surrounding the white matter; therefore the gray matter is called *cortex* (meaning bark).

Fishes have no cortex—only olfactory bulbs and a primitive cerebrum. Amphibia and reptiles have a primitive cortex that is essentially a "smell brain"; this smell brain is called the *paleocortex* (old cortex) or *rhinencephalon* (literally, nose brain). There is another kind of cortex which develops later in evolution than the old cortex. This new cortex (*neocortex*) is concerned with correlation and integration of sensory impulses from all the remaining senses except smell; it also initiates motor impulses. Thus it takes over functions that were served in lower vertebrates by the midbrain.

The evolution of mammalian nervous systems consists largely of the expansion and elaboration of the new cortex. The new cortex first appeared in reptiles, but its greatest development occurred in mammals (see Figure 5.11). In lower mammals such as the rat, the new cortex is mainly a sensory receiving area plus a small motor area; the *association cortex* is very small. It is this association cortex that expands so greatly in higher mammals. It is larger in cats, but the greatest increase is in primates, and the last large jump occurs in the evolution of man. Man's brain is somewhat larger than that of apes, the difference residing in man's tremendously expanded association cortex.

The new cortex is a thin sheet of gray matter that overlies the white matter of the cerebrum. The expansion of the cerebrum during vertebrate evolution provided a larger surface, but the new cortex expanded so much that even the additional surface was insufficient. The solution was a folding of the surface, producing convolutions and therefore a greater surface area. The expansive elaboration of new cortex was necessary because encephalization had shifted neural dominance forward from the midbrain to the forebrain. The cerebral cortex of the highest vertebrates, the primates, consists mainly of new cortex.

Man's Nervous System

The human nervous system is in a sense a museum, containing exhibits of the long history of neural adaptation. This history helps us to understand how it became what it is, especially the simpler origins of extremely complex neural components. But the history lesson is finished, and we turn now to study how the nervous system works in present-day man. As a functioning biological system, the nervous system is organized in three ways: horizontally, vertically, and circularly.

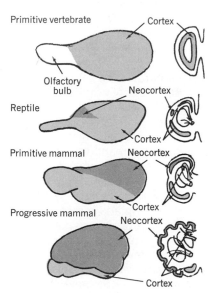

Figure 5.11 Expansion of the neocortex in vertebrate evolution (Simpson & Beck, 1965).

Horizontal Organization

The trend called *encephalization* pushed neural dominance forward toward the head end of the organism. As higher neural structures evolved, they assumed control of older, more primitive structures. This historical stratification has resulted in a horizontal organization of the nervous system (see Figure 5.12).

Both the evolutionary and the functional aspects of the brain have been integrated into a plan devised by Altman (1966). He divides the central nervous system into three levels, from lowest and most ancient to highest and most recent: the spinal cord and hindbrain (*spinomedullary*); the midbrain and the old forebrain (*old brain*); and the new cortex and its associated fiber tracts (*new brain*).[3] Table 5.1 summarizes the plan.

The spinomedullary division consists of the medulla and the core of the spinal cord—neural structures that go back to invertebrates. It controls the *routine maintenance* activities that are necessary for life: visceral functions such as digestion,

[3] *This classification reflects the approach of many investigators to neural functioning; for example, see Bronson (1965).*

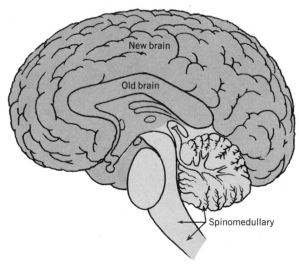

Figure 5.12 *Horizontal organization of the brain.*

respiration, and circulation; body posture; and coordination of the physical aspects of locomotion. These everyday activities comprise the basis of all other animal activities. So vital to life, they are innate activities that depend on inherited neural structures, and as such they are not essentially modified by experience.

The old brain division consists of the next horizontal level of the central nervous system: midbrain, thalamus, hypothalamus, and reticular formation. These structures are present in the' most primitive vertebrates, except for the hypothalamus, which differentiates from the thalamus early in vertebrate evolution. They are concerned with satisfying periodic needs of the body such as the need for food. The label for these activities is *recurrent catering:* metabolic needs such as those for food and water; sexual and parental activities; protection, including defense, attack, and affiliation in social groups; and alternating energy cycles such as sleep-wakefulness and relaxation-arousal.

Recurrent catering activities are performed in essentially the same way by all members of a species, which suggests that these activities are programed into the nervous system. But they can be modified by experience, especially in the details of the way particular acts are executed. In lower vertebrates these activities are largely innate, but in the course of vertebrate evolution they became less innate and more modifiable by the experiences of the individual animal. This trend is parallel and related to the evolution of the new cortex, which renders behavior more plastic, and in higher vertebrates the cerebral cortex exercises considerable control over the old brain.

The new brain division consists of the new cortex and the *direct* sensory and motor pathways associated with it. Of more recent evolutionary origin, this system appears only in mammals. It controls *singular, instrumental* activities: responses to situations that confront only some members of the species. It links highly developed perceptual systems with mechanisms of learning and memory, supplying the basis for solving problems set by new situations. The behaviors that result are acquired by experience and vary considerably from one individual to the next. This division mediates language, logical thinking, and other higher mental processes.

Table 5.1
Neural Organization and Behavior (Altman, 1966)

FUNCTIONAL SUBDIVISIONS	NEURAL SUBDIVISIONS	ACTIVITY CLASSIFICATION	SPECIFIC FUNCTIONS	MODE OF ORGANIZATION
Maintenance	Spinomedullary	Persistent Routine	Breathing Digestion Circulation Posture Locomotion	Stereotyped Innate Impervious to modification
Catering	Old brain	Recurrent Frequent	"Reflex" arousal and motivation Appetite Mating Affiliation Defense "Instinctive" behavior	Species- specific Modifiable
Instrumental	New cortex + pathways	Singular Occasional	Discrimination Skills Exploration "Intelligent" behavior	Personal Unique Acquired

Vertical Organization

Earlier in the chapter we discussed two complementary modes of neural transmission: fast, reliable delivery of messages and slow spreading of the messages for integration and control. The first is accomplished by parallel transmission, the second by divergent transmission. These two modes are arranged *vertically* in the nervous system.

There are nerve tracts (cables of neurons with long axons) from the brain to the spinal cord and on out to the muscles and glands. Other nerve tracts extend from the sense organs through the spinal cord to the brain. These motor and sensory tracts cut across the horizontal stratification of the nervous system, carrying messages up and down the brain and spinal cord. Parallel to these fast-conducting trunk lines of sensory and motor fibers is a *nonspecific system* that transmits impulses slowly, via a circuitous route. These two longitudinal systems comprise the vertical organization (see Figure 5.13).

The inner core of the central nervous system consists of the nonspecific system; the outer periphery comprises the specific, high-speed trunk lines of sensory and motor fibers. The nonspecific core is ancient, having evolved in invertebrates. It is the basic component of the most

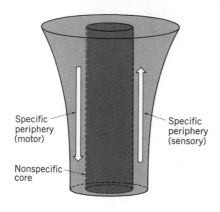

Specific periphery (motor)

Specific periphery (sensory)

Nonspecific core

Figure 5.13 Vertical organization of the central nervous system.

primitive nervous systems, consisting of neurons that are not specialized for fast conduction. The peripheral, specific system is of more recent origin, having evolved as an adaptation for speed and specificity of conduction.

The major component of the nonspecific core is the *reticular formation.* It consists of a network of primarily associative neurons that have short processes and are highly interconnected. The network extends from the hindbrain in the medulla to the edge of the forebrain. The reticular formation is connected to both sensory and motor pathways, and to both higher and lower centers.

The sensory part of the network is called the *ascending reticular activating system* (see Figure 5.14). Surrounding this diffuse core are the peripheral, specific sensory trunk lines from the receptors via the spinal cord. This specific sensory pathway is: sense organ → main sensory tracts → thalamus → sensory cortex. Along this pathway impulses move swiftly and surely from receptors to the cortex. The diffuse pathway is: sense organs → main sensory tracts → collateral neurons to reticular formation → sensory cortex. In this nonspecific pathway, transmission is slow and roundabout. Sensory messages are integrated with neural impulses from other sources, and amplitude is modulated before the message reaches the cortex.[4]

[4] *There is also a* motor *network, which is essential in integrating messages from the brain to muscles and glands.*

Parenthetically, Figure 5.14 does not show the crossing over of sensory tracts. Sensory impulses from receptors on one side of the body are transmitted to the sensory cortex on other side. The crossing of fiber tracts occurs in the brain stem or in the spinal cord, but these details need not concern us here (see Chapter 18).

Circular (Feedback) Organization

The nervous system is also organized in a circular fashion: sensory impulses are sent to brain centers, which are sending impulses to the sensory system that modulates the stimulation being sent to the brain (see Figure 5.15). The sensory inputs to the brain are controlled not only by the strength of the sensory stimuli but also by impulses emanating from the brain itself. Thus the brain has some control over the stimulation that is reaching it through sensory channels. This central control over receptors is an example of circular or feedback organization.

The reticular formation is a key component in such central control over sensory channels. It has been demonstrated that electrical stimulation of the reticular formation reduces the intensity of impulses transmitted from touch receptors to the brain. This finding suggests that one function of this feedback system is to prevent the brain from being bombarded constantly by a chaotic volley of diverse sensory impulses.

A related function concerns attention. Consider

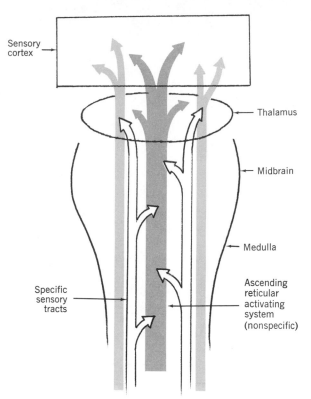

Sensory cortex

Thalamus

Midbrain

Medulla

Specific sensory tracts

Ascending reticular activating system (nonspecific)

Figure 5.14 *Reticular formation and vertical organization of the central nervous system.*

the husband who is so engrossed in a newspaper that he fails to hear his wife's call to supper. Presumably, the sensory impulses from the ears (wife's voice), being irrelevant to the focus of attention, are inhibited. The disturbing message is prevented from reaching the cerebral cortex in sufficient strength to interfere with the focus of attention (newspaper). Thus the reticular formation can arouse the cortex by amplifying sensory impulses to it, or inhibit the cortex by diminishing sensory impulses to it. The cortex exercises similar control over the reticular formation.

We have mentioned feedback loops for sensory mechanisms and attention. Another concerns *posture;* the feedback loop in this case includes the cerebral cortex, the cerebellum, part of the brain stem, muscles, receptors on the muscles and joints, and equilibrium receptors in the head. A fourth feedback loop concerns *emotion* and *recurrent activities* such as feeding, drinking, and mating; the most prominent components of this feedback loop are the cerebral cortex, the limbic system[5] and the hypothalamus.

The three different organizations of the nervous system (horizontal, vertical, and circular) are dia-

[5] *The limbic system is essentially the old cortex or smell brain.*

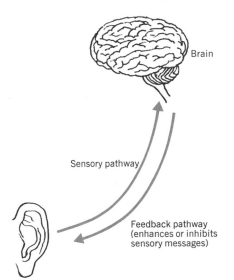

Brain

Sensory pathway

Feedback pathway (enhances or inhibits sensory messages)

Receptor

Figure 5.15 *Sensory feedback.*

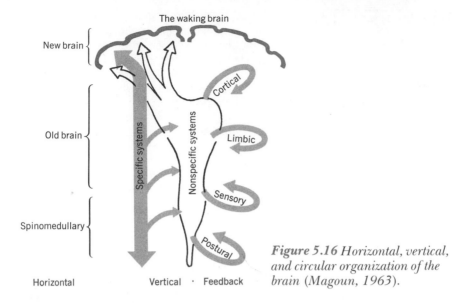

The waking brain

New brain

Old brain

Spinomedullary

Specific systems

Nonspecific systems

Cortical

Limbic

Sensory

Postural

Horizontal · Vertical · Feedback

Figure 5.16 *Horizontal, vertical, and circular organization of the brain (Magoun, 1963).*

grammed in Figure 5.16. All three organizations have an evolutionary history. The horizontal organization reflects the long-term trend of encephalization, with neural dominance progressing toward the head of the animal. The vertical organization reflects a sequence from primitive, nonspecific neural functioning to later specific tracts surrounding the primitive core and offering fast, reliable transmission of sensory and motor impulses. The feedback organization is itself a later evolutionary development, occurring as an adaptive improvement over a simple reflex arc.

The reflex arc has three basic components[6] arranged in the sequence: sensory neuron → association neuron → motor neuron. The stimulus acting on a receptor initiates a sensory impulse toward the central nervous system. The sensory impulse is transmitted first to an association neuron and then to a motor neuron; the motor impulse leads to a very fast response to the stimulus (see Figure 5.17). This primitive stimulus-response mechanism guarantees a quick response to environmental changes but leaves the animal at the mercy of its environment. The animal is

merely a passive responder to changes initiated in the environment, and so long as the reflex arc is the basic neural system, the animal must remain passive.

Obviously it is more adaptive to seek change and to initiate behavior without waiting for an external stimulus. Early in evolution animals progressed from the more passive reflex arc to the more active feedback loop. The animal's current activities determine which stimuli will be allowed to influence the central nervous system, which stimuli will be amplified, and which will be diminished. Thus in all the higher forms, including man, reflex arcs constitute a minor aspect of the nervous system, the major aspect being feedback loops.

The difference between the reflex arc and feedback organizations has implications for the way in which behavior is approached. The relex arc concept assumes that knowledge of the stimulus offers the best way of explaining the response; the implicit assumption is that the organism is a passive responder to the environment. The feedback concept makes the opposite assumption, that the organism is an active responder, controlling the effect of the environment on itself.[7]

[6] *There are also two-neuron reflexes, consisting of only sensory and motor neurons, but the three-neuron reflex is a better representative of the typical reflex.*

[7] *Review the discussion of active and passive models at the end of the last chapter.*

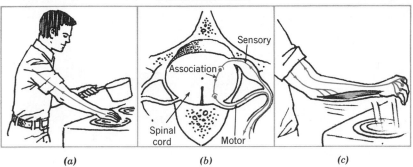

A three neuron reflex

(a) *(b)* *(c)*

Figure 5.17 *A three-neuron reflex.*

The Nervous System and Behavior

Our survey of the nervous system is finished. The account has been brief, and anatomy has been minimized. The emphasis on *function* is in keeping with the nature of this book—the study of behavior.

The aim of the chapter is to introduce the reader to the role of the nervous system in behavior. The word *introduce* needs to be emphasized, for this chapter omits many important details necessary for relating the nervous system to behavior. Instead of presenting all the information about the nervous system here, we shall present it where it is appropriate to the behavior being discussed. Two examples will illustrate this point. In Chapter 7 we shall discuss the neural aspects of biological motivation, including the role of the hypothalamus in hunger and the role of "pleasure" and "pain" brain centers in motivation. And in Chapter 6—the next chapter—we shall consider the roles of the central nervous system and the autonomic nervous system in arousal. The present chapter marks the end of the "background material," and all subsequent chapters will consist of "psychology proper."

section three
arousal and motivation

chapter 6
arousal

*Behavioral arousal — autonomic nervous sys-
tem arousal — homeostasis — central nervous
system arousal — brain waves — stages of
sleep — two kinds of sleep — neural mechanisms
of sleep — dreaming — theories of sleep — wakefulness — the orienting reflex — daytime cycle
of arousal — biological rhythms — the menstrual
cycle — the day-night cycle — perspective*

This chapter and the next one deal with catering activities: the sleep-wakefulness cycle, food-seeking, exploration, and related behaviors. They may be divided into two classes of activity on the basis of *timing.* One class is *rhythmic,* recurring over intervals such as a day (sleep-wakefulness) or four weeks (the menstrual cycle of women). The other class follows no time schedule, occurring in response to tissue needs (seeking food) or simply because the organism is "built that way" (exploring and seeking stimulation).

Both kinds of catering activities involve arousal. The level of behavioral arousal is low when the person is drowsy or satiated with food, and it is somewhat higher when he is wide awake or hungry. In this chapter we shall discuss the concept of arousal, how it is measured, and certain rhythmic catering activities (notably sleep-wakefulness). In the next chapter we shall proceed to more specific and nonrhythmic catering activities.

The Concept of Arousal

Arousal is an important concept but one that needs to be used carefully because of its inclusiveness. We say that someone is aroused when he is excited, tense, and active. Thus arousal may be equated with *activity* or energy output, which varies from a low point in sleep or waking rest to uninhibited frenzy.

Arousal also refers to *reactivity,* which is usually measured by the intensity of stimulation required to elicit a response. Thus a person in a low state of arousal (rest or drowsiness) requires more stimulation to elicit a response than does a person in a high state or arousal (anger or fear).

Finally, arousal may refer to a *temporary* change from the more usual resting state. For example, great excitement occurs only seldom in relation to the more placid, less aroused state that characterizes most of existence. Thus high arousal may be a swift, tension-filled episode set in the more enduring state of low arousal.

In brief, arousal may refer to the intensity of behavior, to reactivity, or to the temporary, phasic quality of behavior. These three characteristics tend to occur together: the enraged person emits intense behavior, reacts to minimal stimulation, and soon terminates this phasic state. However, all three are not necessarily present in every aroused state.

So far we have been discussing *behavioral* arousal, which is easily observed. But the concept of arousal also applies to certain activities of the nervous system, usually (but not necessarily) those accompanying behavioral arousal. For example, as arousal level moves upward from sleep to wakefulness, there are changes in the pattern of *brain activity.* The increase in arousal from calm to great excitement is accompanied by elevations in heart rate, blood pressure, breathing rate, and other physiological reactions; these are controlled by the *autonomic nervous system.* Thus, in addition to behavioral arousal, there are associated states of central nervous system (brain) arousal and autonomic nervous system arousal. The three kinds of arousal are loosely related, especially at the extremes of deep sleep and high excitement, but they are not always correlated. In certain stages of sleep, for example, behavior is at a low ebb, while the central and autonomic nervous systems are firing at high levels. In light of this independence of arousal systems, we shall discuss them separately.

Behavioral Arousal

We can divide behavior into processing of information from the environment (*input*) and responding to the environment (*output*). Input and output vary considerably along the arousal dimension (see Table 6.1, page 100). At the peak of arousal, *strong excitement,* input is often restricted. A person running from extreme danger may be unaware that he has been hurt or simply may not hear the signal that the danger has passed. During high excitement, output ranges from violent activity to shocked paralysis, and behavior is generally inefficient.

In marked contrast are the focused attention and behavioral efficiency of *alert wakefulness,* the middle range of arousal. Even faint stimuli can be sensed, and highly complex responses are delivered quickly.

Lower on the arousal dimension is *drowsiness,* in which there is a sharp reduction of both input and output. Most stimuli are disregarded, and responses are sluggish and uncoordinated.

The bottom of the dimension, *deep sleep,* is marked by the virtual absence of input and output. Very strong physical stimuli do register, which accounts for the prevalent use of alarm clocks. Less intense stimuli are sensed if they possess special importance for the sleeper: a mother tends to waken when her infant cries. Instrumental behavior is largely absent.

Thus both input and output are optimal in the middle range of arousal, alert wakefulness (see Figure 6.1). The relationship looks like an inverted *U.* Both sensitivity to stimuli and efficiency of behavior rise from deep sleep to drowsiness and reach a peak at alert wakefulness, then drop off at the extreme of high excitement. In brief, we function best when wide awake but not over excited.

Autonomic Nervous System Arousal

The autonomic nervous system is phyletically ancient, and it changed little during mammalian evolution. It is concerned with two major physiological functions: the quiet, routine maintenance activities of everyday life and the sporadic, sudden emergencies in response to threat. Consider a man watching his favorite television program,

Table 6.1
The Dimension of Behavioral Arousal

LEVEL OF AROUSAL	INPUT	OUTPUT
High excitement (e.g., panic)	Restricted; some stimuli not noticed; attention poor	Varies from low to high; behavior inefficient; responses may be disorganized, slow.
Wakefulness	All stimuli register; attention good; concentration, focusing excellent	Moderate to high; behavior efficient; organized, quick responding
Drowsiness	Restricted; attention poor; many stimuli not noticed	Low; slow, uncoordinated responses
Deep sleep	Almost no stimuli register; attention poor	Almost no instrumental responding

having just eaten a large meal. While his attention is focused on the TV tube, food is digested, wastes are eliminated, and in general the body goes about its low-arousal business of maintaining life. Suddenly, someone shouts, "The house is on fire!" As the man leaps from his chair, his body prepares him for a massive, high-arousal effort. His heart races, his breathing increases, and his routine digestive processes simply stop. All these physiological reactions are controlled by the autonomic nervous system, which consists of two divisions (see Table 6.2): the *parasympathetic,* involved in low-arousal, routine maintenance activities; and the *sympathetic,* involved in high-arousal reactions to emergencies.[1]

[1] *The two divisions are usually opposed to one another but not always. The present account simplifies an extremely complex interaction between the two.*

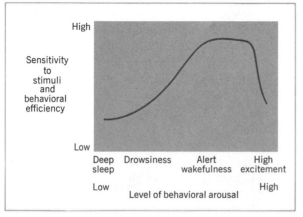

Figure 6.1 *Sensitivity, efficiency, and arousal.*

When a person is threatened, there are immediate physiological preparations for fight or flight. These adaptive reactions are mediated by the sympathetic division. The changes are widespread and diffuse:

1. Breathing rate increases, and the bronchioles of the lungs expand; both processes allow more oxygen to be taken into the bloodstream.
2. The heart beats faster and peripheral blood vessels close down, allowing more blood to flow to the large, action-oriented skeletal muscles.
3. Digestion slows down or stops, and blood is diverted to the skeletal muscles.

These preparations often culminate in violent action, either escape or attack, followed by a return to resting levels. The sympathetic dominance of the emergency period is followed by a parasympathetic dominance, which restores quiescence and normal vegetative functioning. Sometimes the swing is excessive, a phenomenon called *parasympathetic rebound* (see Figure 6.2). In such a case a sudden frightening stimulus initiates sympathetic dominance, which is followed by a rebound of excessive parasympathetic activation; one example is sudden urination. Thus the loss of bladder control in fright is not caused by excessive arousal, but by the *bounce back* from excessive arousal.

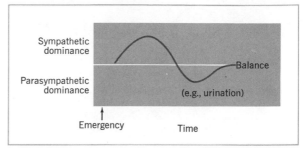

Figure 6.2 *Parasympathetic rebound.*

The parasympathetic division stimulates internal organs in promoting growth and storing energy. These processes, which occur mainly during rest, require *specific innervation.* For example, as food moves through the digestive system, there is successive parasympathetic stimulation of the mouth, the stomach, the small intestine, and so on. Each organ can be activated while the others remain at rest.

In contrast, the sympathetic division prepares the body for sudden, heavy exertion in response to immediate environmental demands. This alarm reaction requires generalized innervation to produce simultaneous, widespread bodily changes. The neural mechanism for pervasive physiological

Table 6.2
Divisions of the Autonomic Nervous System

	SYMPATHETIC	PARASYMPATHETIC
1. Function	Emergency arousal	Vegetative maintenance
2. Control	Diffuse, generalized	Specific
3. Actions	Faster breathing Heart rate increases Digestion stops Sugar is released	Slower breathing Heart rate decreases Digestion starts Sugar is absorbed

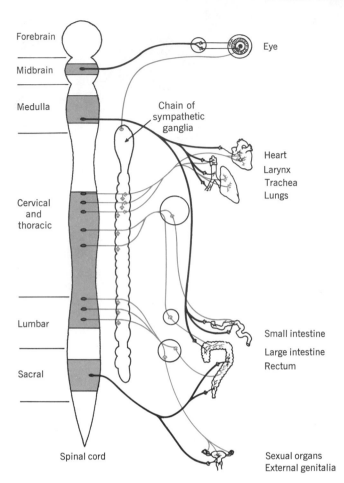

Forebrain

Midbrain

Medulla

Cervical
and
thoracic

Lumbar

Sacral

Spinal cord

Eye

Chain of
sympathetic
ganglia

Heart
Larynx
Trachea
Lungs

Small intestine

Large intestine
Rectum

Sexual organs
External genitalia

Figure 6.3 *The autonomic nervous system.*

change is a *chain of sympathetic ganglia* (see Figure 6.3). This chain, which evolved far back in vertebrate phylogeny (see Chapter 5), spreads the neural message to the appropriate bodily systems (circulation, respiration, and so on).

Loosely speaking, the relationship between parasympathetic and sympathetic is like a man who works hard all month, saves his money, and then spends it all in one glorious, drunken binge. The opposition between the two is not really a struggle for dominance but a way of controlling bodily processes by means of opposing tendencies. In terms of our larger discussion, high arousal is usually mediated by activation of the sympathetic division.

Homeostasis

The joint action of the two parts of the autonomic nervous system tends to keep bodily functions within an optimal range. Whatever temporary deviations from resting level occur (as when the animal is suddenly aroused), there are mechanisms for returning to an optimal range called the *steady state*. The steady state and its related mechanisms are part of the concept of *homeostasis*. The best example is the regulation of temperature, which in man is normally 98–100° Fahrenheit. When exercise or hot weather heats the body, cooling mechanisms are activated. Blood vessels in the skin dilate, allowing the blood to be cooled, and the evaporation of water from the skin also cools the body. At the other extreme, when the body becomes cooler, warming mechanisms are activated. These consist of muscular activity (shivering or exercising), the seeking of warmer local environments, and the seeking of covering for the body.

These are all responses to deviations from the steady state; they are called *homeostatic mechanisms.* We must be careful not to label as homeostatic all adaptive responses to the environment. Birds construct nests, beavers build dams, and men erect houses, all of which offer protection from environment but none of which is homeostatic.

CRITERIA OF HOMEOSTASIS. How do we identify a system as homeostatic? There are three necessary components: a steady state, sensory elements to detect deviations, and effectors to return the system to its steady state. Figure 6.4 shows how these three components function.

1. There is a balanced, steady state. The system (say, temperature) is within the optimal range.
2. An internal or external event alters the system so that it now deviates from the prescribed limits.
3. This deviation triggers sensors (heat-sensing elements), which fire neural impulses.
4. The neural impulses surge through appropriate nervous system channels to effector elements, which reverse the trend, moving the system back in the direction of the steady state (for temperature, sweating would be one effector mechanism).
5. The steady state is restored, the system now being within the allowed limits.
6. The sensors, having earlier been triggered by deviations, are now inactivated by the absence of deviation from the steady state.
7. In the absence of neural impulses, the effectors are turned off.

This is the formal model of a homeostatic system. In their everyday operation, our homeostatic systems may not be so precise; they may overshoot. For example, a high body temperature may lead to so much sweating that the body temperature drops too much. This overcompensation

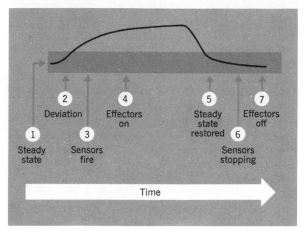

Figure 6.4 Homeostasis.

leads to shivering, which may then restore the steady state of temperature.

THE STEADY STATE. What is the nature of the steady state? It is not merely a static, immobile state but a dynamic equilibrium (Cannon, 1929). The organism is an open biological system, and there is a continuous interaction between organism and environment, with both continually changing over time. The organism's mechanisms oppose environmental variability, maintaining internal systems within strictly defined limits no matter how the environment changes. Does this mean that the steady state is fixed and unchanging? Do homeostatic mechanisms always return the system to the *same* equilibrium point? The answer is a qualified yes. The negative feedback operation that we call a homeostatic mechanism occurs within a relatively brief time of the organism's existence — as, for example, the time it takes for sweating to lower the temperature of an overheated body. But the answer must be qualified because there are shifts in the steady states of some systems. As the organism matures, there may be gradual alterations in equilibrium point, but these occur so slowly that they are not important in everyday functioning. There are shorter cycles of change: for example, body temperature varies during the cycle of day and night and the body temperature of women rises to a peak at ovulation.

Central Nervous System Arousal

Whether we are asleep or awake, relaxed or excited, our brains are continuously active. Though the brain can be stimulated by input from the environment, it functions with virtually no external stimulation. Large groups of neurons fire regularly every hour of the day and night, producing tiny electrical currents. These can be picked up by sensitive electrodes on the surface of the scalp. The minute electrical impulses are amplified and converted into visual form by plotting them on moving paper. This moment-by-moment record of the electrical impulses of the brain is called an electroencephalograph (literally, a chart of brain electricity). We shall refer to such graphs by their abbreviation, *EEGs*, and to the impulses themselves as *brain waves*.

BRAIN RHYTHMS. Brain waves can be rapid or slow, large or small. Small, fast waves are associated with high arousal; large, slow waves, with low arousal (see Figure 6.5). In excitement the pattern is one of irregular, fast, small brain waves. Relaxation with eyes closed produces the *alpha rhythm:* regular, moderately large waves at about 10 cycles per second. If the alpha waves of relaxation are like steady ripples on a lake, the large, slow waves of deep sleep are like the crests and troughs of ocean waves.

It has been speculated (Lindsley, 1957) that the alpha rhythm represents the normal resting state of neurons in the cerebral cortex, firing roughly 10 times per second. In any given area of the cortex, perhaps millions of neurons are synchronized at this rhythm, yielding an electrical signal strong enough to be recorded. When an input comes in from the environment, neurons in different parts of the brain are stimulated, and they fire at different rates. The steady rhythm is broken up, and the fast, small waves of higher arousal begin to appear. This explanation, though simplistic, does account for the relationship between large, slow brain waves and low arousal, and that between small, rapid waves and high arousal.

The alpha rhythm is of special interest because of its *experiential* qualities. Subjects have been trained to elicit alpha rhythms in themselves (Kamiya, 1969; Nowlis & Kamiya, 1970). They report doing this by letting the mind wander, and focusing on the heartbeat, and *not* allowing any visual imagery. Roughly half the subjects find the alpha state to be very pleasant. The subjective reports resemble descriptions of the meditation practiced in Eastern religions, and devotees of Zen are apt at learning to control their alpha rhythms. Such self-monitoring of states of consciousness opens up interesting possibilities for the induction of a variety of self-elicited moods and states of being.

RETICULAR FORMATION. Brain waves derive from cortical neurons, which can be excited by the neural arousal system. The major component of this system is the reticular formation.[2] Its importance in maintaining levels of arousal was established long ago. When the reticular formation of monkeys is damaged, they sleep excessively and are permanently drowsy. In an intact animal, when the reticular formation is stimulated electrically, the brain wave patterns shift from those of a sleeping brain to those of a waking brain (Moruzzi & Magoun, 1949).

The most striking evidence comes from research on cats. Lindsley et al. (1950) interrupted the express sensory paths to the cerebral cortex, leaving the reticular formation intact (see Figure

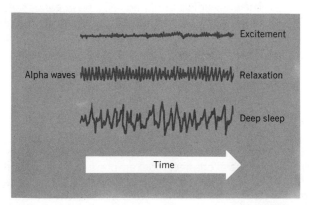

Figure 6.5 *Brain waves in low, moderate, and high arousal (schematic).*

[2] *We discussed the reticular formation at the end of the last chapter. The ascending reticular activating system (ARAS) receives collaterals from sensory pathways, and it relays these messages through a diffuse network to the cortex (see Figure 5.14). It comprises the* nonspecific core *in the vertical organization of the nervous system.*

6.6). The cats showed both the behavior and brain waves of normal wakefulness. Then, using other cats, the researchers damaged part of the reticular formation, leaving the express sensory pathways to the cortex untouched. These cats remained in such deep sleep, in terms of both behavior and brain waves, that it was extremely difficult to waken them. Clearly, the nonspecific core of the reticular formation is necessary to maintain the arousal level of wakefulness. It does something the express sensory pathways cannot: it supplies the cortex with a background level of excitation required for normal functioning.

Sleep

What is sleep? Certainly, it is the lowest ebb of behavioral arousal (aside from coma), though the nervous system remains active. The world is blocked out, and consciousness is lost: we fall asleep, and a moment later—so it seems—the alarm clock rings insistently, though seven or eight hours have passed.

Roughly a third of a man's life is spent in the arms of Morpheus, but until recently there was little reliable knowledge about sleep. It was believed that during sleep the brain rests and rids itself of fatigue and that dreams mainly occur immediately before waking. We now know that both notions are wrong: the sleeping brain is as active as the waking brain, and dreams occur throughout the night.

The breakthrough in sleep research occurred when investigators found brain waves to be related to behavioral measures of depth of sleep. This finding was followed by the discovery of a kind of sleep different from the "orthodox" sleep we have all known about. (Unfortunately, none of the advances in research techniques has led to a resolution of the philosophical question: How do you know that you are really awake, rather than asleep and dreaming that you are awake?)

Stages of Sleep

Anyone who has observed a sleeping person for a few hours knows that the sleeper does not remain inert but occasionally turns, twists, and stretches. This muscular movement is small compared to the neural activity accompanying sleep, as revealed by brain waves. The pattern of EEGs changes often during the night, as the sleeper progresses through various stages of sleep. These patterns have been classified by Kleitman and Dement (Dement, 1965) into a widely used system that includes four stages of sleep. *Stage 0*, which is not part of sleep, is marked by alpha waves of 8 to 12 cycles per second, characteristic of the relaxed, wakeful state. *Stage 1*, which might be labeled drowsiness, contains a mixture of slow and fast brain waves; the sleeper is inattentive and relaxed. *Stage 2*, which is unequivocally sleep, contains *sleep spindles*, irregular, sharply pointed waves of 12 to 16 cycles per second. *Stage 3*, which is called deep sleep, also contain sleep spindles, but moderate

Awake: Midbrain Lesion Afferent Paths

Asleep: Lesion Midbrain Tegmentum

Figure 6.6 Reticular formation and arousal.

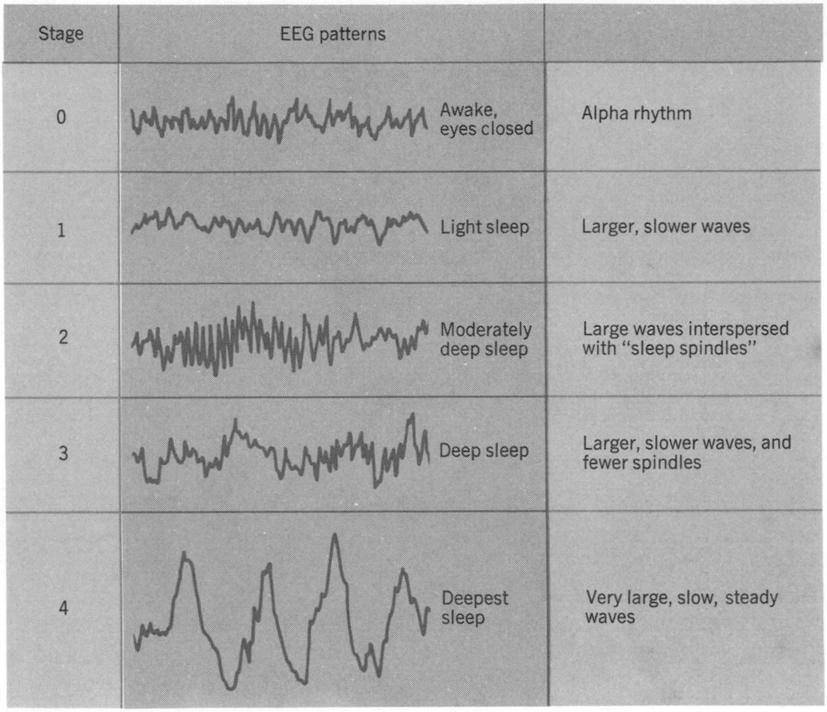

Stage	EEG patterns	
0	Awake, eyes closed	Alpha rhythm
1	Light sleep	Larger, slower waves
2	Moderately deep sleep	Large waves interspersed with "sleep spindles"
3	Deep sleep	Larger, slower waves, and fewer spindles
4	Deepest sleep	Very large, slow, steady waves

Figure 6.7 Stages of sleep.

amounts of slow, large amplitude waves begin to appear. *Stage 4,* deepest sleep, contains large amplitude, slow waves.

These four stages represent the continuum of depth of sleep, with Stage 1 the lightest and Stage 4 the deepest.[3] But what do we mean by *depth of sleep?* The only clear meaning refers to behavioral arousal, in this instance the sleeper's sensitivity to external stimulation. It has been established that the deeper the stage of sleep as marked by the EEG patterns just described, the less sensitive the sleeper is to the world around him (Williams et al., 1966). In one experiment subjects reported whenever they heard sounds presented by the experimenter (Simon & Emmons, 1956). Then the subjects fell asleep. A different system of classifying depth of sleep was used, but the results clearly show that the deeper the stage

[3] *Stages 1 and 2 appear to be lighter phases of Stages 3 and 4, and most sleep researchers concentrate on Stages 3 and 4 as being more representative of the sleeping state.*

of sleep, the less responsive is the sleeper (see Figure 6.8).

During the lighter stages of sleep, especially at the beginning of the night, unusual sensory and motor experiences often occur (Oswald, 1962). There may be hallucinations such as a shot or a crash, a flash of light, or the sensation of electric shock. The most common sensation is of falling, either in familiar surroundings or in empty space. A nearly universal phenomenon at the beginning of sleep, whether recalled or not, is the *nocturnal jerk:* a sudden, uncoordinated jerk of the head, arms, legs, or the entire body.

Two Kinds of Sleep

During the course of the night the sleeper sinks into progressively deeper stages of sleep and then retraces his steps back to lighter sleep. The downward progression toward deeper sleep is smoother, and the upward progression is marked

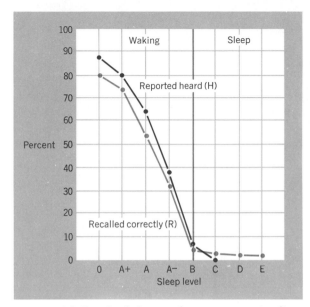

Figure 6.8 Depth of sleep and response to stimuli.

dicates the lightest pattern of sleep. Research with both humans and animals has established that the REM periods are not merely light sleep but *an entirely different kind of sleep* (Aserinsky & Kleitman, 1953). Thus there are two kinds of sleep: one with rapid eye movements (REM) and one without such eye "movements" (NREM). Some of their differences are diagramed in Figure 6.10. In NREM sleep the brain waves are slow and of considerable amplitude, suggesting deep sleep; the eyes remain still or slowly roll in their sockets;

by jumps and sudden shifts. After the initial period of Stage 1 sleep, successive periods of this light sleep are different. They are accompanied by *rapid eye movements* (hereafter abbreviated REMs). Figure 6.9 plots a typical night of sleep. The depth of sleep is greatest early, and as the night progresses, sleep becomes lighter. Each time the sleeper emerges from the trough of deep sleep to Stage 1, the REMs commence. These periods of REMs become longer as the night's sleep takes its course.

REMs occur during Stage 1, when the EEG in-

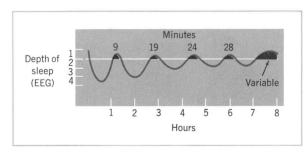

Figure 6.9 Depth of sleep: cycles during the night (Dement and Wolpert, 1958).

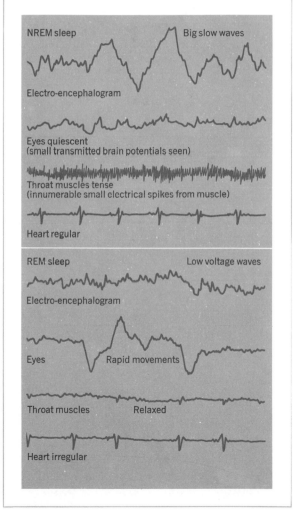

Figure 6.10 REM versus NREM sleep.

Table 6.3
NREM and REM Sleep

	NREM "ORTHODOX"	REM "PARADOXICAL"
Behavioral arousal	Low (except for throat muscles)	Extremely low (sensory blockade)
Central nervous system and autonomic nervous system arousal	Low	Moderate to high (same range as wakefulness)
Occurrence during the night	Tends to occur earlier	Tends to occur later
After sleep deprivation	Recovered first	Recovered last
Eye movements	Slow, rolling, nonconjugate	Rapid, jerky, conjugate
What is recalled	Vague, rambling fleeting images	Vivid, organized sequences ("dreams")
Sleepwalking Sleeptalking	Present More frequent	Absent Less frequent
Penile erection	Absent	Present

the throat muscles are tensed; and the heartbeat is slow and steady; in addition, breathing is slow and deep, blood pressure is normal, and the muscles of the extremities are relaxed. In REM sleep the brain waves are fast and of small amplitude, suggesting light sleep; the eyes jerk back and forth (REMs) as though scanning a visual stimulus; the throat muscles are relaxed; the heartbeat is fast and irregular; in addition, breathing is rapid and jerky, blood pressure is elevated, there are facial and bodily twitches, and in men there are penile erections. Clearly, REM is very different from NREM. It is a paradoxical kind of sleep, one that resembles wakefulness as much as it does sleep.[4] It is not really light sleep—during REM sleep the sleeper is as unresponsive to external stimuli as he is during Stage 4, the deepest stage of NREM sleep. Here is where the paradox lies: if activation refers to sensitivity to external stimuli, then arousal level is *low* in REM sleep, but if activation refers to the functioning of various

[4] *For this reason some sleep researchers use the terms* paradoxical *(REM) and* orthodox *(NREM) sleep.*

brain structures (and perhaps a sensitivity to *internal* stimuli), then arousal level is *high* in REM sleep.

These differences suggest a startling conclusion: when our eyes are closed during the night, two quite disparate processes are occurring alternately, both called sleep. A more complete list of differences between the two kinds of sleep is summarized in Table 6.3. The two kinds of sleep are not evenly distributed throughout the night (see Figure 6.9). NREM sleep predominates during the first hours, but REM sleep increases toward the morning hours. This is especially clear when REM sleep is contrasted with the deepest kind of NREM sleep, Stage 4 (see Figure 6.11).

It might be expected that normal adults, when deprived of sleep, would compensate by sleeping away the hours they missed. In terms of time, there is only partial compensation, the sleep being deeper and shorter than the amount lost. Such sleep is mainly and inordinately NREM, especially Stage 4, and only later is REM sleep recovered. This finding suggests that orthodox sleep is more important in the everyday sleep-wakefulness cycle.

What happens when adults are deprived of paradoxical sleep but allowed orthodox sleep? Such deprivation requires that subjects be wakened as soon as they drift into paradoxical sleep, which is like rolling a stone uphill: the more subjects are deprived of only REM sleep, the more quickly they return to REM sleep. When subsequently allowed unrestricted sleep, they compensate with an excessive proportion of REM sleep.

REM sleep is suppressed by a variety of drugs, both stimulants and depressants. When amphetamine addicts are taking the drug, their sleep is almost exclusively NREM (Oswald & Thacore, 1963). When their usual source of pep (amphetamines) is removed, these addicts become sleepy, and the proportion of REM sleep is twice the normal amount. Thus when persons are deprived of REM sleep, either by drugs or by being awakened in the laboratory, they compensate for only their specific loss. This is strong evidence for two different kinds of sleep.

During both kinds of sleep the eyes move, but in different ways. The eye movements of NREM sleep are slow, rolling, and uncoordinated; one eye might roll to the left while the other remains still.

In contrast, the eye movements of REM sleep are essentially the same as those of wakefulness; the eyes dart rapidly and jerkily, and their movements are synchronized (conjugate). Conjugate movements of the eyes[5] are essential for normal perception of depth. It has been shown that after paradoxical sleep, two-eyed depth perception is improved but one-eyed depth perception is not. Berger (1969) has speculated that one function of REM sleep is to exercise conjugate eye movements, thereby enhancing two-eyed depth perception.

Dreaming

After the original discovery of REM sleep (Aserinsky & Kleitman, 1953), the researchers suspected that the rapid eye movements might be sensory reactions of the sleeper to events occurring in a dream. To check on this speculation, they woke up sleepers during REM and NREM sleep. Dreams were reported 74 percent of the time upon a REM awakening but only 7 percent upon a NREM wakening (Aserinsky & Kleitman, 1955). This dramatic finding was followed by the discov-

[5] *These are the yoked, synchronized movements of the eyes that keep them directed toward the same target.*

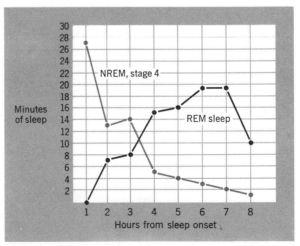

Figure 6.11 Trends in NREM, stage 4 sleep and REM sleep during the night (Webb, 1968).

ery first of an EEG pattern that was characteristic of REM sleep (Dement & Kleitman, 1955) and then a correlation between vertical eye movements and such vertical dream imagery as looking up and down a ladder (Dement & Kleitman, 1957). Thus it appeared that the eye movements of REM sleep were closely tied to dream imagery, and this hypothesis was strengthened by a "blind" matching of recording of eye movements to the events reported in dreams (Roffwarg et al., 1962).

However, subsequent research showed that the relationship between sleep and dreams is not so straightforward. First, rapid eye movements occur even when there is no dreaming—as in the sleep of newborn human infants and cats without a cerebral cortex (Jouvet, 1965). Second, congenitally blind persons, whose dreams contain no visual imagery, have normal amounts of REM sleep (Amadeo & Gomez, 1966). These two facts reveal that there is REM sleep without visual events in dreams.

To add further complexity, dreams also occur during NREM sleep (Foulkes, 1962). There is a lively dispute about how much dreaming actually occurs in NREM periods because the imagery is different from that of REM periods. When sleepers are awakened from NREM sleep, their reports tend to be brief and unexciting; there are few characters, little imagery, and a realistic quality to the mentation. In contrast, the reports of persons wakened from REM sleep are exciting and often sufficiently vivid to frighten the dreamer. Thus there is "dreaming" in both NREM and REM sleep, but much of the mentation that occurs in REM sleep is more like the commonplace idea of dreams than in the mentation that occurs in NREM sleep.[6]

It is no more than common sense to expect that a dreamer might talk or walk in his sleep, but common sense is wrong. Most of the sleep fantasy we call dreams occurs in REM sleep, when virtually all of the body's muscles are so relaxed that the sleeper cannot initiate movements. Moreover, environmental inputs are blocked off and the

sleeper is relatively unresponsive to external stimuli. This is part of the paradox in REM sleep: high *internal* arousal coupled with low *external* arousal. It is during NREM sleep that the talking and walking tend to occur, and they are typically *not* accompanied by fantasy.

Neural Mechanisms

There are three ways in which the sleep-wakefulness cycle might be controlled by neural mechanisms. First, the basic condition might be sleep, and wakefulness would occur only when some stimulus (internal or external or both) jolted the animal from its sleep. Second, the basic condition might be wakefulness, and sleep would occur only when the chemicals that underlie wakefulness are exhausted and can be restored only during sleep. Third, neither state might be basic, but each would be controlled by neural mechanisms that mutually inhibit each other; this possibility is the most likely, if only because it is so typical of biological control systems.

The control circuit for wakefulness is the feedback system between the cerebral cortex and the forward part of the reticular formation. This top part of the reticular formation, or reticular activating system, sends a continuous stream of impulses to the cortex, providing the cortical arousal needed for wakefulness. The cortex, in turn, is capable of stimulating the reticular formation—for example, when exciting thoughts or ideas stir an individual to become aroused.

Reduced to its simplest terms, sleep occurs when the reticular formation is prevented from sending impulses to the cortex. It follows that the sleep system of the brain consists of those structures that inhibit the reticular activating system or at least prevent its impulses from reaching the cerebral cortex. These structures are diagrammed in Figure 6.12. The lower reticular formation inhibits the upper part. The cortex is part of a feedback system with the reticular activating system, and some of this feedback is negative; that is, the cortex can turn off the reticular activating system. The other structures are part of the limbic-midbrain circuit, which is fundamental to the recurrent catering activities of food-getting, flight-

[6] *There has been a recent attempt to account for dreams with a* tonic-phasic *theory (see Grosser & Siegel, 1971). Presumably, dreaming occurs during both kinds of sleep but only during sudden,* phasic *bursts of neural activity, which occur against the background of the more usual, sustained* tonic *activity.*

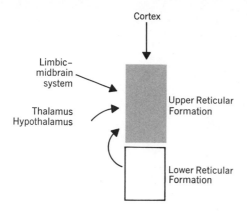

Cortex

Limbic–
midbrain
system

Thalamus
Hypothalamus

Upper Reticular
Formation

Lower Reticular
Formation

Figure 6.12 *Neural mechanisms in sleep.*

fight, and mating. The situation is more complex than can be diagramed. Both the cortex and the limbic-midbrain system not only inhibit the reticular activating system but also may stimulate it; only the lower reticular formation is always inhibitory in relation to the upper part.

The evidence has been summarized by a leading sleep researcher, Jouvet (1967), who concludes that,

. . . sleeping is subject to both active and passive controls. The active type of control consists of the application of a brake on the RAS [reticular activating system] by some other brain structure or structures; the passive type corresponds to a letup on the accelerator in the RAS itself. (P. 67.)[7]

This simplified account of neural mechanisms in sleep derives from a large body of research, most of which is far removed from everyday life. But there are some experiments that furnish information about neural functioning and also make contact with events familiar to all of us. Consider the following.

[7] *Jouvet (1967) has also linked brain neurohumors to the two kinds of sleep. He associates the neural transmitter* serotonin *with NREM sleep and* noradrenaline *with REM sleep.*

Research Report

A British researcher, Ian Oswald (1960, 1966) wanted to corroborate the feedback loop between the cerebral cortex and the reticular formation, especially in its action during sleep. To insure that the cortex would be involved, he required subjects to discriminate among different words. It is well known that sleepers may become sufficiently aroused by novel stimuli to waken from sleep. Thus the country boy is disturbed by city traffic, and the city boy is wakened by crickets and birds. Oswald's solution was to plant meaningful words in a list of words having no special significance. His description is piquant:

We therefore made a very long tape-recording in which fifty-six names were called out one after another, and over and over again in different orders, with several seconds between each name. Having persuaded a volunteer to come and sleep in the laboratory we would attach electrodes to his scalp and to his hands. He was told that if during sleep his own name, say, Peter, was called out, he should respond to it by clenching his hand, and that he should do the same if one other particular name, say, David, *was called. He then fell asleep while the tape recording was played, drowsing off through an endless barrage of words, occasionally clenching his hand as one of the crucial names came. Eventually, he fell asleep, and sure enough, would very often suddenly rouse from sound sleep and clench his fist just after either of the crucial words. . . .*

The upshot of all this was that, whereas spontaneous wakings and movements (which we counted during the period of each ten names that preceded each crucial one) were very rare, fist-clenching after "own" name had been called was so frequent that the difference could not reasonably be attributed to chance. The same was true of the "other" name—Peter responded best to Peter *but was also able, though with less certitude, to pick out* David *during sleep. Furthermore, even if fist-clenching did not occur, the EEG of sound sleep, with slow waves and sleep spindles, was much more often disturbed by a person's own name than by any other name. The electrical responses (called a K-complex) was an indication of a sudden increase in the upflow of exciting impulses from the reticular formation to the cortex. . . .*

Incidentally, some other names during sleep were specially potent in leading to arousal, none more so than the name of a recent girl-friend (Figure 6.13). While Neville slept, the name of his recently acquired heartthrob, Penelope, *would cause a most violent perturbation in his EEG, and a huge "psychogalvanic response," or sudden sweating of the palm (itching too, perhaps).* (1966, PP. 33–34.)

Clearly, the cortex continued to be active after the subject fell asleep. It served to discriminate between the names with no impor-

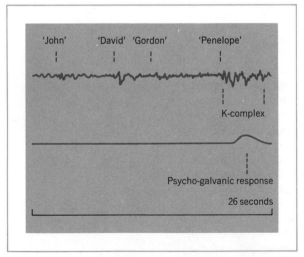

Figure 6.13 Brain wave and autonomic reactions to meaningful stimuli delivered to a sleeping person (Oswald, 1966).

tance and crucial names (the subject's own or his girlfriend's). Significant names resulted in a message to the reticular formation, leading to a momentary arousal. This arousal, reflected in the brain wave and psychogalvanic response,[8] was occasionally intense enough to waken the sleeper. Presumably, an important message alerts the cortex, which in turn temporarily releases the reticular formation from inhibition. This account of Oswald's findings is consistent with our present knowledge of neural mechanisms in sleep.

[8] *This momentary arousal is an example of a* phasic *event, which may be contrasted with the ongoing, background* tonic *events of sleep. (see Footnote 6).*

Theories of Sleep

There are many theories of sleep. We shall limit this account to three. One attempts to explain the origin of sleep in *evolutionary* terms; the second emphasizes *development;* and the third focuses on the *functions* of the two kinds of sleep.

AN EVOLUTIONARY APPROACH. The sleep-wakefulness cycle is closely linked with the evolution of the mammalian nervous system, especially the proliferation of the cerebral cortex, and Kleitman (1963), the pioneer of sleep research, has offered an evolutionary theory of sleep. He distinguishes between *primitive* sleep-wakefulness and *advanced* sleep-wakefulness. The primitive cycle is simply the innate alternation of sleep and wakefulness of those without a functioning cerebral cortex: dogs deprived of a cortex by surgery, children without a cerebrum, and newborn, normal infants. There is an hourly cycle of activity, which coalesces later in development into two-to-four-hour periods of sleep and shorter periods of wakefulness. The 2:1 sleep-wakefulness ratio maintains itself independently of the day-night cycle. In the absence of a functioning cortex, bodily factors determine the onset of waking and of sleep: the animal is awakened by hunger and becomes sleepy after eating. The brief periods of wakefulness are maintained by the reticular activating system through its *descending* paths to receptors and effectors. Sleep is presumably initiated by the lower reticular formation, acting to turn off the reticular activating system.

The advanced cycle evolved together with the cerebral cortex, on which it depends. The sequence of a primitive to an advanced cycle may be seen in human development. The newborn infant, with an essentially nonfunctioning cortex, is barely conscious; but the adult, with a completely functioning cortex, is alert and fully conscious. Kleitman assumes that as an infant develops, consciousness gradually converts the primitive cycle to the advanced one. The cortex becomes part of a feedback system with the reticular activating system, which slowly changes the 2:1 sleep-wakefulness cycle of infancy to the 1:2 cycle of adulthood (see Figure 6.14). The cortex extends the period of wakefulness from a few minutes to roughly 16 hours, presumably because man's curiosity keeps him in continual contact with stimuli that pep up his arousal system. When man is deprived of novelty, as for example by a dull, repetitive lecture, his arousal level falls and he becomes sleepy.

Kleitman assumes that the basic hourly activity cycle of the infant is not lost in the adult. It

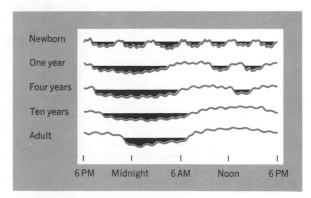

Figure 6.14 Development of the sleep-wakefulness cycle (color-periods of sleep).

stretches to an hour and a half (Hartmann, 1968) and is seen in the waking state as variations in alertness and in the sleeping state as alternations between REM and NREM sleep. This notion requires the further assumption that REM sleep is lighter than NREM sleep, representing the more active phase of the cycle. (Many sleep researchers would not accept this assumption.)

A DEVELOPMENTAL APPROACH. Regardless of the origin of sleep, there are interesting developmental trends during the human life span (see Figure 6.15). The most striking trend is the diminution in sleep from 16 hours in the newborn to less than 6 hours in persons over 70 years old. No less significant is the drop in the proportion of REM sleep, which is 50 percent of sleep in the newborn but only 20–25 percent in 3-year olds. Putting these two trends together, the newborn spends most of his time sleeping, half of it in REM sleep; as the maturing child spends more and more time awake, he spends less and less of his sleeping time in REM sleep. Roffwarg et al. (1966) have suggested that the function of REM sleep is to supply excitation to the developing central nervous system. If the infant is sleeping most of the time, he can take in only small amounts of stimulation, and presumably such stimulation is necessary for normal maturation of the nervous system. If external stimulation is not available, perhaps the internal stimulation accompanying paradoxical sleep can substitute and maintain the proper arousal level needed for neural maturation:

We have hypothesized that the REM mechanism serves as an endogenous[9] source of stimulation, fur-

[9] *Endogenous stimulation originates* internally, *whereas exogenous stimulation originates* externally.

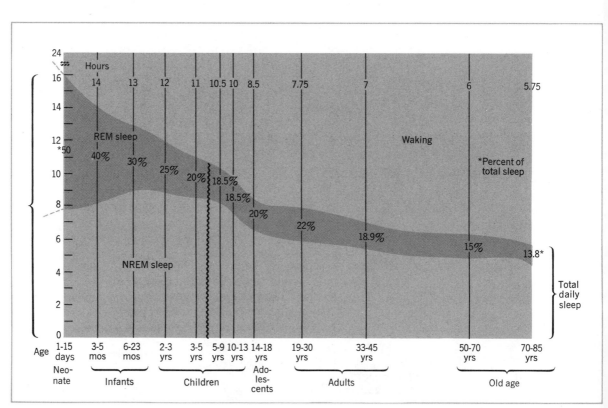

Figure 6.15 Development of orthodox (NREM) and paradoxical (RMM) sleep (Roffway et al., 1966).

nishing great quantities of functional excitation to higher centers. Such stimulation would be particularly crucial during periods in utero and shortly after birth, before appreciable exogenous stimulation is available to the central nervous system. It might assist in structural maturation and differentiation of key sensory and motor areas within the central nervous system, partially preparing them to handle the enormous rush of stimulation provided by the postnatal milieu, as well as contribution to their further growth after birth. The sharp diminution of REM sleep after birth may signify that the mature brain has less need for endogenous stimulation.

(ROFFWARG ET AL., 1966, P. 617.)

If the maturing brain needs internal stimulation to compensate for a lack of waking stimulation, why does the fully mature brain need similar compensation when the individual is awake for 16 hours a day? One possibility is that even a mature brain requires some bare minimum of stimulation. During orthodox sleep the individual is deeply unconscious, the brain receiving virtually no stimulation. Perhaps the cerebral cortex needs to be reinvigorated after orthodox sleep, and paradoxical sleep offers a source of such stimulation (Ephron & Carrington, 1966).

A FUNCTIONAL APPROACH. The basic question here is, "Why do we sleep?" The answer to this question is a theory of sleep. Hartmann (1971) has divided the answer into two parts, one for each kind of sleep. He assumes that NREM sleep fulfills the functions that have always been attributed to sleep: tissue repair, growth, and in general the synthesis of proteins. In contrast, REM sleep presumably consolidates learning and restores the neural processes underlying attention and cognition generally. Hartmann has drawn on a large body of evidence to support his theory; we shall consider only a few of the facts.[10]

NREM sleep appears to be more basic in a biological sense: without rest, the person would eventually collapse. The importance of NREM sleep is reflected in several facts: after deprivation of it, the person is *lethargic* and less able to carry out physical tasks; after deprivation of both kinds of sleep, NREM sleep is compensated for first; and a

variety of drugs that reduce REM sleep have no effect on NREM sleep.

REM sleep, on the other hand, is highly susceptible to drugs, and its deprivation leaves the person *irritable* (rather than lethargic) and poorer at learning and attending. The proportion of REM to total sleep is highest in childhood (see Figure 6.15), which is the period of greatest learning; presumably, less is learned with increasing age, as reflected in the decreased proportion of REM sleep.

There seem to be two kinds of tiredness. The first occurs after strenuous physical work, and it is usually experienced as a pleasant or neutral feeling of drowsiness; presumably, the person needs NREM sleep. The second kind of tiredness occurs often after prolonged mental activity (reading, problem-solving, and so on) or psychological tension (interpersonal conflict, worry over exams, and so on), and it is usually experienced as an unpleasant, taut feeling that is sometimes accompanied by a headache; presumably the person needs REM sleep, but he often finds it difficult to fall asleep.

Finally, there appear to be mood differences associated with the two kinds of sleep. A placid or elated mood tends to go with physical tiredness and a shorter period of total sleep. A tense or anxious mood tends to go with a longer period of sleep, most of which is REM sleep. Long sleepers have no more NREM sleep than do short sleepers, which is consistent with the hypothesis that NREM is a more basic, biologically reparative state that is relatively impervious to psychological disturbance and drugs.

This account has emphasized the differences between the two kinds of sleep. The evidence is not as clear-cut as the theory (it never is). Moreover, the tonic-phasic differences in sleep still need to be explained. However, this functional theory does encompass a large amount of data, and it neatly meshes neural activity with behavior.

Wakefulness

During the waking hours there are two kinds of fluctuations in arousal level. The first is a reaction to stimuli—a phasic alerting response that focuses the person's attention on the source of stim-

---

[10] *For the appropriate research citations, see Hartmann's paper (1971).*

ulation. The second kind of fluctuation is cyclic—a tonic, slow rise and fall of alertness during the course of the day. Both alterations in arousal concern *attention,* which is also involved in the processing of information (see Chapter 19).

Arousal by Stimuli

When men or animals are confronted with novel stimuli, they tend to become aroused. The sense organs are directed toward the source of the stimulation: they sniff and turn the eyes and head, and direct attention to the stimulus. This is *behavioral* arousal. There are also autonomic arousal (changes in heart rate, blood pressure, breathing, and sweating) and central nervous system arousal (changes in EEG, particularly the disappearance of the alpha rhythm). The entire reaction is called the *orienting reflex* (Sokolov, 1963). If the stimulus is irrelevant—that is, has no clear positive or negative consequences—it is subsequently ignored. The orienting reflex wanes each time the stimulus occurs, and eventually the stimulus elicits no arousal (this is called *habituation*—see Chapters 4 and 12).

When stimuli are relevant to the person, he remains in a state of mild arousal. The *pattern* of autonomic arousal depends on the *source* of the stimulation. Lacey (1959, 1963) had subjects perform two tasks involving stimulus *input:* watching patterns of lights and listening to tape recordings of dramatic readings. The heart rates of these subjects *slowed down* (see Figure 6.16). Then the subjects mentally solved arithmetic problems and withstood the pain of holding a hand in ice water. Both of these tasks involve *rejecting* external stimuli, and the subjects' heart rates *accelerated.* In all four tasks, galvanic skin response increased (see Figure 6.16). Thus *attending* to external stimuli leads to one pattern of arousal (heart rate decelerates), and *rejecting* external stimuli leads to another (heart rate accelerates).

A Waking Arousal Cycle

There are variations in body temperature during the daytime. For the average person, the body is coolest in the morning, becomes warmer during the afternoon, and cools again in the evening. This body temperature cycle is directly related to alertness: the higher the temperature, the greater the alertness (Kleitman, 1963). The clearest evidence comes from a task called *choice* reaction time. There are two lights, and the subject is instructed to press a button only when one of the two lights goes on. When the appropriate light

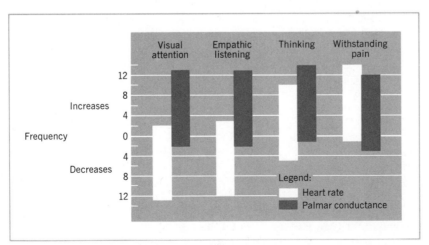

Figure 6.16 Different patterns in arousal when taking in or rejecting stimulus topics (Lacey, 1959).

goes on, he must respond quickly and correctly. The more alert he is, the faster is his reaction time, which is measured in thousandths of a second. The higher the body temperature is, the faster is the subject's reaction time (see Figure 6.17).

There are marked individual differences in the cycle of body temperature—some people are warmest in the morning and others are warmest in the evening. Those whose temperature peaks in the morning tend to wake early and prefer to work in the morning. Those whose temperature peaks in the evening are "evening people": they like to rise late and work best after dark.

Thus the body temperature is clearly associated with alertness, and each person can discover when he is most alert by charting this temperature. Alertness presumably is one aspect of arousal: the person in the middle range of arousal is usually most alert and efficient (see Figure 6.1).

There are also marked individual differences in arousability. Some persons become very aroused (in terms of heart rate and other internal measures) when reacting to stimulation; others become only minimally aroused. These opposed reactions are related to efficiency (Frankenhaeuser et al., 1971). High-arousal subjects perform better when *understimulated,* as in a dull task of watching lights; but low-arousal subjects perform better when *overstimulated,* as when they must perform two tasks simultaneously. Thus both kinds of subjects are most efficient when in the middle range of arousal: a dull task for those who are overaroused, and an exciting task for those who are underaroused.[11]

Biological Rhythms

The daily alternation of sleep and wakefulness is only one of a large number of cycles of arousal. All animals must adapt to fluctuations in the environment, and biological rhythms are adaptations to *regular* changes in the environment over time. The tides ebb and flow twice daily; light alternates with darkness once daily; the moon grows brighter and

[11] *Individual differences in arousal have been studied as a dimension of personality called* sensation-seeking *(Zuckerman, 1971).*

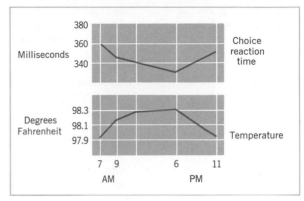

Figure 6.17 Body temperature and reaction time (Kleitman, 1963).

dimmer in a 28-day cycle; and sunlight, temperature, and rainfall vary regularly with the seasons of the year.

Plants and animals have evolved biological rhythms to match the immutable environmental cycles. Some animals are active only during daylight, others only at night. Some animals move about freely while it is warm but hibernate during winter. Most animals breed only during particular seasons of the year. Some species of birds migrate thousands of miles twice each year, moving toward the equator in autumn and away from it in spring.

Man probably has fewer biological rhythms than most animals—as part of his greater independence of the environment. Of the few biological rhythms present in man, two are relevant to behavior: the daily variations in level of arousal (of which the sleep-wakefulness cycle is one example) and the four-week menstrual cycle of women.

The Menstrual Cycle

In animals that reproduce sexually, females have ovarian cycles and they come into heat at regular intervals. Human females do not come into heat, but they do show other behavioral variations during their 28-day menstrual cycle. This cycle, caused by a complex sequence of hormonal changes, can be altered not so much by *physical* changes in the environment as by *psychological* changes in the woman. Thus a woman may begin menstruating early when she is tense or fearful, or she may delay or even skip the menses when she is depressed.

During their normal menstrual cycle, most women show regular fluctuations in mood. Little is known about the positive mood of contentment and happiness, but there is a reliable body of facts about the negative moods of irritability, tension, and anxiety (Bardwick, 1971). These negative moods, which occur during the four days preceding menstruation, have been labeled *premenstrual tension.* It appears to be an especially difficult period for many women. This is the time when a disproportionate number of crimes and suicides are attempted by women, when they have more accidents or become sick, and when they are more likely to seek psychiatric help (Dalton, 1964).

However, the premenstrual period does have one positive feature—increased sexual arousal. Roughly 90 percent of the women in one study reported a greater interest in sex and more orgasms during the four days preceding menstruation (Kinsey et al., 1953). This is of course not the only time women are interested in sex (as it is not the only time they are irritable and have accidents), but it is evidently a period of considerable psychological turmoil and mood change. These cyclic changes in sensitivity and arousal are of course absent in men.

Changing the Cycle

The most important human cycles are not yearly or monthly, but daily. The sleep-wakefulness cycle is obvious, and there are daily variations in the arousal level underlying alertness, giving rise to periodic fluctuations in skill in automobile driving, observing radar, solving problems, and similar tasks requiring close attention. Various bodily chemicals, especially hormones, vary in concentration in a 24-hour cycle. Until recently, few of these periodic fluctuations were of concern to man. He lived completely within nature and could no more alter daily cycles than could other animals. Modern technology, however, has given man the tools to alter some of the cycles of his life. Electric lights can turn night into day, jet air-

plane flights can quickly change one's location (thereby resetting one's day-night cycle), and space flights can remove the day-night cycle entirely.

The basic sleep-wakefulness cycle roughly matches the earth's rotation on its own axis, a period of 24 hours. When men are isolated in caves in the absence of sunlight and clocks, their free-ranging sleep-wakefulness cycle varies around an average of 25 hours (Aschoff, 1965).[12] What would happen if the cycle were changed artificially? Several different researchers have tried shorter cycles (18 or 21 hours) or longer ones (27 or 28 hours) in either caves or northern latitudes (24 hours of sunlight during the summer in the Arctic). After an initial period of adjustment, which varied from one individual to the next, all the men became adjusted to either a shorter or a longer day. This means that there is no "natural" daily cycle:

From the results of these experiments it appears that there is no foundation for assuming that some cosmic forces determine the 24-hour rhythm, aside from "rest, movement, food intake, and sleep." On the contrary, the rhythm seems to be conditioned by activity of the organism which may adapt itself to the astronomic periodicity of day and night. (KLEITMAN, 1963, P. 182.)

That the sleep-wakefulness cycle can be changed is of little practical importance now, but it does have implications for the future. Colonization of the moon is being considered, as are space flights to Mars. Once venturesome man leaves his home planet, he is no longer bound by earth's periods of day and night. For example, the lunar day is two earth-weeks long, which means that man would have to select his own sleep-wakefulness cycle.

A more immediate issue concerns *resetting* the cycle. When workers go on the night shift or return to the day shift, they require up to a week to adjust to the new schedule. The problem is that each of a number of biological processes has its own period of readjustment. Thus water balance might shift quickly; potassium output, more slowly; and body

[12] *Unlike many animals, man is relatively unaffected by changes in the daylight-night cycle. His physiological rhythms are the same with or without light (Aschoff et al., 1971).*

temperature, slowest of all. During the interval of resetting these "biological clocks" they are not properly synchronized. With the various bodily systems out of phase, the individual feels moody and fatigued and cannot attain his usual level of waking efficiency or restful sleep.

Research with animals and man has shown that it is easier to *delay* the daily cycle than it is to *advance* it. Such change is a special problem for someone who flies from one continent to another, over several time zones. When he arrives, his cycle must be reset to the new time zone. The outcome is a period of discomfort and tiredness that ranges from a few hours to several days. This "jet fatigue" is worse when the biological clock is advanced (as in east to west travel) than when it is retarded:

If a traveler leaves on a nonstop flight from New York to Rome (a 7-hour flight, crossing, seven time zones) at 6:30 p.m., he will arrive at 8:30 a.m. local time, which is 1:30 a.m. New York time. He is thus biologically ready to sleep, and not hungry. However, with sufficient conscious effort, he can immediately engage in business meetings, tours, meals, and social functions, but probably at less than peak efficiency for the first 24 hours.

The return flight, after the traveler has become fully adapted to the local time, leaves Rome at 11 a.m. and arrives in New York at 2:15 p.m. after a 10-hour flight. Sleep, which is "due" in 2 or 3 hours, may be delayed for a while, but the "biological clock" starts its awakening process by late evening, and sound sleep, once attained, is hard to maintain. . . . Adaptation after westward flights can thus be expected to take longer than after eastward flights of the same length.

(SIEGEL ET AL., 1969, PP. 1253–54.)

Jet fatigue is merely another in the catalogue of problems facing man as his technology takes him beyond the "natural" environment to which he is adapted.

Perspective

The details discussed in this chapter may have obscured the larger issues involved in arousal. It is true that arousal occurs in three different systems — behavior, the autonomic nervous system, and the central nervous system — but there are theoretical matters that apply to all three

systems and then to the general concept of arousal.

Tonic and Phasic Arousal

One major issue concerns the tonic-phasic dichotomy, which was first raised in an attempt to understand dreaming but which deserves broader application. Thus one kind of arousal may be labeled *tonic* — the longer-lasting states ebb and flow slowly. Tonic arousal includes all the biological rhythms: the sleep-wakefulness cycle, the alternation of REM and NREM sleep, the variations in temperature and alertness during the day, and the menstrual cycle. Tonic arousal also includes several different enduring states that are *not* cyclical; these may be described by the dichotomies *interested-bored, irritable-placid,* and *energetic-fatigued.* These generalized states of being (roughly speaking, *moods*) are usually affected by the person's recent history of successes and failures, activity and rest, and even the ambient temperature and pressure. Weather is recognized as an important determiner of tonic arousal; bright, crisp, sunny days are associated with energy, interest, and buoyancy, whereas dull, gray, rainy days are associated with tiredness, apathy, and low spirits. In brief, tonic arousal includes enduring states that fluctuate cyclically or noncyclically.

Phasic arousal is a temporary state that originates as a reaction to specific stimuli. The best examples are the K complexes of sleep (see Figure 6.13), the orienting reflex, and emotional reactions such as fear and rage (to be discussed in chapter 21). Phasic arousal involves sudden changes from the more enduring, tonic level of arousal that is the more usual state of the person. If the phasic disturbance is sufficiently intense, it may trigger homeostatic mechanisms, which then restore the level of arousal to its more typical tonic ("resting") state. In brief, phasic arousal is a reaction to specific stimuli — external, as in the orienting reflex, or internal, as in dreams. In contrast to tonic arousal, phasic arousal is relatively sudden, short-lived, and specific.[13]

---

[13] *The tonic-phasic distinction helps us to understand fluctuations in attention during long-term vigilance tasks such as making astronomical observations and monitoring radar screens (see Mackworth, 1968). Tonic and phasic differences are also important in reaction time (Porges, 1972).*

Diffuse Versus Directional Aspects

The main quantitative dimension of arousal is *intensity*—variations from low to high arousal. There is no directional component, only a diffuse and usually generalized reaction; this is true of both tonic and phasic arousal. When we know that someone is highly aroused, we do not know whether he will move toward or away from a particular stimulus or goal. We do not know what his needs are or which incentives will spur him to action. All we know is that his generalized reaction (behaviorally or neurally) is intense.

The *directional* aspect of behavior belongs under the heading of *motivation.* To know someone's motivation is to know whether he will move toward or away from a particular stimulus or goal and which incentives will move him. Most motivation (states of need, desires for incentives, and so on) is accompanied by arousal, but arousal does not have a directional component. Moreover, arousal is diffuse, whereas motivation can be diffuse (desire for stimulation) or specific (desire to see a particular movie).

chapter 7

biological motivation

*Programed tendencies — instinct — drive —
classification of motives — hunger (peripheral
and central theories, biochemical factors,
obesity, and food preferences) — curiosity —
pleasure and pain areas in the brain — neural
theory of motivation — push and pull models*

Man, no less than any other animal, must satisfy certain fundamental biological needs. He must supply himself with sufficient food and water to insure good health—or at least to prevent severe weakness or death. He must protect his body against threats, responding to danger by fighting or escaping. And he must find a mate, reproduce, and nurture the next generation, or his line will die out. These biological requirements—vegetative, protective, and reproductive—must be met, for they concern nothing less than the survival of individuals and species. These requirements and the mechanisms for meeting them constitute the subject matter of biological motivation.

Programed Tendencies

It bears repeating that all animals must possess capabilities for individual and species survival. These capabilities can be programed in two different ways. The first is a fixed, rigid tendency to make a specific, adaptive response. For example, certain birds show a full range of the movements and calls characteristic of their species, even when they are raised without parents (Hinde & Tinbergen, 1958). Within a species the pattern is unchanging and inflexible, and one bird's calls differ little, if at all, from another's.

The second kind of programed tendency is more diffuse, flexible, and open to experience. For example, higher animals and especially human beings are curious and tend to explore their environment. This motivation is "built in," but it is shaped and directed to a large extent by the experiences of the individual animal. Consequently, there may be wide individual differences in the exploratory behavior of various members of the same species.

These two kinds of programs—one rigid and specific, and the other flexible and diffuse—define the ends of a continuum that contains many gradations between the extremes. For clarity of exposition we shall contrast the extremes, but the reader should bear in mind the continuous nature of the dimension (see Figure 7.1).

Instinctive Behavior

The highly specific and rigid end of the continuum is called instinct, or more properly, instinctive behavior.[1] Such behavior usually consists of several responses linked together in an adaptive sequence. Instinctive behavior usually begins with a change in the *internal state* of the animal, one that sensitizes it to particular stimuli. These stimuli trigger a sequence of responses that meet a need related to individual or species survival:

Young inexperienced fish and birds manifest in the spring a complex sequence of activities, such as migration, nest building, courtship, displays, mating, brooding, and caring for the young, activities that they never have engaged in before and that are apparently prompted by changing tissue conditions. Signals that they did not heed previously, such as a color patch on the skin or feather (the sex mark of a displaying sex partner or competitor) a leaf or a twig (materials suitable for nest building) become now major attractions, and strenuous acts, such as pro-

[1] *Instinct is usually defined as an inherited tendency or force. It has a long history and carries many different meanings. For this reason, most psychologists prefer the term* instinctive behavior, *which is less controversial and more descriptive. This usage ignores distinctions made by ethologists, which are too complex to be discussed here.*

Instinctive behavior		Drive
Low (insects)	Evolutionary scale	High (mammals)
Rigid		Flexible
Specific		Generalized
Unmodifiable by experience		Modifiable by experience

Figure 7.1 Innate, programed behavioral tendencies.

curing food for the young, become their almost daily occupation. (ALTMAN, 1966, PP. 404–405.)

This example contains one of the criteria of instinctive behavior: *innateness*. The sequence of responses must occur in animals that have not previously been exposed to the situation eliciting the behavior. In other words, the animal has had no individual experience that could serve as a basis of learning. The behavior is presumably pre-programed in the nervous system and is determined solely by the nonexperiential factors: genetic, biological, and psychological-constant (see Chapter 4).

The second criterion is *adaptiveness*. Most instinctive behavior involves mating, rearing of the young, and social interaction (mainly in relation to threats either by or to the animal). These activities are basic to species or individual survival and thus are adaptive—virtually by definition.

The third criterion is that the behavior be *species wide*. Some allowance may be made for variations in the strength or intensity of the behavior, but it should be present in all normal members of the species.

The three criteria—innateness, adaptiveness, and universality—offer an adequate definition of instinctive behavior, but they are not always easy to apply. Instinctive behavior is not qualitatively different from other behavior, and none of the criteria is all-or-none. There is no dichotomy between innate and learned behavior (see Chapter 4); a response may be present in most but not all members of a species; and adaptiveness also varies quantitatively. When there is a continuum of behavior, distinctions, however valuable, must be arbitrary and therefore fallible.

Most instinctive behavior is rigid, sometimes to the extent of being unmodifiable. Consider the behavior of a digger wasp (see Figure 7.2). Without prior experience, it digs a hole, hunts a caterpillar, stings it, and deposits it in the hole. Then it lays an egg, covers the nest, and leaves. The sequence of acts is inflexible, each response following the one before it, with no deviation. Thus, if the stung caterpillar is removed after it has been deposited, the wasp still lays an egg and seals the nest. Of course, in the natural order of things, no one is likely to remove the caterpillar, which means that the rigid sequence is entirely adaptive. But the adaptiveness holds only for a stable environment. The program is for a certain environment and only that one; it cannot cope with shifts in ecology. In this respect, instinctive behavior is less adaptive

in the long run than more open and diffuse programs, which, because they allow for the effects of experience, are flexible and modifiable.

Stimuli play a minimal role in eliciting instinctive behavior. They serve merely to trigger a response sequence that is already primed by internal conditions and ready to fire. For much instinctive behavior the stimulus is analogous to the ignition switch in an automobile: it simply closes a circuit, thereby releasing a chain of reactions that have their own preset mechanisms. Such a stimulus is called a *releaser*. There are circumstances, however, when stimuli also play a guiding role. Courtship in many birds and fishes proceeds in a back-and-forth fashion, with the response of one partner triggering a response in its mate, which in turn elicits a response from the other, and so on. Each stimulus releases the next response in the sequence, and thus stimuli help in *guiding* the partners in the direction of copulation. The role of stimuli here is to maintain the chain of responses that constitute the adaptive behavioral sequence.

Drive

Instinct has been assigned to the low end of the evolutionary continuum of programed behavioral tendencies (see Figure 7.1). The remainder of the continuum falls under the heading of *drive*. Though some psychologists will quarrel with this usage, it appears to fit the notion of drive as it has been used for the past several decades: as basic motivation related to the biological requirements of individual and species survival.

At the drive end of the continuum, response sequences are not completely programed; they develop as the young organism matures. This requires a longer period of development, and, as we saw in Chapter 4, higher animals do take longer to reach maturity. The behavior is not primed to be triggered by specific stimuli. Here the role of stimuli is one of information, providing cues and signs leading to the selection of appropriate responses.

These characteristics lead to the opening up of the tie between biological needs and the responses that meet these needs. Whereas in instinct the link is direct and specific, in drive the link is indirect and generalized. The (mammalian) animal in a state of need becomes aroused and

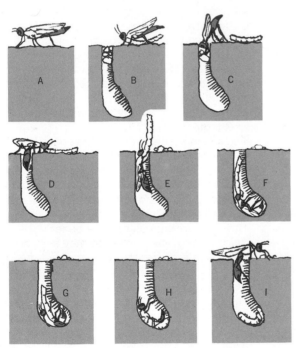

Figure 7.2 *A behavioral pattern in the digger wasp.* A. *Having dug its nest, the wasp captures and stings a caterpillar, paralyzing it.* B. *It transports its prey to the nest.* C. *After depositing its prey nearby, it opens the nest.* D to G. *It packs its victim into the nest.* H. *It lays an egg on its still-paralyzed victim.* I. *It crawls from the nest, reclosing it and leaving it permanently.* (Simpon & Beck, 1965.).

Table 7.1

Differences Between Instinct and Drive

	INSTINCT	DRIVE
1. Programed sequences of responses	Fairly complete, specific patterns	Few such responses and only generalized programs
2. Role of stimuli	Releasers (triggers) of behavior already built in	Cues and signs, providing information needed to select appropriate responses
3. Link between biological need and behavior	Direct, specific	Indirect, diffuse
4. Appropriate model	Reactive organism, relatively unmodifiable	Active organism, relatively modifiable

active, but it does not initially possess the means of satisfying the need. Newborn mammals are so helpless that they will die if not nurtured by a parent. The young animal must *learn* the responses that lead to the appropriate goal. Of course, higher animals are programed to learn, just as they are programed to seek the objects that will satisfy their basic needs.

The trend toward loosening the tie between need and behavior culminates in man. Mason has commented that

. . . *the structure and integration of human behavior has become heavily dependent upon environmental support, and, at the same time, less dependent upon specific forms of experience. Of all the primates, man has gone farthest in an evolutionary venture in which the reliability and efficiency of instinctive patterns have been sacrificed to achieve the behavioral plasticity and the liberation of psychic energies that are so much a part of the human condition.*

(1968, P. 101.)

These distinctions between instinct and drive are listed in Table 7.1. As can be seen, the two kinds of programs lead to different models of the organism. Where instinct predominates, the animal possesses a fixed pattern of behavior; it is turned on or off by specific stimuli (releasers). What they release, of course, is the sequence of behavior already built in. There is little or no room here for the impact of individual experience, and the animal does not act; it *reacts.*

Where drive predominates, there is no fixed pattern of responses leading immediately to the biologically relevant goal. There are general tendencies, but they must be sharpened into specific acts by the honing edge of experience. Thus lion cubs have the essential response components needed for killing prey, but they must learn to put them together to become hunters. Learning, being inserted between the specific behavior and the need that motivates it, must open up the link between the biological requirement and the response specifically relevant to it. This is a rela-

Table 7.2
Classification of Biological Motives

TYPE	GOAL OR REQUIREMENT	MOTIVE
Vegetative	Food Water	Hunger Thirst
Emergency	Escape from threat Eliminating threat	Fear* Rage*
Reproductive	Procreation Rearing young	Sex* Parental nurturance
"Educational"	Stimuli "Knowledge"	Curiosity Exploration (manipulation)

* These drives are also treated as emotions.

tively modifiable program in which the animal does not merely react, but *actively* seeks appropriate goals.

Man's basic motivation—the tendencies built into him—are not limited to behaviors serving individual or species survival. The evolutionary trend toward more open programs has led to motivations that are adaptive only in the broadest sense of the term. These are the motivations that must be built into an active, seeking animal: curiosity and exploration. These two drives may be added to the drives more closely linked to survival (hunger, thirst, and so on) to complete the list of biological drives.

Classification of Biological Drives

Biological drives may be classified into four kinds (Altman, 1966): vegetative, emergency, reproductive, and "educational" (see Table 7.2). Vegetative drives are the oldest and most fundamental tendencies; all living things require nutrition for sustenance, and every animal is programed to ac-

quire the chemicals needed to maintain its own existence. In higher animals the basic vegetative requirements are food and water, and the corresponding motives are hunger and thirst. Though hunger and thirst differ in some obvious ways (for example, the *experience* of hunger is different from that of thirst), as *motives* they are essentially similar. Therefore we shall discuss only hunger, which is more interesting psychologically (for example, the phenomenon of obesity).

The emergency drives are also vital for the survival of the individual. In response to a threat to its existence, an animal can attempt to escape from the danger or eliminate it. In both instances (flight or fight) there is a massive preparatory reaction; one reaction is called fear, the other is rage. Fear and rage are not only motives but also emotions.

The reproductive motive of sex is also an emotion. Sex, fear, and rage will be discussed together with the responses associated with them (rage, for example, is often associated with aggression) in the chapter on emotion and affect (Chapter 21).

The other reproductive motive, parental nurturance, has a special status. In animals it is innate and commonly set in motion by chemical changes, especially in females. Thus immediately after a cat gives birth to a litter of kittens, her internal chemical state drives her to lick and to be rewarded by the smell of her kittens and the by-products of the birth. In humans, however, parental nurturance appears to be entirely learned. Children must acquire the appropriate parental roles as they mature. In spite of the various hormonal changes occurring during pregnancy, there is no *chemical* inducement that could produce maternal behavior. Maternal and paternal nurturance must be *learned;* in some instances the learning does not occur, as we know from cases of child neglect. Parental nurturance will be discussed in the context of social attachment (Chapter 20).

Individual survival requires both the acquisition of food and water (hunger and thirst drives) and an appropriate response to threat (fear-flight or rage-attack). Survival of the species requires both procreation (sex drive) and rearing of the next generation (parental nurturance). All these motives are likely to result in generation after generation of animals that are capable of both surviving and leaving behind sufficient numbers of offspring.

The remaining two drives are not so closely linked with natural selection, but they are adaptive. They move the animal in the direction of novelty, to investigate and "map" its environment. Curiosity and exploration lead to a store of knowledge that is potentially useful in the learning of adaptive responses. Such knowledge might include possible sites of food and shelter, as well as paths to mates or to safety. In higher animals, especially primates, the tendency to manipulate develops motor skills that open up a range of possibilities. Primates can peel bananas and throw sticks, manipulations that are well beyond the capabilities of most animals. But manipulatory potential has been realized to the greatest extent by man, whose propensity for tinkering and handling of objects has yielded manufactured objects of considerable artistry and intricacy.

The tendency of human infants to explore and manipulate develops into strivings for mastery and competence. When these motives are interact with certain socialization practices, a strong need for achievement develops. These various elaborations of the exploratory-manipulating motive are best understood in the context of socialization, which elaborates *biological* drives into *social* motivation (see Chapter 22). Curiosity remains more of a generalized tendency, one that can be studied in both men and animals. We shall discuss it in this chapter, along with hunger.

Hunger

To each of us hunger consists of the *experience* of hunger, usually called hunger pangs. These vague feelings, the result of missing a meal, can cause considerable discomfort. A broader definition of hunger, encompassing a variety of phenomena, is a *readiness to eat.*

It is useful to divide hunger into a sequence of three phases, which may be illustrated by a college student studying late into the night. Suddenly, he decides that he is too hungry to continue studying. He looks for a late-closing diner, buys and eats a hamburger and milkshake, and then returns to his studying with hunger pangs appeased. The sequential phases are (1) appetitive—deprivation of food leads to hunger and foodseeking; (2) consummatory—eating food; and (3) satiation—eating stops and the motivation to seek food disappears.

The adaptiveness of the sequence is clear: men and animals are motivated to seek and ingest the substances they need to sustain life. But this overview offers no clue to the *mechanisms* underlying hunger. When a man has been deprived of food, there must be an internal signal that motivates foodseeking. The signal might originate in the central nervous system, specifically the brain; or the signal might be a change *peripheral* to the central nervous system—for example, salivation or stomach contractions. There must be an internal signal to stop eating and this, too, might be peripheral or central.

We know that men and animals may overeat and become obese. Is obesity caused by a faulty mechanism that turns *on* eating, by a faulty mechanism that fails to turn *off* eating, or by both? Do biochemical factors such as blood sugar level play a role? What about learned preferences? In brief, an understanding of hunger requires exploring these issues: peripheral mechanisms, central mechanisms, biochemical factors, obesity, and food preferences.These issues will be discussed in sequence.

Peripheral Mechanisms

Does the signal for hunger originate in the mouth? One way to answer this question is to bypass the mouth by having food delivered directly to the stomach through a tube. When this was done with rats, they were able to maintain their normal weight on a liquid diet (Epstein & Teitelbaum, 1962). The rats nicely compensated for variations in the density of the liquid food, and the taste of the food proved to be unimportant. Thus the factors of taste, chewing, and swallowing — all sources of signals from the mouth — are not *necessary* for normal feeding.[2]

Perhaps the signal for hunger originates in the stomach. Most of us have experienced both the stomach contractions called hunger pangs — presumably the *trigger* for hunger — and the stomach distension that follows a heavy meal — presumably the *brake* on hunger. The hypothetical sequence is diagramed in Figure 7.3.

The evidence for this peripheral mechanism is more than a half-century old (Cannon & Washburn, 1912). Washburn, a graduate student, was induced to swallow a balloon which, when inflated in his stomach, yielded a mechanical record of contractions (see Figure 7.4). These contractions — presumably caused by the stomach's being

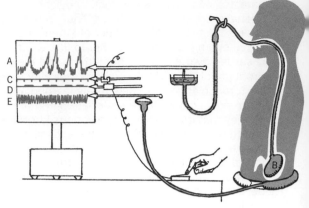

Figure 7.4 *Recording stomach contractions.*

empty — coincided precisely with his reported hunger pangs. Subsequently, it was found that infants have stomach contractions just prior to their usual nursing time (Carlson, 1916).

This research established that stomach contractions can be the signal for hunger, but is this signal *necessary* for hunger? To find out, researchers cut the motor nerves to the stomach of rats and injected them with insulin, which sharply reduces blood sugar level and ordinarily causes hunger (Morgan & Morgan, 1940; Grossman et al., 1947). In the absence of stomach contractions the animals showed the expected hunger after being injected with insulin. When this experiment was tried with human medical patients, they reported hunger sensations and ate normally (Grossman & Stein, 1948). When the *sensory* nerves from the stomach were cut — thereby preventing impulses from the stomach reaching the brain — human patients still reported sensations of hunger after being injected with insulin (Grossman et al., 1947). Thus stomach contractions *may* serve as a peripheral signal for hunger,[3] but they are not *necessary*. Hunger remains even when peripheral mechanisms (mouth and stomach) are prevented from functioning. This means that the basic mechanism must be in the central nervous system, specifically the brain.

[2] *Signals from the mouth may not be* necessary, *but they may be an important* supplementary *factor in feeding, as we shall see below.*

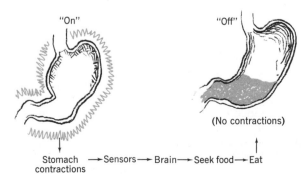

Figure 7.3 *Peripheral theory of hunger.*

[3] *A recent survey of the evidence (Stunkard & Fox, 1971) shows a definite but weak relationship between stomach movements and the experience of hunger.*

Central Mechanisms

As we noted in Chapter 5, recurring catering activities are mediated largely by the old brain, and the role of this neural system has been established for feeding (see Erlich, 1964; Stellar, 1967). The most important structure in this neural system is the *hypothalamus*. The hypothalamus is a complex structure with many nuclei; the parts that concern us here are the *medial* (middle) hypothalamus and the *lateral* (side) hypothalamus.[4]

The role of the hypothalamus in feeding has been established largely by two experimental techniques: electrical stimulation and surgical removal. When rats are allowed to eat until they are satiated, electrical stimulation of the *lateral* hypothalamus causes them to resume eating (Miller, 1958); this suggests that the lateral hypothalamus *turns on* feeding. When rats are in the midst of eating, electrical stimulation of the medial hypothalamus causes them to stop (Wyr-wicka & Dobrzecka, 1960); this suggests that the medial hypothalamus *turns off* eating.

When parts of the hypothalamus are selectively destroyed, the results neatly complement the electrical stimulation research. When only the medial hypothalamus is destroyed, rats eat so much that they become obese (see Figure 7.5); when the lateral hypothalamus is destroyed, the animals stop eating completely (Anand & Brobeck, 1951). The findings from both electrical stimulation and surgical destruction research are summarized in Table 7.3. The simplest explanation of these data is that the lateral hypothalamus is a *hunger* (feeding) center, and the medial hypothalamus is a *satiety* center.

Clearly, the hypothalamus plays a crucial role in hunger and the regulation of eating.[5] Nevertheless, it is best regarded as the major component of a neural circuit in the old brain rather than as *the* regulatory center. This point was made forcefully by Teitelbaum and Epstein (1962), who destroyed

[4] *These labels are only roughly accurate, but we need to simplify some very complex neural anatomy.*

[5] *This conclusion is a majority view; for a minority report see Davenport & Balagura (1971).*

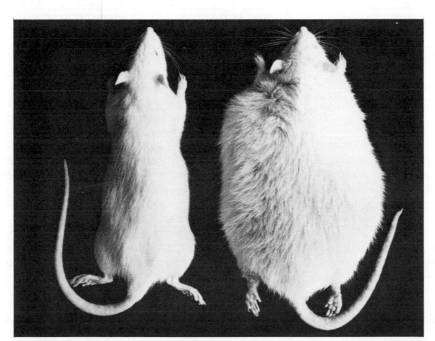

Figure 7.5 *Hypothalamic obese female rat (right) compared with its control.*
(PHILIP TEITELBAUM)

Table 7.3

The Hypothalamus and Feeding

NEURAL STRUCTURE	EXPERIMENTAL PROCEDURE	
	ELECTRICAL STIMULATION	SURGICAL DESTRUCTION
Lateral hypothalamus (hunger center)	Initiates feeding	Stops feeding
Medial hypothalamus (satiety center)	Stops feeding	Initiates feeding

the lateral hypothalamus of rats. These animals would normally have starved to death, but they were kept alive through gastric tube feeding. Gradually, the rats recovered the ability to eat, first only highly palatable food and later all food. There are residual problems—for example, the animals are finicky eaters—but they do eat in the absence of neural impulses from the lateral hypothalamus. This means that other brain centers must also be involved in hunger.

Biochemical Factors

The function of eating is to ingest nutrients. It follows that the neural mechanisms in hunger must themselves be triggered by biochemical factors in the blood. The chemical most likely to affect neural structures—especially the hypothalamus—is *glucose,* which is the prime source of energy for the body. Mayer (1955, 1967) assumes that it is not the absolute glucose level, but the *difference* between glucose levels in arterial and in venous blood. He assumes that when the glucose concentration is higher in arterial blood, the hypothalamus (inhibitory center) fires and there is satiation. When the glucose level is higher in venous blood, the lateral hypothalamus (excitatory center) fires and there is hunger. Though this specific hypothesis about glucose level has not been proved, it has been shown that the content of the

blood is a major determinant of hunger (Davis et al., 1967). First, they deprived rats and discovered how much food they ate normally. Then they again deprived the rats and transfused them with blood from *satiated* rats; now the hungry rats ate only half as much food as they would normally. When the hungry rats were transfused blood from other *hungry* rats, there was no reduction in the amount of food eaten (see Figure 7.6). Thus the blood of a satiated animal must contain a substance that inhibits feeding, a fact that strengthens Mayer's theory.

The major alternative theory assumes that the temperature of the body determines hunger (Brobeck, 1960). Food warms the body; its absence cools the body. When the body is warming up, there is presumably no hunger; but when the body is cooling off, hunger increases. Some animals tend to eat more when the external environment is cold and less when it is hot. It is also known that the hypothalamus regulates body temperature and is sensitive to minute changes in the temperature of the blood. Brobeck's theory attempts to integrate these facts by focusing on body temperature as the major determinant of hunger. Neither Brobeck's nor Mayer's theory has been proved, and it is possible that they are both correct. Thus hunger may be caused by both an arterial-venous glucose differential in the blood and a fall in body temperature.

In summary, several decades of research have

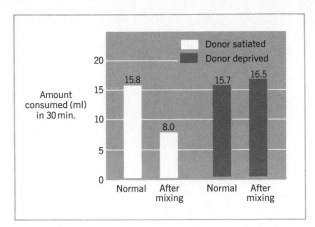

Figure 7.6 Effect on eating of transfusing blood from satiated rats (Davis et al., 1967, p. 1248)

furnished this tentative picture of hunger and food seeking in mammals:

A bout of feeding behavior starts with locomotion in search of food — the appetitive phase. This phase is triggered by activity in the lateral hypothalamic feeding centers and inactivity in the medial satiety centers. The release of the feeding centers from inhibition by the satiety centers, a response to a wide variety of changes in the body associated with deprivation of food, may be the primary step. Changes in the higher brain centers may also release feeding areas from inhibition, allowing for the demonstrable influence of learning on periodic patterns of feeding. After repeated acts of eating and swallowing, followed by arrival of food in the stomach — the consummatory phase — the bout of feeding eventually terminates. Oropharyngeal [mouth and throat] factors play an undetermined but definite role. Stomach distension

plays a critical role, directly activating the satiety center, which then inhibits the feeding center.

(MARLER & HAMILTON, 1966, PP. 129–130.)

Obesity

The feeding mechanism of humans, indeed of most animals, is based on the scarcity of food available under natural conditions. Our biological adaptations concerning eating were never meant to cope with the changed conditions of life in technologically advanced societies: abundance of food, succulence of many of the products of modern cookery, and the diminished energy requirements of a mechanical age. The outcome has been a tendency toward overweight by many adults in societies such as ours. Comparing persons of normal weight with those clearly overweight, do we find differences in their control mechanisms for eating?

Schachter (1968) asserts that overweight and normal persons differ as to whether eating is controlled *internally* or *externally*. He assumes that the normal person experiences hunger and seeks food when his physiological state (empty stomach, for example) indicates deprivation of food. He does not eat because of the sight or smell of food or because of the social aspects of dining. The situation is precisely the opposite for the obese person, who ignores his physiological state as a determiner for eating. His eating is turned on by the sight, smell, or taste of food, the presence of others eating, or a belief that it is mealtime. In brief, Schachter holds that the hunger of the normal person is under *internal* control and that the hunger of the obese person is under *external* control.

Research Report

Schachter confirmed his hypothesis in a series of experiments with overweight and normal persons (see Schachter, 1971*a* and 1971*b*, for reviews of the research). His initial problem was to measure the subjects' eating behavior without their discovering his true purpose. He therefore disguised the experiments as studies of taste preference, in which the subjects judged crackers on several dimensions of taste (salty, cheesy, garlicky, and so on). The subjects could eat as many crackers as they wanted, and the real dependent variable was the number of crackers eaten. All subjects omitted the meal preceding the experiment, so all were hungry.

In the first experiment half the subjects were fed roast beef sandwiches; the other half were fed nothing. When the subjects were hungry, the obese persons ate less than the normals (see Figure 7.7). As Schachter's hypothesis suggests, the normal persons responded more to their internal stimuli (hunger pangs) than did obese persons. As expected, when normal subjects had eaten, they consumed fewer crackers; obese subjects ate as many crackers when full as when hungry (see Figure 7.7).

In the next experiment Schachter frightened subjects, on the assumption that the internal reactions of fear (autonomic arousal) are incompatible with hunger. The hungry subjects were threatened with either mild electric shock (low fear) or severe electric shock (high fear). In relation to low fear, high fear depressed the appetite of normal persons but left the appetite of obese persons unchanged (see Figure 7.8). Again the normal subjects were sensitive to their internal state but the obese were not.

In the third experiment, time was manipulated by speeding up or slowing down the laboratory clock. Subjects started the experiment at 5:05 P.M., and 30 minutes later they were allowed to eat crackers. Half the subjects thought it was 15 minutes later (5:20 P.M.), and the other half thought it was an hour later (6:05 — dinner time). The normal subjects unexpectedly ate less when they thought it was 6:05 (see Figure 7.9), but interviews revealed that this was only because some of them did not want to spoil their appetite for dinner by eating immediately before it. The obese subjects, as expected, ate more when they thought it was dinner time — that is, more when the clock said "6:05" than when it said "5:20."

Schachter's hypothesis leads to several predictions, which have been confirmed by subsequent research. First, Yom Kippur is a

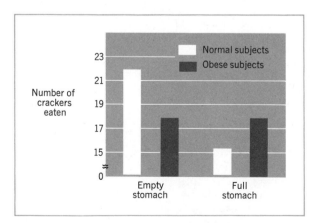

Figure 7.7 Effects of preliminary eating on amounts eaten by normal and obese subjects (Schachter, 1968).

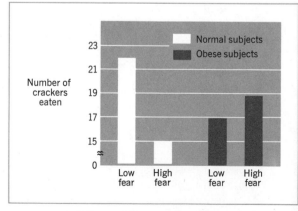

Figure 7.8 Effects of fear on the amounts eaten by normal and obese subjects.

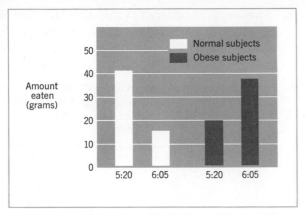

Figure 7.9 *Effects of manipulation of time on the amounts eaten by normal and obese subjects (Schachter, 1968).*

fasting day for religious Jews and therefore controls their eating. As predicted, overweight Jews are more likely to fast on this religious holiday than are normal Jews (Goldman et al., 1968). Second, overweight persons, being controlled more by external factors such as taste of food, should be less tolerant of the bad food in college dormitories; in fact, they are (Goldman et al., 1968). Furthermore, overweight persons eat more ice cream than normal persons only when ice cream tastes good (Nisbett, 1968). Third, normal persons, but not overweight persons, may be expected to buy more food when they are deprived than when satiated. Normals do buy more in a supermarket when they have been deprived, but overweight persons buy more after they have eaten (Nisbett & Kanouse, 1969).

This research offers strong support for Schachter's hypothesis. In normal persons, food deprivation leads to hunger pangs and eating behavior. In obese persons, hunger is turned on not by deprivation, but by external variables such as the presence of others eating, the appropriate time to eat, and the taste and sight of food. Thus in the long run, dieting and losing weight will not suffice for the fat person. He will also have to alter his response to the external cues that turn on his eating.

But what turns off the obese person's eating? If his eating is under external control, he should continue to eat until all the food is gone or it is taken away. Overweight persons certainly do eat larger meals, but they do stop eating even when there is food available. Schachter's hypothesis cannot account for this fact.

His hypothesis also fails to explain one of his own findings. When obese persons are given access to almonds, they eat them if the nuts have been shelled but not if they still have shells on them; normal persons eat almonds whether they are shelled or unshelled (Schachter, 1971a). Why do obese persons refrain from eating when they must work to get at the food?[6]

One possibility is that obese persons have a deficit in response inhibition (Singh, 1973). Once they are making a particular response—say, eating—they have difficulty in inhibiting it and switching to other behavior. Singh (1973) tested this hypothesis under the guise of a taste-

[6] *Overweight newborn human infants also consume less when the nipple of the milk bottle requires greater sucking effort (Nisbett & Gurwitz, 1970).*

preference experiment. Subjects were first trained to move hollow crackers (Pizza Spins) along a twisted steel wire (see Figure 7.10). As each cracker was removed, it was eaten. Subsequently, the subjects were tested under *compatible* or *incompatible* conditions (see Figure 7.11). In the compatible condition, the crackers were moved the same way as in training. In the incompatible condition the crackers were moved in the direction opposite to that of training; thus the subjects had to inhibit their previously learned response.

Both obese and normal subjects were used; they were run under hungry or satiated conditions, but degree of hunger had no effect on the number of crackers eaten. What did affect the amount consumed was whether the test response was compatible with the training response, but only for obese subjects; they ate significantly fewer crackers under the incompatible condition than under the compatible condition. For normal subjects there was essentially no difference in the amounts eaten.

Note that in this experiment there were no differences in either internal or external stimuli. The only difference was in response compatibility, and the obese subjects had difficulty in inhibiting a response acquired previously. There are other data that suggest that the obese person's deficit in response inhibition extends beyond eating to a variety of behaviors (Singh, 1973). In fact, both Schachter and Singh have noted the close parallel between the behavior of obese animals (rats and men) and that of rats without a medial hypothalamus. This leads to the highly speculative but intriguing hypothesis that obese persons may have a malfunctioning medial hypothalamus. Whether or not this guess proves to be correct, the research on humans has established two facts about obese persons. First, they are stimulus-bound and control their eating by external cues (Schachter, 1971a). Second, they have a deficit in response inhibition, which may account for their relative inability to stop eating (Singh, 1973).

Food Preference

So far we have discussed the amount of food eaten and the variables that determine hunger. The other aspect of feeding is *preference*. Most animals prefer some foods to others, and some animals have become so limited in what they will eat that they can exist only in a narrow, specialized environment. The koala, for example, requires the leaf of the eucalyptus tree and cannot survive without it. Of course natural selection rarely hones nutritional needs to so fine a point. The majority of animals, including man, can meet their food requirements in many different ways and can easily shift from one kind of food to another.

If natural selection has shaped food preference, animals should select a beneficial diet when al-

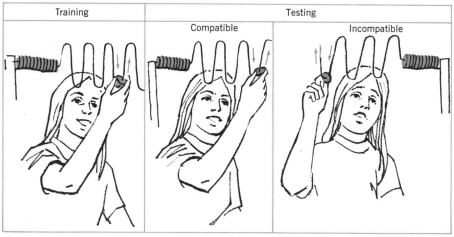

Figure 7.10 Testing for response inhibition (Singh, 1973).

lowed to choose from a variety of foods. Casual observations of such domestic animals as pigs, cows, and chickens suggest that they do select a balanced diet. More systematic observations and reliable data clearly were needed, and Richter et al. (1938) performed the basic experiment. Rats were allowed to select from 11 different pure food compounds (sugar, salt, wheat germ oil, etc.), and the intake of each was measured. There were day-to-day imbalances, but these canceled out and the selections over time were consistent with the rat's nutritional needs.

Can humans do as well? Older children learn many food preferences that lead to severely imbalanced diets, which means that the test should be conducted with infants. Davis (1928) allowed three infants, 6 to 12 months of age, to select food from a large variety of foodstuffs presented on a tray. They were somewhat messier than the rats, but the outcome was essentially the same: the day-to-day variations were substantial, but over time the selections led to balanced diets and normal growth.

If animals are deprived of necessary foods, will they eat these foods selectively to compensate for the deficiency? In most instances, yes. Rats deprived of vitamin B consume more of this substance (Richter & Eckert, 1938). Rats with a salt deficiency — as a result of having their adrenal glands removed — consume more salt and have a lower preference threshold for salt than do normal rats (Richter, 1939). But the evidence is not entirely positive: when rats are allowed to select their own diet, they satisfy nutritional needs, but some of them lose weight (Scott, 1946).

All of this research suggests that animals tend to select foods in proportions that are healthful, but the selection is far from perfect. This is consistent with what we know about the evolutionary mechanism of natural selection: it is a rare mechanism that is maximally efficient. Nature works with what is available, and the results are not perfection but are adaptations that keep the animal reasonably healthy through the reproductive period.

Of course the mechanism does not always work. There are learned preferences that may oppose the animal's needs, and these are especially strong in humans. At one time tomatoes were avoided because of a mistaken belief that they were poisonous. Some religions insist on dietary restrictions; religious Jews do not eat pork. Each nationality has its own dietary idiosyncrasies based on its individual history. Thus Chinese prefer rice and Italians prefer pasta as the major source of starch. Beyond nationality, each of us has favorite foods and pet aversions. In brief, there appear to be two bases for food selection: bodily need and learning.

Curiosity

Curiosity is best defined as the *seeking of novel stimuli*. When a new stimulus appears, an animal tends to look, touch, sniff, or perhaps listen to it or taste it; the human infant usually tries to put it in his mouth. The animal perks up when a new stimulus is presented but soon resumes other activities. New stimuli lose their novelty after repeated occurrences, and they no longer elicit the animal's attention.

Higher animals, including man, are curious about the world around them. Observations of animals in their natural state and of humans in everyday life offer abundant evidence of this tendency to poke, pry, and look for the new and different. Complementing these observations are several lines of laboratory evidence, all converging on the notion of curiosity drive.

ANIMALS PREFER NOVEL STIMULI. Of the various experiments demonstrating this fact, Dember's (1956) is perhaps the most elegant. He placed a rat in a T-maze for 15 minutes, allowing it to see, but not enter, the two goal arms of the maze (see Figure 7.11a). One goal was painted white, one black. Then the animal was removed, and both arms were painted white (see Figure 7.11b). The rat was again placed in the T-maze, but this time it could enter a goal arm. It tended to choose the novel one, the white arm that had previously been black. When the experiment was repeated with two black goal arms, one being changed to white, the result was the same: the rat preferred the novel stimulus.

YOUNG ANIMALS ARE MORE CURIOUS THAN OLD ANIMALS. Welker (1956) presented objects varying in complexity, movement, brightness, and change to 3–4 year old and 7–8 year old chimpanzees. The younger chimpanzees showed more interest in the novel objects than did the older ones. This finding makes sense in the context of

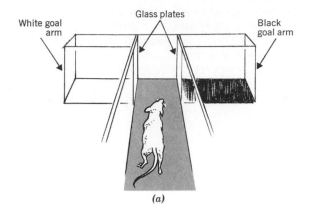

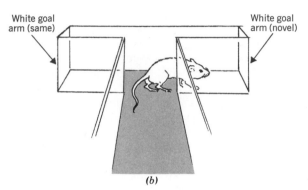

Figure 7.11 Rats prefer novelty (Dember, 1956).

development. The young animal needs information about the nature of its environment: where food might be found, where danger might threaten, which paths lead to safety, and which objects might be sources of pleasure. The older animal has already obtained much of this information, and it is less eager (and has less need) to investigate novelty.

ANIMALS DEPRIVED OF STIMULI SEEK THEM. When visual stimuli are cut off, animals will work to receive even the most minimal kind of stimulation. Kish (1955) kept mice in a dark cage long enough for them to become accustomed to it. There was a bar in the cage. At first, pressing the bar had no effect, and it was pressed very little. Then Kish arranged to have bar pressing followed by the brief appearance of a dim light; the mice quickly learned to press the bar, and they pressed it often. Then the bar was again made nonfunctional, and pressing it no longer turned on the light; eventually, the mice stopped pressing it.

This well-controlled experiment neatly demonstrates that when animals are deprived of stimuli, they will work to receive even the slightest amount of stimulation.

THE LONGER THE DEPRIVATION, THE STRONGER IS THE TENDENCY TO SEEK STIMULI. Butler (1957) placed rhesus monkeys in a dimly lit, enclosed box for 0, 2, 4, or 8 hours. After the time had elapsed, the monkeys could open a small window by pushing against a Plexiglass sheet. When the window was open, they could see other members of the monkey colony. The results are shown in Figure 7.12. The tendency to open the window clearly increased, especially from 0 to 4 hours of deprivation. In general, the longer the period of deprivation, the more times stimulation was sought.

These four lines of laboratory evidence, together with naturalistic observation, make a good case for regarding curiosity as an innate motivational tendency. It may be seen in rats and even more clearly in primates. There is probably an evolutionary progression, especially in the mammalian sequence. Primates are more curious than lower mammals, and man is undoubtedly the greatest seeker of novelty of any creature to roam the earth.

Brain Mechanisms in Motivation

In the last chapter we reviewed the brain mechanisms involved in arousal and earlier in this chapter we noted the brain mechanisms involved

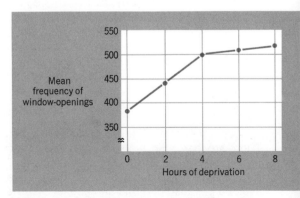

Figure 7.12 Deprivation and stimulus-seeking (Butler, 1957).

in hunger. It is no coincidence that these neural mechanisms are located primarily in the limbic system and reticular formation, which are structures in the old brain. The limbic-midbrain system and the reticular activating and deactivating systems are the neural mechanisms most relevant to motivation, and, as might be expected, there are neural theories of motivation. These theories are based on knowledge of two kinds of brain circuits: those mediating internal need states such as hunger and thirst, and those underlying pleasure and aversion.

Pleasure and Pain Areas in the Brain

During the 1950s James Olds discovered "pleasure areas" in the brain (Olds & Milner, 1954), a breakthrough of great significance. An electrode was implanted deep in the brain of a rat, in the septum, which is at the tip of the brain stem near the hypothalamus. Electric current delivered to

this site caused the rat to act as though it had been rewarded, hence the term *pleasure area.* This technique is called self-stimulation because the animal is taught to make a response that leads to its brain being stimulated. The animal can thus control stimulation of its own brain by making the appropriate response. The technique, which works on a wide range of animals and man, has advanced so far that remote control is now possible (see Figure 7.13).

Subsequent research has established that brain stimulation is an especially strong reward. Just as food will maintain a high level of instrumental responding, so will brain stimulation (Olds, 1969). Similarly, rats will cross a punishing electric grid solely to obtain brain stimulation; in fact, they cross the electric grid more often for brain stimulation than for food, even when they are starving.

Just as there are both positive (food) and negative stimuli (pain), so there are both positive and negative areas in the brain. Electrical stimulation of certain areas is so aversive that animals will

Figure 7.13 Monkey with remotely controlled permanent brain implants.
(FROM PHYSICAL CONTROL OF THE MIND: TOWARD A PSYCHOCIVILIZED SOCIETY BY JOSE M. R. DELGADO, HARPER & ROW, 1969.)

learn an instrumental response to turn it off. Earlier, it was believed that the positive and negative areas might overlap, the outcome being determined by such variables as the intensity of the electrical stimulation and the nature of the instrumental response. It is now known that this view is probably incorrect; the areas yielding positive effects are different from those yielding negative effects.

A Neural Theory of Motivation

The following is a simplified account of a theory formulated by Olds and Olds (1965). The sites of reward and punishment areas in the brain have been mapped, using the technique of self-stimulation. The reward sites are located in a system of fibers called the *forebrain substrate of reward,* and the punishment sites are grouped into a system called the *midbrain substrate of escape* (see Figure 7.14).[7] In an evolutionary vein Olds and Olds speculate that the forebrain, which originated as a ganglion mediating smell, is involved in *voluntary behavior* as the animal moves forward in the environment. The midbrain, which mediates

hearing and touch, is ostensibly involved in *withdrawal and escape behavior* in the face of threat (see Figure 7.15)

. . . it can be supposed that the aversive system may be a device for actual escape from destructive conditions already imposed. Its phylogenetic origin, if the central nervous system may be regarded as a set of invaginated [folded in] receptor systems, would be the somesthetic apparatus and particularly the pain system which warns the organism of imminent threat. Its mechanisms would involve action during stimulation and cessation on withdrawal of the stimulus. By the same reasoning, it could be guessed that the adaptive function of the forebrain system was to lead the organism forward even at times when there was no immediate threat to survival by their lack. Phylogenetically, this system would derive from the olfactory receptor system, placed up front to help the animal to "home" on food. [PP. 341–342]

The theory identifies reward and punishment with activation of the motor paths underlying species-specific consummatory responses (e.g., eating), which implies that electrical stimulation of these sites should elicit motor patterns.[8] It has been shown that stimulation of positive areas elic-

---

[7] *There is controversy over the precise location of reward and punishment areas (see Valenstein, 1966). For simplicity, we are accepting the conclusions of Olds and Olds (1965).*

[8] *This is only one of several theories that relate consummatory responses to centers in the brain (see Glickman & Schiff, 1967; Bindra, 1968).*

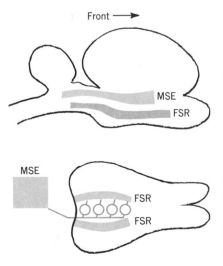

Front ⟶

MSE

FSR

MSE

FSR

FSR

Figure 7.14 Schematic saggital and horizontal sections to show outcome of positive-negative reinforcement mapping study. Pure negative reinforcement behavior was produced by stimulation of the periventricular system of fibers, here labeled MSE (midbrain substrate of escape); pure positive reinforcement behavior was produced by stimulation of the lateral hypothalamic tube, here labeled FSR (forebrain substrate of reward). The nuclei (circled) into which both systems project yielded ambivalent, that is, positive-negative, reactions. (Olds & Olds, 1965)

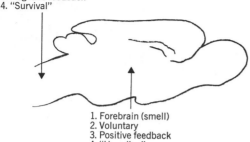

1. Midbrain (touch)
2. Reflex
3. Negative feedback
4. "Survival"

1. Forebrain (smell)
2. Voluntary
3. Positive feedback
4. "Hoarding"

Figure 7.15 Functional differentiation of midbrain and forebrain behavior mechanisms (Olds and Olds, 1965).

its forward movements and stimulation of negative areas elicits freezing or backward movements (Valenstein, 1964). Moreover, certain neurons in positively reinforcing sites become active only when the animal makes particular species-specific responses (Komisaruk & Olds, 1968).

Push and Pull Models of Motivation

There are two general approaches to biological motivation. One assumes a *passive* animal, which is somehow *pushed* in one direction or another by its *needs.* The other assumes an *active* animal, which is *pulled* in one direction or another by *incentives.*

The *push* model assumes that no behavior will occur until it is *impelled* by some motive, usually an internal, vegetative need (see Figure 7.16*a*). Then it seeks a specific goal, one that meets the particular need. This model explains why the animal starts to behave, the assumption being that without a motive there would be no behavior. Presumably, all behavior is motivated by one drive or another, and the basic drives reside in conditions *inside* the organism. The *direction* of behavior is determined by the nature of the need (food, thirst, and so on).[9] When the behavior stops, it is presumably because the motive has been satisfied, and the animal is no longer *driven* to act.

[9] *For an evolutionary account of motivation in terms of the direction of behavior*—approach *versus* withdrawal *and* seeking *versus* avoiding—*see Schneirla (1959).*

The *pull* model assumes an active animal that is usually moving through and exploring its environment (see Figure 7.16*b*). Its motivation is generalized, and there are no specific goals. Some of the stimuli it encounters will prove to be attractive: certain kinds of vegetation may be eaten, certain kinds of animals may be pursued for mating. These stimuli, called incentives, determine the *direction* of the animal's behavior. This model must explain why an animal should *stop* behaving in a given way. It does so by assuming that either (1) the animal becomes fatigued or bored, or (2) new stimuli with incentive value pull the animal in another direction.

It should be obvious that neither model exclu-

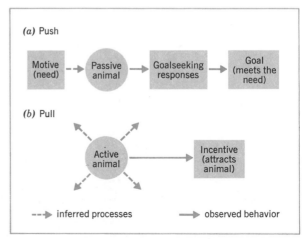

(a) Push

Motive (need) → Passive animal → Goalseeking responses → Goal (meets the need)

(b) Pull

Active animal → Incentive (attracts animal)

---→ inferred processes ——→ observed behavior

Figure 7.16 Push-and-pull models of motivation.

sively applies to all drives. Some drives are linked to vegetative needs, which push the animal to seek particular goals (food, water, or mate). Other drives have no underlying tissue need, and the animal is simply attracted by certain incentives (novel stimuli). The appropriateness of the model varies with the drive under consideration. For vegetative or aversive drives, the push model appropriately emphasizes the reactivity of the organism to internal states or emergency situations. For educational drives, the pull model appropriately emphasizes the incentive value of stimuli in attracting active organisms.

section four
perception

chapter 8
general issues in perception

*Functions of perception—ongoing move-
ments—knowledge—orientation—objects and
events—change—innate response to threat—
damage—arousal—pleasure—evolutionary
trends—specialization—sensitivity—distance
perception—plasticity—perception of relationships—sources of stimulation—threshold—
signal detection—extracting information—
perceptual systems*

Perception involves sensing the world around us, as well as the inside of the body. The information obtained may be used immediately or stored for use later. In this chapter we shall discuss some general issues in perception—its functions, evolutionary trends, sources of stimulation, and so on. The next three chapters discuss in specific detail the various senses and the information derived from the environment.

Functions of Perception

One model of man views him as a sensor, seeking and receiving information from the environment (see Chapter 1). What does he do with this information? Like other animals, he uses it for immediate action, as a basis for later action, for detecting damage, as stimulation needed for arousal, and finally, for pleasure.

Ongoing Movement

Standing on only two legs requires considerable muscular coordination. It has been so well mastered and occurs so automatically that we are unaware of the feedback system needed merely to sustain posture. Infants do not find the task easy, nor do drunken adults.

The task of maintaining balance becomes more difficult during gross movements such as walking, running, leaping, or swinging from a branch. Virtually any movement of the body alters its balance in relation to the force of gravity, and even raising an arm would be enough to cause toppling over in the absence of automatic adjustment. Such adjustments require information about movement, and this information comes from special sensors called movement receptors.

In higher vertebrates, including man, the *cerebellum* integrates all incoming messages from *movement* receptors (see Figure 8.1). The cerebellum receives impulses from movement and stretch receptors throughout the body and from equilibrium receptors in the head. This information is integrated with cortical commands for movement so as to achieve the required action while maintaining balance. The cerebellum also programs the *sequence* of movements, so that a response is smooth and coordinated, rather than a series of jerky, spasmodic movements.

Sequential, coordinated movements require information about equilibrium, as well as what is happening to joints and muscles. Certain actions also require information from *distance* receptors, primarily those involved in seeing and hearing. To pounce on a bird, the cat must gauge the distance before it leaps. The tree-swinging monkey must know precisely how far away the next branch is, or it will suffer injury or death. The bat flying in a dark cave must be able to locate objects by reflected sound waves, or it will crash into them.

In man, *gross* movements are no more balanced or coordinated than those of many animals, but man's *fine* motor coordination far exceeds that of any other animal. It is revealed in such diverse activities as playing a violin, playing billiards, and sewing embroidery. From the very beginning, man has grasped *tools* and used them to do what he could not do with his own biological equipment. The use of tools requires sensory feedback from appropriate receptors, and the way tools are used depends on their function. For example, *a power grip* provides leverage, allowing considerable force to be directed at an object (see Figure 8.2). Successive rotary movements of the tool require feedback from the skin on the palm, from the fingers, wrist, and joints, and from the muscles that grip and rotate the tool. The same sources of stimulation — skin, joints, and muscles — are required when a *precision grip* is used, as in painting or surgery. These skilled acts usually require vision; other skilled acts (playing the piano) do not require vision and blind persons can perform them, relying only on information from skin, joints, and muscles.

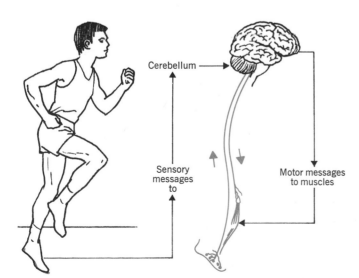

Cerebellum

Sensory messages to

Motor messages to muscles

Figure 8.1 Guidance of gross movement.

Power grip

Precision grip

Figure 8.2 Using tools involves sensory feedback.

Gaining Knowledge

The term *knowledge* includes more than the information picked up first-hand from the environment. It also includes the products of thinking and imagining, topics we shall consider in later chapters under the heading of *cognition.* In the present context, *knowledge* will be restricted to three kinds of information that might guide later action: orientation, objects and events, and change.

ORIENTATION. Locating oneself in space is so fundamental that it usually is done automatically and without awareness. Vision serves this purpose so well that it is all that a man normally uses. His eyes tell him precisely where he is in relation to that tree, that river, that mountain, and the distant horizon. Nonvisual cues are also available—the blind can be taught to walk the city streets by means of hearing, touch, and the counting of steps—but these are poor substitutes for visual information.

Mammals that live in poorly lit locales—bats, porpoises, and whales—use high-pitched sounds to orient themselves. This adaptation, called echolocation, works well in such restricted environments, but it provides less information than vision does. The animals with the best means of orientation are the turtles and birds that migrate thousands of miles to their breeding grounds. These animals use a variety of cues, the birds using mainly sun and stars and the turtles using cues still not known to us (Marler & Hamilton, 1966).

OBJECTS AND EVENTS. The survival of individual animals requires locating and identifying food, water, prey, and predators; the survival of a species requires that animals locate and identify mates. Man's survival in a highly technological society depends on more and finer discriminations:

The world is full of things, to be approached and avoided, to flee from or fight against. The development of perception requires the discrimination of objects such as faces, food, toys, hot radiators, bottles that contain milk vs. bottles that contain medicine, and so on. Sets of objects, such as human faces, and the features that differentiate them must be attended to. The properties and variable dimensions of objects—their colors, texture, shape, and more complex structural variables like the ones that identify different vehicles, or animals, or plants—must be discriminated. (GIBSON, 1969, P. 15.)

Objects may simply remain static, or they may be involved in the sequences we call *events.* Thus a male bird may move through the sequential phases of a courtship dance, and the female of the species must be able to identify each step in the sequence and respond appropriately. In some well-studied animals, the precise sequence of these *innate,* species-specific rituals is known in some detail. Man must *learn* the meaning of court-ship rites, as well as the significance of many other events that might be crucial (for example, the whole range of human facial expression and vocal inflections).

CHANGE. Virtually all living things can somehow detect changes in the environment. With few ex-ceptions, plants and animals follow the cycles of day and night, phases of the moon, or the seasons (see Chapter 6). To follow these cycles, an animal must be capable of perceiving the changes that constitute the cycle. The most important cycles are those involving light, temperature, and mois-ture (important in coastal animals that follow tidal cycles).

Cycles, events, and objects all share a common attribute: they occur over time. Animals must have mechanisms that gauge the passing of time, for these are essential in maintaining cycles of behav-ior. Some humans can set themselves like an alarm clock and wake at a given hour without an external stimulus. Both men and animals can sense the duration of time, but the mechanism is unknown.

A more immediate kind of change concerns the movement of other animals either toward or away from the perceiver. In this world of ever present predators, animals that are preyed on must be capable of detecting predators' movements to-ward them. Most animals are startled into flight by any sudden stimulus: horses by sudden noises, rats by high-pitched sounds, and birds by sudden movements. Ethologists have emphasized the in-nateness of the response of various birds to pred-ators such as hawks.

Research Report

Konrad Lorenz first demonstrated that several species of birds will at-tempt to escape when a certain *model* is passed overhead. The *shape* of the model was critical: short neck and long tail. Tinbergen (1951) followed up by testing a number of models. His best known finding is shown in Figure 8.3. The silhouette of a large bird was passed over birds on the ground. When the direction of flight gave the model the shape of a hawk (short neck, long tail), it caused panic and escape responses. When the model's direction of flight made it resemble a goose (long neck, short tail), there were no panic or escape responses.

Unfortunately, these investigators did not always maintain ade-quate experimental controls (use of subjects with an unknown devel-

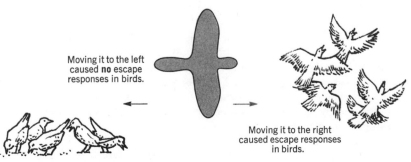

Moving it to the left caused **no** escape responses in birds.

Moving it to the right caused escape responses in birds.

Figure 8.3 Model of a bird of prey.

opmental history, failure to test individual birds). Hirsch et al. (1955), employing appropriate controls, tested the response of chickens to hawk and goose shapes. The chickens showed fear of *both* models, and the significant features of the models turned out to be not shape, but speed of movement and casting of a shadow.

An innate response to a predator should certainly not weaken over time, but the fear response of ducks to both hawk and goose shapes disappears completely after repeated exposure. There does seem to be an innate escape reaction to sudden, fast-moving stimuli, but this general tendency must be sharpened by *experience* until it becomes specific to predators. Marler and Hamilton (1966) cite an experiment by Schleidt (1961) that explains the phenomenon:

Working with turkeys under carefully controlled conditions, he demonstrated that birds exposed to circles or rectangles overhead were at first alarmed and then became habituated. Such birds occasionally exposed to a hawk silhouette gave strong escape responses. Conversely, birds frequently exposed to a hawk silhouette became habituated. When presented with a circle they responded strongly. The initial response to different models was not significantly different. Thus there is general unspecific responsiveness to objects of a certain apparent size and rate of movement. Schleidt concluded that response to a hawk silhouette in birds raised in a free environment results from their habituation to other types of birds flying overhead and from the relative rarity of hawks in the neighborhood. Thus habituation serves to achieve one of the most striking cases of response to a specific stimulus that has been demonstrated. (1966, P. 647.)

In related research, Schiff (1965) studied the effect of a figure moving rapidly toward a subject. He used a screen on which a silhouette expanded so as to simulate approaching the subject, and crabs, frogs, chickens, and kittens all jumped backward or retreated. Young and adult monkeys also leapt rapidly to the rear of the cage in response to a looming figure (Schiff et al., 1962). Thus a wide variety of animals have an innate avoidance reaction to fast-moving, approaching objects. It is not clear whether this holds for man, but casual observation of infants reveals that they become upset and cry when startled by an object suddenly approaching them.

Damage

Animals are subject to harm from either inside (infection, disease) or outside (falls, blows, cuts) the body. The biological integrity of the body requires some way of discovering when there is disease or tissue damage. There are several mechanisms for this, which are traditionally grouped under the heading of *pain.*

Pain is a signal of bodily damage that is imminent or has already occurred. Stubbing one's toe, bumping one's head, and biting one's tongue all result in tissue damage and awareness of being hurt. Extremely intense light in the eyes and excessively loud sounds both threaten immediate danger to sensory mechanisms, again signalled by pain.

In the absence of pain, a person would have to learn indirectly to be wary of hot stoves and sharp knives. Magee et al. (1961) have collected case histories of persons who do not experience pain; several have far exceeded the injury rate of normal persons. Unpleasant as pain is, it is the most effective means of becoming aware of bodily damage.

Arousal

One function of perception is to maintain a minimal level of arousal in the brain, especially the cerebral cortex. There are two neural paths from the receptors to the brain: a high-speed direct system and a slower, nonspecific projective system through the reticular formation (see Chapters 5 and 6). In the latter system, stimuli coming from the environment are converted into neural impulses, which are sent to the reticular formation; this in turn feeds a steady stream of impulses to the cerebral cortex, furnishing the background level of arousal necessary for optimal functioning. When this environmental input is shut off, as in solitary confinement or sensory deprivation research, there are often disturbances in both perceiving and thinking (Bexton et al., 1954).

Pleasure

As we saw in the last chapter, animals (and to some extent, man) are motivated to approach stimuli that will in some way satisfy their drives. When such stimuli are sampled or consumed, we infer that the animal's activity is pleasurable. In man, such consummatory behavior is known directly, through his own consciousness, as pleasurable.

Pleasure is available through all the senses. It may be stimulated by beautiful scenes, tasty food, sexually stimulating perfume, rhythmic or melodious music, the soft touch of fur, and the rough feeling of a massage. There are also the "internal" pleasures, such as a cold drink on a hot day, the muscle-joint-equilibrium joy of bouncing up and down on a trampoline, and the thrill of controlled danger (a roller coaster ride or a parachute jump). Very few of these sensations are relevant to survival of individuals or species. Rather, they are by-products of perceptual systems that *are* relevant to survival. Hail to by-products!

Evolutionary Trends

As generation succeeds generation, an animal species becomes better adapted to its specific habitat. Perceptual mechanisms are shaped by natural selection to obtain information from the local environment. Thus birds, living above ground, require little sensitivity to odors (which do not carry to great heights), but they do need depth perception to navigate in their three-dimensional environment. Bats, living in dark environments, require little sensitivity to light, but they do need a mechanism for detecting distant objects. Regarded in this way, the perceptual adaptations of animals are oriented toward specific, local environments, and there are no broad evolutionary trends.

Nevertheless, all habitats share certain characteristics (gravity, chemical and mechanical stimuli, and so on) or they would not support life. These common features enable us to compare the perceptual apparatus of different species. When the comparison is made across the broad range of animal species, certain evolutionary trends do emerge. We shall consider five trends.

Specialization

A one-celled animal such as an amoeba can sense the presence of food, light, heat, and harmful chemicals. It crudely processes environmental inputs without any specialized receptors. As organisms evolved into a variety of many-celled forms, special organs evolved to perform specific functions. Eyes evolved that were sensitive only to light, ears sensitive only to sound, and so on.

Eyes started to evolve as spots sensitive to light. The eye spot was merely an opening, with light-sensitive elements below it (see Figure 8.4a). To protect these elements, a transparent covering evolved (Figure 8.4b), and eventually it thickened and helped to gather and finally to focus light (Figure 8.4c). The lens itself than required protection, and gradually it was internalized (Figure 8.4d). This specialization led from a crude, light-sensitive area to an eye that could focus light and form an image. A sharp image offers the best information about objects and events in the visual environment.

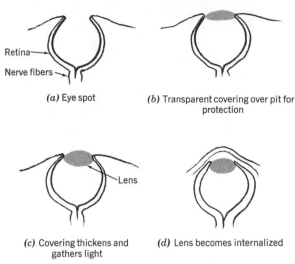

(a) Eye spot

(b) Transparent covering over pit for protection

(c) Covering thickens and gathers light

(d) Lens becomes internalized

Retina

Nerve fibers

Lens

Figure 8.4 *Evolution of the lens of the eye.*

sion would be perceived, and "steady" light would no longer appear steady! A similar state of affairs obtains in hearing, as we shall see: if man's ears were any better attuned, they would be assailed by noises coming from the "dance of the molecules" in the very air in which he lives. (GELDARD, 1953, P. 26.)[1]

Man's acute sight and hearing are not superior to the senses of certain other animals. Dogs have more sensitive ears and can hear higher-pitched sounds; dog whistles are too high-pitched for humans but do summon dogs. Eagles can see farther, and rats have a more sensitive sense of touch in their "whiskers" (vibrissae). But when *all* the senses are compared, man is probably superior to other animals (see Table 8.1). In his sensory mechanisms, as in other adaptations, man is superiority resides in flexibility and comprehensiveness.

One outcome of specialization was an increase in the amount of information extracted from the physical environment. Consider the potential information that can be derived from light. Primitive animals can do no more than distinguish different degrees of *brightness*. More advanced forms can also detect differences in *shape, patterning, size,* and *color.*

Sensitivity

The crude sensors of primitive animals respond only to intense stimuli or large changes in stimulation. As specialized sensors evolved, their sensitivity increased so markedly that animals could respond to the merest trace of stimulation. The sense of smell has evolved to such exquisite sensitivity in lower mammals that dogs, for example, can detect odors of concentrations that do not register on the most sensitive odor-detecting machine yet devised. Primates excel in vision and hearing, and in man sensitivity to light and sound has approached the natural limit:

The visual apparatus is apparently tuned to the highest possible degree consistent with the nature of light energy. If man's eyes were much more sensitive to light than they are the "shot effect" in photon emis-

Perception at a Distance

Primitive animals move slowly, and they respond only to stimuli that actually contact them. The touch of an object does provide information, but if the object is dangerous, the warning may have come too late. An effective signal should arrive early enough to allow time for escape or other action. This requirement calls for a perceptual system that responds when the object or event is still at a distance, some time before it reaches the organism. Sounds and smells can serve as warnings, but sight is the source of the greatest amount of information. Whatever the particular sense modality, it was inevitable that various distance receptors would evolve to provide a margin of safety by signaling danger before it is too late to act.

The appearance of distance receptors marks a significant event in the evolution of behavior. Before these receptors evolved, behavior had to be reflexive. Stimuli were not sensed until they touched the animal, which meant there was no time for anything but a reflexive response. The stimulus elicited the response, with little or no intervening neural action. Distance receptors, by sig-

[1] *The problem of noise is discussed later in this chapter under the heading of* signal detection.

Table 8.1
Approximate Human Thresholds (from Galanter, 1962, p. 97)

SENSE	THRESHOLD
Sight	A candle flame seen at 30 miles on a dark clear night
Hearing	The tick of a watch under quiet conditions at 20 feet
Taste	One teaspoon of sugar in 2 gallons of water
Smell	One drop of perfume diffused into the entire volume of a three-room apartment
Touch	The wing of a bee falling on your cheek from a distance of 1 centimeter

naling impending events before they actually occurred, allowed the animal time for integrative neural activity and the selection of appropriate responses. The central nervous system was provided with two of the basic requirements for computerlike selection of response strategies: information and time to make a decision. Presumably, once these conditions occurred, the way was open for the central nervous system to evolve from a reflexive, telephone switchboard type of operation to a computer type of operation.

Plasticity

In lower animals, perception involves a minimum of processing of the incoming information. As the perceiving animal moves or as the source of stimulation moves, perception of the object changes. Consider a triangle as it is rotated, which yields essentially the same visual input as a animal circling around the triangle (Figure 8.5). For primitive animals, the rotated triangle is entirely different from the unrotated one; the altered perspective changes perception of the object. Higher animals do not have this problem. Their perception is suf-

ficiently plastic to allow for moment-to-moment changes in stimuli, and the object or event is truly perceived in spite of its changes in space and time.

The more veridical perceptions of advanced animals require more processing of the stimulus inputs. Such processing involves *learning* to handle the information flowing in from the senses, and this learning makes the perceptual process more flexible and better able to deal with changes in perspective. Perceptual learning is one of the marks of advanced animals, an evolutionary trend

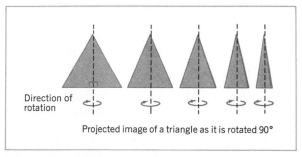

Direction of rotation

Projected image of a triangle as it is rotated 90°

Figure 8.5 *Constancy.*

pointed out by Gregory (1968) with special emphasis on vision:

Perceptual learning is certainly minimal in primitive creatures; and so we must suppose that these special visual patterns have taken on significance through ancestral disasters, just as the development and inheritance of more obvious structural characteristics through natural selection. Some insects do show visual learning — bees, for example, learn key features of the terrain around their nests for navigation — but this ability becomes infinitely greater in mammals and especially the primates. Now what is clear is that perception, as it developed phylogenetically, became less and less tied to specific visual patterns, so that finally a large variety of patterns elicited the same behavior. We may say that perception becomes geared to responding to objects, *no matter how they are presented to the senses.*

(P. 14.)

Stated another way, perception evolved toward perceptual *constancy*. For humans, a triangle is a triangle regardless of its tilt (shape constancy, as in Figure 8.5), and a piece of coal is black even if more light is reflected from it than from a piece of white paper (brightness constancy). This kind of perception allows us to know the environment as it really is: as a stable set of stimuli that do not vary despite the changes in perspective as we bounce, jiggle, and undulate through our usual habitat.

Perception of Relationships

Lower animals can perceive differences in brightness and size, and they can therefore learn to respond to the brighter of two objects or the larger of two stimuli. But can they perceive the *relationship* of "brighter than" or "larger than"? The first psychologist to study this question was Kohler (1925), using the *transposition problem* (see Figure 8.6). He first trained chickens to choose a light-gray stimulus and to avoid the dark-gray stimulus. Then he presented the light-gray stimulus along with an even lighter gray stimulus. The chickens correctly chose the new "lighter than" stimulus.

Animals lower on the evolutionary scale than birds and mammals are, in general, incapable of perceiving such relationships among stimuli. Rather, they learn to respond to a stimulus in terms of its *absolute* properties (size, brightness, and so on), and they cannot transpose (respond relationally) if required to do so. Primates, on the other hand, tend to perceive relationally, and they transpose with ease. Such relational perception is a primitive form of conceptual responding, a cognitive ability we shall return to in Chapters 13 and 1?

Sources of Stimulation

We are concerned here with both the *origin* of stimulation and *how it is delivered* to the perceiving organism.

Imposed and Obtained Stimulation

When perception is studied in the laboratory, it is usually with *imposed* stimulation. The subject passively awaits the delivery of stimuli by the experimenter. This procedure is necessary for experimental control of extraneous variables, but it renders the findings difficult to generalize. Animals rarely wait patiently for stimuli to be imposed, and, except for situations such as waiting for one's name to be called in a physician's office, humans do not passively await stimulation.

In brief, stimuli are less often imposed than they are sought and obtained (see Figure 8.7). Except when sleeping, most animals and humans actively explore the world around them. The air is sniffed, the layout scanned, the surface touched, or the head is turned — all these being attempts to sample the local environment. Most stimulation is obtained in this manner, but higher animals and humans have another means of doing this: *by performing an act* that brings feedback. A man may heft an object to determine its weight, squeeze a piece of fruit to estimate its ripeness (firmness), or bounce on a bed to discover its softness (springiness). With advances in technology, instruments can be substituted for action, and the feedback can be obtained through mechanical means. The dexterity required to obtain such feedback is limited mainly to animals with hands — i.e., primates.

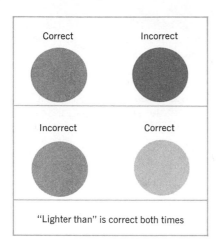

Figure 8.6 Perception of relationship: the transposition problem.

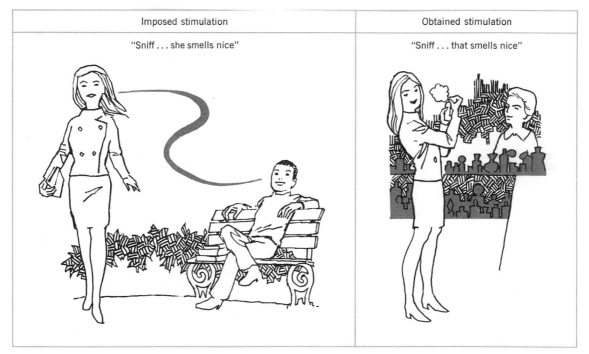

Figure 8.7 Imposed and sought-after stimulation.

Types of Stimulation

Objects and events are sources of information for the perceiver. The information is delivered through energy, which either emanates from the object or is reflected by it. For example, an electric light bulb emanates light, but a person's face reflects it. The physical energy strikes receptor mechanisms, initiating the process of perception. Thus the energy coming from the source is the means by which the perceiver can specify the nature of the source. But the source of the energy (objects and events) is not the same as the energy. Viewed in this way, perception consists of interpreting or making sense of the various kinds of energy in the environment.

Five kinds of energy can be picked up from the environment:

1. *Gravity.* This is a constant, continuous force pulling toward the center of the earth. Its impact on animals is less in the sea, where an animal's comparatively lower density in relation to the medium enables it to float. On land, gravity is a formidable force that requires animals to have rigid supports for their bodies. It presents a special problem for two-legged creatures, necessitating a variety of postural mechanisms merely to maintain an upright posture in opposition to the downward force.

2. *Mechanical Forces.* Gravity is a very special force, one that never ceases to act on any creature on the earth. Most mechanical forces are momentary: one may be pushed, shoved, lifted, or struck. The force can be delivered through immediate contact (a slap on the back) or through the air as vibrations (a loud shout or a sonic boom).

3. *Chemical.* Chemical substances surround us in air and water, and they are sampled in solid objects that are touched or eaten. Land animals have separate senses of taste and smell to pick up information about chemicals, but sea animals need not concern themselves with gases and so have only a single, generalized chemical sense.

4. *Light.* The broad range of energy radiated in the universe has been arranged along an *electromagnetic spectrum* (see Figure 8.8). The energy may be thought of as waves that vary in intensity and length. Most of the energy resonates at wave frequencies too large or too small for man to

sense. What we call *light* is a small fraction of the spectrum between 15 and 30 billionths of an inch in wavelength.

5. *Thermal.* The solid, liquid, and gaseous substances that surround us are either cold or warm in relation to ourselves. In addition, heat can be radiated, as from the sun. Warm-blooded animals must continually sample the air so that homeostatic mechanisms can keep the internal temperatures within the required range.

Sensitivity

Man is sensitive to only a tiny fraction of the electromagnetic spectrum. His receptors have their limits, and light, sound, and pressure must each be of a minimal intensity in order to be sensed. Earlier we mentioned the great sensitivity of man's eyes and ears but did not discuss how this sensitivity is measured. The issue is one of determining the *threshold* of stimulation, the minimal stimulus that can be detected.

Threshold

The study of sensory thresholds, called psychophysics, is one of the oldest areas of psychology. Of the various procedures, we shall examine one of the simplest, the *method of limits.* A series of stimuli is presented to the subject, who responds "Yes, it is present" or "No, it is not." The experimenter starts with a stimulus (say, a sound) too weak to be perceived and increases its intensity in small steps. When the subject reports hearing the stimulus, the series is over. Then a new one is begun, this time with a loud sound, which is softened in graded steps until the subject reports not hearing it. These ascending and descending series are repeated several times to obtain a stable measure.

The notion of an *absolute threshold* assumes that there is a precise point on the dimension of intensity at which the stimulus can be perceived. A stimulus one unit weaker will simply not be sensed. If this assumption were true, the method of limits would yield a curve such as that in Figure 8.9. The subject does not give Yes responses until a certain point, and then he responds Yes 100 percent of the time.

But this kind of curve is never obtained. Laboratory research yields curves more or less like the one in Figure 8.10. The percentage of Yes responses goes up *gradually* as the intensity of the stimulus increases. Thus the sensory threshold is not a single (absolute) point on a stimulus dimension. Rather, the threshold is a *range* of values, and the value called the threshold is an arbitrary choice. The convention in psychology is to select the stimulus intensity at which the subject says yes 50 percent of the time.

In brief, a threshold is not absolute in the sense of specifying a precise stimulus value below which the stimulus cannot be sensed. With the criterion being 50 percent Yes responses, the subject obviously can sense stimuli below the threshold, if only some of the time. Clearly, a sensory threshold is an average measure, representing a range of

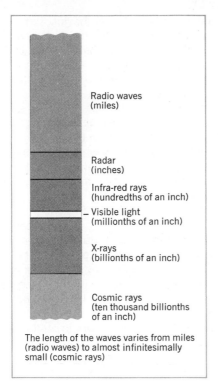

The length of the waves varies from miles (radio waves) to almost infinitesimally small (cosmic rays)

Figure 8.8 *The electromagnetic-spectrum.*

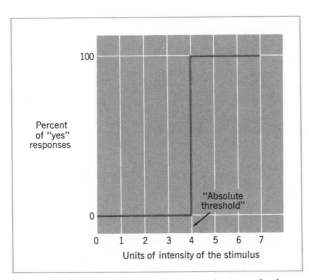

Figure 8.9 *Theoretical curves assuming an absolute threshold.*

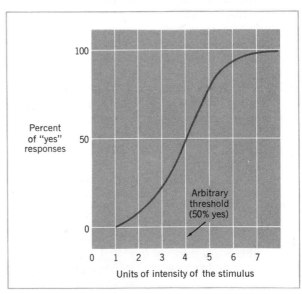

Figure 8.10 *The usual sensitivity curve.*

stimulus values, and it should never be regarded as absolute.

Signal Detection

The method of limits and related procedures in psychophysics implicitly assume that the subject merely responds to the presence or absence of a stimulus. In terms of sound, there would be either a sound that he hears or silence. But absolute silence simply does not exist in the context of measuring sensory thresholds. A laboratory room is noisy, and soundproofed rooms are not free of vibrations. Remember, too, that the subject's own body generates its own sounds, which can be heard when external sounds are deadened: heartbeat, breathing, and digestive gurgling. Finally, the nervous system is spontaneously active, setting up a certain amount of "neural noise," which any sensory message must override.

This conception of ever present background noise to which a stimulus (signal) is added is part of signal detection theory (Tanner & Swets, 1954). This theory nicely accounts for mistakes made in studying thresholds. A subject sometimes says "Yes, I heard it" when no stimulus has occurred. Presumably, he has misinterpreted the internal and external noise, confusing it with a signal. This is especially likely to happen near the threshold, where variations in the level of noise may result in a noise level not very different from the intensity of the stimulus. The opposite error is also made: saying "No, I can't hear anything" when there really is a sound. The explanation is that the intensity of the signal is not greater, or not appreciably greater, than that of the background noise.

The term *noise* refers specifically to sounds, but in the context of signal detection theory, noise refers to *any* background that might interfere with a signal. Thus there are many examples of "visual noise" in everyday life: early morning fog that limits highway visibility, "snow" on the television screen, and the "grain" that appears when a copier does not work properly (see Figure 8.11).

Detecting signals always involves a decision: is it noise alone or noise plus a singal? When a subject makes this decision, there are usually non-sensory determinants of his behavior. Some subjects are bold and tend to report the presence of a signal often; they report too many stimuli. Others are cautious, refusing to report a stimulus unless they are certain; they report too few stimuli. What should a radar observer report when he is not sure of the identity of a blip on the radar screen? What should a soldier on watch do if he is not sure he has heard the password? In these and countless other situations in which the person must decide whether the signal is present, the *consequences* of his decision may be more important than the sensory aspects.

Signal detection theory specifies two major determinants of the perception of stimuli near threshold: the intensity of stimulation (signal plus noise) and the consequences (payoff) of the decision. The theory has led to improvements in the design and analysis of experiments on sensory thresholds, but these complexities need not concern us here.

The ratio of signal to noise, which originated in the study of sensory thresholds, can be applied to other contexts. For example, the pictures sent by television from the moon contained much visual noise. Rather than attempt to increase the intensity of the signal, the space technicians reduced the noise by using computers to reprogram the pictures. The signal-to-noise model may also be applied to laboratory research. The researcher attempts to measure only the response he is focusing on (signal) and not extraneous behavior (noise). The problem of noise is especially troublesome when brain waves are being recorded: is that really an alpha pattern of 8–12 waves per second or merely the random fluctuations of millions of neurons firing?

Extracting Information

Perception, which consists of extracting information from the environment, may be analyzed into four sequential stages (Forgus, 1966). These are (1) the stimuli, which impinge on (2) receptors, which in turn initiate (3) neural activity, which finally results in (4) experience or information (see Figure 8.12). Having discussed the various kinds of energy, we shall proceed to the other three stages.

Figure 8.11 *An example of "visual noise."* (FRITZ HENLE/PHOTO RESEARCHERS)

Receptors

Receptors may be assembled to form a *sense organ* (eyes, ears) or spread throughout the body (stretch receptors, pressure receptors). Their function is to convert the energy of the stimulus into neural impulses. A sense organ cannot be activated by *all* stimuli, only certain kinds within a given range.

Receptors are selective in several ways. First, each kind of receptor is sensitive to a particular form of physical energy. Thus the eyes are specialized to receive light, the ears to receive vibrations in the air or water, the taste buds to receive chemicals in the mouth, and so on. Second, within the physical dimension specific to the receptor, it is sensitive to only a particular range. Thus human eyes see wavelengths of light only in the range of roughly 15–30 billionths of an inch, and human ears hear wavelengths of sound only in the range of 20–20,000 cycles per second. Third, even within the appropriate range, there is selection by

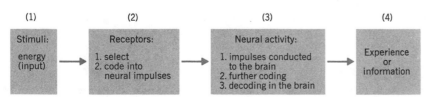

Figure 8.12 *Four stages in perception.*

the receptor. Human eyes do not register the blood vessels lying directly in front of the light receptors in the retina; nor do they react to an immobile retinal image. In brief, the receptors select a sample of stimuli from the much larger population of potential stimuli, and they encode them as neural impulses.

Neural Activity

Sensory impulses proceed from the receptors to the brain, with the neurons synapsing at several junctions along the route. There is some processing of the neural impulses at these junctions, with some impulses being enhanced and others inhibited, but most of the processing and integration occurs in the cerebral cortex.

Each kind of receptor has its own neuron path to the cortex. The nerves from the eye to the brain convey impulses only about light, and this is true whether they are electrically stimulated or are stimulated by light or even by rubbing the eyes. And there is point-to-point projection of the retinal image on the occipital lobe of the cortex (see Chapter 10). Thus different kinds of sensory impulses are kept separate by sending them along distinct and specific routes from the receptors to the sensory areas of the cerebral cortex. There is no danger of confusing being punched on the jaw with being tickled on the soles of the feet.

The final part of the sensory neural circuit is the cerebral cortex, specifically, the rear parts of it (see Figure 8.13). Three areas can be localized; one for vision, one for hearing, and one for body sense (a combination of skin and internal inputs).[2] These areas receive fibers from specific sensory systems (vision, hearing, and so on), and each area reproduces the original (sense organ) pattern of excitation. The representation does not precisely mirror the stimulation received; rather the pattern is distorted in keeping with the importance of the stimulation in the organism's total adaptation. Thus the body is represented in the cortex upside down and with overrepresentation of the face, hands, and feet (see Figure 8.14). In spite of the distortions, adjacent areas of the body are represented side by side, and in general there is a point-to-point correspondence.

These specific areas constitute only one of these components in the functional organization of the sensory cortex. Luria (1970) has distinguished a hierarchical sequence of zones in the cortex, which codes and integrates sensory impulses (see Table 8.2). Each of the sensory modalities (sight, hearing, and so on) has its own three zones.

The first zone is the area in which impulses are received from the receptors and represented in the cortex. Though there is some coding by the primary zone, considerably more coding and organization occurs in the secondary zone. The tertiary zone integrates disparate and sequential information. With each successive zone, there is greater complexity and more processing of information. Table 8.2 also lists the results of injury to the three zones, which is one basis for inferring their various functions.

Experience or Information

The outcome of the processing of stimulus inputs is experience or information. The experience is that of awareness of stimuli: a bright light, an itch, a toothache, the smell of bacon frying, or the beat of a rock band. The information consists of knowledge, which may be used immediately or stored for potential use.

Experience (or information) consists of perceptions, and these are not merely sense data. The preceding sections on receptors and neural activity may give the false impression that perception is merely the recording in the brain of stimulus inputs, as converted by sense organs. But these inputs must be *integrated* with other ongoing stimulation, as well as with the record of earlier experiences that is laid down in the brain. Two kinds of evidence will make this point clear.

First, a single sensory event can result in two different perceptions. Consider the cube in Figure 8.15. It is a reversible figure, which is

---

[2] *These have traditionally been called the* projection areas, *in contrast to the remaining parts of the cortex, which are called the* association areas. *This usage involves theoretical assumptions that have, for the most part, been discarded (Pribram, 1966), and therefore we shall use a different set of terms, as will be seen shortly.*

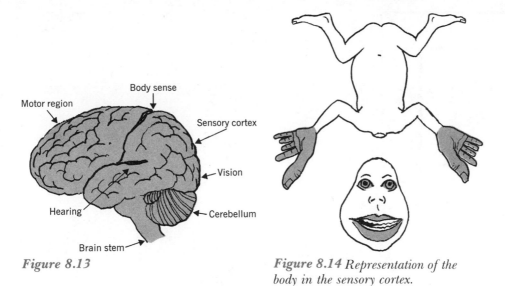

Figure 8.13

Figure 8.14 *Representation of the body in the sensory cortex.*

Table 8.2
Functional Organization of Sensory Areas in the Cortex (Luria, 1970)

ZONE	FUNCTION	RESULT OF INJURY
Primary	Receive, sort, and record sensory information	Cannot see, cannot hear and so on
Secondary	Further codes and organizes sensory information	Trouble in analyzing stimuli
Tertiary	Information from different sources is pooled and integrated	Defects in spatial organization, in handling simultaneous stimuli, and in general, in complex tasks

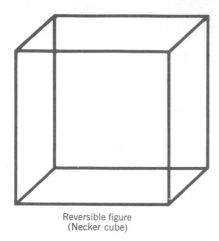

Reversible figure
(Necker cube)

Figure 8.15 One sensory input, two perceptions. The H and the A are identical in the two words but perceived differently.

organized first one way and then another as the viewer continues to gaze at it. A single stimulus pattern gives rise to two perceptions. The bottom of Figure 8.15, consisting of the words *the cat,* illustrates the same thing. The *h* in *the* furnishes an identical sensory input to the *a* in *cat,* but they are perceived differently.

Second, two different sensory events can result in a single perception. Take a sheet of white paper and hold it under a lamp; it appears white. Now move it into a shadow, where the amount of light reflected is diminished. The altered sensory event (the paper is now gray) does not alter the perception of the paper as white.

In brief, perception is a complex process involving both sensory inputs and the organization the perceiver imposes on these inputs. We must understand not only how sense organs work but also how the perceiver organizes his world. This organization obviously involves the kind of experiences the individual has been exposed to, as well as his ongoing motivations.

Perceptual Systems

With our emphasis on adaptation, our focus in perception is on how organisms obtain the information they need. Animals do not passively await stimulation, nor do their receptors function in isolation from each other. It is necessary to understand how each kind of receptor element works, but our interest is not so much in the physiology of sensory mechanisms as in the psychology of perception. This is essentially the approach of Gibson (1966), who speaks in terms of *perceptual systems.* His classification is presented in Table 8.3. These five systems overlap the usual list of sight, taste, smell, touch, and hearing, but there are some differences. Taste and smell are grouped into a single chemical-receiving system, and touch, muscle sense, joint sense, and temperature sense are all included under the haptic system. The basic orienting sense, involving balance, completes the list. All these systems are important, but vision predominates in humans. Visions accounts for most of our information about the environment, and most of the research on perception concerns vision.

Table 8.3
The Perceptual Systems (Gibson, 1966)

SYSTEM	MODE OF ATTENTION	RECEPTIVE UNITS	SENSE	ACTIVITY OF THE ORGAN	STIMULI AVAILABLE	EXTERNAL INFORMATION OBTAINED
Basic orienting	General orientation	Mechano-receptors and gravity-receptors	Vestibular organs	Body equilibrium	Forces of gravity and acceleration	Direction of gravity, being pushed
Auditory	Listening	Mechano-receptors	Ear	Orienting to sounds	Vibration in the air	Nature and location of vibratory events
Haptic	Touching	Mechano-receptors and possibly thermo-receptors	Skin, joints, and muscles	Exploration of many kinds	Deformations of tissues Configurations of joints Stretching of muscle fibers	Contact with the earth Mechanical encounters Object shapes Material states; solidity or viscosity Heat or cold
Taste-Smell	Smelling	Chemo-receptors	Nose	Sniffing	Composition of the medium	Nature of odors
	Tasting	Chemo- and mechano-receptors	Mouth	Savoring	Composition of ingested objects	Nutritive and biochemical values
Visual	Looking	Photo-receptors	Eyes	Accommodation Pupillary adjustment Fixation, convergence Exploration	Light	Information about objects, animals, motions, events, and places

nonvisual perception

Basic orienting system — statocyst — vestibular apparatus — evolution of hearing — human ear — sound waves — sensitivity — theories of hearing — localization — echolocation — feed- back — haptic system — cutaneous, haptic, and dynamic touch — temperature — taste — smell — pain — gate control theory — influences on pain — implications for perception

We have distinguished four nonvisual systems: basic orienting, auditory, haptic, and taste-smell. They will be discussed in turn, with our emphasis reflecting the importance of each system for man. Of the four, hearing is dominant, followed in diminishing order by the haptic, taste-smell, and basic orienting systems. Knowledge about the basic orienting system helps in understanding hearing, and therefore we shall begin with the sense of equilibrium.

The Basic Orienting System

Small primitive animals that float in water need not be sensitive to gravity, but aquatic animals heavier than water and all land animals must respond to the constant downward-acting force. Animals that move must also know where they are and where they are going. Vision, touch, and hearing bring in information, but the major contribution arises from organs specialized to respond to gravitational forces acting on the organism.

The Statocyst

Even primitive organisms are subject to the force of gravity, and early in evolution specialized hair cells evolved that were sensitive to this force. The thin filaments we call hair are well suited to register changes in the surrounding medium because they can be moved by even the slightest physical changes in the medium. This property was exploited with the evolution of a gravity detector basic to all animals, the statocyst (see Figure 9.1). Its two components are the heavy *statolith* and *hair cells*. When the animal is at rest (Figure 9.2a), the statolith presses down, bending the hair cells, which register a pattern of stimulation indicating rest. When the animal is tilted, the statolith changes position (see Figure 9.2b), which causes a different pattern of neural impulses. The organ registers acceleration by both the change in pattern and the increased pressure of the statolith on some of the hair cells (Figure 9.2c).

The basic principle of this organ is simple. The statolith, being heavier than the fluid medium surrounding it, responds to changes in the forces acting on the organism by pressing more heavily or lightly on different hair cells. The changes of pressure on the hair cells initiate descriminable patterns of neural impulses, which furnish information about position and movement.

The Vestibular Apparatus

The statocyst organ evolved into a more specialized and elaborate structure early in the evolution of vertebrates, and there have been virtually no further changes. In the head of the typical vertebrate are two highly specialized statocysts, called *the vestibular apparatus* to distinguish it from the auditory apparatus immediately adjacent. Each member of the paired apparatus in humans has three components: the utricle, the saccule, and the semicircular canals (see Figure 9.3a). The utricle and saccule are essentially statocysts, and in these two chambers there are two statoliths set at right angles to each other. These weights bend the hairs they rest against, the pattern of bent hairs depending on how the head moves. For example, during running the statoliths bounce with each stride.

The semicircular canals register *rotation* of the head, which is a significant adaptation. They work in a different way from the utricle and saccule. The fluid in the canals can circulate freely but is at rest when the head is stationary. When the head rotates, the fluid in one or more canals circulates, deflecting hair cells at the base of the canal (ampulla); these deflections initiate neural impulses. The canals are arranged along the three basic axes of the body: up-down, side-to-side, and front-back

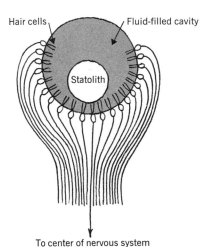

Figure 9.1 *A schematic statocyst.*

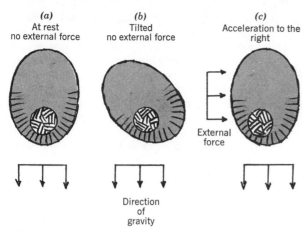

(a)
At rest
no external force

(b)
Tilted
no external force

(c)
Acceleration to the
right

External
force

Direction
of
gravity

Figure 9.2 *The statocyst in three conditions.*

(see Figure 9.3*b*). Thus the pattern of stimulation coming from the three canals yields information about the precise plane of rotation of the head.

Thus the vestibular apparatus provides two kinds of information:

1. The utricle and saccule combine to register the effect of gravity and of acceleration in a line, whether it is up-down, forward-backward, or side-to-side.
2. The semicircular canals register the effect of turning the head, specifying both acceleration and direction.

The most important use made of this information is in maintaining body posture, which is difficult when balancing on only two legs (watch any infant). Information from the vestibular apparatus is fed to the cerebellum, which integrates the muscular adjustments that maintain equilibrium.

There is a close connection between this information and that arising from vision. When a person rotates, his eyes make compensatory side-to-side movements called *nystagmus*. A sudden stop after many turns results in nystagmus lasting long enough to cause dizziness. Ballet dancers compensate by fixating on a spot as long as possible and then whipping the head around to fixate on the same spot. Such head turning not only minimizees dizziness but offers a more stable visual environment for the spinning person. In fact, the visual information overrides the vestibular information, another example of the dominance of vision.

The basic orienting system evolved as an adaptation to the conditions that usually confront animals: active movements and brief passive movements such as short falls (long falls lead to serious injury or death). It is not surprising, then, that the system cannot cope with novel situations that never occur in nature. The system does not register sustained passive movements at a constant speed, such as traveling at high speeds in a train or airplane. Of course, any acceleration or deceleration is immediately sensed, and such changes in the speed of passive movement may result in incorrect perceptions. Thus, after being rotated fast, we sense slowing down as being spun in the opposite direction.

Passive movement can also cause illness. The swaying, swooping, and sudden falling movements that occur in airplanes and ships at sea may in-

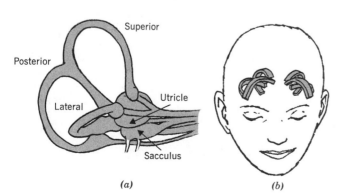

Superior

Posterior

Lateral

Utricle

Sacculus

(a)

(b)

Figure 9.3 *Human mechanisms for equilibrium.*

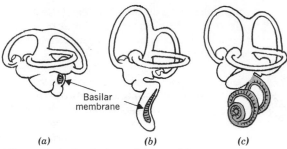

Figure 9.4 *Evolution of the cochlea.*

duce dizziness and nausea,[1] but the same stimulation when self-induced, as in running, leaping, or even spinning, does not lead to any ill effects. Thus whether the person becomes seasick is determined by whether his movements are active or passive, not solely on the presence of stimulation of the vestibular apparatus. The important lesson here is that perception is based not on a single perceptual system operating in isolation (or the neural impulses that come from receptors), but on the total pattern of stimulation coming from all perceptual systems.

The Auditory System

Most events cause vibrations in the medium that surrounds them, for example, a whisper, a handclap, a thunderclap, or an earthquake. The auditory system picks up these vibrations and uses them to *identify* and *locate* an event. In addition, the *feedback* of sound is important in controlling sequences of vocalization, as in bird songs and human speech.

Evolution of the Auditory System

The receptors for hearing are located in the *cochlea,* a coiled structure immediately adjacent to the vestibular system. The cochlea evolved first as an attachment to the saccule and later as an independent organ (see Figure 9.4). Like the ves-

[1] Duration *is at least as important. Shipboard movements last a long time, in contrast to the brief duration of active movements.*

tibular apparatus, the cochlea is sensitive to mechanical forces, especially to the very small vibrations we call sound. During vertebrate evolution the vestibule remained unchanged, but the cochlea increased in size and became coiled to conserve space.

When vibrations in the water strike a fish, its whole body vibrates, and the disturbance in the statoliths results in something akin to hearing. This simple arrangement could not work on land, where the vibrations are transmitted through air. The adaptive problem was to transmit the air vibrations to the water-filled cochlea inherited from sea-dwelling ancestors. The evolutionary solution was twofold: an air canal ending in a tightly stretched drum that vibrates in response to variations in air pressure, and the mechanical conduction of these vibrations to the cochlea. The outcome was the ear man shares with other mammals.

The Human Ear

The human ear may be divided into three parts: outer, middle, and inner (see Figure 9.5). Air vibrations travel through the ear canal to the eardrum (*tympanic membrane*), a tightly stretched structure that resonates to the slightest air vibrations. The eardrum transmits the vibrations to the middle ear, which consists of three bones named for the shapes they resemble: hammer, anvil, and stirrup. The cavity of the middle ear is filled with

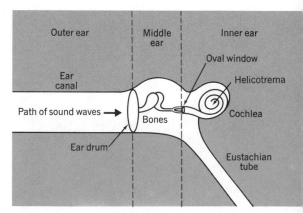

Figure 9.5 *The human ear.*

air, which reaches it through the Eustachian tube. This tube, which is connected to the mouth, helps to keep the air pressure equal on both sides of the eardrum, thereby preventing damage by the energy contained in very loud sounds.

The vibrations pass through the three bones, and from the stirrup they move on the the inner ear, which is filled with fluid (the mechanism first evolved in aquatic animals, and the fluid is a holdover from this ear). Specifically, the foot of the stirrup connects with the tiny *oval window,* which is a fraction of the size of the eardrum. This size differential causes the vibrations coming from the eardrum to be amplified many times at the oval window.

The vibrations of the oval window generate waves in the fluid of the cochlea. Through a sequence too complex to discuss here, the waves eventually reach the *basilar membrane,* on which is the organ of Corti. This pea-sized organ consists of more than 20,000 hair cells, the receptor elements for hearing. The detection of movement by disturbance of hair cells can be traced far back in phylogeny. All of the complex adaptations we have been describing are mammalian devices to conduct air vibrations to a liquid medium containing hair cells.

Stimulation of the organ of Corti initiates nerve impulses, which are carried by the auditory nerve through a series of four relay stations to the brain. Many of the nerve fibers cross to the other side of the brain and eventually terminate in the auditory cortex opposite to the ear from which they originated. Thus each ear is represented neurally on both sides of the brain, an anatomical arrangement which helps the two ears to function as a single organ rather than as two separate organs.

The presence of four relay stations serves two functions. First, there is some coding of the auditory message even before it reaches the cerebral cortex. Second, the ganglionic relay stations can be influenced by impulses coming from the cerebral cortex and other higher brain centers. Thus higher centers, especially the cortex, exercise control over the messages delivered to them so that only relevant or important messages get through.

Though sound waves traveling through the air must be transmitted through the middle ear to the inner ear, there is another route for vibrations. The bones of the skull can be stimulated directly, and the vibrations are transmitted to the cochlea by *bone conduction.* This primitive mode is used by snakes and other animals in close contact with the ground. They have no eardrums, but in their usual haunts ground vibrations (which can easily be transmitted by bone conduction) are more important than air vibrations, which they cannot sense. Bone conduction is not ordinarily used by humans, but its presence causes distortions in self-perception of speech. One's own voice sounds different on a tape recorder than when heard directly because as sound is produced from the larynx, bone conduction contributes qualities not heard when the voice comes from another source. It is a paradoxical fact that it is more difficult to recognize one's own voice than that of another familiar person.

Sound Waves

Sounds are actually pressure waves that move through a medium, which ordinarily is air for humans. The sound waves spread out through the medium the way ripples do when a stone is dropped into a still pond. The speed of sound in the usual human habitat is about 760 miles per hour (1100 feet per second). This velocity increases with temperature at the rate of about two feet per second for every degree of centigrade temperature, and it also varies with the nature of the medium, being faster in water than in air.

The most important properties of sound waves are frequency, amplitude, complexity, and timing. The first three properties are illustrated in Figure 9.6. Pressure waves wax and wane, and each cycle is measured from crest to crest. *Frequency* refers to the number of ups and downs per unit of time, usually expressed as cycles per second (see Figure 9.6a). Cycles per second are now designated *Hz* in honor of Heinrich Herz, a German physicist. The higher the frequency, the higher is the *pitch* of the sound; a soprano voice generates more cycles per second than does a bass voice.

More forceful movements produce more intense vibrations, the vibrating body being displaced more from its resting position. Variations in intensity are plotted as *amplitude* of the wave, the distance from the peak to the trough (see Figure 9.6b). The greater the amplitude, the *louder* the sound; the sound waves generated by a drill

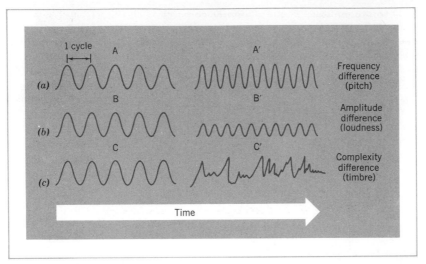

Figure 9.6 *Properties of sound waves.*

sergeant have a greater amplitude than those of a seminar instructor.

Only pure tones can be represented as the simple sine wave shown in Figure 9.6*a* and *b*; virtually all vibratory events produce waves of many frequencies (see Figure 9.6*c*). Variations in complexity are sensed as differences in *timbre,* or the quality of the sound. Voices of the same pitch and loudness can still be distinguished by their tonal quality or timbre, and the differences between muscial instruments (say, violin versus piano) lie mainly in the complexity of the waves they produce.

Sensitivity and Discriminability

It is reasonable to expect that the range of hearing sensitivity is appropriate to the natural habitat of the animal. In general, the smaller the animal, the higher the pitch it can hear. Small animals tend to generate sounds of higher pitch, and their ears must be able to sense these sounds. Man's position in this scheme of things is not clear, but we do know that the range of his hearing is limited to 20 to 20,000 Hz. His sensitivity varies considerably over this range, as may be seen in Figure 9.7. The lower the curve, the greater the sensitivity (the less intensity needed to hear). Man's sensitivity is

greatest in the range of 2000–5000 Hz. so that with intensity held constant, a sound of 3000 Hz seems louder than higher or lower frequencies. Most human speech is pitched much lower, and it has been speculated that the channel of 3000 Hz, which is approximately the pitch of a human

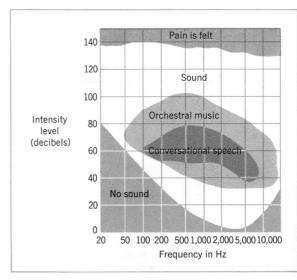

Figure 9.7 *Range of hearing in man.*

scream, has been left open for emergencies (Milne & Milne, 1962).

In modern industrial society man is exposed to huge variations in sound level, as may be seen in Figure 9.8. Like any sensitive instrument, the human ear can be harmed by repeated overloads. It has been known for decades that men working in a boiler plant are likely to become deaf. More recently, some musicians, after repeated exposures to the sounds typical of a rock group, have suffered serious damage to eardrums.

Theories of Hearing

How does the ear code the frequency and amplitude of sound waves so that we hear the pitch and

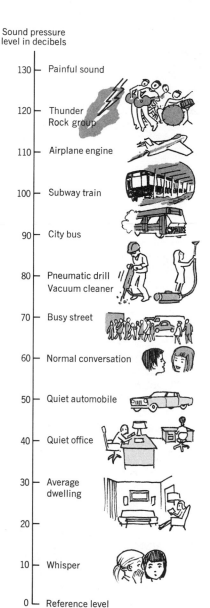

Sound pressure
level in decibels

130 — Painful sound

120 — Thunder
Rock group

110 — Airplane engine

100 — Subway train

90 — City bus

80 — Pneumatic drill
Vacuum cleaner

70 — Busy street

60 — Normal conversation

50 — Quiet automobile

40 — Quiet office

30 — Average
dwelling

20 —

10 — Whisper

0 — Reference level

Figure 9.8 *Some familiar sounds expressed in decibels (a derived measure of loudness).*

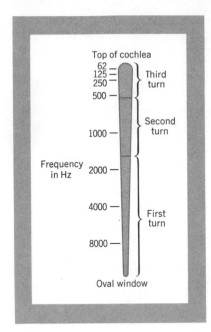

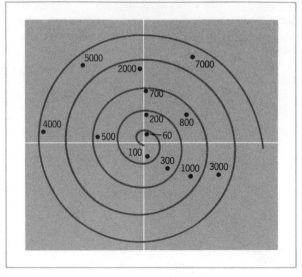

Figure 9.9 *Different frequencies yield optimed cochlea responses at different locations.*

loudness of sounds? The coding must begin in the inner ear, specifically in the basilar membrane of the cochlea, which vibrates when sound waves reach it. There are two major theories of how sound waves are coded. One assumes that the coding mechanism involves *where* the basilar membrane vibrates most (the *place* theory). The other theory assumes that the *frequency* of vibrations of the basilar membrane provides the coding mechanism (the *volley* theory).

The place theory was first formulated 100 years ago, but the modern version is more recent (von Bekesy, 1960). It assumes that sound waves stimulate the entire basilar membrane, but the *maximum displacement* of the membrane occurs at different places, depending upon the frequency of the wave. High-frequency waves (say, from a flute) affect the basilar membrane at the beginning of the cochlea, near the oval window; low-frequency waves (say, from a bass drum) affect it most near the end of the cochlea, near the apex. There is clear evidence for this assumption in the response of an animal's cochlea to waves of different frequencies (see Figure 9.9). The theory neatly ac-

counts for the perception of pitch, which presumably depends on the *place* where the basilar membrane is maximally affected by the sound wave.

The place theory's explanation of loudness is not as good. It assumes that a more intense wave (one of larger amplitude) would excite more hair cells; that is, more of the membrane would be maximally affected by the wave. Ostensibly, the greater the spread of excitation on the basilar membrane, the louder the sound wave is perceived. But if the spread is greater, the sounds of different pitch should be perceived because pitch presumably depends on the *place* maximally stimulated. This means that loud sounds would always be perceived as muddier mixtures of different pitches than would soft sounds. That this is not true weakens the place theory.

The *volley theory* is also very old and has needed modern revision (Wever & Bray, 1930; Wever, 1949). It assumes that sound waves cause the basilar membrane to *vibrate as a whole* in essentially the same way as the diaphragm of a microphone or telephone. The more intense the wave, the more fibers are stimulated, thus accounting for the relationship between amplitude and loudness. The peak of each wave (maximum pressure) excites the hair cells and the nerves fire. The rate of firing is believed to be the same as the frequency of the sound wave. This assumption holds only for low-frequency waves because nerve fibers can fire no faster than 1000 times per second. The theory handles this problem by assuming the nerve fibers do not fire all at the same time but in *volleys* (see Figure 9.10). Thus when the sound wave has a frequency of 2000 Hz, half the fibers fire during one cycle, and the other half during the next cycle; each nerve fiber fires no more than 1000 times per second, but the successive firing of different groups of nerve fibers results in volleys of 2000 firings per second. It is as if two riflemen doubled their rate of firing by having one fire while the other loads, and then reversing roles. This volley principle works well up to 5000 Hz, but beyond that point nerve fibers appear to fire randomly rather than in volleys. Thus the theory cannot account for the perception of high-frequency sounds.

Each theory has been partially supported by data, and each suffers from a crucial weakness. On balance, it would appear that the place theory accounts better for sounds of high pitch and the volley theory accounts better for sounds of low pitch. In addition, coding of sound continues in the auditory pathways to the brain and in the cerebral cortex (Creel et al., 1970).

Localization

One function of the auditory apparatus is to specify the location of vibratory events: movements and vocalizations made by offspring, parents, and mates, as well as by prey and predators. Humans and other primates use their eyes more than their ears to locate objects and events, but in the absence of sight, hearing can be used to detect even silent objects. As we saw in Chapter 2, blind persons can locate obstacles by listening to the echoes made by their own steps or by a cane tapping. For those with normal sight, events can of course be located by the sounds emitted by the events. Such localization involves three aspects: distance, movement, and direction.

DISTANCE. The most important cue for distance is *loudness:* the louder the sound, the closer the object. *Complexity* offers a secondary cue. Sounds lose complexity as they travel, so that the listener hears a simpler sound when it has been emitted from far away. The more complex the sound, the closer the object.

MOVEMENT. We are concerned here only with movement toward or away from the listener; lateral movement involves *direction,* which we shall consider in the next section. Such movement involves a change of distance between the sound source and the listener, and an obvious cue is the *change* in loudness. As the source approaches the listener, the sound becomes louder, and as the

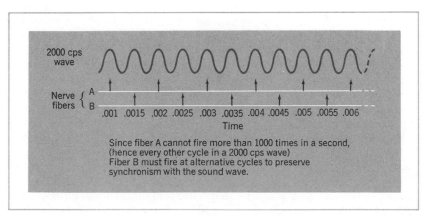

Figure 9.10 Synchronism with the sound wave.

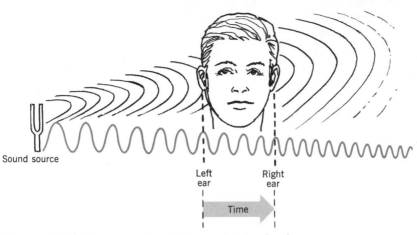

Sound source

Left ear Right ear

Time

Figure 9.11 Three ways in which sound is localized: timing, intensity, and phase.

source withdraws, the sound diminishes in intensity—e.g., an approaching and receding ambulance with its siren blasting. A secondary cue consists of changes in *pitch.* When the second source is moving toward the listener, the sound waves bunch up, increasing the frequency of cycles per second. As the source recedes from the listener, the sound waves stretch out slightly, decreasing the frequency and lowering the pitch of the sound. These changes in wavelength are called the Doppler effect, after the man who discovered them. DIRECTION. The location of the ears on opposite sides of the head results in slight differences in the sound waves reaching them, and these differences furnish *binaural* cues for localizing sound. Specifically, there are differences in the *timing, intensity,* and *phase* of the sound waves reaching the two ears (see Figure 9.11). Suppose the sound comes from the right. The right ear receives the sound waves a fraction of a second before the left ear, and this difference is sufficient for the perception of the direction of the source. The sound proceeds directly into the right ear but must travel around the head to reach the left ear; in the process it loses some intensity, and the intensity difference between the two ears also helps to locate the source of the sound.[2] The

difference in time may also result in the left ear's receiving the sound in a different phase of the wave than the right ear, and again this difference may be sufficient to localize the source. The frequency and intensity differences yield information for precise localization (Mills, 1958). The listener is unaware of discrepancies in time, intensity, or phase; all he has is an impression of the direction from which the sound originates.

These binaural differences have been exploited to yield greater esthetic satisfaction for listeners of music. Music is recorded through different microphones and played back through speakers on either side of the listener. The different sources of the music produce the effect of sound filling the room. An even more striking effect occurs when the listener wears stereophonic earphones: the sound seems to come from the middle of the head.

The direction of sound can also be detected by a single ear, as we know from the reports of persons who are entirely deaf in one ear. Such a listener moves his head, thereby altering the timing and intensity of the sound (Wallach, 1940); such movements can compensate for the absence of a second ear. But a single ear can locate the source of sound even when the head remains still; this is possible because the head "shadows" the sounds that reach the one functioning ear (Perrott & Elfner, 1968). In brief, sound can be localized with one ear and, in most instances, even better with two ears. The cues are summarized in Table 9.1.

[2] *Differences in timing and intensity of sound waves to the two ears are complementary and difficult to separate, but both help in locating the source of sound waves (Green & Henning, 1969).*

Table 9.1
Cues for Localizing Sources of Sounds

ASPECT OF LOCATION	CUE
Distance	Loudness or complexity
Movement	*Changes* in loudness or pitch
Direction	One ear: differences in time or loudness Two ears: differences in time, loudness, or phase

Echolocation

We have been discussing how sounds are located, but earlier we mentioned the possibility of locating silent objects by means of echoes. Such perception, called *echolocation,* is obviously adaptive in environments that severely restrict vision. Cave-dwelling bats and depth-dwelling porpoises and whales clearly need such an adaptation to fly or swim in their usual habitats. They emit high-pitched squeaks (too high for the human ear to hear) and then use the echoes reflected from objects to guide their locomotion. Bats can avoid obstacles in total darkness, and as Figure 9.12 suggests, they can locate and capture rapidly moving prey in the dark (Griffen, 1959). High frequencies—the bat uses up to 100,000 Hz—are reflected better than low ones from small objects, and are used more by bats than by whales or porpoises.

Although there are several types of echolocation, the basic principle is the same. The animal emits a short series of extremely high-pitched sounds and then listens to the pattern of waves reflected back to it. Small differences in frequency, intensity, and phase of the reflected waves are sufficient to serve as cues in localizing objects. Scientists have copied nature, and similar systems are used in navigating through the air (radar) and at sea (sonar).

Feedback

Human speech consists of *sequences* of sounds, and the flow of speech cannot be maintained without proper auditory feedback. As soon as speech is emitted, it is fed back to the person through the channels of air and bone conductions. This flow of information is needed to keep track of what has just been said, which determines what is said next. The speaker's speech flow is paced by his own voice, just as the steps down a flight of stairs are guided by the stepping movements themselves.

The motor aspects of speech may be divided into four parts (see Figure 9.13). The pressure with which the air is expelled, which determines vocal amplitude, is determined by the diaphragm (*A*). The phrasing of speech—the pattern and timing of word sequences—is regulated largely by smaller breathing muscles in the chest (*B*). Pitch and tonal qualities are controlled by the larynx (*C*) and the articulation of consonants by the mouth, tongue, and lips (*D*). The outcome of this complex series of movements is human speech, which is immediately fed back to the ears of the speaker.

If auditory feedback is crucial to the flow of speech, it should be possible to disrupt speech by interfering with the feedback. This is precisely what occurs in *delayed auditory feedback,* the technique developed by Lee (1950). As we saw in Chapter 2, after a few moments of delayed feedback, the subject's speech begins to deteriorate:

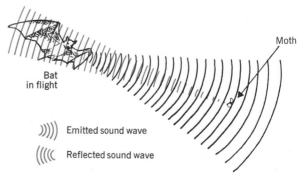

Figure 9.12 Echolocation in the bat.

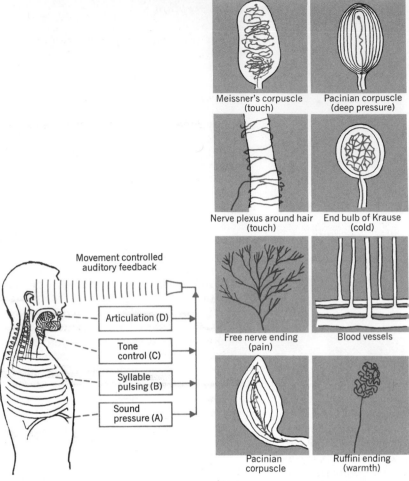

Figure 9.13 *Differential sensory feedback control of the different movement components of speech.*

Labels in Figure 9.13:
Movement controlled auditory feedback
Articulation (D)
Tone control (C)
Syllable pulsing (B)
Sound pressure (A)

Figure 9.14 *Main types of nerve endings and vascular units.*

Labels in Figure 9.14:
Meissner's corpuscle (touch)
Pacinian corpuscle (deep pressure)
Nerve plexus around hair (touch)
End bulb of Krause (cold)
Free nerve ending (pain)
Blood vessels
Pacinian corpuscle
Ruffini ending (warmth)

pitch changes and loudness increases, the rate of speech slows down, repetitions, errors, and stuttering occur.[3] The breakdown of normal speech patterns clearly demonstrates the importance of auditory feedback. Without the return flow of information from one's own utterances, it is extremely difficult to program the complex series of movements that constitute speech. Witness the problems of the deaf in learning to speak: only a small proportion do speak, and their speech has a peculiar cadence.

[3] *The effects make delayed auditory feedback an excellent means for detecting persons who are faking deafness.*

The Haptic System

In everyday language we speak of the sense of touch, which more or less corresponds to the haptic system. This system includes more than what is usually meant by the sense of touch, for it also includes perception of body movement, or kinesthesis. If this description is a little vague, it is because the system is diffuse and spread out through the entire body. Its receptor elements are among the most primitive and phyletically oldest of any found in man.

The Receptor Elements

The receptor elements may be divided into those in the skin and those deeper in the body (see Figure 9.14). Free nerve endings are found everywhere in the skin and also wrapped around tiny blood vessels, which are also sensitive elements. More specialized receptors are located only in certain organs or only where there is hair. Figure 9.14 also shows three kinds of receptors found in muscles and joints. Pacinian corpuscles are believed to be sensitive to movements of joints. Muscle spindles and Golgi organs function in a complementary fashion to record the actions of muscles. Golgi organs are sensitive to *contraction* but not stretching of muscles; muscle spindles record *stretching* but not contraction of muscles.

The hair cells and the free and encapsulated nerve endings, which make up the mechanoreceptors we have been discussing, are found in the skin, joints, muscles, and blood vessels. Information from these locations, singly, or in combination, is the basis for four different haptic subsystems: cutaneous, haptic, dynamic, and temperature (Gibson, 1966).

Cutaneous Touch

Cutaneous touch is more complicated than the sensing of pressure against the skin. When a finger is immersed in a dish of mercury (Figure 9.15), the pressure against the finger is greater at the bottom than at the surface of the mercury, but the skin does not record the gradations in pressure. All that is perceived is the discontinuity at the boundary between mercury and air. Perceptual systems evolved to extract information from the environment, and in most situations it is *discontinuities* that are important to the organism, not continuous gradations.

There has been much research on the ability of the skin to detect stimulation at a single point, such as is delivered by a pin or a hair,[4] but we still

---

[4] *This research has revealed striking differences in the sensitivity of various parts of the body to touch. The tongue, lips, and fingertips are extremely sensitive; the back of the hand and the abdomen are less so; the sole of the foot is very insensitive.*

have little precise knowledge about the skin as a perceptual system. Animals are rarely touched by a single point, and the response to such stimulation yields little information about perception. The skin can be stimulated not only by pressure, but by pulling, squeezing, twisting, and rubbing it. Studying these kinds of stimulation will yield knowledge about the adaptive properties of cutaneous touch, but such research has only just begun (Gibson, 1962).

We do know that the skin can detect differences in the *source* of stimulation, and such information is obviously of adaptive value. Thus a thorn, a leaf, and a crawling insect can be distinguished from each other when they touch the skin; a scratch feels different from a prod or push; and all of these feel different from being stroked, caressed, licked, or gently bitten. The skin can distinguish moving from still stimuli, as well as among such movements as rubbing, scraping, brushing, and rolling against the skin (Gibson, 1966). In short, though cutaneous touch is a passive system, it serves to identify the source of a wide variety of mechanical stimuli that are important to the organism. These include the most intimate social contacts: the two-way skin stimulation occurring between mother and infant and between lovers.

Haptic Touch

Haptic touch combines skin and joint information, whether passive or active. Passive information arises from objects touching the person, who can thereby record the layout of his local environment. Of special importance is information about the angles of the joints, and this may involve no touching at all. The person calibrates the angles of all the various joints in the body, and the integration of this information is a basic requirement for any movement.[5] Receptors in the joints can also supply quantitative information about angles—as when a person shows how large a fish he caught (see Figure 9.16). The distance between his palms can mark off length with little error, whether the eyes are open or closed; the crucial receptors are in the shoulder joints.

---

[5] *Such calibration and integration do not necessarily imply awareness. We are aware of some of these processes and unaware of others.*

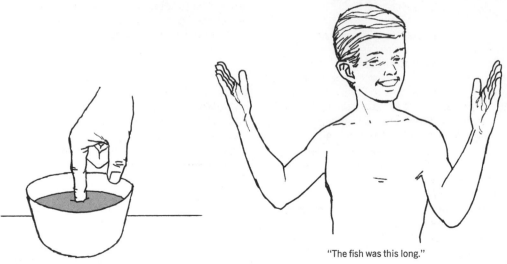

Figure 9.15 *A finger immersed in mercury.*

Figure 9.16 *An example of haptic touch.*

"The fish was this long."

Haptic touch reaches a peak in the active exploration of the world with the hands and fingers, an activity in which primates and humans excel. This ability has been tested in the laboratory, and it has been found that normal, blindfolded subjects can determine many aspects of objects merely by running their hands over them (Gibson, 1962). Haptic touch alone can accurately determine shapes, dimensions and proportions, points and curves, and protuberances (see Figure 9.17).

In addition to geometric properties, objects have *surface texture* that can be discerned by touching. Actually, it requires more than touching to discover whether the surface of an object is hard or soft, or rough or smooth; the object has to be rubbed, and as the hand moves, the minute changes in friction are recorded. It is fairly easy to distinguish different grades of sandpaper (Stevens & Harris, 1962), how slippery a surface is, and how hard or soft the bristles of a brush are. The perception of texture, which has received little attention in the laboratory, is fundamental to the earliest social relationship, that between mother and infant. Primate infants tend to cling to soft, woolly objects, preferring such contact comfort even to hard objects that furnish milk (Harlow & Suomi, 1970). Human infants reveal their primate nature by a preference for soft, cuddly toys and

pillows, and in the extreme case, for a "security blanket."

Dynamic Touch

Like haptic touch, dynamic touch concerns both positions of the body and the identification of objects held in the hand, the distinction being between the hand as a response mechanism and the hand as a perceptual instrument. From the very beginning, man has grasped tools and used them to accomplish what he could not do with his natural equipment. Three sources of feedback stimulation—skin, joints, and muscles—are required in fine motor movement, such as those of a surgeon operating or an artist painting fine details. These skilled acts ordinarily require vision as well as dynamic touch, but dynamic touch is not only essential but can, if necessary, substitute for vision; thus blind persons can be taught to write and to sew, relying only on information from their skin, joints, and muscles.

Even when tools are not used, dynamic touch guides movements of the hand. Picking up a pencil, plucking a guitar, and ripping a sheet of paper all depend on the feedback supplied by a dynamic touch, which is essential to the various

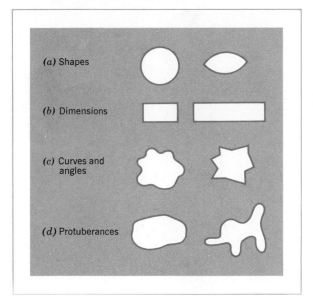

Figure 9.17 Discriminations yielded by haptic touch.

(a) Shapes

(b) Dimensions

(c) Curves and angles

(d) Protuberances

a warm object, other spots register the sensation of warmth. The distribution of warm and cold spots are different, a fact that has suggested to some investigators that there are two temperature senses, one for heat and one for cold (Geldard, 1953).

Supporting this hypothesis is the presence of two kinds of nerve fibers (see Figure 9.19). When an area on the skin is cooled, certain fibers begin firing, but others do not; when the area is warmed, other fibers start firing. The terms *cold fibers* and *warm fibers* refer to the different distributions of firing as temperature varies, but note in the figure that the firing of a warm fiber may yield the sensation of cold, and the firing of a cold fiber sometimes yields the sensation of warmth. Even more peculiar is what happens when a heat grill, consisting of alternating warm and cool pipes, is placed against the skin (see Figure 9.20). The cool and warm stimuli combine to yield a sensation of

hand manipulations that so clearly distinguish humans, and to some extent primates, from virtually all other animals.

When the hand is used as an instrument of perception, dynamic touch yields information about the weight and consistency of objects (see Figure 9.18). The simplest way to determine how much an object weighs is to *heft* it—that is, move the hand up and down to produce a pattern of stimulation from skin, joints, and muscles. Consistency, which is more complex, includes the dimensions of soft-firm and elastic-rigid. Squeezing an object reveals how soft or hard it is, and pulling at it with both hands should establish how elastic it is.

Touch-Temperature

The perception of heat and cold by the skin is poorly understood. There is no agreement about the receptor elements for temperature changes, but the free nerve endings surrounding tiny blood vessels in the skin seem to be the best bet. Most researchers have concentrated on mapping cold and warm spots on the skin. When something cold touches the skin, only some parts of the area register sensations of cold; when this is repeated with

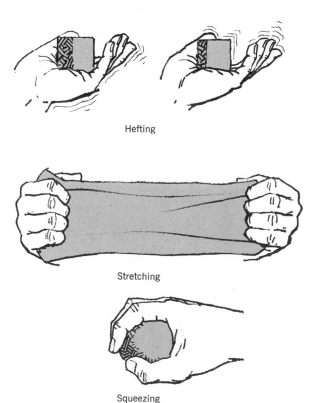

Hefting

Stretching

Squeezing

Figure 9.18 Examples of dynamic touch.

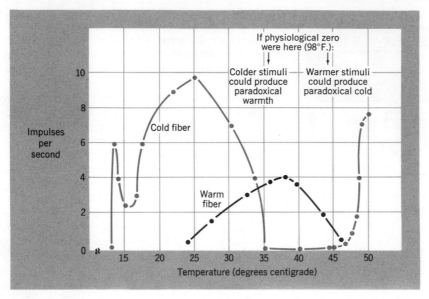

Figure 9.19 *Frequency of discharge of single "warm" and "cold" fibers as a function of temperature.*

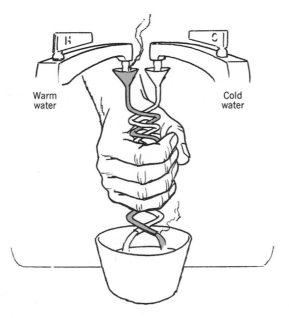

Figure 9.20 *Paradoxical heat.*

intense paradoxical heat, a fact which no theory can explain.

The stimulus for the perception of heat or cold is not the absolute temperature of the object, but the *difference* between the temperature of the object and that of the skin. Warmth is perceived when heat flows (by radiation or conduction) from the object to the skin, and cold is perceived when heat flows from the skin to the object. That this is true is shown by another paradox. The usual temperature of the skin is 91°F; if the left hand is placed in a bowl of water at 110° and the right hand in water at 70°, they register warmth and cold, respectively (see Figure 9.21). The hands soon habituate to these temperatures, and the sensations of warmth and cold slowly disappear. Then if both hands are placed in water that is 91°, it feels cold to the left hand and warm to the right hand. Clearly, the perceptions are determined by the temperature *differential* between the object (water) and the skin, not by the absolute temperature of the object.

The relative temperature of objects is perceived by the haptic system, the receptors providing information about how hot or cold the objects are that touch or are touched by the skin. There is another perceptual system for detecting variations in temperature. As part of the temperature-regulating system of all warmblooded animals, the body detects differences between its internal temperature and that of the surrounding medium. Such perceptions do not ordinarily involve the skin; rather, they are believed to depend on the temperature of the blood, which is monitored by the body's thermostat, the hypothalamus (see Chapter 6).

The temperature of the human environment may be divided into three zones (Winslow et al., 1937). Above 90°F the unclothed person sweats. Below 86° the naked person shivers as his body cools, and between 86° and 90° there is a transition zone. Of course these are average figures, and they do not take into account variations in the usual climate (the Eskimo versus the African tribesman) or gender (women become chilled at higher temperatures than men).

Taste and Smell

Taste and smell are *chemical* senses. In humans these are distinct senses: taste receptors are located in the mouth and smell receptors, in the nose. This difference reflects a difference in function. Taste is part of the eating, or at least the sampling, of food, and it is therefore one aspect of nutrition and digestion. The substances sampled must be in either liquid or solid form and they must obviously be immediately adjacent to the organism; therefore taste cannot be used to detect objects or events at a distance. Smell is part of the breathing mechanism. It picks up information about gases emanating from nearby or some distance away; unlike taste, but like hearing and vision, smell is a distance receptor.

Taste and smell are not separate perceptual systems in all animals. Most sea animals can detect chemicals in their immediate environment, and in the sea there can be no separation of taste and smell. Fish have chemical receptors scattered all over their body as well as in the mouth. It has been speculated that when life emerged from the sea, the taste-smell mechanism diverged to form two anatomically separate mechanisms. Smell as we know it could not occur until the advent of a land animal, and the first animals with a sense of

Figure 9.21 *Perceived warmth or cold depends on the difference between the heat of the object and the heat of the skin.*

smell were amphibians. Aquatic animals can respond mainly to chemicals in their immediate environment. For example when salmon return to their birthplace to breed, they follow rivers upstream by sensing the salinity of the water: less salty water indicates a direction away from the sea.[6] But aquatic animals are for the most part restricted to sampling chemicals nearby because chemicals diffuse slowly and incompletely in a liquid medium. In air, on the other hand, gases spread out quickly and over large areas. The concentration of airborne chemicals is necessarily lower than that of chemicals in the sea, which means that smell must be more sensitive than the more primitive taste-smell combination. The ability of land animals to detect *gaseous* chemical substances allows them to discover objects and events at much greater distances than most sea animals, which are restricted to the combined sense of taste-smell.

Taste

Humans can taste only substances taken into the mouth, and these must be either liquids or convertible into a liquid state in order to be tasted. There are thousands of different tastes, and master chefs and winetasters can distinguish among food substances differing only in delicate nuances of flavor. Underlying the many varieties of taste sensations are four primary tastes: salt, sour, bitter, and sweet. These are of course *human* tastes, and they differ from those in animals. Thus dogs have the same kind of sweet tooth as humans, but cats and chickens do not; we cannot taste pure water, but frogs, chickens, pigeons, dogs, cats, and monkeys can (Zotterman, 1961). There is some relationship between a sweet taste and nutritious substances, but sweetness is no more a guarantee of good food than sourness is of spoiled or poisonous food. Of course, the term *spoiled* is relative: milk that is kept too long is called *sour* and not consumed, but cheese that is kept for a long period is called *aged* and is eaten as a delicacy.

RECEPTORS. The basic receptor, which is found mainly on the tongue, is called a *taste bud*. Each microscopic taste bud consists of 15 to 20 taste cells, and there are roughly 5000 taste buds located mainly in the grooves and pits of the tongue. The regions of the tongue are specialized to receive the four different primary tastes (see Figure 9.22). The tip of the tongue is most sensitive to sweet substances; the back, to bitter substances; and the sides, to salty and sour substances. None of these areas is sensitive *solely* to a given taste, but each is maximally sensitive to the ones just mentioned. Bitter pills are best placed on the front of the tongue and swallowed before they can be tasted by the back of the tongue. Foods can best be savored by tasting them with the entire tongue so as to sample the various flavors in the blend — as, for example, when eating Chinese food cooked in a sweet-and-sour sauce.

There are two types of taste buds (McCutcheon & Saunders, 1972). One type is sensitive to only a single taste; for example, a given taste bud of this type would respond to a sweet solution but not to salty, bitter, or sour solutions. The other type of taste bud is sensitive to several tastes. The presence of both types suggests that at least part of the coding of taste must occur in the pathways to the brain or in the brain itself.[7]

The taste cells initiate impulses in nerves that reach the cerebral cortex by way of three different nerve tracts. These tracts carry fibers from many different locations on the tongue and no one tract carries impulses related to a single primary taste sensation (Pfaffman, 1965). In fact, there is no relationship between either single nerve fibers or groups of nerve fibers and any of the primary tastes. Any given nerve fiber can be stimulated by a range of substances, and these substances cut across the four primary tastes. Thus the basis for the four primary tastes must be some *pattern* of neural impulses that is decoded in the cerebral cortex, perhaps with the aid of the relay stations between the receptors and the brain. This explanation is of course speculative, and there is still no really good theory, embodying both receptors and nerves, for the perception of the four primary tastes by humans.

---

[6] *Chemical sensitivity is probably the principal, but not the only, basis of finding the stream. Temperature of the water might also be used.*

[7] *The problem of understanding the mechanism underlying taste is complicated further by the fact that individual taste receptors have a life span of less than a week.*

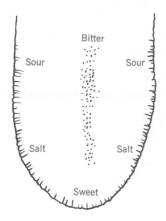

Figure 9.22 *Regions of the tongue where the four primary tastes are dominant.*

ADAPTIVE FUNCTIONS. The taste system in humans, and indeed in all primates, provides information only about ingested substances. Though there are errors, the taste system usually provides the information needed to select a nutritious, nonharmful diet. The perception of *chemical* aspects is only part of the information load imparted by the mouth. There are also receptors for mechanical and thermal stimuli, and the mouth can function as a haptic system. The heat of a substance is important knowledge if the delicate tissues of the upper part of the digestive system are to be protected. The surface texture is important: piecrust is rough, butter is smooth, and lettuce is slippery. Consistency is part of flavor: crackers are crisp and granular; meat is elastic and therefore chewy; butter is soft and peanut brittle is hard; and cheese is firm and tomatoes are soft. The complete perception of food in the mouth includes not only the chemical aspects mediated by taste (and smell) but also the mechanical and thermal aspects mediated by the haptic system. The haptic components are of considerable importance in virtually all of our acquired tastes: we reject bread that is too crisp (stale) as well as toast that is not warm or crisp enough; we accept a soft (not too soft) banana but not a pear of the same consistency; we accept soft vegetables if they are cooked but insist that they be crisp if they are fresh, and we reject food if its temperature is too high but accept such foods as hot peppers, which yield essentially the same uncomfortable sensation of heat. In brief, the sense of taste, as it has developed in human adults, comprises not only chemi-

cal sensitivity but also sensitivity to a range of mechanical and thermal values of the food.

Smell

Odors spread out over a much broader area than liquids do in water, which means that smell can serve as a distance receptor. Of course the widespread diffusion of odors results in very low concentrations, requiring the olfactory apparatus to be extremely sensitive. That smell is more sensitive than taste is a commonplace observation; one estimate suggests that smell is 10,000 times more sensitive than taste in terms of the number of molecules required for stimulation (Moncrieff, 1951).

Many animals, especially lower mammals, use smell the way we use vision: to locate and identify significant objects and events in the environment. They identify their own kind by the odor unique to the species or even the immediate, small group; those with an alien odor are driven off. A mother will accept an alien newborn if it is coated artificially with the proper scent, and will reject its own offspring if it is coated with an alien scent.

Predators such as wolves and lions use smell to seek out prey, and the prey detect their predators by the same means. Hamsters separated from their mothers early in life can still recognize the odor of their worst predator, the polecat. The predator's sense of smell can be turned against it: the skunk's odor.

Compared to most mammals' sense of smell, the human sense of smell is relatively dull, and its main function is to combine with taste in food-sampling. We can understand this directly when a head cold diminishes the sense of smell and renders most foods tasteless. Smell helps us to detect spoiled food, thereby preventing illness or even poisoning.

The sense of smell appears to be one of the least of man's sensitivities. Perhaps because of its dullness, we know little about it. There is no really acceptable classification of odors, and a lock-and-key theory of molecular shape (Amoore et al., 1964) remains without supporting evidence. Much more is known about odor sensitivity in animals, probably because of its greater importance in their lives. In humans, scents are important mainly for their esthetic value: in perfumes, deodorants, wines, and in association with foods.

Pain

Pain can be classified as one of the haptic sub-systems, but pain is not really limited to a single perceptual system. In everyday life most pain is caused by excessive pressure against the skin or penetration of the skin by sharp objects. But pain is also caused by virtually any stimulus that is too intense—for example, a blinding glare of light, a booming explosive sound, a very hot piece of metal, or a strongly acid liquid. As a result of the varied stimuli that can cause pain, there are many different pain *experiences*. As catalogued by Dallenbach (1939), they include:

. . . *achy, beating, biting, boring, bright, burning, clear, cutting, dark, digging, dragging, drawing, dull, fluttering, gnawing, hard, heavy, itchy, nipping, palpitating, penetrating, piercing, pinching, pressing, pricking, quick, quivering, radiating, raking, savage, sharp, smarting, squeezing, stabbing, sticking, stinging, tearing, thrilling, throbbing, thrusting, tugging, twitching, ugly, and vicious. It is clear that some of these terms characterize the temporal aspect of the feeling pattern, others its spatial dimension, others the blend with pressure or temperature, while some appear to have reference to the associated forms of emotional response.* (GELDARD, 1953, P. 193.)

The only common element in the adjectives listed above is their reference to the noxious aspects of the stimulus. Noxious stimuli are usually harmful, and the adaptive function of pain is a warning to withdraw or escape from the source of the harm. But pain is sometimes ignored. Soldiers in battle and athletes in physical contests are often unaware of minor wounds, cuts, and bruises until some time after the engagement. If pain is merely the perception of harm or damage to the body, it is difficult to understand how it can be overlooked.

There are other puzzling facts. Dogs raised in complete isolation do not attempt to withdraw from quite painful stimuli (Melzack & Scott, 1957); and young chimpanzees that are prevented from feeling with their hands or feet (see Figure 9.23) have little or no response to painful stimuli (Nissen et al., 1951). The experience of pain can be diminished in humans by static-like *white noise* (Gardner et al., 1960) and dentists report some success in diminishing pain by playing music. Clearly, pain is a complex phenomenon, and the foremost theory that attempts to explain it is that of Melzack and Wall (1965).

A Theory of Pain

The theory assumes that there is a *gate control system*[8] in the spinal cord. This system receives neural inputs form three sources: (1) small-diameter neurons from receptors, (2) large-diameter neurons from receptors, and (3) neurons from the cerebral cortex (see Figure 9.24). The gate is seen as the synapses in the spinal pathways to the brain. It tends to be kept open by the firing of *small fibers,* which supply a fairly continuous stream of impulses toward the brain. These small fibers have a higher threshold, but they continue to fire longer after being stimulated. The gate tends to be closed by the firing of *large fibers,* which have a low threshold but cease firing quickly.

When a stimulus is applied to the skin, it first excites the large fibers (lower threshold). As the stimulus intensifies, the small fibers start firing, and the gate begins to reopen. With prolonged

[8] *This account of the theory is necessarily simplified. For a more complete account of the theory, see Melzack and Wall (1965, 1968).*

Figure 9.23 Young chimpanzee prevented from feeling with its hands or feet. When the coverings are eventually removed, the chimpanzee does not respond to painful stimuli.

(W. B. SAUNDERS COMPANY, FROM NISSEN, CHOW AND SEMMES, 1951.)

stimulation, the large fibers adapt and the small fibers continue firing. The gate opens wide, and the neural pain message races through to the cerebral cortex; the result is the experience of pain.

The theory is based on neurological evidence

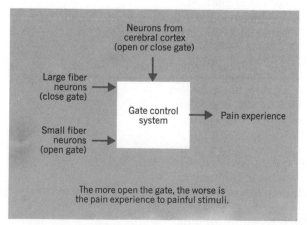

Figure 9.24 Gate control theory of pain (simplified) (Melzack and Walls, 1965).

that cannot be discussed here. What does interest us, however, is the theory's implications for the treatment of pain. In addition to offering therapeutic benefits, such treatments would provide support for the theory.

Research Report

If gate control theory is correct, pain should be reduced by applying a mild stimulus to the skin. The low-intensity stimulation should excite large fibers only, thereby partially closing the gate. This procedure was tried with patients suffering chronic pain from previous accidents and illness (Wall & Sweet, 1967). The mild stimulus was electric shock of such low intensity that it was sensed merely as a tingling feeling. This two-minute electrical stimulation either diminished or eliminated pain in four of eight patients. In one patient who reported chronic burning and painfulness in one hand, the pain was relieved dramatically:

During the stimulation, pressure on the tender area failed to cause any discomfort to the patient. For a period of more than half an hour after the stimulation, the patient reported that the hand felt numb and free of pain, and it could be moved freely. (WALL & SWEET, 1967, P. 108.)

This research only partially confirms gate control theory. Pain was not reduced in half the patients, and it is possible that suggestion may have played a role when pain reduction did occur. Clearly, a more controlled laboratory experiment was needed—one using normal subjects and precise measures of pain.

Higgins et al. (1971) used electric shock as the painful stimulus, and had normal adult men indicate when the shock was uncomfortable, painful and intolerable. The shock was delivered to the left forearm, and there were three different conditions. In one an inflatable cuff—such as is used in measuring blood pressure—was placed on the left arm (below the shock electrode). The cuff was inflated every eight seconds for a three-second period; the pressure was just enough to provide a feeling of being touched. While this mild stimulus was being applied, the subject was shocked. In the second condition the cuff was on the *right* arm—the one opposite to the arm being shocked. In the third condition there was no cuff.

All subjects were shocked during all three conditions, and only the mild stimulus on the same arm had any effect on pain (see Figure 9.25). Note that the tactile stimulus had no effect on the threshold, which was the same in all three conditions. But when the tactile stimulus was applied to the arm that was shocked, it took a more intense shock to make the subject say it was uncomfortable, painful, or intolerable. These findings—taken together with the earlier results in patients enduring chronic pain—provide strong support for gate control theory. Evidently, a mild stimulus can alleviate the pain of concurrent intense stimulus: stimulation of large fibers presumably closes the gate.

Other Factors Influencing Pain

Gate control theory specifies a role for central (cerebral cortex) factors in pain, but the emphasis is neurological. There are several important influences on pain that are best regarded psychologically. One determinant of pain is the social context. For example, when a child falls or is bumped, his reaction often depends on the adult's response. If the adult responds sympathetically and attempts to reassure the child, the child may feel pain; if the adult minimizes the harm and attempts to distract the child, there may be no pain experience. The presence of others is important in adults, too. When electric shock is being shared with a partner (who receives an equal amount), the tolerance for painful shocks is considerably greater than when the shocks are delivered to a single subject (Seidman et al., 1957).

Pain is very much influenced by suggestion, and a *placebo* (inert substance) can be used to relieve pain. Many of the drugs sold without a prescription owe their effectiveness to the belief that they really do work, rather than on any beneficial chemical ingredients. The phenomenon has been demonstrated in the laboratory. Gelfand et al. (1963) tested student nurses for pain tolerance before and after receiving a "pain reliever" that had no active ingredients. They showed a clear-cut placebo response (increased tolerance) in contrast to control subjects, who did not receive a pill.

Even more striking effects occur when persons are hypnotized or strongly motivated to take pain. When a subject keeps his hand in freezing water for three minutes, the cold produces intense pain and irregularities in breathing and muscle tension; but hypnotized subjects report somewhat less pain and irregularities of breathing and muscle tension (Barber & Hahn, 1962). Merely asking subjects to imagine less discomfort ("Imagine that it is a very hot day and the water feels pleasantly cool") reduces pain and physiological reactions as much as hypnosis does. In brief, pain can be markedly diminished by a belief in the power of a drug, by the combination of conditions called hypnotism, and by using one's imagination.

Finally, tolerance for pain can be learned through a program of discipline. Long distance runners (one mile and longer) must learn to bear the extreme discomfort that accompanies peak performance. Athletes in various sports must learn to endure pain as one of the costs of success in competition. These are not merely fictions broadcast by coaches. High school athletes have been found to tolerate considerably more pain than nonathletes; and those who engage in contact sports (football and wrestling) tolerate more pain than those engaged in noncontact sports like tennis and golf (Ryan & Foster, 1967).

Implications for Perception

The susceptibility of the pain experience to a variety of social and personal influences harks back to our discussion of perception in Chapter 8. Perception is something more than the mere reception of stimuli by sense organs and transmission

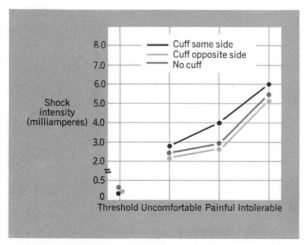

Figure 9.25 *Effect of a mild tactile stimulus on pain (Higgins et al., 1971).*

of neural impulses to the brain. At the neural level, impulses moving *toward* the brain are affected by feedback impulses coming *from* the brain (see Figure 9.24). At the psychologicical level, there are several influences on perception: the state of arousal, motives and needs, the social context, and prior learning. These factors are undoubtedly most influential in complex situations. *Complex,* in this context, means that there is insufficient information coming from the environment, that the information is ambiguous, or that the information requires considerable interpretation. These points will become clearer in the next two chapters on vision.

10

vision: sensory aspects

Evolution of the eye — rods and cones — the lens — eye sockets — frontal eyes — the retina — eye and brain — acuity — accommodation — the pupil — the fovea — dark adaptation — peripheral vision — brightness — satiation — color mixing — theory of color vision — movement — comparator theory — phi phenomenon — auto-kinetic movement — induced movement

Man receives most of his information about the environment through vision, the dominant perceptual system. The dominance of vision shows up clearly when it is placed in conflict with another sense; if an object feels different from what it looks like, the visual information overrides the haptic information. This point was neatly demonstrated by Rock and Harris (1967), who used a distorting lens to make a rectangle look like a square (see Figure 10.1). When the subject was allowed to feel the object without seeing it, he recognized it correctly as a rectangle. But when he was allowed both to feel it and to see it through the distorting lens, he perceived it as a square; that is, distorted vision overrode undistorted touch.

As vision is so dominant in relation to other kinds of perception, it is not surprising that it has been studied more and that more is known about it. Accordingly, we shall devote two chapters to it. The present one deals with the receptor and neural processes underlying the detection of light, color, and movement. The following chapter is concerned with the more organizational and experiential aspects: how shape and space are perceived, and the developmental aspects of visual perception.

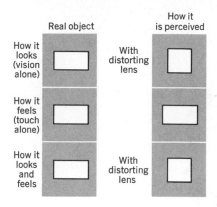

Figure 10.1 *Vision dominates touch.*

The Evolution of the Eye

The human eye is essentially a primate eye, differing only in minor details from the eyes of certain living apes and monkeys. It evolved when primates lived in trees, where both depth perception and color vision confer advantages. There are five features of human eyes that should be examined in evolutionary perspective:

1. There are two kinds of receptor elements, rods and cones.
2. The eyes are simple, not compound.
3. There is a lens, which forms an image.
4. The eyes are set in sockets and can move independently of the head or body.
5. The eyes are directed toward the front and yield overlapping images.

Rods and Cones

Daylight is roughly one million times brighter than night light, which means that night vision requires extremely *sensitive* receptor elements. Accordingly, there was strong evolutionary pressure for such sensitive receptors, which can respond to low levels of light. But sensitive elements yield poor *acuity,* which is maladaptive. Thus there is a conflict between sensitivity and acuity: an animal with good night vision (sensitivity) would have poor day vision (acuity), and vice versa.

One resolution of this problem is excellent day vision but no night vision. Many birds have extremely acute vision but must roost and remain inactive after sundown. Other animals (rats, hamsters) evolved highly sensitive receptor elements that enable them to move around in the murky light of evening. But these nocturnal prowlers must hide in the daytime because their day vision is poor in comparison to that of day animals.

The third solution is the possession of two different light-sensitive elements, and primates are in the small group of such animals. One element, called a rod cell, is extremely sensitive to light but yields poor acuity. The other, called a cone cell, requires considerable light but offers sharp vision. Thus man has the advantages of both kinds of light receptors: sensitivity at night and acuity in the daytime.

A Simple Eye

Eyes began early in evolution as primitive *eye spots,* which merely gathered light on a sensitive area of the body. It was an adaptive advantage to be able to gather more light and extract information from it. One efficient adaptation would be to add more and more eye spots, relying on sheer numbers to register the effects of light. The other possibility is to increase the efficiency of each individual eye spot. But no species could have it both ways. If there are many individual "eyes," then each one must remain small (the alternative—many large eyes—would devote too much of the body to eyes). But if each eye has many light-sensitive elements, then it must become quite

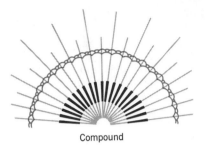

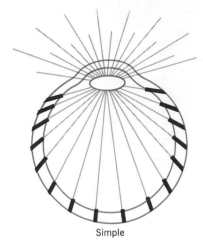

Figure 10.2 *Compound and simple eyes.*

	Group		
	Lizards	Birds	Mammals
Nocturnal	Gecko	Owl	Opossum
Daytime	Chameleon	Pigeon	Chimpanzee

Figure 10.3 *Lenses in eyeballs.*

large. These contradictory pressures led to a fork in the evolutionary road. Some animals tended to multiply eye spots to form a *compound eye,* but the line that led to man took the other path and formed a *simple eye* with many light-sensitive elements. These two solutions account for virtually all advanced visual systems (see Figure 10.2). The compound eye of insects (and others) is convex, presenting a huge surface to the environment. Thousands of facets converge the light toward the center, yielding a mosaic picture of the environment. The simple eye presents a smaller surface to the environment, and the converging light rays are bent by a lens. The lens produces an inverted image on the retina, which consists of light-sensitive elements at the back of the eye.

The Lens

The evolution of the lens from the covering of a primitive eye spot was mentioned earlier (see Figure 8.4). The lens became larger during evolution because a larger lens more efficiently gathers the available light; the principle is the same for eyes as for telescopes. But beyond a given size, a larger lens yields a more blurred image. Again there is a conflict between the need to gather more light and the need for sharp vision. Night animals must have sensitivity and therefore have relatively larger lenses, whereas day animals must have acuity and therefore have relatively smaller lenses (see Figure 10.3). Human lenses are of an intermediate size, representing a compromise between the requirements of day and night vision.

Eye Sockets

In primitive vertebrates such as fishes the eyes are fixed and immobile. During vertebrate evolution the head became mobile, swiveling while the body remained constant. Subsequently, the eyes could rotate while the head remained in place. Human eyes are set in orbits, and muscles move the eyes in various directions, allowing a man to watch a moving object without turning the head or body. There can be fixation on a fixed object while the head moves; when the head rotates, the eyes must make the compensatory movements called *nystagmus* (see Chapter 9). In brief, a series of vertebrate adaptations have made the eyes mobile and able to scan and explore the environment without major bodily involvement.

Frontal Placement

When the eyes are placed laterally, one on each side of the head, the animal can see more of the environment that surrounds it. Optimally, the eyes would be located so that the entire visual field, front and back, would be seen without any blind areas. This ability would be valuable for prey animals in detecting possible predators. But laterally directed eyes offer two separate visual fields with very little overlap. Such overlap, called binocular vision, enhances the perception of depth, which is especially important for predators in determining the distance from themselves to their prey. It is not surprising, then, that predators have frontally directed eyes and prey have laterally directed eyes (see Figure 10.4). Rabbits have panoramic vision (no blind area), and it does no good to try to sneak up on them from behind. Cats, of course, are concerned not with being attacked but with pouncing on their prey. Their frontally placed eyes furnish good depth perception.

Man's frontally directed eyes are a heritage of his primate ancestry. Primates are not especially predatory, but they do need acute depth perception to swing through the trees. Primates can also

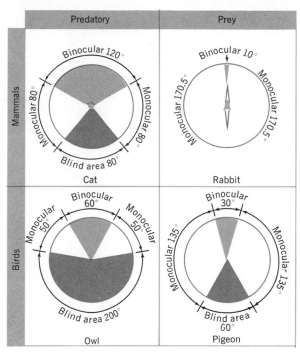

Figure 10.4 *Visual fields in predatory and prey animals.*

manipulate objects with their hands, an activity that is facilitated by binocular depth perception.

The Human Eye

Our interest is not in the anatomy of the human eye but in how it receives and processes visual information. On this basis the eye may be divided into front and back sections, with all of the supporting and nutritive structures omitted (see Figure 10.5). The front section consists of structures that bend light waves or control the amount of light that enters the eye. The *cornea* and *lens* both focus light so as to form a clear image on the back part of the eye. The *iris* is a circular muscle that, by constricting or dilating the opening called the *pupil*, determines how much light enters. These *mechanical* operations, relating to the physics of optics, have two functions: (1) to deliver a sharp image for maximal information, and (2) to insure a balance between sufficient

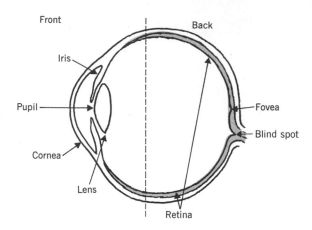

Figure 10.5 *Schematic anatomy of the human eye.*

light for seeing and excessive light that might damage the receptor elements. All these mechanical devices originate developmentally in the ectoderm (skin) of the fetus.

The back section consists of structures that respond to light and those that carry information to the brain. The *retina* contains all the light-sensitive elements that *chemically* transduce the light into neural impulses. Two places on the retina deserve special comment. One is the *fovea, a* small area along the line of sight or *gaze line,* which is packed with receptor elements that guarantee the greatest sharpness (acuity) of vision. The other is the place where the optic nerve originates, which is a *blind spot* on the retina that contains no receptor elements; the optic nerve carries impulses from the eye to the brain. All these receptor and neural structures originate developmentally in the brain of the fetus, and they grow outward toward the skin. In a sense, both the retina and optic nerve are part of the brain. The properties of the two functional divisions of the eye are summarized in Table 10.1.

The Retina

The retina consists of two types of receptor elements: rod cells for sensitivity and cone cells for acuity and color. The cones are heavily concentrated in the fovea; the rods are scattered throughout the entire retina. Light falling on the fovea (along the direct line of sight) stimulates mainly cones, but light falling on the periphery of the retina stimulates only rods.

The greater sensitivity of the rods is the result of two factors. First, each rod cell can be stimulated by lower intensities of light than cone cells can. Second, rod cells are arranged in parallel so that many of them connect to the same neuron (see Figure 10.6a). When light falls on a whole group of rods, the resulting stimulation is *summated* at the single neuron they converge on (a bipolar cell). This pooling of impulses yields greater sensitivity but at the cost of acuity; as Figure 10.6a shows, some information is lost.

Cones are connected to their bipolar neurons in a one-to-one ratio, which renders them less sensitive (see Figure 10.6b). They require higher intensities of light to fire, but they are better able to resolve *stimulus patterns*. Adjacent cones can pick up discontinuities in the stimulus array, and such patterning is retained as information because each cone has its own neuron. This account is an oversimplification for purposes of exposition. Many cones do not have a one-to-one relation with a bipolar neuron, and there are lateral connections between bipolar cells. But these complexities need not concern us here; our emphasis is on differences in the functioning of rods and cones, and not in the detailed anatomy of the eye.

Human retinas are fairly simple in contrast to those of such animals as frogs and rabbits (Michael, 1969). Their complex retinas are responsible for considerable processing of visual information. In man, processing is done largely in the

Table 10.1
Front and Back of the Eye

	FRONT	BACK
1. Parts	Cornea, pupil, lens	Retina (fovea), optic nerve
2. Fetal origin	"Skin"	Brain
3. Function	Admitting, focusing light	Converting light into neural impulses
4. Operations	Mechanical	Chemical

cerebral cortex, another aspect of the twin neural trends of centralization and corticalization (see Chapter 5).

Eye and Brain

Nerve fibers originating in the retina travel to the brain through several relay stations.[1] The fibers

[1] *We are mentioning only the major pathway to the sensory cortex.*

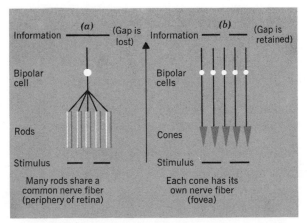

Figure 10.6 Connection of rods and cones to bisolar cells (simplified schematic).

from the nasal (inside) part of each eye cross to the opposite cerebral hemisphere. Those from the temporal (outside) part of each eye do not cross; they remain on the same side. When the eyes are pointed straight ahead, the right visual field falls on the nasal part of the right eye and the temporal part of the left eye; the neural pathway from the nasal part crosses and that from the temporal part remains on the same side, so that both end in the left hemisphere. In brief, the right visual field stimulates the left half of each eye and activates the left hemisphere; the left visual field stimulates the right half of each eye and activates the right hemisphere.

The crossing of only half the nerves from each eye is typical of animals with frontally directed eyes. Animals with laterally directed eyes have nerves that completely cross to the opposite cerebral hemisphere (see Figure 10.7). In such animals the right eye takes in the entire right visual field and the left eye, the entire left visual field. Because the nerve tracts cross completely, the right visual field activates the left hemisphere, and the left visual field activates the right hemisphere. This is probably the simplest arrangement. If an animal is to act on stimuli located in the right visual field, it must use limbs on the right side of the body, and these are controlled by the left cerebral hemisphere. Of course information from one hemisphere is transmitted to the other hemisphere through nerve tracts (the corpus cal-

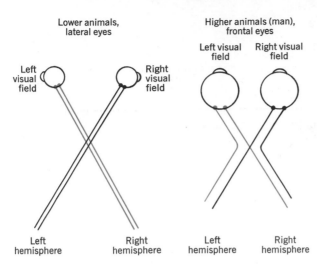

Figure 10.7 *Laterally placed and frontally directed eyes.*

losum), but it is simpler and more direct to have the sensory inflow on the same side of the brain as the motor outflow. Apparently, this arrangement is sufficiently adaptive for it to be maintained regardless of whether the eyes are frontally directed (as in man) or laterally directed (as in many animals).

There are several relay stations in the neural path from the retina to the brain, the most important being the *lateral geniculate body*—a remnant of the once-large midbrain, which dwindled as cor-

ticalization occurred during mammalian and primate evolution. The nerves end in the *occipital lobe,* which contains a projection area in point-to-point correspondence with the retina (see Figure 10.8). The retinal image is represented in the occipital lobe, completing the process that starts when light passes through the cornea. This projection area is not the only part of the brain involved in visual perception, but we cannot present any of the complex details here. The cerebral cortex does not "read" or interpret the retinal

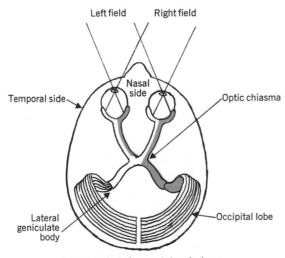

Pattern projected to each hemisphere

Figure 10.8 *Visual neural paths to the brain.*

image the way we scan a photograph. Rather, the retinal image is merely part of a complex perceptual system that starts with light entering the eye, which is converted into neural information and ends up being integrated by several cortical structures. We do not "see" our retinal images; we see objects in the environment.

Acuity

A sharper visual image provides more precise information about objects and events in the environment, and man has several mechanisms that serve acuity.[2] These may be divided into those involving the front of the eye (cornea and lens) and those involving the back of the eye (the fovea).

Light first enters the cornea: transparent curved tissue that bends light and therefore acts as a lens. The cornea is fixed, and light waves passing through it are always bent to the same degree. Light then passes through the pupil and lens, and these can be varied in size or shape to provide a sharper visual image.

Accommodation

When light strikes the eye from very close, it needs to be bent more than when it comes from a distance. Accordingly, the lens flattens when the

[2] *There are different kinds of acuity and different tasks for each. The traditional eye chart measures only recognition acuity.*

eye focuses on distant objects and thickens when it focuses on near objects. These changes in the curvature of the lens, called *accommodation,* are caused by ciliary muscles, which alter the curvature of the lens by contracting or relaxing (see Figure 10.9). These muscles are most relaxed when focusing on distant objects, and prolonged focusing on objects six inches or less from the eye cause considerable fatigue and eye strain.

The ability to accommodate diminishes with age. Children can focus on objects very close to the eye with little strain, a fact that may puzzle adults who are unable to do so. The loss of accommodation continues until about 50 years of age, when the ciliary muscles can no longer alter the curvature of the lens. At this time there is little or no accommodation, and objects closer than two feet do not remain in focus; corrective lenses are usually needed for reading except in those elderly persons with extremely long arms.

Size of the Pupil

The function of the pupil is to maintain an optimal intensity of the light entering the eye. Too little light will not sufficiently excite the sensitive elements in the retina, and too much light will render them inefficient or perhaps even harm them. When there is little available light, the pupil is wide open. When there is much light, the pupil constricts, and a by-product of this constriction is more acute vision. A small pupil admits light mainly to the central part of the lens, the part that provides the best focus; it tends to keep out light

Lens thickens

Near target

Lens flattens

Far target

Figure 10.9 Accommodation—change in curvature of lens.

that strikes the periphery of the lens, such light being focused to a different plane from that coming through the center of the lens. Thus acuity is greatest when the light is very bright and the pupil is very small.

A small pupil also enhances acuity by keeping out extraneous light. Glare reduces sharp vision, as is well known from experience in trying to see in a westerly direction when the sun is setting. Squinting also cuts down the light that enters the eye, thereby sharpening vision. The same effect may be achieved by using a long tube, which yields somewhat sharper images than can be obtained with the naked eye.

Research Report

Light is not the only determiner of pupil size. The pupil also constricts or dilates in response to the *content* of stimuli, and its size evidently varies with ongoing activity. A decade of research has established that the size of the pupil is an excellent measure of arousal.

The research was started by Hess (1965), who noted that magicians doing card tricks often watch the subject's eyes because they know that the subject's pupils will dilate when the correct card turns up. Hess showed a picture of a female face to a man and photographed his pupils in infrared light (our eyes do not respond to the wavelengths in this part of the spectrum). The dilation of one subject's eye is shown in Figure 10.10.

Next, Hess showed men and women pictures of sharks and of male and female pinups. The men's pupils dilated in response to the sharks and still more to the female pinup but not at all in response to

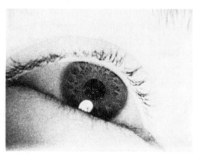
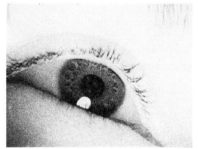
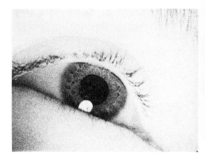
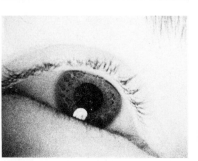

Figure 10.10 Pupil size varies with the interest value of a visual stimulus. These five frames show the eye of a male subject during the first two and a half seconds after viewing a photograph of a pinup girl.

(ECKHARD H. HESS, THE UNIVERSITY OF CHICAGO.)

the male pinup.³ The women's pupils constricted to the sharks and the female pinup but dilated to the male pinup (see Figure 10.11). Hess commented:

These negative responses, exemplified by the reaction of most of our female subjects to pictures of sharks, were not isolated phenomena; constriction is as characteristic in the case of certain aversive stimulation as dilation is in the case of interesting or pleasant pictures. We observed a strong negative response, for example, when subjects were shown a picture of a cross-eyed or crippled child; as those being tested said, they simply did not like to look at such pictures.

(1965, P. 49.)

Subsequent research on pupillary changes yielded intriguing findings. Hess et al. (1965) compared the responses of male heterosexuals and homosexuals to nude and nearly nude pictures of men and of women. The pupils of the heterosexual men dilated more in the response to the pictures of women than of men; the homosexual men showed opposite responses, dilating their pupils more to the pictures of men than of women. Such preferences are not restricted to the area of sex; they extend to political preference as well. Conservatives dilate their pupils in response to a picture of George Wallace and constrict to Martin Luther King; liberals show the opposite pattern (Barlow, 1969).

Finally, mental activity affects the pupils. When a subject is asked to solve arithmetic problems, his pupils dilate and remain that way until the problem has been solved and verbalized (Hess & Polt, 1964). This effect has been confirmed with other tasks, and the pupillary

³ *The effect depends on having a relaxed, friendly experimenter, and it is suppressed by a cold, businesslike experimenter (Chapman et al., 1969).*

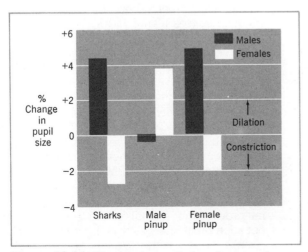

Figure 10.11 Changes in pupil size of men and women to different pictures.

changes are accompanied by increases in heart rate and changes in galvanic skin response (Kahneman et al., 1969). Thus dilation of the pupil appears to be a good measure of arousal, specifically of activation of the sympathetic nervous system.

The Fovea

The light-receptive elements that evolved for acuity—the cones—are concentrated in the fovea. The gaze line directs light to the fovea, which is the area of clearest vision; the remainder of the retina, consisting mainly of rods, is poor in acuity (see Figure 10.12). With only a small segment of the environment in clear focus at any given moment, man must continually scan the environment and shift the gaze line. Man's eyes are constantly and automatically making small, jerky movements that bring in a series of images, each in focus for a brief moment.

Night Vision

Several adaptations have evolved under the pressure of the need to see at night. We have mentioned the variable pupil, which opens wide when the light is poor; the lens which is relatively larger

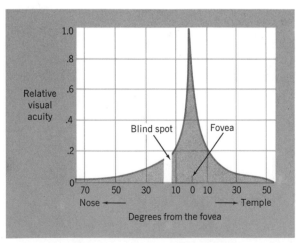

Figure 10.12 *Acuity varies with the part of retina stimulated. Acuity is greatest at the foveal region but falls rapidly as the stimulus moves toward the periphery of the retina.*

in nocturnal animals and of a compromise size in day-and-night animals such as man; and the light-sensitive rod cells. The pupillary response to diminished light is immediate; the receptor shift from cone to rod vision takes longer.

Dark Adaptation

It is common to experience temporary blindness when moving from a brightly lit room into a fairly dark one or when moving from bright sunshine into the dim interior of a movie theater. Gradually the eyes become accustomed to the dark, and one can first discern vague outlines and later, objects. In a dim environment cones function poorly, and vision depends mainly on rods. Adapting to the dark involves chemical changes within the rod cells; specifically, a visual pigment in the rods requires many minutes to regenerate, having been bleached by bright light. Of course if there is a moderate amount of light, the cones can function, but they too require time to adapt to the poorer light condition.

How long does it take to adapt to the dark? Laboratory research has shown that it requires about 20 minutes (see Figure 10.13). The initial increase in sensitivity (or decrease in the amount of light needed to see) occurs in a little more than five minutes. This part of the dark adaptation curve reflects the increasing sensitivity of cones as they adapt to the poor lighting conditions; their maximal sensitivity is of course somewhat less than that of rods. The lower part of the curve represents the adaptation of rods, which require more time to complete their chemical regeneration.

At first glance the half hour required to adapt fully to the dark of night would appear to be maladaptive. A visually deficient animal would surely fall prey to other animals under these conditions, but such rapid changes from light to dark occur mainly in man's technologically advanced civilization. In nature a rapid change from light to dark would occur only when an animal entered a cave, and most animals tend to avoid caves. The *natural*

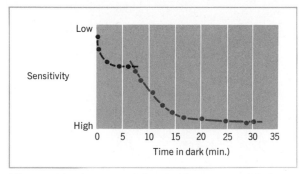

Figure 10.13 *Units of threshold intensity of light.*

transition from light to dark requires approximately 20 minutes—the period of twilight between the sun's setting and darkness of night—and this period matches the time it takes for dark adaptation to be completed.

Peripheral Vision at Night

When there is sufficient light, a man's eyes continually move to keep the image fixated on the fovea, which contains most of the receptor elements (cones) required for acute vision. This strategy must fail when the light is poor because the cones are relatively insensitive to light. Consider the problem of attempting to see a faint star at night. If the viewer focuses directly on the star, the light will fall on the cones in the fovea, and the star will simply not be seen. The correct approach is to fixate on a point to the side of the star (see Figure 10.14). Then the light from the star falls on the sensitive cones in the *periphery* of the retina, and the star can be seen. This solution works not only for faint stars but also for chairs, tables, and other furniture that can stub the toe or bark the shins in a dark room: the trick is to glance to the side and let the available light fall on the periphery of the retina.

Light

What we call light is only a small portion of the electromagnetic spectrum (see Figure 8.9). Light waves vary in frequency, intensity, and purity, and

these three physical attributes correspond roughly to the psychological attributes of *hue, brightness,* and *saturation.*

The wavelength of light is so small that it is difficult to comprehend. It is measured in *nanometers,* or millionths of a meter. The visible spectrum ranges from above 400 to almost 800 nanometers (see Figure 10.15). There is a gross correspondence of hue and wavelength, with violet at the short end and red at the long end of the spectrum, but the perception of different hues is not simply a matter of the eye receiving different wavelengths of light. We can see colors (some of the purples) that simply do not appear on the physical spectrum, and these must therefore be mixtures of wavelengths.

What we see as purple can be obtained from a mixture of red and blue lights. In fact, every discernible color can be produced by lights of only three hues: "blue," "green," and "red." These are called *primary colors* because they can be mixed to derive all others, including white.

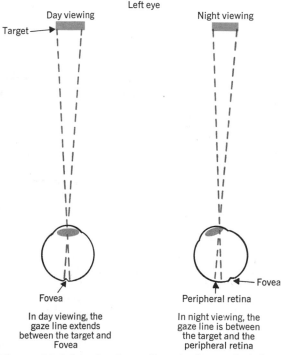

Figure 10.14 *Optimal gaze lines in day-and-night viewing.*

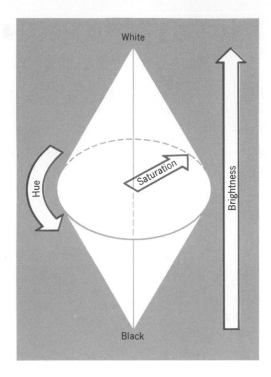

White

Hue

Saturation

Brightness

Black

Figure 10.16

Brightness is directly related to the *intensity* of light. The more intense the light, the more white it appears; the less intense, the more black it appears. But this simple relationship is complicated by hue. For a given intensity, some hues appear brighter than others; yellow, for example, seems brighter than blue.

Saturation corresponds to the *purity* of the wavelengths of light. A single wavelength of light, such as is produced by a laser, appears to be extremely saturated. The addition of other wavelengths makes the hue appear duller and more gray. In fact, the most washed out and desaturated color is gray.

Hue, brightness, and saturation are all related, and relationship can be expressed visually in the form of a color solid (see Figure 10.16). Note that saturation is greatest at a midpoint between white and black. The vertical line through the middle of the solid represents gray.

Brightness

As a general rule, more intense light is perceived as being brighter. One exception—noted above—is that the "hot colors" (red, orange, and yellow) appear brighter than the "cool colors" (blue and green) even when the intensity of light is held constant. The other main exception to the general rule concerns the *patterning* of light—as, for example, the patches of light and shade that occur when the sun shines through the leaves of a tree. Whenever there are patterns of light and shadow, perceived brightness depends on a complex interaction of the brighter and darker parts of the stimulus array.

This point is best illustrated by visual displays. Areas of homogeneous brightness, when placed next to one another, appear to vary in brightness (see Figure 10.17*a*). Each rectangle appears lighter at the border of the adjacent rectangle. The scalloped pattern is not caused by any intensity differences *within* each rectangle; when only one rectangle is exposed (by covering all the others), it

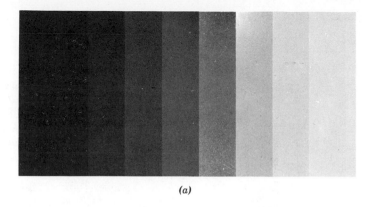

(a)

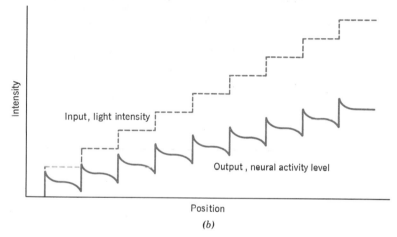

Position

(b)

Figure 10.17 *Intensity and brightness.* (a) *Each rectangle is of a uniform intensity, but the apparent variations in brightness cause a scalloping effect.* (b) *Light intensity and neural output (Cornsweet, 1970).*

is immediately perceived as being of unvarying, homogeneous brightness. There is good reason to believe that the perceived scallops occur because of differences in the neural output of ganglion cells in the retina (see Figure 10.17b)[4]. This theoretical curve of neural impulses neatly matches the scalloping effect perceived in Figure 10.17a. These variations in neural output represent distortions of the step pattern of actual light intensity (upper curve in Figure 10.17a). How do such distortions occur?

The generally accepted explanation is *lateral inhibition* (Ratliff et al., 1963). Receptor elements (rods and cones) in the retina generate nerve impulses in neurons. These neurons transmit the impulses to special neurons, the cell bodies

of which are *ganglion cells.* These ganglion cells are the sensory relay centers[5] that transmit nerve impulses through the optic nerve to the brain. Ganglion cells are functionally linked with one another through synapses, and many of these synapses are inhibitory. The ganglion cells lie side by side in the retina, and each is capable of inhibiting the others; hence the term *lateral inhibition.*

To demonstrate the mechanism of lateral inhibition, we shall assume that a narrow beam of light strikes receptors that excite only a single ganglion cell (see Figure 10.18). When this ganglion cell fires, the neural impulse proceeds to the brain, but at the same time an inhibitory impulse is transmitted to the adjacent ganglion. If both gan-

[4] *Such differences in neural output have actually been recorded in a horshoe crab (Ratliff & Hartline, 1959).*

[5] *It was the fate of early ganglion cells to evolve gradually into brains, as we noted in Chapter 5.*

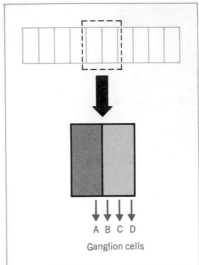

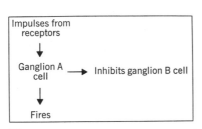

Figure 10.18 *Lateral inhibition of adjacent ganglion cells. Ganglion cells and neural impulse to the brain.*

Figure 10.19 *Lateral inhibition and the scalloped effect. Assume that the light area results in 2 units of inhibition to adjacent ganglion cells, but the dark area results in 1 unit of inhibition. Cell C receives 4 units of inhibition (2 from B and 2 from D). Cell B receives 3 units of inhibition (1 from A [darker area] and 2 from C). Thus cell B is less inhibited, which means that it will signal the presence of more light, and this accounts for the border's appearing lighter.*

glion cells were stimulated they would tend to inhibit one another. Such inhibition does not prevent the ganglion cells to relay neural impulses, but it damps down the firing of such impulses.

How does lateral inhibition explain the scallops in Figure 10.17? Consider only two adjacent rectangles, each of homogeneous brightness (see Figure 10.19). Ganglion cells stimulated by a darker area will inhibit adjacent cells *less* (the less the stimulation received by the cell, the less it inhibits adjacent cells). This means that when a ganglion cell is stimulated by a border area it will receive less inhibition than will cells stimulated by the middle areas of the rectangle. (The details are spelled out in Figure 10.19.)

Lateral inhibition is also believed to cause another interesting effect—Mach bands. These bands—named after Ernst Mach, who first described them more than a century ago—consist of brighter stripes in bright regions bordering on dark regions, or darker stripes in dark regions bordering on bright regions (see Figure 10.20). The explanation is similar to the hypothesis that accounts for the scallops in Figure 10.17, and we need not describe it in detail.[6]

Mach bands and scallops are essentially *mis-*

[6] *Why the effect is stronger when the border between the dark and light areas is fuzzy is still a mystery (see Thomas, 1970, p. 132).*

perceptions, but the underlying mechanism—lateral inhibition—has an important adaptive function: enhancing contour. The *edges* of objects or visual stimuli are perceived more clearly, and objects are better differentiated from the background. In addition, the visual environment is perceived as more patterned (divided into combinations of bright and dark areas) rather than as homogeneous. Thus lateral inhibition helps in extracting more information from the light that strikes the eyes.

The enhancement of contours is another example of a general principle of perception: it is an active process. Sensory inputs are not merely passively received; they are selectively enhanced, diminished, and sometimes distorted. Apparent brightness is determined not only by the intensity of light but also by the stimulus context. Thus if a gray patch of a specific brightness is contrasted with backgrounds that vary in brightness, it is perceived differently. The lighter the background, the darker the central patch of gray appears (see Figure 10.21).

Light and Color

Mixing paints yields different results than does mixing lights. Mixing yellow and blue *lights* results in achromatic gray, but mixing yellow and blue

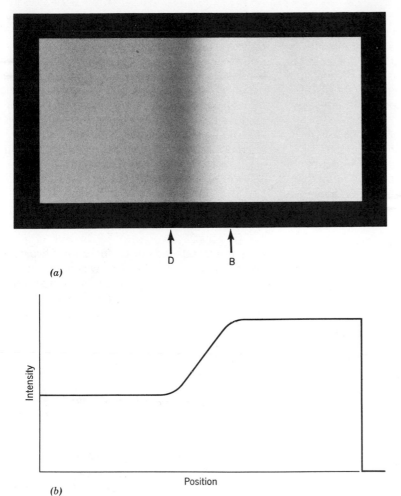

(a)

(b)

Figure 10.20 A mach band pattern. A bright band appears at B and a dark one at D. (Cornsweet, 1970.)

paints yields green. The differences lies in the processes involved in the two kinds of mixtures. Mixing lights is an *additive* process: two or more wavelengths simultaneously stimulate the eye and the effect of one light *adds* to that of the other. On the other hand, paint mixtures combine sub-

stances that selectively absorb and reflect light. What we perceive as color is *reflected* light. When light waves strike an object, some wavelengths are absorbed by the surface of the object more than others. As only the unabsorbed and reflected wavelengths strike the viewer's eye, this is a *subtrac-*

Figure 10.21 The effect of stimulus context on perception.

tive process. When light strikes a blade of grass, most wavelengths are absorbed except those around 510 nanometers, and we see green light reflected from the grass. Similarly a black object (coal) *absorbs* most wavelengths, and a white surface (snow) *reflects* most wavelengths. Additive and subtractive mixtures are compared in Figure 10.22.

The ability to see colored *lights* has no adaptive significance. Both man and animals need to distinguish objects and events, and color undoubtedly aids such discrimination; but it is reflected color, not the color or lights. In nature only *pigments* are important; colored lights are trivial.

Color

Color perception has arisen many times during the course of evolution, and there are no overall phyletic trends. Nevertheless, there is a clear progression within *mammalian* evolution: lower mammals tend not to have color vision, and the closer the animal is to the primate level, the better is its color vision. The color vision of primates is as good as that of any animal, being matched only by that of birds.

Though color vision is a source of considerable esthetic pleasure to man (color television, for example), it is only one aspect of the more general ability to discriminate the composition of surfaces and objects. Color offers another dimension, or set of dimensions, for the pickup of information of considerable importance to the organism, as following examples illustrate.

The prey-predator relationship offers mute evidence of the dynamic changes in adaptation over time. First, the predator develops color vision, which helps isolate the prey from the surrounding terrain. Then the prey develop protective coloration, which helps them to blend into the background. If the coloration is sufficiently protective, the prey will multiply too fast to be adequately concealed by the surrounding vegetation, with the consequence that their numbers will be kept down to optimal size by the everpresent predators.

The preference for a particular color may be a decisive factor in survival. Frogs markedly prefer blue surfaces, which is puzzling until we consider their habitat. They normally reside in the grass at the edge of a pond, the green vegetation bordering the blue pool. A frightened frog will jump away from the threat in the direction of safety, and its reflexive tendency is to jump for blue water.

Finally, color perception and preference is essential to the mating behavior of many species, especially birds. The male bird may lure the female into sexual activity with his proud plumage or colorful nest. Thus the peacock's rainbow colors are irresistible to the drab peahen, and the male bowerbird attempts to entice a mate with nature's counterpart of a bachelor penthouse apartment.

A Theory of Color Vision

Until the last decade or so, there were two competing theories of vision. One was better in explaining how the color receptors (cones) were stimulated by light reaching the retina. The other theory was better in explaining certain facts of color perception; for example, after gazing steadily at a patch of blue color, one sees a yellow afterimage when the blue patch is removed.

These two theories were combined into a single theory by Hurvich and Jameson (1957); they called it the *opponent-process* theory, after the theory developed by the nineteenth century physiologist, Hering. Hurvich and Jameson could not specify the neural processes underlying color vision, for the facts were simply not available in the 1950s. This gap in knowledge was remedied by De Valois and others (1965, 1968), who extended the theory to include two stages: the sensitivity of the receptor elements to various wavelengths of light and the coding of information from these receptors by nerves leading to the brain.

The theory starts with the well-documented fact that there are three kinds of cone cells in the retina (MacNichol, 1964; Sperling & Harwerth, 1971). Each is sensitive to a different range of the visible spectrum, and each has its area of maximal sensitivity (see Figure 10.23). The "blue-violet" cones have their peak sensitivity at 445 nanometers, the "green" at 540, and the "yellow-red" at 570. (The quotation marks are a warning that the cones should not be equated with specific colors. The names, derived from the wave lengths of peak sensitivity, serve to identify the three kinds of cones.) The "yellow-red" cones peak in the yellow part of the spectrum (570 nano-

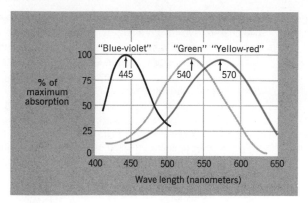

Figure 10.23 Absorption curves of three cone pigments.

meters), but their sensitivity extends into the longer wavelengths that include the red part of the spectrum.

These three kinds of cones initiate nerve impulses toward the brain, and these impulses are presumably coded both in the retina and at neural relay stations. The principal relay station is the lateral geniculate body, about which the theory makes its basic assumptions. It suggests that

there are four kinds of lateral geniculate neurons, consisting of two pairs. Each member of a pair *opposes* the other, so that the neural output of one type of one member of the pair is subtracted from that of the other. The four types of lateral geniculate neurons are:

1. excitatory for red,[7] inhibitory for green (+R−G)
2. excitatory for green, inhibitory for red (+G−R)
3. excitatory for yellow, inhibitory for blue (+Y−B)
4. excitatory for blue, inhibitory for yellow (+B−Y)

The theory assumes that in the resting state, these neurons maintain a low level of spontaneous firing. When they receive impulses from the chain that starts with the three different cones, one of three things happens: the opponent cells are excited and fire more, they are inhibited and fire less, or they are unaffected. The process is illustrated for one pair of opponent cells in Figure 10.24. The +B−Y opponent cell is inhibited by red and yellow light, which presumably causes the

[7] *In this scheme, the yellow-red part of the spectrum is divided into yellow (570 nanometers) and red (660 nanometers).*

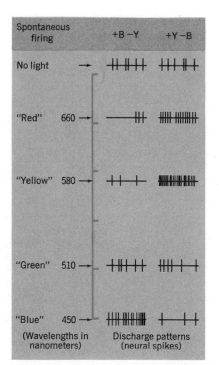

Figure 10.24 Effect of light flashes on two opponent cells in the lateral geniculate body (after deValois and Jabobs, 1968).

"red-yellow" cone cells to send inhibitory impulses to these neurons. But the +B−Y cell is excited by blue light, which should cause the "blue-violet" cones to send excitatory impulses to the cells. For the +Y−B opponent, the light flashes have the opposite effect: excited by yellow light, inhibited by blue light.

Thus the sequence is: (1) light impinging on cone cells, which (2) initiate impulses that (3) either excite or inhibit opponent neurons in the lateral geniculate body. This hypothetical sequence is shown for blue and yellow light in Table 10.2. This sequence also occurs for lights related to the other pair of opponent cells, +R−G and +G−R. Wavelengths of light that excite both opponents in the pair produce no effect; each opponent cancels the other, and the outcome is the perception of white light.

So far, the theory has accounted for *hue:* the color perceived depends on which of the opponents cells are activated and on the resolution of their excitation and inhibition. But the theory also attempts to explain brightness. It assumes that

the lateral geniculate body also contains *broad-band cells,* which give the same kind of response to *all* wavelengths of light. These cells are also divided into an opponent pair. One kind is *excited* by *increases* in light intensity and *inhibited* by *decreases* in light intensity. The other kind is opposite in function: it fires when light dims and turns off when light brightens. The broad-band cells receive stimulation not only from cones but also from rods. Presumably, the output of rods and cones is added together, with the summation probably occurring in the retina.

Summarizing, the theory states that there are two separate systems, one for color vision and one for brightness. The color system consists of two pairs of opponent cells, with each member opposing the other: +B−Y, +Y−B and +R−G, +G−R. The brightness system consists of one pair of opponent cells that are not differentially sensitive to the various wavelengths of light: excitatory for white (+W) and inhibitory for white (−W). This kind of neural coding tends to split perception of light into opposites, such as yellow-blue,

Table 10.2
Hypothetical Processing of Blue and Yellow Light

LIGHT	RETINAL RECEPTOR	ACTION	OPPONENT CELL IN LATERAL GENICULATE
450 Nanometers	"Blue cones"	Excites	+B − Y
		Inhibits	+Y − B
580 Nanometers	"Yellow cones"	Excites	+Y − B
		Inhibits	+B − Y

Sequence →

Figure 10.15 (a) *Dispersion of white light by a prism.* (b) *The visible spectrum.*

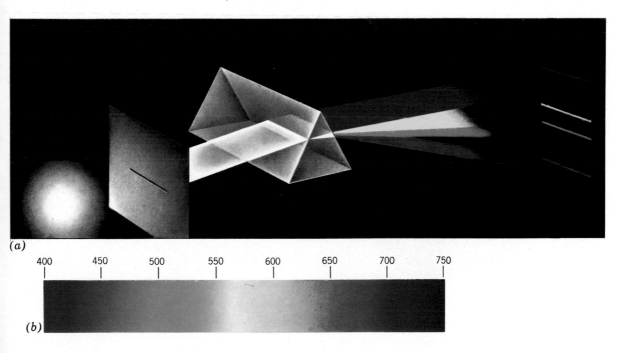

(a)

400   450   500   550   600   650   700   750

(b)

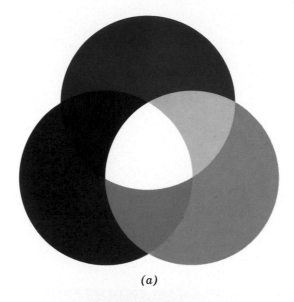

(a)

Figure 10.22 Mixing lights vs. mixing paints. (a) *Additive mixture; total = white*. (b) *Subtractive mixture; total = black.*

(b)

red-green, and black-white. The effect is to enhance contrast, thereby making discriminations
of color and brightness easier.

Finally, the theory has an explanation for each
of the three dimensions of color. *Hue* depends on
which of the spectrally opponent cells (+B—Y,
+Y—B, +R—G, and +G—R) are activated. *Brightness* depends on which of the nonspectral[8] cells
is stimulated (+W or —W). And *saturation*
depends on the balance of excitation between
spectral and nonspectral cells. The more the balance is toward the spectral (color spectrum)
cells, the greater is the saturation.

This modern opponent-process theory has
achieved widespread acceptance as the only integration of data on visual discrimination, chemical properties of cone pigments, and the firing of
neurons in the visual pathways to the brain. There
are no data that contradict it, though—like most
theories—some aspects remain uncertain.

Movement

If an animal possesses vision, then surely it can
detect movement. For some animals, especially
those lower on the phyletic scale, objects are
signals to approach or withdraw *only* if they are in
motion. In fact, certain snakes and amphibians
may perish from hunger while surrounded by stationary food.

The entire retina is sensitive to movement, and
the periphery of the retina is sensitive *only* to
movement. If an object is moving at the edge of
the visual field so that it stimulates only the outer
parts of the retina, we perceive the movement
and its direction but neither the shape nor the
color of the object. This can be checked by standing at a right angle to the street with the eyes directed forward, and watching the movement of
traffic. Neither cars nor trucks will be seen, only
movement.

The periphery of the retina serves as an early
warning system, alerting us to the *presence* of objects. It initiates eye and head movements that
bring the object to the center of the visual field.
Then foveal vision can take over and *identify* the

[8] Spectral *refers to cells in the color system;* nonspectral
to cells in the brightness system.

object. We can specify two visual systems, one to
answer the question "Where is it?," and one to
answer the question "What is it?" (Schneider,
1969). The perception of movement falls mainly in
the *localizing* system.

A Theory of Movement Perception

Any explanation of the perception of movement
must begin with the retina. In certain lower forms,
the retina does most of the processing. Thus the
frog has "bug detectors": retinal cells that trigger a
reflexive tongue thrust whenever they are stimulated by a small, moving shadow (Lettvin et al.,
1959). But in man's visual system, as well as those
of cats and monkeys, the retina is only one element in the system that processes visual information.

One source of information about movement is a
change in the retinal image. When the eye is
directed straight ahead, an object in the left visual
field strikes the right part of the retina see Figure
10.25. If the object moves from left to right,
the retinal image will shift to the left side of the
retina (assuming the eye does not move). Thus
when the eyes are stationary, a change in the position of the retinal image signals that movement
has occurred.

But this is only part of the story. The eyes are
rarely stationary, and once a moving object is located, it is tracked so that the retinal image stays
with the center of acute vision, the fovea. The object is still perceived in motion despite the
unchanging retinal image. Evidently there is another source of information about moving objects:
movements of eyes and head.

Thus there are two systems involved in movement perception: retinal and eye-head. These
must somehow be integrated, and the most generally accepted theory that does this is the comparator theory of von Holst (1954). It starts with
the assumption that there is a *comparator* in the
brain, which performs the function of matching or
accounting for two disparate sources of information: (1) changes in the location of the retinal
image; and (2) commands from the brain to the
eye and head muscles. Note that this is not *feedback* from the muscles, but the *motor impulses*
from the brain that cause the muscles to contract.

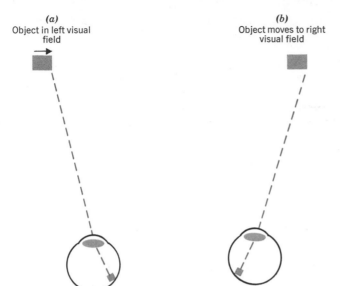

(a)
Object in left visual
field

(b)
Object moves to right
visual field

Figure 10.25 *Movement and the retinal image (⬩
is stationary).*

The theory is diagramed in Figure 10.26. Motor commands from the cortex to the eye and head muscles are monitored by the comparator. This information is matched against changes in the retinal image, and the outcome determines whether movement is perceived. The comparator opposes the two sources of information (retinal and commands to eye/head muscles), and when they are equal, there is no movement perceived; when they are unequal, movement is perceived.

We shall arbitrarily assign a positive value (+) to retinal information and a negative value (−) to eye-head information. Table 10.3 summarizes how the comparator is assumed to function. Suppose the eyes and head are kept still, and an object moves across the visual field (row *a*). The changes in the retinal image are not matched or accounted for by

commands to the head or eye muscles, which means that movement is perceived. Now suppose that the head or eyes, or both, track a moving object (row *b*). The eye-head commands are not neutralized by information from the retina, and the result is perception of movement. Finally, suppose that the head or eyes, or both, are turned while the person is looking at a stationary object; these movements cause the retinal image to change. The retinal change is counteracted by the head-eye commands, and the outcome is no movement perception.

Concerning the factual basis of the theory, the role of retinal images is well documented. The importance of head movements has been substantiated by several researchers (for example, Rock, 1966), and that of eye movements by Mack (1970).

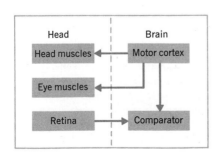

Head   Brain

Head muscles ← Motor cortex

Eye muscles ←

Retina → Comparator

Figure 10.26 *Comparator theory of movement perception.*

Table 10.3
How the Comparator Functions

OBJECT	RETINAL IMAGE	COMMANDS TO EYE/HEAD MUSCLES	OUT-COME	PERCEP-TION
a. Moving	Changes (+)	No (0)	+	Movement
b. Moving	Stationary (0)	Yes (−)	−	Movement
c. Stationary	Changes (+)	Yes (−)	0	No move-ment

Apparent Movement

THE PHI PHENOMENON. If two adjacent lights are quickly flashed one after the other, the lights will not appear to flash on and off; rather, one light will appear to move across to the other. The illusion of apparent motion, called the *phi phenomenon,* may be seen in everyday life in animated neon signs and motion pictures. Movies consist of individual frames of still pictures, which are shown fast enough for us to perceive continuous movement; a slower rate produces flickering. In explaining the apparent motion, the elements of stimulation (a series of still pictures) do not suffice. We must also take into account the visual system of the observer in perceiving the relationship between successive still pictures.
AUTOKINETIC MOVEMENT. When a stationary point of light is viewed in a very dark room, it appears to wander. The lighted tip of a cigarette in an ash tray in an unlit room will seem to move laterally or even to float. The extent of the illusory movement, which can be quite large, is readily influenced by suggestion. The basis of autokinetic movement is largely unknown, and the available hypotheses are too complex to examine here.
INDUCED MOVEMENT. Sometimes the moon appears to move behind stationary clouds, yet we know that it is the clouds that move to cover a stationary moon. Figure 10.27 illustrates a situation in which induced movement can occur. The rectangle and dot are luminous and shown in an otherwise dark room. If the rectangle is moved to the left and the dot is stationary (as shown in *b*), the rectangle is perceived as stationary and the dot appears to move in the opposite direction — actual movement by the rectangle induces movement in the dot. In general, smaller, more enclosed, fixated objects will be seen as moving with respect to other objects.

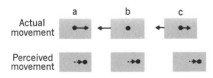

Figure 10.27 Illusions of movement.

chapter 11
vision: perceptual aspects

*Form — figure and ground — Gestalt laws —
perception of faces — depth — monocular cues —
binocular cues — constancy (size, color,
brightness, and shape) — illusions — impossible
figures — objective and subjective approaches —
learning and innate factors — the visual cliff
— perception in infants — active and passive
movement — distorted vision — perspective*

The last chapter showed how the eye works and how we see brightness, color, and movement. Having covered these sensory aspects of vision, we now focus on its perceptual aspects. The perceiver continually seeks meaning in the stimulus array that surrounds him, and he tends to see patterns that make sense rather than the elements that comprise the patterns. Lines, shadings, and textures are integrated to form a meaningful whole. It is not merely light and shadow that are perceived but objects and events, which have distinct shapes and exist in three dimensional space.

Form

Probably the most important feature man uses in identifying objects is their shape or form. Man's visual system seems to be especially attuned to borders; as we learned in Chapter 10, light is processed so as to enhance contrasts of brightness. Such contrast helps in seeing the edges that provide the *contours* of objects. Often, seeing the contour edge of an object is sufficient to identify it, and further information may be superfluous. Consider the profile of a face (see Figure 11.1). A pho-

Figure 11.1 *Three versions of a profile.* (PHOTO, UNITED PRESS INTERNATIONAL)

tograph offers considerable detail, a drawing provides less detail, and a silhouette presents only a border, but the contour of the silhouette provides sufficient information for anyone to perceive a face. This kind of minimal information (contour only) may account for our seeing various forms in clouds in the sky.

Figure and Ground

Objects are seen against a background (see Figure 11.2). Several of the objects in the photograph are touching each other in the two-dimensional array, but they are perceived as separate and distinct. The pen, pencils, book, and notebook all

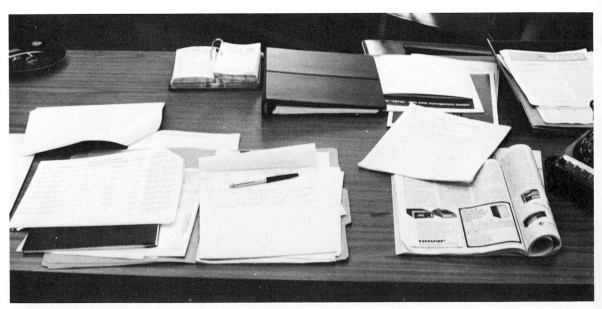

Figure 11.2 *Figure (the objects) against ground (the desk top).*
(WILLIAM H. GRAHAM)

stand out against the desk top. They comprise the *figure* and the desk top, the *ground*. What makes one part of a scene the figure and another the ground? The figure usually has a clearer shape, and seems closer and better defined; the ground is more homogeneous and amorphous, and it appears to spread out continuously behind the figure. When these features are removed, the distinction between figure and ground becomes ambiguous. In Figure 11.3 either the white vase is seen as figure and the dark area as ground, or two faces in silhouette are seen as figure and the white as ground. Reversible figures such as this require that most of the normal components of a visual scene (the features that set figure off from ground) are absent.

The separation of figure from ground is enhanced by contrast. A black panther would easily be seen against a background of snow; a white polar bear would not. It is obviously adaptive for an animal to remain unseen by both its predators and its prey, and many species have evolved coloration or patterns that help them to blend into the background (see Figure 11.4). Some kinds of camouflage work by breaking down the visual separation between figure and ground.

Perceptual Organization

Most scenes consist of several elements; these are perceived not as random components of a visual array but as *groups* of objects. Stimuli are grouped according to certain principles of organization, known as *Gestalt laws*. These principles emerged from research by a group of psychologists[1] who made two basic assumptions about perception. First, they assumed that the basic unit of perception is not an individual sensation (such as a dot or a line) but a *configuration* of elements in a pattern. The term *gestalt* means *whole* or configuration, and presumably perception starts with certain basic forms or wholes. This notion is difficult to grasp abstractly, but it will become clearer when we present concrete examples of the Gestalt principles that underlie perceptual organization.

Gestalt psychologists also assume that perceptual organization is innate—that is, the perception of form, space, and movement is built into man and is not acquired through experience. We shall

[1] *The three leaders of the Gestalt tradition earlier in this century were the psychologists Kurt Koffka, Wolfgang Köhler, and Max Wertheimer.*

Figure 11.3 *A reversible figure.*

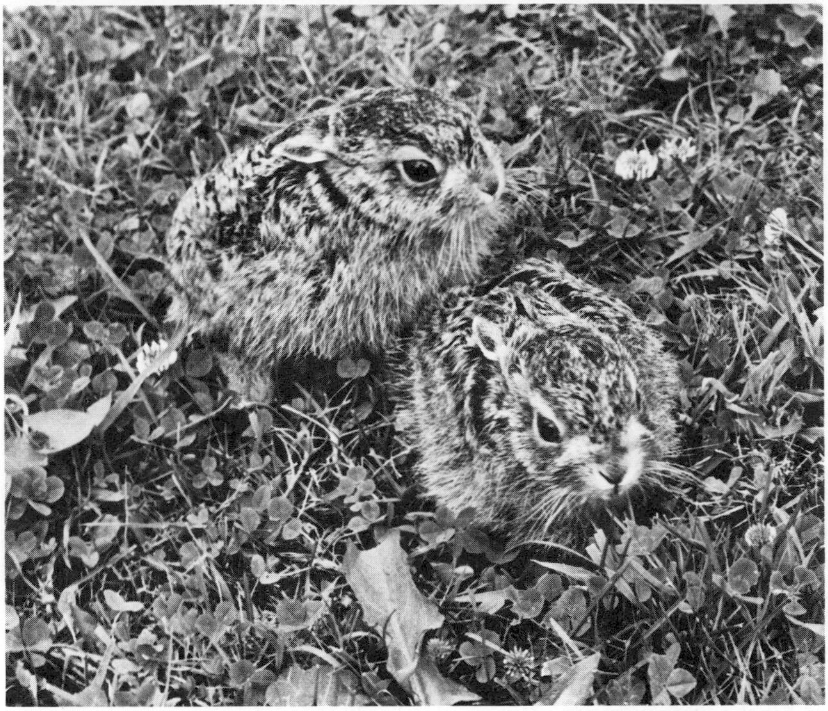

Figure 11.4 *Protective coloration enables these hares to blend into the background.* (S. C. PORTER/BRUCE COLEMAN INC.)

return to this controversial assumption at the end of the chapter.

PROXIMITY. Stimuli near each other tend to be seen as clusters. Equally spaced lines are seen merely as a set of lines, but when they are not equally spaced, they are seen in clusters (see Figure 11.5).

SIMILARITY. Stimuli that resemble one another tend to be grouped together. The elements in Figure 11.6*a* are seen as *rows*, those in Figure 11.6*b* as *columns*. This is similarity of *form*, but the principle also applies to similarity of brightness, hue, saturation, pattern, and complexity.

CONTINUATION. Stimuli may be grouped together because they continue a figure that has already been started. Figure 11.7*a* is usually perceived as

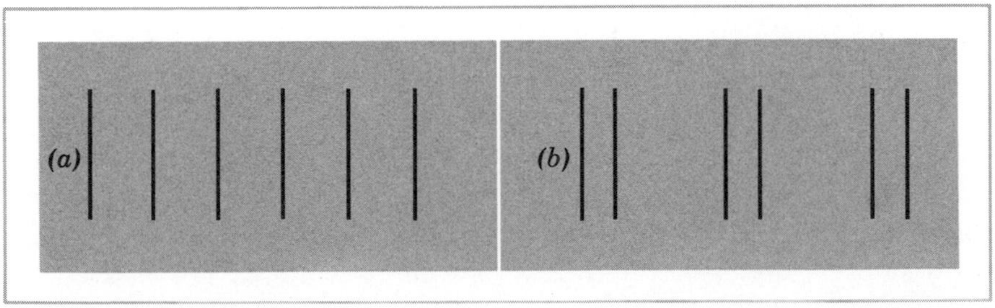

Figure 11.5 *The six vertical lines in (a) are perceived as three groups of vertical lines in (b).*

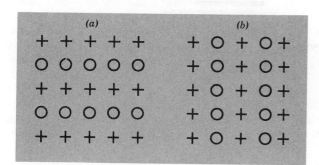

Figure 11.6 In (a), rows of similar elements are seen; columns rather than rows are seen in (b).

a straight line being intersected by a wavy line (Figure 11.7*b*). The figure could also be perceived as presented in Figure 11.7*c*, but it rarely is. Rather, the observer tends to continue the linear parts as a line and the wavy parts as a curve, as in Figure 11.7*b*.

CLOSURE. We tend to fill in blanks and to see complete pictures even when small parts are missing. If the major or crucial parts of the object are present, we respond as if the entire object were present. Thus dotted or dashed lines often substitute for filled ones (Figure 11.8), especially when stimuli are seen only briefly. The tendency toward closure may also account for errors in proofreading: words may be perceived as whole or correct even when a letter is missing or incorrect.

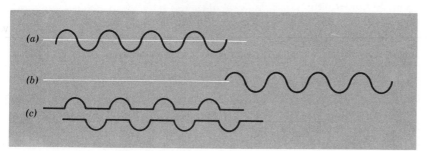

Figure 11.7 The operation of continuation: (a) is usually separated into the two parts shown in (b) rather than those in (c).

Figure 11.8 Examples of closure. Completed figures are perceived. Unconnected lines are seen as letters.

Faces

As man is an extremely social animal, his focus often falls on another face. In fact, the human face is probably the most important object to be perceived in the environment. But what is a face, perceptually? It has color, brightness, shading, texture, and—most important of all—*form*. Its shape is essentially oval, and it has features (eyes, nose, mouth) arranged in a specific pattern. It has been speculated that infants innately attend to a face more than to other objects, but this appears to be untrue. In the first month of life infants tend to look at a checkerboard pattern more than at a face (Thomas, 1965).

The infant does not initially know what a face is and must learn the features that comprise a face. E. J. Gibson (1969) has summarized the research in this area. We can mark off four stages in the infant's learning about faces (see Figure 11.9). In the earliest stage the infant responds only to contours. He can discriminate an oval figure with lines from a rectangle or other shapes. Subsequently, he learns about the distinctive features of the face, and he differentially responds to a face with eyes, nose, and mouth rather than to a featureless oval; but he responds equally to an ordinary face and to a face with scrambled features. In the third stage, he requires an orderly arrangement of features, and he differentiates

between scrambled and unscrambled faces. Finally, he begins to discriminate one person's face from another's, using as cues both the individual features and their arrangement. The infant is now roughly six months old, and he can discriminate familiar faces from the faces of strangers. This developmental trend in learning to discriminate faces appears to be typical of perceptual learning: the child responds first to gross features (contour), then to individual features (including specific contours), and finally to relationships among features.

The Third Dimension

The perception of form involves perception mainly in two dimensions, *height* and *width.* But the world has a third spatial dimension, *depth.* The light reflected off objects around us offers a variety of cues about their distance from the perceiver. It is convenient to divide these cues into those that can be detected by a single eye (monocular) and those that require two eyes (binocular).

Binocular Cues

We have referred several times to the fact that frontally placed eyes yield better depth perception. Man's eyes are roughly two and a half inches apart, which means that each receives a slightly different image (see Figure 11.12). When the object is close, the two images are somewhat dissimilar; the right eye sees more of the right side of the object, the left eye more of the left side. These differences, called *binocular disparity,* provide a powerful cue for the perception of depth.

The two separate images are somehow fused, for we see only a single solid object rather than two overlapping objects. Presumably, the fusion occurs in the brain, but no one understands how. It is known that this depth cue does not require objects, lines, or pictures. Binocular disparity also yields the perception of depth when a subject is presented with apparently meaningless patterns which have been drawn specifically for this purpose (Julesz, 1964).

The other binocular cue is *convergence* (see Figure 11.13). The eyes rotate toward each other to converge on a close object, and they move to an

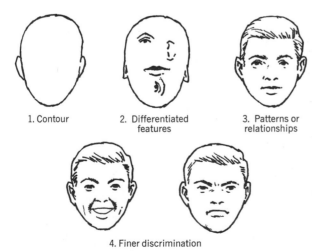

1. Contour   2. Differentiated features   3. Patterns or relationships

4. Finer discrimination

Figure 11.9 Development of discrimination of faces.

Figure 11.10 Motion parallax.   (JAMES ROOS)

almost parallel position when gazing at a distant object. The action of eye muscles in moving the eyeballs offers a cue to distance, primarily for objects closer than 75 feet.[2] We are ordinarily unaware of these movements, which can be sensed when the eyes are extremely converged (fixate on the index finger while it moves toward and touches the nose).

The two binocular cues, disparity and convergence, complete our list of cues for perceiving distance (see Table 11.1 p. 218). Only rarely are all the cues available. For gross perception of distance, the monocular cues usually suffice, with motion parallax and interposition being especially salient. For a more finely tuned perception of depth, especially when hand-eye coordination is involved, binocular disparity is especially useful.

Monocular Cues

Two monocular cues involve activity or movement by the perceiver. The first is *accommodation*:

[2] *There has been some debate about convergence as a distance cue, with some authorities denying its value. Recent research suggests that two-thirds of the population use it and one-third does not (Richards & Miller, 1969).*

changes in the curvature of the lens. As we mentioned earlier, looking at nearby objects causes the lens to thicken, and looking at more distant objects causes it to flatten. These changes in curvature are brought about by relaxation or contraction of the *ciliary muscles*. Such differences in the *tension of the muscles* can serve as cues for distance, but only for near objects.

The second cue is picked up from changes in the retinal image as the eye or head is moved. At the same speed, near objects appear to move fast, and far objects appear to move slowly. This is called *motion parallax*. An airplane that flashes by is usually judged to be closer than one that passes by more slowly. The effect is best seen when the perceiver is driving an automobile. Near objects speed past so quickly that they are a blur, but far objects move past slowly enough to be seen clearly (see Figure 11.10). Motion parallax is probably the most important of all the monocular cues for depth.

The remaining monocular cues require no special action by the perceiver, and therefore they can be represented in such two-dimensional arrays as drawings, diagrams, paintings, and photographs. The seven cues are all present in Figure 11.11.

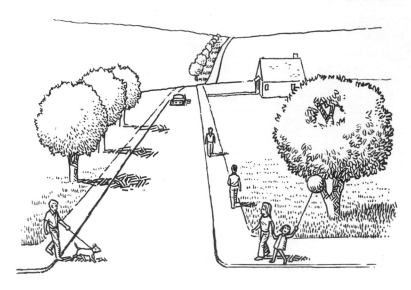

Figure 11.11 Monocular cues for depth.

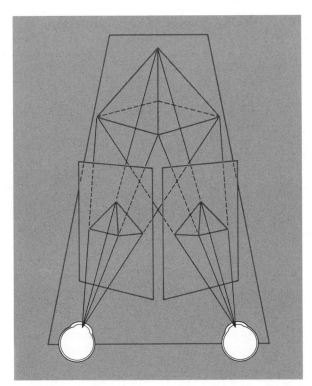

Figure 11.12 The disparate views of an object by the two eyes (from Gibson, 1950).

1. *Interposition.* Objects nearer the perceiver partially block those farther away. The unblocked object is seen as closer and up front; the blocked object is seen as farther and behind. Note the balloon and tree in Figure 11.11.

2. *Apparent Height.* As we view a scene, foreground appears to be low and background appears high. Distant objects appear higher in the two-dimensional plane of the picture than do near objects. Note the near and far trees in Figure 11.11.

3. *Size of Familiar Objects.* If one object appears much smaller than another but we know them to be of equal size, then the first is seen as being farther away. Thus in Figure 11.11 the retinal image of one man is considerably smaller than those of the other men, which makes him appear to be farther away.

4. *Linear Perspective.* As we view a scene, parallel lines appear to converge in the distance (the road in Figure 11.11). Artists use this cue to induce the effect of depth by having apparently parallel lines meet at the horizon of the scene.

5. *Texture.* Most surfaces consist of elements that make the surface look coarse or smooth, grainy or polished, and so on. The closer the object, the coarser its texture appears because the ele-

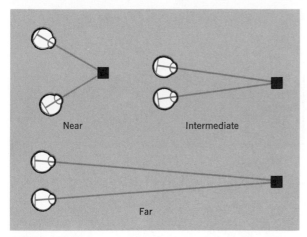

Figure 11.13 Convergence and conjugate eye movements. The eyes move together and toward each other for nearby objects.

ments are spread apart. With increasing distance the texture becomes finer, and this gradient of texture offers a distance cue. Note in Figure 11.11 that the nearby blades of grass are more widely spaced than those farther away.
6. *Clarity.* The closer an object is, the sharper are its details and the more saturated its color. Distant buildings and hills appear to be hazy and their colors seem unsaturated. Compare the low hill in the foreground of Figure 11.11 with the distant hill.
7. *Shading.* When light comes from a strong source, the sun for example, part of an object is in the light and part in the shade. Such shadowing offers an excellent cue for *depth* (not distance). Thus the balloon in Figure 11.11 appears as a sphere rather than a circle because of the shading.

Constancy

There is a real world "out there" beyond our own bodies and sense organs, and it remains the same regardless of how it is viewed. Objects do not change their size, color, shape, or brightness merely because the perceiver changes his own position; standing on one's head does not cause the world to turn upside down. In brief, we see the world as it really is (though we make some mistakes), correcting for distortions caused by our receptor mechanisms.[3]

In a sense, the receptors do not distort; they merely record the stimuli that impinge on them. But even a reasonably faithful reproduction of stimulus energy usually furnishes an incorrect picture of the objects around us. Thus a knowledge of how receptors function is not sufficient; we must also discover what adjustments are needed for perception to mirror the world as it really is.

Size Constancy

How do we perceive the size of objects? In the simplest case, two objects are the same distance from the eye, and the larger one has a larger retinal image. In this respect, the eye functions like a camera, and the retinal image offers sufficient information for the correct perception of size (see Figure 11.14). But the image of an object shrinks as the object recedes into the distance: the image is halved when the distance is doubled. Such changes in images are faithfully recorded by both camera and eye. Though the image is now smaller, the object appears to be virtually the same size. Thus the man is seen as larger than the boy, though the retinal image of the man is smaller (see Figure 11.15).

This phenomenon, called *size constancy*, occurs so often in everyday life that we tend to ignore it. A classroom lecturer appears to be the same size whether he is seen from the first row of seats or the twentieth row. A friend's face does not appear larger as he approaches. We continually make allowances for distance when judging size, even at a distance of half a mile (J. J. Gibson, 1950). This applies to distance along the surface of the earth. Size constancy breaks down when objects are viewed from a great height—perhaps because of unfamiliarity with such a perspective. When a street is viewed from a tall building, the observer is usually surprised to discover that the cars look like toys and the people like ants. This occurs

---

[3] *This statement involves assumptions we shall discuss later.*

Table 11.1
Cues for Perceiving Distance

	NEAR	FAR
Monocular		
Accommodation	Ciliary muscle relaxes, lens thickens	Ciliary muscle contracts, lens flattens
Motion parallax	Objects appear to move fast	Objects appear to move slowly
Interposition	Uncovered	Partly blocked
Apparent height	Lower	Higher
Size of familiar objects	Larger	Smaller
Linear perspective	Parallel lines appear widely spaced	Parallel lines appear narrowly spaced
Shading	Brighter	Darker
Texture	Coarser	Finer
Clarity	More distinct	Less distinct
Binocular		
Disparity	Two images relatively dissimilar	Two images relatively similar
Convergence	Gaze lines tend to converge	Gaze lines tend to be parallel

because the depth cues are poorer in vertical viewing, and the ground appears closer than it really is.

There is a simple but persuasive demonstration of the extent to which we correct for distance. Gaze steadily at a bright light for a few moments and then look at a wall or screen. There will be an afterimage of the light projected on the screen. First look at a near screen, say a piece of blank paper held in the hand. Then look at a far wall. The afterimage, which will be small on the nearby paper, will greatly increase in size when seen on

Figure 11.14 *Retinal image is consistent with actual or perceived size.* (GEORGE ROOS)

Figure 11.15 *Retinal image is* not *consistent with actual or perceived size.* (GEORGE ROOS)

the far wall. The retinal image does not change, but the compensation for the increased distance makes the afterimage appear larger. Under usual conditions of everyday life, such a correction would be necessary to compensate for a smaller retinal image.

We make the same allowance for distance when viewing scenes or pictures, so long as there are cues for depth. In Figure 11.16 the far cylinder is seen as farther away; therefore it appears larger, though its size in the drawing (and consequently the retinal image of it) is the same as that of the near cylinder.

Other Constancies

Perceptual constancy holds also for color, brightness, and shape. As with size constancy, there are limits beyond which these constancies break down. Within these limits, hues appear the same when viewed under different lighting conditions, and the apparent brightness of objects does not change with changes in illumination. Color and brightness constancy are probably more closely related to sensory mechanisms, especially the opponent cells in the lateral geniculate body (see Chapter 10). Size and shape constancy, on the other hand, require the kind of compensation that must originate at a higher level than receptors or neural pathways. The mechanism surely involves a scheme like that of Luria's, with three levels of integration of sensory inputs to the cerebral cortex (see Chapter 8).

Shape constancy is of special interest because it underlies the ability to make the form discriminations so basic to everyday life. An early experiment by Thouless (1931) demonstrated that the shapes we see are really a compromise between the retinal image and the shape as it really is. He showed a subject a circle, placed on a table in various positions so that the angle of viewing

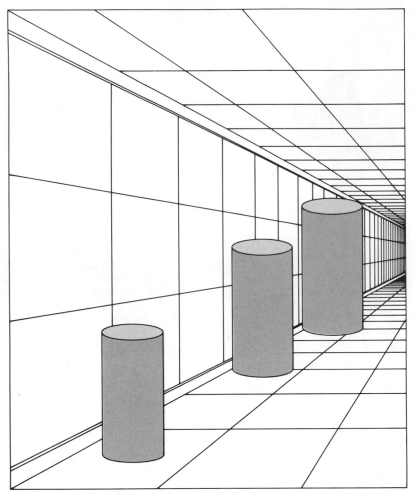

Figure 11.16 An illusion caused by distance cues.

changed drastically (see Figure 11.17). The subject matched a figure to the one he perceived. As Figure 11.17 illustrates, he did not perceive the perspective (retinal) shape but corrected for the angle of viewing. Nevertheless, his correction was not sufficient to compensate for the viewing angle, and the ellipse he perceived was much flatter than the true figure.

   The experiment, together with later research by Bartley (1969), shows clearly that tilt and shape are related. Objects are tilted at various angles from our eyes, and only by compensating for tilt can we approximate the true shape of the objects.

Of course, under normal conditions of seeing, many cues are available, and perception tends to be veridical (not illusory).

Illusions

Perception consists of receiving information from the environment and making sense of it. Most of the time our perceptions are attuned to objects and events, but occasionally we make mistakes. These are called *illusions*. Magicians make their living by inducing an audience to look in the

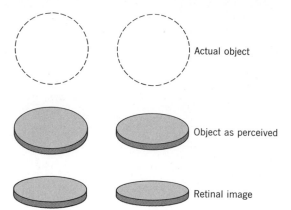

Actual object

Object as perceived

Retinal image

Figure 11.17 An example of shape constancy.

wrong direction or to make faulty inferences. Their feats of appearance and disappearance are properly labeled illusions: they provide the stimulus conditions that induce the observer to make mistakes.

Photographs, paintings, and drawings may also be regarded as illusions. They offer a set of visual stimuli equivalent to those of the real environment. This substitution is effective, and we can perceive depth in a scene depicted on the two dimensions of paper or canvas. Similarly, we perceive movement on a motion picture screen, though there is actually no movement, only cues that induce its perception. The information in pictures is ambiguous. On the one hand, we perceive objects or figures in three dimensions or in movement; on the other hand, we know the picture is merely a reproduction, for we do not reach out to touch the object depicted on paper or canvas. Occasionally an artist will depict a visual dimension (say, texture) so well that we are tempted to feel the surface of the painting (see Figure 11.20, p. 224), but this is the exception rather than the rule.

Psychologists have studied illusions because mistakes often tell us as much as do correct perceptions. Size constancy, for example, requires a correction for the diminution of the retinal image as an object recedes. This automatic compensation can lead to illusions about the size of objects and the length of lines. In addition to illusions of size, there are also illusions of shape, movement, and orientation. In orientation illusions, for example, continuous lines appear broken or vertical lines appear slanted because of tilting of part of

the visual field (see Figure 11.18). There have been separate hypotheses proposed to explain each of the many illusions, but until recently there was no general theory of illusions.

General Constancy Theory

Day (1972) proposed a theory of illusions that is based on visual constancy. As we have already mentioned, perceptual constancy is an important biological adaptation — one that corrects for changes in distance, posture, and movement of the observer. The observer uses some of the stimuli in a visual scene to correct for changes in the retinal image. Thus the observer knows that a cube is still a cube even when it is regarded from an angle (shape constancy) and that the walls of a room are still vertical when the observer tilts his head in looking at them (orientation constancy). Day's theory assumes that illusions occur because of perceptual constancy:

I conclude that any stimulus which serves to maintain perceptual constancy of a property of an object as the visual representation of that property varies will, when independently manipulated with the retinal image not varied, produce an illusion. (1972, P. 1340.)

He is suggesting that the corrections we automatically make for changes in the retinal image will cause distorted perception (illusions) when the size of the retinal image remains constant. Ordinarily, the retinal image would change, and the

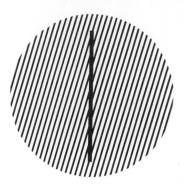

Figure 11.18 *An orientation illusion.*

automatic corrections would yield true perception. When the retinal image is kept constant—as in the drawings that yield illusions—the corrections cause misperceptions.

Consider the Ponzo illusion (see Figure 11.19). In Figure 11.19*a* the two logs are identical in length, but the farther one is seen as larger. This compelling illusion occurs because there is distance information in the drawing: the fence posts and trees are foreshortened as they extend from the observer into the distance. These cues for distance are used to correct the size of the retinal image, and this automatic correction makes the farther log appear larger.

Such corrections are so powerful in determining perception that they occur even when natural features are removed and all that remains is a geometrical drawing. Thus the same kind of size illusion occurs in Figure 11.19*b* and 11.19*c*. The general rule is: *the size of surrounding stimuli determines the perceived size of the object being viewed.* Thus an object surrounded by small stimuli would be perceived as large, and an object surrounded by large stimuli would be perceived as small. The rule applies to a variety of size illusions (see Figure 11.21), including the moon illusion (see Figure 11.22). A horizon moon appears larger than a moon high in the night sky—an illusion that has been pondered since antiquity. Laboratory research has shown that the presence of terrain is crucial, for terrain offers cues for distance (Kaufmann & Rock, 1962). The horizon moon is registered as farther away than the zenith moon. An object that is perceived as more distant is automatically corrected for (the size constancy mechanism), and therefore it appears larger.

Day's theory accounts not only for illusions of size but also for illusions of shape, orientation, and motion. Thus in Figure 11.23*a* the background elements cause the *shape* of the circle to be perceived as distorted. In Figure 11.23*b* the tilts of the surrounding lines distort the perception of the lines, which are parallel but not perceived as parallel; here the tilt causes corrections for *orientation.* Concerning motion, it is not possible to present an illusion in a book. But consider the illusion that occurs when swiftly moving clouds pass over a tall building; viewed from the ground, the building appears to move in a direction opposite to that of the clouds. Or visualize the apparently backward movement of one's own car that occurs when an adjacent car slowly pulls away at a traffic light.

In brief, Day's general theory explains illusions in terms of perceptual constancy. For each kind of constancy (size, shape, orientation, and so on) there should be a class of illusions that occur when the appropriate visual cues are manipulated. The theory does not explain all illusions (see Figure 11.24, for example) but it accounts for most illusions.

Size Constancy as Learned

Presumably, perspective cues are learned in specific environments. We live in a rectangular world of rooms, buildings, and streets. If we lived in a world without such rectilinear features, we would not fall prey to the Müller-Lyer illusion. Similarly, if we lived in an environment that offered no distant vistas with paths and roads retreating toward the

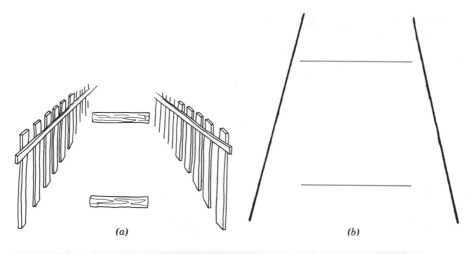

(a)   *(b)*

(c)

Figure 11.19 The Ponzo illusion.   (UNION PACIFIC RAILROAD)

Figure 11.20 *The illusion of texture on a two-dimensional surface:* Napoleon *by Francois Gerard.* (ALINARI/SCALA)

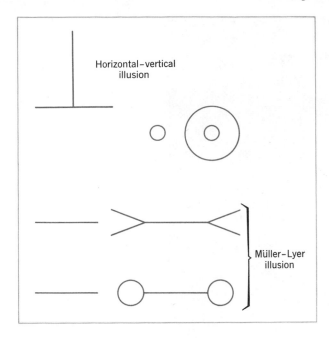

Horizontal–vertical
illusion

Müller–Lyer
illusion

Figure 11.21 *Some illusions of size.*

horizon, the horizontal-vertical illusions would not work.

These two hypotheses were tested by Segall et al. (1966), using American and African subjects. They found that subjects who lived in the rectilinear, "carpentered" environment were much more susceptible to the Müller-Lyer illusion. Concerning the other illusion, their own words suffice:

We offered quite another hypothesis as a source for predicting different cultural susceptibilities to the horizontal-vertical illusions. This hypothesis argues that another aspect of the physical environment of peoples — specifically, the presence or absence of broad, horizontal vistas — is crucial in shaping the visual inference habit that leads to horizontal-vertical illusion susceptibility. If one lives in an environment that provides many opportunities for looking at horizontal expanses, one should become subject to the tendency to infer long-frontal-plane, horizontal distances from short, vertical retinal images. This inference habit, we argued, should contribute to the horizontal-vertical illusion. Accordingly, we predicted that plains dwellers would prove maximally susceptible, urban dwellers moderately susceptible, and groups that live

in restricted environments (e.g., equatorial forests) minimally susceptible to the horizontal-vertical illusion. Again, with just a few qualifications, we found a good fit of our data to this hypothesis.

(SEGALL ET AL., 1966, PP. 212–213.)

Impossible Figures

Pictures and drawings are two-dimensional representations of three-dimensional space. The artist ordinarily seeks to present information so as to suggest a real scene in the environment, but he need not. If he possesses a capricious sense of humor, he can present us with lines and shading that suggest objects that simply cannot exist (see Figure 11.25). The trick is based in part on the limits of our gaze. We can fixate on only one part of the figure at any given moment, and each part makes sense. The figure is nonsense only when all parts are considered together, and this is a kind of afterthought.

Impossible figures and illusions may be explained in terms of either what we learn or how the visual system is innately organized. Learning

Figure 11.22 The moon illusion.

(SCIENTIFIC AMERICAN, JULY 1962; PHOTOS WILLIAM VANDIVERT.)

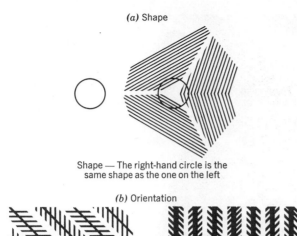

(a) Shape

Shape — The right-hand circle is the
same shape as the one on the left

(b) Orientation

| The diagonal lines are parallel | The vertical lines are parallel |

Figure 11.23 *Illusions of shape and orientation.*

must determine some illusions, as Segall et al. (1966) have shown by demonstrating cultural and environmental influences. But other illusions appear to be universal, and therefore they are not necessarily explained by what is learned.

From a different perspective, illusions and impossible figures may be explained in terms of either properties of the stimuli or how visual information is processed by the perceiver. Thus illusions may be said to arise from contradictory information in a picture or from errors in how we handle sensory inputs. These explanations are not limited to illusions. They are broad theories of perception, and any good theory in this area should account for mistakes as well as for correct perceptions.

Objective and Subjective Approaches to Perception

Psychologists differ in their opinions as to whether the perceiver sees the world directly (the objective approach) or must reconstruct it from sensory inputs (the subjective approach). James and Eleanor Gibson take the objective approach. They assume that the environment is not random and chaotic, but structured and organized; the task of

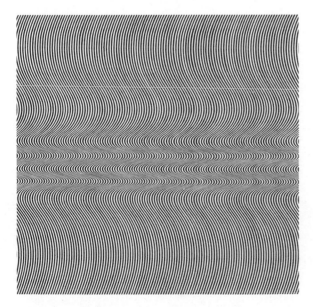

Figure 11.24 *An illusion of movement that is not explained by perceptual constancy:* Current *by* Bridget Riley.
(COLLECTION, THE MUSEUM OF MODERN ART, NEW YORK, PHILIP C. JOHNSON FUND.)

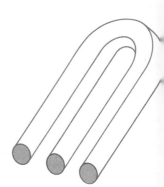

Figure 11.25 Impossible figures (*Left*) Relativity *by M. C. Escher.*
(FROM THE GRAPHIC WORKS OF M. C. ESCHER BY M. C. ESCHER. © KONINKLIJKE UITGEVERIJ
ERVEN J. J. TIJL N. V., ZWOLLE, HOLLAND 1960. © AMERICAN EDITION MEREDITH PRESS, NEW
YORK. REPRINTED BY PERMISSION OF HAWTHORNE BOOKS, INC.)

the perceiver is to discover the important cues
that reside in the environment:

*If the invariants of this structure can be registered by
a perceptual system, the constants of neural input will
correspond to the constants of stimulus energy,
although the one will not copy the other. But then
meaningful information can be said to exist inside the
nervous system as well as outside. The brain is relieved of constructing such information by any
process. . . . Instead of postulating that the brain
constructs information from the input of a sensory*

*nerve, we can suppose that the centers of the nervous
system, including the brain, resonate to information.*

(J. J. GIBSON, 1966, P. 267.)[4]

According to this approach, there is no need for
compensatory processes:

*. . . an object tends to be perceived in its true size
very early in development, not because the organism*

[4] *The extensive use of quotations here is an attempt at
fairness to the theorists, who may not agree with the interpretation of their positions.*

has learned to correct for distance, but because he sees the object as such, not its projected size or its distance abstracted from it.   (E. J. GIBSON, 1969, P. 366.)

Stated another way, the Gibsons suggest that we should ignore how sensory inputs are processed inside the organism and instead pay attention to the properties of *outside* stimuli that determine perception.

The subjective approach directs our attention to the inside of the organism. It assumes that perceptual experience is *constructed* by the perceiver by combining sensory inputs, appropriately encoded, with information already stored in the brain:

Perception seems to be a matter of looking up information that has been stored about objects and how they behave in various situations. The retinal image does little more than select the relevant stored data. The selection is rather like looking up entries in the encyclopedia: behavior is determined by the contents of the entry rather than by the stimulus that provoked the search. We can think of perception as being essentially the selection of the most appropriate stored hypothesis according to current sensory data.

(GREGORY, 1968, P. 75.)

The difference between subjective and objective approaches harks back to the basic split between cognitive and stimulus-response approaches. Cognitive theorists emphasize plans, ideas, hypotheses, images, and similar notions—all inferred as occurring inside the organism and being fundamental in processing sensory inputs and preparing response outputs. Stimulus-response theorists emphasize connections between responses and the stimuli that presumably elicit them; and both stimuli and responses are described objectively, with no recourse to anything as subjective as experience. The Gibsons are not stimulus-response psychologists in the narrow sense of the term, but their refusal to consider how information is processed places them on the side of stimulus-response theory and opposed to cognitive theory. This difference in approach has fortunately not led to needless debate, and it has led to significant research on the special cues that stimuli offer the perceiver (by the objectivists) and

how sensory information is processed within the organism (by the subjectivists).

Learning and Innate Factors

No one suggests that perception is either completely innate or completely learned. Some innate processes must be present at birth, else the infant could not see at all; and certain aspects of perception are learned—as we saw earlier, infants *learn* to discriminate the human face. The argument centers on the *relative* contribution of learning and innate factors. Some psychologists contend that innate perception is extremely primitive and that normal perception requires *some* learning. This approach suggests that the various constancies are slowly learned by the infant. The alternative approach is to assume that constancy is largely innate:

Even after a century of work dominated by psychologists—and before them, philosophers—who believed we learn to see the world the way we do, there is little solid evidence to support this belief. In fact, there now is rather good evidence that form and depth perception are innate, that form and depth are perceptible at birth or soon thereafter.   (ROCK, 1968, P. 27.)

As might be guessed, theorists who emphasize the role of experience in perception do not accept these conclusions. The theoretical dispute has been of value in leading to research on perception in newborn and very young organisms.

Deprivation Experiments

The deprivation experiment eliminates part of the normally-expected environment of the young animal. Thus it is designed to reveal the importance of the psychological-constant factor in development. The task should be one that requires no special experience or training, and the best task in this area tests the depth perception of young organisms. It is called the *visual cliff.*

The visual cliff started with an idea by E. J. Gibson. She wondered, as she gazed across Grand Canyon, whether a newborn infant would fall in or

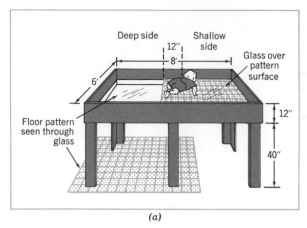

(a)

Figure 11.26 *The visual cliff apparatus.*
(SCIENTIFIC AMERICAN, APRIL 1960; PHOTO WILLIAM VANDIVERT.)

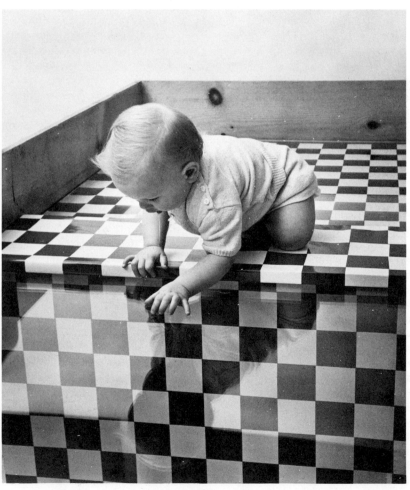

(b)

would possess sufficient depth perception to avoid the drop. This speculation led to the construction of a laboratory apparatus (Walk & Gibson, 1961), which is shown in Figure 11.26. The subject is placed on a board between a shallow and an apparently deep drop-off. There are appropriate controls for brightness, texture, and so on, and glass covers both sides. A preference for the shallow side means that the subject can respond to depth.

The very young of a variety of species have been tested on this apparatus. Showing marked preference for the shallow side were rats, goats, sheep, pigs, cats, dogs, monkeys, and humans. Turtles had only a weak preference for the shallow side, which is consistent with their very short (daily) stay on land. Another water animal, the duck, shows no preference at all. In brief, animals across a broad range of the phyletic spectrum seem to perceive depth very early in life, and land animals avoid a visual cliff.

Experimenters would like to test their subjects immediately after birth, but this is impossible. Subjects cannot be reliably tested for hours or days, and the interval may be crucial in the development of the behavior in question. Thus it is possible that innate depth perception, as revealed by the visual cliff apparatus, requires a brief exposure to the visual stimuli common to all members of the species (the psychological-constant factor). The issue may be resolved by depriving the animal of such stimulation. Newborn animals are kept in the dark from birth until they are tested, in this instance on the visual cliff.

When rats are reared in the dark for one month, or even as long as three months, they still show depth perception; that is, they immediately seek the shallow side of the visual cliff (Walk et al., 1957). But rats are nocturnal animals, and deprivation of light may be of little consequence to them. Presumably, day animals would be more seriously affected by being reared in the dark. This speculation turns out to be correct. When kittens were reared in the dark for roughly a month, they showed no preference for the shallow side of the visual cliff (Walk & Gibson, 1961). With exposure to light, the depth discrimination soon appeared and improved sharply (see Figure 11.27). The same phenomenon has been reported in infant monkeys (Fantz, 1967), and it may well

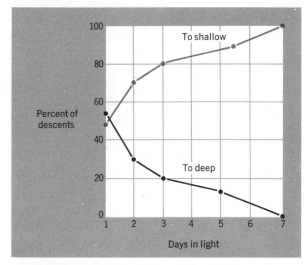

Figure 11.27 *The development of avoidance of a visual cliff by dark reared kittens as a function of days in the light.*

be common to all higher animals including man.

These results reaffirm the importance of the psychological-constant factor in development. Depth perception develops only when the newborn organism is exposed to the normal visual environment common to all members of the species. When denied this stimulation, the organism is incapable of perceiving depth. As the experiments with normal animals demonstrated, depth perception is innate. But innate behavior, as we have been stating repeatedly, usually requires prior experience with the normally expected environment of the animal.

Perception in Human Infants

Can infants perceive depth and achieve size constancy? We know from the visual cliff experiments that older infants can perceive depth, but they are already crawling and moving around in the environment. What about infants who cannot yet locomote?

Bower (1966, 1971) showed that both depth perception and size constancy are present in infants less than three months old. His infant sub-

Table 11.2
Cues to Depth Perception in Infants

CUE	EFFECTIVENESS OF CUE
Monocular movement parallax	Very effective
Static pictorial cue	Ineffective
Binocular disparity	Effective

jects seemed to correct for a diminished retinal image when an object was placed farther away, and this correction requires that distance be perceived.

The next step was to determine which cues were being used to gauge distance. One group of infants had one eye covered, which denied them binocular cues (mainly disparity). Another group looked at slides that contained depth cues but denied them both binocular cues and motion parallax. The third group watched slides through stereoscopic goggles, which allowed the binocular cue of retinal disparity but not that of motion parallax. The findings are presented in Table 11.2. Motion parallax offered the best distance cue; binocular disparity was less effective, and pictorial cues were useless.

This research, as well as the visual cliff experiments, suggests that at least some aspects of perception are innate. Nevertheless, learning plays an important role in the development of perception. Size constancy in infants, for example, is crude

Figure 11.28 The kitten carousel—apparatus for comparing perceptual development in active and passive kittens.   (ALAN HEIN, MIT.)

and primitive. It increases during childhood, as perceptual learning enhances appropriate corrections for distance (Meneghini & Leibowitz, 1967).

The nature of perceptual learning is still a subject of debate. One view holds that the infant has access to very limited information and that perceptual development consists of adding more and more cues. An alternative view holds that infants register as much information as adults, and perceptual development consists of processing more and more of the information. But these two approaches are not incompatible, and it seems likely that they are both partially correct.

Perception, Movement, and Position

No matter what else perception is used for, one of its primary functions is to supply information about position and movement. Stated another way, the sensory-motor linkage is a close one. It may be disrupted at either the motor end or the sensory end, and we shall consider each kind of interference.

Active and Passive Movement

Movement is ordinarily self-produced, and some aspects of perception probably requires self-produced movement. If an animal is prevented from moving actively, its perceptual development should suffer accordingly. Held and Hein (1963) tested this notion by rearing kittens in the dark for two to three months. Then pairs of kittens spent three hours a day in a special apparatus (see Figure 11.28). This was a cylinder with striped walls; one kitten walked around in a circle, pulling the other in a tiny gondola. Thus one kitten moved actively, the other passively, and both were exposed to the same visual stimuli. Held (1965) has summarized the findings:

After an average of about 30 hours in the apparatus the active member of each pair showed normal behavior in several visually guided tasks. It blinked at an approaching object; it put out its forepaws as if to ward off a collision when gently carried downward toward a surface, and it avoided the deep side of a visual cliff. . . . After the same period of exposure each of the passive kittens failed to show these types of behavior. The passive kittens did, however, develop such types of behavior after they were allowed to run about in a normal environment. (P. 94.)

This research demonstrates that *active* movement is needed for normal perceptual development. But movement is not the only important variable; *felt position* also plays a role. In perceiving and responding to stimuli, the person must not only see but also know where his limbs are. The importance of felt position can best be demonstrated when it conflicts with vision, as in distorted vision.

Distorted Vision

Eyeglasses alter the incoming light to correct for visual defects. A new pair of corrective lenses slightly changes the appearance of the world. Spectacles that distort the visual image, by turning it upside down or reversing right and left, radically change the appearance of the world. An inverted world is strange and puzzling, but man can adapt to it. Lower animals cannot adapt to prisms that displace visual targets (Hess, 1956), but monkeys can (Bossom & Hamilton, 1963) and so can humans. Stratton (1897) was the first to wear distorting prisms for long periods. At first he bumped into objects while walking, and he reached incorrectly. When he moved his head, the world appeared to move in the opposite direction (for an explanation, refer back to the perception of movement, Chapter 10). Eventually, he adapted to the changes, and his sensory-motor coordination returned to normal.

Research Report

It is the nature of this adaptation that interests us, and the most compelling hypothesis appears to be that of *felt position* (Harris, 1965). When a subject wears distorting prisms and looks at his arm,

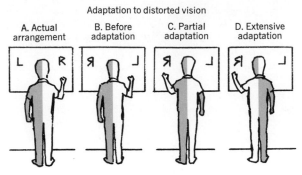

Adaptation to distorted vision

A. Actual arrangement   B. Before adaptation   C. Partial adaptation   D. Extensive adaptation

(Shaded parts = perceived left side of the body)

Figure 11.29 Changes in perception during adaptation to reversing prisms, according to the felt position hypothesis (Harris 1965).

he *sees* it in one place and *feels* it in another. Harris contends that the feeling or position sense changes to match the visual perception. Thus adaptation would consist of altering one's position sense to accommodate to the changes in vision.

Suppose we placed a subject in front of a blackboard on which was written an *L* to his left and an *R* to his right (see Figure 11.29a). After reversing prisms are placed over his eyes, he must adapt to the right-left visual reversal. Before adaptation he should *feel* that his right hand (his writing hand) and the right side of his body are near the end of the blackboard with the backward *L* (Figure 11.29b). But his right hand *looks* near the backward *R* because he views his hand through reversing goggles. As he starts to adapt, his writing hand both looks and *feels* nearer to the backward *R* (Figure 11.29c). After extensive adaptation, he *feels* that the right half of his body is near the hand he writes with; thus he accommodates *felt* location to *visual* location (Figure 11.29d). Having resolved the conflict between felt position and vision, he can now reach, move, and perform coordinated activities correctly.

Harris tested his hypothesis in the laboratory, using prisms that displaced the visual field roughly 11 degrees (about 4 inches at arm's length) to the right or left. Subjects were tested once without prisms, then with prisms, and a third time after the prisms were removed. The task was to point repeatedly with one hand at the center target of five targets in a row (see Figure 11.30). On the first test the subjects pointed correctly; with prisms, they pointed incorrectly to the right. Being able to see the hand pointing to the right, they quickly adapted to the displaced vision and began pointing correctly again. Finally, the prisms were removed, and the adaptation caused incorrect pointing to the left.

The adaptation might consist of a change in either the seen position of the object (vision) or where the hand and arm are felt to be (felt posi-

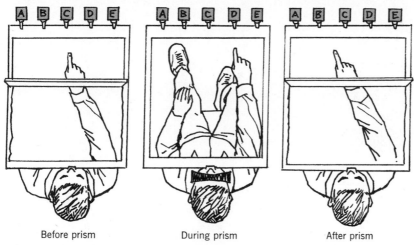

Before prism   During prism   After prism

Figure 11.30 *Adaptation to displacing prisms; subject is to point to center target.*

tion). The kinds of errors made after adaptation should decide between the two possibilities:

1. If it is felt position that adapts but not vision, the subject should err whether he points to a visual object or a source of sound. Subjects do point as incorrectly toward a sound as toward a visual target after adaptation (see Figure 11.31*a* p. 236).
2. If it is vision that adapts, the same mistake should be made with either hand. But if it is felt position that adapts, the unadapted hand should point correctly; it does (see Figure 11.31*b* p. 236).
3. A visual change should yield no effect when the eyes are closed; a felt position change should cause error with eyes closed, so long as the adapted arm is used to point. When an adapted subject is told to point straight ahead with his eyes closed, he incorrectly points off center (see Figure 11.31*c* p. 236).

In this and related research on displaced vision, it has been found that felt position and touch accommodate to vision.[5] Some psychologists (Rock, 1968, for example) have concluded that a visual-haptic conflict is always resolved by the haptic accommodating to the visual. This is not necessarily true. Rather, the resolution of a conflict between two sense modalities depends on which is more important in the particular perceptual situation. Usually it will be vision, our dominant sense. But in perceiving texture, if vision conflicts with touch (as with the graininess of sandpaper), we accommodate vision to touch.

[5] *Subsequent research has partially corroborated Harris' hypothesis (Putterman, 1969; Welch, 1971), but later findings on adaptation to displaced vision have been too complex to be explained by any single hypothesis now extant, including felt position. For example, there is evidence that active movement is important in adapting to prisms (Quinlan, 1970; Hardt et al., 1971).*

Perspective

The term *perspective* is particularly apt in a chapter on visual perception. Note that the chapter has dealt almost exclusively with *human*

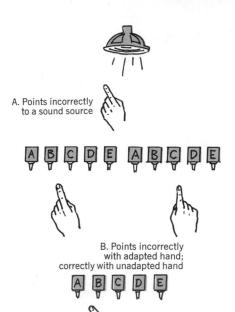

A. Points incorrectly
to a sound source

B. Points incorrectly
with adapted hand;
correctly with unadapted hand

C. Points incorrectly
to "straight ahead"
(using adapted arm)

Figure 11.31 *Evidence for felt position as the change on adaptation to displaced vision (left hand and arm adapted).*

perception. There are two reasons for this preoccupation with humans. First, virtually all researchers in the area of visual *perception*—as distinguished from the sensory aspects discussed in Chapter 10—have used humans as subjects. This is unfortunate because the neglect of perception in animals has left some important questions unanswered. For example, it is not known whether the Gestalt laws of perceptual organization (similarity, closure, and so on) apply to the perception of animals. It would be difficult to discover how a primate organizes the forms in its visual environment, but surely the attempt should be made.

The second reason for the preoccupation with *human* perception in this chapter is our interest in man as an encoder of information. The *sensory* aspects of vision concern how light is received and coded in the nervous system. But the *perceptual* aspects of vision concern how stimuli are *organized* and encoded for retention. Another way

of saying this is that the perceptual aspects of vision involve higher-order psychological processes in comparison with the sensory aspects of vision. This is especially true in the development of perception—as we noted earlier, some of the illusions and the perceptual constancies develop in the context of specific environments (for example, rectangular versus circular environments, or forests versus plains).

As we study man's attempts to extract information from the visual environment, the distinction between perception and cognition becomes blurred. Here man as a sensor is little different from man as a knower. The relationship between perception and cognition will be discussed in the section on cognition. And Cognition—in the way this book is organized—is best regarded as the point at which perception and learning converge. The relationship between cognition and learning will become clear in the next chapter.

section five

learning

chapter 12

varieties of learning

Definition of learning — learning and per-
formance — evolutionary aspects — active-
reactive — simple versus sequential responses
— delay and detour — direct and vicarious
learning — signs and symbols — seven varieties
of learning — habituation and sensitization —
classical conditioning — simple and complex
instrumental conditioning — imitation learn-
ing — concept learning — language

Man is not the only animal that learns, but he is clearly the best learner. The behavior of lower animals is determined largely by innate tendencies; the behavior of man is determined largely by learning. More than any other animal, man can modify his behavior, acquire new responses, and shape himself and his fellows.

Definition of Learning

Learning has been defined in many ways, but the various definitions differ only in minor details. The problem, as with any definition, is to include all relevant phenomena while excluding irrelevant ones. We shall define learning as *a process underlying enduring changes in behavior attributable to the experience of the organism.* Three aspects of this definition require elaboration: that learning is a *process,* that it is an *enduring change,* and that it depends on *experience.*

Learning Versus Performance

Learning is inferred from performance, specifically from changes in performance. We *observe* behavior on two occasions, and from the changes in performance we *infer* that learning has occurred. Consider a hypothetical but realistic example. We start with two groups of school children who read at the rate of 15 words per minute. One group is given special training in reading for a month, the other group no training. When their reading is again tested, the experimental group has doubled their rate to 30 words per minute (see Figure 12.1). The increment in performance suggests that learning has occurred.

Much more is learned than can be inferred from performance. Information may be added and responses acquired, but there may be no call for them. Consider a school examination. Students must master more information than is called for on the test. The examination taps only a *sample* of the student's knowledge, and the remainder is untested and therefore unknown to the teacher. Similarly, we acquire a variety of facts and skills that may never show up in performance simply because the appropriate occasion does not arise.

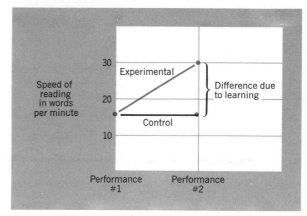

Figure 12.1 *Learning is inferred from changes in performance.*

Learning Endures

In addition to learning, several other variables can induce *transient* changes in performance. Fatigue can cause a decrement in performance, and momentary changes in stimulation can alter responding, but these are merely temporary alterations. The term *learning* is reserved for longer lasting changes. Some well-practiced motor behavior may be retained for many decades. Thus the ability to ride a bicycle or to ice skate does not completely disappear even after 20 or 30 years of disuse.

On the other hand, learning is not permanent. Irregular French verbs, mastered and spoken correctly without hesitation may, after an interval of 10 years, be completely beyond recall. In brief, learning does not ordinarily involve either momentary or permanent changes; rather it refers to the vast middle ground of *enduring* changes in behavior.

Learning Is Based on Experience

As a person moves through his environment, he perceives a variety of stimuli. Some of these encounters lead to changes, and changes in performance brought about by experience are called learning.

What else might cause behavior to change? We have already mentioned *fatigue*. Another cause is *sensory adaptation*. When a person adapts to a dim environment, his eyes at first do not function too well. During the period of dark adaptation, there will be clear improvements in performance until the rod cells are fully functional, but these sensory changes are not considered learning.

Motivation can also cause variations in performance. A football team may be "up" for one game and "flat" for the next, but the resulting fluctuations in performance do not fall under the heading of learning. In brief, fatigue, sensory adaptation, and motivation may all affect performance, but they do not involve learning. The only way to insure that learning has occurred is to eliminate or to control these three variables.

In addition to these short-term variables, *maturation* often leads to changes that may be confused with the effects of learning. As we noted in Chapter 4, maturation may account for dramatic improvements in species wide responses. For example, boys and girls undergo marked biological changes at puberty: a sharp rise in sex hormones and associated changes in body contours and pattern of hair distribution. The increased interest in sexual activities during this period appears to be caused mainly by biological maturation; learning probably plays a minor role.

Controls are needed for maturation, and these can best be instituted in the laboratory. One way to isolate the learning variable is to expose the experimental group to a set of stimuli to which the control group is not exposed. If the experimental group is given practice with stimuli and the control group is not, then any later differences in performance must be the result of learning—assuming that the two groups were matched at the start.

Practice tends to hasten learning and elevate performance. The pupil who studies his lessons masters them quicker and scores better on tests; the actor who studies his lines can recite them so automatically that he can attend to the gestures and interpretations that lead to a superior performance. But practice is not *necessary* for learning to occur. Sometimes a single exposure to a situation is sufficient for enduring retention without practice. Of course the event is likely to be dramatic and linked to strong motivation. Thus some sexual aberrations are acquired in a single experience and retained for many years. For example, some men, after the first sexual experience takes place under a blanket, persist compulsively in having intercourse only when under a blanket. As a general rule, the more meaningful the behavior and the more innate the response, the quicker and more enduring is the learning.[1]

Evolutionary Aspects of Learning

Primitive animals are limited to the simplest kinds of learning; advanced animals are capable of complex learning. This conclusion, so widely accepted as to be a truism, assumes that we can classify learning on a dimension of simple to complex, primitive to advanced. Though most psychologists would agree that such a hierarchy is possible, no one has compiled one.

In constructing an evolutionary sequence of types of learning, it is necessary to specify the criteria of progress. An examination of the various kinds of learning reveals six criteria.

[1] *Each species, including man, seems to have "built in" tendencies that make certain responses easier to learn, others difficult. Such tendencies will be discussed at the end of Chapter 15.*

Active-Reactive

The most primitive animals, far down the evolutionary ladder, tend to be more sluggish than advanced animals. When an animal moves little or not at all, its dominant response mode is *reaction*. It passively awaits stimulation from the environment and then responds reflexively.

The evolution of more mobile animals led to a more progressive type of learning. Advanced animals do not wait passively but actively seek the stimuli they need. They learn which direction to take and which responses are appropriate. Advanced animals can even add novel responses to their behavioral repertoire.

Passive learning is simpler in that it is reflexive. The animal learns only that certain heretofore neutral stimuli are significant and cannot be ignored; they signal an oncoming event. Active learning is more complex in that the animal modifies its *responses*, strengthening the appropriate ones and weakening the inappropriate ones. These responses are instrumental in moving the animal still closer to goals and further away from threats.

The *evolution* of more active learning is paralleled by the *development* of more active learning in human children. Much of an infant's learning is necessarily passive because he is so helpless. The infant's poor motor coordination prevents him from taking an active role in coping with his environment. As he is confined to a passive role, the infant's learning consists mainly of differentiating *input* (see Thompson's critical periods model in Chapter 4). As motor coordination develops, the young child can better manipulate his environment, and his learning becomes mainly differentiating *output*. The shift from differentiating input to differentiating output is essentially the same as the shift from passive to active learning.

Simple Versus Sequential Responses

Obviously, it is easier to learn a single response than it is to learn a sequence of responses. Primitive animals are capable of learning only one response at a time, probably because their nervous systems can process no more than a single stimulus-response connection at a time. As nervous systems evolved, they could store more complex kinds of information, making it possible for an animal to string together *chains* of responses.

The linking of responses in a series—a large step forward in learning—enlarges the animal's behavioral repertoire considerably. A small number of simple responses can be combined in various sequences to yield a large number of complex or multiple responses. It therefore becomes a major task of psychologists in analyzing complex behavior to isolate and identify the component responses that make up complex sequences of behavior.

Single responses are assembled into complex chains very slowly under natural conditions, over years of the animal's life. But the process can be accelerated by laboratory training, which requires only weeks or months to shape a complex sequence in an animal like the white rat (see Figure 12.2).

Delays and Detours

Even a primitive animal can learn to respond immediately when presented with a stimulus. A simple nervous system provides only direct routes for excitation, and a stimulus elicits an immediate response.

But primitive animals cannot learn to make a delayed response, which would require reverberatory neural circuits. Such circuits occur only in advanced animals, for, as Hebb has remarked:

"The capacity for holding an excitation in the central nervous system is the primary mark of the higher animal." (1966, P. 92.)

Therefore, a delayed response involves a higher form of learning than an immediate response does.

Similarly, making a detour involves more complex learning than merely proceeding directly to the goal. When the direct path to a goal is blocked, the learner must learn to move toward it in a roundabout fashion. This may even require moving *away* from the goal at first, and the ability to learn this kind of response is restricted to those animals that possess advanced nervous systems.

Absolute and Relational Learning

In discussing evolutionary trends in perception (see Chapter 8) we noted that lower animals could respond only to the absolute properties of stimuli; higher animals could perceive relationships like *larger than, brighter than,* and so on. The ability to respond to relationships depends on adaptations in both perception and learning. As the task becomes more complex, the perceptual aspects become less important and the learning aspects become more important.

Consider one of the most difficult learning problems, the oddity task (see Figure 12.3). Three objects are presented, two identical and the third different—for example, two cubes and a pyramid. The learner is taught to choose the odd object, in this case the pyramid. Then the task is changed to two pyramids and a cube; now the correct choice is the cube. The stimuli keep changing, but the subject must always choose the odd one. This requires a continual comparison among stimuli and a choice based on their *relationship,* not on their *absolute* identity.

The learning of relationships can be mastered by lower mammals, especially when the task emphasizes perceptual aspects. As the task involves more learning aspects, it becomes more difficult, and very few lower mammals can master oddity problems. The difficulty with oddity problems lies in their *conceptual* nature; the learner is required to follow a *rule* regardless of the absolute properties of the particular stimuli. We shall return to this issue in the discussion of concept learning.

Direct and Vicarious Learning

The learning of lower animals involves direct contact with stimuli and with the consequences of responding. In the commonest kind of learning, the animal learns to respond to a given cue and its behavior is rewarded. Such learning may be called direct in the sense that the behaving animal responds and its response produces certain consequences.

In contrast, in vicarious learning the animal makes no responses, and there are no immediate consequences. Rather, it merely observes another

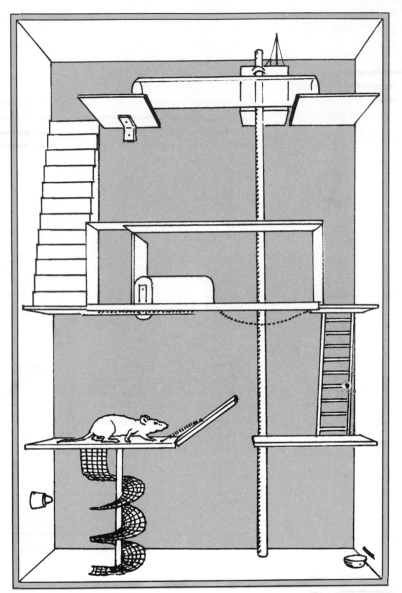

Figure 12.2 *A behavior chain. Upon seeing lit signal the rat* (a) *begins ascending spiral staircase,* (b) *crosses drawbridge,* (c) *climbs ladder,* (d) *pedals car through tunnel,* (e) *runs through tube, and* (f) *pulls chain which starts elevator descending to bottom of demonstration box. There, at the sound of a buzzer, rat depresses lever to receive his food pellet reward.*

(PIERRIEL AND SHERMAN, 1963; THE NEW YORK TIMES)

(a)

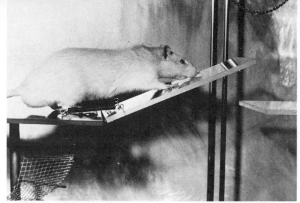

(b)

(c)

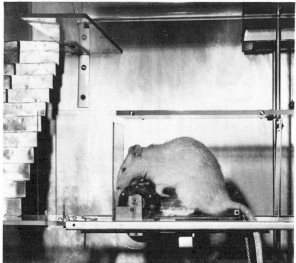

(d)

(e)

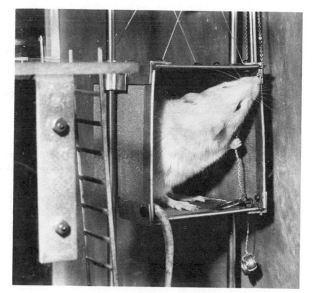

(f)

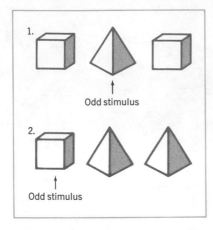

Figure 12.3 *Oddity problems.*

animal (the model) behaving and then imitates the model. Such observational learning is more difficult because it is indirect. The animal must somehow connect the model's behavior with its own situation; the learning occurs without the learner making an immediate response or experiencing its consequences. This kind of learning is seen mainly in birds and mammals, and it reaches a peak in primates and man. The imitative tendencies of primates in zoos is so well known that the word *ape* is a verb as well as a noun.

Signs and Symbols

Animals very low on the phyletic scale are capable of *sign learning,* which involves the pairing of a stimulus with a place or event. If a stimulus is paired with a place, it can come to signal the properties of the place. For men, examples are such places as dentists' chairs and hospitals, which they learn are signals for pain and misery.

Signs are learned through close association with that which they signal. To remain as effective signs, they must continue to be associated with the subsequent event or the place. The simplicity of this learning lies in its dependence on merely a time relationship: a stimulus occurring regularly before a subsequent event comes to be a signal for the event.

Symbol learning, though superficially similar to sign learning, is a much higher form of learning. A symbol is a stimulus that *by convention refers to* object, events, or places. It is not a warning or a signal, and it does not depend on a time relationship. A symbol may be regarded as a representation of the object, place, or event it stands for.

The clearest examples of symbols are found in language. A word or phrase, by convention, represents an object or event, and it can be used to refer to the object or event. But language is not the only kind of symbol, and symbol learning is not restricted to humans. Higher animals, especially primates, are capable of learning symbols, though such learning plays a minor role in their everyday life. Human adjustment, on the other hand, requires considerable learning of symbols, which is basic not only to language but also to the organized play of children.

The various criteria of higher versus lower learning are summarized in Table 12.1. These criteria, taken singly or in combination, can be used to establish an evolutionary continuum of learning.

Seven Varieties of Learning

There has been considerable debate about how many kinds of learning there are. Some psychologists maintain that there is only one kind of learning, which consists of an association between a stimulus and a response. Others insist that there

Table 12.1
Evolutionary Aspects of Learning

CRITERION	LOWER LEARNING	HIGHER LEARNING
Role of learner	Passive	Active
Sequence of responses	Single response	Chains of responses
Time/direction	Immediate/straight line	Delay/detour
Stimulus properties	Absolute	Relational
Contact with stimuli or consequences	Direct (action)	Vicarious (observation)
Sign—symbol	Sign (signals)	Symbol (refers to, represents)

is a second kind, consisting of associations between stimuli. Both views are attempts to explain the many kinds of learning in terms of a single process or only two processes.

Our concern here is not with explaining learning but with describing it.[2] Accordingly, we have listed seven kinds of learning along an evolutionary continuum (see Figure 12.4). The seven varieties can be distinguished on the basis of the task that confronts the learner and how the task is mastered.

There is of course nothing fundamental about the number *seven.* The list might be extended by making habituation and sensitization two separate varieties; or it might be condensed by grouping simple and complex instrumental conditioning. The rationale for these seven varieties of learning lies in the criteria listed in Table 12.1. Each kind of learning differs from every other kind in at least one of the following: the role of the learner,

whether there is one response or a chain of responses, whether there is a delay or detour, the stimulus properties attended to, whether the learning is direct or vicarious, and whether it involves a sign or a symbol.

The placement of the seven varieties of learning on an evolutionary continuum is speculative. Comparative data on learning are sparse and difficult to obtain. Species differ from one another in dominant sense, preferred response, type of nervous system and ecological niche. Thus it would be a mistake to use a visual stimulus to compare learning in rats and birds; smell is the primary sense in rats, vision in birds. In the face of such obstacles to comparison, some psychologists have despaired of ever obtaining truly comparative data on learning (Hodos & Campbell, 1969). But this conclusion seems unduly pessimistic, for it is possible to compare learning across species, taking account of dominant senses and responses. It is important, moreover, to ignore differences in nervous systems and ecological niches. When comparing animals' ability to learn, the basic

---

[2] *Explanations will be discussed in subsequent chapters, as the various kinds of learning are described.*

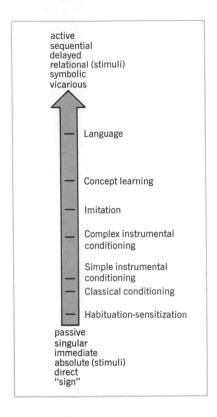

active
sequential
delayed
relational (stimuli)
symbolic
vicarious

— Language

— Concept learning

— Imitation

— Complex instrumental
conditioning

Simple instrumental
conditioning
— Classical conditioning

— Habituation-sensitization

passive
singular
immediate
absolute (stimuli)
direct
"sign"

Figure 12.4 *Evolutionary continuum of learning.*

issues are whether the animal learns and how easily, not whether the particular learning is adaptive to the animal's special environment. As we noted when discussing preadaptation (see Chapter 3), any given adaption to one environment may preadapt the animal to a new environment. Thus when an animal possesses a particular nervous system, the animal may be capable of far greater learning than it shows in the wild. Man has trained animals to do things their species has never done before—for example, a chimpanzee communicating by sign language (see Chapter 28).

A final point about comparative learning concerns available knowledge. Though details are lacking, we do possess *general* knowledge about animal's learning capacities. Thus at the primitive end of the evolutionary continuum, even single-celled animals habituate, but they certainly show no concept learning. The linking of responses into sequences occurs in more advanced animals, as do relational and vicarious learning. In brief,

there appears to be sufficient knowledge to sustain the evolutionary continuum diagramed in Figure 12.4.

The remainder of the chapter consists of a description of the varieties of learning. Habituation and sensitization will be more fully described and not discussed subsequently. The other six kinds will be mentioned briefly and discussed more fully in subsequent chapters.

Habituation and Sensitization

Habituation

A basic task for all animals is to distinguish between harmful and innocuous stimuli. Small, weak animals—being the prey of larger, stronger animals—must react quickly in escaping from danger or they become another animal's dinner. Their survival is aided by the innate tendency to flee from any sudden stimulus, but they must learn that not all sudden stimuli are dangerous. We mentioned earlier that young turkeys scramble for safety when any stimulus moves swiftly overhead, but their escape response gradually wanes (see Chapter 8); this is an example of habituation.

Habituation may be defined as *the waning and eventual disappearance of a natural response to a stimulus.* We use the term *natural* to indicate that the response is either an innate reaction or a strong tendency learned early in life. The adaptiveness of habituation is clear: the animal learns not to react to insignificant stimuli. No organism can afford to waste time and energy on trivial events in the environment, and excessive attention to phantom dangers renders the animal less able to discern real threats.

The disappearance of reactions to inconsequential stimuli may be seen in the very simplest organism. Penard (1948) has offered a naturalistic account of habituation in an Infusorian, a single-celled, microscopic organism:

I began to knock the table on which my microscope was standing and the animal at once shot back into its shell, but almost immediately stretched out again. I knocked again; in it went and then came out; and for a long while I continued repeating the experiment. But—and this is the important point—little by little its responses lost their intensity, until finally they ceased altogether, and the animal remained extended quite undisturbed by what I was doing. (1948, PP. 43–44.)

This example illustrates how an animal's self-protective reactions are turned off when experience reveals the stimuli to be harmless. Such learning evidently occurs throughout the entire phyletic spectrum; it is universal, extending from the most primitive creatures to man. The city man can sleep undisturbed by the raucous clanging of traffic noises, and the farmer can sleep peacefully through the sudden cries of wild animals. Each has stopped responding to the harmless and trivial sounds of his environment by the same process of habituation used by the single-celled infusorian.

Like all learning, habituation must be distinguished from fatigue and sensory adaptation; the major basis is *time*. Habituation is an enduring change in the organism. Fatigue is a temporary state that is soon reversed by rest and the mobilization of energy reserves. Similarly, changes in sensory organs are transient and soon reversed. The problem of isolating habituation from both fatigue and sensory adaptation occurs mainly in higher animals with specialized receptors and an advanced nervous system.

The practical reasons for distinguishing between habituation and sensory accommodation are obvious; for a fairly rapid recovery from stimulation to be ready to respond again is a sine qua non *for efficient sense-organ function. An eye or a nose which remained insensitive to stimulation on Tuesday because it was exposed to it on Monday is either an exceedingly inefficient organ or else it has been overstimulated to such an extent that we can say it has been injured. And so we take it for granted, as a general rule, that the long-maintained waning of response as a result of stimulation must be a kind of learning, and we assume that it is correlated with a change in the central nervous system, not merely with one in the sense organ.* (THORPE, 1956, P. 55.)

Sensitization

Sensitization is precisely the opposite of habituation, and all the properties of habituation apply in reverse to sensitization. In habituation an animal learns not to respond to trivial stimuli; in sensitization an animal learns to respond to weak or ineffectual stimuli as though they were harmful.

To demonstrate sensitization, it is necessary to establish that a neutral stimulus comes to elicit a fear or escape response without any specific training. Grether (1938) did this with monkeys (see Figure 12.5). First he tested them with a bell and found that the sound evoked no special response. Then he frightened the monkeys 10 times with a powder flash or a toy snake that popped out of a box. The animals reacted by jumping backward, struggling, and vocalizing their anguish. Subsequently, the sound of the bell alone elicited the same fear reaction in the absence of the frightening stimuli. Note that the bell and the frightening stimuli were never presented together, which means that this is *nonassociative learning.* Both habituation and sensitization are nonassociative, whereas all higher forms of learning are as-

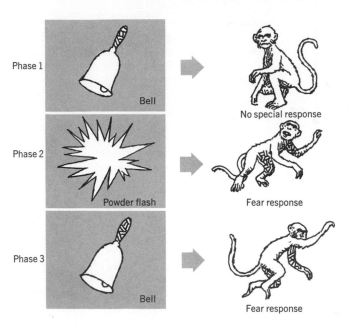

Phase 1	Bell
	No special response
Phase 2	Powder flash
	Fear response
Phase 3	Bell
	Fear response

Figure 12.5 Sensitization in monkeys (Grether, 1938).

sociative: one stimulus is linked to another stimulus or to a response.

Sensitization has been demonstrated with animals throughout the vertebrate series, including humans, primates, cats, and goldfish (see Kimble, 1961, p. 61). Sensitization surely occurs in invertebrates, and there is suggestive evidence of its presence in one-celled animals (Mast & Pusch, 1924). When a process occurs in so broad a range of animals, it must be adaptive, though at first glance sensitization might not appear adaptive. After being exposed to a threatening or harmful stimulus several times, the animal comes to respond to innocuous stimuli as though they were harmful, and in the short run this waste of the animal's time and energy is certainly maladaptive. In larger perspective, however, such sensitization undoubtedly keeps the animal alive longer. When it is repeatedly threatened with danger, the animal *should* react with excessive wariness and caution. The continued or repeated presence of harmful stimuli establishes a temporary tendency to be frightened by and to escape from *any* stimulus. After repeated doses of danger, the animal needs to err on the side of caution; such wariness and suspiciousness is surely adaptive in that it forestalls any further exposure to harm.

Of course the effects of sensitization are not necessarily permanent. Continued presentation of harmless stimuli may elicit less and less intense escape behavior until finally there is no escape response at all (Harris, 1941). This waning of the response is precisely the opposite of sensitization, and the reader should recognize it as habituation.

Both habituation and sensitization are primitive forms of learning: the learner *passively* receives stimuli and makes a *single, immediate* response to the *absolute* properties of the stimulus. The two processes are so primitive that some psychologists refuse to consider them as learning, preferring to limit learning to *associative* processes. Nevertheless, virtually all definitions of learning would include habituation and sensitization, and their nonassociative nature seems to be an arbitrary basis for exclusion.

A Neural Theory of Habituation and Sensitization

The phenomena of habituation and sensitization have been related to the vertical organization of the nervous system (Chapter 5). This organization differentiates between two neural pathways (review Figure 5.14). One pathway of impulses to and from the brain is *direct* and quick; the message gets through fast enough for a rapid response. The other pathway is *circuitous* and slow; the message spreads to various parts of the nervous system, and the level of arousal is elevated.

Groves and Thompson (1970) have formulated a theory that links habituation with the *direct* pathway and sensitization with the *circuitous* pathway. They assume that any effective stimulus excites both neural pathways. Stimuli of low or medium intensity excite the *direct* pathway, and the outcome is a response—usually an orienting response. Repetition of such stimuli causes a *decrease* in neural impulses in the direct pathway, and the behavioral response wanes; this, of course, is habituation.

High-intensity stimuli are assumed to excite the *circuitous* pathway, causing arousal. Mere presentation of such stimuli causes sufficiently strong arousal to elicit a withdrawal response; this, of course, is sensitization.

Sensitization and habituation are opposite processes: one diminishes responses to stimuli and the other enhances responses to stimuli. The theory suggests that they both influence behavioral output:

The two processes of habituation and sensitization occur and develop independently of one another but interact to yield the final response output function. Habituation may be primarily "phasic" in its action on response output, while sensitization may be primarily "tonic." (GROVES & THOMPSON, 1970, P. 441.)

Other Kinds of Learning

Classical Conditioning

The first step in classical conditioning is to start with a reflex such as the pupillary reflex (the pupil of the eye contracts when exposed to an increase in light) or the salivary reflex (the salivary glands secrete when food is placed in the mouth). Reflexive behavior is so constant and dependable that the stimulus can be said to elicit the behavior. The second step is to add a neutral stimulus that does not elicit the response. When this neutral stimulus is paired with the eliciting stimulus, it eventually comes to evoke the reflexive response even when the eliciting stimulus is absent. The original experiments occurred in the laboratory of Ivan Pavlov, the great Russian physiologist, in the latter part of the nineteenth century. Pavlov's experiments *defined* this kind of learning, hence the term *classical* conditioning.

Research Report

Pavlov's subjects were dogs, and the response was reflex salivation. Each dog was placed in an isolated room and restrained by a harness (see Figure 12.6). The isolated room insured control over extraneous stimuli such as noises, lights, the presence of the experimenter, and any other stimuli that might disturb the conditioning process. The recording of salivation presents a special problem. The experimenter cannot simply catch the saliva as the dog drools, and Pavlov's solution was to displace surgically the parotid salivary gland to the outside of the dog's cheek. Then he inserted a tube into the gland, which allowed him to collect and measure the amount of saliva secreted.

When meat powder is placed in a dog's mouth, the dog salivates. Pavlov called the meat powder the *unconditional stimulus* and the salivation, the *unconditional response*. (When these terms were translated into English, they somehow became *unconditioned stimulus* and *unconditioned response,* and this is prevalent usage.) Normally, a dog will *not* salivate when a tone is sounded, though it will turn its head and cock its ears. The conditioning procedure consists of presenting

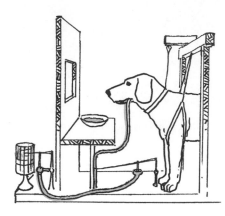

Figure 12.6 Experimental arrangement for conditioning of salivary response.

the tone and the meat powder together at approximately the same time. After repeated pairings of these two stimuli the tone alone comes to elicit the salivation. The tone is called the *conditioned stimulus* and the response to it, the *conditioned response.* The three stages in the conditioning sequence are diagramed in Figure 12.7. The conditioned stimulus initially elicits only an orienting response,[3] but during training when the unconditioned and conditioned stimuli are paired, the orienting response habituates and eventually disappears. After training the conditioned stimulus alone elicits the contioned response, which is not identical to the unconditioned response (a point we shall discuss later).

As training proceeds, the conditioned response becomes stronger—more drops of saliva are secreted. Periodically, the unconditioned stimulus is omitted in order to measure the conditioned response, and the course of its development may be plotted over trials, as in Figure 12.8.

[3] *An orienting response is simply paying attention: the dog cocks its ears, turns its head, and looks for the source of the stimulus (see Chapter 6).*

Classical conditioning is a higher form of learning than habituation or sensitization in that it is associative: two stimuli are paired in time so that one becomes a signal for the other. Nevertheless, classical conditioning is relatively low on the evolutionary continuum. The learner is *passive,* reacting *directly* to the *absolute* properties of a stimulus with a *single* response.

Simple Instrumental Conditioning

It is no more than a truism that man seeks rewards and avoids punishments. When a person is

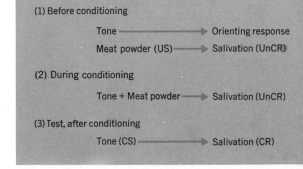

(1) Before conditioning

Tone ⟶ Orienting response

Meat powder (US) ⟶ Salivation (UnCR)

(2) During conditioning

Tone + Meat powder ⟶ Salivation (UnCR)

(3) Test, after conditioning

Tone (CS) ⟶ Salivation (CR)

Figure 12.7 Three stages of salivary conditioning.

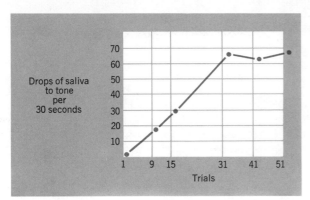

Figure 12.8 Acquisition of the conditioned salivary responses to a tone (Anrep, 1920).

confronted with a particular goal, he tries first one and then another response until eventually one succeeds in attaining the goal; successful responses are then more likely to occur in the future. The entire process of response selection and strengthening is called instrumental conditioning.

Simple instrumental conditioning has been investigated in the laboratory for almost a century as trial-and-error learning. Thorndike (1898) put a hungry cat inside a cage and placed food just outside. The cat had to learn to release a latch to escape from the cage and reach the food. A simpler version of this puzzle box (see Figure 12.9) was later developed by Guthrie and Horton (1946), who made it the basis of an entire theory of learning.

The process of learning can be studied more precisely if the animal chooses between two or more clearly distinguishable choices, and therefore the invention of the jumping stand by Lashley (1930) was an important advance (see Figure 12.10). A hungry rat is placed on a platform; to obtain food it must jump at one of two stimuli. If the jump is toward the correct card, it falls backward, and the rat lands behind it on a feeding platform. If the jump is toward the incorrect card, the rat falls into the net below.

The puzzle box and the jumping stand were designed to discover the course of learning. As the animal learns, it makes the correct response quicker (puzzle box) or it makes fewer errors (jumping stand). These measures are ordinarily plotted against trials (see Figure 12.11). Early in learning the animal makes many mistakes or requires considerable time to make the correct response. As learning progresses, the correct response is made faster or the errors drop to zero or near zero; the learning curve is a quantitative measure of this progress.

Instrumental conditioning involves response se-

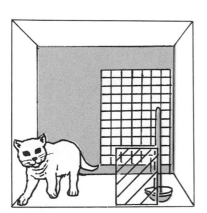

Figure 12.9 Puzzle box for cats (Guthrie and Horton, 1946).

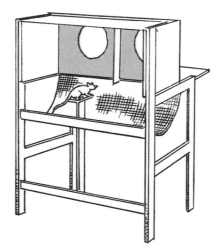

Figure 12.10 Lashley jumping stand.

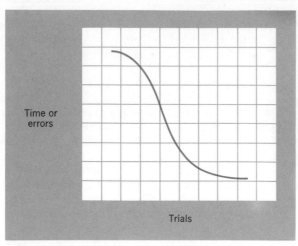

Figure 12.11 Typical learning curve.

lection: the response that leads to a reward (or escapes confinement) is strengthened. This kind of learning is higher than habituation, sensitization, and classical conditioning in that the learner *actively* attempts to solve the task.

Complex Instrumental Conditioning

Complex instrumental conditioning differs from the simple variety in three ways:

1. It involves chains of responses.
2. It involves a delay or detour.
3. The response is to relationships rather than to absolute properties of stimuli.

Examples of two of the three characteristics have been given earlier, and they need to be mentioned only briefly here. The chaining of responses into a sequence is illustrated by the remarkable feats of the rat Barnabus (see Figure 12.2). The learning of relationships among stimuli is illustrated by learning to respond to stimuli as *larger than, brighter than, louder than,* and so on.

A *detour* problem is complex in that the learner must move circuitously toward the goal. A typical task is shown in Figure 12.12. Two bowls are placed behind a slit in a large screen, and the hungry animal eats from the bowl containing food. Then both bowls are quickly moved, one to the left and the other to the right, so that they are no longer seen. The animal must learn to move around the screen on the side of the food bowl. The detour aspects add sufficient complexity to make the task difficult for lower animals, and there is a clear progression from rabbits to cats to dogs in ability to solve this problem (Stettner & Matyniak, 1968).

Imitation Learning

Imitation learning is classified as a higher form of learning because it is vicarious rather than direct. It is not important in the learning of animals lower than primates, but such animals do learn by imitation. One-day old chicks, for example, show evi-

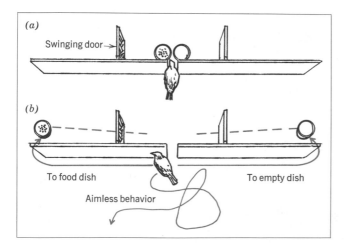

Figure 12.12 The detour problem.

Figure 12.13 How chick observes a mechanical hen pick at grains of food (Turner, 1964).

dence of imitation. Turner (1964) used a mechanical hen as a model when real hens proved to be unreliable at pecking grains of food. Half the chicks saw the mechanical hen peck green grain; the other half, orange grain (the two colors are equally preferred). The chicks were separated from the hen by a wire mesh barrier (see Figure 12.13). Subsequently, the chicks were given access to grains of various colors. They chose grains of the same color as did the mechanical hen roughly two thirds of the time, a preference obviously caused by imitation.

Concept Learning

Concept learning is essentially a special case of relational learning. The simplest relationships, such as *larger than,* seem merely to be forms of perceptual learning, and the term *concept* is conventionally reserved for more abstract relationships. A good example may be found in oddity problems (see Figure 12.3). To select the odd stimulus, the learner must continually compare all three stimuli. An individual stimulus may have many properties (shape, color, size, and so on), but oddity is not one of them. It is not a concrete property of a stimulus but an abstract property involving a relationship among stimuli.

Concept learning involves classifying stimuli on the basis of one or more characteristics and treating all stimuli with such characteristics as the same. This definition includes some of the simpler relationships that fall under the heading of perceptual learning. Thus there is a continuum from simple concrete relationships to complex abstract ones. The latter part of the dimension (the higher

end) is ordinarily reserved for the term *concept,* but the dividing line is arbitrary, varying from one psychologist to the next.

Our interest being in an evolutionary continuum of learning, we shall make the cut-off high. This tactic emphasizes the abstract aspects of concepts and places concept learning at the upper end of the evolutionary scale.

Language

Language, which is unique to man, has two major aspects, words and the rules that govern sequences of words.[4] Words *refer to* objects, events, and places, which means that the acquisition of words is *symbol* learning. Though not all words are symbols (that is, represent real stimuli), most of them are.

In all languages, words are spoken in sequence. There are far too many possible sequences of words for them to be learned by rote. Instead the sequences of words that add meaning to language are governed by rules. Rule learning involves concept learning (classifying words as nouns or verbs), relationships (as between a noun and the adjective that modifies it), and the chaining of sequential responses.

A few higher animals can acquire simple symbols and rudimentary rules, but the abstract symbols and complex rules that underlie language appear to be the exclusive province of man.

*   *   *

We have aligned the varieties of learning on an evolutionary continuum, and the next seven chapters will follow this sequence (see Table 12.2). Habituation and sensitization — the only kinds of learning that do not involve the association of stimuli or responses — have been discussed in this chapter. Classical conditioning, which may be regarded as the substitution of one stimulus for another — will be discussed in the next chapter. Simple instrumental conditioning is covered in two chapters: Chapter 14 deals with the

---

[4] *This sketchy account cannot do justice to these issues. A fuller discussion appears in Chapter 18.*

Table 12.2
Topics of Learning

TOPIC	TYPE OF LEARNING	CHAPTER
Habituation	Nonassociative learning	12
Sensitization	Nonassociative learning	12
Classical conditioning	Stimulus substitution	13
Simple instrumental conditioning	Response selection	14,15
Complex instrumental conditioning	Response selection and rule learning	16
Imitation	Vicarious learning	16
Concepts	Cognitive learning	17
Language	Cognitive learning	18
Memory	All types of learning	19

positive consequences that facilitate behavior, and Chapter 15 deals with the negative consequences that inhibit behavior. Chapter 16 deals with both complex instrumental conditioning and imitation. These types of learning are claimed by both stimulus-response theorists and cognitive theorists.

The remaining three chapters that concern learning (Chapters 17, 18, and 19) comprise the section labeled *cognition.* Concept learning (Chapter 17) shades into thinking and problem solving, and language learning (Chapter 18) is a complex combination of imitation and rule-learning. Finally, memory (Chapter 19), which involves all the varieties of learning, will be discussed in the context of information processing.

chapter 13

classical conditioning

Conditioned flexion — interoceptive condition-
ing — time relationships — adaptive signif-
icance — extinction — higher order condition-
ing — discrimination — stimulus generalization
— the principle of association — emotional
conditioning — conditioning of meaning

Classical conditioning is essentially *sign learning,* and this process accounts for many of the signals of everyday life. Students begin and end classes at the signal of a bell, and a howling siren is the signal for danger or an emergency. Many Londoners who survived the bombing of their city during World War II continued to react with anxiety to the sound of a siren (air raid signal) for many years afterward.

Moods and emotional meanings can also be classically conditioned. Thus slow, lilting music may induce a romantic mood; fast, pulsating music, a mood of excitement; and the college song, a mood of sentimental attachment. Virtually all schoolchildren are taught to revere the flag, and the conditioning is so strong in many adults that they react violently to any disrespect to Old Glory. In brief, classical conditioning accounts for some of our strongest "gut reactions."

Classical conditioning involves the pairing of a neutral stimulus with an unconditioned stimulus until the former comes to substitute for the latter in eliciting a response. The first response to be conditioned by Pavlov was the salivary reflex (see Chapter 12). He and other Russian researchers subsequently studied two other kinds, conditioned flexion and interoceptive conditioning.

Conditioned Flexion

One of Pavlov's contemporaries, Bekterev, originated another kind of classical conditioning—conditioned flexion. He used electric shock as an
unconditioned stimulus and studied the unconditioned withdrawal response of men and animals.
This response consists of flexing the muscles of
the limb so that it retracts from the source of the
pain. In all other respects the procedure is the
same as that used in conditioned salivation. A conditioned stimulus (say, a tone) is paired with electric shock (see Figure 13.1), and initially the tone
elicits an orienting response but not flexion. After
being paired consistently with electric shock, the
tone comes to elicit a flexion response, which is
not identical to the original, unconditioned
response. The conditioned flexion response appears to be a preparatory response, and it does not
possess all the properties of the full-fledged unconditioned withdrawal response to electric shock.

Interoceptive Conditioning

Russian psychology, being Pavlovian in orientation, has emphasized classical conditioning
much more than American psychology has, and
the outcome has been some intriguing research.
Some of the most interesting Russian conditioning
experiments have used stimuli delivered inside
the body. This is called *interoceptive conditioning,*
a procedure that employs an internal stimulus as
either the conditioned or the unconditioned stimulus. Razran (1961) is a major source of information about this research.

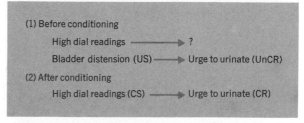

Figure 13.2 Conditioning the urge to urinate to dial readings.

In one experiment the subjects were three patients with urinary bladder fistulas that allowed
access to the bladder from the outside of the
body. Air or fluids could be pumped into the
bladder, thereby distending it; such distension is a
well-known unconditioned stimulus for the urinary
excretion response. Bladder pressure was measured and could be seen on a dial in front of the
subject. Each time the bladder was filled, the dial
reading showed it and the subject had an urge to
urinate. Then the dial was disconnected and,
without the subject's knowledge, controlled by the
experimenter. Subsequently, the dial readings
were manipulated, and the readings seen by the
subject were not related to the fullness of his
bladder. The conditioning process consisted of
first pairing the dial readings with bladder distension and then checking to see whether dial
readings alone would elicit the urge to urinate (see
Figure 13.2).

All subjects conditioned easily. When the
bladder was empty or almost empty but the dial
registered a high reading, each subject reported
an intense urge to urinate. On the other hand,
when the bladder contained more than a normal
amount of fluid but the dial registered low or
empty, the subjects would report no urge to
urinate, nor would they urinate.

The urinary response is only one of a large
number of internal responses conditioned by Russian researchers in both humans and animals. Except for the urge to urinate, the subjects have
been unaware that the responses were occurring.
For example, both constriction and dilation of
blood vessels have been conditioned in man
without the subjects being conscious of these
responses even occurring.

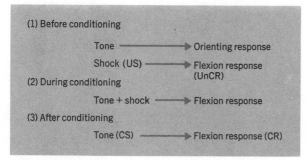

Figure 13.1 Three phases of flexion conditioning.

Time Relationships

In classical conditioning the conditioned stimulus precedes the unconditioned stimulus, and, as with most sequential events, the time relations between these two stimuli are crucial. Conditioning is fastest when the conditioned stimulus is followed almost immediately by the unconditioned stimulus. The optimal interval is 0.5 to 2.0 seconds, depending on the species. The best interval in man is about half a second, which is approximately the optimal interval between the warning stimulus and the signal to respond in a reaction time experiment. Half a second is also roughly the time estimated for the reticular formation to alert the cerebral cortex to its optimal level of arousal for acting on incoming stimuli. All these time relations suggest that the conditioned stimulus acts as a signal that prepares the organism for the oncoming unconditioned stimulus.

At intervals slower than half a second or greater than two seconds, conditioning is slower. In terms of the time interval between the conditioned and unconditioned stimuli, there are three possibilities: simultaneous, delayed, and trace conditioning (see Figure 13.3).
SIMULTANEOUS CONDITIONING. The conditioned and unconditioned stimuli start and end *at the same time,* but very little conditioning results

from this procedure. At very short intervals, say 0.1 or 0.2 seconds, conditioning is slow but more efficient; as the interval approaches half a second, the conditioning becomes faster and more efficient.
DELAYED CONDITIONING. The conditioned stimulus starts *10 seconds or more* before the unconditioned stimulus. When the conditioned response first appears, it occurs immediately after the onset of the conditioned stimulus, but eventually it is delayed until just prior to the onset of the unconditioned stimulus.
TRACE CONDITIONING. The conditioned stimulus *starts and terminates* before the onset of the unconditioned stimulus. Presumably, the response is conditioned to the *neural trace*[1] of the conditioned stimulus, hence the name *trace conditioning.* Trace conditioning has been unequivocally demonstrated only with mammals. This makes sense when we realize that this kind of conditioning requires neural mediation, so that the organism can respond to a stimulus that is no longer present. Only organisms with advanced nervous systems (mammals, for example) can "hold" a stimulus and respond to it after it has terminated.
BACKWARD CONDITIONING. This time relation requires brief mention. In backward conditioning, the unconditioned stimulus *precedes* the conditioned stimulus. Only a few investigators have claimed to obtain this kind of conditioning and then only with great difficulty. Most researchers believe that backward conditioning cannot be achieved, and there is no adaptive function for such an arrangement.

Adaptive Significance

Classical conditioning has been demonstrated virtually throughout the entire animal kingdom, from the lowest form to man. It has been claimed that the one-celled paramecium can be conditioned, but the issue is still being debated. The lowest animal for which there is unequivocal evidence of

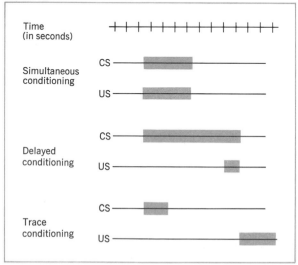

Figure 13.3 *Time relations in classical conditioning.*

---

[1] *The neural trace is inferred from the fact that trace conditioning occurs and from certain facts about the nervous system. For example, stimuli are believed to excite the circuitous, slow neural pathway to the brain (see Chapters and 12).*

conditioning is the flatworm *Planaria,* which has a simple ladderlike central nervous system. If conditioning were merely the passive accompaniment of other adaptive traits, it would be seen in only a few animals. That it occurs in such a broad range of animals attests to its adaptive significance.

The nature of the conditioned response is basic to its adaptive significance. The conditioned response is usually not the same as the unconditioned response. Though there is a close resemblance between the two in salivary conditioning, the conditioned response involves less salivation and does not possess several properties that are part of unconditioned salivation (chewing, swallowing, and so on). The difference between the two responses is clearer in flexion conditioning, in which the conditioned response occurs before the unconditioned response (see Figure 13.4). Note that the conditioned response is weaker than the unconditioned response, which suggests that it represents a half-hearted attempt to avoid the oncoming shock.

In the wild, the animal's struggles to avoid the oncoming harmful stimulus might succeed. The researcher does not allow this to occur in the laboratory, where the animal always receives the unavoidable shock. In everyday life the animal would attempt to avoid the oncoming aversive stimulus, and it would probably succeed. The point is that the conditioned response prepares the animal for an imminent stimulus:

I prefer to think of classical conditioning as particularly appropriate to setting up preparatory responses. This leads to a theory of stimulus substitution in the sense that Pavlov meant it; that is, signalizing, which is fundamentally S-S (stimulus-stimulus) learning. Thus I am arguing for S-S learning, but sophisticated to the extent that in avoidance conditioning for example, the conditioned stimulus stands for "shock-about-to-come," so that the animal makes all sorts of responses which are more or less appropriate in Nature for shock-about-to-come.

(SCHLOSBERG, QUOTED IN KIMBLE, 1961, P. 99.)

This interpretation assumes that classical conditioning is the means by which the animal learns the important signs in its environment. Some of these are stimuli associated with harmful or noxious events: the pain delivered by a predator, a rival, or an experimenter in the laboratory. In na-

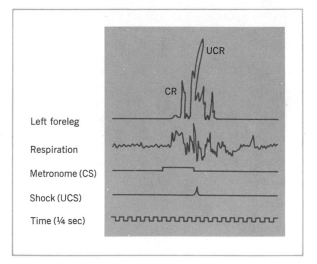

Figure 13.4 Occurrence of conditioned and unconditioned flexion response (Liddell, 1934).

ture the animal learns to associate pain or an uncomfortable state with accompanying neutral stimuli (the conditioned stimuli). Thereafter these conditioned stimuli signify that a harmful event is imminent. For example, when an animal is attacked or threatened in a specific locale, the animal quickly learns to avoid that locale.

Other conditioned stimuli are associated with benign events, as in salivary conditioning. Here the animal learns the stimuli that signify the availability of food and prepares to eat. Previously neutral stimuli come to be valued because of their association with rewarding stimuli. In brief, whether the neutral stimuli are associated with an oncoming positive or negative event, they are *signs* that serve to prepare the animal for what is about to happen (the unconditioned stimulus).

This interpretation of classical conditioning is called *preparatory response* theory (Perkins, 1955; 1968). The theory predicts that when an aversive event (such as electric shock) is unavoidable, subjects prefer to be warned. This prediction has been corroborated many times (see Badia et al., 1967, for example). A preparatory signal (conditioned stimulus) should enhance the attractiveness of forthcoming positive events (unconditioned stimuli). This expectation was confirmed in an experiment on the attractiveness of pictures of women (Wiegal & Rodwan, 1970). The male subjects were either warned before a picture appeared or not warned. The presence of a warning (conditioned) stimulus resulted in the pictures being judged as more attractive. In addition, the longer the duration of the conditioned stimulus (up to 10 seconds), the more attractive the pictures became.

The more time between the signal and the subsequent event, the better the animal can prepare for the event, and this is of special importance when the event is noxious or potentially harmful. Longer preparation time requires a longer interval between the conditioned and the unconditioned stimulus, such as occurs in either delayed or trace conditioning, both of which require a nervous system that can maintain excitation after the stimulus has ceased to act. As we noted earlier, such nervous systems occur mainly in higher animals. Such animals have more time to prepare for oncoming events, which means that they can employ strategy and tactics instead of only reflexes.

Extinction

So long as the conditioned and unconditioned stimuli are paired, the conditioned response is likely to occur, but if the conditioned stimulus is presented repeatedly without the unconditioned stimulus, the conditioned response gradually wanes (see Figure 13.5). The process is called *extinction,* and it continues until there is no longer any conditioned response.

When the organism no longer responds to the conditioned stimulus, it might appear that the effects of the conditioning process are entirely wiped out, but they are not. After a day's rest the conditioned response reappears, though it is weaker. This phenomenon is called *spontaneous recovery.*[2] It may require repeated extinctions to eliminate all the effects of the original conditioning (see Figure 13.5).

Like acquisition, extinction serves an adaptive function. During conditioning the organism learns that a sign (the conditioned stimulus) stands for something (the unconditioned stimulus), and it can prepare for the oncoming event. As time passes, the sign may lose its meaning; that is, the unconditioned stimulus will no longer follow the conditioned stimulus. When the sign is no longer valid, the animal must unlearn its previous conditioning because obviously it is not adaptive to prepare for an event that will not occur. Thus extinction is one of a number of learning mechanisms that allow flexible responding in the face of a changing environment.

Higher Order Conditioning

An unconditioned stimulus is usually part of a stimulus-response reflexive unit that is pro-

[2] *Spontaneous recovery tells us that extinction is not mere forgetting but a disruption of the association between th conditioned stimulus and the unconditioned stimulus. "forgotten" conditioned response would not spontaneous recover.*

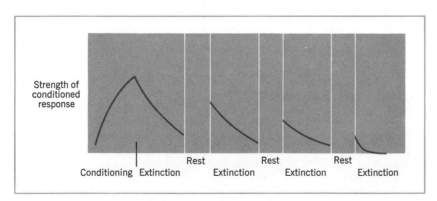

Figure 13.5 Successive extinctions (schematic).

gramed in the nervous system, but this is not always the case. Some unconditioned stimuli are themselves the products of the conditioning process. We have seen how training can convert a neutral stimulus into one that elicits a conditioned response. If the training proceeds far enough, the conditioned stimulus may guarantee that the conditioned response occurs. Any stimulus that can accomplish this can serve as an unconditioned stimulus.

Consider flexion conditioning. First, a tone is paired with electric shock until eventually the tone elicits a conditioned flexion response. Then a light is paired with the tone, omitting the electric shock. The light, through its association with the tone, will eventually elicit the conditioned flexion response, and this is called *higher order conditioning*. It consists of using a previously conditioned stimulus (the tone) as an unconditioned stimulus with which a new, neutral stimulus (the light) can be paired to obtain another conditioned stimulus (see Figure 13.6).

First-order conditioning is nothing more than the process of conditioning we have been describing all along. *Second-order conditioning* consists of using the conditioned stimulus from first-order conditioning as the unconditioned stimulus in a subsequent conditioning procedure. Pavlov has demonstrated third-order conditioning, but it is extremely difficult to obtain.

Higher order conditioning is difficult to accomplish because of the ever present problem of extinction. When the conditioned stimulus is presented without the unconditioned stimulus, the conditioned response extinguishes. Thus, in our example, when the light and the tone are paired, the conditioned response to the tone weakens

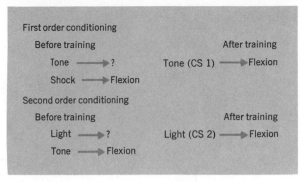

Figure 13.6 Higher order conditioning.

because the original unconditioned stimulus (shock) is absent. This tendency can be counteracted by interspersing trials of first-order conditioning (pairing of the tone with electric shock), thereby strengthening the original conditioned response. These difficulties in obtaining higher order conditioning underscore the limitations of classical conditioning: it cannot be separated very far from the unconditioned stimuli that comprise one half of the innately programed reflexive units.

Discrimination

Survival often involves a choice of alternative responses, and the ability to choose requires the ability to discriminate among objects and events in the environment. Such discrimination is easy to condition, even in so primitive an animal as the flatworm.

Research Report

Griffard and Peirce (1964) conditioned a discrimination in flatworms called *Planaria,* one of the most primitive species in which conditioning has been unequivocally demonstrated. The unconditioned stimulus was just enough electric shock to elicit a vigorous turning response. Planaria escape from such shock by turning away from the anode (positive pole), and in this experiment the source of the shock could be rotated so that it would elicit either a right or a left turn (see Figure 13.7).

Thus there were two unconditioned stimuli, one eliciting a right

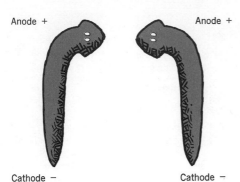

Anode +   Anode +

Cathode −   Cathode −

Figure 13.7 *Placement of poles elicits right or left turn in planaria.*

turn and the other a left turn. There were also two conditioned stimuli, a light and a buzzer. The light was paired with the anode placement for a right turn.[3] When the light shone, the correct response was a left turn; when the buzzer sounded, the correct response was a right turn. There were 200 training trials, with test trials interspersed (on test trails the unconditioned stimulus was omitted). The number of correct response rose steadily as training progressed (see Figure 13.8), furnishing clear evidence of conditioning. This is an important finding in light of a controversy over whether primitive organisms are capable of being conditioned. Some researchers have contended that creatures with so simple a nervous system are capable of sensitization but not conditioning. This contention has been answered in the best possible way, with data:

By conditioning two distinct and homologous responses to the two different CS's, we are in a position to measure learning in terms of both correct and incorrect responses, rather than simply measure the total number of responses. Though it is possible that the subjects of this study became sensitized or pseudoconditioned to the experimental stimuli, neither sensitization nor pseudoconditioning can account for the increasing divergence in the number of the correct and incorrect responses, since there is no way these can differentially affect the responses to the two CS's, and since an equal number of unconditioned turns had been made to each side.

(GRIFFARD & PEIRCE, 1964, P. 1473.)

[3] *This was the experimental setup for half the subjects. For the other half, it was exactly the opposite: light—right turn, and buzzer—left turn.*

Clearly, planaria can be conditioned, and they can distinguish between a light and a buzzer. In fact, such discrimination training is the way we discover whether an animal can discriminate among stimuli.Obviously, we cannot ask the animal, so we must see conditioning as a technique for discovering discriminability. For example, the question of whether a dog can discriminate between certain pitches of sound can be answered by flexion conditioning (Anrep, 1920). The unconditioned stimulus is electric shock, and the conditioned stimulus is a tone of 5000 Hz. After a sufficient number of trials with these two stimuli paired, this high-pitched tone comes to elicit a conditioned flexion response. The next step is to condition a discrimination. A tone of

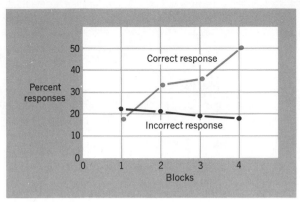

Figure 13.8 Conditioning of a discrimination in planaria (Griffard and Peirce, 1964).

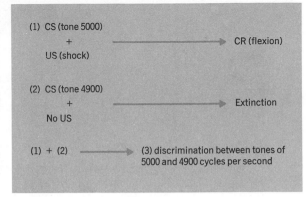

Figure 13.9 Conditioning with discrimination.

5000 Hz is still followed by the electric shock on half the trials, but on the remaining trials a lower tone (say, 4900 Hz) is presented and *not* followed by the shock (see Figure 13.9). This procedure leads to extinction of the conditioned response to the low tone while maintaining it to the high tone, and eventually the conditioned response is made only to the high tone. Having established that the dog can discriminate between tones of 4900 and 5000 Hz, the experimenter then narrows the difference between tones. The pitch of the lower of the two tones is raised higher until finally the animal cannot discriminate—that is, makes the conditioned response to both tones. The smallest difference in tones that yields a difference—presence versus absence of the conditioned response—reveals the limits of the dog's discriminability.

Such a procedure is typical of the way an animal's perceptual abilities are tested, whether it involves a planarian turning right or left, or a dog making or not making a conditioned leg flexion. The basic idea is that the animal makes a differential response, which tells us whether it can discriminate between the conditioned stimuli.

Generalization

Suppose a dog is conditioned to salivate to the sound of a high-pitched tone. When a tone of lower pitch is presented, the dog will still salivate but the response will be slower and weaker. The lower the

tone, the weaker is the conditioned response. Clearly, the conditioned response spreads from the conditioned stimulus to stimuli that have not been conditioned. The less similar these are to the conditioned stimulus, the weaker is the conditioned response. This phenomenon is called *stimulus generalization:* the spread of the conditioned response to stimuli similar to the conditioned stimulus.

An experiment by Bersh et al. (1956) illustrates how stimulus generalization is studied in humans. Mild electric shock tends to diminish heart rate by several beats per minute. If a tone is paired with the electric shock, the tone comes to elicit the drop in heart rate (see Figure 13.10). The tone used in this experiment was 1920 Hz. Once conditioning was established, generalization was tested with lower tones (1020, 480, and 180 Hz). A plot of the strength of the conditioned response (drop in heart rate) against the pitch of tones is shown in

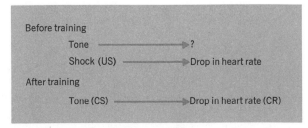

Figure 13.10 Conditioning of heart rate.

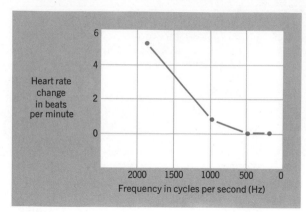

Figure 13.11. The strongest response is that to the
conditioned stimulus (1920 Hz), and the lower the
pitch of the tone, the weaker was the response.
This curve of responding, called the *gradient of
stimulus generalization,* is a quantitative statement of the waning of the conditioned response as
the stimuli become more dissimilar from the conditioned stimulus. The gradient in Figure 13.11
shows stimulus generalization only toward tones
of lower pitch, but generalization also occurs to
tones of higher pitch. When both directions are
used, and this is the usual procedure, stimulus
generalization gradients are bidirectional.

A conditioned response may generalize along
many different dimensions, such as pitch,
loudness, hue, brightness, and size. Animals can
generalize only along physical dimensions, but
man can generalize along dimensions of meaning,
as well. When a person responds in the same way
to words similar in meaning, it is called *semantic*
generalization, a phenomenon that has been demonstrated with many different responses. In one
experiment (Lang et al., 1963) the dimension was
intensity of hostility, and the words were high (*torture*), medium (*scolding*), low (*displeasure*), or
zero (*abstract*) in hostility. The unconditioned
stimulus, electric shock, elicited an unconditioned
response of a change in skin resistance (galvanic
skin response or GSR). The conditioning proceeded in the usual way, using high hostile words
as the conditioned stimuli (see Figure 13.12).

*Figure 13.11 Gradient of stimulus generalization
for the conditioned heart response in man (Bersh et
al., 1956).*

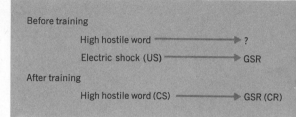

*Figure 13.12 Semantic conditioning of the galvanic
skin response.*

Then the subjects were tested with words that had
not yet been seen, words of medium, low, and zero
hostility, as well as the conditioned stimuli. The
result was a gradient of stimulus generalization
along the semantic dimension of hostility (see Figure 13.13). This gradient offers clear evidence that
a conditioned response (the GSR) does generalize
along a dimension of meaning. Most of the dimensions important to humans vary in meaning rather
than in physical characteristics.

The *adaptive function* of stimulus generalization
is to broaden the effects of conditioning so that a
response conditioned to specific stimuli can also
be elicited by similar stimuli without further
training. It is the exception rather than the rule
that stimuli repeat themselves identically in nature, and it would be maladaptive for an animal to
have to undergo new conditioning for each specific stimulus it might encounter.

Consider the meaning of a flashing red light at a
highway intersection. Previous conditioning has
established that it is a signal for danger, and we
have time to prepare for what might happen. But
flashing lights can be different in several ways: the
rate of flashing may vary, the red hue may be
more or less saturated, the red may tend more
toward the purple or the orange part of the spectrum, or the brightness of the lights may vary.
Regardless of the precise stimulus used in conditioning, our response will be the same to all of
these variations in flashing red lights. We behave
appropriately to the danger signal without further
training; that is, our response generalizes.

If a failure to generalize is maladaptive, so is its
opposite, excessive generalization. It would be
inappropriate to respond in the same way to *all*
the stimuli on a dimension after only a single stim-

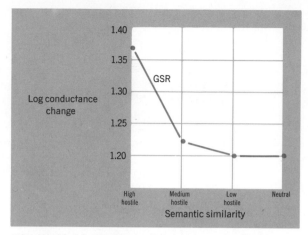

Figure 13.13 Gradient of semantic generalization (Lang et al., 1963).

ulus had been conditioned. This usually does not occur, and as we have seen there is a *gradient* of stimulus generalization: the conditioned response weakens as the stimuli are more dissimilar from the conditioned stimuli, and finally it disappears. In brief, though it is adaptive to generalize, such generalization must also have its limits.

It might be argued that an organism responds similarly to two different stimuli only because it cannot distinguish one from the other. If a dog is trained to salivate to a tone of 10,000 Hz, it will also salivate to a tone of 10,002 Hz because its ears can detect no difference between the two. This argument is true as far as it goes, and if the spread of response were limited only to stimuli too similar for the sensory apparatus to distinguish, there would be no need for the term *stimulus generalization.* However, both humans and animals generalize to stimuli that are easily discriminable. Certainly the words in the Lang et al. (1963) study were clearly distinguishable, yet the galvanic skin response generalized.

To avoid confusion, perhaps stimulus generalization should be defined as the spread of a conditioned response to stimuli that are *discriminably different* from the conditioned stimulus. The response spreads outward from the conditioned stimulus in two steps, as shown in Figure 13.14. The smallest circle (*A*) includes only the conditioned stimulus, which occupies a specific point on several stimulus dimensions; e.g., a tone has a

specific loudness, pitch, and timbre. The conditioned response is made not only to the conditioned stimulus but to stimuli so similar that the organism's sensory apparatus can detect no differences; these stimuli are represented by the next concentric circle (*B*). Stated another way, when the stimulus input is the same (for the organism), the response output is the same. Beyond these stimuli are the generalization stimuli of the last concentric circle (*C*). The organism's sensory apparatus can clearly distinguish these from the conditioned stimulus, but the conditioned response still occurs. Only these stimuli of the outermost circle are truly *generalization stimuli,* for the organism makes the conditioned response to them in spite of their sensed differences from the conditioned stimulus. Of course, the farther out from the center these stimuli are (the more dissimilar), the weaker is the conditioned response to them.

How do we know the limits of an animal's discriminability? We discover these by discrimination training (see Figure 13.9). With human subjects the task is easier, and we can derive fairly precise psychophysical functions, as we saw in Chapter 8.

The relationship between generalization and discrimination is usually reciprocal. When an animal has had only generalization training—conditioning with only a single stimulus—the conditioned response spreads over a broad range of stimuli, as represented by the outermost circle of Figure 13.14. Discrimination training cuts down

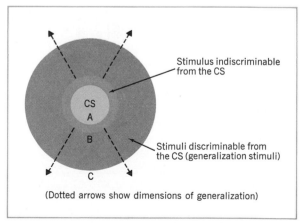

Figure 13.14 Hypothetical relations among stimuli.

this spread of response, constricting the outer-most circle. If discrimination training is carried out to the extreme, the outermost circle is squeezed down until it coincides with the middle circle. The animal manifests no generalization; it discriminates completely.

Association as a General Principle

Classical conditioning is based on the *association* of two stimuli that occur close together in time. The underlying assumption is that whenever *any* two stimuli occur together repeatedly, they will become linked. The learning does not require an immediate response, only repeated joint occur-rence of the stimuli.

The last point was demonstrated in an experi-ment on *sensory preconditioning* in dogs (Brogden, 1939). A bell and a light were presented simultaneously for 200 trials. Then the dogs were conditioned, using the bell as the conditioned stimulus and electric shock as the unconditioned stimulus (see Figure 13.15). Subsequently, the *light,* which had never been paired with shock, was presented. The dogs showed conditioned flexion to the light on a high proportion of trials. A control group, which had no prior pairing of the light and bell but which underwent flexion condi-

tioning, showed virtually no conditioned responses to the light.

Brogden's research shows that stimuli can be associated even in the absence of a specific response. Learning based on mere closeness in time is obviously very simple, and, as we noted in the last chapter, it occurs in very primitive an-imals. Some psychologists believe that this kind of learning, based on the association of stimuli, can explain more advanced and complex behaviors. They assume that classical conditioning is one of the basic building blocks, and that combinations of such conditioning can account for complex behavior all the way to the level of language.

Emotional Conditioning

In Chapter 4 we presented Thompson's scheme of developmental stages. The second stage was called *affective meaning,* in which generalized positive and negative attitudes were acquired through classical conditioning. The original experi-ment was conducted by Watson and Rayner (1920) on an eleven-month-old infant foundling named Albert. Albert had never seen a white rat or a rabbit, and when they were presented to him, he reached for them and seemed to like them. Then conditioning began (see Figure 13.16). When Al-

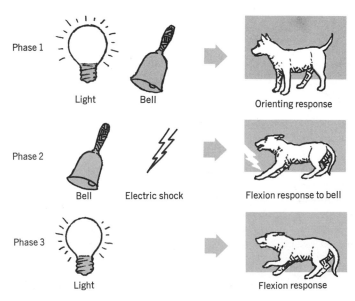

Figure 13.15 *Sensory precondi-tioning.*

Phase 1 — Light — Bell — Orienting response

Phase 2 — Bell — Electric shock — Flexion response to bell

Phase 3 — Light — Flexion response

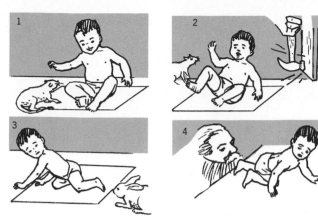

Figure 13.16 Conditioning fear in an infant.

bert reached for the rat, a loud noise startled him and he fell forward on his face. The next time the white rat was paired with the loud noise, Albert whimpered. After seven such pairings, the rat was presented without the noise. Albert's reaction was to cry and withdraw. Further testing revealed that the fear reaction had generalized to the rabbit, a cotton ball, and a variety of furry objects. Unfortunately, Albert was removed from the foundling hospital before his emotional response to furry objects could be extinguished.

Thus a strong emotional reaction was conditioned to a previously neutral stimulus, and this conditioned fear generalized. Two extrapolations followed from this research. First, it was widely assumed that the many fears of childhood are learned through classical conditioning. Second, it followed that positive and negative attitudes could easily be conditioned, a hypothesis that has proved to be correct. Pairing a neutral stimulus with a positive unconditioned stimulus (food) leads to a positive attitude; pairing it with a negative unconditioned stimulus (shock) leads to a negative attitude (Razran, 1954).

These experiments suggest that emotional reactions and attitudes may be acquired through classical conditioning. Undoubtedly some of our affective behavior is learned in this way, but it does not follow that *all* or even most of such behavior is acquired through simple associative learning. Some psychologists insist that classical conditioning nicely accounts for the learning of attitudes and emotions. Others, as we shall see, insist that considerable cognitive learning is involved.

Conditioning of Meaning

Most words are labels for objects and events. Classical conditioning has been used to explain how a word (the spoken sound) comes to refer to an object. Consider the word *doll*. Presumably a child develops several responses to the actual doll: holding it, playing with it, throwing it down, and so on. The sight of the doll may then be considered an unconditioned stimulus for these various responses. Now conditioning begins. Whenever the child holds the doll, the parents say the word *doll* and point to it. Repeated pairing of the doll (US) with the word *doll* (CS) should lead to a conditioned response. The word *doll* will not elicit the response of playing with the *doll*. Rather, it will elicit associations concerned with the *doll*: playing, holding, throwing, and so on.

This account of meaning requires an extension of classical conditioning concepts. An unconditioned response, which originally referred to a reflex, is now extended to such instrumental behavior as playing with a doll. Moreover, the conditioned response involves not an actual response, but an implicit meaning or association.

Many psychologists readily accept such stretching of classical conditioning concepts and find the explanation of meaning quite compelling. Others are uneasy with what they regard as the fast-and-loose shuffling of the definition of such terms as unconditioned response (a reflex *and* an instrumental response) and conditioned response (an overt response *and* an implicit, unseen "meaning" response). The larger question of language acquisition will be discussed in Chapter 18.

Thus classical conditioning has been used as a model for the acquisition of the meaning of words and of positive and negative attitudes. This approach assumes that higher, complex learning consists of simpler components. The complexity is attributed largely to higher order conditioning and the sequential chaining of responses. However, even adherents of this view do not suppose that classical conditioning can account for *all* of learned behavior. Instrumental conditioning is regarded as an equally important building block.

chapter 14

simple instrumental condition-
ing: positive consequences

*Trial-and-error learning — operant condition-
ing —acquisition and extinction —discrimination and generalization — the concept of
reinforcement — incentives — unconditioned
stimuli — information — types of learning —
primary and secondary reinforcers — pharmacological and electrical reinforcers —
magnitude and delay of reinforcement —
schedules of reinforcement — superstition —
autonomic conditioning*

If we had to select one topic of central concern to American psychologists in the 1940s and 1950s, it would be simple instrumental conditioning. They investigated learning in lower animals, mainly the white rat, in relatively simple situations. Their aim was to discover the basic laws of all learning by studying the simplest and presumably the most fundamental aspects of learning. It was implicitly assumed that the laws of learning a single response would hold for *all* responses. Some psychologists went so far as to assume that there is only one kind of learning, and that the apparently different types of learning are merely variations on a theme; this idea has very few adherents today.

During the two decades when learning was of predominant interest, several controversies arose from differences in theory. Is reinforcement necessary for learning to occur? Can learning occur without an overt response being made? Does the subject learn *where* to go or *which response* to make?[1] These questions have either been

---

[1] *These questions can be answered briefly but simplistically. Whether reinforcement is necessary for learning to occur depends on how both reinforcement and learning are defined. Learning can occur without an overt response being made. Subjects learn where to go or which response to make—depending on how they are trained.*

answered with data or simply dropped as being untestable. They are now part of the history of the field (see Hilgard & Bower, 1966; Kimble, 1961) and will not be discussed here.

Instrumental learning includes both trial-and-error learning and operant conditioning. Trial-and-error learning involves tasks such as the puzzle box, the maze, and the jumping stand (see Chapter 12). The focus is on the early phases of learning, when the organism is attempting to discover the response that will lead to the goal: should the learner move to the right or left, stay or run, use the right or left limb, and so on? At first there is considerably variability, as one response is tried and then another. Eventually, the learner selects the right response, the one that leads to reward or avoids punishment. The usual response measures are the number of errors made or the time taken to reach the goal (see Figure 12.11). The characteristics of trial-and-error learning are summarized in Table 14.1.

Operant conditioning is also instrumental learning, but the focus is different. Researchers in operant conditioning tend to ignore the *early* phases of learning, relegating them to the status of a technical problem, called *shaping.* They are interested in the *late* phases of learning, after the learner has selected the response that pays off. In the late phases of learning there is less variability in behavior, for the nonrewarded responses have dropped out. Finally, the usual dependent variable is rate of response (see Table 14.1). Operant conditioning dominates research on instrumental learning.

Operant Conditioning

The basic apparatus used in operant conditioning research, which is shown in Figure 14.1, has been adapted for use with a wide range of subjects, both animal and human. The apparatus is deliberately kept bare to minimize extraneous stimuli. The *light* can serve as a stimulus, but it need not be used. The *key* is the *manipulandum,* the means by which the animal responds. It is used with pigeons because pecking, an innate response, occurs readily in these animals. With rats or monkeys a bar is used, the response being simply depressing the bar. Note that the response is stripped down to its most basic form, a simple

Table 14.1
Comparison of Trial-and-Error Learning with Operant Conditioning

	TRIAL-AND-ERROR LEARNING	OPERANT CONDITIONING
Phase of learning	Early	Late
Aspect of learning	Response selection (from many possibilities)	Response maintenance
Variability.	High	Low
Measure of learning	Time, errors	Rate of responding

(a)

(b)

Figure 14.1 *Operant conditioning apparatus.* [(*a*) KEN HYMAN: (*b*) HARVEY S. ZUCKER.]

movement.[2] It is easy to record and to manipulate, and it can be made to have the same consequence as any other response the animal might make. Pecking the key results in food being dispensed in the food cup. The food is *contingent* on the pecking response: no peck, no food. If the pigeon is hungry and pecking gets it food, the rate of pecking soon becomes steady and high, with the animal pausing only to eat.

Most of the apparatus operates automatically. The food is presented after the key is pecked, and the response is recorded automatically (see Figure 14.2). The *cumulative recorder* consists of a roll of paper, which moves past a pen at a constant speed. Each response causes the pen to move up a notch until it reaches the top of the paper; then it resents and starts upward again. The outcome is a data sheet showing the cumulative number of responses per unit time, usually minutes or hours; this is a graphic record of the *rate of response*. The entire operant conditioning apparatus is usually called a Skinner box, after the man who devised it (Skinner, 1938).

Acquisition and Extinction

A pigeon will not peck a key and a rat will not depress a bar unless it is rewarded; food or water

[2] *The response is arbitrarily selected by the experimenter, who makes his choice on the basis of ease of recording and manipulating.*

is the usual reward. First, the animal is deprived of food or water, and then by making the desired response attains the food or water it needs. In this acquisition phase, the animal achieves a steady rate of responding (see the left side of Figure 14.3). *During acquisition the response is followed by a reward.*

EXTINCTION CONSISTS OF OMITTING THE REWARD. When the animal makes the desired response (pecking or pressing a bar), no food drops in the tray. The absence of a reinforcer slows down the rate of responding, and eventually the animal stops pecking or pressing the bar (see the right side of Figure 14.3). Note that the curve is *cumulative,* each response raising it a notch. The slower responding of extinction is revealed as a flatter slope of the curve, and the total absence of a response is seen as a flat line (zero slope). Each point on the curve reflects the total number of responses made up to that time, and the curve never drops.

The major measure of *resistance to extinction* is the total number of responses made after the reward stops. The final rate of responding has also been used as a measure of resistance to extinction, which itself is an index of response strength. The reasoning is that during acquisition the response builds up strength, which is reflected in the number of responses that are made when the response is no longer reinforced.

The course of extinction parallels that of extinction in classical conditioning. In both instances an

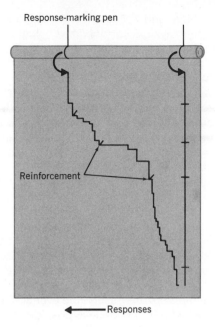

Response-marking pen

Reinforcement

← Responses

Figure 14.2 Cumulative recording of responses.

important stimulus is removed and the response wanes. The phenomenon of spontaneous recovery occurs in both kinds of conditioning. In operant conditioning it is seen as an increase in response rate at the beginning of each new extinction session.

Discrimination and Generalization

We say that an animal discriminates between two stimuli when it responds differently to them. If there are two keys in the apparatus, the animal can be trained to peck one of them but not the other. The training is analogous to discrimination training in classical conditioning. First, the pigeon is presented with two keys, one red and one green, and is rewarded for pecking either key; then the pigeon is rewarded only for pecking the red key. The rate of response to the red key remains high, but the rate of response to the green key drops off sharply, showing the effects of extinction (see Figure 14.4).

We have just described a *simultaneous discrimination,* in which both stimuli are present and the animal can choose between them. But many, if not most, discriminations are successive: only one stimulus is presented at a time, and the animal either does or does not respond. In a typical setup there is only one key. Whenever it is lit red, the reward follows a response; when it is lit green, the reward does not follow the response. Soon the pigeon pecks only when the key is lit red. If this example appears to be entirely removed from everyday life, consider the situation at a traffic intersection. While the red light is on, the drivers do not respond and their cars remain motionless;

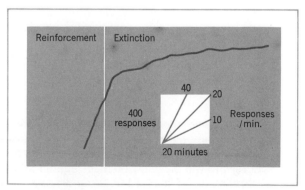

Reinforcement | Extinction

400 responses

40
20

10

Responses / min.

20 minutes

Figure 14.3 Operant conditioning and extinction (cumulative record).

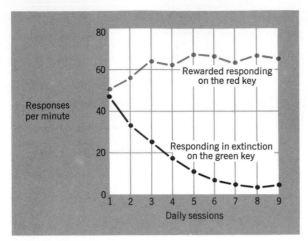

Figure 14.4 Conditioning of a discrimination.

when the green light is on, the drivers respond and their cars move forward. If there is a policeman manipulating the lights, he exercises the same control over motorists as psychologists do over their animal subjects in the laboratory.

Colored stimuli have been used to demonstrate *stimulus generalization* in pigeons (Guttman & Kalish, 1958). These investigators trained pigeons to peck at a disk of approximately yellow-green color (a wavelength of 550 nanometers), with food as the reward. Then they stopped rewarding all pecking responses and presented disks of varying wavelengths. The response had built up to such strength during acquisition that it extinguished slowly, allowing the experimenters to record gradients of stimulus generalization (see Figure 14.5). The rate of responding is high to stimuli near the training stimulus but low to stimuli further from the training stimulus, yielding a typical gradient of generalization.

Reinforcement

In instrumental conditioning, the most important relationship is that between the response and its consequences. Any response that leads to a goal or reward will probably be made again in the same situation (see Figure 14.6). So far we have used the terms *reward* and *punishment* to refer respec-

tively to positive and negative consequences of behavior. In analyzing learning, psychologists have found it useful to include the concepts of reward and punishment under the larger heading of *reinforcement,* a fundamental concept in learning.

Reinforcement is defined most simply as *the strengthening of responses so that they are more likely to recur.* So defined, reinforcement is a necessary condition for learning. Once we define reinforcement in terms of a learning criterion (strengthening of responses), we can no longer ask if learning requires reinforcement. It does by definition.

Reinforcement is a *process* inferred from the fact of learning. Certain events, occurring in association with responses, strengthen the responses. These events are called *reinforcers.* Unlike reinforcement, which is a hypothetical, inferred process, reinforcers are observable events. Three general types of reinforcers have been discovered in research on learning: incentives, unconditioned stimuli, and information.

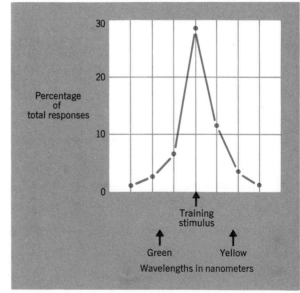

Figure 14.5 Gradients of stimulus generalization to color (Guttman and Kalish, 1958).

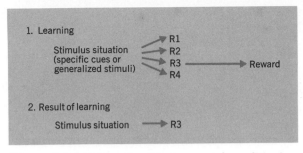

1. Learning

Stimulus situation
(specific cues or
generalized stimuli) → R1
→ R2
→ R3 ——————→ Reward
→ R4

2. Result of learning

Stimulus situation ——————→ R3

Figure 14.6 Schematic of instrumental conditioning.

golf has no prominent stimulus components that serve as reinforcers.

Thus incentives and consummatory responses both contribute to reinforcement, and at present there appears to be no basis for preferring one over the other as *the* reinforcer of instrumental behavior. We shall emphasize incentive *stimuli* because it is these that psychologists typically manipulate and study and because such stimuli can be compared with the other kinds of reinforcers, unconditioned stimuli and information.

Incentives

Incentives are nothing more than the rewards and punishments we have been discussing. *Positive* incentives, or rewards, are valued, and they *strengthen* the instrumental responses they follow; *negative* incentives, or punishers, are avoided, and they *weaken* the responses they follow. In some instances the motivation for seeking an incentive is specific and obvious, as when a hungry animal seeks food. But the motivation may be obscure or generalized, as when an animal seeks novel stimuli. Some incentives *reduce* drive: food diminishes hunger. Others *increase* drive: a sexual object increases curiosity. Whatever the link between these reinforcers and motivation, incentives contribute to reinforcement either positively (reward strengthens instrumental behavior) or negatively (punishment weakens instrumental behavior).

Stimuli are not the only events that serve as reinforcers: *consummatory responses*[3] do also. If the incentives of food, water, and a sexual object are regarded as reinforcers, it makes just as much sense to regard actions such as eating, drinking, and copulating as reinforcers. These examples illustrate the difficulty in separating the effects of positive incentives from consummatory responses: is the reinforcer the food or the consummatory act of eating it? In some situations the stimulus can be isolated as the reinforcer, but there are also consummatory behaviors that appear to be reinforcing without any accompanying incentive: playing a game or sport such as

[3] *For another view of responses as reinforcers, see Premack (1959).*

Unconditioned Stimuli

In classical conditioning the response clearly does *not* produce a positive unconditioned stimulus, nor does it avoid a negative unconditioned stimulus. Initially, the unconditioned stimulus *elicits* the unconditioned response, and after training the unconditioned response merely follows the conditioned response (see Figure 13.1). Nevertheless, the unconditioned stimulus does strengthen the conditioned response, and therefore it is a reinforcer. The pairing of the unconditioned stimulus with the conditioned stimulus does strenghen the conditioned response; the absence of the unconditioned stimulus does cause the conditioned response to weaken. Thus in spite of obvious differences between the unconditioned stimulus in classical conditioning and the incentive stimulus in instrumental conditioning, both contribute to reinforcement.

Information

In acquiring skills, *feedback* is necessary. The individual must have immediate sensory knowledge about his preceding responses, and such information strengthens these responses. The young child who is learning to talk must have immediate auditory feedback from his own speech, and his speech development is enhanced by corrections from his mother. A person who is learning to play the piano must hear the notes if his performance is to improve. If information about responses makes them more likely to recur, then such information contributes to reinforcement.

Of course not all information strengthens behav-

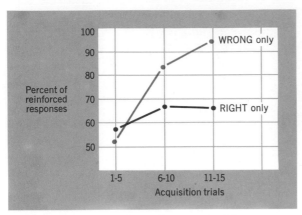

Figure 14.7 *More information conveyed by WRONG than by RIGHT (Buss et al., 1956).*

ior equally. Telling someone that he is wrong after an incorrect response conveys more information than telling him that he is right after a correct response (Buss et al., 1956). It was found that a response was learned faster when incorrect responses were weakened by saying *Wrong* than when correct responses were strengthened by saying *Right* (see Figure 14.7). Subsequent research showed that this holds for a variety of tasks.

Reinforcers and Types of Learning

To summarize, reinforcers are events that strengthen responses and there are three classes or reinforcers: incentives, unconditioned stimuli, and information. Despite their commonality as strengtheners of behavior, the three kinds of reinforcers bear different relationships to the responses they enhance. Each of the three is involved in a different type of learning. Unconditioned stimuli serve as reinforcers in classical conditioning, incentives in instrumental conditioning, and information in a type of learning we shall call *cognitive*, for lack of a better name.

Cognitive learning requires no clear-cut incentive, nor does the learner necessarily respond overtly. One example is the perceptual learning discussed in Chapters 8 and 11. Individuals placed in new surroundings gradually "map" their environment. Other perceptions sharpen in areas

such as music, painting, and perhaps even eating, as some individuals progress from being gross consumers to being connoisseurs.

Cognitive learning is often incidental. Information acquired almost randomly may be retained for many years, and this is the basis of the game of "trivia": recalling minor actors from obscure motion pictures, vice presidents of the United States in the nineteenth century, and so on. Thus an observation casually made today may influence behavior weeks, months, or years from now. In Hebb's terms:

The change of response potential is knowledge; it is not a matter of the specific response to be made to a specific situation, but a modification of response tendency to any of an indefinitely large number of stimulating situations.   (1966, P. 117.)

Cognitive learning also includes *imitation,* which will be discussed in Chapter 16.

Primary and Secondary Reinforcers

A primary reinforcer is an event that innately strengthens a response. No previous learning is required, and a response will be strengthened even the first time it is followed by a primary reinforcer. Such reinforcement helps guide the organism in meeting its basic biological needs: to approach needed substances and avoid harmful events. Thus food is a primary reinforcer for a hungry animal; water, for a thirsty animal; and a mate, for a sexually aroused animal. Avoidance of pain and freedom from confinement are also basic goals, and therefore they are primary reinforcers.

This list is too short to account for all of incentive motivation, and it must be supplemented by learned (acquired) motivation. Presumably, stimuli that are originally neutral can come to be reinforcing, and precisely which stimuli achieve this property is determined by learning. These stimuli are called *secondary reinforcers: stimuli that strengthen a response only because of prior association with a primary reinforcer.* The second reinforcer is a signal or a token for the primary reinforcer, but it is valued in its own right. In one of the earliest experiments on token rewards, Wolfe (1936) taught chimpanzees to obtain grapes by in-

Figure 14.8 *Chimpanzee inserting a poker chip to obtain a grape.*
(YERKES PRIMATE RESEARCH CENTER OF EMORY UNIVERSITY).

serting poker chips into a slot (see Figure 14.8). Then he had them lift a heavy lever, with the reinforcement being a grape or a chip on alternate trials. After this training the animals worked as hard for the poker chips as they did for the grapes. In a followup experiment Cowles (1937) showed that the chimpanzees would learn new problems with only the tokens as reinforcers.

The conditioning of secondary reinforcers is not limited to primates, and an early study demonstrated the phenomenon in rats (Bugelski, 1938). When a rat depressed the bar of a Skinner box and received a pellet of food, a clicking noise accompanied the delivery of the food. Then the delivery of food was stopped, but the clicking noise occurred whenever the bar was depressed. This noise delayed extinction considerably, and the rat

continued to depress the bar for many more trials than it would have ordinarily. The effect of the secondary reinforcer in this study was to delay extinction, which is a weak criterion of the presence of secondary reinforcement. A stronger criterion is the one mentioned above: the subject makes instrumental responses solely to obtain the secondary reinforcer.

The secondary reinforcer, which is initially a neutral stimulus, acquires the power to reinforce behavior by being paired with a primary reinforcer. This is classical conditioning, with the primary reinforcer being the unconditioned stimulus and the secondary reinforcer, the conditioned stimulus. The conditioned stimulus presumably comes to stand for the unconditioned stimulus, thereby acquiring value.

Some secondary reinforcers become associated with several primary reinforcers, so that they eventually stand for a wide range of positive values. They are called *generalized reinforcers,* and the best example is money, which can be a token of food, water, comfort, safety, and even of a potential mating partner.

SHAPING. Secondary reinforcers play a crucial role in the *shaping* of behavior: the "sculpting" of behavior—eliminating unwanted responses and training in wanted responses—until the subject responds in precisely the manner desired by the experimenter. Consider the problem of getting a pigeon to peck the key in a Skinner box. If the pigeon is placed in the box and merely left alone, it may or may not peck the key. The solution is to shape the bird's behavior by successive approximations using secondary reinforcers to move the process forward.

The first step is to make a secondary reinforcer of some easily produced noise. The noise is made and then food is given, repeatedly, until the animal looks for food as soon as he hears the noise. Now when the animal makes any movement toward where you want him to go, you make the noise instantly and follow it with food. After a few repetitions the first part of the movement you want is being made reliably. Now wait until the animal moves a little farther toward the desired goal, then give the secondary reinforcement (make the noise) again, and feed; and so on.

(HEBB, 1966, P. 106.)

Secondary reinforcers are preferable because they can be controlled better than primary reinforcers. If an animal stops to eat, the desired sequence is broken up and the shaping process slows down. Whenever the reinforcer is delayed, learning is retarded—as we shall see later.

Pharmacological and Electrical Reinforcers

Some substances are innately reinforcing because they relate to tissue needs; sugar is a good example. But there are other chemical compounds that are not related to biological needs and are not innately reinforcing, but that acquire strong reinforcing properties. Alcohol, in the form of beer, wine, or hard liquor, can become a potent reinforcer, but it does not achieve this state through association with a primary reinforcer. Alcohol is certainly not a reinforcer the first time it is drunk, and in fact many persons find it distasteful, at least initially. In this respect it is similar to tobacco, another powerful reinforcer that is initially aversive. Both substances come to be valued eventually for their pharmacological effects, though precisely what these effects are has not been determined. To this list we should add mild drugs like marijuana, which is also initially noxious to some persons but which usually comes to serve as a reinforcer.

A more potent source of reinforcement derives from electrical stimulation of the brain (Delgado, 1969). As we saw in Chapter 7, there are specific areas in the brain—principally in the limbic-midbrain system—the stimulation of which is profoundly reinforcing. Some areas are "pleasurable" in that they greatly strengthen the responses preceding their stimulation. Others are "punishing" in that they greatly weaken the responses preceding their stimulation. The effects of electrical stimulation of the brain are so strong that under certain conditions they can successfully compete with the reinforcing power of food to an extremely hungry animal.

Classification of Reinforcers

We have classified reinforcers in several different ways. This section merely recapitulates the ways in which reinforcers may be grouped (see Table 14.2). The type of event includes stimuli or consummatory responses. The type of learning includes the reinforcers appropriate to each: unconditioned stimuli, incentives, and information. The basis of acquisition is either programed into the organism (innate) or acquired through learning. And the nature of the stimulus includes all of the above in contrast to various drugs and brain stimulation.

Magnitude

Common sense tells us that the larger the reward is, the faster the learning will be. Laboratory data confirm that, within limits, the greater the amount

Table 14.2
Classification of Reinforcers

A. Type of Event
   1. Stimuli — food, water
   2. Consummatory response — eating, drinking

B. Type of Learning
   1. Classical conditioning — unconditioned stimuli
   2. Instrumental conditioning — incentives
   3. Cognitive learning — information

C. Basis of Acquisition
   1. Innate — primary reinforcers
   2. Learned (in association with primary reinforcers) —
      secondary reinforcers

D. Nature of the Stimulus
   1. "Psychobiological" — food, water, novel stimuli
   2. Pharmacological — alcohol, tobacco, marijuana
   3. Electrical stimulation — of positive or negative areas of the
      brain

of reinforcement, the quicker is the learning. *Amount* includes both quantity and quality, especially if the reinforcer can be more or less impure, or more or less dilute. For example, rats increase their rate of depressing a bar as the concentration of sugar water is increased (Guttman, 1954).

The effects of both quality and quantity of the reinforcer have been shown in a single experiment (Hutt, 1954). He reinforced rats for bar-pressing with a mixture of flour, milk, and water. To this mixture he added either citric acid to make it sour or saccharine to make it sweet, and the animals were given small, medium, or large amounts of these mixtures. The results, plotted in Figure 14.9, show the separate effects of quantity and quality. That both aspects of the reinforcer affect behavior makes sense from an adaptive viewpoint. The animal needs food to survive, and a concentrated or more nutritious, small amount of food will suffice as well as a dilute or less nutritious, large amount of food.

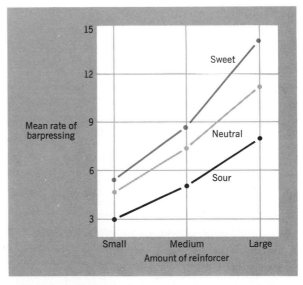

Figure 14.9 Effects of quality and quantity of the reinforcer (Hutt, 1954).

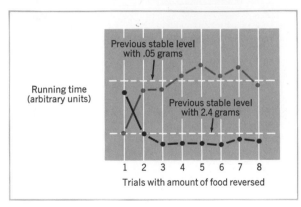

Figure 14.10 Shift in magnitude of the reinforcer (Zeaman, 1949).

What is the effect of altering the amount of reward during learning? If an animal has been reinforced with a small amount of food, will it respond better if the amount is increased? The answer is yes. When the magnitude of reward shifts, there are rapid changes in behavior (Crespi, 1942; Zeaman, 1949). As Figure 14.10 shows, increasing the reward enhances responding, reducing the reward diminishes responding. There is a lively debate over whether these magnitude shifts affect learning or merely performance, but the issues are well beyond the scope of this book (see Capaldi & Lynch, 1967; Spear, 1967).

Delay of Reinforcement

The crucial relationship in instrumental conditioning is the relationship between the response and the reinforcer that follows it. The lapse of time between these two events is an important determinant of the strength of the response: the longer the interval, the weaker the effect of the reinforcer. At very long intervals there is no effect at all; stated another way, the absence of a reinforcer after a response may be regarded as an infinitely long delay. Of course, if there is no reinforcer, the response extinguishes; no payoff, no response.

The effect of delaying reinforcement has been known for many years, and one of the best demonstrations was an early study by Perin (1943). Using rats in a Skinner box, he modified the pro-

cedure to include individual trials. He varied the interval between the bar-pressing response and the subsequent reinforcement, and measured the speed of learning. As Figure 14.11 shows, the longer the delay is, the slower the learning. The retarding effect of delaying reinforcement has also been demonstrated with the T-maze (Wolfe, 1934; Perkins, 1947), and it is clearly a widespread phenomenon.

Schedules of Reinforcement

We have been discussing *continuous reinforcement,* in which a single reinforcer is delivered for each instrumental response. The world we live in rarely pays off with a reinforcer for each response; most of the time it requires many responses to obtain a single reinforcer. A predator may stalk its prey a number of times before capturing it, or stalk a number of prey before capturing a single one of them. A male may make many attempts to mate with a female before succeeding, or try many females before finding a receptive one. A factory worker usually turns out many pieces of work or must work many days before he is paid. In all these situations the reinforcer is delivered less than 100% of the time—*partial reinforcement.*

The most significant effect of partial reinforce-

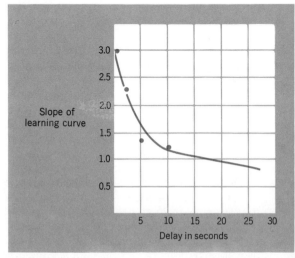

Figure 14.11 Delay of reinforcement (Perin, 1943).

ment is the creation of enduring response strength, as revealed in greater resistance to extinction. In these special circumstances a smaller number of reinforcements (partial reinforcement) results in more resistance to extinction than does a larger number of reinforcements (continuous reinforcement). Psychologists have speculated for many years about this paradoxical fact, but there is no generally accepted explanation.[4]

Nevertheless, the empirical fact is well established. The effect has been neatly demonstrated in humans with a slot machine or "one-armed bandit" (Lewis & Duncan, 1956). Subjects were given disks to insert in the slot machine and told to play as long as they wished. (The disks could be traded in later for nickels.) During acquisition the payoff varied from 0% (no reinforcement) to 100% (continuous reinforcement). The payoffs stopped at the end of training (the beginning of extinction), but the subjects were not told this fact. The lower the percentage of reinforcement was during training, the greater the number of responses made during extinction (see Figure 14.12).

Reinforcers may be scheduled to occur in many different contingencies, and the schedules have been sufficiently varied to fill a rather large volume (Ferster & Skinner, 1957). Two stand out as having the broadest use, *ratio* and *interval* schedules.

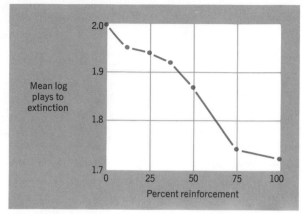

Figure 14.12 *Resistance to extinction in relation to partial reinforcement (Lewis and Duncan, 1956).*

Ratio Schedules

In the partial reinforcement we have been describing, reinforcers are delivered after a specified number of responses. In other words, there is a *ratio* of reinforcements to responses. There are two kinds of ratio schedules, fixed and variable.

A *fixed* ratio schedule is constant: a count is made of the number of responses, and every time this number is reached, a reinforcer is dispensed. The contingency is always the same; if the schedule is 1:30, the organism receives a reinforcer after every 30 responses. The outcome is a stable

[4] *One theory—called frustrative nonreward—attempts to explain both partial reinforcement and extinction (Amsel, 1967). The theory is too advanced to be discussed here, but it has generated both research and controversy (see Bolles & Moot, 1972).*

rate of responding (see Figure 14.13a). It is possible to work up to extremely high ratios of reinforcement but only by gradual stages. First, the subject is placed on continuous reinforcement and then on a low ratio, say 1:3. The number of responses per reinforcer is raised a step at a time until finally the animal may be performing hundreds of responses per reinforcer. At such high ratios the subject often pauses immediately after delivery of the reinforcer, and the rate of response levels off for a brief period.

In a *variable* ratio schedule the reinforcer is delivered after an *average* number of responses. If the variable ratio is 1:30, the animal might be reinforced after 2 responses or after 60, but the average number of responses before obtaining reinforcement is 30. With such a variable schedule, the subject has no way of knowing when a reinforcer might be delivered and has no choice but to keep responding, a situation that leads to extremely high rates of responding (see Figure 14.13b).

Interval Schedules

When the period between reinforcements is determined by time instead of by number of responses, it is called an *interval schedule*. In a fixed interval schedule the time period is constant: the animal is reinforced every minute or every five minutes or

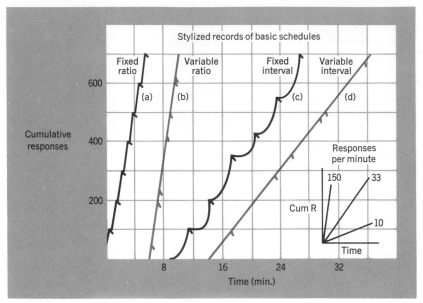

Figure 14.13 *Four schedules of reinforcement.*

every eight minutes, and so on. The animal gradually learns that after every reinforcement there is a "dead period" during which no reinforcement will be given. After each reinforcement the response rate drops sharply, only to accelerate as time elapses. This produces the scalloped curve typical of fixed interval schedules (see Figure 14.13c).

In a *variable* interval schedule the time of reinforcement varies from one reinforcement to the next, averaging out to a particular value. The subject never knows when the next reinforcement will come and so maintains a high and constant rate of responding (see Figure 14.13d). There is a dead period, but its length is so unpredictable that the subject cannot afford to slow down. The outcome is a high, stable rate of responding.

Schedules of reinforcement are not limited to the laboratory; most of us are on one or another schedule in everyday life. The factory hand who is paid on a piecework basis is on a *fixed ratio* schedule. He is paid at the rate of so many cents per item, as is the fruitpicker or vegetable harvester. The best example of *variable ratio* schedules may be found in such cities as Las Vegas (see Lewis & Duncan, 1956). Slot machines are programed to pay off on a variable ratio schedule, and gamblers respond by maintaining ex-

tremely high rates of responding. If the gambler inserts enough coins, there will eventually be a payoff, but he cannot slow down subsequently because the ratio is variable (the payoffs are unpredictable). Compulsive gamblers—seen in this perspective—are merely victims of a variable ratio schedule of reinforcement.

Interval schedules occur less often in everyday life, but the college environment offers some examples. When an instructor announces that there will be a weekly quiz, he is obviously setting up a *fixed interval* schedule, with a good grade serving as a reinforcer. The pattern of students' studying approximates the response rate of rats in a Skinner box. Immediately after a reinforcement (good grade), there is a sharp drop in responding (fewer hours spent studying). After a few days the response rate picks up again, and most of the studying is done just before the next quiz. This pattern of relaxing followed by cramming yields a curve similar to the scalloped curve typical of fixed interval responding in a Skinner box. Unfortunately, the pattern is not conducive to either superior retention or a good education.

Unscheduled surprise tests are rarely used because of their unpopularity with students. If the student never knows when the quiz will be sprung,

Table 14.3

Four Basic Schedules of Reinforcement

	RATIO (depends on responses)	INTERVAL (depends on time)
Fixed (constant)	Piecework	Weekly quiz
Variable (*average* value)	Slot machine	Pop quiz

he must maintain a high rate of studying. This yields the typical response curve of a *variable interval* schedule, in which there are no dead periods and the response rate is high and steady.

The four schedules, together with appropriate examples, are summarized in Table 14.3. They differ in two ways: (1) either the number of responses or time is counted, and (2) the schedule is either predictable (fixcd) or unpredictable (variable).

Superstition

Instrumental responses ordinarily lead to a goal, hence the term *instrumental*. Reinforcers are events that strengthen responses. Sometimes a reinforcer follows a response, but the contingency is *accidental*: the response in no way leads to the reinforcer; it just happens to occur before the reinforcer is delivered. Skinner (1948) offers the example of "body English" after a bowler has thrown the ball. Once the ball is released, the bowler's behavior (bending, twisting, leaning, and so on) obviously cannot affect the course of the ball. Such behavior is reinforced by the few times the ball knocks down the pins. This is *superstitious* behavior: *responses that are clearly not instrumental but continue to be made as if they were.*

If this analysis is correct, it should be possible to produce superstitious behavior simply by random reinforcement of noninstrumental behavior. This is precisely what Skinner (1948) did, using a *fixed interval* schedule. Hungry pigeons

were placed in a Skinner box which had a retractable food hopper:

If a clock is now arranged to present the food hopper at regular intervals with no reference whatsoever to the bird's behavior, operant conditioning usually takes place. In six out of eight cases the resulting responses were so clearly defined that two observers could agree in counting instances. One bird was conditioned to turn counterclockwise about the cage, making two or three turns between reinforcemnts. Another repeatedly thrust its head into one of the upper corners of the cage. A third developed a "tossing" response, as if placing its head beneath an invisible bar and lifting it repeatedly. (P. 168.)

Conditioning occurs because of a time relationship. When a response occurs just prior to the reinforcer, the response tends to be made again. When the reinforcer occurs fairly frequently, the response-reinforcer contingency is likely to occur several times. The superstitious responses are reinforced only some of the time, and this partial reinforcement results in a strong habit.

Many individual superstitions surely arise in this fashion. Bettors often have a special "lucky number," which typically is a number that has been randomly reinforced. Some of the compulsive rituals of neurotics also fall under the heading of superstition, as we shall see in a later chapter.

Random reinforcement may account for *individual* superstitions, but it does not explain *group* superstitions. Avoiding the number 13, breaking a mirror, and walking under a ladder are not learned through operant conditioning or a partial rein-

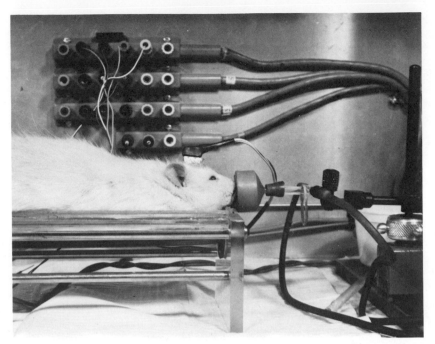

Figure 14.14 *Apparatus for instrumental conditioning of heart rate in a curarized rat. The wires in the background monitor the rat's heart rate; when the rate changes in the required direction, electric current passes through the electrode on the rat's head to the "rewarding" area of the brain.*

(COURTESY NEAL E. MILLER, THE ROCKEFELLER UNIVERSITY; PHOTO BARRY DWORKIN.)

forcement schedule. Whatever their origins in bygone eras, such beliefs are now learned *cognitively:* they are transmitted verbally as part of the culture. Once learned, they tend to be maintained on a low schedule of reinforcement. Thus a rain dance is *sometimes* followed by rain, and a water douser *sometimes* discovers water. In brief, though individual and group superstitions may be acquired differently, both are probably maintained by a *variable interval* schedule of reinforcement.

Autonomic Conditioning

The term *instrumental conditioning* refers to the learning of responses that have an impact on the environment—that is, responses that are instrumental in achieving the learner's goals. Can instrumental conditioning be used to alter the

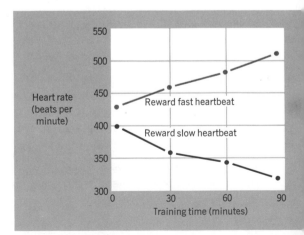

Figure 14.15 *Instrumental conditioning of heart rate increases and decreases in curarized rats (Miller and DiCara, 1967).*

glands and smooth muscles—involved in bodily functions—that are innervated by the autonomic nervous system? For several decades the answer appeared to be no. The few attempts at autonomic conditioning had failed, and most psychologists accepted Mowrer's two-factor theory (1947, 1950). This theory suggested that there are two kinds of learning: (1) instrumental conditioning, which is limited to skeletal muscles (innervated by the central nervous system), and (2) classical conditioning, which is limited to glands and smooth muscles (innervated by the autonomic nervous system).

Not all psychologists accepted this dichotomy.

In the 1960s researchers, starting with Kimmel and Hill (1960), began to use instrumental conditioning to alter the galvanic skin response of human subjects. The data on humans were not clear cut, and a controversy arose (see Kimmel, 1967; Katkin & Murray, 1968). One problem was the possibility of "cheating." A subject can alter his heart rate or blood pressure by increasing or decreasing his rate of breathing. Such voluntary control over breathing involves the *central* nervous system. Thus any changes in heart rate or blood pressure would be caused indirectly by the central nervous system, and they could not be interpreted as examples of autonomic conditioning.

Research Report

Unequivocal demonstrations of autonomic conditioning have been supplied by Miller and his colleagues (Miller & DiCara, 1967; Miller, 1969; DiCara & Miller, 1968; DiCara, 1970). They eliminated any "cheating" with central nervous system control by paralyzing their subjects' skeletal muscles (the subjects were rats). This was accomplished with the drug *curare,* which is used on poison darts by certain South American tribes. In small doses curare does not kill, but it blocks the action of central nervous system transmitter substances. Curare does not interfere with consciousness or the transmitter substances of the autonomic nervous system.

A curarized rat cannot breathe and must therefore be kept alive by a mechanical respirator (see Figure 14.14). The helpless rat cannot eat, drink, or copulate—so the usual rewards could not be used in instrumental conditioning. Instead, electrical stimulation of "pleasure centers" in the brain was used as the reinforcer.

Using this experimental setup, Miller and DiCara (1967) trained rats to increase or decrease their heart rate roughly 20% (see Figure 14.15). This is a striking demonstration of instrumental autonomic conditioning, but these researchers were able to top it with an unusual experiment on specificity of autonomic conditioning. They trained rats to dilate the blood vessels of one ear while leaving the blood vessels of the other ear unchanged (DiCara & Miller, 1968). The results are shown in Figure 14.16.

Many of these findings were later duplicated in noncurarized rats to show that the conditioning was not caused by the effects of the drug. Later research also established that humans can control their heart rate and blood pressure separately—which cannot be accomplished indirectly by controlling respiration (Schwartz, 1972). Remember, too, that EEG alpha waves can be instrumentally conditioned (see Chapter 6).

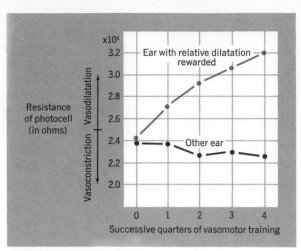

x10⁴

Resistance
of photocell
(in ohms)

Vasoconstriction Vasodilatation

3.2 — Ear with relative dilatation
rewarded

3.0

2.8

2.6

2.4

2.2 Other ear

2.0

0   1   2   3   4

Successive quarters of vasomotor training

Figure 14.16 Instrumental condition of dilation of blood vessels in only one ear of curarized rats (DiCara and Miller, 1968).

Thus autonomic responses can be instrumentally conditioned. This fact does not necessarily mean that instrumental and classical conditioning are the same kind of learning, as some psychologists maintain (Miller, 1969, for example); the two kinds of conditioning differ in other ways — especially in the relationship between the response and the reinforcer.

Also the fact that autonomic responses can be instrumentally conditioned does not mean that it is easy to do so. Elephants can be trained to stand on their two *front* legs, but the training is difficult and arduous, and such behavior never occurs under natural conditions. Similarly, we may question whether autonomic responses are ever instrumentally conditioned outside the laboratory. Is such conditioning pushing against limits set by nature? We shall return to this issue — after discussing negative consequences of instrumental conditioning — at the end of the next chapter.

chapter 15

simple instrumental conditioning: negative consequences

Punishment — suppression of behavior — effectiveness of punishment — avoidance conditioning — two-factor theory — free-operant avoidance — positive and negative secondary reinforcers — Bolles' model of avoidance conditioning — instinctive drift — preparedness — learned helplessness — perspective

Children and other innocent persons tend to think of Heaven as a place where only good things happen; Hell is where bad things happen. In these terms, this chapter is about Hell. In more prosaic terms, the chapter deals with the effects of punishment and with avoidance conditioning. The methods and the explanatory concepts are a little more complex than those of the last chapter.

Punishment

Negative reinforcers weaken a response by their occurrence or strengthen it by their termination. We shall emphasize the first property of negative reinforcers and define punishment as *a stimulus that, when it follows a response, reduces the probability that the response will be made again.*

The Suppression of Behavior

Some psychologists contend that the effects of punishment are more apparent than real and that punishment merely suppresses behavior temporarily but does not abolish it:

Punishment temporarily depresses the rate of responding but does not lessen the total number of responses required for extinction. In the long run, therefore, nothing is gained by punishment. Extinction, rather than punishment, is required to eliminate a habit.
(MORGAN & KING, 1966, P. 101.)

Several experiments have lent credence to this point of view, the experiment most cited being the series by Estes (1944). He reinforced hungry rats with food for pressing a bar and used a schedule of reinforcement to build up high rates of responding. Then he stopped reinforcing with food, and during this extinction period he used electric shock to punish every response. This combination of punishment and extinction virtually wiped out the rate of responding. Finally, the punishment was discontinued, but the extinction procedure remained in force; paradoxically, the rate of responding jumped, though the response still did not lead to food.

This finding has been repeated many times, and Reynolds (1968) demonstrated it again in pigeons with different intensities of punishment (see Figure 15.1). As expected, *intense* punishment depressed the rate of responding more than *mild* punishment. When punishment ended, the response rate climbed rapidly, reaching an even higher level than before punishment. These data were obtained under conditions of reinforcement: the animals were hungry and could obtain food by pecking a key. Thus the positive incentive of food was opposed by the negative incentive of electric shock. With the positive incentive held constant, the stronger the negative incentive, the weaker was the response rate. In this experiment, as soon as the animals were no longer being punished, they could make the instrumental response and be reinforced by food. When both positive and negative reinforcement are being given concurrently, punishment may suppress a response, but as soon as the punishment stops, there is no reason for the subject not to continue responding.

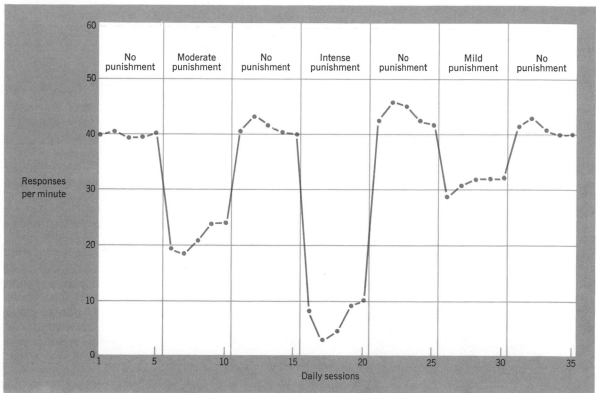

Figure 15.1 The effect of varying degrees of punishment, followed by no punishment on instrumental responding (Reynolds, 1968).

Research Report

This explanation of the temporary effects of punishment does not apply to Estes' study because his animals were not reinforced either during or after punishment, but there is an explanation that carries considerable weight (Azrin & Holz, 1966). In Estes' experiment, there was no punishment during acquisition, but there was punishment during extinction (see Table 15.1). The rats could easily have learned this discrimination: food is associated with no punishment, but the absence of food is associated with punishment. In other words, punishment could have acted as a *discriminative stimulus,* signaling that a response would *not* be followed by a reinforcer. This hypothesis suggests that in the Estes experiment the *stimulus* aspects of punishment were crucial, not the *aversive* aspects.

If this explanation is correct, it should be possible to obtain similar results by substituting a *nonaversive stimulus* for punishment. Azrin and Holz (1966) trained a pigeon to peck at a key illuminated by white light. After training on a variable interval schedule, extinction began. Each response during extinction caused the illumination of the key to change briefly from white to green. This "pseudopunishment" was subsequently discontinued but the extinction period continued. Thus all the conditions of the Estes experiment were duplicated except for the use of an aversive stimulus. The outcome was the same as when punishment was used (see Figure 15.2). During extinction-plus-pseudopunishment the response rate dropped sharply and the animals finally stopped responding. When the pseudopunish-

Table 15.1
Summary of Estes' (1944) Punishment Experiment

PROCEDURE	OUTCOME (as reflected in response rate)
1. Partial reinforcement (food)	High rate
2. Extinction (no food) + Punishment (electric shock)	Very low rate
3. Extinction alone (no food)	High rate

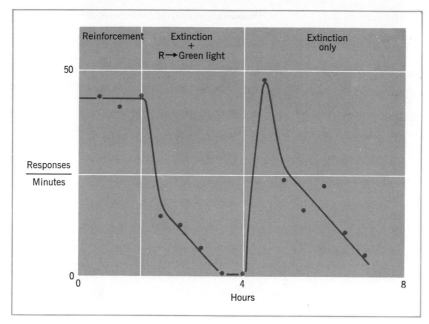

Figure 15.2 Pseudopunishment: the conditioning of a discriminative stimulus (Azrin and Holz, 1966).

ment was discontinued, the response rate climbed back to a level slightly higher than the acquisition level. Of course, since the response was still not being reinforced, it eventually extinguished.

Now green illumination can by no stretch of the imagination be considered a punishing stimulus, but its removal had the same result as the removal of punishment had in all of the earlier research. Clearly, punishment in the earlier experiments served as a discriminative stimulus, and it is this property of punishment that accounts for the *temporary* suppression of behavior. Any stimulus, punishing or neutral, would have yielded the same results when paired with extinction.

Punishment has also been shown to act as a discriminative stimulus for children (Katz, 1971). During acquisition of a hitting response (of a Bobo doll), each hitting response was followed by aversive noise. During the subsequent extinction, more hitting responses were made when the noise occurred than when it did not occur. Thus ". . . an aversive stimulus can acquire a discriminative control function which serves temporarily to maintain, rather than suppress, children's extinction responding" (Katz, 1971, p. 1443).

Are the effects of punishment temporary? They are no more temporary than the effects of reinforcement or of extinction. Reinforcement will elevate a response rate, but only so long as the reinforcement continues. Extinction will depress a response rate, but the rate will increase not only when extinction ceases, but even when the only change is a lapse of time, as in spontaneous recovery.

Effectiveness of Punishment

The effectiveness of punishment depends on a number of factors, the most important of which we shall note briefly (Azrin & Holz, 1966).

1. *Intensity.* The more intense the punishment is, the more it suppresses behavior. This effect is reversible at most intensities of punishment, even when the punishment is fairly severe (see Figure 15.1). Nevertheless, at the highest levels of punishment the animals may stop responding and never start again. In the original Estes experiment (1944) the highest level of shock completely wiped out responsiveness, and subsequent research has repeatedly demonstrated that the animal may never again make the punished response. Masserman (1946) trained hungry cats to make a response for food, and then he airblasted them whenever they made the response. After only a few trials the cats stopped responding, and some of them starved rather than make the punished response.
2. *Frequency.* The more often a response is punished, the more effective the punishment is. The best procedure is to punish after every response.
3. *Immediacy.* The sooner the punishment occurs, the more effective it is. Any reinforcer, positive or negative, works best when it is an immediate consequence of a response. Delay of reinforcement, whether the stimulus is a positive incentive or a punisher, weakens its effectiveness.
4. *Suddenness.* The more suddenly punishment is introduced, the more effective it is. It is least effective when started at a low intensity and gradually made more severe; it is most effective when the maximum amount is given immediately on the first trial.
5. *Brevity.* The briefer the period of punishment is, the more effective it is. Prolonged punishment allows time for adaptation and recovery from the effects of punishment, especially at lower intensities.

In summary, if punishment is to be used in suppressing behavior, the most effective procedure is to deliver a brief, sudden, immediate, in-tense punishment, and to do so every time the response is made. In addition to these factors, the variables that *enhance* behavior also determine how effective punishment will be. If the behavior is strongly motivated and the reinforcement is powerful, the punishment will be less effective. Thus a starving animal may make a severely punished response if it is the only means of obtaining food. Nevertheless, when punishment is administered under optimal conditions—taking account of the five variables just discussed—it is one of the most effective means of weakening or eliminating behavior. Holz and Azrin (1963) compared the success of five procedures in reducing the rate of an instrumental response, the criteria being (1) response rate drops immediately, (2) response rate stays down during the duration of the procedure, (3) response rate drops to zero, and (4) the drop in response rate is irreversible. The procedures compared were *stimulus change, satiation, extinction, physical restraint,* and *punishment.* Punishment was the only procedure to meet all four criteria, and it was obviously the most effective means of weakening behavior (see Table 15.2). These findings, together with those mentioned earlier, show that the widely held view of punishment as merely a weak and temporary suppressor of behavior is incorrect. It is wrong to believe that extinction is the only way to weaken behavior permanently; punishment can accomplish the same end, and for the most part it can do so more effectively. The problem with punishment lies not in its effectiveness but in its side effects: fear and aggression. The punished person may react by avoiding the punishing agent or attacking him, and it is these possible reactions to punishment that limit its usefulness as an inhibiter of behavior.

Avoidance Conditioning

Punishment is not necessarily inescapable. An animal may flee from a punishing stimulus or avoid it. Training an animal to avoid an oncoming negative reinforcer is called *avoidance conditioning,* and the most commonly used apparatus to study it is the shuttle box (see Figure 15.3). Two compartments are separated by a low barrier, and a gate, which can be dropped, prevents the animal

Table 15.2

Comparing Procedures that Reduce Response Rate (Holz & Azrin, 1963)

PROCEDURE	IMMEDIATE EFFECT	ENDURING EFFECT	COMPLETE EFFECT	IRREVERSIBLE EFFECT
Stimulus change	Yes	No	No	No
Extinction	No	Yes	No	No
Satiation	Yes	Yes	No	No
Physical restraint	Yes	Yes	Yes	No
Punishment	Yes	Yes	Yes	Yes

from jumping from one compartment to the other. The procedure is simple. A warning buzzer sounds for one second, and the gate is dropped. Ten seconds later the animal receives a severe electric shock if it is still in the compartment. At first the animal tends to jump only after receiving the shock; this is an escape response. Eventually, it heeds the warning signal and jumps before the shock is delivered; this is an avoidance response. After a brief interval, the warning signal sounds again, and the animal must jump again to avoid punishment.

Using the shuttle box, Solomon et al. (1953) trained dogs to avoid painful electric shock; Figure 15.4 is a record of one of their dogs. On the early trials the dog responded too slowly to avoid the shock—most of its responses occurred immediately after the shock was delivered (at about 10 seconds). Suddenly the animal started jumping sooner, and starting with Trial 13 all of its jumps occurred in less than 10 seconds—quickly enough to avoid the electric shock.

Such training presumably involves both instrumental and classical conditioning. It is *instrumental* conditioning in that the animal makes a response that allows it to avoid (or escape from) a negative reinforcer. It is *classical* conditioning in that a neutral stimulus is paired with an uncondi-

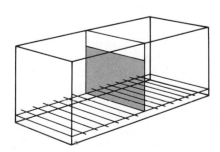

Figure 15.3 Shuttle box for investigating avoidance conditioning.

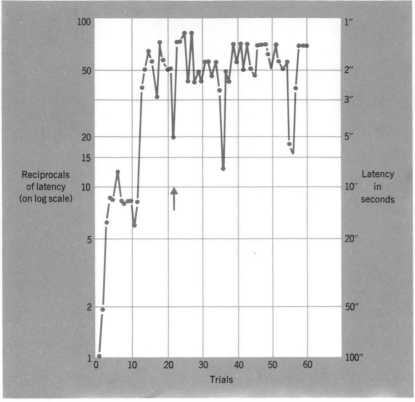

Figure 15.4 *Conditioned avoidance in a dog (Solomon and Wynne, 1954).*

tioned stimulus. The neutral stimulus is the warning buzzer paired with the electric shock that comes 10 seconds later, which makes this an instance of trace conditioning. The procedure is not completely classical in that the animal can avoid the shock.

Once the animal has been trained to jump at the sound of the warning buzzer, this response is extremely difficult to extinguish. So long as the jumping response is reinforced by avoidance of the aversive electric shock, the response should be maintained. But if the animal never experiences shock again, should it not stop jumping? The paradoxical finding that the response does not extinguish, or at best extinguishes very slowly, has been confirmed by many experiments (see Herrnstein, 1969).

Two-Factor Theory

One way of resolving the paradox is to employ the two-factor theory of Mowrer (1939, 1947). Presumably the warning buzzer, through association with the electric shock, comes to evoke the same anxiety as does the shock. When the animal jumps before the shock comes on, it not only avoids the shock but escapes from the anxiety-provoking warning signal. This escape reduces its anxiety drive, thereby reinforcing and maintaining the jumping response. Mowrer's approach specifies two stages in avoidance conditioning (see Figure 15.5). First, the conditioned stimulus acquires anxiety properties through classical conditioning and then the jumping response is reinforced because it provides an escape from this anxiety-provoking conditioned stimulus (instrumental conditioning).

If the animals become anxious, they should manifest autonomic arousal. It follows that the occurrence of the conditioned stimulus (the warning buzzer) should cause a strong autonomic reaction, and it is this aversive state that the animal escapes from when it jumps into the "neutral" compartment. Unfortunately, the data do not support this drive-reduction approach. When peripheral autonomic reactions are blocked, there is still little or no extinction of the avoidance response (Wynne & Solomon, 1955); and autonomic measures such as heart rate are unrelated to the maintenance of the avoidance response (Werboff et al., 1964). Thus anxiety reduction, insofar as it involves autonomic reaction, cannot explain the maintenance of the avoidance response.

Nevertheless, the emphasis on the conditioned stimulus seems well taken. The conditioned stimulus in avoidance conditioning does appear to possess all the properties of a secondary negative reinforcer, and Sidman (1962) has demonstrated the aversiveness of such stimuli. His method, called *free-operant avoidance,* is an important alternative to the shuttle box. An animal can postpone electric shock by depressing a bar in a Skinner box: each response (or each group of responses when a schedule of reinforcement is used) resets a clock, thereby delaying the onset of shock. If the animal continues to respond, it can delay the shock indefinitely; that is, it can avoid the shock. In one experiment (1962), whenever a light was on, a monkey received a shock every 20 seconds unless it pressed a lever; each lever press delayed the shock for another 20 seconds. When the light was off, no shock was delivered, regardless of whether the animal pressed the lever or not. The monkey could turn off the light by repeatedly pulling a chain. This dual procedure was successful: the monkey not only pressed the lever to delay the shock but pulled the chain to turn off the light. Evidently, the light was sufficiently aversive for its absence to be reinforcing.

Terminating the conditioned stimulus is an important aspect of avoidance conditioning. It has been found that if the conditioned stimulus does not turn off immediately after the avoidance response is made, the response will extinguish

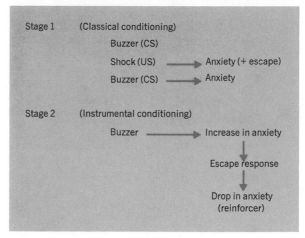

Figure 15.5 *Two-factor theory of avoidance conditioning.*

(Kamen, 1957). Moreover, if the conditioned stimulus is not terminated at all, extinction speeds up (Werboff et al., 1964). This evidence implicates the warning stimulus as the cause of the slow extinction of the avoidance response, but it does not solve the paradox. We know that when a secondary reinforcer is presented without the primary reinforcer, the conditioned response extinguishes. If the avoidance response is really an escape response from an aversive *secondary* reinforcer, why does it not extinguish?

It has been argued that there is no extinction because the animal never *experiences* the absence of the primary reinforcer; it does not wait long enough to discover whether the shock will occur or not. If this were true, then extinction could be accomplished by keeping the animal in the situation and not letting it make the avoidance response. In such "reality testing" a glass barrier prevented dogs from jumping into the other compartment of the shuttle box, so that they were forcibly exposed to the sequence of the warning buzzer without the electric shock following it (Solomon et al., 1953). This procedure had no effect on most of the animals, and the avoidance response returned as soon as the glass barrier was removed. Evidently, being in the situation when the unconditioned stimulus fails to occur does not significantly hasten extinction of the avoidance response.

The explanation for this may lie in the difference between positive and negative reinforcers. All the evidence that the response to secondary reinforcers extinguishes quickly when the primary reinforcer is absent comes from research with *positive* reinforcers. There is no basis for assuming that the same quick extinction would occur with *negative* reinforcers; in fact, the research on avoidance conditioning suggests precisely the opposite. We saw earlier that the effects of punishment can be powerful enough to permanently suppress a response. If punishment can exert such a strong influence, stimuli conditioned to it (secondary reinforcers) should be capable of maintaining an avoidance response with little or no extinction. Of course if the punishment were moderate, the avoidance response should extinguish fairly quickly, and it does (D'Amato et al., 1967). When the punishment is at full strength, as in the typical avoidance conditioning experiment, the secondary negative reinforcer associated with it should be powerful enough to maintain the avoidance response with little or no extinction, and as we have seen, it does.

Viewed adaptively, the difference between positive and negative secondary reinforcers makes sense. An initially neutral stimulus, after being paired with a primary reinforcer such as food, comes to be a signal for the food. The conditioned stimulus prepares the animal for the presence of food, and it can then make instrumental responses that are reinforced by the food. If the association between the conditioned stimulus and the unconditioned stimulus is severed, then the former is no longer a signal for food and the animal must disregard it. Thus it is adaptive for the response to secondary *positive* reinforcers to extinguish quickly.

The sequence of events is similar for negative reinforcers, but only up to a point. An initially neutral stimulus, after being paired with a primary negative reinforcer (such as being attacked by a predator) comes to be a signal for danger. The conditioned stimulus alerts the animal to the impending danger, and it can make preparations for flight. If the association between conditioned and unconditioned stimuli is severed, then the conditioned stimulus is no longer a signal for

danger. The animal need not escape because there is really no danger, but the animal must be wary. Even if the possibility of danger were very low, it would be foolhardy to risk it. It seems likely that natural selection favored animals that were wary, and their descendants are likely to be on the cautious side. In brief, the difference in extinction between positive and negative reinforcers appears to be this: the animal can take the risk of bypassing a reinforcer such as food because it will have other opportunities to obtain food, but it cannot ignore a possible danger because there may be no further opportunities to avoid or escape from the danger.

Bolles' Model of Avoidance Learning

The two-factor theory of avoidance conditioning has required amending and patching in order to survive a variety of experimental onslaughts (for a comprehensive review, see Herrnstein, 1969). Perhaps researchers have been excessively concerned with the laboratory behavior of tamed animals, and we might understand avoidance learning better if we examined the behavior of animals in nature. This is precisely the theme of Bolles' (1970) model of avoidance learning. He suggests that avoidance learning may be of little use to an animal living in the wild:

What keeps animals alive in the wild is that they have very effective innate *defensive reactions which occur when they encounter any kind of new or sudden stimulus. . . . The mouse does not scamper away from the owl because it has learned to escape the painful claws of the enemy; it scampers away from anything that is happening in its environment, and it does so merely because it is a mouse. The gazelle does not flee from an approaching lion because it has been bitten by lions; it runs away from any large object that approaches it, and it does so because this is one of its species-specific defense reactions. Neither the mouse nor the gazelle can afford to* learn *to avoid; survival is too urgent, and the opportunity to learn is too limited, and the parameters of the situation make the necessary learning impossible. The animal which survives is the one which comes into its environment with defensive reactions already a prominent part of its repertoire.* (P. 33.)

Some avoidance responses are conditioned within a few trials, but others require hundreds or even thousands of trials (see Herrnstein & Hineline, 1966). Bolles contends that an avoidance response can be conditioned quickly only if it is a *species-specific defensive reaction* such as running, jumping, or crouching. Thus in the typical experiment on avoidance learning, the animal's immediate response to the electric shock is an innate defensive reaction. The experimenter has arranged that only one of these responses succeeds in removing the animal from the aversive stimulus. For example, in the shuttle box the only way to escape from the shock is to jump into the other compartment (see Figure 15.3). Under these conditions such responses as freezing, crouching, and running are all inhibited during the course of training (see Figure 15.6). This leaves only the jumping response, and the animal needs to learn only *when* to jump: as soon as the warning signal, or conditioned stimulus, occurs. Such learning is usually rapid. In brief, avoidance conditioning is easy only when the avoidance response is part of the animal's innate defensive repertoire.

If *no* innate response leads to escape, then learning is slow. At first the animal tries its innate avoidance responses, and suppression of *all* of them requires many trials. The animal must then learn which response does lead to escape from shock, say a bar-press response. The bar press must then be associated with the warning signal so that the animal *avoids* rather than merely escapes (if it waits too long, the shock comes on). Finally, termination of the warning signal becomes a safety signal: this is analogous to a siren stopping, which signals that the emergency is over. It requires many trials to learn to make the avoidance response on signal and to learn that termination of the warning stimulus signifies safety. Thus avoidance conditioning of a nondefensive reaction tends to be very slow.

Bolles' model of avoidance conditioning neatly accounts for some otherwise unexplained facts. How the model will fare when subjected to experimental test is another matter, but its emphasis on species-specific reactions offers a needed corrective to experimenters who ignore such considerations.

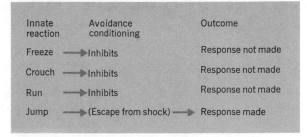

Figure 15.6 *Bolles' (1970) model of quick avoidance conditioning.*

Instinctive Drift and Preparedness

Bolles' message has been piquantly illustrated by Breland and Breland (1961). They applied their knowledge of operant shaping procedures to training animals for displays, exhibits, and entertainment for tourists. Chickens were taught to "dance" or "bat a ball" and raccoons to "deposit money in a bank." But trouble arose when the animal's instinctive tendencies interfered with learned responses. For example, a pig was taught to pick up wooden coins and place them in a "piggy bank." A ratio schedule of five coins per reinforcement kept the pig busy:

At first the pig would eagerly pick up one dollar, carry it to the bank, run back, get another, carry it rapidly and neatly, and so on, until the ratio was complete. Thereafter, over a period of weeks the behavior would become slower and slower. He might run eagerly for each dollar, but on the way back, instead of carrying the dollar and depositing it simply and cleanly, he would repeatedly drop it, root it, drop it again, root it along the way, pick it up, toss it into the air, drop it, root it some more, and so on.

(1961, P. 683.)

The animal was obviously doing what pigs do naturally (root and toss), and this cut into its learned behavior. Learning can overcome innate tendencies, but we should not be surprised if the latter do not remain submerged. The Brelands called this phenomenon *instinctual drift:* a tendency for animals to revert from trained responses to instinctive behavior even when it costs them rewards.

Thus the programed tendencies that an animal brings to a learning situation can eventually undo the effects of learning. But programed tendencies can also enhance or retard the process of learning. As Bolles (1970) noted, some avoidance responses are learned more easily than others. There are many other examples of this phenomenon. To cite two, when cats are placed in a puzzle box, they cannot learn to scratch or lick themselves in order to escape; and—at the other extreme—pigeons learn very quickly in most situations in which the reward response is pecking.

The underlying issue concerns how readily a given response can be conditioned. The concept has been called *preparedness* (Seligman, 1970), and it is best regarded as a continuum (see Table 15.3). At one end of the continuum are responses that the animal is so ready to make that they occur as soon as the appropriate stimulus occurs; the programed tendencies are so strong that no learning is necessary. At the other end of the continuum are responses the animal is programed *not* to make in particular contexts (a cat licking itself to escape from a puzzle box). In the middle of the continuum are responses that can be learned more or less easily. Ethologists and other researchers who lean toward instinct as an explanatory concept tend to study learning at one end of the preparedness continuum; stimulus-response psychologists and behaviorists tend to study learning at the other end. And each finds support for his position in his own research!

The notion of readiness to learn makes sense when applied to animals, but does it contribute anything to the understanding of *human* learning? Seligman (1970) is strongly affirmative: "*Homo sapiens* has an evolutionary history and a biological makeup which has made it relatively prepared to learn some things and contraprepared to learn others" (p. 414). There are certainly enough examples of differences in human readiness to learn, of which a few may be cited. Young children learn to walk quickly, and many infants would learn to swim easily if they were simply placed in water with appropriate precautions. All normal children acquire language with a facility that puzzles adults who must struggle to master a new language.

At the other end of the dimension of preparedness are responses that are difficult to learn. Natural left-handers cannot readily learn to write

with the right hand, and virtually all adults fail in attempts to speak a second language without an "accent." Instrumental conditioning of autonomic responses is also difficult; as we noted in the last chapter, such learning does occur, but many conditioning trials yield only small changes (DiCara, 1970). In brief, not all responses are equally conditionable; some behavior is readily acquired, other behavior is acquired only with great difficulty, if at all.

Learned Helplessness

We have seen that animals quickly learn to avoid imminent pain and that the avoidance response endures. But what happens when the pain is inescapable? It was suggested many years ago that the animal develops a *sense of helplessness* (Mowrer & Viek, 1948). This feeling of futility has been compared to the loss of hope by victims of concentration camps and long-term prisoners.

It might be supposed that the feeling of helplessness is specific to the situation in which it is learned, but recent research has shown that the attitude of passive futility generalizes. Dogs were given many painful shocks while they were restrained in a harness, and a day later they were placed in a shuttle box (see Figure 15.3) for avoidance training (Overmier & Seligman, 1967). They did not learn to avoid the oncoming shock, but merely stood passively and accepted painful shocks each of which lasted almost a minute. A few dogs did jump into the safe compartment on early trials, but they reverted to passive acceptance of shock on later trials. In sharp contrast, a control group—which received no prior inescapable shocks in the harness—quickly learned the avoidance response in the shuttle box.

In a follow-up experiment one group of dogs was allowed to escape from shock in the harness, and another group of dogs was given prior escapable shock in the shuttle box (Seligman & Maier, 1967). Both groups then learned the avoidance response in the shuttle box. In brief, a learned sense of helplessness develops only when there is training *at the start* that shock is inescapable; early training that allows escape prevents a later feeling of helplessness.

This research has implications of our understanding of the various kinds of contingencies that

Table 15.3

A Continuum of Preparedness (Seligman, 1970)

Instinctive responding	Response made on the first trial and consistently thereafter
Somewhat prepared	Response made after only a few trials
Unprepared	Response made only after many trials
Counterprepared	Response made only after hundreds of trials or it is not made at all

can be learned, both in the laboratory and in everyday life:

> *. . . learning theory has stressed that two operations, explicit contiguity between events (acquisition) and explicit noncontiguity (extinction), produce learning. A third operation that is proposed, independence between events, also produces learning, and such learning may have effects on behavior that differ from the effects of explicit pairing and explicit nonpairing. Such learning may produce a subject who does not attempt to escape electric shock; a subject who, even if he does respond, may not benefit from instrumental contingencies.* (SELIGMAN & MAIER, 1967, PP. 8–9.)

The learned helplessness can be overcome by special training—specifically, *compelling* the subjects to escape from the painful shock (Seligman et al. 1968). After the dogs were taught to be helpless, the barrier between the two parts of the shuttle box was removed. Then the dogs were simply dragged to the safe compartment, where they received no shock. Subsequently, they were tested in a regular shuttle box, complete with barrier, and they successfully avoided the shock (see Figure 15.7). Thus they overcame the helplessness by being shown forcibly that something could be done about the shock.

Do human subjects also acquire a sense of helplessness in the laboratory? No one has placed human subjects in a shuttle box, but there have

been experiments that parallel the research on animals. For example, it is known that men prefer predictable shocks to unpredictable shocks—presumably because unpredictable shocks leave them completely at the mercy of an uncontrolled environment (D'Amato & Gumenik, 1960). In addition, variable shocks can reduce human subjects to helplessness. In one experiment, roughly two-thirds of the subjects failed to make even a simple escape response in the face of shock of varying intensity.

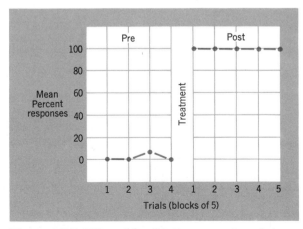

Figure 15.7 *Effect of forcible "treatment" on helplessness (Seligman et al., 1968, p. 260).*

When asked why they did not respond, approximately 60% . . . reported that they felt they had no control over shock, so why try. These subjects reported that they spent the majority of their time in preparation for the upcoming shock. Approximately 35% reported that they, after pushing one or two buttons, abandoned the idea of escape. The other 5% gave no reason for response failure.

(THORNTON & JACOBS, 1971, P. 371.)

Note that the shock was avoidable, but its intensity (if not avoided) was unpredictable, and this condition was sufficient to cause many subjects simply to surrender and passively await shock. This research raises a question about men's behavior in everyday life: can most persons learn helplessness and meekly accept punishing contingencies?

Perspective

Virtually all the concepts discussed in this chapter and the last two are part of the stimulus-response approach. It is in these areas of learning research — classical and simple instrumental conditioning — that the stimulus-response approach originated and works best. Its value lies in the rigor and precision obtained from the study of overt, easily observable events: antecedent conditions (mainly stimuli), responses, and consequences of responses.

Consider only one aspect of learning, time relationships. The timing of the conditioned stimulus in relation to the unconditioned stimulus is a crucial determinant of the speed of classical conditioning. In instrumental conditioning, the time between the response and the reinforcer is equally important. The timing involved in interval schedules of reinforcement is of fundamental importance in understanding how the response is maintained, and the timing of punishment is a major determinant of its effectiveness. All these situations involve overt stimuli, responses, and reinforcers, and in this context the stimulus-response approach has added greatly to our knowledge and understanding of learning processes.

The approach has been especially fruitful in three areas of application. First, it has been used successfully in training animals to engage in behavior never seen under natural conditions. Thus chimpanzees have been taught responses analogous to working arithmetic problems (Ferster & Hammer, 1966). This kind of research tells us that the limits of learning are beyond what they appear to be in nature. One aspect of man's uniqueness may be his control of his own and other's behavior through *training,* as reflected in such changes as the switch from hunting animals to domesticating and raising them.

Second, stimulus-response concepts have proved useful in education. Skinner's early paper (1954) has led to a huge technology on programed learning — so-called *teaching machines* — which has greatly facilitated the mastery of school subjects and other topics (see Glaser, 1965).

A third application has been fruitful in the area of behavior change. Smokers who wish to kick the habit have benefited from a systematic program of punishment, called *aversion therapy,* and persons plagued by phobias have improved greatly with extinction and conditioning procedures, called *systematic desensitization* (see Chapter 27).

Finally, the emphasis on precision has led some stimulus-response psychologists to devise mathematical models of learning (for an early example, see Estes, 1950). Such models are analogous to theories in physics, which generate quantitative predictions. There is some debate about whether our data are sufficiently precise for a mathematical model to work. However the issue is resolved, it is stimulus-response psychologists who are attempting mathematical theories of learning, and this approach is entirely consistent with their emphasis on the precise, quantified investigation of simple, observable responses.

Whether the stimulus-response approach can handle the facts of more complex learning is an entirely different question. An emphasis on observable stimuli and responses may not be the best approach to learning that is largely implicit and covert. If it is necessary to refer to internal, inferred stimuli and responses, then the stimulus-response approach loses much of its rigor and precision. Its adherents insist that it is still preferable to its major alternative (cognitive theory), but this is a matter best left for the chapters on complex learning and cognition.

chapter 16

complex learning and imitation

*Immediacy — delay — flexibility — intradimen-
sional and extradimensional shifts — learning
sets — developmentally early and late learning
— oddity learning — vicarious reinforcement —
imitation learning — theories of imitation
(stimulus-response and social learning) —
determinants of imitation — role of imitation*

The value of the Skinner box in studying learning lies in its inclusion of the basic characteristics of simple instrumental conditioning: a stimulus (specific or generalized), yes-no kind of response (press a bar, peck a key), and reinforcers (rewarding or punishing). This stimulus-response learning, which occurs even in the lowest of animals, may be regarded as a building block in the "construction" of complex learning.

Various criteria of complexity were discussed in Chapter 12. Our interest here is focused on the complex learning lying between simple instrumental conditioning and the symbolic learning exemplified by abstract concepts and language. Four characteristics have been isolated and will be discussed in turn: immediacy, flexibility and strategy, relationship, and vicariousness.

Immediacy

Simple learning involves responding to a stimulus or moving toward a goal that is *here* and *now;* complex learning involves moving toward a goal indirectly or after a delay. We examined the *detour* problem in Chapter 12 (see Figure 12.12); the other basic procedure is the *delayed reaction.*

The delayed response has been studied for many decades. Early in this century Hunter (1913) devised an apparatus to investigate *spatial* delay (see Figure 16.1). The animal is first taught to associate food with an electric light turning on. Then while the animal is in the glass box, the light in one of the three compartments is turned on and then off. After a delay of seconds or minutes, the animal is released and allowed to enter one of three compartments, each having a light (turnedoff).

Mammals easily solve this problem; even the lowly rat can delay several minutes and still respond correctly. The time interval can be bridged by postural cues (the animal simply continues to face toward the correct light) or even by odors. To avoid these solutions to the problem of delay, researchers turned to *nonspatial* delay procedures. They allowed the animal to see which stimulus was correct and then delayed responding with the stimuli temporarily out of sight. With this procedure, rats cannot delay very long, but cats and dogs can delay for many seconds. When the animal must remember a specific object or a particular property of an object, only primates can sustain delays of more than a minute or so (Munn, 1965).

None of this research suggests that lower mammals, such as rats, cannot remember over periods of hours, days, weeks, or months; they can. After a response has been well-learned, it may persevere for long periods. The issue here, however, is not *memory* of a well-learned response but the *learning* of a response when there is a delay between exposure to the stimulus and opportunity to respond. During this delay, the organism must somehow substitute for the absent stimulation (assuming there are not postural or external cues present). It is this substitution, mediation, or *re*-presentation of stimuli that adds complexity to what would otherwise be a simple learning task. Presumably, primates can delay longer than lower mammals because they mediate better, a feature attributable to their larger and better organized cerebral cortex.

Flexibility

Instrumental conditioning is based on a *contingency* between a response and its consequences:

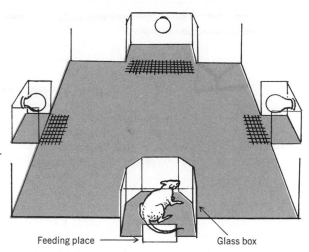

Figure 16.1 *The hunter delayed reaction apparatus (Hunter, 1913).*

Feeding place ⟶   Glass box

When a "correct" response is made, a reward tends to follow. So long as the contingency remains the same, the response is appropriate. But the conditions of life are variable, and yesterday's appropriate response may be inappropriate today. To adapt to changing circumstances, the learner must be flexible enough to alter the *basis* of his responding, the *response* itself, or both.

Intradimensional and Extradimensional Shifts

In studying the flexibility in animals, psychologists have relied mainly on tasks involving the *reversal* of discriminations. For example, an animal is first taught a simple discrimination: respond to a black stimulus but not a white. After the discrimination has been learned, the conditions are reversed. Now the animal must learn to respond to the white stimulus but not to the black.

Reversal learning has been studied in fish, turtles, rats, cats, primates, and man. All these species are capable of reversing discriminations, suggesting that the underlying flexibility of learning is a vertebrate adaptation. There is no evidence that invertebrates can reverse a discrimination, with the possible exception of the octopus (Munn, 1965).

Discrimination reversal has been labeled an *intradimensional* shift: the dimension (say, brightness, as in a black-white discrimination) remains the same, but the correct and incorrect stimuli change places. Flexibility in learning may also be studied by using tasks requiring an *extradimensional* shift: the dimension changes, say, from brightness to size. Mammals can make both kinds of shift equally well, but there are differences in man. The differences are especially important in comparing stimulus-response and cognitive approaches to learning.

In working with humans, especially adults, the discrimination needs to be complicated by extraneous stimulus dimensions; otherwise the learning would be too easy and mastered in a single trial. The first human study comparing the two kinds of shift used blocks of varying size and shape as stimuli (Buss, 1953). The intradimensional shift involved reversing a height discrimination (see Figure 16.2). The extradimensional shift involved a switch from shape to height. Consistent with the animal data, both kinds of shift retarded learning (based on comparison with a control group). The novel finding was that the extradimensional shift was more difficult.

This result, which has been repeated in subsequent research by others, is inconsistent with stimulus-response theory. This theory assumes

that in learning the original discrimination, the response to one stimulus is strengthened and the response to the other stimulus is weakened. When the discrimination is reversed (intradimensional shift), the results of the original learning severely handicap the new learning. In an extradimensional shift, the original learning equally affects the responses to the *new* positive and negative stimuli. Therefore the extradimensional shift should be easier, but the human data oppose the theory: the extradimensional shift is *slower* than the intradimensional shift.

To account for this finding, Kendler and Kendler (1962, 1970) formulated a two-stage theory. In learning a discrimination, humans presumably first learn a covert, implicit response: the nature of the dimension. In the Buss (1953) experiment this would be *height* for one group and *shape* for the other. Then they learn the specific association between the response and the stimuli; for example, short is correct and tall is incorrect. Thus there are two stages in such learning: the nature of the dimension and the specific discrimination within that dimension. When a discrimination is reversed (intradimensional shift), one stage has already been learned (the nature of the dimension); only the specific discrimination needs to be learned. But when the shift is extradimensional, both stages (the dimension and the specific discrimination) must be learned.

This theory has been more or less substantiated by research on children. Young children (kindergarten age and below) make the extradimensional shift quicker. They are responding like animals do, and their performance fits a simple stimulus-response model. Older children (first grade and above) make the intradimensional shift quicker, and the trend continues into adulthood (Kendler & Kendler, 1970). Their performance does not fit a simple stimulus-response model, but it does nicely conform to the Kendlers' two-stage model.

The Kendlers regard their theory as a stimulus-response theory. The implicit, mediational responses presumably lead to internal, inferred stimuli, which in turn lead to instrumental-observable responses. Such mediated responses and stimuli have been inferred by many stimulus-response psychologists (see Osgood, 1953) in an attempt to retain their approach in the face of

	First discrimination		Second discrimination	
	Positive stimulus	Negative stimulus	Positive stimulus	Negative stimulus
Intradimensional shift				
	(Dimension : height)		(Dimension : height)	
Extradimensional shift				
	(Dimension : shape)		(Dimension : height)	

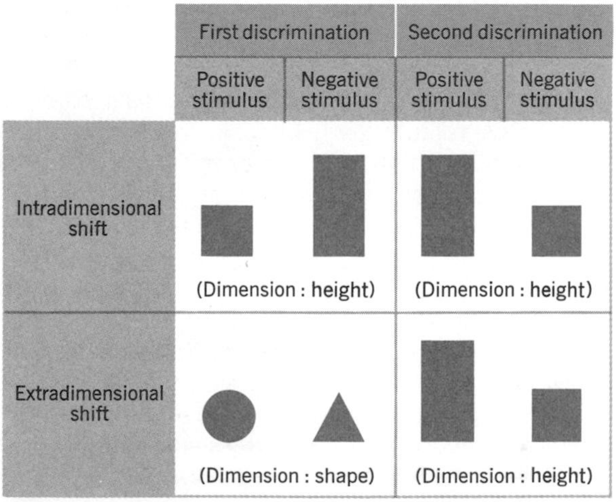

Figure 16.2 Intradimensional and extradimensional shifts (Buss, 1953).

the complexities of higher learning.[1] Thus the Kendlers suggest that the implicit response (the first stage) consists of *labeling* the appropriate dimension. If this is correct, it follows that having the subject *verbalize* as he learns should facilitate discrimination shifts. The evidence on this point is inconsistent: some studies show the effect, some do not, and some show a retarding effect of verbalization (see Wolff, 1967; Stevenson, 1970).

The point of this discussion is that a simple stimulus-response model appears to falter in explaining shift behavior. In an attempt to rescue the approach some theorists have adopted a mediational model that assumes internal covert stimuli and responses, which intervene between the observable stimuli and responses. How different is such mediation from the cognitions inferred by cognitive theorists? The internal, unobserved mediators suggested by stimulus-response theorists are clearly not the same as external stimuli and responses. And once such inferred entities are assumed, the elegant simplicity of the stimulus-response approach disappears. The inferred, covert mediators owe their existence to the inability of a simple stimulus-response approach to handle complex learning. Whether one prefers such mediators or the cognitions of cognitive theorists seems to be largely a matter of taste and training. As learning becomes more complex, abstract, and vicarious, the stimulus-response approach is forced to add inferred, internal processes. When this occurs, the line between stimulus-response and cognitive theories becomes blurred:

The conflict between environmentally based S-R conceptions and cognitive interpretations of behavior represents, in many ways, false dichotomies. When this controversy is considered within the boundaries of discrimination-shift behavior, we note that a single-unit S-R model can be coordinated to the behavior of animals and young children, while a mediational model, involving symbolic representations and possessing characteristics of cognitive formulations, applies to the functioning of older children and adults. In short, single-unit and cognitive control models supplement each other when viewed either within a comparative or a human developmental framework.

(KENDLER, 1971, P. 972.)

[1] *For an alternative theory, emphasizing attention and observing responses, see Zeaman and House (1963).*

Learning Sets

As we have seen, vertebrates are sufficiently flexible to reverse a discrimination or shift to a new stimulus property as the basis of responding. When such shifts are made, the old learning tends to retard the new. When flexibility is required in the face of a changing environment, it is obviously adaptive for a learner to develop a strategy that helps him to know when the old responses are no longer appropriate. Such a strategy could develop only after extended experience with learning problems. It is called learning-to-learn, or, more appropriately, *learning sets.*

The early work was done by Harlow (1951) and his students, mainly with primates. The animal is first trained on a discrimination and then it is reversed, just as in the experiments reviewed in the last section. But instead of a single discrimination reversal, there are hundreds. At first reversal is slow, and the animal makes many errors. But gradually, as trials accumulate, the errors drop out and the reversals are well-nigh perfect (see Figure 16.3).

One way of explaining these data suggests that

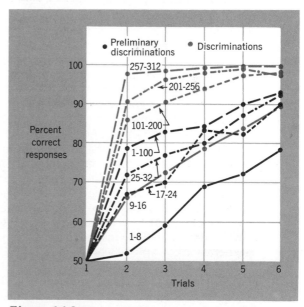

Figure 16.3 *Discrimination reversals in monkeys (Harlow, 1949).*

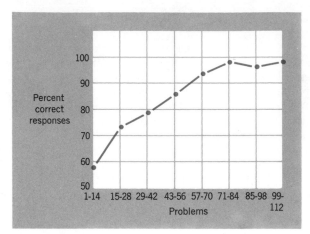

Figure 16.4 Correct responses on the second trial of discrimination reversals (Harlow, 1951).

the animal adopts a strategy of "win, stay—lose, shift." So long as the response is correct, it continues to be made. As soon as it is incorrect, the discrimination is reversed. The animals discovers that the old discrimination is incorrect on the first trial of the new discrimination. This means that the learning set (strategy) should reveal itself on the second trial. A plot of other data of Harlow's (1951) clearly shows the trend (see Figure 16.4). Once primates have acquired the appropriate strategy, they need only a single trial to shift the basis of responding.

A strategy that facilitates quick shifts in responding must be regarded as a higher form of learning. As such, it should show a phyletic sequence, being present in higher but not in lower forms. The evidence agrees. Amphibians and reptiles do not benefit from sustained training on discrimination reversal. Lower mammals can benefit but only a little. Higher mammals develop learning sets, but they do not reach the levels of primates. Figure 16.5 summarizes some of the comparative data. The ability to develop the "win, stay—lose, shift" strategy is directly related to the amount of new cortex in the animal's brain.

As might be expected, learning sets are child's play. Children in the 3- to 5-year range quickly acquire the strategy (Reese, 1965), and the speed of learning depends directly on intelligence (Harter, 1967). With advancing age children ac-

quire many different kinds of learning sets, as their approach to problems shifts from simple rote learning to the use of strategies.

The notion that the entire basis of learning alters during childhood has been used by White (1965) in an attempt to integrate stimulus-response and cognitive approaches. He suggests that early childhood learning is strictly associative (linking of stimuli with responses) and nonrepresentational (few or no cognitions). The outcome is an immediate, impulsive response, which is reinforced by praise or some other incentive. This is rote learning (see Table 16.1).

At roughly five years a transition phase begins, and by seven years the child has added an entirely new mode of learning. It is cognitive, employing many representations (mainly language and imagery). It is reflective, the child inhibiting his immediate rote response in favor of a response based on strategy. And this strategic behavior is reinforced by correctness, rather than by incentives. The addition of cognitive learning does not eliminate associative learning, but the latter is presumably dominated by the former. The earlier kind of behavior occurs mainly when speed

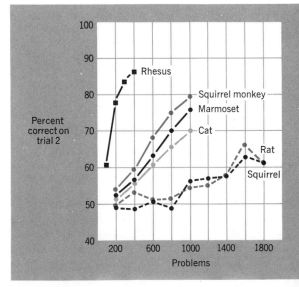

Figure 16.5 Comparative findings on learning sets (Warren, 1965).

Table 16.1

Modes of Learning Early and Late in Childhood (Based on White, 1965)

EARLY	LATE
Associative	Cognitive
Impulsive	Reflective
Few or no representations	Many representations
Rote	Strategy
Reinforced by incentives	Reinforced by correctness

is essential or when inhibition of response breaks down.

No one accepts all of White's assumptions. Some psychologists object that the dichotomy is too sharply drawn; others, that the notion of stages is inappropriate; and still others, that associative learning is not dominated by cognitive learning. Nevertheless, White's synthesis of the two kinds of learning offers an attractive developmental solution to the debate between stimulus-response and cognitive theorists. With both positions having something to offer, perhaps it is better to regard them as complementing rather than opposing one another.

Relationship

This section deals with rudimentary conceptual behavior: comparing stimuli and responding on the basis of one property, while ignoring other, irrelevant properties of the stimuli. The best examples of such relational learning are oddity problems and their opposite, matching-from-sample.

Oddity Problems

On each trial of an oddity problem the subject must select the *different* stimulus from among three or more stimuli (see Figure 12.3). The stimuli are changed from one trial to the next, so that the problem cannot be solved merely by memorizing the correct stimulus. The subject must respond on the basis of a relationship (or concept) — that of oddity — while neglecting all other properties of the stimuli.

Oddity problems were first studied by Harlow (1949) using primates as subjects. Such relational learning is beyond the ability of most lower animals, though rats can master a simplified oddity task with limited stimuli (Wodinsky & Bitterman, 1953). The typical oddity task is so difficult that even primates require hundreds or even thousands of trials to master it. For example, when animals are given 4800 trials in which to learn an oddity problem, monkeys and chimpanzees can do so but cats and raccoons cannot (Strong & Hedges, 1966).

To cap this phyletic sequence, children can master in only a few hundred trials oddity problems of the type used with animals. Young children (preschool age) have considerable difficulty, but school age children master oddity problems with ease (Lipsitt & Serunian, 1963; Gollin & Shirk, 1966).

To pile complexity on complexity, the oddity problem can be made *conditional*. Suppose, for example, that the stimuli vary in both shape and color. The subject could be required to select the odd-colored stimulus when given a color cue but the odd-shaped stimulus when given a shape cue (see Figure 16.6). This task adds a discrimination task to the oddity problem, rendering it extrmely difficult. Monkeys require as many as 6000 trials to master this problem (Harlow, 1951). When children are allowed only 200 trials to learn this task, their mastery varies directly with age: 10% of four year olds, 50% of six year olds, and 100% of twelve year olds are successful (Hill, 1965).

Matching-from-Sample

The oddity problem requires selection of the different stimulus. Matching-from-sample requires a

(a)   (b)

Figure 16.6 *A conditional oddity problem. The light-colored tray (a) is cue for odd shape and the dark-colored tray (b) is cue for odd color.*

(HARRY F. HARLOW, UNIVERSITY OF WISCONSIN PRIMATE LABORATORY).

Figure 16.7 *Examples from matching familiar figures test for reflection-impulsivity (Kagan, Pearson and Welch, 1966).*

match between a sample and one member of an array of stimuli. The two tasks are merely opposite sides of the coin of relational learning.

The matching task is illustrated in Figure 16.7. The top drawing is to be matched to one of the six below, and five of these differ in at least one way from the sample. The difficulty of the problem depends on how many properties are allowed to vary and how subtle the differences are. By manipulating these variables, Raven (1938) was able to develop an excellent nonverbal intelligence test, which consists entirely of matching-to-sample problems (the Progressive Matrices Test).

Matching-to-sample has not been used with lower animals, presumably because they lack the ability to learn the task. It has been used mainly with monkeys and chimpanzees, principally by Harlow and his students. In the simplest version, the animal merely matches the sample to one of two or three stimuli; this task requires as much as 1000 trials to learn. Complexity may be increased by adding a delay period. After the sample is shown, the animal must wait 5–20 seconds before the remaining stimuli are presented.

The task can also be made more difficult by requiring a generalized response (Weinstein, 1945). Thus when the sample is red the animal learns to select *all* red stimuli (see Figure 16.8*a*). The basis of selection is the color of the stimuli, regardless of their size, shape, or postion. Weinstein trained one monkey to go beyond matching and into humanlike conceptual responding. When the sample was an unpainted triangle, the monkey learned to select red stimuli (see Figure 16.8*b*). Later this learning was turned around, the animal selecting triangles when the sample was red. This represents a large step up from stimulus-bound learning. An unpainted triangle is perceptually unrelated to red objects, which means that the basis of matching cannot be mere visual similarity but must be a relationship between two stimulus *categories:* triangularity and redness.

The two kinds of matching illustrate one aspect of the concrete-abstract dichotomy. A match based on perceptual similarity — selecting red stimuli when the sample is red — is *concrete* in the sense that it depends directly on physical properties of the stimuli. A match based on a learned relationship — selecting red stimuli when the

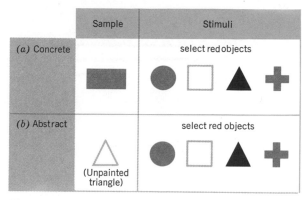

Figure 16.8 *Matching to sample: concrete and abstract.*

sample is an unpainted triangle — is *abstract* in that physical similarity is irrelevant. The learner must ignore the perceptual relationship and respond only to the learned one: that a triangle "represents" red objects.

Observational Learning

All the learning discussed so far has been *nonsocial.* The stimuli preceding the behavior *might* be other organisms, but they might also be, and usually are, objects or events. Observational learning is *social* in that another organism must be involved: after observing the behavior of a *model,* the *observer* changes his behavior, and this change is relatively enduring.

This broad definition includes several variants of observational learning. The key difference depends on reinforcement during acquisition: to the model, to the observer, or to both (see Table 16.2). If both the model and the observer are reinforced, the model's behavior serves as a cue for the observer's response, just as any nonsocial stimuli might serve as cues. The observer's task is simply to match his behavior to that of the model, hence the name *matched-dependent learning.* If only the model is reinforced, the observer cannot experience the reinforcement directly, hence the name *vicarious reinforcement.* Finally if neither the model nor the observer is reinforced during acquisition, any learning that occurs must be attributed

Table 16.2
Types of Observational Learning

	ACQUISITION	
	MODEL REINFORCED	OBSERVER REINFORCED
Matched-dependent learning	Yes	Yes
Vicarious reinforcement	No	No
Imitation	No	No

solely to the contiguity of the two organism, one behaving and the other observing. This variant of observational learning we shall call *imitation*.

Matched-Dependent Learning

The matching of one's behavior to another's occurs frequently in everyday life, especially in children. Witness the simple game of follow-the-leader. Miller and Dollard (1941) demonstrated that rats can also play the game. They first trained rats to turn one way in a simple T-maze to reach food. Then untrained rats were allowed to follow the trained ones through the maze, with both animals being reinforced for a correct response. On the first trial, the observer rats responded randomly, but by roughly 50 trials they had learned to match their responses perfectly to those of the models. Nor was the matching behavior specific to the model or the situation. It persisted, in both rats and children, when both the observer and the specific learning situation were altered.[2]

Such learning is instrumental conditioning in that the learner makes a response and is then rewarded. But it is a special kind of *relational* learning: the observer's response must be the same as the model's. The only difference between

matched dependent learning and other kinds of relational instrumental conditioning is that the cues for the observer's response are not objects or events but the behavior of the model.

Vicarious Reinforcement

When only the model is rewarded, any effects of the reinforcement on the observer must be vicarious. Presumably, such substitute reinforcement offers information about either the reinforcer (its nature, magnitude, and occurrence in relation to preceding behavior) or the model's reaction to the reinforcer. However it works, vicarious reinforcement does lead to the acquisition of new responses by the observer (Berger, 1961).

The basic variable obviously must be what happens to the model, and an experiment by Bandura et al. (1963a) neatly demonstrates the effects. Their subjects were nursery school children who first watched models on film and, after a delay, were tested for imitation. In the film seen by one group the model was rewarded, and in another the model was punished. A control group saw no film. The children in the model-reinforced condition copied more behavior than did the children in the control group, but there was no reliable difference between the model-punished and the control groups.

Many students have confirmed this effect (see

[2] *For a review of subsequent research on matched dependent learning, see Aronfreed (1969).*

Flanders, 1968), but only a few have determined its magnitude. Vicarious reinforcement has been found to yield better learning than direct reinforcement (Berger, 1961), but this may be a special case. In other research (Kanfer & Marston, 1963) the two have yielded roughly equivalent learning, though adding direct reinforcement to vicarious reinforcement did not enhance learning.

Though vicarious and direct reinforcement have essentially similar effects on *acquisition,* their effects on *extinction* are different. The effect of *partial* direct reinforcement during acquisition is well known: the lower the percentage of reinforcement, the greater is resistance to extinction. This effect simply does not hold for vicarious reinforcement (Lewis & Duncan, 1958). In fact, the greater the percentage of vicarious reinforcement, the more copying there is in both acquisition and extinction (Bisese, 1966). Thus reinforcing a model may yield different results from reinforcing an *observer.* This finding is a reminder that the term *reinforcement* is broadly defined and includes several different processes (see Chapter 14).

Imitation

We have reserved the term *imitation* for the learning that occurs when neither the model nor the observer is reinforced during acquisition. Though many lower animals imitate, such learning is most easily observed in primates. The best-documented reports have come from researchers who raised chimpanzees in a human environment. Thus the chimpanzee Viki — reared with humans — spontaneously applied cosmetics to her face in front of a mirror, pried lids off cans, and inserted a pencil into a sharpener and turned the handle (Hayes & Hayes, 1952). Such activities usually involve a long delay between observation and subsequent performance, and they occur without reinforcers being delivered to either the model or the observer. A more recent example, the chimpanzee Washoe, can imitate more "human" behavior:

From the beginning of the project she was bathed regularly and according to a standard routine. Also, from her 2nd month with us, she always had dolls to play with. One day, during the 10th month of the project, she bathed one of her dolls in the way we usually bathed her. She filled her little bathtub with water, dunked the doll in the tub, then took it out, and dried it with a towel. She has repeated the entire performance or parts of it, many times since, sometimes also soaping the doll. (GARDNER & GARDNER, 1969. P. 666.)

The only startling aspect of such behavior, which is common in human children, is that a young chimpanzee was capable of it. Perhaps we should not be surprised, for imitation learning evidently occurs in lower animals. But it is in primates, and especially humans, that imitation plays such an important — perhaps even dominant — role during development.

Research Report

An experiment by Bandura (1965*a*) demonstrates not only imitation under the controlled conditions of the laboratory, but also the effects of reinforcement to the observer and the model. The subjects were nursery school boys and girls, but we shall examine only the girls' data, which are more clear-cut than the boys'.

All subjects first watched a film of a man behaving as follows:

The film began with a scene in which the model walked up to an adult-size plastic Bobo doll and ordered him to clear the way. After glaring for a moment at the noncompliant antagonist the model exhibited four novel aggressive responses each accompanied by a distinctive verbalization.

First, the model laid the Bobo doll on its side, sat on it, and pinched it on the nose while remarking, "Pow, right on the nose, boom, boom." The model then raised the doll and pommeled it on the head with a mallet. Each response was accompanied by the verbalization, "Sockeroo . . . stay down." Following the mallet aggression, the model kicked the doll about the room, and these responses were interspersed with the comment, "Fly away." Finally, the model threw rubber balls at the Bobo doll, each strike punctuated with "Bang." This sequence of physically and verbally aggressive behavior was repeated twice.   (BANDURA, 1965a, PP. 590–591.)

The remainder of the film differed for the two experimental groups. One group of children saw the model *rewarded* with candy and soft drinks. The second group saw him *punished* by another adult, who bawled him out and sat on him. A control group, labeled *no consequences,* saw no film.

Immediately after the film, each child was taken to a room with many toys, including the ones used by the model. The experimenter told the child that he could play with anything and then left, ostensibly to bring back more toys. Each child's behavior was observed for ten minutes through a one-way mirror (first performance). Finally, the experimenter returned and promised the child a variety of incentives (pretty picture, fruit piece) for each activity of the model that the child could reproduce (second performance).

The findings are shown in Figure 16.9, which shows only the girls' data. During the first performance, when there was no incentive, there was as much imitation when the model was not rewarded (no consequences) as when he was, but punishment to the model drastically diminished imitation during the second performance, eliminating differences among the three groups.

These data demonstrate the importance of distinguishing between *learning* and *performance.* The child clearly learned some novel responses merely by observing the model: in the *no consequences*

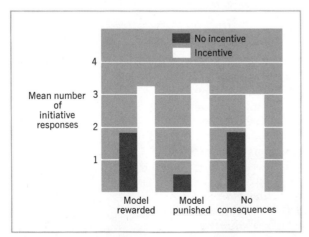

Figure 16.9 *Imitation with and without incentives under varying conditions of model-reinforcement (Bandura, 1965).*

group, neither the model nor the observer was reinforced as of the first performance. But when incentives were supplied, their *performance* increased. We know that the incentives affected only performance because there was no opportunity for further learning between the first and second performance. In brief, observation of a model, without any reinforcement, is sufficient for imitation to occur, but the performance of imitated acts is enhanced by reinforcement.

There are two major approaches to imitation. The first is the traditional stimulus-response learning view, which emphasizes reinforcement and assumes that the tendency to imitate is itself learned. The second is a "social learning" approach, which emphasizes contiguity and the encoding of cognitions[3] and implicitly assumes that the tendency to imitate is innate.

Stimulus-Response Theory

Though there have been several attempts to formulate a stimulus-response theory of imitation (see Miller, 1959; Rosenbaum & Arenson, 1968), the most comprehensive theory is that of Gerwitz (1968; Gerwitz & Stingle, 1968). He attempts to account for four sequential aspects of imitation, or, in his terms, *matching responses:*

1. Initial occurrence of matching responses.
2. How matching responses are learned.
3. Development of a general tendency to match behavior.
4. How matching behavior is maintained with minimal or no reinforcement.

The theory is outlined in Figure 16.10. The first matching responses are usually seen early in development. They may occur merely by chance, by physical assistance from an adult, or by direct training (operant shaping procedures). However they first occur, matching responses are strongly reinforced by praise from adults or by achieving a reward. As time passes, many different matching responses are reinforced in many different situations. This learning is analogous to the matching-to-sample behavior discussed earlier. Gradually

the various matching responses coalesce into a general tendency to imitate the behavior of others. Such behavior is reinforced only part of the time, and it is well known that partial reinforcement leads to behavior that is extremely resistant to extinction. The endpoint is a generalized tendency to imitate, which can be sustained with little or no immediate reinforcement.

This theory certainly accounts for what is known about imitation. Its strength lies in its ability to explain imitation on the basis of learning principles already well established: reinforcement, partial reinforcement, and matching-to-sample learning. But it does have two weaknesses. First, it neatly explains imitation but only after the fact: it accounts for what is already known, but it offers no suggestions that would lead to further knowledge. As we noted in Chapter 2, a good theory not

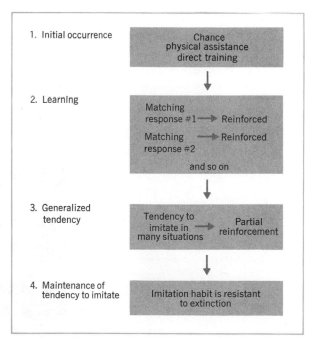

Figure 16.10 Stimulus-response theory of imitation.

[3] *Though this approach is labeled* social learning, *it leans heavily toward the cognitive side of theorizing. Thus the two views of imitation are the familiar opponents, stimulus-response and cognition.*

only explains old facts but leads to the gathering of new facts.

The second weakness is the heavy burden placed on the learning of very young organisms. The theory assumes that the tendency to imitate is a product of learning, but imitation appears very early in life. This means that an infant who imitates must have previously been reinforced for a variety of matching responses, a notion that strains credulity. One way of testing this hypothesis is to determine whether a young animal with little or no prior learning can imitate. Turner (1964) used chicks only 30 hours after hatching; each chick observed a mechanical hen peck at grains of food (see Figure 12.3).[4] After this observation the chicks were allowed to feed on various-colored grains of food and tended to choose the same color as the mechanical hen. A 30-hour chick simply has had no time to learn to imitate, and therefore such imitation must be innate.

Social Learning Theory

This theory assumes that imitation learning, like classical or instrumental conditioning, is an innate

[4] *This experiment was described in Chapter 12 (see p. 244).*

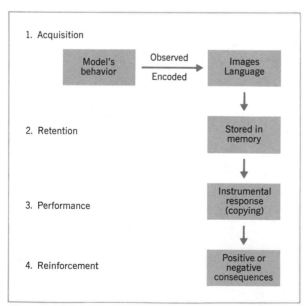

Figure 16.11 *Social learning theory of imitation.*

capability of the organism. It focuses on the details of imitation, especially the encoding of observations for later use. As outlined by Bandura (1965b; 1969), there are four sequential steps: acquisition, retention, performance, and reinforcement (see Figure 16.11).

Acquisition starts with observation of the model's behavior. Our focus being on imitation rather than on vicarious reinforcement, we assume that the model is not reinforced. The observer encodes what he sees, as images or language representations. These are stored in memory until there is an opportunity to perform the behavior. When the imitation response is made, it can be strengthened by positive reinforcement or weakened by negative reinforcement. This last phase is no different from any other stimulus-response learning.

The theory makes a sharp distinction between acquisition and performance. *Acquisition* of matching behavior is assumed to occur mainly through *contiguity*: the mere presence of an observer when the model is responding. *Performance* of imitative acts is thought to be determined by *reinforcement* of either the model, the observer, or both. Linking acquisition with performance are the observer's symbolic representation of the model's behavior.

The cognitive aspect of the theory—the encoding of observations as images or language—clearly distinguishes it from stimulus-response theory, and this cognitive emphasis is one of the strong points of the theory in that it has led to new facts. For example, the theory predicts that any procedure that facilitates encoding of observations of the model's behavior should enhance imitation. This prediction was tested with three groups of young children who watched a film (Bandura et al., 1966). One group described the film as they watched it (*symbolization*); the second group merely observed passively (*passive observation*); and the third group counted numbers as they watched (*competing symbolization*). On a subsequent (reinforced) test of copying the model's behavior, the symbolization group imitated most, the passive observation group next, and the competing symbolization group least. With the passive observation group clearly being a control (no special encoding), these results demonstrate that imitation is *enhanced* by helping symbolic encoding and *diminished* by interfering with symbolic encoding. Score another point for the cognitive approach.

Determinants of Imitation

The variables that influence imitation may be grouped under headings relevant to social learning theory, which has sparked most of the research in this area: the model, the observer, encoding, rehearsal, and performance (see Table 16.3 for a summary).

THE MODEL. The model's various responses comprise the stimuli displayed to the observer. These stimuli should be easier to encode when they are simple, discrete, and presented at a reasonable rate; and presumably the easier the encoding, the better the retention and subsequent imitation.

The consequences of the model's behavior comprise a powerful determinant of copying behavior. Vicarious reinforcement enhances imitation, vicarious punishment diminishes it.

One model tends to vary from the next in gender, age, and a variety of other characteristics. The relationship of the model and the observer, established on the basis of their prior interaction, clearly influences imitation; we shall discuss this issue under the heading of *identification* in Chapter 24. Of more immediate relevance are the competence and success of the model. Celebrities, affluent persons, and those with demonstrated competence tend to be imitated more than others (see Bandura, 1969). Power, in the form of control over rewards, exerts a strong influence on imitation (Bandura et al., 1963b).

THE OBSERVER. The observer must possess sufficient cognitive ability to record and store his observations for later use. This involves being able to focus attention, encode what is perceived, and eventually retrieve it for performance. Vision appears to be the most efficient sensory channel for the perception of complex stimuli, and it is no accident that visually dominant animals tend to imitate more than others. Of course, hearing is also an excellent channel, and we know that birds and humans easily mimic the calls and other sounds of those around them.

On the motor side, the observer must have the appropriate response components available. Watching a skilled violinist or surgeon will not facilitate imitation by an inexperienced observer.

Table 16.3
Determinants of Imitation

Model

Behavior:
simple
clearly distinguished
slow enough to be observed

Reinforcement:
model rewarded
model punished
no consequences

Characteristics:
competent
successful
powerful

Observer

Cognitive capabilities:
attention span
encoding abilities
retrieval (memory)
Motor capabilities:
sufficiently mature
response availability

Encoding
Imagery
Language
Other symbols

Rehearsal
Re-presenting stimuli
Practicing responses

Performance
Appropriate occasion for the response
Reinforcement

Nor has man succeeded when his attempts at flying have been exact imitations of birds' flight. A final example concerns speech. Primates cannot imitate human speech in spite of having some of the cognitive abilities underlying language; they simply do not have the necessary vocal apparatus. Parrots, on the other hand, can mimic human

speech — but only as sounds, not as language.
ENCODING. It is not known how animals encode their observations of the model's behavior. Human encoding consists primarily of visual and auditory images and language; other symbolic codes, such as music or dance notation, are rare.

We saw earlier that encoding enhances imitation (Bandura et al., 1966). Gerst (1971) extended these findings, comparing coding by concrete description, summary labels, and vivid images. When delayed imitation was tested, summary labels proved best; imitation was substantially poorer when imagery or concrete verbalization was used.
REHEARSAL. After the observations have been encoded, they may be rehearsed by re-presenting the stimuli: calling up an image of the model's behavior or repeating to oneself the summary labels. On the other hand, the model's responses themselves may be rehearsed, and the observer may actually practice the behavior along with the model. Berger (1966) found that observers practiced performing the hand signals of a model, though observers had not been instructed to do so. Such rehearsal cannot be attributed to the anticipation of later performance and reinforcement, for it occurred even in subjects who believed that they were no longer in the experiment (and therefore anticipated no subsequent performance or reinforcement).
PERFORMANCE. Finally, the extent of imitation is determined, as is any learning, by the opportunity to perform what has been learned. The more a situation calls for, or is appropriate to, responses that have been previously observed in a model, the more likely are imitative responses. Once such responses occur, they are subject to the consequences that follow any instrumental behavior; reward strengthens them, and punishment and nonreward weaken them.
THE ROLE OF IMITATION. Imitation learning is much more efficient than instrumental conditioning in speed and breadth of learning (Bandura, 1969). Most of the complex sequential acts we acquire are learned through imitation. Consider a common skill such as driving a car. If the learner's behavior had to be shaped by the slow process of differential reinforcement, he would need many months of intensive training to master driving — and many persons would never learn to drive. Imitation learning bypasses most of the early trial-and-error phases of acquisition, and the learner can start early to make correct responses. The ability to copy allows most persons to learn to drive in only a few hours.

Driving a car is a trivial skill in comparison with speaking a language. All normal children acquire the language that they hear spoken. There is some reinforcement for speaking correctly and with the local accent, but no child could ever learn to talk solely on the basis of instrumental learning. Without imitation, children do not acquire speech, which accounts for the failure of deaf children to learn to talk.

There are analogous situations in animals. Many species of birds have particular calls that are acquired by the young through imitation. The penguins of Antarctica often gather on the ice at the edge of the water and try to push one penguin overboard. This seemingly playful activity is designed to discover whether there are seals in the water (seals eat penguins). Thus only one unlucky penguin is risking its life, while the remainder of the group can learn by observation. Thus observational learning can play an important role in the survival of highly social animals, including man:

The provision of social models is also an indispensible means of transmitting and modifying behavior in situations where errors are likely to produce costly or fatal consequences. Indeed, if social learning proceeded exclusively on the basis of rewarding and punishing consequences, most people would never survive the socialization process. Even in cases where nonsocial stimuli can be relied upon to elicit some approximation of the desired behavior, and errors do not result in perilous outcomes, people are customarily spared exceedingly tedious and often haphazard trial-and-error experimentation by emulating the behavior of socially competent models. In fact, it would be difficult to imagine a socialization process in which the language, mores, vocational and avocational patterns, the familial customs of a culture, and its educational, social, and political practices were shaped in each new member by selective reinforcement without the response guidance of models who exhibit the accumulated cultural repertoires in their own behavior. To the extent that people successfully match the behavior of appropriate societal models, the social-learning process can be greatly accelerated and the development of response patterns by differential reinforcement can be short-circuited. (BANDURA, 1969, P. 213.)

section six
cognition

chapter 17

concepts and cognitive development

Concepts — basis of equivalence — affective, functional, and formal categories — percepts and concepts — uses of concepts — rules — conjunctive, disjunctive, and relational rules — a hierarchy of rules — cognitive development — two views of knowing — Piaget — assimilation and accommodation — stages — sensorimotor period — representative intelligence period (preoperational and concrete operations subperiods) — conservation problems — formal operations period — perspective

Concepts and cognitive development are separate but related topics. Research on concepts has been mainly an American enterprise, influenced strongly by the stimulus-response approach and typically using adults as subjects. The aim of the research has been to understand the *content* of the concepts and the *rules* of their use.

Cognitive development has been, until recently, the focus of European psychologists—under the influence of Jean Piaget. The theoretical approach has been extremely cognitive, the research approach less laboratory-oriented, and the subjects mainly children.

Concepts

Each object or event is unique in that it differs in *some* way from all others. In both science and everyday life uniqueness is ignored; we explicitly or implicitly assign the object or event to a *class* or the basis of shared properties of attributes. Such classes are called *concepts,* and they are the basic tools used to impose order and meaning on an environment that bombards us with stimuli.

Basis of Equivalence

To treat two objects as members of the same class — for example, to say that an apple and a pear are both fruits — is to assume or decide that they are in some way similar. Obviously, apples and pears can easily be discriminated, but in some contexts they are treated alike; that is, they are examples of the concept *fruit*. What is the basis of such equivalence? Bruner et al. (1956) suggest that there are three bases, yielding three broad classes of categories: *affective, functional,* and *formal.*

AFFECTIVE CATEGORIES. Objects and events may be linked because they evoke the same mood or affect. Affective reactions often occur at a nonverbal level, and some can be traced back to early childhood (a preverbal period). Affective categories are therefore difficult to verbalize, and they are usually discussed by using connotations and indirect description. It is difficult to describe precisely which paintings, songs, stories, plays, or movies make us laugh, but they are linked by the common response, laughter; others may induce sadness or melancholy.

The category may also be time-defined. The songs, movies, and dances of a particular year tend to be grouped and remembered nostalgically by those who experienced them together when young. A surprisingly large number of men include a professional football game in the class "Pearl Harbor Day" because the Japanese attack was announced during the radio broadcast of the football game.

FUNCTIONAL CATEGORIES. The large majority of concepts are functional, the class linking objects of events in terms of common consequences. A bicycle, an automobile, a wagon, and a bus are alike in that they serve as vehicles of transportation. Similarly, a rifle, a cannon, a knife, a whip, and a club all deliver physical punishment and thus are included under the concept of weapons. These disparate objects are linked solely by their function.

That functional concepts are common and easily understood should not surprise us. Most behavior is instrumental in that it has an impact on the environment, and the most important aspect of adjustment to the environment is "getting the job done." We have been naturally selected to stay alive (acquire food and ward off danger) and raise the next generation. These functions break down into the thousand-and-one instrumental tasks of everyday life. Small wonder, then, that our concepts tend to be utilitarian.

FORMAL CATEGORIES. Beyond functional categories are classes defined by properties that are less concrete and utilitarian. Such classes, which specify *intrinsic* attributes, are called *formal* categories. They are less stimulus-bound and more abstract than the functional concepts common to everyday usage and thought. Thus the physical concept of *force* is somewhat more abstract than everyday notions of force. Similarly, the psychological concept of *reinforcement* is abstract and inclusive, including three general kinds of events (see Figure 17.1). Formal categories are widely used in science but not in everyday life; this is one reason why laymen find scientific explanations so difficult to understand.

The Perceptual-Conceptual Dimension

The discerning reader will have noticed that categories occur not only in using concepts but also in perception. When an object is perceived as being red or as being large, it is in a sense classified by the perceiver. Though classification is involved in both perceiving and conceptualizing, percepts and concepts do differ: they lie on opposite ends of a developmental continuum. The infant can perceive but cannot conceptualize. As he progresses through childhood, he becomes better able to classify and categorize. Beyond the age of 10 years, most new learning is probably conceptual (Gagné, 1968).

Percepts and concepts differ in four ways[1] (see Table 17.1). We perceive the *concrete* properties of objects — their color, size, weight, hardness, smell, and so on. But we may conceptualize *abstract* qualities such as beauty and democracy.

Perceiving is facilitated by *redundancy:* repeated information or the same stimulus input presented in different ways. Thus, when there are

---

[1] *The last three distinctions (redundancy, selectivity, and contiguity) were suggested by Wohlwill (1962).*

Table 17.1
Differences Between Percepts and Concepts

	PERCEPTS	CONCEPTS
Concrete-abstract	Concrete	Abstract
Redundancy	Repeated information is often needed	Repeated information is rarely needed
Selectivity	Difficult to distinguish relevant from irrelevant	Easy to distinguish relevant from irrelevant
Contiguity	Stimuli must be near in space and time	Stimuli can be distant in space and time

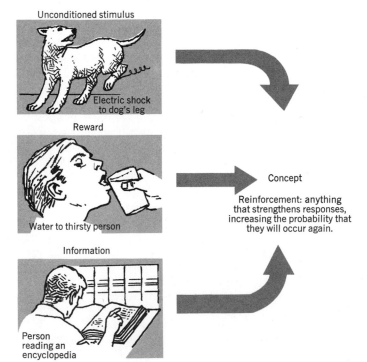

Unconditioned stimulus

Electric shock to dog's leg

Reward

Water to thirsty person

Information

Person reading an encyclopedia

Concept

Reinforcement: anything that strengthens responses, increasing the probability that they will occur again.

Figure 17.1 A formal category.

many cues, the figure-ground distinction is easily perceived; when there are few cues, figure can become ground, and ground can become figure, as in reversible figures (see Figure 11.3). In contrast, concepts require little extra information. Once the object or event has been classified, no more information is needed; this is one of the advantages of concepts over percepts.

The third dimension is *selectivity*. Perception alone does not suffice to separate relevant information from irrelevant information. Thus, if water in a wide glass is poured into a narrow glass, it rises higher in the narrow glass. Young children, perceiving the increased height of the water (irrelevant), say there is now more water. Older children attend not to the dimensions of the glasses but to the operation of pouring water (relevant), and this tells them that the amount of water is unchanged. Concepts make it easier to distinguish the relevant from the irrelevant.

Finally, perception requires that stimuli be *contiguous* in space and time. We have already noted how proximity affects perception (see Chapter 11), and it is obvious that to be perceived, a stimulus must be here and now. But concepts can refer to stimuli that are widely spaced (for example, the concept of the capitals of countries) or separated in time (the concept of historical causation — a present event causing a future event).

In brief, the developmental sequence from *perceptually* dominant cognition to *conceptually* dominant cognition confers several advantages: more efficient processing of information (less redundancy needed, relevant easily distinguished from irrelevant) and capability of dealing with a broader range of stimuli (more abstract, more distant in time and space). The perceptual end involves simple, concrete properties of stimuli, such as color, size, weight, hardness, smell, and all the various attributes discussed in the section on perception. These are the characteristics that allow us to identify most of the objects and events in the environment. Some objects and events are complex, possessing several properties, and their identification borders on the conceptual end of the dimension. Finally, there are classes of objects and events that involve complex and *abstract* properties (for example, *beauty* or *democracy*), and these may be placed at the conceptual end of the continuum.

Though percepts and concepts differ in several ways, the process of categorizing is essentially the same for both (Bruner et al., 1956). The emphasis here will of course be on the conceptual end of the continuum.

The Uses of Concepts

What good are concepts? They have four uses. First, they help to *identify* objects and events. This is extremely important, for most of us greatly fear the unknown. An approaching object may cause some trepidation so long as it is strange and unidentified ("Do I stay, run, or approach it?"). Once identified as a dog, it no longer elicits fear.

Second, concepts help to simplify complex stimuli. Objects that are in many ways dissimilar can be grouped together on the basis of one or more similarities. Thus hundreds of different objects can be subsumed under a more manageable number of categories.[2] For example, in spite of a great variety among dogs — compare a dachshund with a Saint Bernard — the many breeds may be classified under a single concept, dog (see Figure 17.2).

Furthermore, if concepts are available, one need not continually learn about new stimuli. Novel stimuli can be assigned to a class of stimuli already known. For example, if one were to encounter a relatively rare breed of dog — say, a Mexican Chihuahua — the animal is sufficiently doglike to be so labeled; there would be no need to learn about an entirely new stimulus (the Chihuahua). Thus concepts provide ready-made categories into which new information is fitted, and this is a major way of imposing meaning on the environment.

Finally, concepts help to distinguish between appearance and reality. A very young child, who has only a vague concept of what a dog is, might believe that a man dressed as a dog is really a dog (see Figure 17.2). But an older child, who knows precisely what a dog is, would not be fooled. Similarly, older children can distinguish between the imaginary world of myths (Santa Claus, elves,

---

[2] *This process also leads to stereotypes, one basis of prejudice (to be discussed in Chapter 30).*

(*a*)

goblins, and dragons) and the real world of animals and humans.[3]

RULES. So far we have been dealing with only one aspect of concepts, *attributes*. Attributes, as we have seen, may be properties (red, large, heavy) or functions (cuts, moves, transports, shelters). Some are more concrete (colors, sounds), and some are more abstract (democracy, beauty).

The other aspect of concepts is the *rules* that state which attributes constitute the concept and how they are to be combined. The rule defining the concept may be extremely precise—for example, *widow* or *parallelogram;* or it may be fuzzy and imprecise—for example, the concepts of *creativity* or *intelligence*. The rule may be laid down to include many instances—for example, *crystals;*

---

[3] *This example suggests that concepts may also* confuse *appearance with reality. Preconceived notions—such as ghosts or the stars' influence on events—have served to obscure reality for those who believe in these notions.*

or it may be restricted to include fewer instances for example, *diamonds*. Thus some concepts are precise, others not; some concepts are more inclusive, others more exclusive.

TYPES OF RULES. There are three basic ways in which attributes can be combined to form concepts: conjunctive, disjunctive, and relational (Bruner et al., 1956). The three types of rules are summarized in Table 17.2. *Conjunctive* categories require the joint presence of two or more attributes. Thus a bachelor is both male and unmarried; a priest is both male and Catholic. *Disjunctive* categories involve *either-or* rules. Thus a single person may have never married or may have married but no longer be married (as a result of divorce or death of the spouse). *Relational* categories require that attributes be in some way linked. Thus first cousins must be the children of siblings (*sibling* is a disjunctive concept meaning brother *or* sister).

Of course, attributes do not have to be com-

(c)

Figure 17.2 *Uses of concepts: (a) identify objects; (b) deal with complexity; (c) deal with new stimuli, avoid need for constant new learning; (d) distinguish between appearance and reality.*

[(a) SELDA SCHARIN/MONKMEYER: (b) WALTER CHANDOHA:

(c) V. D. MEID/MONKMEYER: (d) FRIEDMAN-ABELES]

(d)

Table 17.2
Types of Conceptual Rules

TYPE	BRIEF DEFINITION	EXAMPLE
Conjunctive	*Both* attributes	Bachelor (both male and unmarried)
Disjunctive	*Either* attribute	Single person (unmarried, divorced or widowed)
Relational	*Relationship* between attributes	Cousins (parent of one child is brother or sister of parent of other child)

bined. The concept can be defined solely in terms of a single property. Thus all vertebrates have a backbone, and all birds have wings.

A HIERARCHY OF RULES. The various rules can be arranged in a hierarchy of use: lower-level rules are necessary in order to use higher-level rules. Neisser and Weene (1962) arranged simple, conjunctive, and disjunctive rules into three such levels (see Table 17.3). The simplest level involves only a single attribute, which is common to all members of the class. The second level consists of *conjunctive* rules (*both* attributes), *disjunctive* rules (*either* attribute), and elaborations on these; these rules are combinations of the simpler rules of the first level. The third level consists of rules comprising combinations of rules at the second level. In the example given in Table 17.3, the level-3 rule is a combination of a level-2 rule, disjunction (*either* attribute) and a level-1 rule, negation (not present).

The hierarchy presents a logical ordering of conceptual rules from simple to complex. It follows that the simpler concepts should be learned faster than the more complex ones. This is precisely what Neisser and Weene (1962) found: level-1 rules were learned faster than level-2 rules, which were learned faster than level-3

rules. Thus the hierarchy of complexity is reflected in difficulty of learning: the more complex the rule, the more difficult it is to learn. Subsequent research has confirmed this fact in adults (Haygood & Bourne, 1965) and children (Bourne & O'Banion, 1971).

Bourne (1970) extended the scheme of Neisser and Weene, showing that it was part of a larger hierarchy. He moved subjects through a sequence that began with properties of objects and ended with a complex, inclusive system of classification. The subjects were shown objects, each with several *attributes.* The objects were linked by common attributes to form a *class concept.* These concepts were combined by various *rules* (conjunctive, disjunctive, and combinations of these). Finally, the rules could be assembled to form a *system.* From lowest to highest, the hierarchy consists of attributes, objects, class concepts, rules, and system.

*   *   *

Much has been learned about concepts in the absence of any particular theory, but no scientist can be satisfied with a mere catalogue of facts. They must be integrated as part of a coherent

Table 17.3
*A Hierarchy of Conceptual Rules**
(from Neisser & Weene, 1962)

RULE	DESCRIPTION	EXAMPLE
Level 1		
presence	Single attribute must be present	Vertebrate: must have a backbone
absence	Attribute must *not* be present	Invertebrate: must not have a backbone
Level 2		
conjunction	Both attributes must be present	Wife: must be both female and married
disjunction	Either attribute must be present (or both together)	Citizen: must be born here or married to someone who is already a citizen
Level 3		
either/or	*Either* attribute must be present but *not both* together	Negative product: either factor negative $(-1 \times +1 = -1)$ but not both $(-1 \times -1 = +1)$

* These are examples of each level; the complete list has 10 rules.

system that not only explains what is already known but directs the search for new information. In this endeavor the few attempts by American psychologists to create a comprehensive theory have been overshadowed by the monumental work of Jean Piaget.

Cognitive Development

Piaget's theory (1926, 1952, 1954, 1970) embraces not merely concepts but all of cognition. His ideas, at first neglected by most psychologists,

have loosed a torrent of research and controversy during the past two decades.

For the past 50 years Piaget has studied the *development* of thinking and conceptualizing, which until recently were neglected by American psychologists. His contributions had little impact, not so much because most were written in French but because his approach to *knowing* is so different from the empirical tradition. Moreover, the many *inferred processes* he believes to be important were alien to psychologists imbued with a behaviorist tradition. Finally, his emphasis on a *stage* theory of development was counter to the

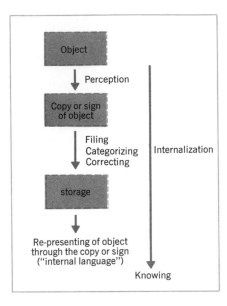

Figure 17.3 *Common, empirical view of knowing.*

cumulative learning model implicitly assumed by American psychologists, whose environmental bias was stronger than it is now. In brief, Piaget's approach diverged from mainstream American psychology in the areas of *knowing, basic processes,* and *developmental stages.* These are suitable headings for describing the theory.

Knowing

Piaget's view of knowing may be contrasted with the commonly accepted view (Furth, 1968). In the prevailing empirical view, knowing involves implicit signs that copy and represent reality (see Figure 17.3). Perception of an object presumably leads to a kind of *internal sign,* which is filed in an appropriate category. Subsequently, this sign can be re-evoked, enabling the person to think about the object despite its absence. Thus to know about an object is to possess something like a carbon copy, which stands for the object. Previously overt reactions to overt stimuli are replaced by covert reactions to covert, mediating stimuli. Thus the process of knowing involves internalizing what was originally external.

Piaget's reaction to the common empirical view of knowing is forthright. He rejects it:

But this passive interpretation of the act of knowledge is in fact contradicted at all levels of development and, particularly, at the sensorimotor and prelinguistic levels[4] of cognitive adaptation and intelligence. Actually, in order to know objects, the subject must act upon them and therefore transform them: he must displace, connect, combine, take apart, and reassemble them. . . .

Knowledge, then, at its origin, neither arises from objects nor from the subject, but from interactions— between the subject and those objects. (1970, P. 704)

Knowledge, then, is not something extracted from the environment but something that arises from the person-environment interaction (see Figure 17.4). The infant can know something at only a practical level, when he "*acts*" directly on the object or event—that is, when he handles it or actively looks at it. Gradually, these overt acts become unnecessary, and the child can know an object without acting on it. Instead he performs *operations,* which are implicit "mental acts" roughly analogous to thinking and conceptualizing. Thus there is a progression from ex-

---

[4] *These are the earliest eras, including the first 18 months of life, before language is available.*

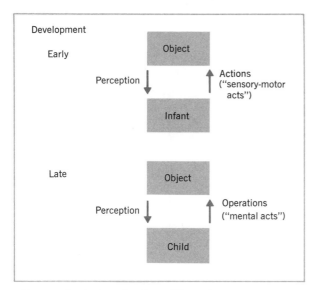

Figure 17.4 Piaget's view of knowing.

ternal to internal knowing that is comparable to *internalization* in the usual empirical view. But the developmental process, as seen by Piaget, is not at all comparable, and Furth (1968) has suggested the term *interiorization:*

What I like to call functional interiorization *is thus the specific condition of a knowing in which the external motor reaction is no longer an essential prerequisite. . . . As compared to a sensory-motor act, what is interiorized is not the structure that is always internal, but the result of this inner structure. In the case of an active sensory-motor scheme[5] there issues an external act, in the case of an operational scheme an internal knowing.*   (P. 149)

Stated in its simplest terms, the major difference between Piaget's and the common view of knowing resides in whether the stimulus or the response is emphasized. In the common view, the *stimulus* is somehow internalized and can subsequently be re-presented as a sign or as part of an internal language. In Piaget's view, the *action* is internalized (more precisely, *interiorized*), and this transformation results in mental *operations*.

[5] *The term* scheme *is roughly equivalent to* functional concept.

Piaget is arguing that one can know the world only by constructing it from perceptions, actions, and operations. This is similar to the constructionist view of perception, encountered in Chapter 11. To illustrate it, Piaget describes how a child learns about the permanence of objects.

Piaget assumes that at first there are no permanent objects, only fleeting perceptions. Gradually, the infant looks for an object at the place where it disappeared, such looking usually being successful (the object usually reappears in the same spot, as in the peek-a-boo game). At this point there is still no objectivity: the child believes that the presence of the object literally depends on his actions. (This is equivalent to believing that this book ceases to exist when the reader is not looking at it.) There follows a period during which the child looks at and handles objects as they vary in position and time. He gradually learns that objects sometimes move or are moved even when he cannot see or feel them while they are moving. The child learns that he does not have to "act" (see or feel) in order to know that the object is there; that is, he learns that the object exists independent of his actions.

The child is now roughly one year old, and he can start to deal with his own egocentricity. As long as objects have no objective existence, the child can be the passive center of the universe. Once the child sees that objects have an independent existence, he can no longer make this God-like assumption. By the age of 12 to 18 months the child realizes that he is only one of many mobile objects in space. Piaget has compared this insight with the "Copernican revolution," in which it was recognized that the earth is not the center of the universe but merely one of many planets revolving around the sun.

Basic Processes: Assimilation and Accommodation

Piaget explicitly rejects the notion of *association* as the basic element in behavior. His fundamental processes, not only in behavior but in biological adaptation, are *assimilation* and *accommodation*.

No behavior, he points out, starts from absolute

Table 17.4
*Comparison of Assimilation with
Accommodation*

	ASSIMILATION	ACCOMMODATION
Consequence of input	Input is absorbed or changed by internal structures	Input changes internal structures
Adaptive function	Cope by using present mechanisms	Cope by changing in the face of new situations and problems
Examples Perceptual	Shape constancy: perceiving the same shape in spite of different inputs	Adapting to new eye glasses
Motor	Suckling at mother's breast	Learning to drink from a cup
Science	A theory incorporates known facts	A theory is modified by new facts

zero; it always becomes a part of inner structures[6] already present (innate or previously learned). The stimulus inputs feed into an organization already present, one that invests the environment with meaning. This point is in keeping with Piaget's view of knowing as an interaction, the person acting on and being acted on by objects and events. *Assimilation,* then, consists of taking in information and "translating" it by means of programs already present (see Table 17.4). The input is incorporated and modified, just as food is assimilated by the body. This process involves the use of present structures to cope with problems, whether novel or familiar. Thus a cube is perceived as a cube regardless of the angle of regard, and a hungry infant responds to its mother's breast by suckling (and assimilating the milk). Assimilation also occurs in science: a theory encompasses facts already known, sorting them into appropriate categories.

Accommodation represents the other side of the coin. While input is being altered by the inner structure (assimilation), the inner structure is being altered by input (accommodation). Assimilation assures continuity and stability in the face of a complex and changing world, but accommodation leads to the changes in inner structure needed for adaptation to new circumstances. Thus vision must adapt to the addition of eyeglasses, the motor

---

[6] *We shall use the term* inner structures *to include several of Piaget's concepts (including* scheme *and* schema*), which have been defined vaguely, ambiguously, or differently at various times in Piaget's long career.*

system of an infant must adapt to the switch from breast to cup, and a scientific theory must change when new facts so dictate.

Assimilation and accommodation are complementary; one cannot occur without at least some of the other. The process of incorporating stimuli into the inner structure (assimilation) always results in at least a small change in the structure (accommodation). And no learning can occur (accommodation) unless there has been at least a partial assimilation of the new material.

When assimilation and accommodation are balanced, behavior is most adaptive. But such an equilibrium is not the usual state; it is the temporary endpoint of a developmental sequence:

This idea is that structures continually move toward a state of equilibrium, and when a state of equilibrium has been attained, the structure is sharper, more clearly delineated than it had been before. But that very sharpness points up inconsistencies and gaps in the structure that had never been salient before. Each equilibrium state carries with it the seeds of its own destruction, for the child's activities are thenceforth directed toward reducing those inconsistencies and closing those gaps. (PHILLIPS, 1969, P. 10)

This notion of moving toward an equilibrium that itself is dynamic and unstable is a basic axiom in Piaget's theory. Development is assumed to consist of a sequence of stages, each starting with an imbalance and ending with a temporary equilibrium.

There are two kinds of imbalance that involve assimilation and accommodation. In the first, assimilation dominates accommodation: only stimuli consistent with momentary interests are attended to, with the result that thought processes are self-centered and unrealistic. Cognitive processes are too subjective, failing to take account of the complexity and flux of the environment. In the second kind of disequilibrium, accommodation overrides assimilation. Stimulus inputs too easily bring about change, and behavior is largely imitative. Piaget (1970) assumes that this imbalance leads eventually to imagination: from imitation of present persons, to deferred imitation, and finally to mental images. Such denial of self cannot last, and an increasing tendency to assimilate (and assert the self) leads to equilibrium.

Stages of Cognitive Development

The details of Piaget's theory are contained in his account of the *development* of cognition. It is a description of the child's achievements in understanding objects and events, as well as an explanation of these achievements. The child must develop concepts about four closely related aspects of the environment: objects, space, time, and causality. We have already described how the young child progresses from a completely egocentric view of *objects* to a conception of objects as existing in their own right. His concept of *space* develops in a parallel fashion. At first there are many individual "spaces," each linked to a separate action by the infant. This yields to a mature conception of space as a single, objective "container" that includes both objects and the child himself. Concerning *time,* at first there is nothing more than a vague, personal feeling of duration, with no awareness of such dichotomies as before versus after, or now versus later. The child slowly becomes aware of time as a dimension, like space, in which events can be arranged in sequence; there is not only a present but also a past and future.

The development of notions of *causality* follows a similar path from a distorted, subjective view to a correct, objective view. At first the notion of cause is based on either the infant's own actions (a kind of wish fulfillment) or on two events that occur at the same time (correlation implying causation). With increasing cognitive maturity, these primitive notions become *psychological* causality (the thought or wish precedes and may lead to the act) and *physical* causality (one object moves or changes another).

The Three Periods

Piaget's theory is so rich in detail that his general themes tend to become blurred. An overview of the developmental sequence will help to keep them in focus. Following Baldwin (1915), who postulated three successive stages in the interpretation of reality (prelogical, logical, and hyperlogical), Piaget laid out three broad periods of cognitive development. The salient characteristics of each are presented in Table 17.5.

Table 17.5
*Overview of Piaget's Developmental Periods**

PERIOD	AGE RANGE	COGNITIVE ACTS	MODEL
Sensorimotor	0 to 1-½ or 2 years	Sensory and motor acts in response to stimulation; self is separated from "other."	Intelligent animal
Representative Intelligence	1-½ to 11 years	Representation of reality through symbols; thinking about objects and events	Practical man
Formal Operations	11 to 15 years	Manipulation of symbols, representations; thinking about thoughts; considering possibilities; separating form from content; deducing	Scientist

* The age limits are approximate, and they have not been maintained consistently. These are the ones mentioned recently by Piaget (1970).

The *sensorimotor* period, spanning roughly the first two years of life, starts with a helpless infant and ends with a young child who can walk, talk, and manipulate objects. The emphasis is on actions, mainly the instrumental and perceptual responses that enable the child to know his environment. The child discovers that there are permanent independent objects and that space contains both these objects and himself. This first period sees considerable development of the perceptual constancies and motor coordination. In brief, the child develops many of the perceptions and instrumental acts he needs to cope with the immediate environment. Though his responses are limited to the here-and-now, they are appropri-ate—in the same sense that an intelligent animal can respond appropriately to its environment.

During the second period, *representative intelligence,* cognition develops in ways that are uniquely human. The objects and events of the environment can now be *coded* by means of symbols—in words and in images. Knowing is based no longer on actions but on internal representations and "operations" (see Figure 17.4). The focus is still on the here-and-now, but this immediate reality can be re-presented, mainly through codified symbols (principally language). These shared symbols enable the child both to think about objects and to communicate his thoughts to others. In brief, he can "manipulate" reality through internal symbols, and though the manipulations are implicit and "mental," they are still directed toward the external world. This is the mark of the practical man, who uses his intelligence to master everyday problems.

The last period, *formal operations,* occurs between the ages of 11 and 15 years. (The possibility that adult intelligence develops further is left open.) The operations of the representative intelligence period are *concrete* in that they refer to immediate reality; the operations of the final period are *formal* in that they are detached from reality and are therefore content-free. The clearest examples may be found in mathematics. Thus the term $x^2 - 1$ can be factored into $(x + 1)(x - 1)$, an operation that refers to no particular content; it consists only of manipulating symbols.

The divorce of form from content and of thought from immediate reality enables the adolescent to consider all possibilities. Thus when most persons thought the real world was flat, some could speculate that it was round. And today, when most physicists consider the speed of light to be a real upper limit of velocity, some can conceive of particles traveling faster than the speed of light. Reality is treated as only one of several possibilities that might exist. This is the final phase of a developmental sequence that starts with actions in response to the environment (sensorimotor), moves to thoughts about the environment (representative intelligence), and ends with thoughts about thoughts (formal operations).

The Sensorimotor Period

This first period is marked by *preconceptual* behavior, and therefore our description will be brief. The infant starts life with essentially reflexive behavior and an inability to make sense out of a chaos of stimulation. As he explores the world with his senses, he gradually differentiates its main aspects, the first achievement being a separation of self from other. Objects, which at first are linked only to his actions, become independent of his actions and therefore permanent. The movement of objects can be followed in both space and time. The notion of causality develops from a more primitive notion that things just happen to a more sophisticated realization of cause and effect. Consider what happens when an infant's shirt catches on a nail (see Figure 17.5). At less than a year old the infant, being action-oriented, simply *pulls* away. When older than a year, the in-

Figure 17.5 Infant with clothing caught on nail pulls away from nail. An older child would try to detach clothing from nail.

fant, realizing that he is being *acted upon,* moves *toward* the nail to detach himself. These various achievements are the result of *experimentation:* the infant repeatedly handles, drops, bounces, and retrieves objects as he learns about the world through his *actions.*

The sensorimotor child, like an intelligent animal, has extremely primitive cognitions. He is limited in five related ways.

1. He perceives sequences of events much like a series of flickering individual pictures. His cognitions, being tied to his actions, must be run off in strict, slow-moving sequence.
2. He is fixed on the concrete reality of here-and-now and therefore cannot even consider what has been or might yet be. He is stuck in the immediate present (and perhaps the very brief past), and neither past nor future has any meaning for him.
3. He pursues only concrete goals, as opposed to seeking knowledge. Stated in the terms of Chapter 14, reinforcement is defined solely by rewards for instrumental acts, rather than by knowledge for cognitive acts.
4. His cognition, being confined to his own actions, is personal and private, in contrast to later socially oriented cognition, which can be shared through language.
5. He is incapable of symbolic functioning, being unable to differentiate a sign from what it signifies. Thus when events signify other events, the two are part of the same cognition: "pajamas-on-going-to-sleep" rather than "pajamas-on" (sign) separate from "going-to-sleep" (significate).

The Representative Intelligence Period: The Preoperational Subperiod

The period of representative intelligence is divided into two periods, *preoperational* (roughly 1½ or 2 to 7 years) and *concrete operations* (7 or 8 to 11 years).

SYMBOLIC FUNCTION. Piaget subsumes language and related internal representations under the heading of *symbolic function.* It develops mainly through accommodation, specifically imitation. The *overt* imitation of the sensorimotor period is followed by *internal* imitation of the preoperational subperiod. These "mental imitations" take the form of images, each image being a *signifier* of an object or event in the environment. Objects and events are of course the *significates* that give the signifier its meaning: the image of a rose is the signifier, the flower itself the significate.

Once the child can symbolically represent objects and events in his environment, his cognitive development leaps forward. He is no longer restricted to the immediate present but can recall the past and plan for the future. His thought processes are no longer retarded by the slow pace of action, and he can mentally run through events as if they actually were happening. In brief, he can represent reality rather than merely acting on it overtly.

In spite of this achievement, the child's cognitions are limited. His representations remain closely tied to concrete reality, and he is still incapable of the transformations called *operations* (hence the name for this subperiod, *preoperational*). These limitations are revealed in the startling answers children give to *conservation* problems, which require them to go beyond their immediate perceptions.

Research Report

Consider the following problem. There are two glass containers of milk, one wide and one narrow, and the level of milk is higher in the narrow container (see Figure 17.6*a*). Which container has more milk, or are the amounts equal? This question poses a difficult perceptual problem, one that cannot be solved without measuring instruments.

Of course if the subject had seen the milk poured from containers with known amounts of milk, he could easily make the judgment. This is essentially what is done in a conservation problem (see Figure 17.6*b*). First the child sees two containers (*A* and *B*) of equal width

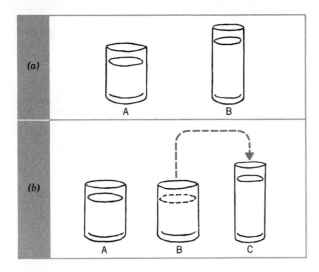

Figure 17.6 Conservation of volume.

and an equal level of milk. Then the experimenter pours the milk from *B* into container *C*, which is taller and narrower, taking care not to spill any. Are the amounts in *A* and *C* equal? A five year old will say "No, there is more in *C*." When asked why, he replies that the column of milk in *C* reaches higher than that in *A*. He does not realize that merely pouring the milk into a differently shaped container does not alter the amount of milk.

But perhaps this conclusion is premature, and the reason for the child's error lies in a misunderstanding of the question. For example, a five year old might think that *more* means *higher*. The way to find out is to ask the question differently. Now the child is asked what will happen if the milk from *C* is poured back into *B*. The child points to a level *higher* than the original level in *B*. The error is not based on a misunderstanding but on a failure to realize that the quantity of milk is conserved.

A final reservation: perhaps the problem is that the child only passively watches the transformations rather than doing them himself. A child of five may spill liquids while pouring, so beads are used (see Figure 17.7). From a pile of beads the child picks up one bead in each

Alternate placing in two containers
Even-numbered
pile of beads

Figure 17.7 Conservation of number.

hand. He is told to put the one in his left hand into container *A* and the one in his right hand into container *B*, and repeat until the pile disappears. Container *B* is taller and narrower than *A*, and the column of beads rises higher. When asked, the child says that *B* has more beads (some children say that A has more "because it's wider," but none say that they are the same). This task, involving conservation of *number,* shows that the five year old fails to conserve even when he carries out the manipulations.

The conservation problem is typical of Piagetian research. The child is given a task that requires certain kinds of cognitive activities and subsequently is asked the basis for his answers. Piaget and his colleagues have been clever in constructing problems that not only interest children but require them to go beyond their perceptions. Note how the conservation problem requires the child to distinguish between appearance (the substance is *higher* in one container and therefore *appears* to be greater) and reality (the two containers have equal amounts). The preoperational child cannot loosen himself from his immediate perceptions. The older, operational child can, and he *knows* that the amount or number is the same because the problem is no longer perceptual; he is capable of the cognitive operations needed for conservation.

LIMITATIONS OF THE PREOPERATIONAL CHILD. Conservation problems illuminate the low level of thinking of the preoperational child, which we shall consider under four headings: centering, irreversibility, egocentrism, and states and transformations.

1. *Centering.* The preoperational child can attend to only one aspect of a situation at a time and can shift only with difficulty. Thus in the liquid conservation problem (see Figure 17.6) he *centers* on the heights of the containers, neglecting the widths. The older preoperational child may be able to shift from height to width but cannot take both into account simultaneously. He cannot *decenter,* which is one of the reasons he does not know about conservation.
2. *Irreversibility.* The other reason for failing the conservation problem is *irreversibility.* When a liquid is poured from *A* to *B*, the preoperational child cannot comprehend that it can be poured back. Consider an example using plastic clay. Two balls of clay are presented and the child agrees that they are equal in size (see Figure 17.8a). Then, as the child watches, one ball is rolled into the shape of a sausage (see Figure 17.8b). Now the child says that one has more clay than the other (the sausage because it is longer or the ball because it is higher). He cannot understand that the transformation of the ball into the sausage is *reversible.*
3. *Egocentrism.* The preoperational child is tied to his own view of the world. His representation is so clearly linked to external objects and events that he cannot take a point of view other than his own. This egocentricity shows up clearly in the *three-mountain* task (see Figure 17.9). Three mounds, one larger and two smaller, are placed on a table to represent mountains. The child sits in one position and is asked what he would see

(a)   (b)   *Figure 17.8 Conservation of substance.*

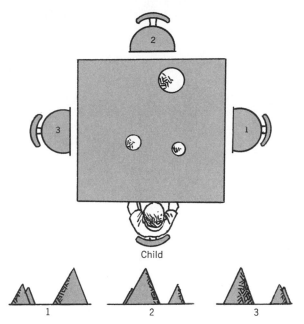

Figure 17.9 *Test for representation of objects (Piaget and Inhelder, 1956).*

The Representative Intelligence Period: The Concrete Operations Subperiod

During this subperiod (7 or 8 to 11 years) the child develops the cognitive skills that enable him to master conservation of substance, length, areas, weight, and number. He can classify objects into appropriate groups, revealing an ability to attain concepts (see the first part of this chapter). These achievements are the result of *operations: internal, cognitive acts that are parts of a coherent, integrated system of such acts.* Piaget refuses to consider operations singly, and sees them only as a part of a system of related operations.

Piaget uses logic and mathematics as models for thought, and his description of operations is largely nonpsychological. For this reason we shall not discuss operations in detail but will merely illustrate a few simple ones. Consider first the arithmetic operations of addition and subtraction. When two different things are regarded as similar in some way, they can be added together to form a higher class. Thus cats and dogs can be assigned to the supraordinate class of mammals (see Table 17.6). To extract the original members from the class, one separates or subtracts them.

Now consider the operations of equality and placing in order (see Table 17.6). Equality involves a symmetrical relationship, with one member substituting for the other. Thus if $A = B$, then $B = A$. Placing in order involves an asymmetrical relationship. Thus if A is larger than B, B is definitely not larger than A.

These simple operations can be combined to yield rather complex cognitive manipulations. These occur as part of a structured system, which impresses stability and coherence on the world of reality.

ACHIEVEMENT. The older child masters virtually all conservation problems and has a more-or-less adult conception of time and space. Having already noted the various problems he can master (see the section on the preoperational child), we

from each of the other three positions. He can draw or select from drawings such as those in Figure 17.9. The five year old simply cannot visualize the scene from another position; the ten year old can do it easily.

4. *States and Transformations.* Another aspect of the young child's concreteness is his fixation on each stage of a sequence rather than on the entire sequence as it unfolds. Consider the falling over of a vertical pencil, as it would appear in a series of still pictures (see Figure 17.10). The child can neither draw the sequence nor recognize the drawings when they are shown to him. As Flavell (1963) has commented:

Preoperational thought, then, is static and immobile. It is a kind of thought which can focus impressionistically and sporadically on this or that momentary static condition but cannot adequately link a whole set of successive conditions into an integrated totality by taking account of the transformations which unify them and render them logically coherent.

(P. 157)

Figure 17.10 *States and transformations — a pencil falling.*

Table 17.6
Simple Concrete Operations

SYMBOL	MEANING	LOGICAL RELATIONSHIP	EXAMPLE
+	Add, combine	Form a supraordinate class	cats dogs ↘ ↙ mammals
−	Subtract, separate	Reconstitute original members from class	mammals ↙ ↘ cats dogs
=	Equality, substitution	Symmetrical relationship	Fred is Bill's brother; Bill is Fred's brother
>	Place in order	Asymmetrical relationship	Tom is Jack's father; Jack is not Tom's father

shall consider only one more example. It involves the composition of classes and illustrates several of the operations mentioned in Table 17.6.

The child is shown a box containing 20 wooden beads, 18 brown and 2 white (see Figure 17.11). He is told that a necklace will be made of the beads and is asked whether a necklace made of *brown* beads would be longer, shorter, or the same length as one made of *wooden* beads. The answer requires an ordering of brown and white beads to the larger class of wooden beads. The preoperational child of five years cannot arrange such parts into a conceptual whole, but the operational child of eight years can and therefore answers correctly. He *knows* there are more wooden beads because he can use the operations of combining and separating (see Table 17.6). He has a coherent set of *reversible* operations that allow him to integrate disparate perceptions and to distinguish appearance from reality.

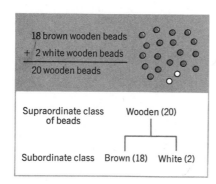

Figure 17.11 Composition of classes — parts and wholes.

LIMITATIONS. In spite of these achievements, the thought of the older child is still limited. First, his operations are directed toward objects and events that are in the present or the immediate past. His cognitive acts organize concrete reality and rarely explore *possibilities.* Second, the close link between his concrete operations and reality sometimes leads to confusion. He cannot sufficiently detach his representation from present objects and events to sort them and deal with them one at a time. Faced with several dimensions or variations in stimuli, he is overwhelmed by complexity. He has yet to divorce form completely from content. Third, though he has a number of cognitive structures, they are isolated and uncoordinated. They have yet to be organized into an integrated whole, which would rescue the child from unmanageable complexity.

The Formal Operations Period

The concretely operational child is sufficiently advanced to discover inconsistencies in his own solutions. His own sharpening operations immediately reveal gaps and contradictions in his thinking. Spurred by knowledge of his own deficiencies, he moves forward to the period of *formal operations* (11 to 15 years).

This stage marks the culmination of a developmental trend toward increasing dominance of central thought processes over the more peripheral processes of perception and thought. The adolescent can finally detach himself from the tight grip of reality. He can separate form from content: he can think of the possible as well as the actual. Consequently, he can imagine possible outcomes and reason with propositions such as "if . . . then." Thus in the conservation problem involving balls of plastic clay, he can reason: "*If* no clay is added or subtracted, *then* the amount of clay in the new shape (sausage) is still the same."

The adolescent integrates various operations into an organized system. He can think about *all* possible combinations of variables and run them off sequentially, knowing that he has exhausted all possibilities. Thus he can construct complex classifications and follow the logic of classifications that are given to him—for example, the classification of animals from species to phyla.

Lastly, he learns a new set of operations—those of logic, hence the name for this period, *formal operations*. The structures of logic and mathematics are well beyond the scope of this book, but one example should illustrate what is learned.

We shall use the transformation called *reciprocal,* which in effect nullifies or cancels a previous transformation. Consider the movements of head and eyes when watching a fixed point (see Figure 17.12*a*). If the head moves to the left, the image shifts to the right on the retina. This effect can be cancelled by appropriate eye movements in the opposite direction to the head movement, returning the image to its original place on the retina. Here the eye movements are reciprocal to the head movement.

A similar transformation is used in experimentation. In testing a drug, merely the act of injecting a substance may have an effect. Therefore we add a control group that receives an inert substance (see Figure 17.12*b*). The control group in effect cancels or neutralizes any effects of the injection procedure.

The adolescent acquires this reciprocal transformation along with a variety of other transforma-

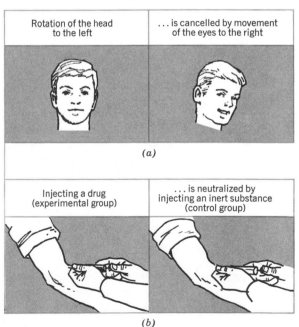

Figure 17.12 The reciprocal transformation.

Table 17.7
Sequence of Cognitive Processes

COGNITIVE ACT	PROCESS	PERIOD
1. Receive information from environment	Perception	Sensorimotor
2. Organize information into classes, categories	Concrete operations	Representative intelligence
3. Transform the content into propositions which can be combined to form hypotheses	Operations on operations	Formal operations

tions and combinations of formal logic. He cannot verbalize these tools of logic any more than he can clearly state the rules of grammar. Nevertheless, just as his speech more or less follows the rules of grammar, so his thoughts follow the rules of logic.

The appearance of formal operations does not cause the thinking of earlier periods to disappear. The cognitive processes of childhood not only exist side-by-side with those of adolescence but enter into the logical thought processes of adolescence. They occur early in the sequence (see Table 17.7). The first step is to discover the objects and events of reality, a process that begins in the sensorimotor period. The information is organized by means of the the operations that develop during the period of concrete operations. These operations are transformed by the operations of the period of formal operations to yield hypotheses. The final step is to test the hypotheses against reality, thereby initiating another sequence. Such sequences embody the essentials of scientific thinking.

The potency of the adolescent's logical thought processes causes an unexpected egocentricity. Piaget points out that the person is self-centered three times during development. The infant believes that he is the center of the universe, and that it depends on his actions for its existence.

The young child believes that his point of view and his representations are the only ones possible. Finally, the adolescent believes that his newly established powers of logic must predominate over the environment. His inner world is logical and therefore the outer world must conform. This combination of logic and omnipotence yields the idealistic schemes that adolescents construct for solving universal problems.

Perspective

The period of formal operations closes the circle by returning to adult concepts discussed in the first part of the chapter. If less space has been devoted to the more traditional approach to adult concepts, it is because it embodies the behaviorism discussed in previous chapters. Piaget's theory, on the other hand, is less familiar in its assumptions about knowledge, its emphasis on cognitive structure, and its insistence on stages of development.

As mentioned earlier, Piaget has inspired a rich outpouring of research in this country,[7] which is

[7] *Especially since the publication of two books summarizing his work (Hunt, 1961, and Flavell, 1963).*

adding to the voluminous data generated by himself, his colleagues, and his students. One goad to research was the surprising nature of Piaget's findings. Another was his methods of investigation, which often lacked the rigor of adequate controls, proper recording, or quantification. Still another was his ingenious tasks, which have opened up new areas of investigation.

But the greatest stimulant was the theory itself. Piaget laid out the development of cognition in terms both general (his stages of development) and specific (the particular actions and operations of each stage). His hypotheses have drawn investigators to the laboratory to seek either confirming evidence for a theory they bought or opposing evidence for a theory they rejected.

So much research has emerged on so many different facets of Piaget's theory that several volumes might not do it justice, but we can summarize one small piece of it. Piaget originally believed that cognitive development, being invariant, could not be hastened. This doctrine was an anathema to American psychologists, most of whom believe that special training can produce strong effects (see Gagné, 1968, for example). A decade of research on special training in such things as the operations needed to solve conservation problems has yielded the kind of answer that emerges from most research: in some instances special training greatly accelerates the acquisition of cognitive operations; in other cases the acceleration is slight; and in some instances there is no effect.[8]

Of course, some of Piaget's ideas, being interpretations of a large domain of behavior, are not really subject to empirical evaluation. Thus his insistence on discrete periods (or stages) of development cannot be confirmed or disconfirmed in the laboratory; it is merely one way of looking at how cognition develops.

Similarly, his downgrading of the importance of language cannot be tested, though it certainly is not universally accepted. Bruner (1964) echoes many psychologists when he states that ". . . language shapes, augments, and even supersedes the child's earlier modes of processing information." The power and predominance of language as a cognitive tool is certainly evident during development, but there are compelling evolutionary arguments also, as we shall see in the next chapter.

---

[8] *For reviews, see Bruner et al. (1966), Elkind and Flavell (1969), Elkind and Sameroff (1970). An interesting shift has occurred over time. Earlier research suggested that special training does not accelerate mastery of conservation problems (Mermelstein & Meyer, 1969), but later research suggested that it does (Brainerd & Allen, 1970).*

chapter 18
language

Cognition and communication — words and sentences — speech and sound — meaning and reference — meaning in sentences — rules and meaning — competence and performance — sentence structure — surface and deep structure — language development — child's first grammar — regularization — transformations — biological aspects — brain asymmetry — electric shock and drugs — splitbrain — asymmetric hearing — brain waves — a critical period of language acquisition

Language can be a powerful *cognitive* tool. The person who can cast propositions in the "if . . . then" mold is capable of solving rather difficult problems of reasoning. He can try out various possibilities "in his head," rather than having laboriously to act out each possible response.

But language, in either speech or writing, is also a powerful means of *communication*. It can be used to convey instructions, information, and emotional states. Thus language has two faces. Viewed one way, it is part of cognition and belongs with imagery and various "operations" discussed in the last chapter (see Figure 18.1*a*). Viewed another way, it is part of communication, along with gestures, facial expressions, and nonlanguage vocal expressions such as screaming and laughing (see Figure 18.1*b*). The two aspects are best treated separately, and we shall discuss language as cognition in this chapter and language as communication in Chapter 28.

All normal children acquire language, just as all normal children develop the cognitions discussed in the last chapter. Nor are children limited to a single language. When more than one language is spoken by those around them, children acquire several languages with equal facility. Thus the

(a) Cognitive

(b) Social

Figure 18.1 Language: cognitive and social aspects.

children of immigrants to this country usually learn both English and the native language of their parents; many Swiss children become proficient in German, French, and English.

Language is acquired so readily and so universally that we must wonder if there is an innate disposition to do so. Many students of language assume that speech is no less a biological aspect of our species than is two-legged locomotion, and the development of the brain offers some confirming evidence.

What is it that children learn in acquiring language? Briefly, they learn how to understand the speech of others and how to speak themselves. To accomplish these things, they must learn to connect meaning with sounds, to connect words with what they signify, and to master the rules that determine how words are combined to form sentences.

Words and Sentences

Words, taken singly, fall into three categories. The first consists of proper names: *Harry, Nancy, Rover, Indianapolis,* and so on. These simply identify a particular person, animal, or place. They *refer* to particular things and have no meaning

beyond this; merely pointing to the person or place would be equivalent.

In the second category are words that *sound like* that which they signify: *buzz, bang, zing,* and so on. Again, such words serve to identify an event, and they rarely possess any meaning beyond "sounds like."

The vast majority of words are not proper names, and they do not sound like that which they signify. Any sound can be associated with any meaning, and a given meaning is likely to be represented by different words in different languages. Thus we say *horse,* the French say *cheval;* we say *dog,* the French say *chien.* The sound, being arbitrary, is different; the meaning is the same.

Most words should be regarded as concepts. The meaning of the word *dog* is a set of properties flexible enough to include a French poodle and a Great Dane. Even the words for everyday objects such as *table, chair, spoon, house,* and *car* are conceptual in that each includes a class of objects with certain common properties.

If language consisted merely of single words, it surely would not be one of man's unique features. Some animals have the requisite ability to attain concepts, and one chimpanzee has developed a fair vocabulary in sign language (Gardner & Gardner, 1969). But words taken alone constitute only a small part of language, for the meaning of a word usually depends on its context. Thus the word *pen* means one thing in the phrase *ballpoint pen* and another in *play pen,* and the word *drinking* clearly means two different things in *drinking companions* and *drinking glasses.*

Words are assembled to form sentences, and the combinations and sequences are strictly determined by precisely the kind of rules we discussed in the last chapter. Though we often violate the rules ("I am here, *aren't* I?"), there are rules of speech in every language. Thus there are rules for singular and plural nouns, for present and past tenses of verbs for positive and negative statements, and so on.

Miller's Seven Admonitions

In the past, psychologists have attempted to explain language in terms of classical conditioning, mediated responses, and imitation of sounds.

These approaches assumed that language consisted of chains of words, just as a motor sequence (e.g., the running broad jump) consists of a chain of single responses. Psycholinguists, who study the psychology of language, have pointed out that language is considerably more complex than mere chains of single verbal responses. Miller (1965) has summarized seven aspects of language that any student of the subject needs to know.[1]

1. "*. . . not all significant features of speech have a physical representation*" (p. 17). There are important components in language that do not show up in sound alone. Thus two identical sounds can have entirely different meanings, depending on the words that accompany them in a sentence. In the sentence, "You can stay, BUT do not BUTT in," the words *but* and *butt* have identical sounds but different meanings. Similarly, the sentence, "THEY'RE going THERE in THEIR car," has three words that cannot be distinguished by their sounds but have different meanings.

2. "*The meaning of an utterance should not be confused with its reference*" (p. 17). Reference is essentially *denotation*. We can refer to a table by pointing at it or by saying, "that table." To name an object or event is to refer to it. Thus language can substitute for pointing, and in so doing it can clarify the intended referent. Saying, "It's the third tree from the left" indicates the referent more precisely than merely pointing does (see Figure 18.2a). Of course language can be ambiguous in its denotation. If there are three men present, saying "the man" is clearly less precise than merely pointing at the man (see Figure 18.2b).

When language is used to denote, it can refer not only to objects and events that are immediately present but to those of the past and the future. Pointing is limited to the here and now, but language opens up vast possibilities of reference by being capable of denoting our history and our possible future.

But meaning is not the same as reference.[2] The word *table* may be used to refer to a particular article of furniture, but it also possesses *meaning* as a concept: an object with at least three legs and a

---

[1] *Miller's admonitions have been edited.*

[2] *For an opposing view, see Olson (1970). Reference is an essential part of language as a tool of communication (see Chapter 28).*

(a)

(b)

Figure 18.2

flat top on which objects may be placed. Insofar as words are concepts, they have meaning that transcends their reference to any particular object or event. This is true of any concept: it has meaning beyond its application to any particular instance.

The distinction between reference and meaning becomes even sharper when we examine sentences. These are sentences that have meaning but no physical referent: "See that unicorn over there." And there are sentences that convey something even when, in terms of reference, the sentence is redundant. Consider: "George Washington was the first president of the United States." The first and last parts of the sentence have the same referent, but the sentence is not pointless (as "George Washington was George Washington," would be). The significance of the sentence clearly cannot reside in reference; it must reside in something else—namely, *meaning*.

3. "*The meaning of an utterance is not a linear*

sum of the meanings of the words that comprise it" (p. 18). The meaning of a word can alter drastically when it is placed in different contexts. An earlier example was *pen* in *ballpoint pen* versus *play pen. Venetian blind* means something very different from *blind Venetian.* In brief, this admonition warns us to distinguish sharply between words and sentences: the meaning of a sentence is something more than the meanings of the individual words.

4. *The rules governing how words are grouped will largely determine the meaning of a sentence.* A sentence is a *rule-defined* sequence of words, and the listener can extract meaning only if he knows these rules. Consider the sentence "They are buying gloves." The words *are buying* are linked as the verb, some action that *they* are doing. Such a grouping is different from "They are boxing gloves." Here *boxing* is linked not with *are* but with *gloves;* it refers not to what *they* are doing but to a particular property or use of gloves. We can easily extract the meaning of these two sentences because we know the rules governing how the words are grouped (regardless of whether we can *verbalize* the rules).

5. *"There is no limit to the number of sentences or the number of meanings that can be expressed"* (p. 18). The speaker has a limited number of *sounds* he can utter; there are approximately 45 different sounds in English. These are used to form words, and there is an upper limit — probably in the thousands — to the vocabulary of any speaker. These words can be combined to form an *infinite* number of acceptable sentences. In fact, there is no theoretical limit to the length of a sentence: it could run on so long that the species would die out before the sentence did. The limits on *spoken* sentences are set mainly by the *memory* of the speaker or the listener. Who can remember the beginning of a spoken 50-word sentence when he reaches the end?

How can a *finite* number of words be combined to yield an *infinite* number of *acceptable* sentences? The only way is by using rules to generate sentences. This *generative* aspect of language has important implications for the acquisition of language. It means that the child cannot learn a language through classical conditioning or discrimination learning. Rather the child must master the rules that give sentences their structure, a topic

we shall pursue in the last section of this chapter.

6. *"A description of a language and a description of a language user must be kept distinct"* (p. 18). Each of us, having a command of speech, has "internalized" a set of rules governing how words are combined. Thus when presented with two sentences — (1) *She is yet not ready,* and (2) *She is not yet ready* — we know that the first is incorrect, and the second is correct. Regardless of whether the appropriate rule can be verbalized, each of us knows where the word *not* belongs in the sentence. It may be *inferred* that we implicitly possess the rule governing negative sentences. In general, we understand what sentences mean, and the meaning depends upon the structure of the sentences. In a sense, then, we "know" the rules that generate sentences (though we do not always use them correctly).

The necessary distinction is between *competence* and *performance,* which harks back to an earlier distinction between learning and performance. The learner knows more than he can ever perform, his performance being limited by such transient factors as fatigue, motivation, and inhibitions. Similarly, the native speaker has considerably more competence than is ever revealed in his speech (which is limited by memory and other factors). Performance, being concrete and observable is easier to understand; competence, being abstract and inferred, is more difficult. Two quotations may help:

. . . *"competence" refers to the ability of the idealized speaker-hearer to associate sounds and meanings strictly in accordance with the rules of his language.*
(CHOMSKY, 1967, P. 398)

Competence . . . represents the knowledge a native speaker of a language must have in order to understand any of the infinitely many grammatical sentences of his language; it represents a mature speaker's linguistic intuitions — his realization that the man hit the ball is grammatical but the man virtued the ball is not.
(MCNEILL, 1966, P. 17.)

Competence refers to abstractions about language, intuitions that we all use in speaking and understanding sentences. Competence is properly the subject matter of linguists, who study the rules that generate an infinity of acceptable sentences.

Table 18.1
Language Competence Versus Performance

COMPETENCE	PERFORMANCE
Idealized speaker or listener	Actual speaker or listener
Knowledge (intuitions) about language	Actual sentences
Inferred, abstract	Observable, concrete
Population of possible sentences (infinite)	Sample of actual sentences (finite)
Language only	Language plus nonlanguage factors (e.g., memory)
Linguistics	Psycholinguistics

Performance refers to the actual speaking or understanding of language, which involves the addition of psychological variables. It is properly the subject matter of psycholinguists, who study how language is acquired and used, but who rely on linguists to tell them what language is. These properties of competence and performance are summarized in Table 18.1.

7. *"There is a large biological component to the human capacity for articulate speech"* (p. 18). In accord with this statement, there is evidence for a critical period of speech development (see the last section of this chapter). It has also been suggested that as a species we are especially attuned to the speech code (Liberman et al., 1967). Furthermore, underlying the acquisition of language are cognitive capacities, common to language and other behaviors, that appear to be unique to man (Chapter 17). Finally, there appear to be certain features that are present in all languages, a fact that suggests a strong biological component in language development.

Grammar

Miller's admonitions comprise an introduction to modern linguistics, which is dominated by the formulations of Noam Chomsky (1965, 1967). In Chomsky's view, a grammar is best regarded as a theory about the competence of native speakers of a particular language. It consists of a system of rules that reveal the structure of sentences and that link sound to meaning.

THE STRUCTURE OF SENTENCES. Sentences are analyzed by breaking them down to their component parts. Like concepts, sentences are organized hierarchically, with higher levels including levels beneath them. The sentence, "The boy caught the ball," may be diagrammed as a hierarchy of levels, starting with words and working upward (see Figure 18.3). In this sentence, *The* and *boy* are parts of a noun phase, which is one of the basic components of the sentence. The remaining words, *caught, the,* and *ball* are all parts of the verb phrase, which is the other basic component.

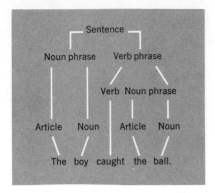

Figure 18.3 Diagram of a sentence (a phrase marker).

This splitting of a sentence into its components yields its *structure,* the diagram of which is called a *phrase marker.* This structure is the result of *rules of syntax,* which we shall discuss below.

Before the reader concludes that this page was left over from an English grammar text and in-serted by mistake, we had better demonstrate the psychological importance of the structure of sentences (called *phrase structure*). The evidence comes from research on how listeners process the sentences they hear.

Research Report

The research started with the discovery that it is difficult to locate a click sound when it occurs in a sentence (Ladefoged & Broadbent, 1960). One hypothesis for this finding was that the errors were caused by the natural breaks within sentences that occur between their grammatical components. For example, in the sentence, "The men watching me were fools," there is a break between "The men watching me" (noun phrase) and "were fools" (verb phrase). Presum-ably, clicks sounded while the sentence was being heard would tend to be located at the break. To test this hypothesis, Fodor and Bever (1965) had subjects listen to a sentence delivered to one ear while a click was delivered to the other. There were 30 sentences in all, and for each sentence there were 9 different locations of the click. For ex-ample, in the sentence

That he was happy was evident from the way he smiled
↑ ↑   ↑   ↑↑↑   ↑↑   ↑

the arrows point to the location of the clicks. Each sentence was repeated nine times, each time with a different click location. The subjects listened, wrote down the sentence, and placed a slash mark (/) where they thought the click had occurred. Only one click occurred at the boundary between the major components of the sentence (for example, between *happy* and *was*).

The subjects tended to locate the clicks around the major boundary of the sentences. When the click preceded the break, it was usually reported as occurring later; when the click followed the break, it was usually reported as occurring earlier.

In spite of attempts to control for intonation and pauses when the sentences were tape recorded, such variations in how the sentence was spoken might have occurred. A subsequent study (Garrett et al., 1966) eliminated any such possibility. This time one phrase was used in two different sentences in such a way that the major break was different in the two sentences. Thus the clause *George drove furiously to the station* appeared in the sentence, "In order to catch his train George drove furiously to the station," and in, "The reporters assigned to George drove furiously to the station." The click sound coincided with *George* in both sentences. As predicted, subjects located the click earlier in the first sentence (major break between *train* and *George*), and later in the second sentence (major break between *George* and *drove*).

These findings attest to the reality of phrase structure in sentences. It might be argued that the results were confounded by having the subjects write down the sentences, but a subsequent experiment yielded the same results when subjects merely listened and reported click locations without writing down the sentences. Nor is there anything special about click sounds as stimuli: the same shifts in location toward the major break occur when the intruding stimuli are mild electric shocks (Kirk et al., 1965) or flashing lights (Bever et al., 1965). These experiments demonstrate that listeners attend to the *structure* of sentences. Stated another way, phrase structure is no mere linguistic abstraction; it is an important aspect of the *psychological* processing of speech.

SURFACE STRUCTURE AND DEEP STRUCTURE.
The click experiments showed that the structure of sentences determines where the breaks are perceived. The placing of pauses, intonation, and stress are all part of the way a sentence is spoken, and they offer clues to the *surface structure* of the sentence. But there is also an underlying structure to sentences, called *deep structure*. Consider three sentences:

(1) *They are drinking highballs.*
(2) *They are drinking glasses.*
(3) *They are drinking companions.*

The phrase structure of the first sentence is different from that of the last two:

(1) (they) (are drinking) (highballs).

versus

(2) (they) (are) (drinking glasses).
(3) (they) (are) (drinking companions).

The difference is said to be in *surface structure.*

Sentences (2) and (3) are alike in surface structure, but they are different in *meaning*. This is clearly revealed when we paraphrase, which is to state the meaning in other words. Thus we can say, *They are the glasses for drinking,* but not, *They are the companions for drinking.* On the other hand, we can say, *They are the companions that drink,* but not, *They are the glasses that drink.* Thus the difference between sentences (2) and (3) lies in the allowable *transformations,* those that do not change their meaning.

Other examples help to drive the point home:

John is easy to please.
John is eager to please.

Both sentences are the same in surface structure

but different in the way they can be paraphrased.

> *It was finished by John.*
> *It was finished by noon.*

Again, the sentences are indentical in their *surface* structure but different in their underlying or *deep* structure.[3]

Language Development

The normal child starts to say words toward the end of his first year. At approximately a year and a half he puts words together into two-word sentences. During the next 30 months he learns enough about his native tongue to speak grammatical sentences most of the time. He learns the correct forms for questions, negative statements, future and past tense, and various other forms.

The very young child listens to speech, mainly adult speech, and abstracts the rules underlying it. Using these rules, he first comprehends what is spoken and then gradually uses the rules in his own speech. As others correct his speech or as he notices discrepancies, he learns both more advanced rules and the exceptions to rules common to all languages (for example, *came* rather than *comed*).

We saw in the last chapter that children develop considerable conceptual skills. Those skills required for abstracting and using the rules of language may be further advanced than other comparable skills in the young child. Such precocity can be attributed to strong evolutionary pressure for early communication, but even if we accept this speculation, language acquisition is not so easily explained. The speech the child hears is fragmentary and often ungrammatical. When everyday speech is recorded, it is found to be full of interjections, interruptions, false starts, and mistakes in grammar ("I did, too, tell the truth. I'm right, aren't I?"). The child, though exposed only to such error-laden utterances, still manages to

acquire the appropriate rules. Moreover, psycholinguists believe that children acquire the underlying structure of their language first. This implies that they master the most abstract relationship— that between surface and deep structure— before they acquire grammar.

How does the infant relate meaning to sound? Recall that by the second year of life, he has already observed many regularities in everyday life. The sensorimotor child understands the relationship between his own activities—both perceptual and motor—and the status of objects and events around him. Concerning the question of connecting meaning to sound,

> *The answer must be that the infant is able to relate sound and meaning because he is able to tell what the speaker is speaking about independent of the speaker's language.*   (MACNAMARA, 1972, P. 10)

Presumably, the infant already knows what the speaker is referring to, and therefore the infant can use this knowledge to decipher the speaker's speech code. This hypothesis makes sense, but it does not suggest any details of the deciphering process. Thus the puzzle remains as to how young children extract meaning and rules from the fallible speech samples they hear.

The Child's First Grammar

At roughly eighteen months the average child starts putting two words together. At first such utterances are rare, but six months later there are thousands of them (see Figure 18.4). The two-word utterances convey meaning but in many instances only when the context is well defined. Thus *baby toy* means that the child wants the toy when it is not easily available, but it simply locates or identifies the toy when the child is holding it. Similarly, *Mommy sock* can refer to either the mother's sock or to the mother's putting a sock on the child's foot. Other two-word combinations are unambiguous; *allgone milk* clearly means that there is no more milk.

Concerning such two-word utterances as *allgone milk,* there are two aspects that merit our attention. First, the child must have *invented* them, never having heard such combinations from

---

[3] *Some sentences are ambiguous as stated, and their meaning can be extracted only from the context in which they occur (see Suls & Weisberg, 1970). For example, "Phil likes racing cars at the show." could mean either that Phil likes racing or Phil likes cars, depending on the sentences that precede or follow it.*

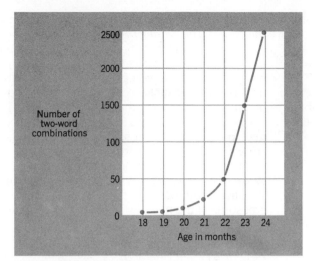

2500

2000

1500

Number of
two-word
combinations

100

50

0

18 19 20 21 22 23 24

Age in months

Figure 18.4 Two-word combinations as a function of age (After Braine, 1963).

others. Second, they constitute a primitive system for combining words to yield meaning—the child's first grammar. Having sampled adult speech, the child has abstracted certain elements and then constructed his own grammar. It is simpler than that of adults, as well as clumsier and poorer in communication. But—and this is crucial—it is not merely a reflection of the speech he has heard but an invention of his own.

Regularization

"Regularization" appears to be the best word to describe children's tendency to adhere strictly to rules as they acquire speech. Consider the past tense of a class of frequently occurring words called *strong verbs: ran, went, sat,* and *broke.* The young child learns these individually and at first uses them correctly; he has no rules for using them, and in fact there is no rule in our language. Then the child learns a simple rule for past tense: add *-ed* to the verb. He applies this rule equally to weak and strong verbs, and he starts saying *runned, goed, sitted,* and *breaked.*

These novel, rule-directed words can be observed in the everyday speech of children, but this is a tedious, time-consuming way of studying them. An easier and more systematic method was devised by Berko (1958). She showed the child a small "animal" and then two of them (see Figure 18.5). She said, "This is a wug; now there are two of them. There are two _____." The child's answer reveals whether he has mastered the rules of pluralization. Berko found, as did Ervin (1964) that there is also regularization in pluralizing, yielding such words as *foots, mouses,* and *tooths.* As children develop, they gradually exempt the irregular verbs and nouns from the general rules, and their speech approximates that of adults. But when they first start using rules, they use the rules strictly and stubbornly resist attempts to change them. McNeill (1966) offers this piquant example:

Child: Nobody don't like me.
Mother: No, say "nobody likes me."
Child: Nobody don't like me.
*   (eight repetitions of this dialogue)*
Mother: No, now listen carefully; say "nobody likes me."
Child: Oh! Nobody don't likes me.

(P. 69)

Even the child's deliberate attempt to imitate failed because he could not relinquish the rule he had mastered.

Transformations

The use of negatives and the past tense involves *transformational rules,*[4] the last aspect of

---

[4] *Such rules alter word sequences and add and delete words without changing the underlying meaning of the sentence.*

This is a wug.

Now there is another one.
There are two of them.
There are two _____.

Figure 18.5 Method of studying pluralization rules in children (Berko, 1958).

grammar acquired by children. Such rules involve agreement on gender and tense, sequence of words (especially auxiliary verbs such as *can, do,* and *is*), and deletions. Thus it is no surprise that a sentence with the form, "It's a nice day, isn't it?" is mastered later rather than earlier. Similarly, children make mistakes like, "Why not me break that one," and the one made by the child using double negatives, "Nobody don't like me."

We are as interested in the child's *comprehension* of transformations as we are of his *production* of them. Fraser et al. (1963) originated a method especially useful for comprehension. They used either objects or pictures to illustrate two opposing meanings of a given sentence. Thus to a child, "The boy is washed by the girl," might mean that he washes her or that she washes him (see Figure 18.6). The child points to the picture described by the sentence. Three-year-old children tend to treat passive sentences as active ones. Thus the sentence above is interpreted to mean that the boy is washing the girl. This seems to represent an early strategy in decoding sentences:

treat the first noun as the *actor* and the second as the *object.* The strategy works well for active, declarative sentences ("The boy hits the girl"), but it obviously fails in passive sentences ("The boy was hit by the girl"). Sentences like the latter can be understood and spoken only when transformational rules have been mastered.

The child learns these increasingly complex rules presumably because they allow him to generate sentences with more meaning and less ambiguity. Moreover, he is continually made aware of the discrepancy between his own constructions and those of adults. Under the twin pressures of the need for better communication and the need to match his own utterances to those of others, the child takes the final step in acquiring syntax: learning transformational rules.

Biological Aspects of Language

The two hemispheres of the adult human brain are not equivalent. This left-right asymmetry of the

(a)

Figure 18.6 These two illustrations could be used in testing a child for comprehension of the passive sentence "The boy is washed by the girl." Most three-year olds, accustomed to the active-voice pattern of subject-verb-object will point to (a).

(GEORGE ROOS)

brain is especially important for language. It is probably no coincidence that man is the only animal with language and also with *lateralization* of motor function (one side dominates, the right for most of us).[5] A man is not born with one hand dominant, nor with one side of the brain dominant. Such lateralization develops during childhood and is fully accomplished by puberty. This age period matches the full development of speech, which suggests a connection between language development and lateralization. Thus we have two issues to discuss: (1) language in relation to the two sides of the adult brain, and (2) maturation of the brain and the acquisition of speech in the *child.*

The Asymmetrical Human Brain

For most adults, an intact left cerebral hemisphere is essential for normal language. When the left hemisphere is damaged — by lesions, disturbances in brain circulation, or other abnormalities — the ability to understand and produce speech and writing is impaired. Language disturbance (called *aphasia*) has many forms: inability to speak, to understand speech, to write, to understand the written word, and so on. Though there are exceptions, most aphasic patients have undergone damage to the left hemisphere, specifically to what is called the speech area in the left cerebral hemisphere (Penfield & Roberts, 1959).

For more than a hundred years, knowledge of brain-language relationships accrued largely through studying aphasics. More recently, researchers have devised means of studying the relationship in adults whose language is normal. ELECTRIC SHOCK AND DRUGS. Electric shock of sufficient intensity to cause a convulsion has been used for many years to treat depressive patients. One of its negative by-products, transient memory loss, has been used to demonstrate the different functions of the two cerebral hemispheres. Cohen et al. (1968) studied the effect of convulsive electric shock on depressed women whose brain and speech were normal. One group of patients re-

ceived shock only on the left side of the brain; one group, only on the right side; and a third group, on both sides. All patients first learned a language task (word associations) and a nonlanguage task (drawing from memory), and they were tested several hours after the shock treatment. The results are shown in Table 18.2 (p. 352): shock to the left brain impairs language memory; shock to right brain impairs nonlanguage memory; and shock to both sides impairs both kinds of memory.

The same kind of effect occurs when a depressant drug (sodium amytal) is injected through an artery in the neck into one or the other side of the brain. Such drug-induced depression of the left hemisphere virtually eliminates the processing of language (production and comprehension) for several minutes and causes errors for up to an hour. Depression of the right hemisphere leaves language function essentially intact (Milner et al., 1964). In brief, when either drugs or electric shock interfere with the functioning of the left cerebral hemisphere, language is disturbed.
SPLIT BRAIN. Serious epileptic seizures can be controlled by surgery that severs the corpus callosum (the band of fibers between the hemispheres), thereby cutting off direct communication between the right and left hemispheres. The study of patients with split brains has yielded conclusive evidence of brain asymmetry (Gazzaniga, 1967; Sperry, 1968). In one task the subject touched and held common objects that were behind a curtain (see Figure 18.7).

When an object was held in the right hand, from which sensory information is sent to the left hemisphere, the patient was able to name and describe the object. When it was held in the left hand (from which information goes primarily to the right hemisphere), the patient could not describe the object verbally but was able to identify it in a nonverbal test — matching it, for example, to the same object in a varied collection of things. (GAZZANIGA, 1967, P. 25)

In testing the effects of the visual stimuli, the experimenters blindfolded one eye of the subject and had him fixate the other on a midline between two stimuli:

If two different figures are flashed simultaneously to the right and left visual fields, as for example a

---

[5] *Most sensory and motor tracts cross, innervation from (and to) the brain being to (and from) the opposite sides of the body. Thus the left hemisphere is dominant for motor activities in right-handed persons, and the right hemisphere is dominant for motor activities in most left-handed persons.*

Table 18.2
Memory Loss After One-Sided or Two-Sided Electro-Convulsive Shock (Cohen et al., 1968)

	LEFT HEMISPHERE ONLY	RIGHT HEMISPHERE ONLY	BOTH HEMISPHERES
Word associations (language)	Severe loss	Essentially no loss	Severe loss
Visual forms (nonlanguage)	Very slight loss	Severe loss	Severe loss

"dollar sign" on the left and a "question mark" on the right and the subject is asked to draw what he saw using the left hand out of sight, he regularly reproduces the figure seen on the left half of the field, that is, the dollar sign. If we now ask him what he has just drawn, he tells us without hesitation that the figure he just drew was the question mark, or whatever appeared in the right half of the field.

(SPERRY, 1968, PP. 725–726)

The reason for this weird confusion may be seen in Figure 18.8. The left hand, commanded by the right hemisphere, draws what that hemisphere sees: a dollar sign. When the patient is asked what he drew, the question can be deciphered only by the left hemisphere, the side specialized for language. This hemisphere saw not a dollar sign but a question mark, so that is what the patient verbalizes.

Severing the corpus callosum does not result in a completely split brain. The two hemispheres are still connected through the brain stem. Neutral factual information cannot be communicated from one hemisphere to the other, but affective reactions can be communicated. Consider what happens when a male patient is shown a slide of a nude woman in the left visual field and nothing in the right visual field (see Figure 18.9). The right hemisphere perceives the nude, but the left hemisphere does not. The patient starts to laugh, but

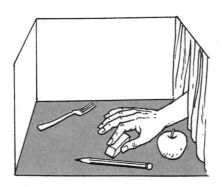

Figure 18.7 *Manual test for split-brain patient.*

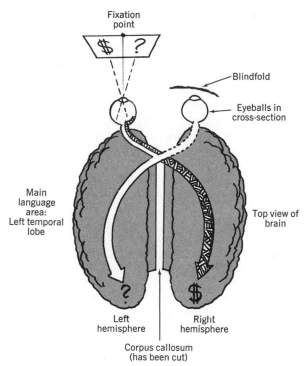

Figure 18.8 *Visual paths in a split-brain patient (from Sperry, 1968).*

UNEQUAL HEARING. In persons with normal hearing, one ear is as sensitive as the other. But when each ear receives different inputs, the right dominates for certain sounds and the left for others. The explanation for such differences does not reside in anatomy: there are sensory nerves from each ear to *both* hemispheres. In explaining the phenomenon, we must look at the way the brain functions, not at its anatomy.

First, sensory messages from the *opposite* ear tend to dominate those from the ear on the same side as the hemisphere. This has been neatly demonstated in split-brain patients by Milner et al. (1968).

Second, sounds involved in listening to language are picked up better by the right ear than by the left. This should not be a complete surprise in light of the dominance of opposite-sided hearing. Thus with the left hemisphere being specialized for language, it follows that the right ear should dominate the left when speech is being decoded.

The basic experiment involves feeding different sounds, equated for loudness, into each ear. For example, the word *pit* would be delivered to the left ear and the word *pin* to the right ear (a difference of consonants); or *pin* could be delivered to one ear, *pan* to the other (a difference of vowels). The subject resolves this competition between the ears by reporting the one word he hears. The data, which have come from several laboratories, are summarized in Table 18.3. The right ear/left brain is dominant for digits, words, nonsense syllables, and consonants. These are all characteristics necessary for proper decoding of speech. Vowels, which are less important in

cannot explain why. The "talkative" left hemisphere does not know why—only that something is funny. This could occur only when one side of the brain does not know what the other is doing, as in a split-brain patient under restricted experimental conditions, but the phenomenon has a frightening, science-fiction quality.

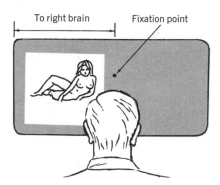

Figure 18.9 *Shared effect in a split brain patient.*

Table 18.3

Left Ear/Right Brain Versus Right Ear/Left Brain*

MATERIAL	DOMINANCE
Digits	Right ear/left brain
Words	Right ear/left brain
Nonsense syllables	Right ear/left brain
Consonants	Right ear/left brain
Vowels	No dominance
Melodies	Left ear/right brain
Environmental sounds	Left ear/right brain

* The findings are from Kimura (1961, 1963, 1968); Shankweiler and Studdert-Kennedy (1967); and Palmer (1964). They apply only to right-handed persons

speech perception, are heard equally well by the two ears. But the left ear/right brain dominates for music and environmental sounds.

Third, there are left-right differences in the effects of delayed auditory feedback (for right-handed persons). While a subject was reading, his speech was fed back—after a delay of 1/5 second—to either his right or left ear. The interference with speech was more disruptive when the feedback was to the *right* ear than to the left ear (Bradshaw et al., 1971). Precisely the opposite effects were found when the task was playing a piano: feeding back the music to the *left* ear produced more disruption in playing.

BRAIN WAVES. When normal persons listen to speech and decode it, there are brain wave differences between the two hemispheres. The amplitude of the major component in the EEG is larger when brain waves are recorded from the left temporal lobe than from the right temporal lobe (Morrell & Salamy, 1971). The left hemisphere evidently is specialized to analyze language. When subjects discriminate between words, their brain waves from the left hemisphere are different than when they discriminate between sounds; the right hemisphere shows no difference in brain waves between language and nonlanguage acoustic discriminations (Wood et al., 1971).

The left hemisphere is also specialized for speech production. In one experiment, subjects pronounced syllables and made nonlanguage motor responses (spitting and coughing). The brain waves of the left hemisphere were different from those of the right hemisphere when the speech sounds were made, but there were no left-right hemisphere differences in brain waves for the nonspeech motor acts of spitting and coughing (McAdam et al., 1971).

The general conclusion that emerges from the research on brain waves, hearing, electric shock, drugs, and split-brain patients is that the left hemisphere is specialized for the production and comprehension of language, and the right hemisphere is specialized for several nonlanguage functions (music, spatial perception).[6] This conclusion holds for (right-handed) adults but not for young children, whose brains are not yet asymmetrical. Specialization of the left hemisphere, called *lateralization,* occurs during childhood, roughly matching the development of speech. Both are more or less complete by puberty, suggesting the possibility of a critical period of language acquisition.

The Critical Period Hypothesis

All normal children acquire a language starting in the second year of life, master most of its components by the fifth year, and slow down markedly

---

[6] *The left hemisphere of most adults is slightly larger than the right hemisphere (Geschwind & Levitsky, 1968). For this and related brain asymmetries, see Geschwind (1970, 1972).*

Table 18.4

Correlation of Motor and Language Development
(Lenneberg, 1969)

AGE (years)	MOTOR MILESTONES	LANGUAGE MILESTONES
0.5	Sits using hands for support; unilateral reaching	Cooing sounds change to babbling by introduction of consonantal sounds
1	Stands; walks when held by one hand	Duplicates syllables; signs of understanding some words; applies some sounds regularly to signify persons or objects—that is, uses first words
1.5	Prehension and release fully developed; gait propulsive; creeps downstairs backward	Repertoire of 3 to 50 words not joined in phrases; trains of sounds and intonation patterns resembling discourse; good progress in understanding
2	Runs (with falls); walks stairs with one foot forward only	More than 50 words; two-word phrases most common; more interest in verbal communication; no more babbling
2.5	Jumps with both feet; stands on one foot for 1 second; builds tower of six cubes	New words every day; utterances of three and more words; seems to understand almost everything said to him; still many grammatical deviations
3	Tiptoes 3 yards (2.7 meters); walks stairs with alternating feet; jumps 0.9 meter	Vocabulary of some 1000 words; about 80 percent intelligibility; grammar of utterances closely approximates that of colloquial adult; syntactic mistakes fewer in variety, systematic, predictable
4.5	Jumps over rope; hops on one foot; walks on line	Language well established; grammatical anomalies restricted either to unusual constructions or to the more literate aspects of discourse

in the ability to learn a new language after puberty. Combining these facts with those of lateralization of the brain, Lenneberg (1966, 1969) argues strongly that there is a critical period for language acquisition. It starts when there has been sufficient maturation of the brain, and it ends when the brain has become completely organized, with the language center located in the left cerebral hemisphere.

MATURATION. It has been established that much of motor development follows a more or less constant sequence in children, which is determined largely by innate factors (see Chapter 4). If language acquisition follows a similar, more or less fixed sequence, the case for a maturational hypothesis of language is strengthened.

The relevant information is assembled in Table 18.4. Just as many motor skills advance through a sequence of milestones, so language skills advance from cooing and babbling to basically grammatical speech. The point is not that language depends on motor skills but that it follows a similar maturational sequence. The orderly development of language is neither slowed down by motor problems nor accelerated by special, intensive training (Lenneberg, 1966).

DEVELOPMENT OF BRAIN LATERALIZATION. The brain of an adult is asymmetrical, with the left brain dominant and specialized for language. The brain of an infant is symmetrical, with no specialization for language. Lateralization of the brain occurs during childhood, paralleling the acquisition of language.

The most compelling evidence has come from observing children with brain damage. During the first year or so of life, before the onset of speech, damage to one or the other cerebral hemispheres may cause a delay in the acquisition of language but no permanent deficit. When one side of the brain is damaged between the ages of two and four years, language is temporarily lost, but the process of acquisition starts again and leads eventually to normal speech by late childhood. From four to ten years, the brain specializes in function, with the left side becoming increasingly crucial for speech. Thus in children of this age range left-brain damage results in temporary language disturbance in 85% of the cases, whereas right-brain

damage results in disturbance in only 45% of the cases (Basser, 1962). The deficits are all wiped out in two year's time, and normal speech ensues. The picture changes markedly after puberty, and 96% of adults with permanent speech deficits have damaged left brains; damage to the right hemisphere in adults rarely results in permanent speech disturbance (see Geschwind, 1970, for a summary).

OTHER ASPECTS OF LANGUAGE DEVELOPMENT. It is rare for children who are born deaf to acquire speech, and children who become deaf before the advent of speech fare little better. If there is a critical period during which language is normally acquired, children who lose their hearing *after* starting to speak should be retrainable.

. . . those who lost hearing after having been exposed to the experience of speech, even for as short a period as one year, can be trained much more easily in all language arts, even if formal training begins some years after they had become deaf. On the other hand, children deafened before completion of the second year do not have any facilitation in comparison with the congenitally deaf (based on personal observations). It seems as if even a short exposure to language, a brief moment during which the curtain has been lifted and oral communication established, is sufficient to give a child some foundation on which much later language may be based.

(LENNEBERG, 1966, P. 155.

Other observations relevant to a critical period hypothesis come from language learning in those with normal hearing. The easy, automatic acquisition of language by children yields to a more difficult and laborious learning of language after puberty. Foreign languages can be learned by adults only with considerable effort. Moreover, a second language learned as an adult is almost never learned completely, and mistakes show up in grammar and accent. A foreign accent is extremely difficult to eradicate in a language learned after childhood, and even regional speech accents stubbornly persist after puberty.

In brief, the theory of a critical period of language acquisition is supported by several kinds of evidence (see Table 18.5):

Table 18.3

Development of Language and the Nervous System (Lenneberg, 1966)

AGE	USUAL LANGUAGE DEVELOPMENT	PHYSICAL MATURATION OF CNS	LATERALIZATION OF FUNCTION	EXPLANATION
Months 0–3 4–20	Emergence of cooing	About 60-70% of developmental course accomplished	None: symptoms and prognosis identical for either hemisphere	Neuroanatomical and physiological prerequisites become established
21–36	Acquisition of language	Rate of maturation slowed down	Hand preference emerges	Language appears to involve entire brain; little cortical specialization with regard to language, though left hemisphere begins to become dominant toward end of this period
Years 3–10	Some grammatical refinement; expansion of vocabulary	Very slow completion of maturational processes	Cerebral dominance established between 3–5 years but evidence that right hemisphere may often still be involved in speech and language functions About ¼ of early childhood aphasias due to right hemisphere lesions	A process of physiological organization takes place in which functional lateralization of language to left hemisphere is prominent; "physiological redundancy" is gradually reduced and polarization of activities between right and left hemispheres is established As long as maturational processes have not stopped, reorganization is still possible
11–14	Foreign accents emerge	A limit is reached on almost all parameters; exceptions are myelinization and EEG spectrum	Apparently firmly established but definitive statistics not available	Language markedly lateralized and internal organization established irreversibly for life; language-free parts of brain cannot take over except where lateralization is incomplete or had been blocked by pathology during childhood
Mid-teens to old age	Acquisition of second language becomes increasingly difficult	None	In about 97% of the entire population language is definitely lateralized to the left	

1. Brain maturation, especially lateralization.
2. The outcome of brain damage during childhood and adulthood.
3. The trainability of children deafened at different ages.
4. The difficulty of learning a language after puberty.
5. The easy shifting of linguistic accents before puberty versus their relative permanent after puberty.

chapter 19

attention and memory

Information processing — attention — doing two things at once — selective attention — model of attention — filter theory — response bias theory — memory — sensory store — short-term store — effects of brain damage — adaptive aspects — long-term store — proactive and retroactive inhibition — verbal encoding — tip-of-the-tongue phenomenon — imagery encoding — eidetic imagery — retrieval — search versus reconstruction — perspective

In Section 4 we discussed man as a *sensor,* searching for and receiving stimulation from the environment. In Section 5 we discussed man as a *learner,* adapting himself to the changeable and recurrent events that confront him. In Section 6 we have been discussing man as a *knower,* organizing his world into meaningful entities. All three approaches converge on man as an *information processor,* focusing on particular stimulus inputs (attention) and storing them for later use (memory).

The information to be processed may be stimulus inputs, memories, or even fantasies (daydreams, nightdreams, images, and "thoughts"). In this chapter we are concerned mainly with inputs from the environment. In each person some of these inputs are selected for *attention,* and some of those attended to are encoded for *storage.* Subsequently, the "memory bank" is searched, and the information is *retrieved* from storage.

This three-stage process is analogous to the way libraries operate (see Table 19.1). *Input consists* of receiving a particular book which is marked according to a classification system and *stored* in a particular location. To retrieve the book from storage, the librarian uses appropriate markers

Table 19.1
Information Processing

PROCESS	IN MAN	IN LIBRARIES
Input	Attention to particular stimuli	A book is received
Storage	Encoding by organizing and "placed" in the nervous system	The book is classified, using a system, and placed in a specific location
Retrieval	Memory is searched, and the trace is decoded (alternatively, the event is "reconstructed")	The library shelves are searched, using the number (code) of the book, and the book is retrieved and made available for use

(title, author, content, classification number) to locate the book.

This chapter treats attention and memory together because the two processes are closely linked. One memorizes only what one attends to,[1] and which stimuli one attends to is determined to a considerable extent by what is already stored in memory . This circle must be broken somewhere to start the exposition, and we shall begin with attention.

Attention

Attention has been likened to a flashlight probing a dark room. The light illuminates first a chair, then a couch, then a table, and so on. At any given moment, only a small part of the room can be seen; the rest cannot be seen or is only dimly perceived. This description implies that we attend

to stimuli only one at a time, all others going unnoticed. If this were true, we could not engage in more than one activity at a time. Let us examine this proposition in its simplest form—simultaneously performing two acts.

Doing Two Things at Once

Can we do two things at one time? The answer is an unequivocal *yes*. The reader can not only scan these words but at the same time scratch his head or listen to the radio. It is commonplace to speak while walking or driving, and translators at the United Nations simultaneously speak one language while listening in another.

Of course, if stimuli are presented at extremely fast rates, it becomes difficult or impossible to do two things at once. The original demonstrations occurred 50 years ago (see Woodworth & Schlosberg, 1954, p. 90). Subjects are presented with two different discriminations, one involving the eyes and one the ears. Each discrimination is so easy that it can be made perfectly at extremely

---

[1] *This statement applies only to long-term storage, as we shall see below, but it is roughly correct in the present context.*

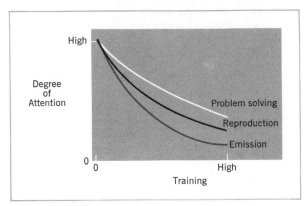

Figure 19.1 Hypothetical curves showing degree of attention and training on three different tasks (Peterson, 1969).

high rates of stimulus presentation. But when both discriminations must be made simultaneously, there is a sharp drop in efficiency and many errors occur. Presumably, if the stimuli were presented sufficiently fast, performance would drop to chance level. Thus, if the term *at once* means a precise instant of time, then we *cannot* do two things simultaneously.

The fact remains, however, that in all but extremely high rates of response production, we *can* do two things at once. And this holds better for some activities than for others. Performance that requires considerable attention will obviously suffer more from ongoing simultaneous responses than will performance requiring little attention.

Verbal activities have been classified into three levels on the basis of how much attention they require (Peterson, 1969). The lowest level, called *emission,* includes counting numbers and reciting the alphabet. Performance is self-guided, with virtually no external cues. The next level, *reproduction,* includes reading and copying (handwriting or typing). Such activities combine the self-guided acts of emission with the simultaneous perception of stimuli; in addition the person must match output to input. The third level, *problem solving,* includes arithmetic computing and mastering puzzles. Here the input must be subjected to the kinds of "operations" described in Chapter 17. Inputs are not merely reproduced but

transformed, and transforming inputs requires more attention.

This classification assumes that the efficiency of doing two things at once depends mainly on the nature of the activity, and this is precisely what Peterson (1969) found. Subjects were asked to solve a word puzzle (anagrams) while simultaneously counting (level 1), while repeating spoken messages (level 2), or while adding (level 3). As predicted, concurrent counting yielded the fewest errors, reproducing speech was next, and adding yielded the largest number of errors. These findings strengthen the classification scheme.

Not to be ignored is *training.* The unskilled person must attend so closely to one task that he cannot perform another simultaneously. A skilled person can "automate" his actions to some extent, thereby reducing the degree of retention required. For example, the inexperienced car driver usually cannot drive and talk simultaneously because he must attend closely to controlling the car. Thus the efficiency of simultaneous performance depends on both the nature of the task and the extent of training (see Figure 19.1). An infant just learning to walk (emission) would have to attend more to his task than would a moderately skilled typist (reproduction). A typist, in turn, might have to attend more closely to typing than would a highly skilled accountant when checking figures (problem solving).

Selective Attention

Doing two things at once involves *divided* attention—that is, handling two inputs. One way to cope with conflicting inputs is to focus on one input and ignore the others—a phenomenon called *selective attention.* Thus the reader engrossed in his novel may not hear the call to dinner, and the avid girl-watcher may trip over an unseen (unattended) obstacle. One of the most stringent tests of attention may be found in a crowded room with conversations occurring all around the listener. (The name given to the phenomenon, the *cocktail party problem,* identifies the initial researcher, Colin Cherry, as a member of the older generation.) The problem is to shut out all the intruding voices and the noise in favor of the one conversation of interest. How is this

Figure 19.2 The shadowing experiment (Cherry, 1953).

accomplished, and under which conditions do intrusions occur?

Though a party may be just the place to formulate ideas, the laboratory is a better place to test them. The most common method of studying selective attention is that of *shadowing* speech (Cherry, 1953). The subject listens to recorded speech and attempts to repeat it aloud just as it is heard, following the speaker closely (that is, "shadowing" him). Then two separate messages are fed in, one to each ear, and the subject is instructed to shadow only one of them, say the one directed to the right ear. This he does easily (see Figure 19.2). His report is accurate but delivered in a monotone, and often he has little idea of the content of the message.

The fate of the rejected (nonshadowed) message is especially interesting. It was recognized as speech, but no words or phrases could be indentified. The language could not be identified as English, and a switch from English to German and back again was unnoticed in the message delivered to the left (rejected) ear. But physical properties of the rejected speech were noted: a switch from speech to a pure tone or from a male to a female voice was almost always noticed. In brief, the subject's attention was focused on the shadowed message, and all but the few gross physical properties of the rejected messages went unnoticed.

The shadowing experiment forces the subject to attend to the messages coming into one or the other ear. But a person can attend selectively even when the same set of messages reaches both ears, as at cocktail parties and in similar situations. The listener extracts one message from the apparently meaningless babble by using such cues as voice quality, loudness, and localization (see Neisser, 1967, p. 207).

Basic Model of Attention

The facts of divided and selective attention may be explained in different ways, but all theories share four assumptions. They can be stated as aspects of a basic model of attention (see Figure 19.3):

1. *Input channels.* Information processing begins with impulses coming from the senses. The messages come from many sources (eyes, ears,

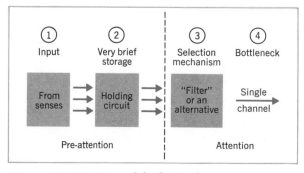

Figure 19.3 Basic model of attention.

nose, skin, and so on), and they vary along many dimensions. Sound, for example, varies in loudness, pitch, and quality, as well as in meaning. Thus there are many different sources of the information pouring into the nervous system, all competing for attention.

2. *Very brief storage.* The various inputs are all held in storage momentarily. We saw earlier that attention could be divided, two tasks being performed at the same time. This presumably is accomplished by switching attention rapidly from one to the other. But while inputs from one task are being attended to, inputs from the other must be held momentarily so that they can receive attention as soon as the person switches back to them. Such switching requires time, probably hundredths of a second, and therefore two fast-paced tasks cannot be performed simultaneously, as we saw earlier.

3. *Selection mechanism.* Of the various messages competing for attention, only one is selected at a time. The selection mechanism might operate like a filter or a radio tuner, or it might operate in some other way (theories differ sharply on this point).

4. *Bottleneck.* There must be a selection mechanism because of the bottleneck in processing inputs: only one input can receive the focus of attention at any given moment. Various inputs can be stored momentarily and even tentatively analyzed (the basis of selection), but only one at a time can get through. This assumption is consistent with the facts of divided and focused attention, as well as the intuitions each of us has about his own attention. Precisely where the bottleneck is has been a matter of considerable dispute, as we shall see.

Filter Theory

The first theory along the lines of our basic model of attention was that of Broadbent (1958). He made two fundamental assumptions (see Figure 19.4). First, the filter works on an all-or-none basis: if two channels are coming through, one is rejected and remains unattended; the other is attended and is further processed. Second, the pre-attention processing is only on the physical properties of the events that give rise to the inputs (loudness, pitch, timing, and so on). Such processing is necessary for the filter to operate. Thus if the listener is instructed to attend to the higher-pitched voice, the sounds must first be processed for pitch before the filter can reject the lower-pitched channel.

This theory neatly accounted for the early research of Cherry (1953), but subsequent shadowing experiments proved to be its undoing. First, Moray (1959) demonstrated that a subject will attend to the message in the unattended ear when his own name is suddenly mentioned. Thus *meaning* (one's name) must be processed *before* reaching the filter, not *after* as in Broadbent's theory (see Figure 19.4).

Then Gray and Wedderburn (1960) again dem-

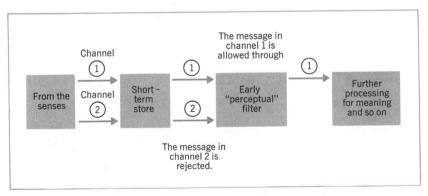

Figure 19.4 Broadbent's filter theory of attention.

onstrated that a subject would switch channels on the basis of meaning. They divided words and presented them alternately to the two ears. If the subject attended to only one ear, he would report a series of nonsense syllables, but if he switched back and forth, he would report a series of words. The outcome was a switching back and forth, indicating that meaning was determining attention. Another way to demonstrate switching is to feed "mice-5-cheese" to the left ear and at the same time feed "3-eat-4" to the right ear. Subjects often report hearing "mice eat cheese," indicating that they are switching attention from one ear to the other and back again on the basis of meaning.

Finally, Treisman (1960) interchanged channels so that the message going to the attended ear (say, the right ear) now went to the unattended (left) and vice versa. Thus in the following lines a slash (/) shows where the messages were interchanged, and capital letters indicate the subject's responses:

(right ear) . . . SITTING AT A MAHOGANY/
                 three POSSIBILITIES . . .
(left ear) . . . Let us look at these/
                 TABLE with her head . . .

Note that the subject switched attention to the left (unattended) ear because the word *table* was expected. Clearly, in this and the other experiments the *meaning* of the rejected message must somehow be registered. It follows that Broadbent's all-or-none, early filter theory cannot be correct, as he himself has admitted (Broadbent & Gregory, 1964).[2]

The original filter theory could not cope with the fact that *unattended messages* may be processed for meaning. It was therefore modified by Treisman (1960, 1964, 1967, 1969) in two ways: (1) a single filter was replaced by a series of filters acting in sequence, and (2) the all-or-none property of the filter was replaced by *attenuation* or a weakening of the message. Thus an unattended message would not be completely rejected but merely diminished in intensity. This theory is too complex to discuss here, and its status is

controversial (see Norman, 1969; Lewis, 1970; and Moray, 1970).

Response Bias Theory

Why is attention selective? Everyone agrees that the potential load of information to be processed is excessive and must somehow be reduced. Less important information needs to be screened and rejected so that more important information can be focused on and fully processed. One solution to the problem is to assume an *early* filter (Broadbent, 1958) or a sequence of filters (Treisman, 1960).

Another possibility is the processing of *all* messages whether they are attended to or not. This theory assumes that ". . . a message will reach the same perceptual and discriminatory mechanisms whether attention is paid to it or not . . ." (Deutch & Deutch, 1963, p. 83). Such automatic processing would allow the message to be matched with some representation already in memory. Only then would one or another message be selected for attention. This notion assumes extensive pre-attention processing before selection. The initial suggestions of Deutch and Deutch (1963) were elaborated into a more complete theory by Norman (1968, 1969), who accepted the idea of a *late* filter:

> *An alternative theory of selective attention requires us to move the selection mechanism back a bit. That is, suppose we admit that every incoming signal does indeed find its match in memory and receive a simple analysis for its meaning. Then we let the selective attention mechanism take over from there.* (1969, P. 33)

Selection is based largely on *pertinence,* which is determined by the subject's prior expectations and the relative importance of the messages. The subject presumably has a response bias that directs him to attend selectively to certain messages. Thus certain kinds of inputs, such as his own name or that of his girlfriend, are highly pertinent, and will therefore receive preferential attention.

Norman's scheme is outlined in Figure 19.5. Note that the crucial arena is the storage system. Stimulus inputs are matched against their repre-

---

[2] *Some researchers do not find the opposing evidence so formidable and retain the notion of an all-or-none filter, but they do not study meaningful messages (see Swets & Kristofferson, 1970).*

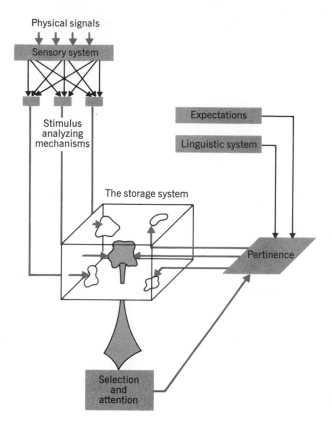

Figure 19.5 Norman's response bias theory of attention (1969).

sentations in storage, and from the other end, expectations and previous analyses act (through pertinence) on their representations in memory. The outcome at any given moment is attention to a single stored representation.

At present there are no crucial data that allow us to choose between late-filter and early-filter theories of attention. Both theories assume that there is considerable analysis of sensory inputs before selective attention occurs. Both recognize that a simple-filter view of attention will not suffice and that there are pre-attentional processes that analyze stimulus inputs automatically and without awareness. Thus it has been established that information is automatically extracted from visual stimuli one dimension at a time (say, color, then brightness, then texture) and that recognition depends on a hierarchy of sequential tests (Egeth, 1967; Neisser, 1967). Finally, it is now acknowledged by all attention theorists that prior expec-

tations and material in storage are both determiners of attention, which brings us to the topic of *memory*.

Memory

In everyday life we store items for varying periods of time. Clothes just returned from the cleaner may be stored in a closet for a day or so until used, or they may be put away for an entire season (until appropriate weather returns). We store milk in the refrigerator, and frozen juice may be kept in the freezer for months. In recent years psychologists have found it useful to distinguish among several kinds of information storage on the basis of *duration* of storage: from less than a second to permanent storage.

In the last section, several diagrams indicated that input coming from the senses is fed into a

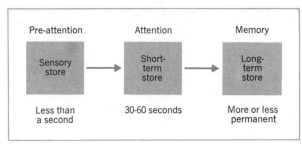

Figure 19.6 *Three kinds of storage.*

short-term store. Everyone knows that there is also a long-term store, yielding memories lasting for as long as several decades. Thus there appear to be three kinds of storage: sensory, short-term, and long-term (see Figure 19.6). The sensory store merely holds incoming information while it is being initially processed and moved on to the short-term store. Presumably, while information is in the short-term store, it is either attended to or not. If it is attended to, it may be encoded for the long-term store, where presumably it reposes permanently.

The three kinds of storage differ not only in duration of storage but also in how the information is processed. Sensory store consists of stimulus inputs that are held momentarily while undergoing preliminary perceptual analysis. Such analysis is automatic and out of awareness. Short-term store consists of inputs coming from the sensory store. Some of these inputs are selected for further processing—that is, they are attended to. Long-term store consists of inputs that have been attended to and somehow processed so that they can be retained for long intervals. Strictly speaking, memory should refer only to long-term store (the term *pre-attention* being more appropriate for sensory store and *attention* for short-term store). However, current usage includes all three stores under the heading of memory.

Sensory Store

When a light bulb is turned off, the glow of the filament fades quickly, but it is retained for just a moment. There is an analogous phenomenon in perception: when a stimulus is turned off, we retain an impression of it for just a moment. Presumably, the input is held, or it reverberates, in the *sensory store.*

The clearest evidence comes from work initiated by Sperling (1960). He presented arrays of letters so briefly (1/20 second) that eye movements did not occur. There were three rows of letters (see Figure 19.7), and after a tone sounded the subject was to repeat one row of letters. A high tone meant that he should repeat the top row; an intermediate tone, the middle row; and a low tone, the bottom row. When the tone occurred immediately (as soon as the letters were turned off), accuracy was almost perfect. But the longer the tone was delayed, the more accuracy decreased. Beyond one second, further delays made no difference. These findings suggest that the visual input was retained very briefly (less than a second), so that the subject could "read off" one part of it even after it had been turned off.

This extremely transient storage of visual inputs was verified by subsequent research (Averbach & Coriell, 1961; Posner & Keele, 1967), but is there an analogous sensory store for *sounds?* On logical grounds, there must be:

Perhaps the most fundamental fact about hearing is that sound is an intrinsically temporal event. Auditory information is always spread out in time; no single millisecond[3] contains enough information to be very useful. If information were discarded as soon as it arrived, hearing would be all but impossible. Therefore we must assume that some "buffer," some medium for temporary storage, is available in the auditory cognitive system. (NEISSER, 1967, PP. 199–200)

[3] *A millisecond equals a thousandth of a second.*

Presented for 1/20 second	Variable delay	One of three tones presented
RZT		← High pitch
PFN		← Intermediate pitch
RSD		← Low pitch

Figure 19.7 *Experiment on visual sensory store (Sperling, 1960).*

Table 19.2
Sensory Versus Short-term Store

	SENSORY STORE	SHORT-TERM STORE
Duration	A second or so	30–60 seconds
Rehearsal	No	Yes
Coding	Simple, if any	Complex
Information processing	Minimal processing (pre-attention)	Considerable processing (attention and rehearsal)

There have been a number of studies demonstrating an *auditory* sensory store, but the most direct evidence has come from Massaro (1970*a*, *b*; 1972). In his research a sound was "retained" for approximately ¼ second, but he admitted that the retention period might be longer, depending on the task.

Estimates of the duration of the sensory store have varied from a fraction of a second to several seconds, but a reasonable guess limits it to one second. So far only vision and hearing have been tested, but surely the inputs coming through the other senses are held momentarily in a sensory store.

Short-Term Store

Short-term store is less transient than sensory store, but a distinction between the two involves other differences (see Table 19.2). Material in short-term store can be *rehearsed* (for example, one repeats a telephone number to oneself). The inputs in sensory store are not rehearsed; they are primitive "images" of the stimuli impinging on the senses. They are either uncoded or relatively uncoded, whereas the material in short-term store undergoes complex processing (Posner & Boies, 1971). Thus sensory store involves automatic, pre-

attentional processing of stimulus inputs, but short-term store involves selective attention — that is, awareness or consciousness.

Having distinguished short-term store from sensory store, we must complete its description by contrasting short-term with long-term store. There is strong debate on this issue. Some theorists insist that there is only one kind of memory, and any distinction between short-term and long-term memory is both arbitrary and unnecessary. Others insist that the distinction is both fundamental and required by the facts, and this is our position. There are two ways in which short-term and long-term store differ: capacity and effects of brain damage.

CAPACITY. Long-term store contains a vast array of memories. Everyone knows this from everyday experiences, and observations of actors and poets, who can recite by the hour, drive home the point. Short-term store, on the other hand, contains only a few memories of the events that have just occurred. A United Nations translator can retain sentences he hears for a few seconds, but they are forgotten soon after he translates them. A typist can briefly remember what she is typing, but by the end of the page she cannot recall material at the beginning of the page (unless she has paid special attention to the material). Similarly, looking up a telephone number produces a memory

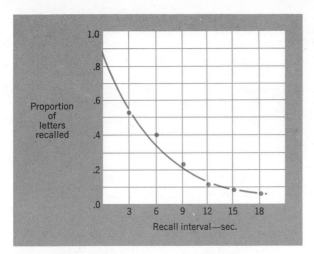

Figure 19.8 Short-term memory with rehearsal blocked by a competing activity (Peterson and Peterson, 1959).

that lasts the few seconds needed to dial the number. After even a brief telephone conversation, the number is usually forgotten. To be remembered for more than a few seconds, the telephone number must be *rehearsed*—that is, somehow coded for long-term store.

Because rehearsal encodes material for long-term store, it is necessary to prevent rehearsal when studying short-term tore. The most frequently used technique is to block rehearsal with a competing activity (Peterson & Peterson, 1959). Three letters are read to the subject. He repeats them once and then starts counting numbers backward by threes. A few seconds later he is asked to recall the letters. The longer the interval, the fewer letters he remembers (see Figure 19.8). After only 18 seconds he remembers very little.

Short-term store is commonly regarded as a "leaky bucket" (see Figure 19.9). Items come into short-term store as water drops into a bucket. It fills rapidly and then starts leaking. Why are items forgotten? There are two theories, one passive and one active. The passive theory suggests that memories merely fade away from disuse, just as items passively leak out of the bucket. The active theory suggests that memories suffer *interference* from

other memories, that is, old items do not merely leak out but are *pushed out* by new items.

A *decay* theorist would interpret the data in Figure 19.8 as forgetting due to rapid decay of the memory trace. An *interference* theorist would note that rehearsal was prevented by having the subject count backward. Clearly, this competing task would cause forgetting by *interfering* with brief storage of items. Most psychologists lean toward the interference interpretation (see Tulving & Madigan, 1970).[4]

The capacity of long-term store is so large that it is difficult to estimate, but the capacity of short-term store is small enough to be specified. It is between five and nine items, or, to use Miller's (1956) apt label, seven plus or minus two. The usual limit for perfect recall of single letters or numbers is nine, and a sequence such as 2014538697 proves extremely difficult to repeat back without error. But, as Miller has pointed out, we tend to group individual items into clusters called *chunks,* and such organization of the material enhances memory. Thus the above number can be broken down into three chunks and treated as a telephone number, the sequences being area code, exchange, and individual telephone: 201-453-8697. Grouped this way, the ten digits can easily be recalled.

Similarly, we read *groups* of letters (words), not

[4] *The opposing theories have proved very difficult to test definitively because of problems of method too complex to discuss here.*

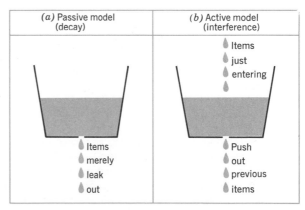

Figure 19.9 Short-term store as a leaky bucket.

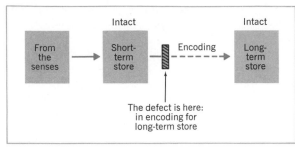

Figure 19.10 *Effect of damage to the brain (the hippocampus) on memory.*

individual letters, and three groups are just as easy to remember as three letters (Murdock, 1961). Given the limitation of short-term store (7 ± 2 items), the solution is to group items into chunks, thereby increasing the total number of items that can be remembered (as, for example, in converting a ten-digit telephone number into three chunks). In essence, the person *recodes* the material, increasing the *size* of memory units without increasing the *number* of units (the chunk becomes the unit). This processing of stimuli bears on the distinction between short-term and long-term store:

When presented with a meaningful sequence of letters, subjects perceive words, not separate letters, and words are stored in short-term memory. The perceptual processing which takes place when these chunks are formed is quite automatic and seems to require a minimum of time and effort. In fact, one of the main differences between short- and long-term memory appears to lie in the way in which material is encoded for storage. Chunks are stored in both short- and long-term memory, but the chunks of short-term memory are the result of very superficial perceptual processing, while the units of long-term memory are based upon higher level analyses, which require time and often considerable effort. (KINTCH, 1970, P. 175)

In brief, stimuli probably undergo some processing for their brief tenure in short-term store, just as new library books may be temporarily stored prior to being catalogued. For long-term storage, stimuli undergo longer and more complex processing, just as library books are appropriately classified and cross-classified before being labeled and permanently shelved.

EFFECTS OF BRAIN DAMAGE. One kind of brain damage—to the *hippocampus,* which is part of the forebrain system—causes an unusual kind of memory loss (Milner, 1959). The patient can remember the immediate past, and he has no trouble either in remaining aware of what is happening or in understanding long sentences. Thus his short-term memory is unimpaired. In fact, he may repeat material continuously in order to keep it in short-term store, a device used by such patients to avoid forgetting.

Nor is long-term retention of older memories impaired. The patient retains memories learned before the brain damage: the names of friends and families, the places he formerly frequented, and the tools he was accustomed to use. But no matter how much he rehearses, he cannot retain new material. He can no longer encode information for long-term storage. Yesterday's jigsaw puzzle is just as novel today, and he cannot remember where he left the lawn mower. Consider a hypothetical sequence of how information is stored (see Figure 19.10). Messages from the senses move to short-term store, where they are processed; this is intact. Then they are encoded for long-term store; this is the process that is knocked out by the brain damage.[5] New information never gets programed for long-term store and is therefore forgotten. The long-term store itself is intact, and memories that preceded the brain damage are retained.

The hippocampus can be rendered temporarily ineffective by disruptive electric shock. When such shock is administered to rats, their short-term memory (roughly, one minute) is not affected, but their long-term memory (24 hours) is seriously disturbed (Kesner & Conner, 1972). Thus in both rats and men disruption of the functioning of the hippocampus interfers with long-term store but not short-term store. This fact suggests that the two kinds of storage are different.

ADAPTIVE ASPECTS. Stimulus inputs are held in short-term store only briefly, and they can be re-

[5] *This point is disputed by Warrington and Weiskrantz (1970), who believe that the crucial deficit in amnesia is in retrieval from long-term store, not in encoding. Whether the deficit is in encoding or retrieval, amnesic persons have problems with long-term store but not with short-term store.*

tained for more than about a half minute only by rehearsal (for example, after looking up a telephone number, keep repeating it). The information in short-term store undergoes further processing or it is promptly forgotten. What are the uses of such a brief memory? There are three (Hilgard & Bower, 1966).

First, an immediate memory is needed to comprehend events that last more than a second or two but less than half a minute. The best example is human speech, which includes sentences that may take many seconds to be spoken.

Second, information can be temporarily shelved so that attention can be focused on new material. A U.N. translator needs to listen to new sentences while he is translating the sentence heard a moment ago (and held in short-term store). Thus short-term store offers a "working space" for recent inputs and for internal thoughts and cognitions as well (such as doing arithmetic "in one's head").

Third, short-term store allows time for the encoding of material to be placed in long-term store. As we shall see, inputs must be organized and somehow "located" in long-term store, and such processing can occur while the inputs are in short-term store.

Long-Term Store

Most psychologists believe that forgetting is caused by *interference:* one group of memories somehow blocks recall of another group of memories. This belief is founded on a solid factual basis, notably the repeated demonstration of two kinds of interference, *proactive* and *retroactive.* The interference of earlier material with later material is called *proactive.* When later material interferes with earlier material, this is called *retroactive.* Consider a problem of memorization that has confronted virtually everyone. You arrive at a party early, are introduced to six persons, and try to memorize their names. An hour or so later another group arrives, and you try to memorize their names. As might be expected, the first list of names causes trouble in your memorizing the second (proactive interference), and the second list causes forgetting of the first (retroactive interference).

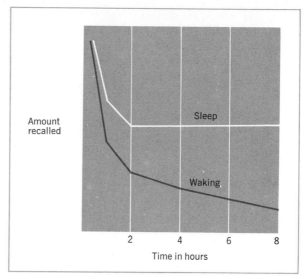

Figure 19.11 *Forgetting after sleep and waking (after Jenkins and Dallenbach, 1924).*

During every waking hour we take in and store information, whereas virtually no new information is taken in during sleep (see Chapter 6). It follows that learning followed by sleep should yield better recall than learning followed by wakefulness. This was confirmed in a classic experiment by Jenkins and Dallenbach (1924). Their subjects learned a list of ten nonsense syllables and were then tested for recall after varying amounts of sleep or wakefulness (see Figure 19.11). After eight hours of sleep they recalled about half the items; after eight hours of waking activities they recalled only about one-tenth. Clearly, most, if not all, forgetting must be attributed to interference from extraneous stimulus inputs.

Two aspects of this research merit attention. First, the measure was the amount of material *recalled,* which is the most common way of measuring retention. An alternative is to determine how much is *recognized.* Students are well aware of the two types of measure. Essay and short-answer examinations are measures of recall, whereas true-false and multiple-choice examinations are measures of recognition.

Second, even after sleeping, the subjects forgot much of what they had learned. This comes as no surprise to students, who have been known to forget what they learned not only as long ago as a year or a month but as recently as a week, a day, or even an hour. But the very fact of forgetting seems to contradict an assertion made earlier, that long-term storage is permanent. The paradox may be resolved by distinguishing between *encoding* and *retrieval.* Materials must somehow be encoded for long-term storage. Once this occurs, the material is permanently *available.* Subsequently, it must be retrieved from storage. Some encoded material is easy to retrieve, some difficult. If material in long-term storage is not *accessible,* we say it has been forgotten. Thus in terms of our model of memory, material may be available but not accessible (Mandler, 1967*b*). Consider books stored in library stacks. Once a book is placed in a given location, it is available for retrieval. But if the file card is lost or the file card is incorrectly filled out, the book may be inaccessible.

Thus there are two separate but related aspects of long-term store: *encoding* and *retrieval.* Material in short-term store must be processed so that it can be placed in long-term store. It must be tagged so that subsequently, when memory is searched, it can be retrieved for use. If a given sensory input is to be remembered later, it must usually be rehearsed in short-term store and then encoded in a way that will make it accessible to retrieval. There are many different ways of encoding information, and psychologists have barely scratched the surface of this topic. But two ways are well known, and they may well be the dominant ways of encoding for storage: verbal (meaning) and imagery.

VERBAL ENCODING. After language has been acquired, a large proportion of stimulus inputs consists of words and sentences. This verbal material has many dimensions—associative, referential, grammatical, and meaning, to name a few—and presumably all these dimensions are involved in placing the material in long-term store:

. . . when a person hears or sees a word, the process of perceiving this word consists of encoding it within a number of different aspects, attributes or conceptual psychological dimensions. I assume that when a person hears the word "horse," it is encoded into the broader categories of beasts of burden, warm-blooded animals, and finally animals in general. In short, I suspect that the encoding process functions in the manner of a good player of Twenty Questions, but in more or less the reverse direction. (WICKENS, 1970, P. 1)

TIP-OF-THE-TONGUE PHENOMENON. Most of us have experienced the "tip-of-the-tongue" phenomenon, in which we are searching for a word whose definition we know, but the word momentarily escapes us. Investigation of such lapses in recall has shown that subjects know what the target word sounds like, its meaning, its synonyms, the number of syllables, and the first letter (Brown & McNeill, 1966). All those aspects must be part of the way the word is encoded in long-term store. Note that the word being sought is only temporarily lost; it can be *recognized* immediately if spoken, and it is almost always recalled subsequently. Thus such a word is available but temporarily not *accessible.*

ORGANIZATION. One of the most difficult tasks that can be assigned is the rote memorization of unrelated words, syllables, or numbers. The difficulty lies in the lack of *organization,* for when material is in some way connected or associated, it is easier to retain. There are many ways to organize verbal material (see Wickens, 1970, for a summary of research), but we need only one example to illustrate how it is done.

As Mandler (1968) has shown, verbal units can be classified and placed in a hierarchy. Mandler assumes that no *chunk* can contain more than five units—the lower end of Miller's (1956) seven plus or minus two. The hierarchy is shown in Figure 19.12*a*, and it works as follows:

At the lowest level of organization, each set contains five words. These basic sets are organized into categories so that each category subsumes five of these words. At the second level of the hierarchy there is again a set of five categories which belong to a single set. This organization continues upward in the hierarchy, but any five categories belonging to a category set are subsumed under a superordinate category.

(MANDLER, 1968, P. 112)

Starting from the top of Figure 19.12*a*, each cate-

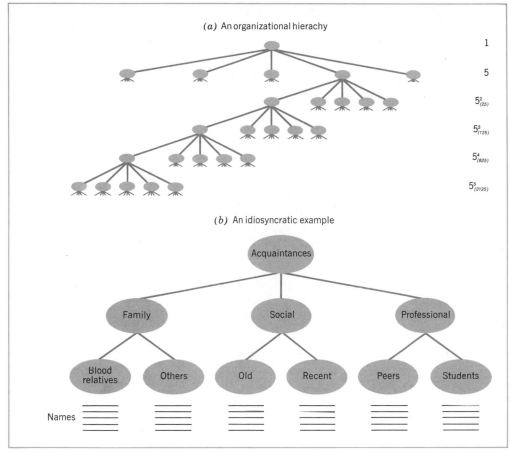

(a) An organizational hierachy

1

5

$5^2_{(25)}$

$5^3_{(125)}$

$5^4_{(625)}$

$5^5_{(3125)}$

(b) An idiosyncratic example

Acquaintances

Family   Social   Professional

Blood relatives   Others   Old   Recent   Peers   Students

Names

Figure 19.12 *An organizational hierarchy (Mandler, 1968).*

gory contains five subunits, yielding a total of 3125 units in the entire system (space limits us to showing only enough of these units to demonstrate the organization).

Figure 19.12*b* shows how a list of acquaintances could be organized hierarchically. The discerning reader will have linked this kind of organization to the conceptual hierarchies discussed in the first half of Chapter 17, where we noted that concepts were major cognitive tools used to organize the chaotic flux around us. Such organization is equally important in memory, and the grouping of stimuli into hierarchical categories yields large gains in retention (see, for example, Bower et al., 1969).

IMAGERY ENCODING. Verbal encoding plays such a dominant role in everyday life, especially in the life of a student, that it obscures the role of imagery in memory. We must possess fairly good auditory imagery in order to sing, play, or recognize melodies and other aspects of music, or even to identify different voice qualities and accents in speakers. The importance of visual imagery in memory can easily be established by a simple test. If you are not at home, locate where the bed is in your bedroom; or if you are at home, locate where your psychology lecture room is on campus. Any such simple request will call up a visual image of the object in its usual surroundings.

With vision being the dominant sense in man, it comes as no surprise that most imagery is visual. Individuals vary considerably in the sharpness and retention of visual images, and at the extreme is the rare person with *eidetic imagery* ("photographic memory").

Research Report

It is no easy task to identify a person with eidetic imagery, and in recent years there has been only one large-scale attempt — by Haber and his colleagues (Haber & Haber, 1964; Leask et al., 1969; Haber, 1969). Children were shown a picture for 30 seconds, and then they gazed at a neutral gray card and described what they had seen. Out of 500 children, 20 described enough details to suggest they might have eidetic imagery. But there was no way to be sure; the 20 children might have been superior memorizers, not eidetic children.

What was needed was an unequivocal test, a task that could be solved by an eidetic person but not by someone with only a superior memory. The solution is to present a pattern of dots to one eye and have the subject later superimpose it over the pattern exposed to the other eye. This was done with one of the patterns that Julesz (1964) developed to study three-dimensional vision (see Chapter 11). The experiment was performed by Stromeyer and Psotka (1970), using a woman with remarkable visual imagery. One paired set of stimuli contained the letter "T" in it, but only when viewed with both eyes. One member of the pair was presented to the subject's right eye. After a brief interval, the other pattern was presented to her left eye, while she superimposed an image of right-eye pattern. Without hesitation, she identified a "T" that seemed to be coming toward her. This is the normal perception of a person looking at both patterns *simultaneously,* but only a person with eidetic imagery could bridge the *time gap.*

This basic experiment was repeated with two variations of special interest. First, the time interval between exposing the two patterns was increased to 24 hours (with a different pattern of course), and the subject still showed evidence of eidetic imagery. Second, there was a double-blind variation, with neither experimenter nor subject knowing what pattern should be seen. With this control for cues from the experimenter (see Chapter 2), the subject still reported the appropriate pattern. For further details of the talent of this unusual woman, see Stromeyer (1970).

True eidetic imagery rarely occurs, but all normal persons possess visual imagery and use it in retention. Such imagery, when not linked to verbal encoding, leads to a common problem: visualizing a past event or object but furnishing only a vague, impoverished account of it. But imagery does help recall: when material is imagery-encoded and placed in long-term store, it is more accessible. Several experiments have documented this assertion, one of the clearest being reported by Paivio (1969). He presented two groups of subjects with ten nouns presented in series and then

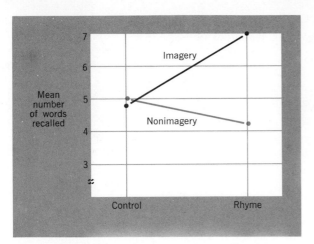

Figure 19.13 Effect of imagery on recall (after Paivio, 1969).

tested for recall; this was the Control condition. Then both groups were instructed to use rhymes in learning another set of ten nouns; in this Rhyme condition one group was told to use mental images, the other was not. The results are shown in Figure 19.13. In the Control condition recall was roughly the same for both groups, but in the Rhyme condition imagery significantly increased recall.

These laboratory findings confirm what has been known for thousands of years: that the best schemes for improving recall are those involving imagery (see Yates, 1966). For example, the learner can use familiar places or objects to "park" items to be remembered. Suppose the following grocery list is to be memorized: sugar, ham, bananas, carrots, and bread.[6] Each of these would be "located" on or against a familiar object, such as might be found in one's own bedroom. Anyone can easily call up an image of the bed, chair, desk, window, and closet in his bedroom. It is a simple matter to visualize each item on the grocery list superimposed on an object in the bedroom (see Figure 19.14). To recall the items on the grocery list, one would need only to visualize the room and then recognize the objects placed in various parts of it. Schemes such as this may seem farfetched and unworkable to anyone who has not tried them,

[6] *Such a short list would not require a device to aid recall, but it will suffice to illustrate how the device works.*

but they do work. Long before psychologists studied memory, students of the art of memory perfected devices for improving recall.[7] In the days before the invention of the printing press, anyone who aspired to learning had to rely mainly on his memory.

DEVELOPMENTAL ASPECTS. Imagery yields recall that is *concrete* and seems more *real* to the individual, perhaps because the memories contain an *affective* tinge (happy-sad, angry-fearful, and so on). Verbal encoding yields a more *abstract summary* of objects and events, with less of their" feel." Concerning the sequence of development during childhood, the traditional view assumes that imagery encoding occurs first:

During the pre-adolescent period of physical and cerebral maturation the increased capacity for abstract thought is stimulated and encouraged in most school subjects. In accord with this trend, linguistic skills in oral and written expression take precedence over the inexpressible image. Though some personally experienced events may continue to be registered with something of their original sensory-affective quality,

[7] *The schemes improve retention of any given set of memories, but they do not improve memory in the sense of "sharpening the mind."*

Figure 19.14 Imagery as an aid to memory.

such events are also categorized in more abstract terms. Language is used more and more to compress, to represent and to express our experience.

(RICHARDSON, 1969, P. 40)

This account fits neatly into Piaget's description (see Chapter 17) of the child's progress from the sensory-motor and preoperational stages (mainly imagery) to the two later stages involving *operations* (manipulation of symbols, mainly language symbols).[8]

Research with children has supported this developmental theory of information processing. Younger children tend to retain stimulus inputs in the visual sensory store longer than older children and adults; and younger children transfer inputs into short term store more slowly than older children and adults (Gummerman & Gray, 1972). The processing of visual information speeds up rapidly at eleven to twelve years of age—coincidental with the beginning of Piaget's period of formal operations.

RETRIEVAL. Most psychologists see retrieval as a *search* for stored memories. The main reasons for forgetting are assumed to be (1) interference from other memories and (2) problems in locating the stored items. Having discussed interference earlier, we shall focus on problems of locating material. Again, the library analogy may help. Suppose you are in a very large library, seeking a book. Any information that narrows the range of the search will hasten the search—especially the author's name, the topic of the book, and its title.

Similarly, anything that narrows the range of possible responses will facilitate retrieval. This is why rhymes are easily recalled: the list of possible responses is limited to words that sound alike (Bower & Bolton, 1969). And this is why the structure of language helps: the words in a sentence must fit into specific grammatical categories. Thus if a sentence begins "The boy . . . ," the next word is likely to be a verb. Such narrowing of possibilities is akin to knowing that a library book is fiction—it saves searching in the wrong place.

The tip-of-the-tongue phenomenon (Brown & McNeill, 1966) shows that verbal material is encoded in several different ways: sound, initial

[8] *For an opposing minority view, see Rohwer (1970).*

letter, length, meaning, and associations (the stimulus *table* commonly elicits the association, *chair*). Such encoding specifies several "addresses," which help the retrieval process. It is precisely this aspect of retrieval—specifying a location—that makes memory schemes work. Consider the imagery scheme of locating grocery items in one's bedroom. Memorizing the items together with the bedroom images actually *adds* to the burden of memory, but it facilitates recall. If recall is better when there is *more* to remember, the added material must have a function. This function is twofold: to make an item easy to locate, and to outline a sequence of locations that can be followed in recalling a list of things. In brief, memory schemes work because they guarantee better retrieval.

Viewing retrieval as a *search* implies that the objects of the search are passive *memory traces,* which need only be located. Locating the trace would activate it, and the item would be recalled. Opposing this view is a minority position that suggests that all memory is *reconstruction* (Bartlett, 1932). Presumably, it is not the full-blown memory that is stored, but only elements or components out of which a memory can be constructed. Thus each recall consists of assembling a cognition out of traces of past cognitions—in effect *re*constructing the original object or event. The appropriate analogy is to a scientist reconstructing an entire animal from a few bones:

. . . *we store traces of earlier cognitive acts, not of the products of those acts. The traces are not simply "revived" or "reactivated" in recall; instead, the stored fragments are used as information to support a new construction. It is as if the bone fragments used by the paleontologist did not appear in the model he builds at all—as indeed they need not, if it is to represent a fully fleshed-out, skin-covered dinosaur. The bones can be thought of, somewhat loosely, as remnants of the structure which created and supported the original dinosaur, and thus as sources of information about how to reconstruct it.* (NEISSER, 1967, PP. 285–286)

The two opposing positions, search versus reconstruction cannot easily be tested. There have been attempts but no agreement on the outcome.

Figure 19.15 Search versus reconstruction views of memory.

Therefore, all we can do is state the two contrary approaches.[9] The search view emphasizes first how inputs are encoded and then how they are retrieved. Once the memory trace is located, there is some kind of match between what is sought and the trace; recall is automatic, that is, it occurs when the trace is found in storage. The basic model is that of a library (see Figure 19.15a).

The reconstruction view emphasizes first the *constructive* aspects of perception (see Chapter 11) and then the assembling of memory traces into a *re*presentation. The process of recall is assumed to be essentially the same as the process of perception except that the elements of the cognition are assembled from memory rather than from the senses. The retrieval process is seen not as a search but as a construction of cognitions. The basic model involves reconstructing an animal (object or event) from the bits and pieces of

its bones (memory traces)—as shown in Figure 19.15b.

Perspective

One advantage of the *search* view of memory is that it fits more easily as a component of information processing. Accordingly, we shall summarize attention and memory, using models borrowed from several sources, mainly Norman (1969) and Schiffrin and Atkinson (1969).

The basic diagram should be familiar by now (see Figure 19.16). Attention starts with stimuli, which are initially analyzed by the senses (pre-attention). The message, now translated into neural impulses, stays only a moment in sensory store and automatically moves to short-term store. If it is "irrelevant," it is not attended to and is forgotten as though it had never occurred. Relevant messages are attended to only if they somehow connect to material already in long-term store. The major determinant of relevance is what is already in long-term store. While an input is being attended to, it is in conscious awareness; thus consciousness is equivalent to the short-term store.

Rehearsal can keep inputs in short-term store beyond the normal half-minute or so. Rehearsal also serves to encode messages for placement in long-term store. The better and more complete the encoding the easier it will be to retrieve the memory from long-term store.

Recall starts with either a self-instruction or a stimulus that somehow activates the retrieval

[9] *One way of integrating the two approaches is through the two different types of encoding. Imagery encoding is fairly complete; it omits so few details that reconstruction is not necessary: the memory is sufficient as it has been stored. Verbal encoding, in contrast, is extremely abbreviated and omits most details. Such details would have to be reconstructed from the minimal information in the verbal memory. Thus the search model might be appropriate for memory images and the reconstruction model might be appropriate for verbal memories.*

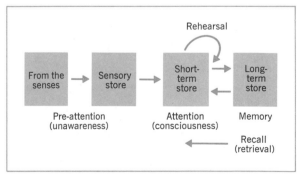

Figure 19.16 A model of attention and memory.

mechanism. A search is initiated, and it continues until the item is located or the attempt is given up for attention to other matters. Recalled material becomes the focus of attention, which means that it is temporarily in short-term store. In this model the focus of attention—whether of stimulus inputs or of memories retrieved from long-term store—is the material in short-term store. Thus short-term store has two faces, like the god Janus: one faces toward the future (stimulus inputs being perceived) and the other faces toward the past (memories being retrieved from long-term store).

section seven
socialization

chapter 20

attachment

Like any newborn mammal, the helpless human infant cannot survive alone and would soon perish of hunger, thirst, heat, or cold. He needs an adult, typically his mother, to feed, nurture, and protect him. Beyond these requisites for survival, the human infant seems to require the kind of stimulation that only another human can offer: the comfort, affection, and give-and-take of close personal relationships. On the basis of such parental behavior and the infant's response, there develops the close parent-infant bond called *attachment.*

Our interest in attachment centers on three questions: how, when, and so what? We want to know *how* the newborn develops a close social bond with the mother. Is it solely in response to the mother's behavior, or is the infant also active in initiating the relationship? And how does the infant relate to other familiar humans and to strangers? Is the infant socially oriented at birth, or does social interest develop out of nonsocial or asocial, innate tendencies?

Concerning *when,* we want to know the sequence of attachment. When does it begin, what is its course, and does it ever terminate? Finally, concerning *so what,* we want to know the outcome of this first social bond. It has been suggested that infants, when sufficiently loved by their mothers, confidently anticipate good things in subsequent encounters with human beings. This may be an oversimplification, but it is essentially correct. As the first social bond, the mother-infant tie may well set the tone for subsequent relationships. But we cannot neglect the roles of the infant's own predispositions and the pressures of socialization, as we shall note in subsequent chapters.

Stages of Attachment in Mammals

Man shares with all other mammals a period of helplessness in infancy during which maternal care establishes a close tie between infant and mother. By examining the mother-infant relationships of other mammals, we can discover both the general trends that appear to hold for all mammals and the features unique to man.

Cats

The mother-infant tie among cats is close for eight weeks, during which there are three sequential stages: approaches by the mother, mutual approaches, and rejection by the mother (Schneirla et al., 1963). Figure 20.1 schematizes the sequence.

MOTHER APPROACHES (1–3 WEEKS). The mother initiates most of the feedings. If the kittens are asleep, she licks them until they are awake. Licking is also necessary for the kittens' urination and defecation. In fact, licking of the kittens is the mother's major nonnutritive response in binding her infants to her, leading to a strong attachment.

At first the kittens are inefficient at rooting out the nipple and beginning to suckle. They cannot see and must grope blindly. Nevertheless, they learn quickly, and in two to three days are efficient at locating their preferred nipple. During this stage it is the mother that initiates all contacts. She evidently receives gratification from being suckled and from the sight, the touch, and especially the smell of her kittens.

MUTUAL APPROACHES (4–5 WEEKS). The mother continues to approach the kittens, offering them the opportunity to suckle, but more frequently the kittens seek out the mother, interrupting her resting or feeding. They can see (since

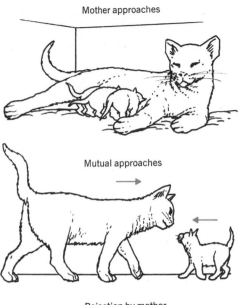

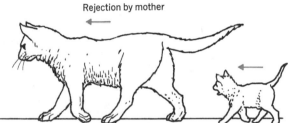

Figure 20.1 *Three stages in cat–kitten attachment.*

the beginning of the second week) and move around well. When approached, the mother helps by stretching or moving into a position that makes it easier for the kittens to suckle. There is much mutual stimulation through the media of sight, touch, smell, and to a lesser extent hearing.

The mother tolerates the kittens playing over and around her, and occasionally she participates. However, toward the end of this period, she tolerates less play and appears less interested in the kittens. Sometimes when they approach her for feeding, she avoids them.

REJECTION BY MOTHER (5–8 WEEKS). The mother no longer initiates feeding. All feeding is instigated by the kittens, who follow the mother around and pursue her if she attempts to avoid them. If she is lying down, they nuzzle her until they can get at the nipples. The mother, on her part, keeps the feeding brief, and appears to be relatively disinterested in the kittens. They are encouraged to eat solid food, and the basis is laid for weaning.

Dogs

Essentially the same three stages can be distinguished in dogs, though the time sequences are not the same. For the first week the mother approaches the pups, licking and suckling them. There is mutual approach for the next two weeks. Subsequently, the mother starts to avoid the pups, leaving the litter more and more, and she stops licking them. All feeding is initiated by the pups at this stage, but sometimes the mother punishes them for approaching her.

Figure 20.2 *Monkey infant clinging to its mother.*
(UNIVERSITY OF WISCONSIN PRIMATE LABORATORY).

Primates

Moving from dogs and cats to primates is a long step toward man. The mother-infant relations of primates differ from those of dogs and cats in these ways:

1. There is no litter, so that all the mother's attention is focused on a single infant, which leads to a close tie.
2. Odor cues are reduced, the smell of the offspring being only weakly attractive to the mother; there is little licking.
3. In line with the greater visual and tactile sensitivity of primates, sight and touch are more important in the mother-infant relationship.
4. There is increased communication between mother and infant, especially by vocal and facial expressions.

Harlow and his collaborators (1959, 1961, 1962, 1963, 1965) have collected much information on the mother-infant affectional system in rhesus monkeys, and most of their findings apply to primates in general. They distinguish three stages, parallel to the stages seen in dogs and cats: maternal attachment and protection, ambivalence, and rejection.

ATTACHMENT AND PROTECTION. The mother initially keeps in close and intimate contact with the newborn infant. She cradles it, and the infant monkey clings to her (see Figure 20.2). Clasping and clinging are reflexive in newborn primates, and their responses result in an extremely close bond between infant and mother. Both clinging and cradling decline steadily throughout the first three months. Nutritive suckling follows the same course: at first it is very frequent, but its frequency declines to a low point during the third month, and it remains low. The same general curve describes the course of clinging, cradling, and nutritive suckling (see Figure 20.3).

The mother's manipulation of her infant is not restricted to cradling and holding. She grooms the infant, smoothing and parting its hair and removing dirt and parasites from its skin. Grooming increases during the first 30 days but then declines to a low point at 90 days. Except for the initial increase, grooming follows the general curve shown in Figure 20.3.

AMBIVALENCE. The period of ambivalence starts in the third month and continues for about a year. The positive response of seeking and protecting the infant, grooming, clinging, and clasping all continue, but at a low frequency. The other aspect of ambivalence—negative responses—increases steadily during this stage. More and more the mother tends to threaten or roughly push her infant as the months pass by, and the initial period of attachment yields to increasing rejection.

REJECTION. Harlow and his collaborators did not observe complete rejection by mothers of their maturing offspring. They attributed the absence of rejection to both the captive status of the animals and the absence of subsequent offspring. But there have been field studies of langurs (Jay, 1963) and baboons (DeVore, 1963). In both these primates the stage of maternal ambivalence is followed by a stage of rejection, during which the infant is weaned. Jay writes of langurs, starting with the eleventh month:

It takes about 4 or 5 months before the infant no longer tries to nurse or cling. Early rejection is mild. At first the mother avoids her infant by moving away, after jumping from one tree to another so that the infant must maneuver long distances down to the ground and up into her tree. When the infant catches up with her, she merely turns away, and only after the infant persists in trying to nurse does she hold it off with outstretched arms. (1963, P. 297)

The rejection becomes more severe with time, and a persistent infant langur is likely to be slapped or pushed hard by an irritated mother. In spite of tantrums and severe frustration, the young langur is weaned by the age of 15 months. By then the mother has resumed the estrus cycle and is more and more the subject of attention from adult males. When the juvenile langur is two years old, its mother gives birth again. The mother's preoccupation with her newborn then completes the process of rejection. Subsequently, it is as if the juvenile had no particular mother. This sequence of weaning and rejection is essentially the same as that seen in baboons.

The adaptiveness of the three-stage sequence should be evident. Initially, the helpless infant needs to be soothed and protected. Eventually, it must be pushed out to make its own way in the world.

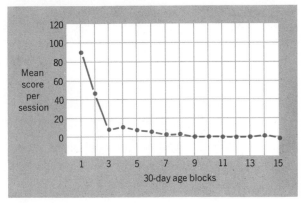

Figure 20.3 *Developmental curve for cradling, suckling and clinging in monkeys (Harlow et al., 1963, p. 259).*

Humans

The stages of attachment, ambivalence, and rejection can be discerned in the early development of cats, dogs, and primates. Is there a similar sequence in humans? The answer must be a qualified yes. There are comparable stages, but human beings are sufficiently different to suggest caution in analogizing.

The initial stage, *attachment,* starts at birth and may last from one to several years, depending on the society and the particular mother. The mother tends to be loving, nurturing, and protecting during this period, and at first she makes no demands. The first important maternal demand is for weaning, which in our culture commonly occurs between 6 and 14 months. In some cultures the infant may nurse for several years— for example, among Eskimos.

Weaning is only the beginning of maternal demands, and the stage of *ambivalence* comes to full flower with demands for control of bladder and bowels. This ordinarily occurs in the second year. Moreover, where birth control is not practiced, the infant's second year of life is likely to be accompanied by the mother's subsequent pregnancy.

The last stage, *rejection,* is not as clear-cut in humans as it is in other mammals. Mothers nurture their children for many years, in keeping with the protracted period of childhood among

Table 20.1
Three Stages of the Mother-Infant Bond in Humans

STAGE	DESCRIPTION	EXAMPLE
Attachment	Mother nurtures infant, makes no demands	Infant is fed on demand
Ambivalence	Mother still nurtures infant, but makes demands	Toilet training
Rejection	Nurturance is reduced, demands are increased; less permissiveness, more punishment	Appearance of new baby, or young child sent to nursery school

humans. But there are at least partial rejections, the major one being the dethronement of the young child by the mother's next child. The three stages are summarized in Table 20.1.

This brief account reveals similarities as well as differences between humans and other mammals. The similarities, as might be expected, are in broad evolutionary trends. The mother must initially protect and nurture her offspring, but gradually she frees herself for other, increasingly important activities. And the infant initially requires the mother's nurturance, but his need wanes and gradually conflicts with needs for exploration and autonomy. The young of animals tend to have autonomy thrust on them through increasingly sharp rejection by the mother. The human child, in contrast, suffers somewhat less rejection; autonomy is something he seeks rather than having it forced on him through maternal rejection.

Concerning other differences, humans mature slower, which means that the period of helplessness and attachment is longer. All human societies require toilet training or similar training, and there are many childrearing practices—varying within and between societies—that have no counterpart in animals.

The Infant's Repertoire

The infant is no mere passive recipient of the mother's attention and affection. He has available six responses that bring her to him, maintain the contact, or bring him to her.

1. *Crying* indicates discomfort and usually brings the mother quickly.
2. *Smiling* entices the mother to closer contact and usually elicits a smile from her.
3. *Vocalizing,* in the form of cooing and (later) babbling, often elicits attention.
4. *Suckling* maintains contact.
5. *Clinging* also maintains contact, especially reciprocal clasping by the mother.
6. *Following,* usually by creeping or crawling after the mother, occurs later than the other responses, and it marks the beginning of much more *active* seeking of the mother.

Note the first three responses (crying, vocalizing, and smiling) bring the mother to the stationary infant, the next two (suckling and clinging) maintain proximity, and the last one (following) brings the infant to the mother.

We have outlined three stages of early social relationships: attachment, ambivalence, and rejection. The remainder of the chapter will deal with the first stage, attachment.

We shall be concerned with the three questions mentioned earlier: when, how, and so what? *When* involves the *sequence* of attachment from its nonsocial origin to the close mother-infant bond. *How* concerns the *explanations* psychologists have offered, as well as the issue of whether there is a critical period for attachment. Finally, *so what* involves the *consequences* of attachment for later relationships and future socialization.

The Sequence of Attachment

There may be no better introduction to attachment than Bowlby's:

When a baby is born, he cannot tell one person from another and indeed can hardly tell person from thing. Yet by his first birthday he is likely to be a connoisseur of people. Not only does he come quickly to distinguish familiars from strangers but amongst his familiars he chooses one or more favorites. They are greeted with delight; they are followed when they depart; and they are sought when absent. Their loss causes anxiety and distress; their recovery, relief and a sense of security.

(1967, FOREWORD)

In understanding the sequence of attachment it is helpful to divide it into three phases.[1] In the earliest phase, social objects are not distinguished from nonsocial objects; in the second phase, such discrimination occurs, but persons are not distinguished from one another; and in the third phase, persons are distinguished from one another.

Asocial Phase

The human infant, even more than his primate forebears, is an intensely curious animal. From the beginning, whenever he is awake, he searches his environment. Soon he can control head and

[1] *These come from Schaffer and Emerson (1964). Other possibilities are the five-phase sequence of Ainsworth (1967) and the four-phase sequence of Bowlby (1969).*

eye movements, and his visual perception becomes more efficient. As we noted in Chapter 8, one of the functions of perception is arousal, and, as we shall document later, the infant seeks stimulation perhaps to maintain an optimal state of arousal.

His primary source of stimulation is the visual world around him. He looks at objects, especially moving objects, and attempts to locate the sources of sounds. When placed on his belly, he raises his head to look around. When picked up, he swivels his head right and left to observe what is going on. When he grasps an object, he looks at it.

Other sources of stimulation are not entirely neglected. The infant responds to sounds and to being touched, stroked, handled, and carried. But vision is the dominant sense, and, so long as the infant is not uncomfortable, visual stimulation is what he seeks.

In this earliest, *asocial* phase he does not discriminate between human and nonhuman stimuli. Both kinds arouse his interest, and both kinds seem to keep him occupied and satisfied. He will attend as quickly to a simple moving toy or to a rattle as he will to a smiling human face. If either kind of stimulation—human or thing—is removed, as when the room is darkened and everyone leaves, he often protests by crying. But he does not cry for the presence of others, only for stimulation.

Indiscriminate-Social Phase

It takes only a few weeks for the infant to start preferring humans to things. Beginning with the second month of life, he increasingly looks at humans longer, seeks them more often, appears more satisfied in their presence, cries more when they depart, and in general reacts more intensely to them than toward nonhuman objects. This preference comes about because social stimuli are intrinsically more interesting than nonsocial stimuli.

Consider the human face, especially a mother's (see Figure 20.4). As a visual object, it immediately commands attention. There are well-defined *contours,* the components form a *complex* array, and the eyes are *bright*. Contour, complexity, and

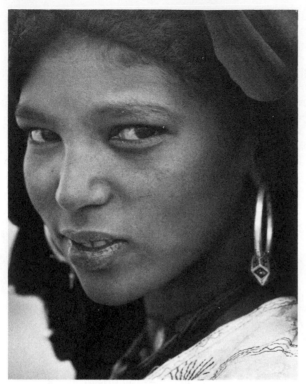

Figure 20.4 Why the face is interesting.
(VICTOR ENGLEBERT/PHOTO RESEARCHERS)

brightness all attract visual attention. From the face there emerge sounds, either language or nonlanguage, that vary in *pitch* and *loudness.* Finally, the human face offers *feedback.* If the infant smiles, the mother usually smiles back; if he vocalizes, she usually responds in kind or with gestures or language. Ultimately, it is the *responsivity* of other humans that is decisive. Other objects can be made interesting on the basis of appearance or sound, but only humans offer the give-and-take that defines a social relationship and is necessarily absent in a nonsocial one.[2]

Thus the infant develops an attachment for human beings, starting in the second month of life. It is no coincidence that social smiling starts

[2] *Later in childhood, pet animals can also offer feedback, though not to the same extent as humans. For some persons, a relationship with a dog may substitute for a human social relationship.*

at almost the same time, smiling being the best example of a purely social response—that is, having no other function than to initiate friendly intentions. The attachment is not specific: the infant smiles at all humans and needs no *particular* caretaker to nurture and comfort him. His social response remains somewhat *indiscriminate* during the next several months, but during this time he gradually learns to discriminate familiar humans from strangers.

Specific-Social Phase

By the age of six months the infant clearly differentiates some humans from others. He smiles more at his mother than at anyone else, though he also bestows the smile on his father and any other adults he sees often. But he does not smile at strangers, and he may react to an unfamiliar human with avoidance, tears, and perhaps even fright.

Two *social* phases of attachment have been marked off in the first year of life (Schaffer & Emerson, 1964). In their research, the first phase—*indiscriminate-social* attachment—was present at the earliest time it was assessed (at 5 to 8 weeks), and it changed little during the first year (see Figure 20.5). *Specific* attachments started at about six months and reached a maximum in the last quarter of the first year.

Note that attachment to the mother follows the

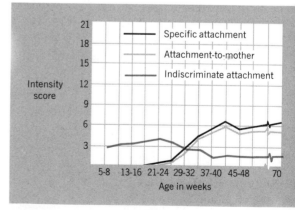

Figure 20.5 Social attachment in infancy (after Schaffer and Emerson, 1964).

same trend as attachment to other known individuals (specific attachment). But this finding may be misleading in that it is based solely on reaction to separation. When other measures of attachment are considered—differential smiling, following, clinging, and reaching to be picked up—the infant undoubtedly prefers his mother over all others (Ainsworth, 1967).

Nevertheless, the infant does develop strong attachments to other familiar figures, especially during the second year of life. Foremost among these is the father, who comes to exert a stronger influence on the child with each passing month. By 18 months the attachment to the father may equal that to the mother (Schaffer & Emerson, 1964).

Theories of Attachment

The human infant starts life with no specific attachments and, in fact, does not discriminate

humans from objects. During the first year of life he gradually limits his attachments to specific individuals, and often one crucial figure stands out, his mother. Why is the infant so clearly tied to his mother—seeking her, crying when she leaves, and becoming calm when she returns? Several theories have attempted to answer these questions.

Secondary Reinforcement

One explanation ascribes this close attachment to the mother's becoming a secondary reinforcer. The primary reinforcer is food, though contact may also be considered a primary reward. The mother, an initially neutral stimulus, is paired with these primary, unlearned rewards. It is mainly she who feeds and holds the infant. Food and comfort are innately reinforcing, and the pairing of the mother with these primary reinforcers eventually makes her a reinforcer (see Figure 20.6):

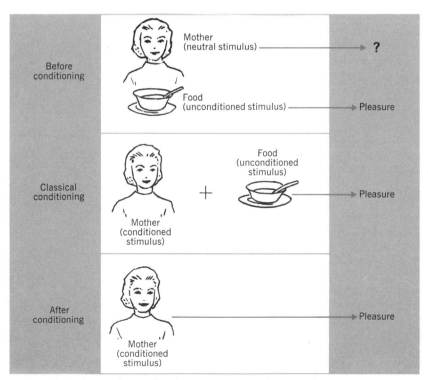

Figure 20.6 How the mother becomes a secondary reinforcer.

Initially, the child feels pangs of hunger and cries in response to this need. The mother then holds and feeds the child. As the rewarding stimulus of food and tactile contact are being received, the child is surrounded by all the visual, olfactory, and auditory stimuli that are an integral part of the feeding situation. According to the laws of learning, any new stimulus that is associated in time with a reward (food and skin contact, for example) acquires reward value itself. Thus, the mother, as a stimulus, comes to signify, through learning, pleasure, and contentment, —in short, something positive. The mother becomes a cue which stands for pleasure and gratification in much the same way that the buzzer became a cue for food in Pavlov's dogs. Furthermore, the infant will learn that to approach and search for this source of pleasure will lead to effective gratification of his needs with minimal delay. The child is learning the important response of looking for and approaching his mother when he is hungry.

(MUSSEN, CONGER, & KAGAN, 1963, PP. 157–158)

The emphasis on the feeding situation stems from two divergent sources: psychoanalysts and animal learning psychologists. Starting with Freud, psychoanalysts have pointed to feeding as the most fundamental kind of social relationship (the infant metaphorically "incorporates" other persons). The earliest era of life is called the *oral* stage, and presumably stimulation of the mouth and lips is innately reinforcing.

Animal-learning psychologists, in attempting to motivate rats and pigeons to learn laboratory tasks, have used hunger drive. Typically, they deprive an animal of food and then reward the hungry animal for making the desired response. Reinforcers such as food are labeled *primary* reinforcers because, being biologically necessary, they are innately reinforcing. Extensive research has shown that initially neutral stimuli, when paired with a reinforcer such as food, acquire reward properties of their own; that is, they are *secondary* (learned) reinforcers (see Chapter 14).

When two approaches as different as psychoanalysis and learning theory converge on the same theoretical point, it would appear to be a good hypothesis. Nevertheless, the notion that an infant becomes attached to his mother principally because she feeds and cares for him appears to be wrong. The available data refute it.

It has been found that when there are many caretakers, infants develop close ties with some of them but not with others; infants do not prefer certain caretakers because they are better at feeding and caring for the infants (Ainsworth, 1963). Furthermore, infants develop attachments to adults who are never their caretakers (Schaffer & Emerson, 1964). We know that infants form a close social bond with their fathers, especially in the second year. If this bond formed only because of secondary reinforcement, the tie would be closer to fathers who fed and cared for their infants than to those who do not. There is no evidence that this is true. Thus feeding is not a necessary condition for the formation of a social bond.

Research with primates strengthens this conclusion. In experiments to be described in more detail later, Harlow (1962) raised monkeys without a real mother. Each infant monkey had access only to artificial "mothers," one constructed of wire mesh and one of terry cloth (see Figure 20.7). Infant monkeys preferred the terry cloth figure for its better contact comfort. In one experiment the wire mesh "mother" supplied milk, the other none. The infant monkeys still spent most of their time clinging to the terry cloth figure, moving to the wire figure only when hungry. This finding is precisely the opposite to what the secondary drive hypothesis predicts.[3]

Association

If the secondary reinforcement approach to attachment does not work, is there another learning approach that does? Cairns (1966) has offered a theory emphasizing sheer association. He assumes that attachment behavior is determined by (1) the amount of time the infant spends with the potential object of attachment, and (2) the relative *cue weight* of the object. Concerning the second assumption, we have shown that social objects (other animals) are more conspicuous, interesting, and capable of feedback. These factors favor

[3] *See Scott (1962) for comparable results with dogs. Concerning monkeys, they prefer as "mothers" not only objects they can cling to but also objects that are warm and that can be set in motion (Harlow & Suomi, 1970).*

Figure 20.7 Wire mesh and terry cloth "mothers."
(UNIVERSITY OF WISCONSIN PRIMATE LABORATORY.)

social over *nonsocial* attachments.

Concerning the first assumption, Cairns refers to the phenomenon of *imprinting*—the tendency of young animals to follow those they are associated with. As he notes, an animal of one species that is reared with another species later comes to prefer the alien species. For example, pet dogs have been known to prefer their human masters to other dogs.

Cairn's theory appears to be correct as far as it goes, but it omits two important factors. First, being a theory of *mammalian* attachment, it neglects important response dispositions common to *primates*. Infant primates have a strong need for *contact comfort,* and they prefer to cling to soft, fuzzy objects. Thus Harlow's monkeys preferred a terry cloth substitute mother to a wire mesh one (see Figure 20.7). Human infants have a well known preference for soft, cuddly dolls and toys, the most famous example of which is the "security blanket."

Second, infant animals (and probably humans),

when deprived of mothers or live mother-substitutes early in life, never develop adequate attachment and suffer serious disruption of later behavior. Moreover, separation of infants from mothers leads to stronger, not weaker, attachment, a finding that opposes the association explanation. The facts of deprivation and separation are better handled by the notion of critical periods.

Critical Period of Attachment in Animals

Long before scientists studied attachment, dog trainers knew that there is a critical period for attachment in dogs. A dog must be exposed to humans during its first three months of life if it is to become a pet. If the puppy associates only with other dogs during this period, it cannot subsequently be tamed. But dogs are a long distance from humans on the evolutionary scale, and evidence with primates is obviously more relevant.

Research Report

Harlow and his collaborators (1959, 1961, 1963, 1965) have demonstrated the importance of contact with the mother and with peers by
depriving infant monkeys of such contact. One group of infants was
separated from their mothers at birth and raised in a wire cage. There
infants could see and hear other monkeys but could not touch or be
touched by them. Some of the monkeys were isolated for almost
three months, some for six months, and the remainder for two years.
A second group was raised with a mother; of these, some had their
real mothers and also played with peers, and others had their real
mothers but never had contact with other infants. Monkeys of a third
group were raised alone with a surrogate mother, which consisted of a
wire cylinder plus head or the same structure covered by a soft cloth
(see Figure 20.7); the remaining monkeys were raised four infants to
a cage, with neither real nor surrogate mothers.

These three groups of monkeys subsequently were tested for ade-
quacy of behavior in the areas of play, defense, and sex. The results
are shown in Table 20.2. These data show that isolation (visual and
auditory contact but not tactile contact) is disastrous for the infant
monkey's later behavior. After two years of isolation there was no
social behavior, and after six months, almost none. Harlow and
Harlow report that the monkeys raised in isolation:

> . . . *sit in their cages and stare fixedly into space, circle their cages in a
> repetitive, stereotyped manner and clasp their heads in their hands or arms
> and rock for long periods of time. They often develop compulsive habits,
> such as pinching precisely the same patch of skin in the chest between the
> same fingers hundreds of times a day; occasionally such behavior may
> become punitive and the animal may chew and tear at its body until it
> bleeds.* (1962, P. 138)

Isolation for less than three months (80 days) causes severe deficits in social behavior, but they are reversible. Once the monkey
begins to associate with peers, it slowly acquires the social behaviors
typical of its age group. Note in Table 20.2 that three months of isolation followed by a period of contact leads to almost normal play,
defense, and sex behavior. There are individual differences—some
monkeys benefiting from adult social contacts, others not (Missakian,
1972).

The data on total isolation suggest that there is a critical period for
the development of social behavior in rhesus monkeys—between
three and six months of age. Six months of no physical contact with
other monkeys renders the monkeys unfit as social animals. Two to
three months of isolation is harmful, but the effects are reversible.
Harlow and Harlow (1962) note that two to three months in the
rhesus monkey is comparable to six months in the human infant.
They suggest that the total isolation of their monkeys is comparable
to human infants being reared in the impersonal situations that obtain in orphanage institutions or homes with indifferent mothers.

Table 20.2
Effect of Infant-Rearing Conditions on Later Behavior (adapted from Harlow & Harlow, 1962)

EXPERIMENTAL CONDITIONS		BEHAVIOR			
		NONE	LOW	ALMOST NORMAL	NORMAL
Raised in total isolation	2 years	Play Defense Sex			
	6 months	Defense Sex	Play		
	almost 3 months			Play Defense Sex	
Raised with mother	normal mother, no peers	Sex	Play		Defense
	normal mother, peers				Play Defense Sex
Raised with peers	four together				Play Defense Sex
	surrogate raised, peers				Play Defense Sex

Of the remaining subjects in the experiment, only those deprived of contacts with peers showed deficits in social behavior. Infant monkeys with their real mothers but no access to other infants were inadequate in both sex and play behavior. This is surprising but even more so is the normality of those raised without a real mother but with access to peers. All the monkeys raised with peers showed normal play, defense, and sex behavior. Evidently, the crucial determiner of normal social behavior in these animals is the presence of peers, not the mother.

Figure 20.8 A depressed infant monkey — following separation from its mother.
(UNIVERSITY OF WISCONSIN PRIMATE LABORATORY.)

This conclusion is perhaps too sweeping. In the Harlow and Harlow experiment the infant monkeys were deprived of their mothers at birth. What is the effect of removing the infant from the mother after a period of normal attachment? Kaufman and Rosenblum (1967; 1969) answered this question by separating infant macaque monkeys from their mothers when the infants were five to six months old. The reactions of the infants during the four weeks of separation may be divided into three phases.

1. *Agitation.* There was considerable pacing, and the infants searched everywhere. They cooed, which is the distress call of the infant macaque, and they sucked and mouthed their fingers, toes, and other parts of the body. This lasted from a day to a day and a half.

2. *Depression.* The cooing and searching dropped sharply.

Each infant sat hunched over, almost rolled into a ball, with his head often down between his legs. Movement was rare except when the infant was actively displace. The movement that did occur appeared to be in slow motion, except at feeding time or in response to aggression. The infant rarely responded to a social invitation or made a social gesture, and play behavior virtually ceased. The infant appeared disinterested in and disengaged from the environment. (1969, P. 1030)

The depression lasted for five or six days (see Figure 20.8).

3. *Recovery.* Thereafter the infant started to resume upright posture, exploration of the environment, and contact with peers. Although there was still some depression, there were also periods of play and increased activity. Nevertheless, at the end of the four weeks of separation the infants did not show normal behavior for their age. During the month of separation there was more self-directed behavior and less play, both social and nonsocial.

Then the infants were reunited with their mothers. Thereafter the mother-infant pairs were virtually inseparable. The usual measures of mother-infant attachment rose steeply: clinging, protective holding, and contact with the nipple. Note that the infants were now six to seven months old, an age when normal monkeys are being weaned and rejected by the mother. Thus the absence of a real mother *after a period of attachment* appears to be cause of a depression and a drop in social behavior (see also Suomi et al., 1970). *When there is no mother from birth,* such absence causes neither depression nor a deficit in social behavior so long as there is contact with peers.

All the research with primates has emphasized the importance of contact comfort, and, as Harlow demonstrated, infant primates prefer mother substitutes that they can cling to. But in the natural environment the mother plays more than a passive role. She interacts with the infant, carrying it, pushing it, shoving it, and in general *responding* to it. Mason (1968) demonstrated the importance of responsivity by using a "robot mother," which provided some interaction for the infant primate (see Figure 20.9):

Since the movements of the robot are essentially unpredictable, it can withdraw from the infant without warning, or sneak up on it from behind and deliver a gentle rap on the head; its comings and goings demand adjustments from the infant that are not required of the animals reared with stationary devices. The robot stimulates and sustains interaction: it is withdrawn from, pursued, pounced on, and wrestled with. (P. 89)

When robot-reared animals were compared with stationary-reared animals, it was found that the robots produced more normal primates. The monkeys spent more time in contact with the robot, engaged in virtually no stereotyped self-rocking, and moved around much more in exploration. Above all, they were quicker to approach and interact with people (see Figure 20.10). These findings underline what we have said about mothers and mother-substitutes as *responsive* agents. It may well be that the single most important factor in social situations is the mutual feedback of the interacting parties. Even a nonliving object can partially substitute for another animal if it moves about in a responsive manner.

Critical Period of Attachment in Man

Harlow and others demonstrated the devastating effects of depriving infant monkeys of their mothers. Similar experiments of course cannot be conducted with human infants, but there are "nature's experiments": events similar to those that might be manipulated in experimental research. Many human infants are raised as foundlings in institutions. They are placed in institutions at birth or shortly thereafter, and they remain without a specific mother unless they are placed in a foster home.

Goldfarb (1943, 1945) traced children who had resided from birth to three years in an institution. The children showed deficits in learning, conceptual ability, self-control of behavior, and inability to tolerate frustration. Of particular relevance to our present discussion was their inability to achieve close relationships with adults or peers. Spitz and Wolf (1946) observed babies who spent their first year of life in institutions that provided insufficient care and nurturance. Toward the end of the year about 15% of the infants developed an *anaclitic depression:* eyes open but apparently not perceiving, indifference to the environment, and complete lack of emotional expression. These findings have been challenged because of lack of control subjects and problems of sampling, but the observations have been sustained by later, detailed studies. For example, Provence and Lipton (1962), studied infants reared in institutions for the first two years of life. They found an interesting divergence in the development of motor skills, harking back to the distinction (Chapter 4)

Figure 20.9 *"Robot mother" offering movement stimulation.*   (WILLIAM A. MASON)

between species-wide skills (dependent on maturation) and individual skills (dependent on practice). Species-wide motor skills developed normally, but individual skills were retarded. Of particular interest were the retardation of both the tendency to approach and reach out to persons and objects, and the ability to modulate muscular acts in the interest of smooth motor sequences.

We should add a note of caution here. Not all children are seriously affected by the deprivation that occurs in such institutions, and only a small minority is so severely affected as to develop anaclitic depression. Some infants can survive neglect; others cannot. The outcome of maternal deprivation depends on the child (presumably, innate tendencies), when the deprivation occurs, for how long, and the quality of postseparation care.[4]

[4] *For details, see the summary of research in Maccoby and Masters (1970).*

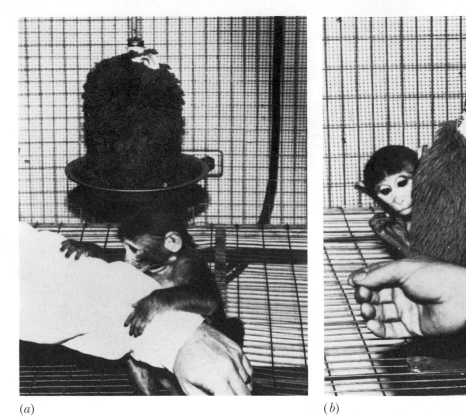

(a)   (b)

Figure 20.10 *Reaction to humans of (a) robot-reared and (b) stationary-reared monkeys.*   (WILLIAM A. MASON)

Can these observations be fitted into the framework of the critical periods hypothesis? Yarrow (1964) suggests that they can:

In direct analogy with the data on imprinting in animals, one might hypothesize that there is a specific developmental period during which vulnerability to separation is greatest. The most sensitive time may be the period during which the infant is in the process of establishing stable affectional relationships, approximately between six months and two years. A break in the relationship with a mother figure during this period would presumably be most traumatic. (P. 122)

Comparable data on monkeys were supplied by Kaufman and Rosenblum (1967) who separated infant monkeys from their mothers at about five months of age. As we noted above, during the month of separation the infant monkeys became agitated and then depressed, before finally starting to recover. Human infancy is longer, and similar reactions would presumably occur until two years of age. If we also analogize from the Harlow and Harlow (1962) findings on *total* isolation, deprivation from birth to about one year of age would permanently damage the child's ability to achieve close personal relationships. Thus the following speculations seem reasonable:

1. Human infants deprived of their mothers or mother-substitutes for the first year of life never develop the capacity for close relationships and therefore never become properly socialized.
2. Human infants deprived of their mothers after 6 to 24 months of age suffer severe anxiety and

in some instances, depression. But they recover and can be socialized, though there may be lasting psychological scars in some children, which impair their capacity for friendship, love, and the development of conscience.

Arousal Level

In attempting to understand attachment, we have emphasized the infant's disposition to seek out and remain close to its mother. But this is only half the story, for the infant must also be separated from the mother in order to explore the environment and try out new responses. Thus two very strong tendencies are set in opposition: the need for *security,* as manifested in proximity-seeking and clinging, versus the need to *explore,* as manifested in detachment behavior and manipulation.

In general, the need for security dominates; only when it is secure will an infant venture from its mother—that is, so long as she is within sight and potentially recoverable. Harlow (1961) demonstrated this need hierarchy in monkeys with terry cloth "mothers." When presented with a novel stimulus, the infant monkey's first response was to cling to the cloth figure (see Figure 20.11*a*). Once it was secure, it ventured forth to explore the novel object, so long as the "mother" was in sight (see Figure 20.11*b*).

The same kind of behavior can be observed in the response of a young child to a stranger. At first, the child clings to the mother and may even hide behind her skirts. With time and patience, the child may be induced to approach the stranger. In a novel environment the young child uses his mother as a base: he leaves her to explore but returns repeatedly to "touch home base" or at least to make sure that she is in sight; when separated, the infant cries and searches for his mother (see Ainsworth & Bell, 1970; Rheingold & Eckerman, 1970).

The two opposing tendencies, security and curiosity, may be related to arousal level. Novelty arouses the infant, security pacifies it. Let us assume that there is an optimal range of arousal (see Chapter 6). When the infant is below this level, as when he is secure, he seeks stimulation. When he is above this level, as when he has had excessive stimulation, he seeks security.

This is essentially Mason's (1965*a,b;* 1970) formulation, and he tested it with infant chimpanzees. Each infant had access to two experimenters, each with a distinctive costume and head covering (see Figure 20.12). One experimenter always held the animal and let it cling to him (soothing); the other never held the animal but roughly played with it (arousing). The chimpanzees were allowed to choose one of these two figures. At first there was no preference, but grad-

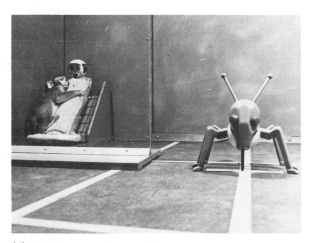
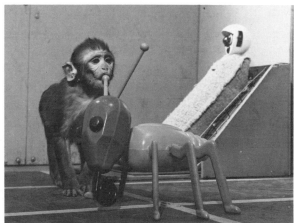

(*a*)   (*b*)

Figure 20.11 *Security (a) and exploration (b) in an infant monkey. (University of Wisconsin Primate Laboratory).*

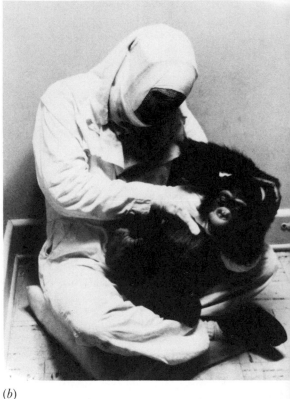

(a)   (b)

Figure 20.12 *Clinging versus play in chimpanzees:* (a) *costume associated with clinging;* (b) *costume associated with play.*   (WILLIAM A. MASON)

ually the animals came to prefer the playful, arousing figure. This tendency was reversed whenever the animal was initially aroused. Thus when it was placed in an unfamiliar room, separated for a period from its fellow animals, or administered an activating drug (amphetamine), the animal tended to choose clinging and soothing over play and arousal.

There is similar, if indirect, evidence in human infants. Crying infants visually explore the environment more after soothing (being picked up and held) than without such soothing (Korner & Grobstein, 1966). Presumably, during high arousal (crying) the infant is too uncomfortable to seek stimuli and will do so only when arousal level is lowered.

These facts add another dimension to the mother as an attachment figure. Not only is she

interesting in terms of stimulus complexity and responsivity and available as an object of association (see Cairns, 1966), but she also is an object capable of soothing the infant, thereby diminishing an excessively high arousal level.

Integration

Each theory of attachment contributes to our understanding, but the contributions are not all of equal importance. The notion of an optimal range of arousal is fundamental in that it encompasses and at least partially accounts for two innate tendencies: security and comfort versus curiosity and excitement. Moreover, this approach—which derives from Schneirla's (1959) broad theory of approach-withdrawal—specifies the conditions under which one or the other tendency prevails.

The idea of critical periods is almost as important. The mother-infant bond is so crucial to the survival of the young of *all* mammals that we must assume some continuity with our fellow mammals. Therefore we must assume the presence of a critical period of human attachment analogous to that present in lower animals, and there is some evidence for this assumption.

The theory that sheer association yields attachment has some merit. Other things being equal, the mother normally is the object most frequently in contact with the infant, and certainly association strengthens attachment. But the theory neglects the role of soothing and the infant's need to cling, so well documented in primate research. Furthermore, sheer association (time spent in contact) predicts the wrong outcome of separation: attachment is stronger, not weaker, after separation.

Finally, the secondary drive notion, which derives attachment from such primary drives as hunger, has little to offer. So long as the infant is fed, it matters little *who* feeds him. The really important factors are stimulation, association, and the capability of soothing.

Consequences of Attachment

At the beginning of the chapter we asked three questions about attachment: when, how, and so what? The first two have been discussed; now, a brief comment about the consequences of attachment.

The normal human child emerges from infancy with strong affectional ties to his mother, father, and perhaps a few other familiar figures. These figures, largely adults, can manipulate his behavior of offering or withdrawing affection, by using extrinsic rewards (candy, toys) or punishments, and by providing appropriate models for the child to imitate. These are all part of socialization, which in the present context may be divided into three aspects. The first concerns emotions such as fear and rage, and affects such as love and melancholy; these are discussed in the next chapter. The second concerns *social motives* such as sex, aggression, competence, and achievement (see Chapter 22). The third aspect of socialization concerns how behavior is inhibited, and the development of shame, guilt, and a code of morality; these are discussed in Chapter 23.

The normal child, emerging from infancy, is also a member of a family group—minimally himself and two parents. He is already communicating with them, and subsequently he makes great progress in the precision and extent of communication, both verbally and nonverbally (see Chapter 28). He is exposed and introduced to a variety of groups, and he learns to become part of these groups both in terms of his contribution and what he derives from others (see Chapter 29). At the same time that reactions to members of the in-group develop, so do reactions to members of outgroups, especially the reaction called prejudice (see Chapter 31). In brief, attachment marks the beginning of social behavior, and its consequences involve the extension and proliferation of social behavior during the course of development.

chapter 21

emotion and affect

Emotions — the arousal continuum — affects
— evolutionary considerations — physiology
of fear, rage, and sexual arousal — theories
of emotion — feelings — cognitions — self-per-
ception — autonomic feedback — metaphors —
integration — emotion as a disorganizer

Emotion and affect probably arose late in evolution. They are present in mammals and birds but absent in the reptiles from which mammals and birds evolved and absent from animals lower on the evolutionary scale than reptiles. Thus on the grand scale of evolutionary time, emotions and affects are a recent development. But on the more restricted time scale of mammalian evolution, emotions and affects are very old—representing two of man's oldest forms of behavior. There are good reasons for distinguishing emotion from affect—specifically, differences in level of arousal and in adaptive function.

Emotions Versus Affects

Emotions

Emotion was mentioned in the context of motivation in Chapter 7, where two emergency drives (rage and fear) and one reproductive drive (sex) were labeled emotions. Rage, fear, and sexual arousal are not called emotions simply because they are motives (other motives such as hunger, thirst, and curiosity are not considered emotions).

All emotions may be regarded as motives, but not all motives are emotions.

How do emotions differ from nonemotional motives? Most psychologists agree that *emotions are states of high arousal—specifically, autonomic arousal.* The other two kinds of arousal—central nervous system and behavioral—sometimes accompany emotional reactions, but arousal of the autonomic nervous system is believed to be crucial in emotion.[1]

The Arousal Continuum

There is general agreement that emotions are aroused states but aroused in comparison to what? If (NREM) sleep is taken as a baseline, all waking activities must be regarded as states of arousal. Clearly, the baseline for determining arousal must be normal waking activity. Thus

[1] *The autonomic arousal that accompanies physical effort—as in work or athletics—is excluded from the definition of emotion.*

when a person peers through a telescope or attempts to solve a problem in mathematics, he is mildly aroused—as measured by his heart rate, blood pressure, and galvanic skin response (see Chapter 6). But no one would suggest that concentrating and solving problems are emotional reactions. *Emotions involve arousal above that of normal wakefulness.*

So defined, emotions occupy the top of the arousal continuum (see Figure 21.1). Wakefulness occupies the large range between the high end of emotion and the low end of sleep. The emotional reactions of fear, rage, and sexual arousal are relatively infrequent, but their intensity makes them memorable. We tend to forget the thousand-and-one routine responses of daily life but easily recall the rarer moments of panic, rage, and sexual excitement. The basic assumption of this approach to emotions is that only these three reactions—fear, rage, and sexual arousal—attain a level of arousal beyond that of normal wakefulness. Normal wakefulness includes such states as alertness and attention, which are accompanied by at least a moderate degree of au-

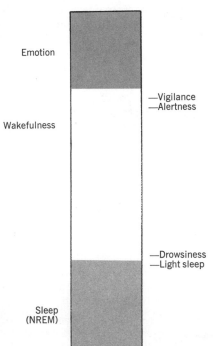

Figure 21.1 *The arousal continuum.*

tonomic arousal (Lacey, 1956). An elated person is definitely aroused but no more so than when he is attending closely to stimuli. As we would not label attention an emotion merely because of its moderate arousal level, so we cannot call elation an emotion merely because of its *moderate* arousal level. Only the three reactions of fear, rage, and sexual arousal exceed the *moderate* arousal seen in attention, and therefore only these three should properly be called emotions.

Affects

If the reactions of joy, grief, disgust, love, shame, and jealousy are not emotions, what are they? They are best regarded as *affects: positive or negative feeling states or moods.* Affects represent evaluative reactions that deviate from neutrality ("I couldn't care less, one way or the other"). They may be aligned along three bipolar dimensions: approach-withdrawal, acceptance-rejection, and pleasure-unpleasure. Each dimension is a different aspect of the positive versus negative evaluations that define affects.[2] We seek out and are delighted with persons and objects that we accept and that make us happy. We avoid and are disgusted with unpleasant things that cause sadness or shame. In brief, there is no middle ground; all affects are either positive or negative feelings, or both.

Affects have one defining characteristic: explicit or implicit evaluation (either positive or negative), which is reflected in the term *feelings.* Seen in this light, rage, fear, and sexual arousal are affects. Fear is a negative affect (preparation for withdrawal), and sexual arousal is a positive affect (preparation for approach). Rage is both positive and negative; the events that elicit it are noxious, but rage is preparation for approach, and the *feeling* of rage is not necessarily aversive to the person who experiences it.

But rage, fear, and sexual arousal are also emotions—that is, they involve arousal beyond the range of normal wakefulness. Thus all three emotions are affects, but none of the other affects is an emotion. Affects have a single defining charac-

teristic (positive or negative evaluation), whereas emotions have two defining characteristics (evaluation and arousal beyond the normal range).

Evolutionary Considerations

Does it matter whether we distinguish between emotions and affects? Why not lump them all into a single category: feeling states that vary in level of arousal? There are two arguments for maintaining the distinction. First, arousal level is an important issue. As we shall see below, psychologists disagree about whether emotions disorganize ongoing behavior. Disorganization can be caused only by excessive arousal. If some affects cause disorganization and others do not, we have a valid reason for distinguishing between the two types—reserving the term *emotion* for the affects that can disorganize behavior.

The second argument concerns the adaptive functions of emotions and affects. Emotions are components of reactions that concern survival of the individual or of the species. When an animal (or a man) is threatened by imminent injury or death, it can attempt to escape or fight off the attacker. The emergency requires a maximum effort, and the preparation for such effort is mediated by the autonomic nervous system. The terrified animal requires a high level of activation for its dash to freedom; the enraged animal requires high activation for a ferocious attack on the foe. Animals capable of rapid escalation of arousal level in preparation for massive action tend to survive and produce members of the next generation. Animals without this adaptation tend not to survive, and their line becomes extinct.

Fear and rage are preparations for coping with attack, and therefore their adaptive function is related to survival of the *individual animal.* Sexual arousal, in contrast, is related to survival of the *species.* Sexual arousal prepares the organism physiologically and psychologically for mating, and any adaptation that enhances mating will easily hurdle the barriers of natural selection. In brief, the three emotions are adaptive in the most fundamental sense: survival of individuals or species. It is not surprising, then, that they are present in all mammals.

Affects, in contrast, are present only in the more

---

[2] *The three dimensions are closely related. For example, in Table 21.1* admiration *involves both approach and acceptance;* contempt *involves both withdrawal and rejection.*

Table 21.1
Three Dimensions of Affects

BIPOLAR DIMENSION	POSITIVE AFFECT	NEGATIVE AFFECT
Approach-withdrawal	Delight Admiration	Disgust Contempt
Acceptance-rejection	Love Pride*	Hate Shame*
Pleasure-unpleasure	Elation Hope	Grief Despair

* Pride and shame are *self*-evaluation—pride involving acceptance of self and pleasure, and shame involving rejection of self and unpleasure.

social mammals. Consider two of the most important affects—elation and grief. When a primate infant is separated from its mother, both mourn their loss; when the two are reunited, both are elated. Dogs have been known to mourn their dead masters, and all dogs wag their tails vigorously to indicate joy. Dogs and primates are highly social animals. Cats are less social, and they have little or no affect. Cats have been reported by owners to show mild elation or depression, but there have been no precise, reliable observations. If cats do show affects, these are minimal in comparison to affects displayed by dogs and primates.

The adaptive role of affects is different from that of emotions. The most important affects (elation and grief) facilitate group cohesiveness and interaction among individual animals. Joy appears to be a universal reaction *among social animals* to acceptance of affection from other members of the group, especially those to whom there is a strong attachment. Grief is a reaction to separation from or rejection by others (Averill, 1969).

Thus affects are essentially reactions to the outcome of social interactions. This observation is entirely consistent with the way affects are defined. Consider the three dimensions outlined in Table

21.1. Approach-withdrawal, acceptance-rejection, and pleasure-unpleasure all reflect reactions to social situations. Positive affects derive from and enhance close social contacts; negative affects derive from social separation and rejection, and negative affects lead to further separation and rejection. This difference between emotions and affects is essentially a difference in *consequences*:

Although both feelings and emotional behavior involve psychological interactions between organism and environment, a useful and important distinction between the two can be made on the basis of the localizability of their principal effects or consequences. Emotional behavior seems most usefully considered as part of a broad class of effective interactions, the primary consequences of which appear to change the organism's relationship to its external environment. Feelings or affective behavior, on the other hand, can be distinguished as a generic class of interactions, the principal effects of which are localizable within the reacting organism rather than in the exteroceptive environment. Many different subclasses of feelings may be identified within this broad affective category, but emotional behavior seems uniquely definable in terms of a change or perturbation, characteristically

Table 21.2
Emotion and Affect Compared

	EMOTION	AFFECT
Arousal	High	Low to moderate
Occurrence	In all mammals	In social mammals
Adaptive function	Survival of the individual and/or the species	Group cohesiveness and solidarity of interaction
Kind of behavior	Preparation for massive action (motivational)	Reaction to acceptance, rejection, etc. (mood)

abrupt and episodic, in the ongoing interaction between organism and environment. (BRADY, 1970, P. 70)

Affects are essentially moods (reactions to events) rather than motives (goads to actions). The differences between emotions and affects are summarized in Table 21.2.

Autonomic Aspects of Emotion

Most research on the physiology of emotions has concerned fear and rage, probably because of the intense arousal that occurs in these states. Joy, grief, and all the other affects involve no more arousal than do neutral, nonaffective reactions. (It is interesting to note that those psychologists who insist on classifying such affects as elation and melancholy as emotions simply ignore them when discussing the physiological aspects of emotion.)

Fear and Rage

In both fear and rage the sympathetic nervous system clearly predominates, as the individual prepares for a massive emergency effort. The pupils of the eyes dilate, letting in more light;

breathing speeds up and the bronchioles of the lungs dilate, both of which allow more oxygen to enter the bloodstream; the heart beats faster and blood pressure mounts so that skeletal muscles receive more blood; clotting agents in the blood increase; secretion of saliva and digestive juices stops, and digestion stops or at least slows down; and in general, the vegetative processes of the body are turned off and the instrumental processes (largely skeletal muscular) are augmented.

The neurohumors, *adrenaline* and *noradrenaline,* are important here; they not only mediate neural transmission but cause widespread autonomic changes. Adrenaline increases heart rate and the amount of blood pumped at each stroke, and it raises blood pressure by constricting peripheral blood vessels (the effect being blanching). Noradrenaline causes either no change or a slight drop in heart rate and stroke volume, but it markedly constricts the peripheral blood vessels (Wenger et al., 1960). Thus both neurohumors elevate blood pressure but in different ways—adrenaline mainly by acting on the heart and noradrenaline by acting on the peripheral blood vessels.

This difference in the effects of adrenaline and noradrenaline has been suggested as a basis for distinguishing between fear and anger (Funken-

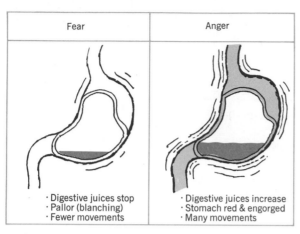

Fear	Anger
· Digestive juices stop · Pallor (blanching) · Fewer movements	· Digestive juices increase · Stomach red & engorged · Many movements

Figure 21.2 Reactions of the stomach to fear and anger (Wolf and Wolff, 1947).

On the basis of current data it may be concluded that while adrenaline secretion provides a sensitive index of the intensity of the emotional reaction, it is not related to the quality of the emotion. Instead, both pleasant and unpleasant emotions are accompanied by increased adrenaline output. Noradrenaline secretion does not seem to be systematically related to either emotional intensity or quality.

(FRANKENHAEUSER, 1971, P. 258)

Thus at present there is no good evidence that fear differs from anger autonomically. This conclusion suggests that the person experiencing the emotion does not identify it on the basis of internal bodily changes. The discrimination between fear and anger must be accomplished by means other than perceiving differences in autonomic patterns.

stein, 1956). That the two are different physiologically is suggested by an older study of stomach changes (Wolf & Wolff, 1947). A patient had part of his stomach wall exposed, and changes inside could be observed directly (see Figure 21.2). When he was frightened, the secretion of digestive juices slowed down, blood flow decreased (making the stomach wall appear pale), and there were fewer stomach movements. His reaction to anger was different: greater flow of digestive juices, greater blood flow (a red, engorged stomach wall), and more stomach movements. This study of a single organ in one subject is highly suggestive of a physiological difference between fear and rage, but for more conclusive evidence research needed to be conducted with other organ systems and with a large number of subjects.

Ax (1953) and later Schachter (1957) devised the appropriate experiments. They used a variety of physiological measures to test reactions to danger (fear) and extreme provocation (anger), and they demonstrated that the fear pattern differed from the anger pattern. The fear pattern was more or less adrenaline-like, and the anger pattern was more or less noradrenaline-like. Nevertheless, the differences between fear and anger were rather small, and there was considerable overlap.

Though the earlier research suggested autonomic differences between fear and anger, later research has failed to sustain this hypothesis:

Sexual Arousal

There are obvious ethical and practical problems in studying sexual behavior in the laboratory, and they were overcome only recently in the pioneering research of Masters and Johnson (1965, 1966).[3] These researchers divide sexual arousal into four phases: excitement, plateau, orgasm and resolution (see Figure 21.3).

The excitement phase is initiated by any of the stimuli that can sexually arouse humans, and there appears to be an endless variety of such stimuli.

From the excitement phase the human male or female enters the second or plateau phase of the sexual cycle, if effective sexual stimulation is continued. In this phase sexual tensions are intensified and subsequently reach the extreme level from which the individual may move to orgasm. The duration of the plateau phase is largely dependent upon the effectiveness of the stimuli employed, combined with the factor of individual drive for culmination of sex tension increment. If either the stimuli or the drive is inadequate or if all the stimuli are withdrawn, the individual will not achieve orgasmic release and will

---

[3] *Most laboratory research on sexual arousal has been on the effects of sexually arousing stimuli rather than on the sex act itself (Zuckerman, 1971).*

drop slowly from the plateau-phase tension levels into an excessively prolonged resolution phase.

(MASTERS & JOHNSON, 1966, P.6)

Failure to achieve orgasm results in an extension of the physiological arousal and in many instances physical discomfort (see Pattern *B* in women, Figure 21.3). Note that women are capable of rapid, multiple orgasms (Pattern *A*), but men have a refractory period during which the level of excitement drops rapidly. It takes time to restimulate a man, and with increasing age his refractory period lengthens considerably. There are no reliable data on humans, but male rats can be rearoused after apparent satiation resulting from repeated copulation by replacing the first partner with a new one. Fisher (1962) reported prodigious sexual feats in some of the males so treated.

During the four phases there is a marked elevation of several aspects of autonomic functioning. The arousal goes well beyond that seen in the normal range; the specific bodily reactions are summarized in Table 21.3 (p. 406). These bodily changes have been interpreted in terms of competition between the sympathetic and parasympathetic divisions of the autonomic nervous system:

The initial phase of sexual excitement, leading to tumescence of erectile tissue, is mediated primarily by the parasympathetic nervous system. As the emotion approaches the point of climax, the sympathetic nervous system becomes dominant in some functions. Finally, during postorgasmic relaxation, a secondary phase of parasympathetic nervous system dominance may develop through overcompensation.

(WENGER ET AL., 1968, P. 469)

One other aspect of physiological arousal requires comment, largely because of the mythology surrounding it: the question of whether there are substances (called *aphrodisiacs*) which, when ingested, cause sexual excitement. There have been many "love potions" down through the ages, and the best-known aphrodisiac of modern times is called *Spanish fly,* a preparation of the crushed dried bodies of a species of beetles. It does not work, nor do any of the hundreds of other substances put forth by the ignorant or superstitious. With sexual excitement so easy to condition, individuals can easily be aroused by a wide range of

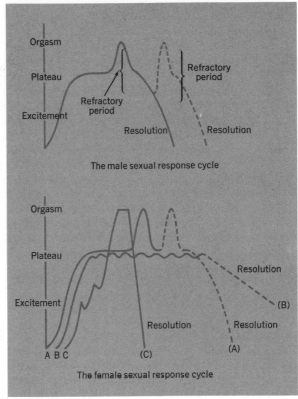

Figure 21.3 *The sexual response cycle.*

psychological stimuli, including suggestion. Thus any effects that seem to be caused by a chemical are no doubt due to the placebo effect (see Chapter 2).

Theories of Emotion

Feelings

For some psychologists the essential element in emotion is *feelings.* Psychologists who maintain this position (Arnold, 1960, for example) more or less adhere to the James-Lange theory, which was a combination of two highly similar views. James (1890) asserted that we do not run because we are afraid; rather, we are afraid because we run. He focused on the perception of skeletal and vis-

Table 21.3
Physiological Aspects of Sexual Arousal
(Masters & Johnson, 1965, p. 517)

	MEN	WOMEN
Excitement phase	Nipple erection (30% of subjects)	Nipple erection Sex tension flush (25%)
Plateau phase	Sex tension flush (25%) General muscle tension Rapid breathing Rapid heart rate	Sex tension flush (75%) General muscle tension Rapid breathing Rapid heart rate
Orgasmic phase	Specific muscle contractions Rapid breathing Very rapid heart rate	Specific muscle contractions Rapid breathing Very rapid heart rate
Resolution phase	Sweating reaction (30–40%) Rapid breathing Heart rate dropping to normal	Sweating reaction (30–40%) Rapid breathing Heart rate dropping to normal

ceral events inside the body and theorized that this perception—the feeling component—defined emotion.

The hypothetical sequence is diagramed in Figure 21.4*a*. A threatening stimulus triggers widespread arousal of the viscera: the heart races, the blood pounds, and breathing accelerates as the body prepares for emergency action. This action—fighting or running away—occurs almost simultaneously. The next step in the sequence is awareness of these visceral and muscular activities, and it is this awareness of bodily arousal that James called emotion.

The James-Lange theory was attacked by Cannon (1929) on a number of grounds, most of which are of only historical interest now. But the main thrust of Cannon's criticism was correct. He insisted that the viscera are too insensitive and slow-acting to yield the sensations required by the James-Lange theory. Moreover, there is insufficient *patterning* of visceral arousal to provide a basis for different emotions solely on the basis of sensations arising within the body.

Cannon offered a theory that locates emotion *centrally,* specifically in the thalamus and neocortex (see Figure 21.4*b*). A threatening stimulus triggers the firing of impulses by the thalamus, which both initiates bodily arousal and alerts the cerebral cortex. The cortex in turn releases the thalamus from inhibition, and the ensuing massive discharge from the thalamus is registered by the cortex as the *feeling* of emotion. In opposition to James, Cannon would say that we run because we are afraid.

Cannon's theory has been rendered obsolete by modern research on the nervous system. We now know that the thalamus plays a minor role in arousal; the major neural components in arousal are the hypothalamus and the reticular formation (see Chapter 6). Cannon was correct in principle (the neural basis of emotion is central, not peripheral) but incorrect in the details (see also Fehr &

Stern, 1970). He was also correct in denying that emotion consists of nothing more than *feelings*—the awareness of bodily changes.

There are two issues here, one theoretical and one empirical. Theoretically, it may be unwise to focus on feelings as being central to emotion. Feelings can be communicated only through language, and language is a poor vehicle for such communication. Animals and very young children are unable to communicate feelings, but no one would deny that they have emotions. Thus feelings should not be made the crux of emotions.

The empirical issue is more complex, but the central problem is straightforward. If awareness of bodily arousal defines emotion, then there should be a different pattern of bodily arousal for each emotion. If the same pattern of bodily arousal gives use to different feelings, then awareness of internal states—though necessary—cannot be the essential element in emotion.

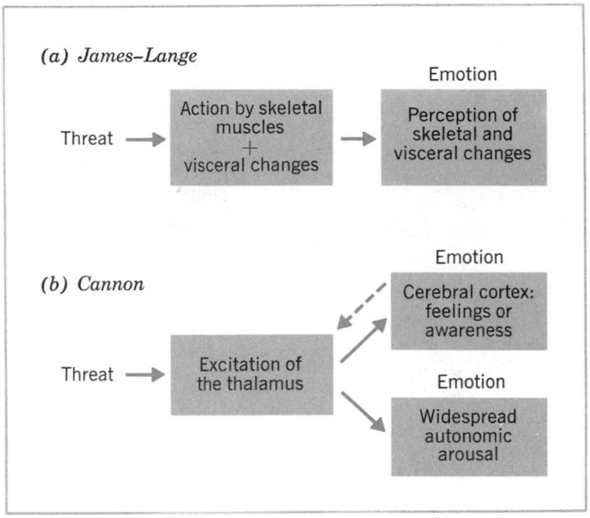

Figure 21.4 Two theories of emotion.

Cognitions

We have mentioned two kinds of perception that occur in emotional reactions. The first is perception of the threatening or emotion-arousing stimulus; the second is perception of one's own bodily reactions (heart pounding, muscles tightening, and so on). In everyday life the stimulus situation usually explains the bodily arousal. Thus, upon being called a "Fascist pig," an enraged police officer would have a ready explanation for the autonomic reactions of tension, sweating, and flushing.

A single pattern of visceral reactions may give rise to somewhat different affects when the situation is different. For example, a child who becomes slightly dizzy in an airplane that descends suddenly would probably assume that the situation was dangerous and react with fear and tears. If the same sensation of dizziness occurred on an amusement park joy ride, the child would interpret the dizziness as a delightful feeling and seek more of the same. In brief, in emotional reactions there are not only situational stimuli and autonomic arousal but also an interpretation involving a causal connection between the two. This point has been demonstrated in a clever experiment.

Research Report

The experiment was designed to produce physiological arousal comparable to that seen in emotion but in the absence of a clear psychological stimulus for such arousal (Schachter & Singer, 1962). Subjects, who were told that a drug was being tested, were injected with adrenaline, which causes rapid heartbeat, muscular tremors, and other effects that mimic sympathetic stimulation. Some subjects were told what the physiological effects would be (Informed), and others were given erroneous information (Misinformed). Then they waited for 20 minutes with another ostensible subject who was really an experimental accomplice. This confederate acted out a series of

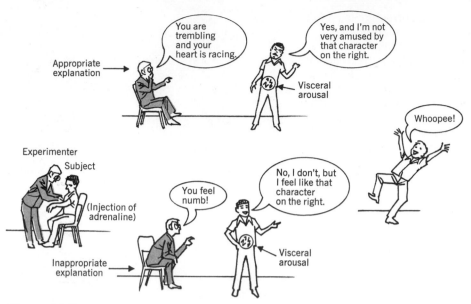

Figure 21.5 *Cognition and affect (Schachter and Singer, 1962).*

wild antics: doodling, making and flying a paper airplane, and using a child's hula hoop. The entire effect was one of playfulness and childish happiness. When the subjects were asked to rate themselves, the Misinformed subjects reported being happy but the Informed subjects did not (see Figure 21.5).

Other subjects waited with a confederate who simulated extreme anger, making derogatory remarks to the experimenter and finally ripping up a questionnaire he was supposed to fill out. Some of the subjects had been informed about the drug, and others had been given no information. The Ignorant subjects reported being quite angry, but the Informed subjects did not.

Schachter and Singer (1962) interpreted their findings in the framework of a cognitive approach:

It has been suggested, first, that given a state of physiological arousal for which an individual has no explanation, he will label this state in terms of the cognitions available to him. This implies, of course, that by manipulating the cognitions of an individual in such a state we can manipulate his feelings in diverse directions. Experimental results support this proposition for following the injection of epinephrine,[4] those subjects who had no explanation for the bodily state thus produced, gave behavioral and

[4] *Epinephrine is another name for adrenaline. Note also that this research involved both an emotion (anger) and an affect (happiness). Cognitions would be expected to influence affects more strongly.*

self-report indications that they had been readily manipulable into the disparate feeling states of euphoria and anger.

From this first proposition, it must follow that given a state of physiological arousal for which the individual has a completely satisfactory explanation, he will not label this state in terms of the alternative cognitions available. Experimental evidence strongly supports this expectation. In those conditions in which subjects were injected with epinephrine and told precisely what they would feel and why, they proved relatively immune to any effects of the manipulated cognitions. In the anger condition, such subjects reported themselves as far less happy than subjects with an identical bodily state but no adequate knowledge of why they felt the way they did.

(P. 395–396)

This research neatly separated autonomic arousal from the usual conditions that cause it. Such separation rarely occurs in everyday life; one example is diffuse anxiety—a nameless fear that is more frightening than most fears because its cause is unknown. More commonly the emotionally aroused person knows why he is scared or angry or sexually aroused.

Self-Perception Theory

It is easy for an experimenter to manipulate a subject's verbalizations about his internal bodily processes. The trickery may involve false instructions, as in the experiment just described, or it may involve fake dial readings, as in the classical conditioning of the urge to urinate (see Chapter 13). Internal events, whether they occur in emotional or neutral states, are often vague and diffuse. Our internal sensors are dull compared to our external sensors, and we have only blurred impressions of what is happening inside the body. If a precise label is required for an internal state, we turn to the stimuli around us; for example, one knows he is afraid because his hands shake and his heart races. Thus our feelings are determined less by internal sensations than by external stimuli.

This view—which also accounts for the Schachter and Singer (1962) findings—has been called *self-perception theory* (Bem, 1970):

In identifying his own internal states, an individual partially relies on the same external cues that others use when they infer his internal states. In other words, we may think that we are always reading our internal states directly, but we "cheat" and peek outside to look at the same clues that others *look at when they want to know our internal states. Furthermore, we are usually unaware that we do so.*

(P. 50)

Like Schachter, Bem believes that each person develops cognitions (explanations) about his internal events, but Bem specifies that the source of the explanation is external. He insists that in *self-perception* we use the same external cues that we use in ordinary perception. In this view, ". . . most self-knowledge must still come to us from without."

FEEDBACK. If self-perception theory is correct, it should be possible to influence self-perception by using misleading external cues. This was done in an experiment on reactions to sexually arousing stimuli (Valins, 1966). While men watched semi-nude photographs from *Playboy,* their heart rate was recorded and amplified so that they could hear the beats. What they actually heard were heart sounds of other people that had been prerecorded. Thus the experimenter could manipulate the *perceived* heart rate of the subjects, and the latter would be using *external* cues (the amplified heart sounds) to infer their *inner* reactions.

Half the pictures were accompanied by a marked change in the amplified heart rate; for the other half there was no change. The pictures for

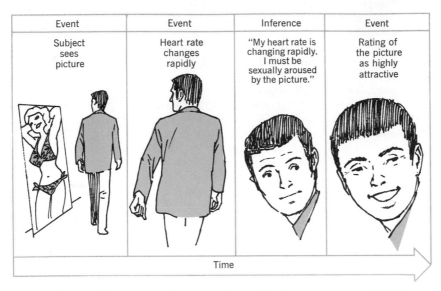

Event	Event	Inference	Event
Subject sees picture	Heart rate changes rapidly	"My heart rate is changing rapidly. I must be sexually aroused by the picture."	Rating of the picture as highly attractive

Time

Figure 21.6 Self perception interpretation of Valins' experiment (1966).

which the heart rate seemed to change were rated by the viewers as much more attractive and were selected by the subjects to take home with them. A month later the men still preferred these pictures.

Bem interprets these findings in terms of self-perception (see Figure 21.6). There are three sequential events: the subject sees a picture, his heart rate apparently changes, and he rates the picture as highly attractive. Bem would infer that the subject described his *internal* reaction based on the *external* cue of the amplified, spurious heart sounds.

Persons may be expected to vary considerably in their use of external cues to infer internal reactions; they do. College students with high anxiety (as measured by a questionnaire) were much more affected by the spurious heart rate changes rating *Playboy* pictures than were the students with low anxiety (Valins, 1967). Recall also that obese persons tend to use external cues to gauge hunger, whereas persons of normal weight tend to use internal cues such as hunger pangs (Schachter, 1968).

External cues are used not only in states of high arousal (emotion) and moderate arousal (affect) but also to states that have been called mystical

or transcendental. Weird, ecstatic, and apparently supernatural experiences are common; the way they are reported depends upon the person's usual external environment (Bourque, 1969). Deeply religious persons, especially those of fundamentalist sects, describe their experiences i religious terms. Nonreligious persons describe the experiences in esthetic terms ("far out," "peaceful," or "indescribable." As far as can be determined, the experiences appear to be the same, but they are described differently— presumably because of the different cues in the person's usual environments.

. . . the esthetic ecstatic-transcendental experience occur among a group which society often seems t characterize as acceptably middle class, well educated white residents of the suburbs. In contrast, religiou ecstatic-transcendental experiences appear to occu most frequently among those whom society has ig nored, namely, the poorly educated, older, rural Negro populations. (BOURQUE, 1969, P. 159

METAPHORS. Self-perception theory correctly identifies an important problem about feelings: how does a child come to identify and communicate his inner, private states? Bem suggests that part of the answer lies in metaphors. Thus a headache may be described as feeling like "a tight band of steel is pressing on the skull"; the internal sensations of fear may be described as "butterflies in the stomach." Most of us have experienced inner events that may loosely be described in such terms, and therefore we can understand each other's feelings. But most internal events are difficult to describe; physicians know how difficult it is for a patient to communicate and localize his symptoms.

The problem is more severe when there are no clear bodily reactions. Consider the affect of romantic love. How does a lover communicate his passion to the loved one? Everyday language is arid, and we must rely on poets to furnish the appropriate metaphors. The issue is well illustrated in a passage from Cyrano De Bergerac, a play by Edmund Rostand. Two men love the heroine, Roxanne. Christian is handsome, but he cannot communicate his passion to the heroine who wishes to be wooed with words.

CHRISTIAN: (After a silence) *I love you.*
ROXANNE: (Closes her eyes) *Yes, Speak to me about love.*
CHRISTIAN: *I love you.*
ROXANNE: *Now, be eloquent.*
CHRISTIAN: *I love —*
ROXANNE: (Opens her eyes) *You have your theme. Improvise! Rhapsodize!*
CHRISTIAN: *I love you so!*

At this point Roxanne becomes bored and soon leaves in disgust. Contrast Christian's prosaic repetitions with Cyrano's poetic metaphors:

ROXANNE: *What words with you?* . . .
CYRANO: *All those, all those, all those*
That blossom in my heart, I'll fling to you —
Armfuls of loose bloom! Love, I love beyond
Breath, beyond reason, beyond love's own power
Of loving! Your name is like a golden bell
Hung in my heart; and when I think of you,

I tremble, and the bell swings and rings —
"Roxanne!" . . . "Roxanne!" along my veins . . .

Cyrano is making his passion manifest, and we can all appreciate the metaphors, but what is he describing? The metaphors tell us only one thing: that Cyrano loves deeply. Beyond intensity, the poetry adds nothing descriptive, and this is precisely the problem in attempting to communicate *any* private experience. It is not that poetry does not offer delights to the ear and mind; it is that metaphors and images simply cannot adequately describe the rich complexity of private experience.

The recurring problem is that feelings can be communicated only through language and, as Mandler (1962) has noted, *"We often consider a statement emotional if it begins with 'I feel' and then makes references to unobservable, private events or states"* [p. 229]. Such language behavior is slowly acquired during childhood, and the ability to make fine distinctions in referring to inner feelings may owe more to verbal training than to acute perception. In brief, the references we make to internal states seem to be controlled not so much by internal events *per se* as by external cues in the environment.

Integration

Five theories of emotion[5] have been discussed: those of James, Cannon, Schachter, Bem, and our own evolutionary hypothesis. Each of them enhances the understanding of emotion. James pointed out that emotion is a *reaction* to external and internal events, though his view was too simple; we do not merely perceive our bodily reactions in emotion. Cannon noted that peripheral autonomic changes cannot be perceived as sufficiently different to be a basis of distinguishing different emotions. Schachter revised James by demonstrating that emotion consists not only of perceptions of external stimuli and bodily changes

[5] *This list does not include* all *theories of emotions — only the major ones (see Goldstein, 1968; Arnold, 1970).*

but also of cognitions that causally link the two events. Bem specified how bodily events are perceived and interpreted: as inferences made largely on the basis of *external,* not internal, stimuli.

How do these theories relate to the evolutionary approach, which distinguishes between affect and emotion on the basis of level of arousal? The more recent theories—those of Schachter and Bem—focus on two components: bodily changes and cognitions about the cause of these changes. As has been demonstrated by Schachter and Singer (1962) and Valins (1966), cognitions play a more important role in *affective* behavior. Thus when arousal level is moderate—after injection of a mild dose of adrenaline or exposure to *Playboy* pictures—cognitions play a major role in the subject's affective reaction, and bodily changes play a minor role.

What happens when arousal level is extremely high, as in emotions? There is no direct evidence, because it would be unethical to inject sufficient adrenaline to drive arousal up to the level of emotions. Nevertheless, it seems likely that when arousal level is high enough to be labeled *emotional,* cognitions play a minor role in the person's reaction. There is evidence to sustain this hypothesis.

Valins (1966) showed pictures of nude women to his male subjects. Goldstein et al. (1972) showed pictures of both nude women and nude men to their male subjects. Though the pictures of nude men probably did not elevate arousal to an emotional level, the pictures of men did cause a much higher level of arousal than did the pictures of women:

A number of the subjects reported that they were "grossed out" by the male nudes, and, overall, subjects who had viewed the male nudes in the experiment reported being offended by the experiment significantly more than subjects who had viewed only female nudes. (P. 50)

When only female nudes were shown and subjects heard their heart rate change rapidly (as manipulated by the experimenter), they rated the pictures as being more attractive; this repeats Valins' (1966) results. But when male nudes were shown and the heart rate apparently changed, offensiveness of the pictures did not change. Instead the rated offensiveness of the male pictures varied directly with subjects' *actual* changes in heart rate.

Goldstein et al. (1972) interpret these findings in a way that is entirely consistent with our distinction between affect and emotion. When arousal level is low, the person uses information (the apparent heart rate) about his physiological arousal as a cue in making judgments. This is consistent with Schachter's and Bem's views. But when arousal level is high, the person's *actual* physiological arousal largely determines his affective reaction:

Thus in the case of potent emotional situations, it is not the cognition of physiological arousal that is crucial in mediating emotionality; rather it is actual physiological arousal. (P. 51)

This observation is consistent with our distinction between affect (low arousal) and emotion (high arousal).

Emotion as a Disorganizer

Emotion can be a potent disorganizing influence on behavior, especially the peaks of emotion attained in terror and extreme rage. Actors may become rigid with stage fright; automobile drivers may freeze at the controls of their cars and helplessly crash when an accident might have been avoided; and soldiers have been known to remain immobile under attack and not fire a single shot at the advancing enemy. Boxers and football players may hurt their own cause by wild and uncontained violence when they become enraged. But the picture cannot be this one-sided, for if emotion were so unequivocally maladaptive, surely it would not have survived natural selection. Emotion must not only disorganize behavior; it must also facilitate it. The facilitation occurs only when the behavior is appropriate to the emotion: when flight follows fear, when attack follows rage, and when mating follows sexual arousal.

Fear enhances flight	Fear disorganizes flight
The frightened person runs faster.	The frightened person does not coordinate his actions well. He stalls the car or drives poorly in his haste to escape.

Figure 21.7 Emotion both enhances and disorganizes behavior.

Fear is part of the generalized reaction to threat, and the widespread physiological arousal that occurs in fear helps prepare for the oncoming flight. An aroused person can mobilize his full bodily resources to escape from the immediate danger. Thus fear energizes escape behavior. Rage may also be a reaction to threat. Fighting requires tremendous energy to lend strength and speed to the person's attack. The enraged person is sufficiently aroused to strike with his utmost force, and thus rage energizes aggressive behavior. Concerning sexual behavior, it simply will not occur unless the person is first sexually aroused. Clearly, in both men and animals the three emotions are adaptive. Those better prepared to escape or to defend themselves are more likely to survive; those better prepared to mate are likely to leave behind more offspring. Thus emotions are adaptive in the situations most relevant to natural selection: survival of the individual and of the species.

Situations involving defense and mating, important as they are, occupy only a small part of life. Defense of self is a response to an emergency sit-

uation; soon the emergency is over, and arousal level returns to normal. Emotions enhance responses to emergencies, but emergency mechanisms are inefficient in everyday nonemergency situations. If there is no need for a quick, explosive response, the high arousal level associated with emotion is likely to interfere with ongoing behavior. The situation might call for single-minded concentration to solve an abstract problem, for vigilance in the face of oncoming stimuli, or for inhibition of response and the ability to wait and tolerate delay. In such situations emotion, as a massively aroused state, is a disturbance that disorganizes behavior.

Clearly, emotion is not intrinsically enhancing or disorganizing (see Figure 21.7). It energizes appropriate behavior in emergencies and in mating situations; it disorganizes behavior in the everyday tasks calling for quiescence, concentration, and steadiness. In our present civilization most situations are of the latter type. There are few emergency situations, and even these do not require massive arousal because we have mechanical aids for flight and for fight. Fear can ruin the driving skill of someone fleeing a pursuer; rage can spoil the aim of an aggressor firing a rifle, or it can reduce the intended invective of the enraged person to sputtering incoherence. Modern man neither escapes nor attacks the way his forebears did. He uses mechanical devices that require highly developed skill; thus in man emotion is often a disorganizing influence on behavior, even behavior for which the emotion may be appropriate.

chapter 22
social motivation

Social versus biological motivation — sex — evolutionary trends — masturbation — coitus — incest taboo — double standard — homosexuality — hormones and development — aggression — animal aggression — evolutionary trends — human aggression — angry versus instrumental aggression — antecedents of aggression — inhibitors of aggression — catharsis — mass media and violence — competence — development of competence — locus of control — achievement motivation — self-actualization

Social motivation may be distinguished from biological motivation on the basis of the impact of socialization. Consider the four classes of biological motivation: vegetative, emergency, reproductive, and educational.[1] The vegetative drives of thirst and hunger are only slightly affected by socialization practices, but the other three classes are strongly affected by socialization practices.

This chapter deals with areas of behavior associated with drives that are highly socialized: sex, aggression, and competence. These three areas are the focus not only of training by parents and other agents of socialization but also of the conflicts that inevitably arise between parents and children—the so-called *generation gap*.

Sexual behavior and aggression are familiar to everyone, but competence requires a brief introduction. *Competence* involves mastery of the environment. It includes the desire to explore and manipulate—educational motives mentioned in Chapter 7. Competence has been described as a ". . . process whereby the animal or child learns to interact effectively with his environment"

[1] *These four classes of biological motivation are discussed in Chapter 7.*

Table 22.1
Overview of Human Social Motivation

MOTIVATION	BEHAVIORAL EXAMPLE	SOCIAL INTERACTION	SOCIALIZATION STARTS
Sex	Sexual intercourse	Cooperative	Late*
Aggression	Slapping someone	Antagonistic	Early
Competence	Inventing a better mousetrap	None necessary**	Early

* Socialization of *gender role* starts early, and there are early prohibitions of masturbation. But socialization of the main *adult* sexual activity (intercourse) starts relatively late.
** Competence may involve solitary activities such as solo airplane flights, painting, composing music, and writing. Nevertheless, these activities and all those related to competence motivation are shaped by socialization agents.

(White, 1959, p. 329). Early in life it may be seen in the infant's movements away from its mother to see what is on the other side of the room or in his grasping objects and putting them in his mouth. Later in life it may be seen in the adult's attempt to understand his world, to discover what lies beyond the next mountain, or even to compete against a standard of excellence, overcoming obstacles to reach a goal.

All three motivations are strongly shaped by agents of socialization: parents, teachers, adult models, police, and children in the peer group. Table 22.1 provides a brief overview. Sex involves cooperative behavior (we except for the moment such behaviors as masturbation and rape), and it is usually socialized late (end of childhood, beginning of adolescence). Aggression is of course antagonistic, one person punishing another; controlling and directing aggression is a major task of child-rearing from the time the young child can control his movements sufficiently well to hurt another. Competence does not necessarily involve *social* responses, but the push to master and excel starts very early ("my son walked early," "my daughter already speaks in sentences," etc.).

Sex

We have come a long way from the Victorian prudery that was violently rocked by Freud's insistence on sex as a basic drive. In this country the pioneer sex researchers were Alfred Kinsey and his colleagues (1948), who assembled statistics on sex practices. In the face of considerable suspicion and hostility, Kinsey and his colleagues interviewed men and women in the 1940s, when even a double bed in the bedroom of a married couple could not be shown in motion pictures.[2]

Though Kinsey investigated a wide range of sexual behavior, he never defined it. Some equate coitus with sexual behavior, neglecting not only homosexuality and masturbation but also such nonorgasmic forms as kissing and fondling. Some animal psychologists insist on including *all* aspects of reproductive behavior, including courting and nestbuilding. The problem of defining human

[2] The New York Times, *reflecting the censorship of the day, refused to carry a conservative, nonsensational advertisement for Kinsey's book in 1948.*

Table 22.2
Evolutionary Trends in Sexual Behavior

	LOWER MAMMALS	PRIMATES
Link between sexual behavior and reproduction	Very strong	Weak
Link between sex hormones and behavior	Strong	Weaker, variable
Arousal	Smell is crucial	Sight and manipulation are important
Social variables and individual experience	Relatively unimportant	Very important

sexual behavior is complicated by our extreme conditionability. Thus some men develop a *fetish,* becoming sexually aroused when handling female garments; others become aroused by beating another person and still others by being beaten themselves.

In brief, human sexual arousal can be conditioned to so many stimuli and associated with so many responses as to defy definition. We shall discuss only the three major human outlets: masturbation, coitus (heterosexual intercourse), and homosexuality. But first, sex must be considered in evolutionary perspective.

Evolutionary Aspects

If we follow our line from lower mammals to man, there is a progression in motivation from more direct, specified programed sequences of behavior (instinct) to more indirect, diffuse programs (drive) that require considerable learning. The evolution of sexual behavior reflects this trend (see Table 22.2).

The link between sexual behavior and reproduction is very close in lower animals, an obvious fact that follows from selection pressure: the genes of animals that leave more offspring behind tend to predominate in the population. In lower mammals, coitus is determined mainly by the female. If she is not in heat, the male tends not to be aroused; even if he is, the nonovulating female rejects him. If she is in heat (the peak of fertility), her smell attracts and arouses the male, as any cat or dog owner can attest. But the close tie between reproduction and coitus loosened during mammalian evolution. Nonhuman primates represent a midway point between man and a mammal such as the dog; there is some nonreproductive coitus in primates, though the peak of activity occurs during ovulation.

Whether or not there is a similar cycle of sexual arousal in women is controversial. Some researchers have reported a paradoxical peak of sexual arousability in women during the premenstrual period, when fertility is at a low ebb:

It is not that women can be sexually aroused only during this time. Rather, most women report a more spontaneous interest in sex, an increased conscious sexual desire, an increased ease in reaching the plateau level of arousal, and an increased ease in reaching orgasm. Thus women appear to have a biologically based cyclic increase in sexual drive based partly on the erotic effects of endocrines.

(BARDWICK, 1971, P. 45)

In contrast, other researchers have reported a peak of arousability during ovulation. In comparison to the premenstrual period, the period of ovulation is one of greater reported arousability and pleasure in sex (Moos, 1969) and of higher "sexiness" ratings for *Playboy* pictures of men and women (Luschen & Pierce, 1972).

There is presently no ready explanation for these opposing findings. Individual women may vary in their interest and excitability in relation to their ovarian cycle, but there is apparently little consistency from one woman to the next. Moreover, such nonhormonal factors as specific mating habits, deprivation (relative abstinence during menstruation), and satiation (having had enough after a "sexual binge") are probably much more important in determining frequency of coitus.

This brings us to the second trend, concerning the link between hormones and sex behavior. Sex hormones determine secondary sexual characteristics at puberty: those anatomical differences that sharply differentiate human males from females (breasts, hips, body hair, and so on). And sex hormones must be present *during development* for normal sexual behavior to occur in adulthood. These facts hold for all mammals.

Nevertheless, hormonal influences vary greatly from lower mammals to man, waning in importance as we ascend the ladder of mammalian evolution. If the ovaries of rats, cats, dogs, horses, or cows are removed, the lack of hormones eliminates sexual behavior. If a female adult chimpanzee's ovaries are removed, her sexual behavior declines sharply but does not completely disappear. The link between hormones and behavior is even weaker in women, many of whom maintain sexual interest and responsiveness after their ovaries cease to function during the age decade of the forties or the fifties:

The human female appears capable of marked sexual excitability without the physiological stimulation pro-

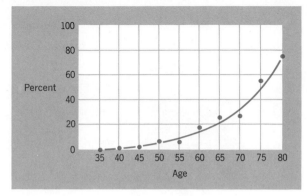

Figure 22.1 *Age of onset of impotence (Kinsey et al.,* 1948, p. 236).

vided by the ovarian hormones. She may be sexually aroused before puberty and after menopause. Very often the surgical removal of the ovaries has no effect upon the enjoyment of sexual relations.

(FORD & BEACH, 1951, P. 253)

For males the effect of hormones on sexual behavior is similar, up to a point. Lower mammals such as rats, rabbits, and guinea pigs lose interest and capability soon after their testes are removed, but injection of male hormones restores sexual potency. The effect of castration on adult men is variable: some completely lose interest, some show a drop in sexual behavior, and others report continued interest and potency for several decades.[3]

The male role in sexual behavior is more active, requiring as a minimum an erect penis. There is no abrupt cessation of functioning of the testes in men, as there is of the ovaries in women. Rather, the output of male hormones gradually wanes with old age. Interest in sex may or may not diminish, but sexual potency (capability of erection) slowly fades (see Figure 22.1). Injection of male hormones has proved to be helpful, indicating at least some connection between hormones and sexual behavior. But male hormones are of somewhat less importance to the sexual behavior of men than to that of lower mammals.

[3] *They are of course incapable of fertilizing an ovum, but this does not prevent sexual behavior or enjoyment.*

Table 22.3
Sexual Tendencies Common to Humans and Mammals

1. Gender similarity	Sex initiated by either gender
2. Gender differences	a. Females vary in interest; males always interested b. Males more sexual in that they masturbate more and engage in more homosexuality
3. Development	a. Innate reflexes: swelling of genitals, pelvic thrusts b. Sex play occurs

The last two evolutionary trends may be dealt with briefly. Lower mammals become sexually excited by the *smell* of a potential mate, primates by *sight* and manipulation. Social variables are of little importance in the sexual behavior in lower mammals, the important determinant being hormones. As the link between hormones and behavior weakened during mammalian evolution, both social variables and individual experience increased in importance. Thus not only humans but all primates require the usually expected social contacts during development for normal adult sexual behavior, as Harlow and others have demonstrated (see Chapter 20).

FEATURES MAN SHARES WITH OTHER MAMMALS. Though the evolutionary trends just discussed tend to make man's sexual behavior different from such animals as cats and dogs, there are still several shared features that reveal our mammalian heritage (see Table 22.3). First, there is the tendency for either gender to initiate sexual contact, indicating by body position, facial expression, or vocal communication an interest in copulating.

Second, there are behavioral differences between males and females that are common to all mammals. Females show variation, usually cyclic, in interest and excitability, whereas males are virtually always actively interested or easily excited. Males are somewhat more sexual than females, as revealed in self-stimulation and same-sexed contacts. That mammalian males are more homosexual and masturbate more than females suggests that their sexual motivation is stronger.

Third, all mammals share certain developmental trends. All have two innate sexual reflexes: swelling of the genitals (more easily seen in males) and pelvic thrusts. Moreover, sex play is universal in mammalian young, and in primates it is a necessary precursor to normal adult sexual behavior. In man, childhood games of the "doctor and nurse" variety may facilitate the development of sexual behavior after puberty.

FEATURES UNIQUE TO MAN. Whatever man's mammalian heritage, his species possesses characteristics shared with no other animal (see Table 22.4). First, human foreplay involves kissing of various kinds, including tongue insertion, as well as fondling of the female breasts (which are relatively large in comparison to those of other mammals). Face-to-face coitus is so much preferred that it is the dominant mode; this may be

Table 22.4
Uniquely Human Sexual Features

1. Coitus:	a. Type of foreplay b. Face-to-face as the dominant mode
2. Privacy:	A universal desire
3. Arousal:	Through symbolic modes
4. Orgasm:	In women as well as in men

have been rapid changes in sexual attitudes during the last decade, and women are challenging traditional notions, which they believe are not only excessively puritanical but demeaning to women. Perhaps in another decade women will be turned on as much by pictures of nude men as men are by pictures of nude women; or possibly nudity will no longer excite either gender.

Fourth, mammalian males routinely achieve orgasm, which is marked by the ejaculation of sperm. Orgasm in female cats, rats, dogs, and other mammals is unknown. In human females, however, orgasm is fairly common. A minority of women seem never to experience orgasm, but it is not necessary for sexual enjoyment, in spite of a mythology that has sprung up on the basis of pronouncements of "experts."

partly anatomical, the vagina being located farther forward as part of the rearrangements necessary for man's two-legged stance.

Second, the need for privacy while copulating or masturbating, which is conditioned during socialization, appears to occur in all societies. There are exceptions in each society, but the majority of humans avoid prying eyes or ears when sexually active.

Third, men and women are sexually excited not only by sensory stimulation but also by the language and imagery of symbolic modes. We can be turned on sexually by *cognitions,* and in our society there is an interesting gender difference. Consider magazines showing partially or completely nude human bodies. Whether the pictures are of men or of women, the purchasers are almost exclusively male. Men are sexually excited by *visual* stimuli, especially naked or (preferably) nearly naked women. Women's sexual interest is focused more on the *relationship.* Thus women buy magazines depicting *romance,* the mutual love of the partners exciting their sexual interest. Men are more visually oriented (Sigush et al., 1970), and imagery is more important in their love-making and masturbation than it is in women.

These and other differences in sexual attitudes and behavior refer to the traditional sex roles played by American men and women. But there

Sexual Practices and Attitudes

As part of socialization each child learns the ways of his culture and subculture concerning sex. He learns the conditions under which sex is permissible: when, how, and with whom.

MASTURBATION. Self-stimulation is assumed to be universal, though many persons refuse to admit having practiced it because our society frowns on it. Each generation of children and adolescents acquires the usual myths that are presumably designed to scare them: that masturbation causes insanity, stunted growth, or warts. Our society regards masturbation as childish, and most adolescents and adults react with shame to their own self-stimulation. The feeling of shame does not seem to inhibit masturbation any more than does the guilt of persons with a religious orientation. Psychologists agree that masturbation is in no way harmful, and the taboo against it makes no biological or psychological sense.

COITUS. All societies place restrictions on sexual *partnerships.* Though practices vary widely, there is one shared by all societies: the *incest taboo.* No society tolerates parent-child or brother-sister relationships. The principal reasons for this universal inhibition appear to be the likelihood of sexual jealousy within the family and the problem ensuing from the kinship of the offspring. Thus when a father and daughter mate, the baby's father is simultaneously its grandfather (its mother's father); such complications would play havoc with inheritance of property and with the customs surrounding kinship (how does a man act toward his sister's child when it is also his own, as a father or as an uncle?). It has been speculated that the incest taboo represents an adaptation designed to prevent the genetic flaws that may accompany inbreeding (Lindzey, 1967).

Some societies encourage sex before marriage but discourage extramarital sex. Others discourage premarital sex but provide unofficially for extramarital sex (the more affluent men have mistresses). Our society, taking a Victorian view, is on record as being against both premarital and extramarital sex. Actually, sex prior to or outside of marriage is not only frequent but the source of a flourishing business, the "oldest profession" of prostitution.

Like most societies, we have a double standard: one for men and a more restricted one for women. Women have traditionally been assigned a lower status than men. For more than a century they were denied the vote as well as acceptance into most professions. They have always been granted less freedom than men, and this includes sexual freedom. Around the reality of male dominance there are several myths regarding female sexuality. One is that women are not really interested in sex and are useful only as the passive instrument of men's urges. A related masculine myth assumes that there are two kinds of women: "those you have fun with and those you marry."

A more realistic basis for the double standard was a fear of pregnancy.[4] It is a strange paradox that evolutionary adaptations designed to propagate the species should cause problems: unwanted children at the personal level and overpopulation at the societal level. We provide poorly for the children of unwed mothers, and "illegitimacy" remains a serious stigma. And if a woman has a child by any man except her husband, it may be sufficient cause to destroy the marriage. Moreover, paternity is a very serious issue in de-

ciding kinship and inheritance of privilege and property. Finally, the masculine image is prideful, and men's sexual jealousy is intense; a significant proportion of men would still prefer to marry a virgin.

Whatever the role of pregnancy in fostering a double standard previously, in this era of safe contraception it no longer offers a rationale. Where women are granted essentially the same sexual rights as men, as in Sweden, adolescent girls initiate coitus at the same age as boys and with only slightly lower frequency (Linner, 1967). In this country we have been moving toward such equity, but progress is retarded by the inertia of tradition and the bigotry of male chauvinism.

HOMOSEXUALITY. Sexual behavior with members of the same gender is an adaptive dead end (no children), and not surprisingly most members of society are heterosexual. In fact, there are very strong restrictions on homosexuality, and in most states it is illegal. England recently passed more permissive laws, and U.S. laws are being enforced more laxly.

There are few reliable statistics on homosexuality, the best being those collected by Kinsey for men (see Table 22.5). As the table shows, exclusively homosexual men constitute a small minority (4%), but the frequency of homosexual acts is somewhat higher than this figure would suggest. Thus more than one third of all men have had at least one homosexual experience, and for unmarried men the frequency is 50%.

These figures are now 25 years old, and there may be more homosexuals per capita at present than there were previously. A recent estimate was 2.5 million to 4 million American men (Socarides, 1970). Certainly homosexuals are more visible than previously, as witnessed by the attempts of men to obtain marriage licenses, the greater number of homosexual bars, and the militancy of the Gay Lib movement.

Virtually all children are taught to despise homosexuals, and the ensuing prejudice has fostered and been fostered by two myths. The first is that male homosexuals behave like women (hence the terms *queen* and *fairy*), and female homosexuals behave like men. It is true that a *minority* of homosexuals show transsexual behavior. There are men who dress like women, act like women (copying effeminate gestures), or both; and there

[4] *Fear of pregnancy, surprisingly, is the reason given by men more than by women for restraint; women give as reasons for restraint not losing the man or fear of feeling ashamed or guilty afterward (Driscoll & Davis, 1971).*

Table 22.5
Incidence of Male Homosexuality in the United States (Kinsey et al, 1948)

CATEGORY	PERCENT
Exclusively homosexual throughout life	4
Exclusively homosexual for at least three years in adulthood	8
More or less homosexual for at least three years in adulthood	10
More homosexual than heterosexual for at least three years	13
At least some homosexual experience to the point of orgasm during adulthood	37
Men who remained single until 35 years and have at least some homosexual experience	50

are women who dress like men, act like men (masculine stride, gruff talk), or both. But by all accounts these make up a small minority of homosexuals, and the overwhelming majority cannot be distinguished from heterosexuals by their behavior or by psychological tests (Hooker, 1962).

One reason for the myth is a confusion between sex outlet and gender identity. *Sex outlet* refers to particular sex acts, as defined mainly by the *direction* of the sexual behavior. Thus sexual acts can occur alone (masturbation), with an opposite-sex partner (coitus), or with a same-sex partner (homosexuality). There are essentially no gender differences in the direction of sexual response, both men and women engaging in a wide variety of sexual behavior (see Table 22.6). *Gender identity* refers to the psychological characteristics that define masculinity and femininity. These consist of (1) the *preferences* shown in sports, hobbies, and so on, and (2) the *personality traits* usually as-

sociated with masculinity and femininity. These properly fall under the heading of personality, and they will be discussed in Chapter 25.

The second myth assumes that all homosexuals have some kind of hormonal abnormality—that homosexual men, for example have either too much female hormone or insufficient male hormone. There is a grain of truth in this assertion, though not enough to sustain the myth. Earlier attempts to demonstrate hormonal differences in homosexuals failed to do so, but a recent attempt succeeded (Kolodny, et al., 1971). Young men (18–24 years old) were classified by the Kinsey system, as follows:

0. exclusively heterosexual.
1. predominantly heterosexual but incidentally homosexual.
2. predominantly heterosexual but more than incidentally homosexual.

Table 22.6
Sex Outlet Versus Gender Identity

	TYPICAL BEHAVIORS
Sex outlet	Coitus, homosexual acts, masturbation

Gender identity
  Preferences
  Personality traits
	Clothes, sports, vocations
	Aggressiveness, achievement,
	   compassion, dependence

3. equally heterosexual and homosexual.
4. predominantly homosexual but more than incidentally heterosexual.
5. predominantly homosexual but incidentally heterosexual.
6. exclusively homosexual.

The degree of homosexuality (as per Kinsey) was found to correlate negatively with both amount of testosterone and sperm count. The relationship between testosterone and degree of homosexuality is shown in Figure 22.2. Note that even those who were classified 4 (predominantly homosexual) had testosterone in the normal range. Note also that there is a clear relationship and that it is a *correlation.* The researchers were keenly aware that the testosterone-homosexuality relationship might be causal in either direction:

There is no suggestion that endocrine abnormalities will be found in the great majority of homosexuals or that endocrine dysfunction is a major factor in the pathogenesis of male homosexuality. In fact there must be speculation that the depressed plasma testosterone levels could be the secondary result of a primary homosexual psychosocial orientation. . . .

(KOLODNY ET AL., 1971)

There are rare individuals whose biological gender is mixed. Briefly, there are two bases of biological gender: heredity and early development. At conception the determination of gender is

made: males have an XY pair and females an XX pair of chromosomes (see Chapter 3). But there are rare chromosomal anomalies involving an additional chromosome, the usual cases being XXY or XYY. They result in a variety of bodily abnormalities, which occur early in development (see Federman, 1967; Money, 1970).

The other kind of biological abnormality also occurs early in development. The young fetus,

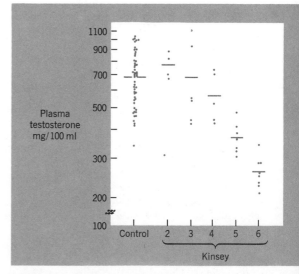

Figure 22.2 Plasma testosterone levels in heterosexual and homosexual men (Kolodny et al., 1971).

whether male or female, has undifferentiated external sex organs. Differentiation is determined mainly by the presence or absence of male hormone. A normal fetus synthesizes the male hormone that leads to a full-sized penis and testes; in the absence of male hormone, female genitalia develop. In the exceptional case the hormones do not match the gender. Thus if a male fetus fails to synthesize male hormone, it will be born with female external genitalia. Similarly, a female fetus may have male hormones, either synthesized by an abnormal adrenal cortex or triggered by antimiscarriage hormones sometimes administered to pregnant women. They retain their ovaries but develop a penis.

What bearing do these facts have on homosexuality? First, such biological anomalies are rare and therefore cannot account for the vast majority of homosexuals. Second, even when there is a *biological* problem of gender identity early in development, the outcome depends mainly on *psychological* factors. Persons with these problems can have their biological sex changed. If it is done early in development, the usual childrearing practices yield a sexually normal adult:

The data from the study of those individuals who have had a change of sex imposed on them at various ages suggest that a significant degree of gender-role development coincides with the development of language — from 18 months to two years of age. Clinical experience indicates that a change in the sex of rearing of a child can be successfully imposed on a child prior to this age. These findings are schematically represented in Figure [22.3]. Thereafter one invites varying degrees of psychological risk.

(HAMPSON, 1965, P. 125)

The important point here is that the child will follow its assigned gender role: if treated as a boy, it will become a man; if treated like a girl, it will become a woman. This has clear implications for homosexuality. Most of us are taught to inhibit sexual advances or responses to members of the same gender, and our sex motivation is channeled toward the opposite gender. Homosexuals, for reasons not entirely clear, are either frightened of sex with the opposite gender or excessively stimulated by sex with the same gender. This is entirely understandable in light of the conditionability of

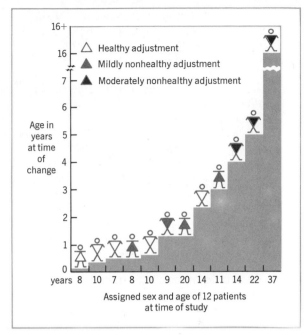

Figure 22.3 Change of sex imposed at different ages (*Hampson, 1965, p. 126*).

sexual behavior, as illustrated by the bewildering array of fetishes and deviant sexual acts seen in at least some members of all societies.

Male homosexuals cannot be treated by injections of androgen (the male hormone), for it serves to *increase* sex motivation without regard to outlet; both men and women may find their sex drive heightened by injection of androgen, though the effects are variable (Money, 1970). Nor is estrogen (the principal female hormone) effective in treating female homosexuals. If it has any effect at all, it is toward *diminishing* sex drive in general.

There is a definite minority of homosexuals who are strongly predisposed to become homosexuals by either genetic deviance (XXY chromosomes, for example) or early hormonal imbalance. These may be what Money (1970) calls *chronic* and *obligatory* — as opposed to biologically normal homosexuals, who might be called *transient* and *optional*. The latter probably constitute the majority of homosexuals. How did they become homosexuals? One way is through childhood sexual contacts with members of the same gender.

Homosexual men tend to become sexually active somewhat earlier than heterosexual men (Manosevitz, 1972). Same-sex contacts may direct the child toward later homosexuality:

If a child's object choice is undifferentiated — that is, directed toward both males and females, and if he is sexually precocious while most of his social relations are with males, then it is possible that many of his early sexual experiences will be with same-sexed partners. It is entirely probable that these early sexual experiences may affect subsequent development and adult sexual preferences. (MANOSEVITZ, 1970, P. 401)

A final point concerns sex motivation in general. In the normal course of events, each of us inherits a male or female gender. During development, biological maturation yields appropriate gender-related hormones, external genitalia, and a sexual arousal system. This arousal system is part sympathetic, part parasympathetic, and its physiological aspects are now known (see Chapter 21). The arousal system is biological, but the sexual acts themselves are essentially psychological. We can learn to be aroused by an endless variety of stimuli. Most men are strongly aroused by women's breasts, but this is *learned.* Moreover, the *object* of the sexual act can be almost anything that is physically appropriate: another person of either gender, oneself, animals, or inanimate objects. The *direction* of sexual behavior is determined mainly by society's rules and the individual's own experience. Most human motivation is diffuse and undifferentiated at the start; the appropriate behavior is shaped, directed, and focused by the events of each person's life. With respect to sex, the diffuse, background factors are *biological,* but the specific, directional factors are *psychological.*

Aggression

As a topic, aggression shares several features with the topic of sex:

1. It is socially important and is especially relevant to a society such as ours, which has been labeled *violent.*
2. The many forms of human aggression pose serious problems in defining aggression.

3. There are physiological and hormonal aspects.
4. There are marked gender differences.
5. There are clear evolutionary trends.

Aggression is easier to study in animals because it is more open, direct, and adaptive than in humans. Therefore, we shall start with animal aggression, then describe evolutionary trends, and finally move on to human aggression.

Animal Aggression

Three questions need to be answered: what, how, and why? *What* is animal aggression? This problem involves defining aggression and excluding noninstances of the class of responses. *How* do animals aggress? This question asks for a description of the various responses labeled aggression. *Why* do animals aggress? This question concerns the conditions under which aggression occurs and its unusual consequences.

DEFINITION. Animal aggression consists of attacking or fighting with another animal: "An animal acts aggressively when it inflicts, attempts to inflict, or threatens to inflict damage on another animal" (Carthy & Ebling, 1964, p. 1). Harm to the victim is an essential part of the definition of aggression, but harm is not inevitable. Thus the animal may *attempt* harm but fail to do so because of its own inability (old age, illness, or injury). Or it may merely threaten to do harm, attacking only if its opponent fails to yield or run away.

Excluded from the definition are food-getting responses by predators. Animal researchers agree that carnivorous animals such as lions, sharks, and snakes are not being aggressive when they hunt down and kill their prey: ". . . a hawk swooping down on a small bird is no more aggressive than the family butcher engaged in his livelihood" (Carthy & Ebling, 1964, p. 2). There is of course no evidence that butchers are more aggressive than, say, accountants. Thus flesh-eaters are no more aggressive in their food-gathering than are vegetarians, who also kill living things (plants). This is not to say that carnivores are not aggressive, for they are. Any animal with the teeth and claws needed for hunting prey is also well equipped for fighting others of its kind. Attacks against other species (except prey) are rare, and

Table 22.7
Varieties of Animal Aggression

Biting	Wolf
Clawing	Tiger
Goring	Bull
Poisoning	Rattlesnake
Kicking	Horse
Butting	Goat
Pecking	Chicken
Stinging	Wasp
Hugging	Bear
Squeezing	Boa constrictor
"Shooting"	Porcupine
Spraying	Skunk

virtually all animal aggression consists of fights between members of the same species.

VARIETIES OF ANIMAL AGGRESSION. Many different modes of inflicting harm have evolved in animals. The dozen listed in Table 22.7 are the major forms, though there are variations on these themes in the animal kingdom. Whatever the specific means, all the responses have a single function: to inflict serious injury, perhaps to the point of killing the victim. It follows that if animals with such deadly natural weapons used them often against members of their own species, the species might die out. Clearly, some natural control over aggression is necessary, a point that will be considered below.

OCCASIONS FOR FIGHTING. When an animal is threatened, it can either attempt to escape or try to subdue the attacker. Not all prey merely turn and run in the face of a predator; some turn and fight. Thus aggression may be defensive, a response to threat.

Male animals of the same species often fight to win a position of social dominance or to seize or retain a piece of ground. Achieving dominance or territory leads to such basic rewards as food and mates. The dominant male, or the one with its own territory, often has first choice of available food and mates. In some species—the walrus, for example—a dominant bull fights to keep his harem of females; during the mating season he is often so busy fighting and mating that he has no time to eat.

In brief, all animal aggression is *instrumental* in that it leads to one of two kinds of reinforcement. Either the aversive stimulation of being attacked is turned off or the animal competes successfully and wins important rewards (food, mate, and so on). In this respect aggression has the same goals as *any* instrumental response: eliminating aversive stimuli and achieving rewards. But aggression differs from other instrumental behavior in its punitiveness. Aggression succeeds because it harms or threatens to harm another animal, thereby forcing it to yield. We have already seen that strong punishment tends to inhibit behavior (see Chapter 15). The source of punishment is typically the aggressive response of another animal.

Virtually all aggression between males of the same species is competitive. Thus two animals may butt heads to determine which is dominant (see Figure 22.4), but neither will ordinarily attempt to kill or maim the other. As we noted above, there must be built-in restraints to intraspecies aggression, else the males will kill each other off. Most species use one of two adaptations (Lorenz, 1966a). The first is well-developed defensive maneuvers that enable the usual method of attack—which is typically species-specific and therefore stereotyped—to be successfully parried. The second is *ritualized* fighting, in which the antagonists do not unleash their most dangerous weapons. Thus lions may not fully unsheath their claws, and snakes of the same species may coil around each other but do not attack with fangs. Threatening postures and menacing gestures are also part of ritualized aggression: competition, with the danger of serious harm minimized. Of course animals do fight seriously, and often one is in a posi-

Figure 22.4 *Intraspecies animal aggression: fighting but no maiming or killing.* (TOM MCHUGH/PHOTO RESEARCHERS)

tion to finish off its antagonist. Typically the loser adopts a submissive posture, which is usually sufficient to turn off the victor's attack. Intraspecies fights ordinarily are not fatal.

Thus though intraspecies fighting is commonplace, there are sufficient restraints to keep the animals from killing themselves off:

Indeed on examining intraspecific fighting more than superficially it is at once apparent that an important part of animal behavior, at least in mammals, is directed towards avoiding intraspecific aggression. The weapons are potentially so dangerous that fighting is ritualized into display, threat, and submission or appeasement, so that fights are generally no more than trials of strength followed by disengagement and rapid withdrawal by the weaker. This does not mean that fights never end fatally, for a threat that is never carried out loses its meaning, but fighting to the death rarely happens in the normal environment. (MATHEWS, 1964, P. 24.)

GENDER DIFFERENCES. Fighting is a predominantly male activity. Females will fight to defend a nest or their young, but otherwise females—with rare exceptions—constitute the peaceful gender. They generally do not compete for dominance, and in virtually all highly social species defense of the group is handled by adult males.

The relative aggressiveness of males is determined by two related factors: size and hormones. When two animals of the same species fight, the larger one almost always wins. It has been estimated that in puppies one-half pound is sufficient to tip the balance in favor of the heavier dog (Scott, 1958). With rare exceptions (hamsters, for example), mammalian males are larger, heavier, and stronger than females (see Figure 22.5). The message is clear to animals and observers alike: the male is bigger and stronger and therefore a better fighter than the female.

One of the reasons males are larger is the predominance of male hormone.[5] Male hormone also induces greater aggressiveness, as is well known by farmers and ranchers: a castrated male calf develops into a docile steer, not a ferocious bull. When *adult* males are castrated, the outcome is variable; most animals become less combative, but some persist in being aggressive.

The effects of castration need not be permanent if male hormone is replaced. Early research by Clark and Birch (1945) demonstrated that injections of male hormone makes chimpanzees more aggressive. First they castrated two adult chimpanzees and had them compete for peanuts. After

[5] *This statement oversimplifies complex relationships between hormones and growth, but it is essentially correct.*

Figure 22.5 *Sexual dimorphism of primates.*   (T. FULLER/ANIMALS, ANIMALS)

some initial fighting, one chimpanzee emerged as dominant. Then the subordinate one was injected with male hormone. He promptly rebelled, defeated his opponent, and remained dominant even after the hormone was stopped.[6] Thus male sex hormone is a major determiner of the aggression of animals, just as it is a determiner of their sexual behavior.

Evolutionary Trends

The trends for aggression are similar to those for sexual behavior. First, hormones play a decisive role in the aggression of animals but have little or no effect on human aggression. The presence of male hormone does masculinize boys, who are certainly more aggressive than girls, but this difference may be attributed to *learning*, not directly to hormones. Boys are expected to compete intensely and to play roughly, and they are shaped to be physically assertive. Thus, unlike male animals, the human male seems to be more aggressive because of training, not hormones.[7]

Second, in line with the waning of instinct during vertebrate evolution, aggressive tendencies are less innate. As Lorenz and other ethologists have amply documented, the aggression of many birds and fish is turned on only by specific stimuli. These stimuli act as *releasers*, unleashing the inflexible aggressive behavior that is characteristic of the species. In species closer to man, aggression is less instinctual and more learned.

Third, there is an evolutionary trend toward more varied instrumental behavior, so that species closer to man possess a wider response repertoire for coping with the environment. One consequence of this trend is a greater variety of aggressive behavior, and as we shall describe below, the human repertoire is extensive.

Another consequence is the availability of non-aggressive responses in social situations. As we noted earlier, animals (especially males) compete in contests of strength. To the victor go the spoils: dominance, a preferred mate, extra food, and so on. There are analogous contests of strength in most human societies, but they are not the major

---

[6] *For recent research on the role of hormones in aggression, see Garattini and Sigg (1969).*
[7] *There has been a report of a correlation between self-reported aggression and testosterone (Persky et al., 1971), but the findings are equivocal. There was a strong correlation for men under 28 years of age but no relationship at*

all between testosterone and aggression for men over 31 years old. The sample size was small, and the discrepancy is puzzling. Clearly, the correlation for young men requires confirmation, but if it is confirmed, it will reverse current opinion about hormones and aggression in man. Incidentally, it has been established only that men are physically more aggressive than women (e.g., Buss, 1963, 1966b).

Table 22.8
Varieties of Human Aggression

	ACTIVE		PASSIVE	
	DIRECT	INDIRECT	DIRECT	INDIRECT
Physical	Punching the victim	Practical joke, booby trap	Obstructing passage, sit-in	Refusing to perform a necessary task
Verbal	Insulting the victim	Malicious gossip	Refusing to speak	Refusing consent, vocal or written

determinants of male status. In most societies males compete for high position in less directly aggressive ways or in nonaggressive ways. Thus physical beauty is more likely to win a preferred mate than is fighting ability or sheer size and strength. Social dominance is achieved far more often by skill and manipulation than by ferocity.

Human Aggression

The aggression of animals is physical and direct: fighting that inflicts pain or damage. However cunning the animal, its aggression is limited by the teeth, claws, and other natural equipment. But human aggression is not limited by the restrictions of natural equipment. Our fingernails are poor substitutes for claws, and our teeth are too short and dull for serious damage (though our saliva is sufficiently germ-ridden to cause infection).

Human aggression spreads out in several directions, overcoming the limits of time, space, and natural weaponry. Thus man has invented weapons (club, knife, gun) that inflict more damage than tooth or claw. Man has transcended physical aggression, extending punishment into the sphere of language: the "bite" of verbal aggression may be as sharp (psychologically) as the proverbial serpent's sting. Man conquers time and space by leaving *booby traps* for the unwary: from letting air out of the tires of a neighbor's car to placing land mines for the enemy to explode. The aggressor may even punish his victim by *inactivity,* as in stubborn refusal to go along.

The varieties of human aggression may be subsumed under eight classes of behavior (see Table 22.8). These are generated by three dichotomies: physical-verbal, active-passive, and direct-indirect. Most animal aggression is active, physical, and direct, consisting principally of fighting. Humans fight less than they aggress verbally, but fighting is a more serious problem for society.

Indirect aggression is a prime example of the human propensity for devious behavior. The aggressor attacks his victim in a roundabout fashion by spreading nasty stories about him or setting his house on fire. In both instances the aggressor does not confront his victim directly: in one case he attacks verbally without being present; in the other he attacks physically, destroying something of value to the victim. Indirect aggression may offer the aggressor less satisfaction, but he often escapes detection and therefore is less concerned about retaliation.

Passive aggression is the least noxious form of aggression, especially when it is indirect. Its punishing aspects reside in blocking of the victim's behavior, as in student *sit-ins* (which block the normal operation of the college). It is often the weapon of choice by subordinates against authority, and it is commonly used by children against their parents—usually without much success.

Table 22.9
Angry Versus Instrumental Aggression

	STIMULUS	EMOTION	RESPONSE	REINFORCER (INTENT)
Angry aggression	Anger-inducers: insult, attack, annoyers, etc.	Anger	Aggression	Discomfort of the victim: pain, suffering, embarrassment, etc.
Instrumental aggression	Competition, a reinforcer possessed by another person	(none)	Aggression	Acquisition of the reinforcer: victory, food, money, status, etc.

Sequence →

The passive and indirect forms of aggression may sometimes be so mildly aversive that they shade into nonaggressive behavior. They are the borderline instances that no definition can easily handle, which may be a problem for the victim who cannot decide whether he should retaliate. ANGRY AGGRESSION AND INSTRUMENTAL AGGRESSION. Aside from the form of the aggressive response (one of the eight categories just described), it is useful to distinguish two broad classes of aggressive behavior in terms of the *stimuli* that elicit them, the accompanying *emotion,* and the consequences (Buss, 1961). The first class, *angry aggression,* is commonly incited by insult, attack, or annoyances. The usual emotional reaction is *anger,* which is often followed by aggression that causes the victim to suffer. The usual consequence of angry aggression is pain and discomfort of the victim. Stated another way, the intent of the aggressor is to harm the victim. (Note that we infer intent from the usual consequences of the behavior.) In brief, angry aggression is defined in terms of its antecedents (aversive stimuli), emotion (anger), and usual consequences or intent (the victim's suffering).

The second class, *instrumental aggression,* is initiated by competition or by any of the usual incentives that motivate behavior (dominance, food,

mate, and so on). There may or may not be an emotional reaction (anger), but it is not a necessary part of the sequence. The unusual consequence is success in competition or attainment of the incentive; any harm to the victim is incidental.

These two classes of aggression are compared in Table 22.9. The description of instrumental aggression reveals that it is essentially the same in humans and animals. In fact, virtually *all* animal aggression, being oriented toward incentives, is instrumental. It is *angry* aggression that is uniquely human. Animals fight for status, territory, or mates, but they do not aggress solely to harm their victims. The inflicting of pain on a victim in the absence of an extrinsic reward is peculiarly human. Presumably such cruelty is learned during development, but there are no really good explanations for it, only speculation.

We conventionally exclude certain kinds of punishment from the class of instrumental aggression. These are punishments delivered in the context of a social role in which the punishing agent is working for the punished person's own good. Thus a dentist may cause pain when repairing teeth; a physician, when injecting healing drugs; or a parent, when disciplining his child. All such situations involve aversive stimuli, but they are delivered for the ultimate good of the recipient, not the punisher. Of course the punishing agent can hide behind his social role, and there is a small minority of sadistic dentists and parents. Some teachers and bosses also misuse their positions to aggress against subordinates, and it is difficult to separate legitimate punishment from angry aggression. Such a distinction requires an estimate of how much punitiveness is required by the social role; any excess may be attributed to angry aggression. Thus a teacher may legitimately criticize a stu-dent's exam paper; calling him stupid constitutes angry aggression.

LABORATORY RESEARCH. Given the nature of aggression, there are ethical and practical problems in studying it in the laboratory. Human subjects cannot be harmed, but if the measure of aggression is to have any meaning, there must be a victim. It is also desirable to measure the aggression quantitatively, which presents problems: how many light taps equal one punch?

Research Report

One solution to these problems is the *aggression machine* (Buss, 1961). The mode of aggression is electric shock, and the procedure involves deception in placing the subject in an appropriate role for giving shock. He is instructed that he will participate with another "subject" (actually an experimental accomplice or confederate) in a learning experiment. The ostensible purpose of this "experiment" is to test the effect of punishment on learning, and for this reason both experimenters and subjects need to be sampled. In the bogus learning task the accomplice, playing the role of learner, makes mistakes. Each time he errs, he is shocked by the subject, playing the role of experimenter. The confederate makes 35 mistakes for each subject, which means that there are 35 opportunities to shock. The confederate surreptitiously turns off the shock and therefore receives none. He secretly watches how much shock is given, and for very high levels he gasps or groans appropriately.

The apparatus is shown in Figure 22.6. The subject, playing the role of teacher, presents patterns of stimuli to the accomplice, who responds by pressing one of the two response switches. The two lights on the stimulus-control panel tell the subject whether the accomplice is correct or not. If the response is correct, the subject switches on the "correct" light; if the response is wrong, he presses one of the 10 shock buttons.

The intensity of electric shock increases steeply from button 1 to button 10. The subject is first given shock from buttons 1, 2, 3, and 5 so that he will know the painfulness of the shock he later delivers. The shock from button 1 can barely be felt; that from button 2 is mild; that from button 3 hurts; and that from button 5 is rather painful. He is told that the intensity increases at the same rate for buttons 6 through 10. By extrapolation the shock from button 10 would knock the victim out of his chair, but these circuits are not even connected. Fuses protect against any possibility of real harm, and of course the accomplice does not actually receive the electric shock.

Pain sensitivity is one determinant of the intensity of shocks administered (the greater the sensitivity, the less intense the shock

Figure 22.6 Aggression machine (Buss, 1961).

given later), and it must be controlled. Each subject rates the shock from button 5 on a scale ranging from "Can't Feel It" to "Extremely Painful." If the rating is either extremely high or extremely low, the subject is told that there has been some "drift" in the apparatus and that it must be reset. A rheostat is then adjusted, lowering the voltage for pain-sensitive subjects and raising it for pain-insensitive subjects. Shock is again administered from buttons 1, 2, 3, and 5, and again the subject rates the shock from button 5. The rare subject who does not then rate it in the middle range is not used in the research. This procedure has been found to eliminate the relationship between pain sensitivity and intensity of shock (the correlation was −.01).

The delivery of electric shock to another person is certainly punishment, but why call it aggression if the subject is so instructed? It is true that the subject is instructed to give shock, but only as a signal that the victim's response is incorrect. All the subject need do is give shock from button 1 or 2 (not noxious), and he fulfills his obligation as experimenter. Shock from buttons 3 and higher deliver painful stim-

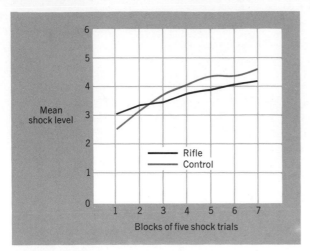

Figure 22.7 *Effect of firing a weapon on aggression in the laboratory (Buss et al., 1972).*

uli, and they are clearly more intense than is needed merely to signal an incorrect response. The situation is analogous to a parent disciplining his child or a teacher criticizing his student's work, and the delivery of punishment more intense than is warranted by the social role should be called by its proper name, aggression.

The aggression machine and its modifications have helped to standardize research on human aggression in the laboratory. One study on the effect of firing a weapon will illustrate the results in yields (Buss et al., 1972). Men in an experimental group first fired a small rifle at a target in the laboratory and then were given 35 opportunities to shock (in their role as experimenter). A control group were given 35 opportunities to shock, without first firing the weapon.

The 35 shocks were grouped into 7 blocks of 5 each, and their intensities were recorded (see Figure 22.7). The Rifle (experimental) subjects started off with a higher level of shock intensity, but the Control subjects caught up and surpassed them. The differences between the two groups were small and may be attributed to chance. In brief, this experiment demonstrated that merely firing a weapon does not intensify aggression.

ANTECEDENTS OF AGGRESSION. Instrumental aggression can be set in motion by a wide variety of incentives or by competition (see Table 22.9).[8] Whenever there is a conflict over dominance, aggression is a likely response. Whenever there is a

[8] *Like any instrumental behavior, aggression can be learned in various ways, including instrumental conditioning and imitation (see Chapters 14 and 16).*

reinforcer possessed by one person and desired by another, the probability of aggression increases. It is not that aggression is inevitable, for nonaggressive responses often achieve the reinforcer or the victory in competition. The problem is that in the usual nature of things aggression, more than any competing response, tends to *guarantee* achieving the desired goal. This holds for animals as well as for men, the difference being that men tend to regulate aggression through codes and laws.

The antecedents of angry aggression are more restricted, in the main consisting of frustration and attack. *Frustration* may be defined so broadly as to include both stimulus conditions (*any* failure to achieve satisfaction) and emotional reactions ("I feel frustrated"). This will not do. We cannot have one term, *frustration,* refer to both a stimulus and a response; it would lead to statements such as, "I feel frustrated because I am being frustrated." Therefore we shall restrict the term *frustration* to stimulus events and exclude emotional reactions.

This restriction removes ambiguity, but frustration still comprises a variety of events: *the blocking of behavior that has previously led to reinforcers.* The blocking can occur in any part of the sequence of (1) instrumental response, (2) presentation of the reinforcer, and (3) consummatory response. Consider the behavior of a thirsty student who attempts to obtain a soft drink from a dispenser. The instrumental response is depositing coins in the appropriate slot; he might be blocked by having insufficient money. The reinforcer is the cold drink; he might be blocked if the machine jams and the drink fails to appear. The consummatory response is drinking; he might be blocked if the drink slipped or was knocked to the ground.

Thus there are three different aspects in a behavioral sequence that might involve frustration. When a person is prevented from reaching his goal, he usually seeks an alternative route. He may become angry and perhaps aggress, but these are less likely than persistent attempts to solve the problem by *non*aggressive means. In fact, the temporary blocking of behavior is the major stimulus for problem-solving behavior: if there were no frustration, there would be no problem to solve.

An emphasis on frustration as an antecedent of aggression dates back to the *frustration-aggression* hypothesis of Dollard et al. (1939). They assumed that frustration inevitably leads to some form of aggression. In the face of strong criticism, the hypothesis was amended to read that frustration leads to many types of responses, including aggression (Miller, 1941). But it was also asserted that all aggression is caused by frustration, and

this hypothesis flies in the face of strong opposing data. In both humans and animals, aggression is easily elicited by attack, and an attack in no way constitutes a frustration. Frustration is only *one* of the antecedents and by no means the most potent one (Buss, 1969a).

The most powerful inciter of aggression is attack itself. An early experiment (Gillespie, 1961) demonstrated that attack elicited more intense aggression and did so more consistently than frustration, but the measures of aggression were indirect. Later experiments with the aggression machine confirmed that attack elicits more aggression than does frustration (Geen & Berkowitz, 1967; Gentry, 1970).

Clearly, attack by means of insult or physical aggression is a stronger antecedent of aggression than is frustration. Some of our urban riots have been interpreted as stemming from frustration suffered by the ghetto residents. This interpretation appears to be mistaken on two counts. First, it neglects many ghettoes that have had no riots in spite of many frustrations. Second, it fails to consider incidents not only of police brutality but also of consistent insult and derogation directed toward blacks. Martin Luther King's assassination was widely regarded by blacks as an attack on all of them, and the ensuing riots were more widespread than any before or since. The lesson seems clear, at least for this country in these times: when searching for the determinants of aggression, seek out attack as the principal antecedent.

INHIBITION OF AGGRESSION. The control of aggression occupies an important place in socializing children, and considerable effort is expended in attempting to inhibit it. For the most part, aggression can be inhibited by punishment, prosocial training, codes of morality, and the affects of shame and guilt.[9] Punishment as an inhibitor of aggression deserves some comment.

Punishment can inhibit any response it follows, and aggression is no exception. But the situation is complicated by the special relationship between aggression and punishment: when a person is punished, he is being attacked. Attack, as we have seen, is the most potent antecedent of aggression. Therefore the inhibiting effects of pun-

---

[9] *These inhibitors of aggression will be discussed in the next chapter.*

ishment are countered by its inciting effect. Imitation further complicates the effects of punishment. The punisher serves as a model whose behavior may subsequently be copied by the punished person: the attempt to *reduce* aggressive behavior being punished.

In brief, the inhibiting effects of punishment may be canceled or even outweighed by (1) its attacking aspects, which may incite anger and aggression, and (2) its modeling aspects, which may lead to imitative aggression. One solution is to employ punishment that does not attack. Thus the aggressor can be denied privileges, have affection withdrawn, or be rejected from a group. These are certainly aversive conditions, but the attacking aspects are minimized and there is less incitement to anger and aggression.

Another solution, if physical punishment must be used on children, is to use a response that is difficult to imitate. When a parent slaps, beats, or whips a child, these behaviors can easily be copied by the child. But spanking is difficult for a child to imitate on two grounds. First, it has (or should have, if done correctly) a ritualistic quality that is absent in everyday aggression. Second, most children would find it difficult to sprawl their victim in a position appropriate for spanking. Summing up, if aggression is to be punished, the punishment should be as nonaggressive as possible, ritualistic, and difficult to imitate.

CATHARSIS. The concept of catharsis is part of a hydraulic model of personality. The underlying notion is that impulses or tendencies build up and demand release. Thus the tendency to aggress might escalate like fluid in a reservoir, with the pressure building until the impulses burst through. Once the reservoir is thus drained, the pressure is temporarily lowered. This model has been adopted by both psychoanalysts and some ethologists. Lorenz (1966*b*), for example, believes that aggressive tensions build up in both animals released. In this formulation, any aggressive act is a *catharsis,* lowering the tendency to aggress subsequently.

There is evidence that when angry persons are allowed to aggress, their autonomic arousal subsides quicker (Hokanson et al., 1963, 1966, 1968). Thus aggression apparently reduces *anger* level. Is there also a drop in the tendency to aggress?

The answer here is a definite *no.* If an aggressive response has any effect on subsequent aggression, it is to *elevate* it, not reduce it (for reviews of relevant research, see Buss, 1961, and Berkowitz, 1964). The conclusions of a more recent review of research on catharsis are apt:

The traditional energy model of aggression is clearly inadequate to account for many of the findings I have reported here. Not only is this conventional analysis much too simple, but it has also impeded recognition of the important role played by environmental stimuli and learning in aggressive behavior. Above all, this energy model and the associated catharsis doctrine have helped to justify the expression of aggression and have delayed our recognition of an important social principle: Aggression is all too likely to lead us to still more aggression.

(BERKOWITZ, 1970, P. 6)

Violence and the Nature of Man

In recent years there has been much hue and cry about violence in this country. Some commentators, pointing to assassinations, kidnappings, and riots, have claimed that this nation is becoming more violent. Like all newsworthy comments, this one has been enlarged and reverberated by the mass media until is appears to be no less than common sense. But the claim is probably false. This nation has always had its share of violence, and there have been assassinations, kidnappings, and riots throughout the history of the country. And we have practiced something akin to genocide on the Indians whose lands we pirated. To suggest that violence is greater now than in the past requires that we ignore our history.

Thus we are probably as violent as we have always been. Two radically different explanations have been offered for the prevalence of aggression. The first assumes that man has an instinct to aggress (Freud, 1927; Lorenz, 1966*b*). This assumption strongly appeals to those who believe that man is basically animallike, with all the motivations of animals. Ethologists are especially fond of citing evidence of animal aggression and then drawing analogies to human aggression.

The theory that man is instinctively aggressive

appears to rest on faulty analogizing. As indicated earlier in this chapter, as well as in Chapter 7, the evolutionary trend is toward diminishing the role of instinct. As we ascend the phyletic ladder toward man, specific and built-in programs yield to diffuse programs that depend mainly on individual experiences.

The second explanation for the prevalence of human aggression is that it is *learned*. Our society reinforces aggression in many ways. Many political candidates have won elections by unfairly attacking their opponents. Senator Joseph McCarthy made a career in the 1950s by accusing many citizens of being "soft on communism," and more recently Spiro Agnew achieved notoriety by attacking (among others) the mass media.

We socialize boys to be aggressive. In spite of some changes in the last decade, the stereotyped masculine male is tough, competitive, hardhitting, dominant, and in a word, *aggressive.* The association of aggressiveness with masculinity guarantees that many men will be aggressive.

Another reason for our aggressiveness may be the mass media. Newspapers, magazines, books, radio, movies, and television are filled with violence. Psychologists have documented the fact that observing violence in films leads to imitative aggression (Bandura et al., 1961; Berkowitz, 1965, 1971; Hartmann, 1969; Eron et al., 1972; Liebert & Neale, 1972). The effects of violence, especially as portrayed on television, are complex and depend on several factors: (1) the age, gender, and socioeconomic status of the subjects, (2) the context of the violence—as part of realistic fiction, cartoons, or real-life reports; (3) the justification for violence; (4) the reward or punishment of those engaging in violence; and (5) the frequency of violence. Whatever these complexities, a national commission has concluded that the mass media foster violence, the general effect being, ". . . to extend the behavioral and attitudinal boundaries of acceptable violence beyond legal and social norms currently espoused by a majority of Americans" (Lange et al., 1969, p. 375).

Thus it is possible to account for prevalence of aggression in this country without invoking an instinct to aggress. We offer both children and adults a variety and profusion of aggressive models. We generously reward aggression, and our national myths sustain pride in an image of

aggressiveness ("We have never lost a war"). These facts do not bode well for any immediate attempts to reduce violence, but they surely obviate the need to invoke instinct as a cause.

Competence

It is widely assumed that we are all lazy and will not work unless tempted by incentives or goaded by aversive stimulation. Consider a choice between working for a reward and merely doing nothing, letting it drop into one's lap. The prediction is straightforward: a preference for doing nothing. But experiments with rats have demonstrated that the prediction is wrong. When allowed a choice—press a bar to obtain food versus merely eating the food from a cup—rats prefer to work rather than "freeload" (Jensen, 1963; Neuringer, 1969).

Perhaps rats are different from humans in this respect: humans, being more intelligent, know a good thing when they see it and will therefore freeload rather than work. This argument was answered by Singh (1970, 1972), who gave boys and girls a choice of working for marbles or merely receiving them without working. The children preferred to work rather than freeload. Nor are adults essentially different. Some politicians have claimed that those on welfare are simply too lazy to seek work. This assumption has been shown to be false, the vast majority of welfare clients being ill, handicapped, mothers of large families, and in general *unable* to work. Furthermore, research in industrial situations has shown that workers can be motivated much more by meaningful work than by better pay or shorter hours (McGregor, 1960).

The Concept of Competence

The preference for work may be explained by the concept of *competence*. This notion was suggested by White (1959) to include the drives of exploration, manipulation, and curiosity. These are the educational drives that are necessary for organisms like man, in whom there are few (if any) preprogramed tendencies designed to meet basic needs (see Chapter 7). With so much to be learned by each person, we should not be surprised to discover in man the motivation to interact with and master the environment.

Interestingly, this motivation does not have the driving urgency of such drives as hunger or sex. As White (1959) points out,

. . . it might therefore seem paradoxical that the interests of competence should be so much entrusted to times of play and leisurely exploration. There is good reason to suppose, however, that a strong drive would be precisely the wrong arrangement to secure a flexible, knowledgeable power of transaction with the environment. Strong drives cause us to learn certain lessons well, but they do not create maximum familiarity with our surroundings. (PP. 326–327)

This point harks back to several facts mentioned earlier in the book: (1) a highly aroused organism may become disorganized (Chapter 21); (2) traumatic avoidance learning leads to very strong inhibitions on exploratory behavior (Chapter 15); and (3) infants will not leave their mothers to explore unless they are secure and thus in a state of low or medium arousal (Chapter 20). In brief, competence motivation rarely competes with the more potent drives that relate to problems of survival of the individual or the species.[10] Rather, it comes to the fore during periods when such drives are at an ebb and make few demands on the organism.

Developmental Aspects

Part of socialization consists of directing the child toward greater independence, but in many areas the child wishes to "do for himself" before the parent begins to apply pressure. Thus young children may concentrate and persist in play activities without any parental reinforcement, and especially during the second year of life there is a strong tendency to resist being helped. The activities called *play* have an important function:

[10] *A hungry rat that is offered food in a novel environment will explore before it eats, but its apparent curiosity is more wariness in the face of possible danger than a simple manifestation of exploratory drive.*

The child appears to be occupied with the agreeable task of developing an effective familiarity with his environment. This involves discovering the effects he can have on the environment and the effects the environment will have on him. To the extent that these results are preserved by learning, they build up an increased competence in dealing with the environment. The child's play can thus be viewed as serious business, though to him it is merely something that is interesting and fun to do. (WHITE, 1959, P. 321)

As an educational drive, competence emphasizes the exploratory and manipulatory aspects of behavior. The complete picture includes the more perceptual side of things, as manifested in curiosity drive (see Chapter 7). The more cognitive aspects have been investigated by Piaget and his followers (see Chapter 17), and Hunt (1965) has suggested a developmental sequence of the young child's cognitive approach to his environment (see Table 22.10).

Developmental Outcomes

As the young child interacts with his environment, he learns something about his place in the larger scheme of things, and his competence motivation becomes shaped by socialization agents. These events lead to a variety of developmental outcomes, of which we shall discuss three: control, achievement, and self-actualization.

LOCUS OF CONTROL. Early in development the child learns to walk. Later he acquires control of his bowels and bladder, and he rapidly masters language. These events, together with continued exploration and manipulation of the environment, should gradually instill a feeling of confidence in his own ability. If a child is allowed contact with graded problems, he will see that his mastery extends to more and more difficult tasks. If he is praised for his efforts, he gains confidence in his ability to act. If his environment is relatively stable, he will become more and more aware of the contingency between his behavior and its consequences. Such a child will believe that the world is reasonably orderly and that he can influence the course of events.

On the other hand, if the young child's immediate environment is unstable and chaotic, he will

Table 22.10
Development of Informational Interaction
(Hunt, 1965, 1969)

STAGES	BEHAVIOR
1	Reacts to changes in stimulation
2	Attempts to maintain contact with *familiar* stimuli
3	Becomes interested in novel stimuli
4	Acquires information through language and perception of reality

learn that many outcomes are uncertain at best. If he is not rewarded for his instrumental behavior or if he has little ability at games with toys, then he will fail to develop confidence in his own instrumental behavior. He will feel helpless and uncertain, unable to control what happens, and at the mercy of an unpredictable fate.

There are two extremes of a dimension that has been labeled *locus of control* (Rotter, 1966). At one end are individuals who firmly believe that their own actions determine what happens to them. Their locus of control is *internal* and they label as *true* statements like, "What happens to me is my own doing."

At the other end are those whose locus of control is *external*. They cannot rely on their own ability, and they believe that their plans will come to nothing. Their future is determined by luck, chance, or fate, and they label as true the statement, "Most people don't realize the extent to which their lives are controlled by accidental happenings." In brief, an internal or external locus of control, which may be a consistent and enduring disposition, is one outcome of the impact of early environment on an individual's competence motivation (see Rotter, 1971, for a review of research).

ACHIEVEMENT. Competence motivation can develop in the direction of social interaction, and this path is usually taken by women.[11] More than men, they use their abilities to teach, to nurse, to give comfort, to raise children, and in general to offer nurturance to others. Another more or less feminine tendency is to develop sensitivity to the esthetic aspects of life: flowers, music, art, clothes, and so on.

The more masculine mode is to direct one's abilities toward success in competition, excellence in whatever tasks are undertaken, and the meeting of challenges (whether from others or the environment). Pursuing success, overcoming obstacles to reach a goal, and competing against a standard of excellence all fall under the heading of *achievement motivation* (McClelland et al., 1953). Its manifestations abound in everyday life. Boys and young men learn to compete in games and athletics, and men are expected to allow nothing to interfere with success in business. Men are expected to work hard, persist, and show courage in meeting competition. When there are no competitors, they compete against some standard, as in challenging par on a golf course.

[11] *We are referring to traditional roles in today's society. In spite of changes by a minority of young persons, traditional masculine and feminine roles predominate.*

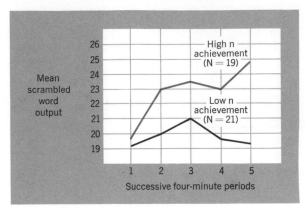

Figure 22.8 Performance of high and low achievers (Lowell, 1952).

The origins of achievement motivation have been spelled out by Heckhausen (1967). It starts of course with competence motivation. As the child masters tasks, he gradually becomes pleased not only with solving the problem but also with himself for doing so. During the fourth year of life, the child develops self-attitudes based on his success and failures. His native abilities are important, but so is the rigor of the standards set by parents and later, by school authorities. Gradually, the generally successful child begins to seek challeges and test himself; his achievement motivation increases. The unsuccessful child, lacking reinforcement for competing, gradually avoids the risks of competition; his achievement motivation drops, and he tends to fear failure.

Research on achievement motivation, almost exclusively with men and boys, has proliferated in a number of directions, including industry and the economic development of nations (see McClelland, 1961). An early experiment illustrates how achievement motivation has been studied. Lowell (1952) had subjects make up stories in response to pictures (the Thematic Apperception Test). The stories were analyzed for achievement themes and the subjects divided into high and low achievers. Then each subject was presented with scrambled words (for example, TESA for EAST) and told to unscramble them. The high achievers started out at the same rate as the low achievers,

but they increased their rate rapidly, whereas the low achievers showed little improvement (see Figure 22.8).

High achievers also volunteer more for experiments, take a more active role in college, try harder to obtain knowledge of results, and consider themselves more responsible for outcomes (Atkinson, 1964). This last, suggesting that high achievers have an internal locus of control, should come as no surprise. They believe that they will win, and that they can influence the course of events or they would not be high achievers. Though research on achievement and research on locus of control emphasize different aspects of competence motivation, they seem to converge on the belief that one can effect changes in the environment.

SELF-ACTUALIZATION. A third and related outcome of competence motivation is *self-actualization*. This concept, which looms large in *humanistic psychology,* was formulated by Maslow (1943). He attempted to establish a hierarchy of needs, from lowest to highest: physiological, safety, love, esteem, and self-actualization. After the first four needs are satisfied, the individual is free to self-actualize. Maslow's description of self-actualization reveals its relationship to competence motivation:

It refers to the desire for self-fulfillment, for full flowering of the capacities and potentialities of the person, to the tendency for him to become actualized in what he is potentially. This might be phrased as the desire to become more and more what one is, to become everything that one is capable of becoming.

The specific form that these needs will take will of course vary tremendously from person to person. In one individual it may take the form of the desire to be an ideal mother, in another it may be expressed athletically and in still another it may be to paint pictures or create inventions. (1943, P. 384)

Note that the self-actualizer uses his abilities in effecting changes in the environment—through creating new products or works of art, through competing where skill decides the issue, or through acts of social good. This is the best we can expect from competence motivation, and for most persons it is an ideal rather than a reality.

chapter 23

self-control and morality

Three reaction systems — stimulus-response theory — timing and intensity of punishment — problems concerning punishment — impersonal and personal punishment — cognitive theory — moral development — moral judgments — Kohlberg's theory — suffering and separation — development of guilt and shame — perspective

A major aspect of socialization is the acquisition of self-control. Infants are not expected to exercise any control over their own impulses or behavior, but, starting with toilet training, children are expected to control more and more of their behavior as they mature. Such self-monitoring is necessary for the effective functioning of groups of persons. No society can rely completely on the "cop on the corner" to inhibit behavior deemed deviant or harmful by the society. Its citizens must be taught to inhibit responses harmful to others even in the absence of a punishing agent.

In Western societies the acquisition of self-control has traditionally fallen within the province of morality. The child is taught a code of ethics by parents, teachers, and clergy, and this code is expected to govern his behavior. It is a well-known but unacknowledged fact that most adults mouth the moral code but suit their behavior to self-interest. But some members of society do act entirely ethically, and most of us are occasionally deterred by moral considerations.

Linked to morality are the affective reactions of *guilt* and, to a lesser extent, *shame.* These negative self-reactions are needed to complement the rules that make up the moral code. When rules are broken, there must be aversive consequences, and in the absence of punishing agents, the vio-

Table 23.1
Three Approaches to Self-Control

THEORY	REACTION SYSTEMS EMPHASIZED	MEANS OF ACHIEVING SELF-CONTROL	RESULT OF LOSS OF SELF-CONTROL
Stimulus-response	Instrumental	Instrumental learning	Fear of punishment
Cognitive	Cognitive	Learning of concepts, codes, and rules	Cognitive conflict
Dynamic	Affective	Identification, "internalization"	Shame, guilt

lator must punish himself. Thus a guilt reaction to transgression results in the condemnation of *self* as sinful, evil, and unworthy.

Both moral codes and guilt may be regarded as examples of *internal* control. The child learns a set of rules that he must apply to his own behavior, and he learns a set of self-reactions—punishment to be administered by himself to himself after breaking the rules. But self-control need not be *internal,* for it may be achieved through *external* punishment. The contingencies of behavior (antecedents and consequences of responses) can be arranged so that the child learns that it is *never* safe to transgress. If certain responses inevitably lead to punishment even when made in the absence of a punishing agent, these responses are unlikely to occur. The individual will inhibit them even in the absence of the "cop on the corner," and such inhibition is the essence of self-control. Thus self-control can be achieved *externally,* through manipulation of the consequences of behavior. This is as true for animals when properly trained as for humans. Human self-control is distinguished by the cognitions of moral codes and the affective reactions (guilt and shame) usually associated with them.

Thus three reaction systems are involved in self-control:[1] instrumental, cognitive, and affective.

[1] *The four reaction systems, first mentioned in Chapter 1, are instrumental, affective, cognitive, and perceptual. Only the first three are relevant here.*

There are three theoretical approaches to self-control, each emphasizing a different reaction system (see Table 23.1). The *stimulus-response* approach focuses on the *learning* of self-control through punishment for socially forbidden responses. Imitation learning supplements instrumental conditioning in building up inhibition. The *cognitive* approach focuses on the *rules* governing behavior, the concepts of morality mastered by the child during the course of development. The emphasis is on *intellectual* factors: the child's understanding of the way abstract concepts affect his and other's behavior. Finally, the *dynamic* approach focuses on *affects:* the acquisition of negative self-reactions and their relation to transgressions. Here the emphasis is on the mood and emotional state of the sinner and how these might deter future sinful behavior.

The Stimulus-Response Approach

This approach, as might be expected, uses *behavioral* criteria of self-control: resisting temptation or engaging in *prosocial* behavior. The first one is more commonly used by researchers, and in the typical experiment a subject is tempted to make a response that satisfies an immediate want but is socially or morally wrong.

Almost all the research has been conducted with children as subjects and with attractive toys

Figure 23.1 *A typical experiment of self control (Aronfreed and Reber, 1965).*

as the temptation. An experiment by Aronfreed and Reber (1965) illustrates the procedure (see Figure 23.1). There are two toys, one attractive and the other unattractive; the toys are changed on each trial. The child is told to pick up one of the two toys and tell the experimenter all about it. The last instruction is that some of the toys are only for older boys and that he is not to choose these. Then there are nine training trials during which the experimenter says, "No, that's for older boys," when the child picks up the attractive toy. After training, the experimenter leaves the room on a pretext, allowing the child to be alone with two new toys, one attractive and one unattractive. The measure of self-control is resistance to temptation: does the child pick up the attractive toy and if so, how soon does he do so?

This experiment (Aronfreed & Reber, 1965) concerned the *timing* of punishment. In one experimental group the child was punished as he reached for the attractive toy (*early* punishment); in a second experimental group he was punished after handling the toy for two or three seconds (*late* punishment); a control group received no punishment. Then each child was left alone for five minutes and observed surreptitiously. All of the *control* subjects picked up the attractive toy. The punished subjects showed some resistance to temptation: one-third of the late-punished boys

refrained from touching the attractive toy, as did two-thirds of the early-punished boys.

Timing of Punishment

That the *timing* of punishment should affect resistance to temptation should surprise no one. Earlier we mentioned that punishment is most effective when it is immediate, and delay of punishment may weaken it to the point of ineffectiveness (see Chapter 15). A response sequence may be divided into an early preparatory phase (reaching for the attractive toy) and a later consummatory phase (handling and playing with the toy). As Aronfreed and Reber (1965) demonstrated, punishment *early* in the sequence links aversiveness with the *initiation* of the act and is therefore more effective on later occasions. Punishment *late* in the sequence is less effective because it is opposed by the rewarding effects of consummatory behavior (playing with the toy). Thus the timing of punishment determines which aspects of the response sequence will be suppressed (see Figure 23.2). If the punishment is early, the child will inhibit *initiating* of the response. If the punishment is late, the child may not inhibit the response but may become fearful (of the impend-

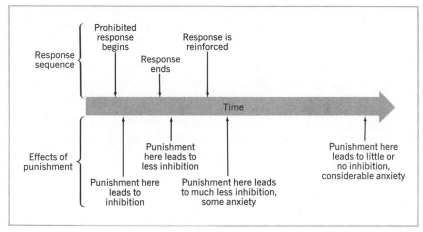

Figure 23.2 *Timing of punishment.*

ing punishment) after he makes the forbidden response.[2]

This issue confronts parents and child caretakers with a serious problem. Transgressions are usually discovered some time after they occur, and both everyday observations and laboratory research agree that it serves little purpose to punish the child hours later — other than to allow the parent to vent his anger. The solution is to use the child's own cognitive abilities. A child sufficiently mature to be punished for transgressions already possesses excellent imagery. The parent can use the child's imagery to reinstate the situation leading to the transgression. Thus a parent might ask his child to imagine that he is opening the desk drawer in his father's study and about to steal the dollar bill that is lying there. When the child can visualize this scene, the parent promptly slaps the child's hand. From the child's point of view, this is an unfair use of his own imagination. From the parent's point of view, it is the only means of turning back the clock and rendering the punishment effective by making it contingent

on the *initiation* of the forbidden behavior. Such use of imagery has also produced remarkable therapeutic results in dealing with phobias and other neurotic behavior (see Chapter 27).

Intensity of Punishment

The stronger the punishment, the more a response is inhibited. In the extreme case, traumatic avoidance conditioning may permanently eliminate a response (see Chapter 15). Research with children in temptation situations has confirmed earlier research with animals and adult humans. For example, Parke and Walters (1967) used a combination of rebuke ("No, that's for the other boy") and an annoying buzzer whenever their subject touched a forbidden toy. The buzzer was either very loud (intense punishment) or softer (mild punishment). Then the subjects, boys of 6–8 years, were left alone with the toys for 15 minutes. Those who had received high-intensity punishment resisted temptation more and for longer periods than those who had received mild punishment. This finding confirmed earlier research (Aronfred & Leff, 1963) and was in turn confirmed by later research (Parke, 1969). *Stronger punishment does lead to greater resistance in temptation.*

---

[2] *See Aronfreed (1966), Parke and Walters (1967), Walters and Parke (1967), Parke (1969), and Hoffman (1970) for confirmation of the effects of timing on punishment. That these researchers study the effects of the timing of punishment does not mean that they are adherents of the stimulus-response approach.*

Problems Concerning Punishment

Punishment unequivocally inhibits behavior, but it does not always lead to *self*-control. The child may learn when it is safe to transgress and when it is not. When he is likely to be caught and punished, the child may resist temptation; when punishment is unlikely, the child tends to give in to temptation. The learning of such a discrimination obviously defeats self-control: the child inhibits behavior only part of the time.

One solution to this problem is to make punishment inevitable, to convince the child that it is never safe to transgress. Thus parents can become expert detectives, rooting out all transgressions and solving all crimes in the household. Did the child watch television when he was forbidden? Feel the television set to ascertain if it is still warm. Did the child get into the cookie jar? Count the cookies before and after. Given a sufficiently determined parent, the young child can be convinced that it is never safe to transgress, and he may exercise self-control. But older children become crafty, and parents cannot maintain a sufficiently high level of sleuthing. In such a context, the child must eventually win, and when he learns how to escape detection, inhibition of behavior occurs only when there is a "cop on the corner."

One parental alternative is to turn to religion. With appropriate religious training, children can be taught that they are continually under God's surveillance ("His eye is on the sparrow"). The reward for virtue is Heaven, the punishment for sin is Hell. It is never safe to transgress, for all behavior is being transcribed in the Book for the final evaluation on Judgment Day.

In previous eras—and even today in some parts of the country—this Fundamentalist faith was widely taught and believed. We can only conjecture how effective it was in sustaining self-control, but we do know that churches have never lacked sinners. It is difficult today for children to believe in a literal Hell, and the notion of an omniscient, all-seeing God is too abstract and far removed from everyday behavior. No doubt such beliefs lead to self-control in some individuals, but for most of us Hell proves no deterrent to transgression.

It appears, then, that we are forced to reconsider punishment. Perhaps better detection (removing "safe" transgressions) and more intense punishment are the answers. But such answers are unacceptable on two grounds. First, a police state would reduce transgressions, but only at the cost of freedoms cherished by most of us. Second, the toll in increased anxiety would be formidable. One of the side effects of punishment is fear: fear of the tempting situations and fear of punishing agents. Children are disciplined mainly by their parents, and severe punishment may lead to fear of avoidance of the parents. Another side effect is anger, and intense punishment may cause a child to become hostile and rebellious.

Thus there are serious problems associated with the use of punishment to achieve self-control. This does not mean that it should never be used, only that it should be used with caution. The real solution may lie in the kind of punishment employed. All punishment is noxious to the recipient, but some varieties may be more effective in achieving self-control.

So far we have considered only physical and verbal punishment (see Table 23.2). Physical punishment by parents or caretakers is ordinarily limited to slapping and spanking; verbal punishment usually goes no further than criticism, insulting remarks, and threats. The third variety of impersonal punishment, *withdrawing rewards,* is usually successful in inhibiting forbidden behavior, but, like the other kinds of impersonal punishment, it usually does not lead to self-control. Unlike insults or spankings, depriving a child of privileges does not make him fearful, and anger that does occur is likely to be less intense.

The remaining two kinds of punishment are *personal* in that both require a social bond. In punishment by *rejection,* the child is temporarily cast out of the group, as, for example, when he is told to leave the dinner table because he is unfit to continue eating with the family. In punishment by *withdrawal of affection,* the child is told that the parent temporarily does not like him. Both kinds of personal punishment run the risk of either angering or depressing the child, but no punishment is free of negative side effects. As with any disciplinary technique the issue is whether gains in socialization—in this instance the development of self-control—are worth the price of the child's discomfort.

Personal punishment may be more effective than impersonal punishment in developing self-

Table 23.2
Types of Punishment of Children

Impersonal	Physical	Slapping, spanking
	Verbal	Threats, criticism, derogation
	Withdrawal of reward	No television, no allowance
Personal	Rejection	Removal from the group
	Withdrawal of affection	"I don't like you any more."

control, perhaps for two related reasons. First, the punishment usually lasts longer: a child can be denied a place in the group or parental affection for rather long durations. Second, the end of the punishment can be made contingent on a particular response of the child: admitting wrong-doing, self-punishment, or even a compensatory response to make up for the harm done. But this issue, as well as the issue of affect (fear, anger, and depression), is taking us well beyond the stimulus-response approach, and we shall defer further discussion of it until after discussing the cognitive approach to self-control.

The Cognitive Approach

The young child is essentially without morality. Over the course of childhood his understanding of codes of conduct deepens, and by adolescence he can comprehend the more abstract aspects of justice in the affairs of men. As Piaget (1948) has commented, he moves from earlier *egocentrism* and *concreteness in action* to a more dispassionate view and an understanding of morality as a set of abstract ideas concerning justice and equity.

Piaget studied the development of children's understanding of moral codes in two ways. The first was to describe various transgressions and discover why the child thought the act was wrong. The child might be asked which is more wrong: breaking five cups accidentally while trying to

open a door or breaking one cup while pilfering jam from the cupboard. The second was to interview children in detail about their marble games: how the rules originated, why they should be adhered to, and whether they might be changed.

Six Aspects of Moral Development

On the basis of these two kinds of observations, Piaget outlined six aspects of the development of moral judgments.[3] Piaget believed, probably correctly, that mature concepts of morality begin to develop between eight and ten years of age. Accordingly, for purposes of exposition, we will contrast the moral judgments of younger children (below eight years) and older children (above ten years) (see Table 23.3).

1. The intentions of the transgressor are unimportant for young children, most of whom say the boy who breaks five cups accidentally is worse than the boy who breaks one while getting at the jam; older children (nine years and beyond) say the one with sticky fingers is more to blame.

2. With regard to relativism, young children are *absolutists* and are unable to tolerate ambiguity. They insist that there is only one correct viewpoint and that an act is either right or wrong. Older children realize that there are different perspec-

[3] *There are actually eleven aspects, but, following Kohlberg (1964), we shall include only the six that have shown clear developmental trends.*

Table 23.3
Development of Judgments of Morality

ASPECT	YOUNGER CHILD (below eight years)	OLDER CHILD (above ten years)
1. Intentionality	Act is bad because of its consequences	Act is bad because of intent to do harm
2. Relativism	Act is either right or wrong; adult view is always right	Can see degrees of right and wrong, as well as diverse points of view
3. Basis of evil	Act is bad because it leads to punishment	Act is bad because it breaks a rule or causes harm
4. Reciprocity	No consideration or placing of self in role of others, no gratitude	Consideration and placing self in role of others, ideal reciprocity
5. Restitution	Severe punishment, no restitution	Mild punishment, restitution to the victim, hope of reforming the sinner
6. Causality	Misfortunes are seen as punishments for wrong-doing	No confusion between accidental misfortune and punishment

tives, and they are aware of two different answers to the question: who is worse, the person who cheats on an exam or the one who deliberately lets him copy?

3. In judging morality, *punishment* is uppermost for young children, who judge an act as evil because it is punished. Older children recognize that an action may be good even if it is unfairly punished; bad acts are those that harm others or break rules.

4. Young children are *self-centered* and locked into their own selfish concerns. If they are sinned against, their reply is based on anticipating retalia-

tion or favorable treatment. In concrete terms, this is "an eye for an eye." Older children can comprehend an *ideal reciprocity*, which requires a denial of self-interest or at the very least, being able to take another's viewpoint.

5. The aftermath of transgression should be *automatic* and *severe* punishment, according to young children. Older children focus more on the sinner and the possibility of his eventual *reform;* thus punishment should be tempered by the requirements of reeducation. Older children are also concerned with restitution to the victim and therefore favor compensation by the transgressor,

rather than merely his punishment.

6. Finally, perhaps because of a Bible-oriented education, many children believe that *accidental misfortune is punishment* for past misdeeds. (This attitude has engendered such cynical adult aphorisms as, "Married persons deserve each other.") Older children recognize the accidental nature of most misfortune (and therefore would not suppose that marital trouble is punishment for past sins).

These various aspects of the child's developing morality are believed to reflect sequential stages of broad cognitive processes. As we saw in Chapter 17, cognitive development starts with an egocentric orientation, direct action, and concreteness. With increasing maturity, the child can better recognize that other viewpoints exist, his thought processes depend more on internal "operations," and he can grasp abstract rules and principles.

These broad trends have been accepted by cognitive psychologists, but some have objected on empirical grounds to the details of Piaget's theory of moral development. The leading theorist in this area is Kohlberg (1964, 1969), whose revision of Piaget's theory offers an account of the development of morality among American youngsters.

Kohlberg's Developmental Theory

Kohlberg and Kramer (1969) interviewed children, presenting them with moral dilemmas and classifying their answers. The result was a developmental sequence of six stages, which were ordered to three sequential levels: premoral, conventional morality, and self-accepted morality (see Table 23.4 p. 450).

Level I. The premoral level is so named because of the young child's *external* orientation. Standards are handed down from above (from parents and other authorities), and the penalty for disobedience is automatic, external punishment. There are two sides of the coin: avoiding punishment and seeking rewards. The first stage reflects one side of the coin, obeying rules to avoid punishment; this is aversive control of behavior. The second stage reflects the other side of the coin, conforming to achieve rewards. Now the young child actively seeks reinforcement by being good, and he believes implicitly (and insists firmly) that his favors be reciprocated. In brief, the first level con-

sists of *instrumental behavior,* as the child learns which responses are punished (stage 1) and which pay off (stage 2).

Level II. The second level reflects a more *social* orientation, with the child conforming to what is expected of him. The child is now extremely *other-directed.* In the third stage he becomes sensitive to what others think of him, and the severest punishment is disapproval by a respected adult or peer group. Now acts can be separated from intentions, and a bad act might be justified by the good intentions of the transgressor. There may be strong and persistent attempts to explain to others why they should still approve of the sinner in spite of his apparent immoral behavior.

It is a short step from avoiding disapproval from others in stage 3 to avoiding censure from institutionalized authority in stage 4. Children are taught to respect parental authority in the home, religious authority in the church, and political authority in school. An older tradition teaches respect for the law and those who enforce it; a newer tradition, outside of the usual institutions of education, teaches disrespect for many laws and those who enforce them ("policemen are *pigs*"). The clash of these majority and minority views will split the country for some time to come. If there is a single word that characterizes this second level, it is *shame.* The young person wishes not to be caught by others in a compromising situation, else he will lose their approval (stage 3). He wants to do his duty and obey the laws, lest he feel the full weight of institutionalized punishment and dishonor (stage 4).

Level III. This is the most advanced level, the one in which judgments of behavior are based on moral *principles.* But to *which* principles should the mature person appeal in evaluating behavior? There are two broad kinds, one underlying stage 5 and one underlying stage 6.

The cardinal rule of stage 5 is *social responsibility:* there are democratically oriented laws that must govern us all and to which we owe allegiance. The basic notion is one of a social contract among consenting persons, which demands conformity from those in the group. Acts are evaluated in accord with both written laws and society's welfare. Presumably, ethical judgments can be made rationally, on the basis of existing laws and codes, with an ultimate appeal to the general good.

The cardinal rule of stage 6 is the *higher law of personal conscience:* there are ethical "laws" that

Table 23.4

Classification of Moral Judgment into Levels and Stages of Development (Kohlberg, 1969)

LEVEL	BASIS OF MORAL JUDGMENT	STAGE OF DEVELOPMENT
I Premoral	Moral value resides in external, quasi-physical happenings, in bad acts, or in quasi-physical needs rather than in persons and standards.	Stage 1: Obedience and punishment orientation. Egocentric deference to superior power or prestige, or a trouble-avoiding set. Objective responsibility. Stage 2: Naively egoistic orientation. Right action is that instrumentally satisfying the self's needs and occasionally others'. Awareness of relativism of value to each actor's needs and perspective. Naive egalitarianism and orientation to exchange and reciprocity.
II Conventional morality	Moral value resides in performing good or right roles, in maintaining the conventional order and the expectancies of others.	Stage 3: Good-boy orientation. Orientation to approval and to pleasing and helping others. Conformity to stereotypical images of majority or natural role behavior, and judgment by intentions. Stage 4: Authority and social-order maintaining orientation. Orientation to "doing duty" and to showing respect for authority and maintaining the given social order for its own sake. Regard for earned expectations of others.
III Self-accepted morality	Moral value resides in conformity by the self to shared or shareable standards, rights, or duties.	Stage 5: Contractual legalistic orientation. Recognition of an arbitrary element or starting point in rules or expectations for the sake of agreement. Duty defined in terms of contract, general avoidance of violation of the will or rights of others, and majority will and welfare. Stage 6: Conscience or principle orientation. Orientation not only to actually ordained social rules but to principles of choice involving appeal to logical universality and consistency. Orientation to conscience as a directing agent and to mutual respect and trust.

transcend any human contracts or codes. These are not employed in a rational fashion against the criterion of a consensus. Each individual must judge acts according to his own scruples, using intuition rather than reasoning. This orientation rejects social contracts and established codes as a basis of morality. It argues that we must not accept man as he is but as he should be.

These differences between stages 5 and 6 may seem overly abstract or perhaps of merely academic interest, but further analysis suggests otherwise. The underlying principles lead not only to differences in *judging* behavior but also to basic differences in life style. The *social* orientation of stage 5 is typical of the well-socialized, over-30 adult who has "made it" in today's world and who defends its institutions as rational and organized for the general welfare. The *personal* orientation of stage 6 is typical of the idealistic, radical younger person who is painfully aware of all the injustice of current laws and institutions and who breaks "unjust laws."

Research Report

The relationship between ethical principles and political attitudes has been demonstrated by Hogan (1970). He presented college and non-college adults with 16 moral dilemmas, of which the following is an example.

T. E. Lawrence, author, historian, and special English agent, fought with the Arabs against the Turks during World War I. The ragged Arab army which he advised camped for an evening at an oasis. During the night one of his most trusted sergeants, Hamed the Moor, was alleged to have murdered a member of an Arab tribe taking part in the army. The relatives of the dead man, according to the ancient desert code, demanded Hamed's death.

The events surrounding the Arab's killing were quite muddled, yet due to the circumstances there was no chance for a trial. Hamed fervently declared his innocence, and Lawrence believed him. However, Lawrence's first duty was to maintain unity in the army; and it was clear that to preserve unity Hamed had to die. Lawrence shot Hamed. (HOGAN, 1970, P. 267)

The subjects were asked whether they would justify or condemn Lawrence's act and to say why. In addition, they were asked to agree or disagree with items involving moral principles. The first set espoused personal conscience:
—Rebellion may be a sign of maturity.
—A man's conscience is a better guide to conscience than whatever the law might say.
—There are times when any man should break the rules.
—All civil laws should be judged against a higher moral law.
The second set espoused social responsibility:
—Right and wrong can be meaningfully defined only by the law.
—Without law, the life of man would be nasty, brutish, and short.
—Civil riots are always bad.
These items were given to two divergent groups of adults in the San Francisco Bay area: members of Students for a Democratic Society, the Free Speech Movement, and other left-oriented groups (political activists) versus police officers. The political activists tended to agree strongly with the first set of items and disagree with the second set; thus they took a stand based on personal conscience and a higher

law. The police officers disagreed with the first set of items and agreed strongly with the second set; thus they took a stand based on social responsibility to existing institutions.

Finally, a sample of college men was administered the above sets of ethical items and a self-report personality inventory. The relationship between the two led Hogan to conclude:

Persons whose moral appraisals are grounded on considerations which regularly transcend the dictates of law and custom may be unconventional, liberal, and progressive; however, they may also be capricious, undependable, and anticonforming. On the other hand, persons whose moral judgments are guided by rational and legal considerations are often thoughtful, considerate, and honest, yet they may also be conventional and overconforming. They have a strong need for structure and order and tend to gravitate to positions where support of rules of conduct is viewed as positive behavior.

(1970, P. 211)[4]

[4] *For similar findings, using Kohlberg's entire developmental scheme, see Haan et al. (1968).*

Comment

Both Piaget's theory and Kohlberg's extensive revision make considerable sense and impose a reasonable order on the development of moral judgments. Kohlberg's classification of sequential stages helps us to understand how children progress toward adult morality, the cognitive processes being essentially those described by Piaget (see Chapter 17). Nevertheless, the formulation has some faults.

First, children's judgments of moral situations can easily be shifted toward maturity merely by having an adult make appropriate comments as the child acts (Bandura & McDonald, 1963; Turiel, 1966). This finding suggests that the stages are not as fixed as the theory assumes and that advances in moral judgment need not await basic changes in the child's cognitions.

Second, the sequence of stages, especially the late stages of morality, is not as rigid as the theory suggests. As can be seen in the Research Report, radical college students can move from conformity to others' expectations (stage 3) directly to the personal conscience of a "higher law" (stage 6) without going through the intervening stages. Moreover, middle-class children probably advance through a different sequence than lower-class children do, and surely other societies have not only different sequences but different outcomes at adulthood.

Third, the notion of stages should not mislead us about the nature of *adult* judgments of morality. Some adults never operate at the final level of morality (stage 5 or 6), and those who do cannot maintain the level consistently:

Even the person whose conscience is capable of operating at the heights of moral philosophy will often judge alternatives of conduct on less exalted ground because he is subject to constraints of information, intensity of affect, and decision-making time.

(ARONFREED, 1968, P. 265)

Finally, though cognitions are an essential part of morality, they constitute only part of the picture. The missing parts are the *instrumental* aspects (self-control, as in resistance to temptation) and the *affective* aspects (guilt and shame).

The Dynamic Approach: Guilt and Shame

Guilt and shame are negative affects closely linked to socialization, morality, and self-control. As part of our everyday, nontechnical vocabulary they are often misused, the most common mistake being a confusion of one with the other. Thus a daughter might say, "I feel so ashamed that I did not treat my mother better while she was alive," when she obviously is experiencing guilt. Or a visi-

Guilt	Shame

Figure 23.3 Guilt versus shame.

tor might say to her hostess, "I feel so guilty about being clumsy and accidentally breaking your vase," when she obviously is experiencing shame. To clear up such confusion, the exposition will emphasize the differences between guilt and shame.[5]

Guilt and Shame Compared

Guilt and shame both are negative affects in which the person directs aversive cognitions or feelings against himself. In guilt the feeling is of sin or evil ("I am bad; I have transgressed"), whereas in shame the feeling is of embarrassment or clumsiness ("I have made a social error; I have done something really dumb"). In brief, guilt involves self-hatred, and shame involves social anxiety (see Figure 23.3). This and five other distinctions between the two affects are summarized in Table 23.5 (p. 454).

Guilt is triggered by a violation of the moral code, and except for religious dogma, there is only one kind of action that constitutes a transgression: harming someone else. The damage can be direct and against a single person, or indirect and against large groups or even society as a whole. The worst transgression and the one usually causing the most intense guilt is hurting a loved one. *Shame* is more closely tied to modesty and

failure to perform. On the one hand, there are many actions (bathing, eliminating, making love) that are strictly private, and any exposure to an audience results in acute embarrassment. On the other hand, there are situations involving failure while being watched (missing two foul shots, thereby losing the basketball game) or of being clumsy in a formal social setting (spilling soup on the lady next to you at a dinner). Both kinds of situations elicit acute social anxiety, often accompanied by blushing, sweating, and similar signs of autonomic arousal.

The public-private dichotomy offers the clearest distinction between guilt and shame. Guilt is essentially private, and the best test of whether an individual is truly experiencing guilt is whether anyone else knows of his transgression. In true guilt, no one need know; it is private, a matter of one's own conscience, and therefore there is no escape. Shame is essentially public: if no one else knows, there is no basis for embarrassment. When seen by others, the embarrassed person can diminish shame only by running from the group. Perhaps this is why the ashamed person casts his eyes down or covers his face.

How is the stigma removed? The problem for the guilty person is to convince himself of his worth by instituting reform. Children are taught early that evil must be punished; therefore the transgressor punishes himself. Self-punishment not only evens the score ("an eye for an eye . . .") but serves to reform the evil-doer. The problem for the ashamed person is to convince others of his worth. This he accomplishes by succeeding when previously he had failed, by showing

---

[5] *The exposition will also be controversial in light of the variety of moral and religious training in the general population. There may be as many opinions on these matters as there are persons.*

Table 23.5
Comparison of Guilt and Shame

PROPERTY	GUILT	SHAME
Feeling	Sin, evil	Embarrassment, self-disgust
Basis	Harming someone, violating moral code	Private behavior seen in public, disappointing the group
Inner-outer	Private; no escape	Public, escape by hiding
Expiation	Self-punishment (convince self)	Succeeding, being competent (convince others)
Basis of control	Submission to authority	Conformity to (peer) group

skill and competence when previously he had been clumsy and incompetent. The group needs to reverse its earlier evaluation, and if it does, the person experiences *pride,* which is the opposite of shame. (The opposite of guilt is *self-virtue.)*

Finally, both shame and guilt are involved in the control of behavior. Guilt involves submission to authority, the appeal being to the authority of legal codes (Kohlberg's stage 5) or to a "higher law" (stage 6). Shame involves submission to the evaluation of the appropriate reference group, usually one's peers (Kohlberg's stages 3 and 4). Doing one's duty, being competent, and maintaining the public-private distinction in one's acts are judged by the group, the issue being *conformity,* not submission.

Self-Control

Other things being equal, guilt is more effective in insuring self-control than is shame. The transgressor who harms someone presumably will feel guilty whether or not he is caught. The incompetent or clumsy person will not experience shame unless he is exposed: so long as he avoids being caught, he is safe. Thus we all learn the public-private distinction, and shame does not lead to self-control *in private.*

Nevertheless, in our society shame is probably stronger than guilt. Religion is waning as a moral force, and most of us easily rationalize our transgressions. Even murder and torture can be squared with conscience. The Nazis who sent Jews to gas chambers said that they were "just following orders," a self-justification also used by American soldiers who killed Vietnamese elderly persons and children in cold blood. Similarly the barbaric treatment received by prisoners in many penitentiaries is justified: "They deserve it." In addition, there is a widespread tendency to believe in a just world, in which the good are rewarded and the bad are punished. When a victim suffers and an observer can do nothing about it, the observer tends to derogate and blame the victim for his misfortune (Lerner & Simmons, 1966).

Most of us are trained to fear censure from the group, and the most severe punishments are being laughed at, being pitied, and being rejected as a failure. All these involve shame: a failure to be competent or to keep private acts from being made public.

One difficulty with shame and guilt as deterrents is that they ordinarily occur *after* the forbidden responses have been made. The problem is the familiar one of the timing of punishment—in this case, self-punishment. The solution is the same as before: cognitions. The person must think of the transgression he is about to commit and then imagine how he will punish himself, "I am stupid, I am bad, I am evil and unworthy." If these aversive feelings can be linked with the anticipated act, the negative feelings may inhibit the act.

Suffering and Reparation

No one wishes to remain in a state of guilt, suffering from his own accusations of unworthiness and evil. One solution is to suffer the consequences of transgression and take the punishment that is due—in this instance self-punishment. If he is religious, the sinner can expunge guilt by suffering and begging God's forgiveness. If he is not religious, he may still make himself suffer to wipe out the stain of guilt—though this is rare in nonreligious persons.

The alternative is to compensate the victim for his pain or loss. If the victim of the transgression can be restored to his previous state—his suffering eliminated or his loss regained—then the transgression is nullified and there need be no guilt. Thus reparation can remove guilt, and it is certainly preferred to self-punishment, as attested to by its more common occurrence. Of course reparation can also be used to reduce shame, the ashamed person making up for his stupidity or clumsiness by rendering aid or engaging in altruistic behavior.

Ideally, expiation through suffering should be studied by allowing the subject to transgress and then giving him a chance to punish himself. But, though subjects have been made guilty, there has been no research on expiation through self-punishment. Guilt has been induced by permitting subjects to lie (Freedman et al., 1967), harm another subject (Berscheid & Walster, 1967; Carlsmith & Gross, 1969), or harm a rat (Regan, 1971). In each instance the means of alleviating guilt was

an altruistic response—reparation, not expiation by self-punishment.[6]

In all the laboratory research the subjects' transgressions were public—that is, known to the experimenter—and this of course introduced an element of shame. Not surprisingly, the outcome of such studies was similar to that of experiments on shame: subjects attempted to make reparations.

Shame has been manipulated in the laboratory mainly by having the subject accidentally damage equipment (Brock & Becker, 1966; Wallace & Sadalla, 1966) or accidentally knock over a pile of sorted data cards (Freedman et al., 1967). Presumably, the subject would experience shame because of his public clumsiness.

In these various studies, guilty and ashamed subjects have volunteered to make various kinds of reparations. Some have been direct compensation to the victim (allowing him to win money, or giving him bonus green stamps), others have been contributing to worthy causes (being a subject in subsequent research or telephoning people for a save-the-redwoods campaign). In brief, when subjects cause damage or harm, they will attempt to make restitution. Note that this occurs only when the event is public. If the transgression is not discovered, subjects do *not* make reparations, as for example by volunteering for subsequent research (Wallace & Sadalla, 1966; Silverman, 1967). This fact reinforces a conclusion drawn earlier: it is mainly *public* transgression that leads to negative affect and perhaps self-control, not *private* transgression. If our society must be characterized, it is marked by shame, not guilt.

Development of Shame and Guilt

How are children trained to experience shame and guilt? The following formulation, though speculative, is consistent with the facts of socialization. The issue may be framed in terms of a question: if we deliberately set out to produce shame and guilt, how would we proceed?

As a prologue we shall first discuss the reward systems used by parents in socializing their children. The major reward a parent can bestow on a

[6] *In these and related studies the altruistic responses sometimes involved effort or even mild discomfort, but the self-punishing aspects were minimal or absent.*

child is his attention and affection, and these can be given unconditionally or conditionally. The earliest common parental response, especially by the mother, is to love the child unconditionally—not for what the child *does* but simply because he *is.* To the extent that the child imitates the parent, the child learns that he is worthwhile regardless of what he does or fails to do. Later, when training begins, conditional love is necessary, the parent bestowing affection only if the child is good or if he achieves. If conditional love is begun too early or is too pervasive, the child will learn by imitation that he is not intrinsically worthwhile but of value only for what he does. His esteem will always depend on being good or on achieving the goals set by parents. Thus to the extent that conditional love predominates, the child will be predisposed to develop excessive guilt and shame.

SHAME. The first step is to institute a regime of conditional love as early as possible. The child is taught that his parents' affection depends on what the child does: precocity in motor development, obeying rules, toilet training, etc. This should make the child dependent on parental support to maintain his self-esteem; later his self-esteem will depend on what he achieves. He will have little intrinsic self-esteem and will have to achieve and obey rules or suffer from a lack of worth.

Second, the parents set lofty goals for the child, goals difficult to attain but possible of attainment at least part of the time. This means the child is placed on a schedule of low percentage of reward for achieving the parental goals, a schedule that helps resist extinction. He learns that the goals are within his reach and that reaching them is the major avenue of parental affection, and later, of self-esteem. Similarly, the parents establish a strict code of social conventions, with many restrictions and complex rules to follow. Third, failure to achieve and failure to be socially correct are punished by withdrawal of affection and by ridicule. The ridicule is essential because the child must learn that the parent not only temporarily does not love him but is also disgusted with him. The child is held up to scorn, and his disgrace is observed by others; he learns that failure to achieve or a breach of conduct leads to scorn and debasement. If the standards are so high that they cannot always be obeyed, then the child cannot conform to parental expectations. Therefore there will be many occasions on which he is labeled *inept, dirty, stupid,* or *clumsy,* and he will feel

shame. So long as the child is held in the parental bind (needing love for self-esteem and later needing to fulfill parental goals taken over as his own), he cannot escape a pervasive feeling of shame. He must continually doubt his own worth and feel that he does not measure up to his (his parents') standards.

GUILT. Conditional love is instituted very early, and the child, who needs parental affection in order to maintain self-esteem, learns that he will receive it only if he is good. He need not achieve, but he must not engage in forbidden behavior. Next, he is taught a moral code so strict that it must be broken in the course of everyday living. Optimally, the set of rules prohibits behaviors strongly motivated in children and adolescents, especially sexual and aggressive behaviors. These are labeled *bad,* and when the child engages in such behaviors, he is labeled *evil.* The child learns to respond to himself as his parents do; whenever he transgresses, he labels himself sinful. Since violations must occur with some frequency because of the strict moral code, the child finds himself making negative self-labels fairly often. Copying negative parental attitudes is not the only imitation that can lead to guilt. The parents themselves may act guilty when they transgress, thus serving as models for the child. If the modeling effect occurs, the child will respond to his own transgressions with a reaction of guilt, just as his parents do. Thus imitation of either parental attitudes or parental guilt reactions can lead to a pervasive sense of guilt and evil.

The type of punishment used by the parents is crucial. Physical punishment should never be attempted; instead parental affection should be withdrawn. Hill (1960) has pointed out that withdrawal of parental affection usually lasts until the child has made an expiatory response. As soon as the child admits his errors and asks forgiveness, parental love is reinstated. When parental punishment is physical, the noxious stimuli are delivered and then end; the punishment is transitory and does not endure until the child makes an expiatory response. Therefore physical punishment is less likely to lead to guilt.

There is another difference between the withdrawal of love and physical punishment: the child's immediate reaction. Withdrawal of love is a form of rejection; the parent says, in effect, "You are bad and therefore undeserving of my love." The child is thus cast out of the circle of parental nurturance and at the same time labeled as aversive. The child's immediate reaction is likely to be dejection because he is temporarily unloved. In physical punishment the element of rejection is either absent or minor, and the child's immediate reaction to the adult's "aggression" is likely to be anxiety, anger, or both. Fear of painful stimuli and anger at being hurt are both incompatible with guilt feelings. The child is likely to become more secretive in engaging in the forbidden behavior, as well as truculent in his approach to his parents, but he is unlikely to punish himself for having transgressed. Thus the crucial difference between physical punishment and withdrawal of love may be not how long they last but their immediate consequences. Physical punishment tends to provoke anger, imitation of parental aggression, and anxiety rather than guilt; withdrawal of love tends to induce dejection and self-blaming responses.

Inducing guilt in the child is facilitated by the parent's behaving as though he were hurt. If the parent can convince the child that the child's transgressions have in some way harmed the parent (disappointment, sorrow, illness, etc.), this will enhance the negative labels. The child would then learn that his transgressions cause harm to a beloved person. To the extent that the child loves and identifies with the parent, he cannot help but attack himself. If another person caused harm to the parent, the child would become angry and perhaps attempt to attack the other person. When the child learns that it is he who is causing the harm, he has no recourse but self-recrimination.

Finally, the reward of parental forgiveness is made contingent upon the child's admission of guilt and an appropriate penance, with the parent insuring that the admission and the penance are not perfunctory. Note that guilt need not involve embarrassment. The child learns that he is evil whether or not anyone else discovers his transgressions. In guilt the child attacks himself for being evil (sometimes for "harming" the parent), whereas in shame the child is ridiculed by others.

One of the major differences between the development of guilt and shame is the kind of label used by the parents. If the parents brand the child as inept or disgusting, the child becomes ashamed; if the parents brand the child as evil, the child becomes guilty. These distinctions may be blurred during the development sequences. If parents use both kinds of labels and if they react

to the child's behavior by being both disgusted and hurt, then both shame and guilt will occur and be difficult to distinguish. However, in most homes probably one or the other predominates. If the parents are religious, the moral aspect and evil will be emphasized, and guilt will develop. If the parents are upwardly mobile and relatively nonreligious, then their emphasis on attaining goals and conforming to social conventions (together with scorn for failure or clumsiness) will lead to shame.

Perspective

Each of the three approaches to self-control and morality—stimulus-response, cognitive, and dynamic—adds to our understanding of the issues. The stimulus-response approach, by focusing on resistance to temptation, offers a detailed account of how forbidden responses are inhibited. The cognitive approach, by insisting on the importance of concepts and codes of morality, offers a detailed account of how moral judgments develop. And the dynamic approach, by emphasizing shame and guilt, offers a detailed account of the consequences of transgression, especially the affective consequences (shame and guilt).

Each approach makes its unique contribution but omits significant aspects of morality and self-control. Thus no single approach is sufficiently comprehensive to do the job, and we seem to need all three. With each theory examining a different aspect of moral behavior, they are not so much competing as complementary theories. Thus it appears futile to set them up in opposition, and it is preferable to use each for the insights it offers.

A greater error than fixating on one approach to the exclusion of others is that of equating reality with morality. This is the stance assumed by those who legitimize the status quo, as, for example, the parent who says to the child, "Do it because I say so." In the larger context of society this approach attempts to justify present conditions on the basis of a reality-oriented morality:

As has often been noted, tradition prevents change. What "is" takes on the character of "ought" with the consequence that we fail to see abuses and we become apathetic to them.   (KELLY, 1971, P. 299)

section eight
the person

chapter 24

individual differences

Traits — consistency — temperament — evolutionary aspects — human temperaments — activity level — emotionality — sociability — impulsivity — developmental outcomes — intelligence — mental age — deviation IQ — problems in using tests — models of intelligence — nature of intelligence — inheritance of intelligence — comment

The study of personality requires a vantage point different from that taken in the study of other aspects of behavior. Until now, we have viewed behavior in terms of the independent-variable–dependent-variable formula: how does an environmental event affect the responses of the behaving organism? Any differences among individuals must in this context be regarded as a nuisance, for they merely mask or water down the effect of the independent variable (environment) on the dependent variable (behavior).

In the study of personality the differences among individuals are no longer an annoyance but are the focus of attention. Now we are interested in the various ways one person differs from another, for it is the study of individual differences that leads to an understanding of those features that mark each person as unique:

A person cannot be unique without differing from others. He is, of course, similar in some respects. But considering his whole pattern of characteristics, he is different from all others. It is in individual differences, then, that we find the logical key to personality. . . . (GUILFORD, 1959, P. 5.)

Thus each of us may be regarded as a unique

combination of characteristics (traits), and this pattern is the individual personality.

As noted in Chapter 2, science treats uniqueness by assigning each instance to a class of similar instances. As a fingerprint can be identified on the basis of a small number of dimensions, so can the personality of each person. But which are the crucial dimensions of personality? The answer is in considerable dispute, largely because of different theoretical positions and gaps in knowledge. One theoretical issue of immediate consequence concerns traits.

Traits

A trait is an enduring characteristic of an individual. In the present context we are concerned only with *psychological* traits and therefore neglect a large class of physical traits (color of eyes, ability to run fast, and so on).

No single trait can distinguish one person from all others—any more than one aspect of a fingerprint makes it unique. Thus a student may achieve an IQ that places him in the top 1% of the population of this country. His IQ distinguishes him from 99% of the population, but he shares his IQ with 2 million others. He derives his uniqueness from a *combination* of other personality traits. Thus he might be guilt-ridden, aggressive, domineering, sociable, impulsive, moody, and so on, and this combination of traits presumably would be different from that of any other person.

Consistency over Time

The second part of the definition of traits concerns their consistency over time: a trait is an *enduring* characteristic. Consider two men who bowl (see Figure 24.1). The consistent bowler is reliable over time; his scores vary within a fairly narrow range. He can be described as a good bowler, and the description will fit his performance in any given week. The inconsistent bowler is unreliable, and his scores fluctuate wildly from one week to the next. There is no way of describing his performance accurately because the scores range from a low of 120 to a high of 190. It is not meaningful to regard the inconsistent bowler's performance as a trait, but it is meaningful to treat the consistent bowler's performance as a trait.

This example has an important implication for personality: *we cannot assume the presence of a trait unless there is evidence of consistency over time.* It is assumed that there is consistency for many behaviors and for most persons, and to the extent that this assumption is true, traits have meaning. Nevertheless, at least a minority of persons may be so variable in any particular behavior that it would be illogical to say that they were manifesting a trait.

Some characteristics are known to be stable over time, and therefore we do not question them as traits. For example, intelligence (as reflected in the IQ) is an enduring characteristic that varies little from one month to the next. But other characteristics are stable over time for some persons but inconsistent for others. For example, some persons are consistently aggressive; others vary considerably in how aggressive they are. It follows that aggressiveness is a trait for some people but not for others. There undoubtedly are other characteristics that are traits for only a part of the population but not for the entire population.[1]

[1] *Many psychologists equate behavioral characteristics with traits, and they would therefore reject the notion of a trait for some persons but not for others. Logic, however, suggests that our position is correct, not theirs: traits are inferred on the basis of consistency, not the mere presence of behavior on some occasions.*

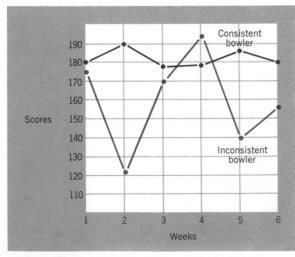

Figure 24.1 *Variability (of bowling) overtime.*

Consistency Across Situations

The notion of traits requires consistency not only over time but also across situations. Suppose a girl is extremely competitive in swimming, training hard and going all out at swimming meets; but in no other area is she competitive—not in other sports, in grades, in beauty contests, or in dating boys. With her competitiveness limited to a single activity, there would be no sense in regarding it as a trait. We would be justified in doing so only if she were competitive in several or all of the contests mentioned.

It is a rare person who behaves consistently in all or even most situations. Most of us are inconsistent, varying the response with the situation (see Figure 24.2). Consider the responses labeled social dominance: giving orders, taking responsibility for the group, winning arguments, controlling the behavior of others, and so on. Perhaps only one man in a thousand will dominate those around him in virtually all social contexts, including home, family, work, play, and friends. The most familiar examples of such persons may be found in the ranks of national leaders, especially in the military—say, Napoleon, Charles DeGaulle, or General George Patton. At the opposite end of the scale are the few meek individuals who are subordinate in most contexts, being dominated by spouses, friends, and even their children. But the vast majority of persons fall in between and vary their behavior according to the demands of the sit-

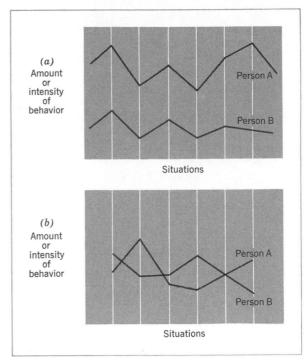

Figure 24.3 (a) *Variability of behavior consistent with the notion of traits.* (b) *Inconsistency of position, which denies the notion of traits.*

uation: submissive with a boss, egalitarian with friends and fellow workers, and dominant over subordinates. Social dominance, then, is not a *general* trait seen in *all* situations. Rather it may be seen in particular contexts (home, work, play, and so on). When so limited, social dominance must be considered a trait because there is some consistency over a *narrow* range of situations.

Even if an individual's behavior varies across situations, it may be meaningful to invoke the notion of traits. Remember that the personality approach implicitly compares two or more persons. If both vary from one situation to the next but *do not alter their relative positions,* the trait notion is worthwhile (see Figure 24.3a). For example, if one person (A) is *always* more socially dominant than another (B) regardless of both their fluctuations, this consistency of position is sufficient to establish the trait of social dominance. This is of course the optimal case. If the converse were true (see Figure 24.3b), it would be useless to invoke the trait notion. Reality lies between the poles

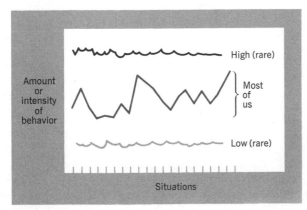

Figure 24.2 *Consistency and inconsistency across situations (hypothetical).*

represented by Figure 24.3. When individuals are compared, there is *some* consistency of their positions along various dimensions, enough to suggest that traits are meaningful but not as much as is usually assumed by most persons, including psychologists.

Each person implicitly believes that his behavior is self-consistent, and this belief is fostered by emphasizing consistency when it occurs and ignoring inconsistency. Psychologists have in the past assumed consistency of behavior across situations because this assumption simplifies the task of studying personality: if behavior is consistent, then knowing about responses in one or two situations reveals the person's usual behavior over many situations.

Recently, psychologists have challenged this simplifying (some would say simple-minded) assumption, and Mischel (1968) has documented the case against it. After reviewing hundreds of studies, he concluded,

. . . it is evident that the behaviors which are often construed as stable personality trait indicators actually are highly specific and depend on the details of the evoking situations and the response mode employed to measure them. (P. 37.)

Mischel's review of the facts provided a much needed corrective to the view that most behavior is consistent across a wide range of situations. Nevertheless, his conclusion that there is virtually no generality of behavior appears to be too sweeping. The issue is still being debated (see Alker, 1972; Bem, 1972), and we shall take a moderate position on it, as follows. First, there seem to be very few traits that span a wide variety of situations; intelligence is one example. Second, there seem to be many traits that span a small number of situations; aggressivness and guilt are examples. Third, for any given trait there is probably a small number of persons for whom there is generality across most situations; but for most persons the range of situations is narrow.

Determinants of Traits

The determinants of behavior may be classified into four factors (see Chapter 4): genetic, biological, psychological constant, and psychological variable. The first three add up to *innateness,* and the last one is equivalent to *individual experience.* To simplify the discussion, let us assume that all traits are determined by innate variables or by experimental variables.

An example of an innately determined trait is *intelligence.* As will be documented later in the chapter, intelligence has a strong inherited component, and individual differences in brightness appear in young children as early as intelligence can be measured. Of course, the experiences of childhood are also important, and it is known that IQ can be enhanced by an enriched environment or diminished by an impoverished environment. Nevertheless, intelligence represents one of a number of traits that originate *constitutionally;* that is, the infant starts life with a strong predisposition to act in certain ways.

On the other hand, guilt is an example of an experientially determined trait. Children surely are not born with a tendency to be guilty. It is something that requires specific training (see Chapter 23) and in some societies simply does not exist. Many traits are similarly determined by specific training by agents of socialization or by the experiences of everyday life. Such determinants have been discussed in other contexts in previous chapters—especially the section on socialization—and will be further discussed in the last section of the book. This chapter concentrates on the *innate tendencies* that underlie many personality traits.

Temperament

"The innate tendencies that underlie personality traits" is a rough description of temperaments.[2] A more precise definition is difficult because the tendencies are broad and diffuse. If temperaments are innate, it follows that they should be in

[2] *Temperament was tentatively defined as the organism's general levels of arousal and emotionality in the discussion of Thompson's model of development in Chapter 4. We are broadening the definition to include not only arousal and mood but other, nonaffective, psychological tendencies as well. The logic of this inclusive definition will become clear shortly.*

Table 24.1
Four Temperaments in Evolutionary Perspective

	FEARFULNESS	AGGRESSIVENESS	IMPULSIVENESS	SOCIABILITY
Rats	yes	yes	no	a minimum
Cats	yes	yes	yes (inhibitory control)	a little
Dogs	yes	yes	yes	yes
Chimpanzees	yes	yes	yes	yes

evidence at birth or soon after and that they should be the most pervasive aspects of any individual's personality. Another implication is that temperaments have an evolutionary history.

Evolutionary Aspects

After reviewing findings about the personality aspects of a variety of mammals (including man), Diamond (1957) concluded that there are four basic temperaments in these animals: fearfulness, aggressiveness, affiliativeness, and impulsiveness. *Fearfulness* includes both the autonomic reactions involved in fear and the tendency to avoid or withdraw from dangerous situations. *Aggressiveness* is the tendency to fight other members of the species and to defend against attacks from others. *Sociability* (affiliativeness) involves the seeking of contacts with others and the avoidance of being alone. *Impulsiveness* includes both a lack of inhibitory control (very quick response to stimuli) and a high level of activity (these two aspects should really be kept separate, as will be discussed below).

These four temperaments are not necessarily present in all mammals, but Diamond believes that they are the four major constitutional tendencies that have been found in mammals. Consider the evolutionary sequence of rats, cats, dogs,

and chimpanzees (see Table 24.1). Diamond discerns only two temperaments in rats, fearfulness and aggressiveness: "In the life history of each rat, these original dispositions to fearful withdrawal from danger and to aggressive attack against victims or competitors are often in conflict, and undergo many modifying experiences" (1957, pp. 49–50). Thus the two temperaments in rats are shaped not only by life experiences (some rats become very aggressive, others very fearful) but also by conflict with one another (a given rat may vacillate between flight and fight).

To the two temperaments seen in rats, a third is added in cats. This is the opposite of impulsiveness: *inhibitory control*. Cats are capable of sustained attention and suppression of responses to distracting stimuli. Their control shows up best when they are stalking prey, at which times their patience and caution provide a good model for any hunter. Most dogs, on the other hand, tend to be more impulsive and distractible. Their activity level is higher, and they are less patient.

Perhaps the most fundamental difference between cats and dogs is in *sociability*. In the wild, cats tend to be solitary, but wolves (the immediate forebears of dogs) are highly sociable. Domesticated cats are friendly if fed and petted, and they may seek the company of others or even show minimal affection toward their owners. But domesticated dogs are considerably more affectionate

(a)

and loyal. A dog becomes closely tied to his master and in a sense, extremely dependent on him; a cat may develop a loose bond with its owner but is too independent to be thought of as having a *master.*

These differences in temperament may be attributed to patterns of hunting that evolved over millions of years in the forebears of cats and dogs (Colbert, 1958). The ancestors of today's cats were solitary stalkers that ambushed and overpowered their prey (see Figure 24.4*a*). Early in their history these predators became anatomically specialized for killing, and to this day they mostly hunt alone, using their climbing ability, claws, and teeth.

The ancestors of dogs, like the wolves of the present era, hunted in packs (see Figure 24.4*b*). They became specialized for running long distances and for holding victims in their jaws; otherwise they were relatively unspecialized meat-eating mammals. But the requirements of group hunting gradually shaped them to be cooperative (in pursuit and in dividing spoils) and sociable (in attaching themselves to other members of the pack). Colbert summarized the differences this way:

Dogs are plastic in their behavior because they are relatively unspecialized physically, while at the same time they are highly intelligent and have a heritage of being very social animals. Cats are fixed in their behavior because they have been highly specialized carnivores, indeed the most highly specialized of land-living predators, for some forty million years. They are intelligent, but they have a long history of non-social behavior, of living by themselves. (1958, P. 41.)

This passage seems relevant to *human* temperament. Like dogs, primitive man is believed to have

(b)

Figure 24.4 Hunting patterns in cats and canines: (a) cats (opposite page) are solitary stalkers note leopard in tree; (b) dogs hunt in packs.

(NORMAN MYER/BRUCE COLEMAN)

hunted in packs, using legs and guile, not claws and slashing teeth. Like dogs, man is highly social, seeking close attachment to others. And like dogs, he is relatively unspecialized anatomically, depending on his intelligence and flexibility to cope with environmental challenges.

The greater sociability and impulsiveness of dogs is also seen in most primates, the chimpanzee being our example. Diamond (1957) has charted a developmental sequence of the four temperaments in the chimpanzee:

Dependent-affiliative behavior is at its peak in early infancy. Avoidance, or fearfulness in response to external objects as opposed to the panic of desertion, seems more frequent and intense at a somewhat later period. The peak of impulsivity or hyperactivity is probably reached in still later childhood. Aggressive tendencies, although they show themselves early in dominance testing, continue to grow in strength and probably do not reach their peak before sexual maturity. (PP. 91–92.)

This developmental sequence might easily be applied to humans, whom it seems to fit.[3]

Human Temperaments

Each infant presumably starts life with a set of temperaments that form a major basis of his behavioral individuality. Ostensibly they have evolved as part of man's adaptation to his environment, and therefore they should be related to the most basic aspects of behavior. Though there may be many different temperaments, we shall discuss only those that are part of man's evolutionary heritage: activity level, emotionality, impulsiveness, and sociability.[4] Each relates to a fundamental as-

[3] *Diamond (1957) has applied it to humans, except that for humans he places fearfulness first. It seems more reasonable to place sociability first, in light of evidence on social attachment (see Chapter 20).*

[4] *A good case can be made for a fifth temperament, which will be discussed subsequently.*

Table 24.2
Human Temperaments

TEMPERAMENT	EXTREMES OF THE DIMENSION	ASPECT OF BEHAVIOR
Activity	active — lethargic	how much
Emotionality	emotional — impassive	intensity
Sociability	gregarious — detached	how close to others (proximity seeking)
Impulsiveness	impulsive — deliberate	quickness of response

pect of responsivity: how much behavior, how intense (level of arousal), how quick, and how close to other persons (see Table 24.2).

Aggressiveness has been omitted and *activity* substituted for it (the reasons will be discussed below). Level of activity refers to the sheer energy output of an individual. The active person is usually involved in a wide range of situations. He is the one who rushes to meet new challenges, and who wants to keep going when others are tired or wish to relax. It is as if the idler of his engine were set very high, and his sheer energy output is higher than that of persons around him. Those on the high end of this temperament scale thrash around more as infants, show restlessness in the classroom as children, and reveal strong enterprise as adults.

Emotionality includes not only fearfulness but also the tendencies to become angry, to laugh easily, and to be moved to tears. As the name implies, emotionality refers to the *affective* aspects of behavior and is therefore linked to both level of arousal and intensity of response. The highly emotional person has a labile autonomic nervous system: for any given arousing situation, his autonomic response tends to be of greater than average intensity. Such a person may be expected to cry more in infancy, to be irritable and "dif-

ficult" during childhood, and to be moody (anxious, irritable, or easily moved to laughter or tears) as an adult.

Sociability is virtually self-defining. It refers to the desire to be with others, to mingle closely, and to form close affectional bonds. At the opposite pole is the need for distance from others ("breathing room") and the tendencies to ignore social rewards and to resist group pressures in favor of independence. The highly sociable person tends in infancy to seek a very close tie with his mother and other significant adults, cries more when left alone, and requires the presence of his mother as a security base more than most infants. During childhood he is relatively easy to train, being strongly susceptible to social reinforcement, and he does not oppose his parents or assert his own independence as much as most children. During adulthood, the highly sociable person is known as a good mixer, prefers the company of others to being alone, seeks a consensus before acting, and tends to conform to group norms.

Impulsiveness includes several aspects of responding. Foremost is latency; impulsive persons tend to react so quickly that their behavior at times appears reflexive. Another aspect is *distractibility*: the impulsive person seems to be at the mercy of the stimuli that impinge on him, and each new stimulus pulls his attention away from the old. The highly impulsive person has continual difficulty in inhibiting behavior. In infancy he cannot wait to be fed, to have his diaper changed, or to be picked up and played with. In childhood he tends to be distractible and restless, and his tolerance for frustration is low. In adulthood he hates to be kept waiting and tends to do things on the spur of the moment; more than most persons he seeks excitement, and (if intelligent) cannot suffer fools gladly. As can be seen from this description, impulsivity is related to activity level in that both share components of excitement-seeking and restlessness. Nevertheless, the highly active person may have excellent inhibitory control, and the impulsive person may have a low energy level; therefore the two temperaments are best regarded as separate.

Aggressiveness has been omitted as a temperament for two reasons. First, it refers mainly to boys and men. There are variations in aggression among girls and women, but aggression is of lesser importance among females.[5] Second, the tendency to be aggressive may be derived from combinations of three of the temperaments (Buss, 1961, pp. 201–203). Thus a tendency to aggress is more likely to be present in a person with a high activity level (more behavior, more energetic responses), who is emotional (higher level of anger arousal, more intense responses) and impulsive (reacts quickly, fails to inhibit responses). As aggressiveness is derivative, there is no need to include it with the four basic temperaments.

Research on Temperaments

Temperaments are broad dispositions, which makes them difficult to measure. Moreover, these tendencies do not go untouched during socialization and even after, which means that they are subject to change. In spite of these difficulties, there is research demonstrating the presence of the four basic temperaments. The findings orig-

inate from three sources: self-reports of older children and adults, observations of twins (whose similarities have a definite hereditary origin) and observations of infants and children over time. SELF-REPORTS. The four temperaments have all been found in analyses of personality questionnaires.[6] The standard procedure is to correlate each item with every other item on the questionnaire. Then, through statistical procedures too complex to discuss here, the factors underlying the correlations are derived.

The three psychologists most closely associated with the approach just outlined are Guilford, Cattell, and Eysenck. Guilford (Guilford & Zimmerman, 1956) reported—among other factors—the presence of four factors that match activity, emotionality, sociability, and impulsivity; his factors were called General Activity, Emotional Stability, Sociability, and Restraint. Similarly, Cattell (1957) found factors he called Ergic Tension and Surgency (activity), Ego Strength and Self-Sentiment Control (emotionality), Schizothymia-Cyclothymia (sociability), and Superego Strength (impulsivity).

Eysenck (1947) has not attempted to assess activity level, and his factor of Neuroticism includes much more than emotionality. But his other two factors are sociability and impulsivity, which he combines to form *introversion-extraversion*. The correlation between impulsivity and sociability was originally thought to be moderate; Eysenck and Eysenck (1963) reported a coefficient of .47. However, subsequent research by Farley (1970) yielded a somewhat lower correlation, as did unpublished research by the author. In brief, impulsiveness and sociability appear to be separate temperaments. RESEARCH WITH TWINS. There is little research with twins that bears directly on the issue of temperaments.[7] One exception that is directly relevant is Scarr's (1966; 1969) studies of twins. Activity,

---

[5] *This comment applies mainly to* physical *aggression, which is relatively low in girls and women. But it is physical aggression that Diamond (1957) has included as a temperament, and we cannot assume the presence of a temperament that would hardly apply to women.*

[6] *Factors other than the four temperaments have also emerged from these analyses, but we shall not consider these other factors. Also, the names given to the temperaments differ from one study to the next.*
[7] *Virtually all of the twin studies have used self-report measures, and the items on the questionnaires were not relevant to the four temperaments being discussed. Other twin studies have had extremely small samples of subjects.*

Table 24.3
Temperament Questionnaire

Sociability	Child makes friends easily. Child tends to be shy. Child likes to be with others. Child is independent. Child prefers to play by himself rather than with others.
Emotionality	Child cries easily. Child gets upset easily. Child is easily frightened. Child has a quick temper. Child is easy-going or happy-go-lucky.
Activity	Child is always on the go. Child is off and running as soon as he wakes up in the morning. Child cannot sit long. Child fidgets at meals and similar occasions. Child prefers quiet games such as coloring or block play to more active games.
Impulsivity	Child gets bored easily. Child tends to be impulsive. Child goes from toy to toy quickly. Child learns to resist temptation easily. Learning self-control is difficult for the child.

sociability, and impulsivity were each found to have a definite inherited component—based on ratings of identical (one-egg) and fraternal (two-egg) twins. In a very large-scale study (232 pairs of twins, one to five years of age) Wilson et al. (1971) reported that emotionality had a strong inherited component. They did not use the term *emo-tionality,* but the behavior pattern seemed to fit this temperament: temper intensity, irritability, and crying.

How does research on twins yield estimates of heritability? The following research report describes the most common method.

Research Report

The study attempted to determine the heritability of the four temperaments.[8] The first step was to construct a questionnaire for each

---

[8] *The research—by the author, Robert Plomin, and Lee Willerman—is being prepared for publication.*

Table 24.4
Correlations Between Twins for the Four Temperaments

	BOYS		GIRLS	
	IDENTICAL (28 PAIRS)	FRATERNAL (28 PAIRS)	IDENTICAL (26 PAIRS)	FRATERNAL (11 PAIRS)
Activity	.86	.20	.64	.22
Emotionality	.74	0	.74	0
Sociability	.74	.27	.51	.06
Impulsivity	.86	.15	.81	.69

of the temperaments (see Table 24.3). The questionnaires were administered to the mothers of twins, who rated their children on each item—using a scale of 1 (least) to 5 (most). The next step was to determine how much alike the twins were in each temperament—keeping boys and girls separate and keeping identical twins and fraternal twins separate. All twin pairs were of the same gender, and the age range was 2–13 years.

The measure of relationship between the twin pairs was the *correlation;* the data are presented in Table 24.4. For all four temperaments the correlations for identical twins were higher than those for fraternal twins. In seven out of eight comparisons (four for boys and four for girls) the correlation was much higher for identical than for fraternal twins.

It is known that identical twins share essentially the same heredity, whereas fraternal twins have roughly half of their genes in common (the same as for children of the same family born at different times). Other things being equal, if identical twins are more alike than fraternal twins are, it is because their common inheritance is greater. For all four temperaments identical twins were considerably more alike (higher correlations) than fraternal twins were. It follows that these temperaments have a strong inherited component. Let it be said immediately that the presence of a strong inherited component does not deny the role of environmental factors. In fact, that the correlations were somewhat less than 1.00 means that environmental factors must be present.

Table 24.5
Developmental Trends in Temperaments (from Thomas et al., 1970)

TEMPERAMENTAL QUALITY	RATING	2 MONTHS	6 MONTHS	1 YEAR
Activity level	High	Moves often in sleep. Wriggles when diaper is changed.	Tries to stand in tub and splashes. Bounces in crib. Crawls after dog.	Walks rapidly. Eats eagerly. Climbs into everything.
	Low	Does not move when being dressed or during sleep.	Passive in bath. Plays quietly in crib and falls asleep.	Finishes bottle slowly. Goes to sleep easily. Allows nail-cutting without fussing.
Emotionality (intensity of reaction)	Intense	Cries when diapers are wet. Rejects food vigorously when satisfied.	Cries loudly at the sound of thunder. Makes sucking movements when vitamins are administered.	Laughs hard when father plays roughly. Screamed and kicked when temperature was taken.
	Mild	Does not cry when diapers are wet. Whimpers instead of crying when hungry.	Does not kick often in tub. Does not smile. Screams and kicks when temperature is taken.	Does not fuss much when clothing is pulled on over head.
Threshold of Responsiveness	Low	Stops sucking on bottle when approached.	Refuses fruit he likes when vitamins are added. Hides head from bright light.	Spits out food he does not like. Giggles when tickled.
	High	Is not startled by loud noises. Takes bottle and breast equally well.	Eats everything. Does not object to diapers being wet or soiled.	Eats food he likes even if mixed with disliked food. Can be left easily with strangers.
Sociability (approach/ withdrawal)	Positive	Smiles and licks washcloth. Has always liked bottle.	Likes new food. Enjoyed first bath in a large tub. Smiles and gurgles.	Approaches strangers readily. Sleeps well in new surroundings.
	Negative	Rejected cereal the first time. Cries when strangers appear.	Smiles and babbles at strangers. Plays with new toys immediately.	Stiffened when placed on sled. Will not sleep in strange beds.
Impulsiveness	Low	If soiled, continues to cry until changed. Repeatedly rejects water if he wants milk.	Watches toy mobile over crib intently. "Coos" frequently.	Plays by self in playpen for more than an hour. Listens to singing for long periods.
	High	Cries when awakened but stops almost immediately. Objects only mildly if cereal precedes bottle.	Sucks pacifier for only a few minutes and spits it out.	Loses interest in a toy after a few minutes. Gives up easily if she falls while attempting to walk.

2 YEARS	5 YEARS	10 YEARS
Climbs furniture. Explores. Gets in and out of bed while being put to sleep.	Leaves table often during meals. Always runs.	Plays ball and engages in other sports. Cannot sit still long enough to do homework.
Enjoys quiet play with puzzles. Can listen to records for hours.	Takes a long time to dress. Sits quietly on long automobile rides.	Likes chess and reading. Eats very slowly.
Yells if he feels excitement or delight. Cries loudly if a toy is taken away.	Rushes to greet father. Gets hiccups from laughing hard.	Tears up an entire page of homework if one mistake is made. Slams door of room when teased by younger brother.
When another child hit her, she looked surprised, did not hit back.	Drops eyes and remains silent when given a firm parental "No." Does not laugh much.	When a mistake is made in a model airplane, corrects it quietly. Does not comment when reprimanded.
Runs to door when father comes home. Must always be tucked tightly into bed.	Always notices when mother puts new dress on for first time. Refuses milk if it is not ice-cold.	Rejects fatty foods. Adjusts shower until water is at exactly the right temperature.
Can be left with anyone. Falls to sleep easily on either back or stomach.	Does not hear loud, sudden noises when reading. Does not object to injections.	Never complains when sick. Eats all foods.
Slept well the first time he stayed overnight at grandparents' house.	Entered school building unhesitatingly. Tries new foods.	Went to camp happily. Loved to ski the first time.
Avoids strange children in the playground. Whimpers first time at beach. Will not go into water.	Hid behind mother when entering school.	Severely homesick at camp during first days. Does not like new activities.
Works on a puzzle until it is completed. Watches when shown how to do something.	Practiced riding a two-wheeled bicycle for hours until he mastered it. Spent over an hour reading a book.	Reads for two hours before sleeping. Does homework carefully.
Gives up easily if toy is hard to use. Asks for help immediately if undressing becomes difficult.	Still cannot tie his shoes because he gives up when he is not successful. Fidgets when parents read to him.	Gets up frequently from homework for a snack. Never finishes a book.

Longitudinal Research

Of the many studies that have examined the personality characteristics of children for periods of years (some from birth to adulthood), most did not attempt to measure the four temperaments; or if there were appropriate measures, they do not bear directly on the four temperaments we have selected. For example, Kagan and Moss (1962) assessed *passivity,* which consisted of a combination of emotionality (reaction to frustration) and impulsivity (responding versus withdrawing).

Only a few studies bear directly on the four temperaments. Activity level shows up strongly in longitudinal research (Fries & Woolf, 1953; Escalona & Heider, 1953), and so does emotionality (Escalona & Heider, 1953).

The most relevant long-term research is that of Thomas et al. (1968, 1970). They reported individual differences along several dimensions that are more or less the same as the four temperaments described here.[9] The developmental trends are shown in Table 24.5. Note that their approach-withdrawal dimension is only a very rough match for sociability, and two of their dimensions fall under the heading of emotionality.

The developmental trends reveal that the range of responses increases tremendously during childhood. The life of the two-month old infant revolves around feeding, sleeping, and being held. The life of the ten-year-old child extends beyond food and sleep to a variety of school and play situations, in which he has acquired a large repertoire of responses. This huge range of behavior multiplies the problems of assessing temperament, which is easier to observe in the more restricted behavior of the young child.

Developmental Outcomes

Some of the temperaments are shaped more during the course of socialization than others, and they may tentatively be ordered from least to most socialization pressure: activity, emotionality, sociability, and impulsivity. Activity level is usually left alone by agents of socialization. Parents may complain of too-energetic infants and teachers may

[9] *They also described dimensions—such as mood and rhythmicity—that do not appear to be temperaments.*

despair of pupils who cannot sit still, but no one tries to do much about it. Any attempt to alter activity level is discovered to be futile in any event, and parents and teachers learn quickly to do no more than direct the child's energies into socially acceptable channels.

Emotionality clearly receives attention from parents and others, starting early in childhood. Most parents try hard to diminish the young child's tendency to cry and become upset. Later, boys are trained to suppress fear and girls to inhibit anger. In our society there is a clear gender separation in emotionality, with expression of affects generally allowed in women and denied in men.

Sociability is strongly rewarded in all human groups for the obvious reason of obtaining group effectiveness and solidarity. Infants are strongly reinforced for smiling and young children for talking. The young child requires help from adults to survive, and therefore social contacts are doubly associated with rewards. As demands are made on the child (for achievement and self-control), interaction with others acquires negative properties, thereby opposing the pressure for social contact. About this time the child starts being involved in groups (play or nursery school, followed by grammar school). These groups inevitably pressure their members to conform and yield to the dictates of a group consensus or a group leader. Subsequently, the developing child and later the adult are subject to strong pressures to act in concert with others, to go along with the group, and even to sacrifice individual incentives for those of the group. All these trends during socialization are in the direction of sociability and away from independence. Of course the demands for achievement and the male role of independence run counter to these group pressures. Thus, though most socialization pushes the child toward closer contacts with others, some aspects direct him toward solitary activities (especially males).

Impulsiveness is the focus of much socialization, probably because group life requires considerable inhibitory control by members of the group. The first control demanded of a child is control of his bowels and bladder. Subsequently, he is expected to achieve self-control (suppression of impulsivity) in a variety of contexts, some involving morality and some not (see Chapter 23). Most of the punishment that occurs in childhood is an attempt to diminish impulsiveness: teaching the child to resist temptation, delay gratification, wait patiently, sit quietly, etc.

What happens to temperaments during the course of development? The following speculations seem reasonable. At birth the individual is predisposed toward one part of the dimension of any given temperament: let us say that he has the potential to be average to high (see Figure 24.5). Assume also that the high end is undesirable in the group that is socializing him. Members of the group will selectively reward behaviors consistent with less of the temperament and punish behaviors involving more of the temperament. Gradually the range of this temperament will become narrower, as the individual is shaped by parents, teachers, and others who control his behavior.

Each person presumably starts life with a *potential* for a given range of temperament. The impact of life experiences molds this tendency, selecting that part of the range most appropriate to the person's particular family and subculture. Thus the *origin* of temperament is constitutional, but its final outcome depends on modification by the environment. Note, however, that any given individual may resist the pressures of socialization. Thus, if a child of very low sociability is required to knuckle under to the demand for group conformity, the outcome is likely to be not conformity but rebellion. The further socialization requirements are from the individual's temperament, the more likely is an *enhancement* of the temperamental characteristics rather than a modification of them. Most psychologists now agree that the child enters life with his own individuality—the potential to develop within a given range of temperament. Parental practices modify these tendencies but obviously cannot create them. If we had to choose one direction of causality, it would be that parental practices are determined by the child's initial personality (essentially temperaments) rather than the child's personality being deing determined by parental practices (see Bell, 1968).

Intelligence

Most of what we know about intelligence has come from research with intelligence tests, but this does not mean that there is nothing more to intelligence than what the tests measure. On the

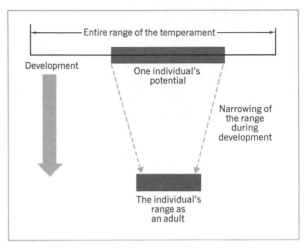

Figure 24.5 *Modification of temperament.*

contrary, intelligence tests omit important aspects of intelligence, for example, the behavior loosely denoted by the term *creativity*. Nevertheless, not only are intelligence tests useful but, when used appropriately, they are informative.

Mental Age and IQ

Intelligence testing originated with Alfred Binet at the beginning of this century. He was instructed to devise a measure that would identify those children who would benefit little or not at all from schooling. Together with another Frenchman, Theodore Simon, he assembled a group of tasks that did the job. Thus the first intelligence test was used to predict success in school, and since then virtually all such tests have been related to school performance.

It is no more than common sense that older children can perform tasks that younger children cannot. Binet used this fact as a basis for the concept of *mental age:* that during childhood at least, intelligence increases with age. Accordingly, test items were assigned to different age levels on the basis of the percentage of children at each level who passed the item. For example, a given item might be passed by 10% of the 5-year olds, 40% of the 6-year olds, 60% of the 7-year olds, and by all older children; it would be assigned to the 7-year level, at which a little more than half the children passed it.

Table 24.6

Items Assigned to the 8-year Level on Form L of the 1937 Stanford-Binet Intelligence Scale

1. Defines words from a vocabulary list that begins with *orange*.

2. Remembers most of a simple story.

3. Can say why statements are absurd. (Example: They found a young man locked in his room with his hands tied behind him and his feet bound together. They think he locked himself in.)

4. Distinguishes between pairs of words, such as *kite* versus *airplane*, and *river* versus *ocean*.

5. Understands such things as what makes a sailboat move.

6. Can repeat a long sentence.

Binet's test was translated into English by Lewis Terman, who, with colleagues at Stanford University, undertook extensive revisions and the collection of data on American children. The outcome was a series of revised tests (called Stanford-Binet) in 1916, 1937, and 1960 that became standards for intelligence testing. A measure of *relative* brightness, the *intelligence quotient* (first used by a German psychologist, W. Stern), now came into wide use. This measure is merely a ratio of mental age to chronological age, multiplied by 100 to eliminate decimals:

$$\frac{\text{mental age (MA)}}{\text{chronological age (CA)}} \times 100$$
$$= \text{intelligence quotient (IQ)}$$

Thus a child of 10 years with a mental age of 8 years has an IQ of 80, and a 10-year old with a mental age of 12 years has an IQ of 120. The intelligence quotient derives from *mental age,* a fact that should not be forgotten.

As described above, items are assigned age levels on the basis of the percentage of children at each chronological age who pass them (see Table 24.6). When this is done properly, the average mental age of children should equal their chrono-

logical age. These facts have two important consequences. First, the average IQ is set at 100 by the way tests are devised, not by any natural law. Second, mental age is a score on a test, derived from placement of test items according to difficulty level. The meaning of mental age and IQ rests on assumptions to be spelled out shortly.

Adult IQ

The concept of mental age is based on the fact that as children mature, they have more information and can solve more difficult problems. This is especially true for language-related and school-related items. After adolescence, however, increases in age are not necessarily accompanied by increases in learning or in the ability to solve problems. In tests that require speed and close concentration, performance levels off early in adulthood and then *declines* throughout maturity and old age. On the Stanford-Binet, increments in *chronological age* not accompanied by increments in *mental age* would lead to a successive lowering of any individual's IQ. This problem was handled by fixing chronological age at 16 for all persons this age or older. This solution kept IQs from artificially declining, but it did not solve the more fundamental problem: the mental age concept does not apply to adults.

The answer was the deviation IQ, devised by Wechsler (1939). It is based on two properties of frequency distributions, the *mean* (average) and the *standard deviation.* Frequency distributions vary considerably in the *spread of scores* around the mean, as was noted in Chapter 2. The standard deviation is a measure of the spread of scores around the mean: the wider the spread of scores, the larger the standard deviation. Thus when two distributions have the same mean, the one with the larger spread has a bigger standard deviation (see Figure 24.6).

When the mean and standard deviation of a frequency distribution have been computed, they can be used to determine how well an individual has done. Suppose a person scores 120 in the upper distribution of Figure 24.6. This is 20 points above the mean of 100. With the standard deviation of this distribution at 10, his score is 2 standard deviations above the mean. Now consider the same score, 120, on the lower distribution of Figure 24.6. The mean is also 100, but the standard deviation is 20; this means the score of 120 is only 1 standard deviation above the mean. Thus in terms of *relative standing* a score of 120 on the lower distribution is not as good as 120 on the upper distribution. What we have just done is to compare scores from two different frequency distributions by expressing them in standard deviation units in relation to their means. So long as a score is expressed in standard deviation units above or below its mean, it can be compared with *any* other scores expressed the same way.

These facts about means and standard deviations form the basis of the deviation IQ. Wechsler tried out items on adults of varying ages. For each age group (20-year olds, 21-year olds, and so on) he arranged their scores (number of items passed) in a frequency distribution. After computing the mean and standard deviation for the distribution, he expressed each person's score in terms of standard deviation above or below the mean. This yielded both positive scores (above the mean) and negative scores (below the mean), as well as decimal scores. To eliminate both signs and decimals, as well as to make the scores com-

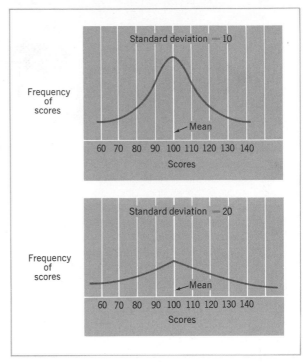

Figure 24.6 *Hypothetical distributions with different standard deviations.*

parable to IQs derived from the Stanford-Binet, Wechsler simply multiplied by 15 and added 100. He thereby set the mean IQ at 100, with a standard deviation of 15.

The deviation IQ is not a *quotient.* No mental age is involved, merely a score expressed in standard deviation units. Thus a man with a score 1 deviation *above* the mean of his distribution receives an IQ of 115 [100 + (1 × 15)]; a man with a score 2 standard deviations below the mean receives an IQ of 70 [100 − (2 × 15)]. Note that each person is compared with his own age group: 25-year olds with the 25-year-old group, 30-year olds with the 30-year group, and so on.

Problems in Using Intelligence Tests

The use of intelligence tests involves assumptions that, if ignored, lead to serious misinterpretations. Some assumptions are obvious and straight-

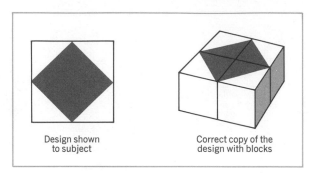

Design shown
to subject

Correct copy of the
design with blocks

Figure 24.7 Block design problem.

forward: the person being tested should be in good physical health, not handicapped in any way that would interfere with performance (being blind, paralyzed, and so on), able to understand the instructions, and not too tired to perform. Other assumptions involve sampling either the various aspects of intelligence or the population of persons on which the test will be used.

SAMPLING DIFFERENT ASPECTS OF INTELLIGENCE. Some intelligence tests consist mainly of verbal items—the kinds of problems and information learned largely in school—for example, arithmetic and vocabulary. Such items predominate in the Stanford-Binet, which accounts for its close relationship with success in school.

Many intelligence tests also include nonverbal items in which language and school learning play only a small role. The Wechsler Scales, for example, include five such subtests, grouped to yield a separate IQ for Performance (as contrasted with a Verbal IQ). These include Block Design (see Figure 24.7), Picture Arrangement, Picture Completion, Object Assembly, and Digit Symbol. These nonverbal tasks have time limits or are scored for time taken, and of course they are scored for errors. This places a premium on speed and sensori-motor skills. When an intelligence test has many such items, it penalizes older persons—who are slower and less alert. As a result, the age trends for intelligence appear to show a clear-cut decline in maturity and old age (see Figure 24.8a). This decline has fostered the myth that intelligence reaches a peak in early adulthood and thereafter declines. When nonverbal items are separated from verbal items, the age trends are distinct (see Figure 24.8b). Nonverbal performance certainly declines with age, older persons

becoming slower and slower in solving problems; but language-related items continue to show increases throughout adulthood. Vocabulary level, which is considered the best single subtest in intelligence tests,[10] continues to increase throughout life.

Thus the purported intellectual decline of older persons results from the way intelligence tests are constructed. They have been devised mainly for young persons, especially those attending school. School subjects are mainly verbal, but students are usually under considerable time pressure. The younger person can solve problems quicker than the older person: there is clearly a decline in speed with age, once maturity has been reached. But the older person can compensate by continuing to accumulate information and perhaps even wisdom. Thus it makes no sense to talk of a change in intellectual functions with age unless the intellectual functions are specified: some decline, some remain constant, and some increase. If intelligence tests were constructed principally for older persons, younger persons would be penalized. The present situation is opposite: most intelligence tests penalize older persons.

SAMPLING DIFFERENT POPULATIONS. Intelligence tests commonly assess both information and skill, both content and process. What is sampled is the residual of the individual's past learning: the information he has acquired and the skills he has attained. Thus in inferring intelligence from an IQ score, it is assumed that the subjects taking the test have had equal opportunity to acquire three things: the *knowledge* and

[10] *The vocabulary subtest has the highest correlation with the total score (IQ) on most intelligence tests.*

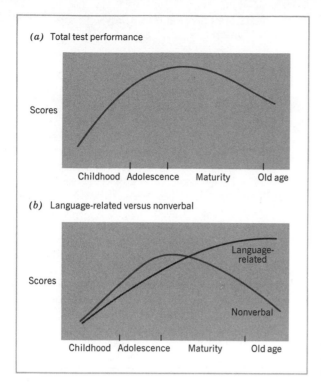

(*a*) Total test performance

Scores

Childhood   Adolescence   Maturity   Old age

(*b*) Language-related versus nonverbal

Scores

Language-related

Nonverbal

Childhood   Adolescence   Maturity   Old age

Figure 24.8 *Age trends in intelligence (composite based on several sources).*

skills to be assessed, and the *motivation* to perform. The standardization groups[11] of most intelligence tests include only native-born individuals. If an intelligence test is administered to a person who was born elsewhere or who was reared in a home where English was not spoken, he is at an obvious disadvantage. The typical Mexican-American child cannot fairly be compared with a native-born American child on intelligence tests. The American child has grown up in a home where English is spoken, where he is presented with problems of the sort that might be found on an intelligence test, and where school achievement is strongly pushed. The Mexican-American child clearly suffers with respect to access to information and skills, and motivation to perform.

Motivation to succeed in competition is extremely important. In some cultures, children are taught to cooperate with one another, not compete. Within our culture, children are taught to compete, but some drop out of competition early. Black children often lack the motivation to succeed in school-related tasks (the usual context of an intelligence test). First, most lack the advantages of white children in both intellectual stimulation and push by parents. Second, they are often labeled as intellectually inferior, if not by teachers then by white fellow students. Third, the usual rewards for intellectual achievement, which accrue naturally to white children, historically have been denied to black children. Lacking a payoff for intellectual efforts, they tend not to bother.

For these reasons it is not fair to compare the intelligence of whites with that of blacks. There have been hundreds of studies comparing the two, and the results are consistent in showing white superiority. Such comparisons are invidious because the tests themselves are unfair. As intelligence tests that are constructed for young persons must be unfair to older persons, so intelligence tests that are constructed for members

[11] *Intelligence tests are first tried out with a sample of subjects that presumably is representative of the population. This sample is called the standardization group, and the results of the tryout yield the norms needed to compute IQ.*

of the native-born, white community must be unfair to blacks, Mexican-Americans, or any other group that is not part of the dominant culture. None of this denies the possibility that ethnic groups differ *inherently* in intelligence. Rather, the differences that have been found might be explained by environmental differences. For the past few years there has been bitter controversy over the issue of black-white differences in intelligence,[12] and two geneticists have suggested that continued research involves risks:

In the present racial climate of the U.S. studies on racial differences in IQ, however well intentioned, could easily be misinterpreted as a form of racism and lead to unnecessary accentuation of racial tensions.

(BODMER & CAVALLI-SFORZA, 1970, P. 29.)

Some psychologists have attempted to construct *culture-free* tests. But intelligence tests assess the residuals of previous learning, which can occur only within a cultural context, and therefore the notion of culture-*free* tests is nonsense. Attempts to construct a culture-*fair* test are at least reasonable, if difficult. The content of the test must be common to several cultures, which poses a formidable obstacle. A farming culture shares little with an urban culture, and both diverge from a hunting culture. We saw in Chapter 11 that different visual environments can so alter perception as to yield different visual illusions. Surely, different cultures pose different problems to solve. Thus an Eskimo boy, adept at hunting and making tools for hunting, would be inept at solving such nonverbal problems as Block Design (see Figure 24.7).

In brief, intelligence tests reflect the dominant culture in which they are constructed, just as athletic abilities do. Americans laugh when they watch a European try to throw or catch a baseball, but Europeans are just as amused to watch an American try to pass and kick a soccer ball. To assess a black or Mexican-American with a standard intelligence test is like comparing a European to an American in baseball skill. Intelligence tests are useful and fair only with the populations for which they are devised.

Models of Intelligence

We have referred to different abilities in young and old persons, as well as in different cultures. How many different abilities does intelligence comprise, and are they all related to one another as merely different aspects of a single superability, intelligence? For many decades psychologists have been trying to answer these questions by administering batteries of intellectual tasks and analyzing the correlations among them. As noted above, the mathematical technique for analyzing correlations is called *factor analysis*. Stated simply, its aim is to discover the minimum number of dimensions (factors) that account for the relationships (correlations) among the various tasks. Unfortunately, there is no general agreement on how this is best accomplished, so that two different techniques of factor analysis of the same set of correlations can yield different sets of factors. Moreover, the outcome of a factor analysis depends on which particular tasks were used as intelligence tests. But these problems are no more serious than those confronting researchers in any domain of behavior, and factor analysis has yielded valuable information about the dimensions of intelligence.

SPEARMAN'S MODEL. The simplest model of intelligence accounts for performance on any given task mainly in terms of a general factor of intelligence. This was the first model (Spearman, 1927). Spearman assumed, and claimed to have evidence for, a general factor, *g*, which is the main determinant of intelligent performance. In addition, each task requires one or several highly specific skills (*s*'s), which are minor determinants of performance. Thus Block Designs require both general intelligence (*g*) and spatial relations ability (*s*).

THURSTONE'S MODEL. Spearman and his followers were British. The American tradition in factor analysis rejected *g* as a solution and opted for several *group factors*. As the British factor analyses yield a large *g* factor, so the American factor analyses yielded a number of group factors. Thurstone

---

[12] *For a summary of the controversy, see Scarr-Salapatek's two articles (1971a and 1971b).*

(1938) called them *primary mental abilities:* Verbal, Number, Spatial, Memory, Reasoning, Word Fluency, and Perceptual Speed. He assumed that these factors, in combination, could account for performance on any intellectual task. GUILFORD'S MODEL. Rejecting both *g* and group factors, Guilford (1967) has outlined a model containing 120 factors. These are divided into four contents of intellect, five operations, and six products. The model is too complex to be described here, and the evidence for it is still in dispute (see Cronbach, 1970). Nevertheless, it has already had two beneficial effects. First, it has linked the study of intelligence to the mainstream of psychology by using knowledge of learning, psycholinguistics, thinking, concepts, and so on, in devising intellectual tasks. Second, it has located areas of intellectual functioning that are poorly represented on standard intelligence tests. For example, most intelligence tests assess *convergent thinking:* solving a problem that has only one correct answer. Thus to the question, "What is the name of a hard, semiporous substance, manufactured in blocks, often colored red, and used in constructing buildings and walls?" there is a single answer, *brick.* Lacking in intelligence tests are tasks involving *divergent* thinking: "Name as many unusual uses for bricks as you can" (answers may include: *weapons, doorstop, ballast,* and *ruler*). This kind of thinking, which requires the fanning out of cognitive

processes in many directions, appears to be more closely involved in creativity than convergent thinking is.

THE HIERARCHICAL MODEL. A compromise model, which attempts to include the others,[13] assumes that more specific factors may be subsumed under broader factors to form a hierarchy (Burt, 1949; Vernon, 1950). One attempt at such a model is diagrammed in Figure 24.9. The most general factor is general intelligence, *g*, which accounts for *part* of performance on the vast majority of intellectual tasks. It may be subdivided into two higher group factors, called (loosely) *verbal* and *nonverbal*, which are kept separate on such intelligence tests as the Wechsler scales (Verbal versus Performance subscales). These higher factors in turn ostensibly subsume Thurstone's Primary Mental Abilities. Note that his Verbal factor is omitted (replaced by the higher-order verbal factor), and Memory belongs under both the Verbal and Nonverbal higher factors. Finally, the Primary Mental Abilities subsume specific factors that relate to particular tasks. Thus performance on a Piagetian problem of conservation of volume (see Chapter 17) would presumably require both general intelligence and an ability

[13] *It cannot incorporate Guilford's model because he refused to acknowledge a broad, overall factor* (g).

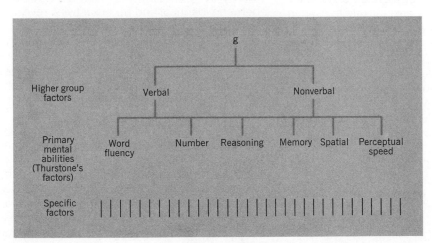

Figure 24.9 *Hierarchical model of intelligence.*

specific to *conservation* tasks (perhaps even specific to conservation of volume).

The Nature of Intelligence

Intelligence may be regarded as a temperament: a quasi-biological behavioral tendency, constitutional in nature, which marks off individuals from one another.[14] There is clear evidence for its inheritance, it appears relatively early in life as a basis of individual differences, and it is a generalized tendency out of which more specific abilities emerge. Figure 24.9 may be regarded as a developmental sequence moving from top to bottom. Early in life the young child possesses only general intelligence, g, undifferentiated and plastic. As he interacts with the environment, his intelligence becomes differentiated. Piaget offers clues about the process of differentiation, and surely the advent of language plays a role. As the child matures, he is called on to master diverse tasks and acquire knowledge in many areas. He begins to specialize, becoming more skillful and knowledgeable in some fields than in others.

Nevertheless, an individual's generalized intelligence remains as part of his individuality, for we can still distinguish one adult from another on the basis of general intelligence. Such differences show up only when they are large — say, a difference of 25 IQ points. The person with an IQ of 75 and one with an IQ of 100 have different patterns of abilities, and they are unlikely to overlap in any specific ability. The person with the 100 IQ will perform better on virtually any task than will the one with the 75 IQ. Similarly, the person with an IQ of 130 will outperform the one with a 100 IQ in virtually every area. The difference may be attributed to different levels of general intelligence.

On the other hand, when the difference in IQ is small, say 10 points or less, general intelligence is relatively unimportant. Here specific abilities come to the fore, the pattern of one person's abilities being different from that of other's.

INHERITANCE OF INTELLIGENCE. The basic method for determining the inheritance of intelligence is to examine the IQs of individuals differing in blood relationship. The IQs of unrelated persons should be uncorrelated; those of distant blood relationship (cousins) should show a definite but low positive correlation; those of siblings (children of the same parents) should show a higher correlation; and finally, those of monozygous (identical) twins should show a very high correlation. A strong trend toward higher correlations as blood relationship becomes closer indicates that intelligence is inherited.

For many years researchers have been studying the IQs of related individuals, and their findings lead to the inescapable conclusion that heredity is a major determinant of intelligence. About 10 years ago 52 studies were selected for review on the basis of subjects used and care taken in establishing blood relationships (Erlenmeyer-Kimling & Jarvik, 1963). The results of these studies, taken together, show a clear trend toward higher correlations as blood relationship increases from distantly related persons to siblings to identical twins. A number of studies yielded the following correlations: .53 for fraternal twins, .75 for identical twins not reared together, and .87 for identical twins brought up together. The .12 point difference between identical twins reared apart and those reared together suggests that environment plays a role, but the much larger difference between identical and fraternal twins reveals the importance of heredity.

These findings were later supplemented by results from England (Burt, 1966), which are presented in Figure 24.10. Note the steady increase in correlations for IQ as blood relationship becomes closer. The jump from correlations in the .50s for siblings and fraternal twins to correlations of roughly .90 for identical twins is especially significant: it is precisely the increase expected for an inherited trait.

What seems to be inherited is a general tendency to do better on a variety of tasks loosely defined as "cognitive." As Burt (1972) has written

Two main conclusions we have reached seem clear and beyond question. The hypothesis of a general factor entering into every type of cognitive process

---

[14] *Some psychologists insist that temperaments must somehow involve only the "emotional" aspects of behavior, and this approach eliminates intelligence as a temperament. But we prefer a broader approach, for intellect is as much a part of personality and a determiner of individual differences as the other temperaments are.*

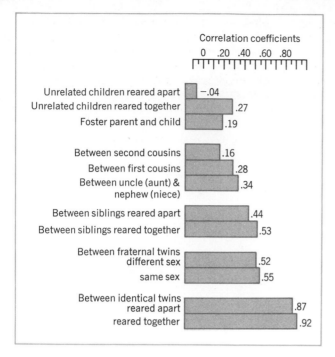

Correlation coefficients

0   .20   .40   .60   .80

Unrelated children reared apart −.04
Unrelated children reared together .27
Foster parent and child .19

Between second cousins .16
Between first cousins .28
Between uncle (aunt) & nephew (niece) .34

Between siblings reared apart .44
Between siblings reared together .53

Between fraternal twins different sex .52
same sex .55

Between identical twins reared apart .87
reared together .92

Figure 24.10 Correlations for IQ among persons of different blood relationships (after Burt, 1966).

tentatively suggested by speculations derived from neurology and biology, is fully borne out by the statistical evidence; and the contention that differences in this general factor depend largely on the individual's genetic constitution appears incontestable. The concept of an innate, general, cognitive ability, which follows from these two assumptions, though admittedly a sheer abstraction, is thus wholly consistent with the empirical facts. (P. 188.)

Comment

With man's background as a planner and problem-solver first in hunting and later in husbandry, agriculture, and eventually technological pursuits, intelligence is obviously adaptive. Inevitably, it has a strong inherited component, as revealed by the evidence just presented. Two points about this evidence require comment.

First, when individuals were compared on intelligence tests, they were from the same populations. Americans were compared with Americans, British with British, and so on. There were no comparisons across nationality or ethnic groups. Such comparisons would be invidious because, as noted earlier, IQs have meaning only for the populations with whom the tests are standardized. Second, environment clearly plays a role in determining IQ. Very few persons would seriously doubt this, but it is reassuring to have evidence for it.

A final comment concerns early development. It seems reasonable that a child's intelligence can be affected by his early cognitive development. Like all innate components, intelligence establishes a *potential* that may or may not be achieved. The child with excellent motor coordination may go on to become a superb athlete if he is encouraged to develop his potential and if he learns the appropriate skills. Similarly, the child with a potential for high intelligence may realize this potential if he is rewarded in the cognitive sphere and if he acquires the appropriate cognitive skills and information.

There is some indirect evidence for the last assertion. In spite of the level of television programing, television has proved to be an educational boon for children. Today they are exposed to a wider range of environmental events than was a previous generation with radio (and that generation was more knowledgeable than a preradio generation). One effect of television may be the higher scores attained by today's children and adolescents in subtests of Vocabulary and Information than the previous generation achieved. Inheritance appears to place a ceiling on an individual's intelligence, but few persons reach this ceiling. Cognitive stimulation early in development should bring intellectual *achievement* closer to intellectual *potential* not only for disadvantaged persons but also for those who presently suffer no special disadvantages (middle-class white children, for example).

chapter 25

the self

*Sense of self (over time, across situations) —
roles (achieved and ascribed) — role conflict —
expectations and performance — masculine
and feminine — identification — imitation and
empathy — theories of gender identification
(Freudian, social learning, and cognitive) —
self-esteem — Coopersmith's study — body image
— body boundary — theories of self — Freud —
Erikson — Rogers — comment*

Man is unique in his self-consciousness. Each person is aware of an individual self, different from all other persons, and each can react to himself as an object. Of course the perspective from which he views himself is different: it is a subjective view, from "inside." It is this subjectivity that makes the self so elusive; one has a keen awareness of self, but what is it that one is aware of? Allport (1961) outlined the problem:

The psychology of personality harbors an awesome enigma—the problem of self. The self is something of which we are immediately aware. We think of it as the warm, central, private region of our life. As such it plays a crucial part in our consciousness (a concept broader than self), in our personality (a concept broader than consciousness), and in our organism (a concept broader than personality). Thus it is some kind of core in our being. And yet it is not a constant one. Sometimes the core expands and seems to take command of all our behavior and consciousness, sometimes it seems to go completely offstage, leaving us with no awareness whatsoever of self. (P. 10)

Some aspects of the self have remained mysterious because they are so private. The sense of identity over time, possessed by all of us, appears to be a vague feeling that there is a constant core of "self-hood," which remains stable in the face of change. Thus the 70-year-old man may feel that he is essentially the same person he was at 20, though his physique, his responses, his attitudes, and in fact most of the cells of his body are no longer the same. What can we say about this sense of continuity except that it exists?

One aspect of the self is not mysterious but puzzling; this is *identity.* During World War II there were Nazis who tortured and murdered helpless Jews but who were also good husbands, fathers, and pillars of their residential communities. Which was their real identity: mass murderer or good family man? The answer is that these men were *both,* but this raises the issue of consistency. How could the Nazis square their sadistic behavior with their role as pillar of the community? Gergen (1972) suggests that

> . . . *inconsistency in concepts of self may be perfectly natural and widespread. At the same time there may be a generalized tendency to reduce inconsistency. The extent of this tendency will largely depend on the individual's awareness of the inconsistency, the functional value of the concepts at stake, and the amount of training he has had in avoiding in consistency.*
>
> (P. 22.)

The issue of identity is primarily one of the *social self:* the *roles* each person plays in relation to others. Roles are played with varying degrees of awareness: the very young child whose principal role is "baby of the family" is surely less aware of the role than is his mother of her maternal role.

The self may be regarded as *an object* that is valued and esteemed. Self-esteem is not a single and fixed valuation but a mixture of different kinds of self-evaluations that may vary over time.

We have mentioned the *social self* and the *self as object.* There is also the self as *subject,* which consists mainly of the feeling each person has about his body. This *body image* is personal and usually private, and it tends to be different from the way others view the person's body. In brief, we have suggested that there are three kinds of self, each involving a different psychological perspective: roles, self-esteem, and body image. The sequence just mentioned moves from public to

private and from more social to more personal. We shall begin with the most public part of the self — roles.

Roles

A role is a *pattern of responses displayed in particular contexts, usually in social situations in relation to other persons playing reciprocal roles.*[1] Thus a woman may play a warm, nurturant, loving, attentive role in relation to her dependent, helpless infant; or she may play a brisk, efficient, helpful subordinate role as secretary to her employer. These examples point up three important aspects of roles: (1) they consist of *patterns* of behavior rather than single responses; (2) they are *social,* involving at least one other person; and (3) they are called for in *specific contexts,* so that an individual typically plays a variety of roles during the course of everyday living. Adjustment to the normal demands of adult living requires flexible role-taking. Thus a woman college student plays a subordinate role in relation to her teacher when in class, an egalitarian peer role when with her boyfriend, and a superordinate role when she babysits with a neighbor's child (see Figure 25.1).

Ascribed Versus Achieved Roles

Every person is assigned a place in society. This occurs regardless of any specific talents or achievements, and it is based largely on gender, kinship, and age. There are patterns of behavior associated with being male or female, being a member of this family or that, and being an infant, child, or adolescent. These are *ascribed roles:* the person is expected to play the appropriate role because of his niche in society. *He does not earn the position; it is assigned to him.*

In contrast, *achieved roles must be earned.* Society recognizes individual differences in talent and accomplishment, and it rewards those who have more to contribute. With the necessary combination of ability and willingness to work, it is pos-

---

[1] *This definition seems most appropriate for the psychological approach to behavior, but others are possible (see Biddle & Thomas, 1966).*

(a) Subordinate role

(b) Egalitarian role

(c) Superordinate role

Figure 25.1 *The same persons play several roles during the day.*

sible to climb the heights to become a movie or television star, a senator or even president, or a Nobel prize winner. Each of these positions has a roughly defined set of behaviors linked with it. There is sufficient latitude for the individual personality to make its mark, but each role carries with it certain expectations about how the person will behave. For example, a movie star can have a well-publicized love life that would be strongly condemned in a president.

The gender roles—which are present in all societies—are both ascribed and achieved. The biologically assigned role of male or female is often marked in our society by dressing male infants in blue and female infants in pink. Throughout life each of us can maintain this assigned role merely by meeting certain norms of dress and appearance—though gender differences in clothes and hair have been diminishing.

But the masculine and feminine roles must be *achieved* by adopting the expected patterns of behavior. The traditional norm for men includes self-reliance, aggressiveness, competitiveness, toughness, and in general an achievement orientation. The traditional norm for women includes being affectionate, nurturant, compassionate, helpful, soft, and in general a *social* orientation. Men and women earn the masculine or feminine role by adopting the behavior patterns associated with it.

Role Conflict

As children mature, they learn a variety of roles applicable in a variety of social situations. When confronted with a novel context, the child may become apprehensive because of ignorance of the role expectations or inability to meet the demands of the role. The first day of school often frightens the young child who is unsure of what is expected and may not possess the required responses. The experience may be repeated in diminished intensity when a high school graduate first steps onto a college campus. From the social point of view, the development of personality consists of acquiring successively more complex and demanding roles:

Our culture encourages children to play roles that are most likely to be required of them as adults, meanwhile discouraging certain others which may be disruptive to current or future development. Through such role-playing, children learn what to do and what not to do, what role elements are proscribed, falling into the realm of behavior to be avoided. The role-playing is carried out under conditions of play or practice, with little or no censure, so that the first faltering learning trials take place in a nonpunitive environment.

Early role-playing is a transient, unorganized process. Expectations for performance in various roles differ, of course, and the separate learning situations are not systematically related. The understanding is, one might say, of a series of dyads,[2] rather than of a

[2] *A dyad is a two-person group.*

society. It is when the child, growing older, finds him-self in more complicated situations in which he must respond to the expectations of several people at the same time, must balance these demands, must assign them priority and integrate them, that the further development of personality takes place. (BRIM, 1966, P. 12.)

Clearly, adjustment to the social demands of everyday life requires that each person apportion his time and energy to the various roles he is called on to play. Ordinarily, it is possible to keep roles separate, playing one role in one situation and a different one in another situation. Occasionally, a single context calls for two opposing roles, and this is called *interrole conflict*. Thus when a student is called on to proctor an examination that his friend is taking, the role of proctor may conflict with the role of friend. If he sees his friend cheat, should he report the cheating or remain silent? Which takes precedence, the role of proctor or that of friend? Presumably, it is by resolving such conflicts that young persons discover their own values, thereby attaining maturity.

Interrole conflicts are rare, but they may reach tragic proportions. For example, a policeman may have to arrest his own son, a soldier may have to disobey an unfair order (such as murdering civilians, as at the My Lai massacre in Vietnam), or a banker may be forced to turn down a loan to a relative.

The other kind of role conflict occurs within a single role, hence the name *intrarole* conflict. It usually occurs when a role is ill-defined and especially when a role has contradictory elements. Consider the stereotyped masculine role in our society: competitive, aggressive, tough, and unsentimental. When a young man in the full bloom of masculinity falls in love with a young woman, he may be called on to show tenderness and perhaps even sentiment. This places him in a bind. On the one hand, he regards himself as a hard, no-nonsense, stoical American male, but on the other hand, he is expected to reveal a soft side of himself to his woman. Many American men became acutely embarrassed and may feel that their masculinity is treatened by any sentimental gesture. Too often tenderness is taken as a sign of lack of masculinity.

Role conflict is pervasive, extending well beyond masculinity and femininity:

A great deal of what we commonly think of as the friction, the maladjustment, the occasional turmoil of growing up and living with others is a consequence of strains which are so often precipitated by our efforts to take on roles whose lines do not seem to have been written for us specifically. We protest, we rebel at times, and in every age there are the few who seem never to be able or willing to adapt themselves to society's central roles. (NISBET, 1970, P. 149.)

One aspect of the widening gap between generations is the unwillingness of many young persons to fit easily into the niches prepared for them. They protest that they do not wish to become corporation lawyers, highly paid physicians, or a variety of other occupations whose main goal is acquiring money. They also reject roles in the community as home-owners, PTA members, and volunteer workers. In brief, the past decade has added a new dimension to role conflict: a rejection by the young who are being socialized of the basic values of the adults who were socialized a generation earlier.

Expectations and Performance

A distinction needs to be drawn between role *expectations* and role *performance*. Society has expectations or norms for each role: the pattern of responses prescribed for individuals playing the role. Such norms vary in clarity; in our society the feminine role is less clearly defined than the masculine role. Whatever the norms, each person brings his own talents and experiences to his role-playing. Role expectations are stereotyped and fairly rigid, whereas role performance differs markedly from one individual to the next. Thus a Supreme Court justice is expected to be dignified, reserved, and perhaps even a little stuffy in appearance and behavior. In their role enactment recent Supreme Court justices have varied in style from the conservative demeanor of Felix Frankfurter to the flamboyance of the mountain-climbing, much-married William O. Douglas.

A discrepancy between expectations and performance may be the source of acute discomfort. Consider an adolescent boy who wishes to impress a girl by playing the stereotyped adult masculine role. This role calls for a deep voice, ease in making conversation, and a certain dash in behavior. If the young man has a voice that occasionally breaks, a stutter in his speech, and a tendency to be clumsy in his movements, he will be made uncomfortably aware of the gap between role performance and expectation.

As performance of a role varies so much from one person to the next, little can be said about it. But role expectations are stereotyped and sufficiently fixed for their patterns to be described. One of the most basic set of roles in any society is the masculine-feminine pair.

Masculine and Feminine Roles

How do we identify ourselves? To the question "Who are you?" one of the first answers is often "I am a man" or "I am a woman." Very early in life, each of us discovers and is told that he is a male or that she is a female. *Male* and *female* are biological labels, referring to anatomical and physiological differences between the two genders. To become masculine, a boy must develop certain gender-associated characteristics, especially behavioral tendencies; to become feminine, a girl must do the same. Thus masculinity and femininity are initially set apart biologically, but they are ultimately defined psychologically.

What is considered masculine or feminine varies from one culture to the next. In some societies men kiss each other and are emotionally demonstrative; in many sectors of our society such behavior would be considered feminine. During socialization, each child in the culture is expected to learn the set of behaviors appropriate to his gender. To state it another way, boys are expected to learn the *masculine role* and girls, the *feminine role.*

TRADITIONAL ROLES. The difference between traditional masculine and feminine role norms[3] in

[3] *The distinction between masculine and feminine roles is deliberately sharpened for ease of exposition. It is easier to describe behavior in terms of* contrasts, *but the reader should be aware of the distinction involved. Simplifying the exposition does not render the behavior less complex. Some of the details — in all their complexity — are explored in Garai and Scheinfeld (1968) and Rosenberg and Sutton-Smith (1972).*

Table 25.1
Traditional Roles

MASCULINE (INSTRUMENTALITY)	FEMININE (EXPRESSIVENESS)
Aspiring	Understanding
Achieving	Sympathetic
Competitive	Affectionate
Independent	Nurturant
Assertive	Compliant

our society has been summarized by a dichotomy: *instrumental* (male) versus *expressive* (female) modes (see Table 25.1). Men are expected to seek lofty goals, to accept challenges, and to solve problems. Their curiosity is directed toward mastery of the environment, as in (1) exploring new lands in previous centuries or space in this century; (2) creating new products and services, as in engineering and invention; and (3) discovering new facts and solving mysteries, as in science. The masculine norm is to welcome any challenge, especially those that come from other men, and the unfortunate truth is that those who win in competition are usually considered more masculine.

Men are also expected to assert their individuality against the group if it is necessary. The "rugged individual" who stubbornly goes his own way is an important American folk hero, deriving from an earlier pioneer era. It is also part of our heritage to expect individuals to resist the tyranny of government, but this is expected of men, not women. In brief, men are expected to stand their ground and to get the job done, whatever the odds. The latter aspect offers a name for the masculine role: *instrumentality.*

Women are of course expected to work, but the stereotype includes only two kinds of work: helping men and managing the home. Women are expected to cook, sew, clean house, and rear children. In these traditional activities, all done within the home or very local environs, the women are expected to be understanding, sympathetic, and helpful. These norms are reflected in the vocations typically assigned to women: nurse, social worker, domestic worker, secretary, and teacher. The vocation of teacher is especially instructive about the feminine role. Nursery schools and kindergartens are taught almost entirely by women; grammar school teachers are predominantly women; high school teachers are mainly women, but men constitute a large minority; college teachers are predominantly men. This progression neatly matches gender roles. Women, being nurturant, teach very young children, who need sympathy, understanding, and a personal relationship with a parental figure. As these requirements wane and mastery of subject matter becomes the major goal of school, men gradually replace women. As a sidelight, teaching in the higher grades and in college offers higher status, and this naturally attracts more men.

Women are expected to *express* their emotions and affects. A fearful man may be branded a coward, but a fearful woman can expect help from others, especially men. Women can cry and can hug and kiss each other; men must suppress tears and refrain from gestures of affection except when celebrating great victories (such as winning a football game).

In general, women are expected to seek rewards in personal relationships. The ideal woman in our society is a sweet, nurturant mother, a loving wife and daughter, and a sympathetic, understanding friend. It is essential to her self-esteem that she be liked by friends and loved by her family. Developing girls are expected to be "good," which means an absence of defiance and aggression, and a minimum of the assertion of individuality. If a woman does compete, it is to be the most popular or to snare the most successful husband. This is in sharp contrast to the independence and competiveness of men, whose self-esteem requires solving, mastering, and succeeding against the challenges of others. A man cannot achieve status through his wife's accomplishments, but a woman can through her husband's successes.

The norms for men and women are reflected in the ideal personality traits associated with each gender. Jenkin and Vroegh (1969) asked men and women to describe the most masculine and the most feminine persons they could imagine:

Active, emotionally stable, adventurous, confident, vigorous, energetic, and ambitious were the items most descriptive of most masculine imagined. Affectionate, charming, appreciative, attractive, courteous, graceful, and gracious were among the items most characteristic of most feminine imagined. (P. 693.)

CHANGING ROLES. This exposition not only enlarges differences between masculine and feminine roles but also describes the role norms as they have existed for some time in this country. But they are changing. Women's Liberation is a tiny organization, but it is only the tip of the iceberg. Women are becoming increasingly restive about their subordinate status, their roles as wives and mothers, and the close link between femininity and compliance.[4] They are slowly forcing a reevaluation of expectations for women, and the generation gap between mothers and daughters is probably even larger than that between fathers and sons. Without a crystal ball, no one can safely predict how soon any large changes will occur, especially in the face of masculine resistance to women's insistence on equal status. Nevertheless, it is safe to predict that the present description of masculine and feminine norms will be obsolete in a few decades. How much change is possible is a moot question, the answer to which involves assumptions about the innateness of behavioral differences between the genders.

The domination of males over females is well-nigh universal among humans. Males are larger and stronger; they can easily subdue women and they are the obvious choice for defense against attack and for hunting animals for food. Women must bear children and, at least in nontechnological societies, nurse them. In hunting or primitive agricultural societies, the traditional gender roles make sense. Men must handle the larger, tougher, more challenging and aggressive tasks, and women must stay with their young

[4] *To say that women tend to be more compliant than men does not deny that they can subtly control men by techniques of persuasion and influence that are not immediately obvious to men.*

and perform tasks requiring less strength and ferocity.

But such primitive societies belong largely in the past and have little relevance for the present time, in which a woman eight-months pregnant can drive her children to school and shop for family groceries. In our highly technological society, strength is needed for only a few occupations, ferocity for none. As for defense, the invention of pistols and rifles has eliminated the need for great physical strength. In brief, whatever *societal* needs once underlay the difference in gender roles, they are no longer present in our society today.

Still unresolved is the question of innate gender differences in personality (aggressiveness, for example) and intellect (men's superiority in numerical skills, women's in language skills). Some psychologists believe these enduring gender differences are genetic or hormonal (see Broverman et al., 1968); others just as stoutly maintain that socialization practices produce all *psychological* differences between men and women. The evidence is so conflicting that there appear to be no clear trends. Those who emphasize heredity and are biologically oriented assume that all or perhaps most gender differences in personality are innate. This is vehemently denied by those who emphasize environment and are socially or sociologically oriented. Similarly, men who are interested in asserting the superiority of their own gender lean toward the hereditary hypothesis, and some women agree. Women who are protesting their inferior social status insist that socialization practices produce personality differences between the genders, and some men agree. As with racial differences in intelligence, gender differences in personality may be too explosive an issue for psychologists to cope with. It is difficult to accrue knowledge when an issue generates more heat than light.

The Concept of Identification

How does an individual progress from mere biological gender at birth to a complete realization of the appropriate gender role in adulthood? The anatomical characteristics of each gender provide the starting point, but the gender-appropriate responses must be acquired during development.

The concept most commonly used to explain this aspect of socialization is *identification*.

Is it necessary to have a separate concept of identification? Some psychologists (Bandura, 1969, for example) deny its necessity, pointing out that identification is essentially the same as imitation. Certainly the boy who wishes to grow up to be like his father will imitate some of the father's behavior, and such father-son relationships are the clearest examples of identification. If the copying of behavior were the only criterion of identification, there would be no need for the concept. But identification involves the sharing of affects and feelings. Consider a movie or a television play. The viewer often reacts to tragedy on the screen with sorrow, to a happy ending with joy. When he cries in the face of another's sorrow or laughs with along happiness, he is in part reacting as though the events were happening to himself. These partial reactions, which involve a sharing of affect, are called *empathic* reactions and the sharing process is called *empathy*.[5]

It is empathy that distinguishes identification from imitation. If behavior is copied without any shared feelings, the appropriate label is *imitation*. If there is a *vicarious* experiencing of feelings (empathy), whether or not behavior is copied, the appropriate label is *identification*. This distinction implies that imitation can occur without empathy, or empathy without imitation. Of course the two can occur together.

These three possibilities are illustrated in Figure 25.2. *Imitation* without empathy is common in everyday life. Children learn to write the alphabet by copying the teacher's script (see Figure 25.2*a*), and regional speech accents are acquired by the child's imitating the speech of those around him. But there are many situations in which the observer cannot or does not imitate behavior but does share feelings. Thus a boy too small to play tennis will cheer on his tennis-playing father (see Figure 25.2*b*), being happy when he wins and sad when he loses; this is *empathy* without imitation. Of course imitation can occur with empathy, as when a son decides to become a physician, just

---

[5] *The term* sympathy *applies mainly to shared sorrow, whereas empathy includes both shared sorrow and shared joy. We are making a fine distinction but one that may help to clarify the role of affect in identification.*

like his father, and this is *identification* (see Figure 25.2c).

Identification involves an extension of self to include others. When a mother is upset at her child's being hurt, her reaction is similar to what it would be if she were hurt. This is a special case of *vicarious reinforcement* (see Chapter 16), with an emphasis on feelings rather than learned responses. It is especially important in close personal relationships: with one's best friend, with one's spouse or lover, with one's child, or with one's father or mother. Vicarious affects in children have been neatly demonstrated in the laboratory by Kagan and Phillips (1964).

In such relationships the empathy often has a behavioral component, *altruism*. The clearest examples of altruistic behavior are those in which one person sacrifices self-interest for another. Thus a mother may deny herself to feed her child when there is insufficient food, a husband may protect his wife by exposing himself to danger, or a man may risk his life to rescue a close friend from drowning or being burned.

Identification is not limited to two-person relationships; it is an important aspect of group membership. Young athletes are encouraged to work for a team victory, and they are often willing to sacrifice self-interest for group goals. In some societies, individuals have so closely identified with their country that they have voluntarily sacrificed their own lives in wartime: for example, Japanese Kamikaze pilots deliberately crashed their airplanes into American warships in the Pacific during World War II.

(a) Imitation without empathy

(b) Empathy without imitation

(c) Imitation plus empathy

Figure 25.2 *Imitation and empathy.*

Research Report

Identifying with a group means that one is willing to work or even to endure discomfort for the sake of the group. This implication offers a means of testing the strength of identification with a group: the greater the discomfort endured, the stronger is the group identification. This point was tested in an experiment on pain tolerance (Buss & Portnoy, 1967).[6] First, college students ranked the strength of their identification with various groups: how strongly committed they were, how important it was to belong, and how strongly they felt as members of the group. The ranking contained no surprises (see Table

[6] *This experiment followed up an earlier one by Lambert et al. (1956) on religious identification.*

Table 25.2
Mean Rankings of Group Identi-fications (Buss & Portnoy, 1967)

REFERENCE GROUP	MEN*	WOMEN*
American	2.3	2.5
Gender	3.3	3.2
Religion	3.4	3.0
Vocation	4.3	3.0
Age	5.0	5.2
College	5.3	5.0
Club	5.7	6.4
State	6.5	6.2

* The study was based on the replies of 167 men and 186 women. Stronger identification is indicated by a lower numerical rank.

25.2). Nationality was most important, followed by gender and re-ligion, and so on down to weaker identification with ones club or state. As might be expected, the women's rankings differ from the men's. This survey was conducted in 1964, and it would probably yield different results today, especially on nationality.

The experiment itself was run on a new sample of college students, all men. They were tested for how much pain they could stand—in the form of electric shock delivered to a finger. After the first trial the subjects were given false norms about the pain tolerance of other subjects. One group was told that Russians have a greater pain toler-ance than Americans; the second group was told women tolerate more pain; and a third group was told that Penn State students toler-ate more pain (the study was run at the University of Pittsburgh, a traditional rival of Penn State). A control group was told nothing. Then all subjects were again tested for pain tolerance.

The change scores (differences between first and second tests) are presented in Table 25.3. The control subjects tolerated slightly *less* pain, and the experimental groups tolerated *more* pain. The stronger

Table 25.3
Mean Change in Pain Tolerance* (Buss & Portnoy, 1967)

American	3.9
Gender	2.8
College	1.9
Control	−0.3

* In milliamperes.

the identification, as ranked in Table 25.2, the greater was the increase in pain tolerance. Evidently, the men were willing to endure real discomfort because of their identification as Americans, as males, or as students at the University of Pittsburgh.

Theories of Gender Identification

Boys acquire their masculine behaviors largely by imitating their fathers, older brothers, male friends, and even heroes of movies and television. Several theories assume that such imitation derives from identification:

The identification notion, then, implies that behavior derives from a general conception of the real or ideal self molded on the child's conception of a particular person, i.e., that imitation arises from a perceived conceptual similarity between the self and the model rather than from a conception of the situationally or socially appropriate, and accordingly is resistant to situational reward. The identification concept also implies that this generalized and intrinsic tendency to imitate another's behavior rests upon the existence of a strong emotional attitude or tie to another, i.e., upon the relationship of love for, or control by, the model. (KOHLBERG, 1966, P. 125.)

There are three major theories of gender identification, and for simplicity we shall discuss only their accounts of masculine identification: Freudian, social learning, and cognitive. Freud's concept of identification is deeply imbedded in his psychoanalytic theory of personality. Each boy unconsciously desires to possess his mother, a childish sexual desire that precipitates the Oedipal complex. It is only natural for the boy to fear retaliation from his father. To resolve the Oedipal complex, the boy temporarily renounces his mother, thereby avoiding retaliation. But he does not give up the quest permanently, only until he can become as powerful as his father. This he attempts to do by emulating his father, copying the latter's behavior and trying in every way to resemble him. In identifying with his father with the eventual goal of overthrowing him, the boy acquires his masculine identity (see Figure 25.3a).

Social learning theory (Bandura, 1969) views identification as an outcome of imitation and reinforcement (see Figure 25.3b). The father is one of the two crucial adults in the boy's life (the other is his mother). As a principal controller of rewards and punishments, the father is a powerful figure to be admired and imitated. Of course reinforcement

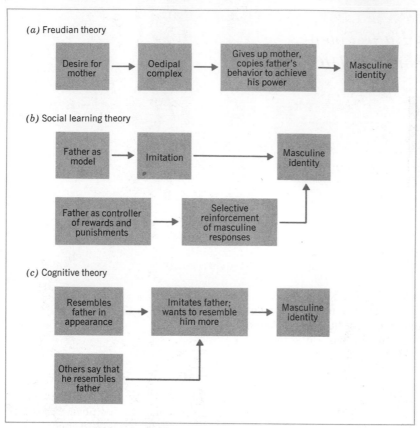

(a) Freudian theory

Desire for mother → Oedipal complex → Gives up mother, copies father's behavior to achieve his power → Masculine identity

(b) Social learning theory

Father as model → Imitation → Masculine identity

Father as controller of rewards and punishments → Selective reinforcement of masculine responses →

(c) Cognitive theory

Resembles father in appearance → Imitates father; wants to resemble him more → Masculine identity

Others say that he resembles father →

Figure 25.3 Three theories of masculine identity.

is not sufficient, else boys reared by their mothers alone would have a feminine identification; while such boys may be less masculine, they are clearly not feminine (Biller, 1971). Moreover, when given a choice, boys imitate a man without rewards more than a woman (Bandura et al., 1963).

The missing ingredient is provided by cognitive theory (Kohlberg, 1966). The boy discovers very early that he is a male "like Daddy." Others tell him that he looks like his father, and that he is "Daddy's boy." Thus he discovers that his identity is essentially the same as that of his father, and this cognition leads him to imitate his father's behavior. Such imitation leads to greater sensitivity between the boy and his father, and this brings about a close affectional bond (see Figure 25.3c).

None of the three theories offers a complete

explanation of gender identity. Freudian theory requires an acceptance of certain basic assumptions (a universal Oedipal complex, for example) that most psychologists reject. The social learning and cognitive theories, when combined, yield a comprehensive account of gender identity. Social learning theory emphasizes rewards, and one of these may be affection bestowed by the father. Children tend to identify with those who love them. Of course this includes the mother, which makes it necessary to add a cognitive component. The boy initially may identify with both parents, but knowledge of his maleness inhibits imitation of his mother's behavior. Thus he identifies with his mother, as with any loved person, in his empathic response to her. She is in part an extension of self: he is glad when she is happy, sorrowful when she

Table 25.4
Adjectives Describing Self-Esteem (From Buss & Gerjuoy, 1957)

Self-exalting	Too much
Pompous	
Conceited	
Boastful	
Vain	
Cocky	
Confident	
Modest	
Humble	
Self-doubting	
Self-effacing	
Self-deprecatory	
Self-abasing	Too little

These adjectives were ranked by 42 psychologists, and the list reflects the average rankings.

verbalized. We also evaluate ourselves in a similar fashion, except that the judgments are usually implicit and unverbalized. There are two kinds of self-judgments, one temporary and other enduring. Temporary self-evaluation refers to specific behaviors to particular situations: "That was stupid of me," "I played very well today," or "I really out-maneuvered them this time." These transient reactions, limited in time and place, are of less interest to the student of personality than are the more generalized and enduring evaluations each person makes of himself. The latter evaluations are more central to the self and represent the residuals of some of the most fundamental life experiences: affection from others and one's own achievements.

As with many aspects of personality, self-esteem may be regarded as a dimension with two extreme poles: too much and too little self-esteem (see Table 25.4). Persons whose sense of self-worth exceeds their real worth, as judged by others, arouse annoyance and hostility in those around them. Nevertheless, they are usually fairly well adjusted and are no more abnormal than persons in the middle range (*confident, modest*). Those with very little self-esteem arouse sympathy and pity in others, probably because low self-evaluation is accompanied by melancholy. The extreme low end of self-esteem may be part of an abnormal depression of mood, such as is seen in neurotics or psychotics (see Chapter 26).

A Model of Self-Esteem

Consider what happens when a series of misfortunes occur to one person within a brief period of time. A man is deserted by his wife and family, shunned by his friends, fired from his job, and realizes that he will not achieve his ambition to be a successful writer. These calamitous events would temporarily rob him of much of his self-esteem, leaving him with little feeling of self-worth. But he does have a residual core of self-love, a feeling that he is still worth something as a human being, and this feeling is usually enough to get started again with the business of living. The point here is that there is a core of self-esteem, possessed by virtually everyone, which does not depend on current affection or achievement.

is sad. But he does not imitate her, because she is not a male. His identification with his father includes both empathic and imitative components.

Self-Esteem

Each person continually evaluates those around him, judging others as being strong or weak, good or bad, wise or foolish, bright or dull, and so on. Such evaluations are usually explicit and often

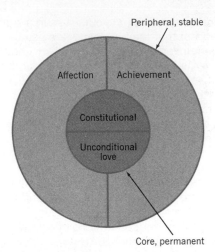

Peripheral, stable

Affection   Achievement

Constitutional

Unconditional love

Core, permanent

Figure 25.4 A model of self-esteem.

Superimposed on this core is a more peripheral self-esteem, which, though fairly stable, fluctuates with important life events: affection and rejection, success and failure.

The model is diagrammed in Figure 25.4. It consists of a core of more or less permanent self-esteem, originating in constitutional factors and unconditional parental love; and a periphery of stable self-esteem, which varies with long-range affection and achievement.[7]

THE CORE. It seems reasonable to attribute the core of self-esteem to constitutional determinants and the earliest parent-child interactions. Concerning innate factors, we can only speculate that there may be individual differences in the most central part of the self, the feeling that one is worthwhile. Of the temperaments mentioned in the last chapter, sociability is probably the most relevant. The highly sociable infant has a strong need for the company of others and for the *social* rewards that come from others. Presumably, he needs reassurance that his existence is justified: he has value because others care about him. All infants need parental attention and affection, but the highly sociable child needs it more than the independent child, who may well have an advantage in possessing more of the core self-centeredness or egotism.

[7] *The most peripheral aspects of self-esteem would involve daily or weekly events, and these are omitted from the model because of their random, unstable character.*

The core is also formed by the unconditional love of the parents. The mother and father love the child because he is theirs. Initially they make no demands and place no conditions on their affection. Under this benign regime, the infant learns that the most important figures in his life think him valuable merely because he exists. He need not be beautiful and he need not be accomplished (demands for achievement will come later). Thus love without conditions forms a major part of the core of self-esteem. Presumably, the highly sociable infant needs more of such affection, whereas the highly independent child needs less. Whatever the infant's needs, when there is sufficient unconditional love, the residual should be a permanent feeling of self-love and the expectation that others will offer affection.

THE PERIPHERY. Peripheral self-esteem also consists of two parts. The first concerns affection of different kinds. There is the continued affection of the parents, now with conditions laid down: more love when the child is good, less when he is bad. There is the affection of other members of the family and, as the child matures, the affection of a wider sphere of friends. Later there are close bonds with a few friends and adult, heterosexual love. During the intense infatuation phase of love between a man and a woman, there is a huge increase in self-esteem. There is some truth to the adage that love is blind, at least in the early stages of the relationship. Each partner gladly overlooks the other's faults, and each basks in the glow of the other's adulation. This is a partial reinstatement of unconditional love, this time from a peer instead of a parent. Whatever other aspects of romantic love are rewarding (sex, for example), one of the most rewarding must surely be its enhancement of self-esteem. Finally, there is the person with children of his own, and their affection is another source of self-esteem.

The second part of peripheral self-esteem derives from accomplishments. One can be beautiful, talented, popular, or all three, and this knowledge contributes to a realistic evaluation of self-worth. At first the child performs to please his parents, but gradually his goals are based more and more on group norms. To these group norms are added individual aspirations, which often cut across gender-related or other group expectations. Each person evaluates his accomplishments in relation to his aspirations, the outcome being a positive or negative contribution to self-esteem. Of course aspirations do not exist in a vacuum. They derive from a vague appreciation of one's own talents, together with one's knowledge of past successes and failures. A history of past successes usually leads to high aspirations and the expectation of further achievement; a history of failure leads to lower aspirations in the hope of at least some success in the future.

INDIVIDUAL DIFFERENCES. By middle childhood, one's core of self-esteem has effectively been established. If the core is sufficient, the person will always be able to fall back on a reserve of self-love. But what if the core is insufficient because of either a constitutional deficiency or a relative lack of unconditional love? Such a person will always be driven to seek affection or to demand respect for achievement. To seek affection and to achieve are normal and adaptive, but not when carried to excess. The person who seems *driven* to appeal for love or *driven* to accomplish requires inordinate esteem from others to compensate for his lack of self-esteem. Without a sufficient core of self-esteem, he needs continual assurance of his own worth.

The perceptive reader may already have discovered a gender difference in peripheral self-esteem. The main avenue for men is through achievement. Men are the explorers, the scientists, and, if nothing else, the breadwinners. They seek self-esteem through success in competition,

and in most cultures there are appropriate rituals that celebrate male accomplishments (success in war, politics, athletics, or science). There are also rituals for successful women, but they are restricted largely to a few incidental sports and such minor activities as baking and beauty contests.

Traditionally, the main road to self-esteem for women is through affectional relationships. To be liked by others for one's friendliness and empathy is a major goal of women.[8] If a woman is rejected by friends and loved ones, the drop in self-esteem is disastrous. Women who cannot turn to achievements as a substitute must therefore reinstate the old affectional ties or develop new ones. A man's role is a little easier; where vocational or other failures threaten his self-esteem, he can fall back on the love of his family or friends. If he is rejected by his wife and friends, he can bury himself in work, with the ultimate aim of reinstating self-esteem through accomplishments or success in competition.

The gender differences have been documented in a study that tested boys and girls twice, once in the sixth grade and again in the senior year of high school (Carlson, 1965). There were no gender differences in *amount* of self-esteem at either testing, but there were differences in self-image. High school senior girls were most concerned about appraisals from others—a *social* orientation; boys were more concerned about appraisals involving personal achievements—a *nonsocial* or *personal* orientation. These differences reflect the outcome of adolescent socialization, which specifies one route to self-esteem for boys and another for girls.

Coopersmith's Study

The most comprehensive research on self-esteem is a study by Coopersmith (1967) on fifth- and sixth-grade boys and girls. They filled out a questionnaire and were also rated for self-esteem by teachers. The differences between those high and

[8] *Again, this is the traditional woman's role. Many women are rebelling against tradition, and as women's roles change, so will the bases of their self-esteem.*

those low in self-esteem are presented in Table 25.5.[9]

CHARACTERISTICS OF THE SUBJECTS. The children were entirely realistic about their abilities and hopes for success. Those high in self-esteem achieved high grades and higher scores on intelligence tests than those low in self-esteem. Realistically, the children with more ability should have higher aspirations, and they did. In spite of these differences, the two groups of children agreed on the various characteristics they deemed important:

In such important areas of preadolescent life as academic performance, athletics, friendliness, attractiveness, intelligence, and independence, we find that groups differing in their level of esteem hold these and other values equally important.

(COOPERSMITH, 1967, P. 139.)

Clearly, the two groups had adopted the same social norms and evaluated themselves against a common set of criteria. Those with the requisite ability, attractiveness, and so on, realistically rated themselves high, and those deficient in these attributes rated themselves low.

FAMILY BACKGROUND. As all the children came from middle-class homes, social class was not an important variable. Nevertheless there were predictable differences: high-esteem children were more likely to come from upper-middle-class homes than low-esteem children. Subsequent research has shown that self-esteem correlates with social class (Kaplan, 1971). In addition, the fathers of high-esteem children had better work histories and fewer absences from the home than the fathers of low-esteem children.

Order of birth was a significant variable, with high-esteem subjects tending to be first or only children. This finding is much stronger for boys than for girls, which suggests the possibility of a special position for the first-born male:

Apparently the tradition that the male is heir to family aspirations and maintains the family name results in greater attentiveness, concern, and deference to only-child males. Such treatment presumably gives

[9] *These are only a small part of Coopersmith's data, which include other groups and measures.*

these children a sense of significance that is not attained by the only-child females who are reared under similar physical circumstances.

(COOPERSMITH, 1967, P. 153.)

The last family background measure, parental personality, varied as expected. The parents of high-esteem children had greater personal stability and higher self-esteem than the parents of low-esteem children.

PARENTAL PRACTICES. There was more love in the home of high-esteem children, the mother being closer to the children and more loving than the mothers of low-esteem children. But the parents of high-esteem children were *not* more permissive. On the contrary, they were firmer and made more demands, but their punishments tended to be just. The parents of low-esteem children seemed to be less concerned and were less strict, but their punishments were harsher and less fair; presumably, the children had fewer rules to guide them and developed less self-esteem under a regime of permissiveness coupled with harsh punishment.

COMMENT. Coopersmith's study shows that self-esteem is a pervasive characteristic. Children with high self-esteem tend to be brighter, more able, and more aspiring; they come from more successful homes and their parents have lavished more attention and affection on them; and they have benefited from child-rearing techniques that emphasize regularity, clear rules, and just punishment. Small wonder, then, that such children value themselves highly. Endowed with the requisite abilities, secure in parental affection, and reared in a stable home atmosphere, they emerge fully equipped to adapt to the demands of middle-class life.[10]

This description may have a familiar ring. We have already described two personality dimensions that are linked to adaptiveness: competence and achievement. Body boundary will be discussed below. We may speculate that these three dimensions converge on self esteem. Thus the highly competent achiever, who believes he can control his fate, and who has a definite body

[10] *Coopersmith's data were correlational—self-esteem related to ability, parental affection, and so on—but we have inferred a causal relationship.*

Table 25.5
Subjects High Versus Low in Self-Esteem (from Coopersmith, 1967)

CHARACTERISTICS OF THE SUBJECTS	HIGH SELF-ESTEEM	LOW SELF-ESTEEM
1. Ability	Higher I.Q. and grades	Lower I.Q. and grades
2. Aspirations	Higher	Lower
3. Values	No difference	
Family Background		
4. Social class	More in upper middle	More in lower middle
5. Work history of father	Regularly employed	More likely to have had periods of unemployment
6. Absence of father from home	Rare	Moderately often
7. Ordinal position of child	First or only	Other
8. Parental personality	More stable and higher self-esteem	Less stable and lower self-esteem
Parental Practices		
9. Mother's affection	Mother closer, more loving	Mother distant, less loving
10. Child rearing	Demanding; firm, just punishment	Fewer demands; less guidance, harsher punishment

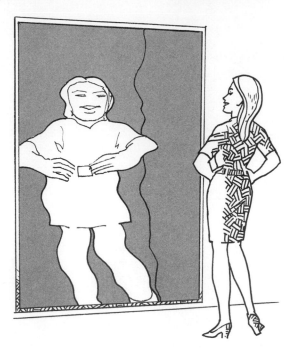

Figure 25.5 *Visual distortion of one's body.*

boundary, is likely to evaluate himself highly. This hypothesis is probably too simplistic, but it does integrate knowledge about various aspects of personality by emphasizing adaptiveness. The developing child must acquire certain skills and attitudes if he is to adapt successfully to the adult world. Success in this endeavor is likely to be associated with higher ability, an achievement orientation, and a firm body boundary. The child with these characteristics will almost certainly value himself highly.

Body Image

The commonsense approach to body image is to define it as ". . . the picture of our own body which we form in our mind, that is to say the way in which the body appears to ourselves." (Schilder, 1935, p. 11.) But this definition tells us nothing about this image or how to study it. Is the body image a distortion of the body's actual proportions? Does it involve satisfaction or despair about one's own body? Are the different regions of the body implicitly regarded in different ways? All

three questions are relevant to body image, and each has been investigated in a different way.

Visual Perception

The most straightforward approach is to have a subject look at himself in a mirror that distorts his reflection, much in the fashion of amusement park mirrors (see Figure 25.5). This technique was first used only with the face, and it was found that subjects made large errors in identifying their own image unless they were first shown an accurate image of their own faces (Schneiderman, 1956).

Subsequently, Traub and Orbach (1964) devised a mirror that systematically distorted different parts of the entire body. The subject's task was to adjust the mirror until it provided a true picture of himself. Subjects accepted rather distorted reflections as true images of their own bodies (Orbach et al., 1965). This is not as surprising as it might seem, for each person can view himself — even in a mirror — from only one fixed perspective.

One variation of the mirror technique is to show

men nude pictures and ask them to select the one that most closely resembles their own bodies (Schonbuch & Schell, 1967). All subjects made errors, but the greatest distortions were those of underweight and overweight men, both of whom *overestimated* the size of their bodies. Evidently, those who are too slim see themselves as being closer to normal, whereas those who are too fat exaggerate their obesity.

Another variation is to have subjects estimate the size of various parts of their bodies (see Wapner & Werner, 1965; Shontz, 1969). Most of the findings are extremely complex and limited too much to specific conditions of measurement.[11] But there were two facts of general interest: (1) the width of the head and the length of the forearm are *over*estimated, whereas the lengths of the hand and foot are *under*estimated; and (2) women overestimate the size of the waist more than men (Shontz, 1969). The first fact is not readily explained, but the second may be attributed to the desire of virtually all American women to be slim and their resultant dissatisfaction with their waist size.

Attitudes Toward the Body

Attitudes toward one's own body are shaped largely by cultural norms. In our society, men are ideally large, trim, and well-muscled, and those who deviate very far from this picture tend to be at least somewhat dissatisfied with their bodies. There is more emphasis on female beauty, though the proportions change from one generation to the next. A generation ago the ideal woman had a larger bust and hips, curviness being emphasized. Today women aim at slimness, with an emphasis on trim waist and legs. Women are more attuned to their appearance and bodily proportions than are men, and they are more dissatisfied and concerned about their bodies (Secord & Jourard, 1953; Jourard & Secord, 1955).

Unfortunately, there is little known about an attitude toward one's own body that may be called *dependability*. All through childhood and early

[11] *The Wapner and Werner (1965) research attempted to test their* sensory-tonic *theory of perception, and they were not interested in body image per se.*

adulthood, each person gradually comes to know the strengths and weaknesses of his body, as it increases in size and changes in proportions. Most persons discover that there are bodily reserves: when sick, the body restores itself; when bruised, it heals itself. Most persons discover that they are more or less as healthy, strong, and well-proportioned as those around them. But this is not true for a minority. Some are especially strong or weak, and some especially healthy or sickly. Thus for some persons the body is a source of great enjoyment for the attention or the rewards it brings. The supreme confidence of the superb athlete or beauty contest winner derives from a sure knowledge that his body is valued. At the other extreme, the feelings of dissatisfaction and inferiority of the puny male adolescent or very plain girl reflect the low valuation placed by others on their bodies.

In short, we know that attitudes toward one's own body are determined in large part by the performance of the body in relation to health and to cultural values, but we do not know more than this generality. What is the developmental course of this attitude? What happens as the person ages and can depend less and less on his body? Can the impact of cultural norms on those with less-valued bodies be defeated by loving friends and family? These questions are as yet unanswered.

Body Boundary

The most interesting facts about body image have come from indirect measurement of it: the Rorschach Ink Blots (see Figure 25.6). In this technique for studying personality and abnormal persons, the subject is asked what he sees in the ink blots, what they remind him of, or what they might be. Fisher and Cleveland (1958) scored subjects' responses for their protective or boundary-defining aspects—for example, *cocoon, mummy wrapped up, man in a robe, and knight in armor*. A count of such responses yielded a *barrier* score for each subject. Persons with a high barrier score should focus more on the exterior of the body (skin and muscles) than on the interior (stomach and heart); the opposite should hold for persons with a low barrier score. These assumptions were tested and for the most part were confirmed.

In one series of experiments the Rorschach-

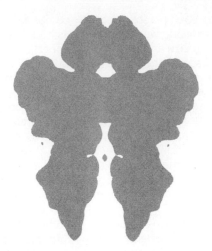

Figure 25.6 *An ink blot similar to the ones used by Rorschach.*

derived barrier scores were related to body sensations (Fisher & Fisher, 1964). In the first experiment subjects merely sat still for five minutes and reported *exterior* sensations (skin and muscle) and *interior* sensations (heart and stomach). The number of interior feelings was subtracted from exterior feelings to yield a score indicating the relative dominance of exterior sensations. This score was moderately correlated with the Rorschach barrier score: the higher the barrier score, the greater the dominance of exterior over interior sensations.

In the second experiment subjects recalled their body experiences when angry, tired, afraid, and so on. In the third experiment they swallowed an inert pill that supposedly produced many symptoms and sensations, and they reported their reactions. In both experiments the reported sensations (external versus internal) were related to barrier scores.

In the fourth experiment subjects were shown phrases related to skin, muscle, stomach, and heart, and then they were asked to recall as many as possible. The kinds of phrases they remembered (skin-muscle versus stomach-heart) were related to their Rorschach barrier scores. Thus the barrier scores, derived from responses to ink blots, were definitely related to body sensations reported in various experimental contexts.

Strong supporting evidence emerged from a conditioning experiment on high-barrier and low-barrier subjects. Armstrong (1964) paired an electric shock (unconditioned stimulus) with a tone (conditioned stimulus) until the tone alone elicited the response (see Figure 25.7). There were two different responses conditioned simultaneously, both arousal reactions to electric shock: galvanic skin response (see Chapter 6) and increased heart rate. Armstrong found that for high-barrier subjects the galvanic skin response (exterior) conditioned better, whereas for low-barrier subjects heart rate conditioned better. Thus the definiteness of body boundary is a decisive determinant of body reactivity, a definite boundary being associated with exterior (skin) reactivity and an indefinite boundary with interior reactivity (heart).

Barrier scores, as measures of the definiteness of body boundary, should obviously relate to the kind of psychosomatic illnesses[12] seen in patients. They do. Patients with exterior symptoms such as arthritis have higher barrier than those with internal symptoms such as ulcers (Fisher & Cleveland, 1955; Cleveland & Fisher, 1960; Williams & Krasnoff, 1964).

The body-boundary concept has been extended beyond body sensations and autonomic reactivity. For example, high-barrier subjects can tolerate more pain than low-barrier subjects can (Nichols

[12] *These are clusters of physical symptoms that have strong psychological determinants involved in their origin, their flare-up, or both.*

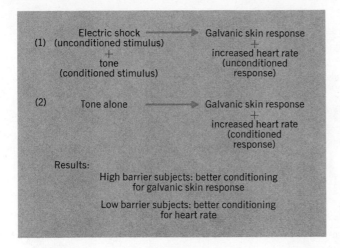

Figure 25.7 *Simultaneous conditioning of galvanic skin response and heart rate.*
(ARMSTRONG, 1964.)

& Tursky, 1967). Body boundary is also related to how persons act in groups, high barrier subjects tending to be more friendly, communicative, and active when in a social group. These and a large number of related findings are summarized elsewhere (Fisher, 1963; Fisher & Cleveland, 1968). Taken together, they offer a convincing argument for the importance of the body boundary.

Theories of Self

Maslow's (1943) notion of self-actualization, mentioned in Chapter 22, is part of his theory of the self, and Rogers (1959) has emphasized the self in his humanistic approach. But the most influential theory of self may be found in the psychoanalytic formulation of Freud and his followers.

Freudian Theory

Freud's theory includes much more than the self, but the other aspects will be ignored here.[13] He divided the self into three parts: the *id,* the *ego,* and the *superego.* The id may be regarded as the residual of evolutionary trends. It consists of the primitive biological urges, especially sexual and aggressive urges, present in virtually all higher animals. In addition it is a kind or reservoir of all

[13] *Freud's approach to abnormal behavior will be discussed in Chapter 27.*

infantile wishes and longings, which demand expression in behavior. They set up tensions that are presumably aversive; relief of the tensions is pleasurable, and the id operates solely on a *pleasure principle.*

The self of the newborn infant is assumed to be all id. As this primitive self comes into contact with the environment, part of it becomes modified to form a buffer. This buffer between the desires of the id and the demands of the world is the ego. Its function is to effect a compromise that will allow id impulses to be expressed in a form acceptable to society, which involves the timing, intensity, and style of the responses being emitted. Psychoanalytic theory specifies a number of ego mechanisms and defenses, some of which will be discussed in Chapter 27.

The self is also called on to strive for lofty goals and police itself according to the prevailing moral code. As we saw in Chapter 23, self-control and morality develop gradually throughout childhood and adolescence. The internalization of goals and morals results in the third part of the self, the superego, which splits off from the ego and eventually makes its own independent demands on the ego.

Psychoanalytic theory implies that the ego is a *core self,* mediating the internal demands of the other two structures, the id and the superego. On the other hand, the id pushes for expression of primitive or infantile wishes, and these are strongly opposed by the superego. The

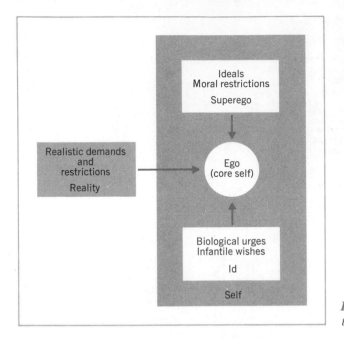

Figure 25.8 *Freudian model of the self.*

twin sets of demands converge on the ego, which must resolve the conflict. Thus the self consists of three parts, but the ego is the core (see Figure 25.8). In addition to demands from within the self, there are demands and restrictions from the environment. The ego cannot ignore these, and it must somehow resolve the conflicting demands of both id and superego with those of the real world. To state it another way, the ego (unlike the id) operates on the *reality principle.*

What happens to the self during development? The id continues to supply the underlying push or motivation, intensifying its strivings (as in the upsurge of sexual urges at puberty). The superego develops out of the ego and gradually matures as the child identifies with appropriate adult figures. It is the ego that undergoes the most sweeping and complex changes, in normal development emerging from the status of office boy (virtually helpless in the face of id urges) to that of executive (neatly managing the demands of id, superego, and reality).

Freud specified five psychosexual stages during development, each involving a successively more mature ego or core self (see Table 25.6). The first stage is *oral* both literally and metaphorically. The

nursing period involves suckling and exploration of objects with the mouth, but the infant is also "taking in" psychologically, in the sense of receiving care and affection. The infant's profound selfishness and self-centeredness is called *narcissistic,* after the mythical character Narcissus, who fell in love with his own reflection.

The second stage is called *anal* because of the battle between parents and child over toilet training. The metaphor for this era involves a conflict between "holding back" and "letting go." The immature self gains strength by willfully and stubbornly asserting "I won't" or "I'll do it my way."

The metaphor for the *phallic* stage is "aggressive thrusting," as the child explores the environment and develops better modes of expressing aggression. Childhood sexuality is focused on the mother, and this precipitates the Oedipal conflict. As noted earlier, the conflict is resolved by the boy's temporarily giving up his mother and identifying with his father. This ushers in the *latency* stage, which is marked by play with same-sexed peers and development of skill in both cognitive and motor activities.

This relatively asexual adjustment is terminated by a sudden increase of sexual wishes in puberty

Table 25.6
Freud's Psychosexual Stages and Development of Self

PSYCHOSEXUAL STAGES	DEVELOPMENT OF SELF
Oral (0—1 year)	Passive, dependent, narcissistic self
Anal (1—2,3 years)	Assertion of self by resistance, negativism
Phallic (2,3—5 years)	Assertion of self by exploration, aggression, and childhood sexuality
Latency (5 years— puberty)	Assertion of self by learning, activities, developing skills
Genital (adolescence— adulthood)	Assertion of self by mature assertiveness, sexuality, responsibility, and intimacy

(genital stage), and from then on the person must "put it all together." True maturity requires the taming of sexual and aggressive urges, allowing their release in socially acceptable ways. The self must be sufficiently mature to surrender itself to another and achieve true intimacy.

Erikson's Revision

Freud's developmental sequence was revised by Erikson (1963), whose approach is more social and ego-oriented. He expanded the developmental sequence into eight stages, making two assumptions:

. . . *(1) that the human personality in principle develops according to steps predetermined in the growing person's readiness to be driven toward, to be aware of, and to interact with, a widening social radius; and (2) that society, in principle, tends to be so constituted as to meet and invite this succession of potentialities for interaction and attempts to safeguard and to encourage the proper sequence of their unfolding.*[14]

(1963, P. 270.)

The eight stages are summarized in Table 25.7. BASIC TRUST VERSUS MISTRUST. Regularity of care and affection brings with it a confidence that things will turn out all right: hunger will be assuaged and discomfort removed. That an infant can trust his mother to leave, knowing she will return, implies that presence of a primitive sense of ego identity, a sense of continuity and sameness. The alternative to trust is mistrust of others, which prevents the infant from developing confidence in

[14] *If these assumptions have a familiar ring, it is because they are similar to those of Piaget and other stage theorists.*

Table 25.7
Erikson's Developmental Sequence

PERIOD	ESSENTIAL CONFLICT
Oral	Basic trust versus mistrust
Anal	Autonomy versus shame and doubt
Phallic	Initiative versus guilt
Latency	Industry versus inferiority
Puberty and adolescence	Identity versus role diffusion
Young adulthood	Intimacy versus isolation
Adulthood	Generativity versus stagnation
Maturity	Ego integrity versus despair

Genital brace covers Puberty and adolescence through Maturity.

himself and sets the stage for lifelong low self-esteem.

AUTONOMY VERSUS SHAME AND DOUBT. The young child is required to master his own impulses, starting with control of his own bodily functions. As he gradually acquires this mastery, he develops stronger sense of *self*-control. To the extent that he fails, he is made ashamed of his immaturity and he comes to doubt his own ability to function independently.

INITIATIVE VERSUS GUILT. As the child's developing locomotor and manual skills open up new worlds to explore, he actively seeks stimuli to manipulate and conquer. But his actions may be intrusive and troublesome to others, and invariably moral codes are invoked against him. This is the classic conflict between the animalistic desires of the id and the rigidly moral demands of the early superego.

INDUSTRY VERSUS INFERIORITY. All societies require that children be taught the prevailing technology, whether primitive or advanced. Thus in our society, children attend school to learn such basic skills as the three "R's" and such basic knowledge as our history and myths. If the child cannot master the rudiments of the prevailing technology, he may feel profoundly inferior—a special problem for minority groups who are not attuned to the middle-class values that prevail in schools.

IDENTITY VERSUS ROLE DIFFUSION. The adolescent must face two basic problems of identity. First, puberty is marked by rapid changes in body size and secondary sexual characteristics. In just a few brief years, the individual's appearance changes from that of a child to that of an adult. This poses a problem of continuity of self for the part-child–part-adult adolescent. Second, there are many *role models* (peers, older persons, mass-media heroes), and the adolescent busily tries on different identities as he would different clothes. Thus identity can become confused by com-

plexity, by rapid change, and by multiple expectations. In the past the solution in our society lay in
selecting a stable identity through marriage,
career, and place in the community. For many
young people today, this solution is no longer
workable, and role diffusion has become an
enduring problem.

INTIMACY VERSUS ISOLATION. When the self is
secure in its identity, it can merge with other
selves and even temporarily give up its independence. The readiness to let go and abandon oneself to another is presumably a precondition for
the intimacy of true genitality:

*In order to be of lasting social significance, the utopia
of genitality should include:*

1. *mutuality of orgasm*
2. *with a loved partner*
3. *of the other sex*
4. *with whom one is able and willing to regulate
   cycles of*
   a. *work*
   b. *procreation*
   c. *recreation*
5. *so as to secure to the offspring, too, all the stages
   of a satisfactory development.*

(ERIKSON, 1963, P. 266.)

The alternative is self-centeredness and an isolation from really close contacts with others, sometimes seen in the phenomenon of "jumping in
and out of others' beds."

GENERATIVITY VERSUS STAGNATION. Everyone
starts out as a dependent infant and progresses
toward independence. Erikson suggests that the
endpoint is one step beyond independence: caring
for and guiding the next generation. Of course
producing and *creating* need not be limited to procreation, for it may also include invention, art, and
production of goods and services. In brief, the
adult needs to be *useful* to society in ways that go
beyond his own needs. The alternative is to stag-
nate in the prison of one's own selfishness.

EGO INTEGRITY VERSUS DESPAIR. The person
who has resolved the conflicts of the first seven
stages has presumably developed a mature identity, which extends beyond his immediate self. He
can identify with his immediate family and
friends, and to a lesser extent with all human
beings. He sees order and continuity beyond his

own mortal life span. The alternative is the despair
that is most clearly reflected in a profound fear of
death—as opposed to an acceptance of one's own
life cycle.

Roger's Self Theory

The outstanding nonpsychoanalytic theory of self
is that of Rogers (1959, 1961). His emphasis is on
awareness and experience. Presumably, it is optimal to be in close contact with immediate experience, and through perception one first develops
an *awareness of self* and then a need for positive
regard. This need is so strong that the child may
learn to seek it from others even at the expense of
his own experience. Thus a child may do something not because it gives him satisfaction, but
because it pleases his mother. Stated another way,
conditional love makes the child dependent on
performing for self-esteem, rather than depending
on the core self-esteem that arises from unconditional love.

Rogers' theory is a variation on the theme "To
thine own self be true." He insists that the only adjustive mode is self-acceptance of all feelings, impulses, and attitudes. This does not mean that one
can or should behave in any way he pleases,
disregarding the rights of others. Rather, it means
that all *experience* that is part of the self is
regarded positively. Thus bad thoughts are as
acceptable as good thoughts, though bad thoughts
should perhaps not be expressed in behavior.

In this framework, man's basic conflict is
between his own experience and positive regard
from others. The more an individual is motivated
only to please others and thereby obtain positive
self-regard, the more he denies his own experience and becomes alienated from his true self.
The solution, Rogers believes, is positive *self-
regard*. The infant, in his self-centeredness, is in
closest touch with his experience and suffers least
from the distortions caused by seeking positive
regard from others (Rogers, 1959). Thus the ultimate answer to problems in adjusting to the
world is more and more positive self-regard. This
can be brought about only by others accepting
and loving the person as he is, without conditions.
Under these conditions, the individual will grow
psychologically and self-actualize.

Comment

These theories of self represent a tradition that emphasizes inner man, inner experience, and the goals of life. As such, they are part of a humanistic orientation that opposes more objective and experimental approaches. These self theories derive mainly from clinical situations in which troubled persons are seeking help for problems that will be discussed in the next chapter. The theories are perhaps as much social philosophy as they are conceptions of behavior. Whether this approach enhances or detracts from their value depends on what one thinks a theory should be. In brief, these self theories are attempts to describe the unique nature of man, and their value is determined by one's training and experience not by one's objective fact-finding.

chapter 26

abnormal behavior: description

Criteria of abnormality—discomfort (anxiety, depression, and existential problems)—bizarreness—inefficiency—continuity of normal and abnormal behavior—instrumental symptoms—affective symptoms—cognitive symptoms—social symptoms—neurosis—psychosis—schizophrenia, depression, atypical psychosis, and paranoia—conduct disorders

In the last few chapters we have been discussing man as a person: differences among individuals and various aspects of the self. This chapter continues in the same vein but with an altered emphasis. Here the focus is on adjustment and the normative aspects of behavior. All societies require stability in the role-taking of individual members, and the give-and-take of societal processes (work, socialization of the young, and so on) requires that each person keep his behavior within certain acceptable bounds. Thus there are prescribed *norms* and expectations, and persons who seriously violate them are usually ridiculed or punished. Individual adjustment requires at least a minimum of conformity—a compromise between one's own demands and those of the community. Rebellion against societal norms is usually deemed criminal, and this issue is best left to those with special knowledge (largely sociologists and criminologists). Inability to conform properly falls under the heading of abnormal behavior, and here psychologists can claim to have special knowledge. There is more to abnormal behavior than deviance; we shall also consider the misery and sense of failure that often accompany abnormality.

Criteria of Abnormality

Abnormality is, by definition, a deviation from normality, which means that there must be a *statistical* criterion. Normality must comprise whichever behaviors are prevalent in the population, which is essentially what a *norm* is. Abnormality, by definition, must comprise behaviors that are rare or uncommon in the population. Most of us have full color vision, but a small minority is color-blind, and therefore color blindness may be deemed abnormal and color vision normal. However, if virtually all humans had no color vision and only a tiny minority had full color vision, then full color vision might well be called abnormal.

If the reader is reluctant to accept the conclusion stated in the last sentence, there is a good reason. We generally do not use the term *abnormal* to describe uncommon behaviors that are helpful or in some way worthwhile. Thus individuals of very low intelligence may be labeled abnormal, but geniuses are not. Therefore the statistical criterion of abnormality is necessary but not sufficient. It offers one basis for labeling behavior as abnormal — that it is uncommon. But we must also know the content of the behavior, for some acts that are rare will never be called abnormal (for example, the creative acts of an Einstein or a Beethoven).

In searching for criteria of abnormality, it is perhaps best to be practical. The concept of abnormality has led psychologists into a morass of verbiage when they have tried to pin it down scientifically. Perhaps it is better to regard it as an everyday, rule-of-thumb concept, which is fuzzy and imprecise but still useful, especially in practice of clinical psychologists and psychiatrists. This approach still demands a search for criteria, but the question is a practical one: what are the reasons for labeling someone as abnormal? There are three practical criteria of abnormality: discomfort, bizarreness, and inefficiency.

Discomfort

No one escapes discomfort during the course of life. Everyone has transient episodes of anxiety, depression, and feelings of worthlessness. Brief, specific discomfort, being common, is by definition normal. Only when discomfort is *frequent, repetitive,* or *chronic* does it indicate abnormality. This criterion applies to all abnormality: it refers to enduring tendencies rather than brief, specific behaviors.[1]

ANXIETY. Some persons spend many of their waking hours in a state of tension, as they fret and worry about real and imagined problems. The pattern is so familiar that it has been exploited in aspirin advertisments in the phrase "PAIN, TENSION, HEADACHE." These are the bodily or somatic aspects of anxiety; the cognitive aspects involve apprehension about immediate events (forthcoming examinations) or vague feelings of impending doom.

DEPRESSION. Variations in mood occur as a normal part of everyday life, and everyone has experienced melancholy over rejection, loss, or failure. But a depression that outlasts the normal period of mourning or a melancholy that is out of proportion to the failure or loss is usually considered abnormal. A person may become so despondent that he feels he can end his misery only by ending his own life, and suicide is a clear and present danger in anyone with severe depression.

EXISTENTIAL PROBLEMS. Related to depression is a pattern of problems concerning the meaning of life. Most of us pause at some time during the life cycle, usually during adolescence and middle age, to ponder about larger goals and values. Does life consist merely of the pursuit of materialistic goals? Why bother to do anything constructive when it will only fade and wither away after death, if not before? It is common to question and doubt oneself and the meaning of life from time to time, but chronic indifference, doubting, and apathy are sufficiently serious to be labeled abnormal. Maddi (1970) has called the pattern an *existential neurosis* and described its cognitive, affective, and instrumental components:

The cognitive component of the existential neurosis is meaninglessness, or chronic inability to believe in the truth, importance, usefulness, or interest value of any

---

[1] *There are some exceptions to this statement. For example, a man who goes berserk and kills or wounds several persons need do so only once to be judged abnormal.*

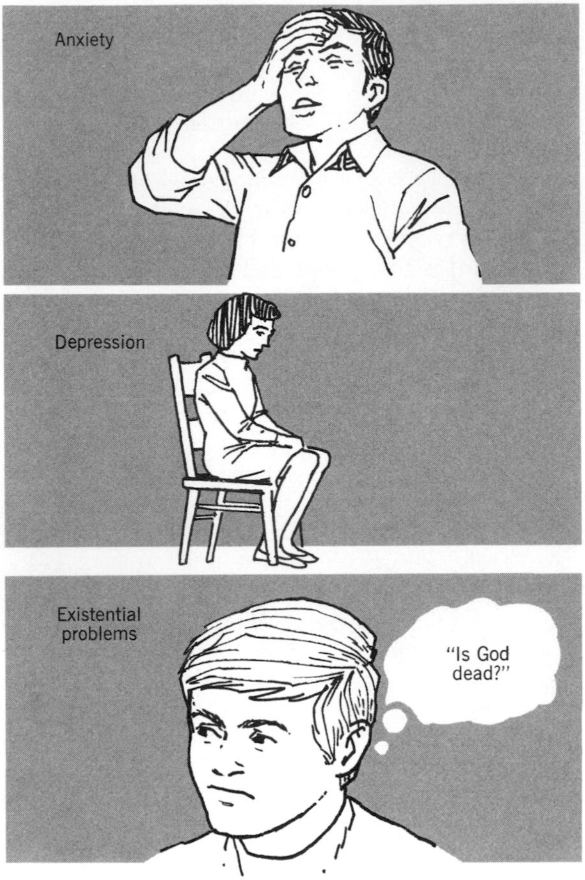

Figure 26.1 *Three kinds of discomfort.*

of the things one is engaged in or can imagine doing. The most characteristic features of affective tone are blandness and boredom, punctuated by periods of depression which become less frequent as the disorder is prolonged. As to the realm of action, activity level may be low to moderate, but more important than the amount of activity is the introspective and objectively observable fact that activities are not chosen. There is little selectivity, it being immaterial to the person what if any activities he pursues.

If there is any selectivity shown, it is in the direction of ensuring minimal expenditure of effort and decision making. (P. 313.)

In brief, one criterion of abnormality is human misery, which is manifested in being scared, depressed, or bored (see Figure 26.1).

Bizarreness

Bizarreness is socially defined. Each community, subculture, and society defines the behavior it will tolerate, as opposed to the behavior that will be labeled weird and crazy. The issue is very complex, and members of society are required to make some very fine discriminations. For example, children must be taught that it is acceptable to be naked inside the bedroom or the house but not outside. Men and women can prance around entirely unclothed in public, but only if the context is a stage play or movie. Women are not allowed to go topless unless they work in special restaurants or night clubs. Gender differences in allowable nakedness are well known, and of particular interest is exposure of the genitals. If a woman exposes herself to a man, she might be breaking the law, but she would not necessarily be considered abnormal. If a man exposes himself, he is not only breaking the law but in danger of being institutionalized as a bizarre sex offender.

One of the most serious bizarre behaviors, *hallucinations,* is the one most commonly associated with *crazy* people. Most hallucinations involve hearing voices that are not there or seeing persons or objects that are not there. Interestingly enough such behavior is not branded bizarre in all contexts. If a lecturer suddenly started talking to another, but nonexistent, lecturer on the platform with him, he would be considered a candidate for institutionalization. But for those who believe that the spirit lives on after death, a seer conducting a seance would not be considered abnormal if he described a dead person in detail and conversed with its ghost (see Figure 26.2). In some cultures, and certainly in some previous historical eras, those who heard voices or reported visions were accorded special status, not censured.

As part of socialization, each child learns what is acceptable in his own culture and subculture. Topless waitresses are acceptable in San Francisco but reprehensible in Dubuque, Iowa. Masturbation is considered quite normal among intellectual members of the middle class but a mild perversion among most members of the lower class. Most communities tolerate minor eccentricites of their members, and the issue of abnormally bizarre behavior does not occur frequently. Moreover, with each passing decade, most persons are becoming more tolerant of minor deviations in behavior, dress, hair styles, and so on. But major misperceptions of reality, especially hallucinations and sudden, senseless acts, are so clearly bizarre as to be recognized by virtually everyone as a sign of abnormality.

Inefficiency

A lack of efficiency is one of the ills of modern technological society. The average new automobile has more than 25 defects (according to the magazine *Consumer Reports*), and most of the products we use suffer from some shoddiness in manufacture. In their personal and professional lives many persons make errors, waste time, and generally do not perform as well as they might. Why, then, should we consider inefficiency as abnormal?

The criterion of abnormality here is the *degree* of inefficiency. Every adult has at least one role to play in society, whether at work or in the family or community. The housewife is expected to take care of the house, care for the children, and cook the meals. The businessman is expected to sell goods or services, pay his employees, and make a profit. *Gross* inefficiency, especially when it is sudden, is usually a sign of abnormality. Thus the housewife who leaves the dishes in the sink, fails to cook, ignores the children, lets the dirty laundry pile up, and merely sits staring at the floor is abnormal enough to be hospitalized. In brief, adults are expected to manifest at least a minimal degree of efficiency in playing their roles; less than minimal efficiency may be considered abnormal.

The Normal-Abnormal Continuum

It is traditional in courses in abnormal psychology to take the students on a tour of a mental institution. There one can see the most bizarre and extreme cases of disturbed behavior: patients having hallucinations, insisting that they are really historical figures such as Napoleon or Woodrow

Figure 26.2 Hearing voices may or may not be bizarre.

Wilson, or sitting immobile for hours on end. Such deviant behavior appears to be so different from that of normal individuals that it appears to fall into a qualitatively different category. But appearances are sometimes deceiving, for abnormal behavior is on a continuum with normal behavior. The behavior of disturbed individuals is nothing more than an exaggeration of the every day behavior of any of us.

Consider the hallucination of hearing voices. Everyone is taught to attend to the "still, small voice of conscience," and it is commonplace for normal individuals to "hear" a parental admonition to be good and to resist temptation. Those with especially good imagery can vividly recall the speech of others, complete with vocal timbre and intonations. The essential difference between

Table 26.1
Words Connoting Impulsivity
(Buss & Gerjuoy, 1957)

	INTENSITY*	ABNORMALITY**
Incontinent	2.1	7.8
Reckless	2.2	7.0
Rash	2.7	6.3
Impetuous	2.8	5.8
Excitable	3.6	5.1
Hasty	3.9	5.0
Abrupt	4.1	4.5
Restless	4.4	4.8
Mobile	4.7	3.8
Spontaneous	4.8	1.8
Self-possessed	5.5	2.1
Cool-headed	5.7	2.0
Deliberate	5.9	3.0
Controlled	6.0	2.8
Restrained	6.6	4.2
Staid	6.6	4.3
Over-cautious	7.3	5.5
Retarded	7.8	6.8
Sluggish	7.8	5.8

* For intensity, the more impulsive words have a lower numerical value.
** For abnormality, the higher the number, the more abnormal is the behavior indicated by the word.

such normal responses and hallucinations is that the person knows that the voice is not real, but recalled or imagined. Nevertheless, it is a short step from imagination to a belief that the voice is real and present.

The same point holds for obsessive thoughts, which preoccupy a person and may frighten him with their intensity and persistence. These are present not only in disturbed individuals but also in weaker form in normals. Certainly, many adolescents and sex-deprived persons tend to become preoccupied with sexual thoughts and fantasies; these may be different in some ways from the obsessions of neurotics, but they surely lie on the same dimension. In brief, normal and abnormal behavior are best considered as being on a single continuum rather than as qualitatively different.

There is a tendency for normality to be associated with moderation, abnormality with exaggeration (too much or too little of any behavior). Thus a normal person will occasionally become fearful as he confronts some of the frightening events of everyday life. The abnormal person is usually excessively fearful (intense or frequent anxiety), but he may be at the other extreme and respond with no fear at all when the situation is truly threatening. Thus too much *or* too little behavior is typically abnormal, with normality represented by a middle ground of moderation.

A quantitative example of the link between moderation and normality may be found in the research of Buss and Gerjuoy (1957). Clinical psychologists scaled words along dimensions of personality such as *impulsivity* (see Table 26.1). The words were scaled once for intensity, ranging from minimal to maximal impulsivity, and a second time for abnormality (higher numbers representing more abnormality). Note that abnormality is represented by both extremes of the intensity dimension. The relationship between intensity and abnormality is asymmetrical: it is more abnormal to be too impulsive than it is to be insufficiently impulsive.

Reaction Systems

In Chapter 1 we examined several models of man and discussed four reaction systems involving nonsocial behavior: *instrumental, affective, cogni-*

tive, and *sensory.* The sensory reaction system has little relevance to abnormal behavior; though disturbed persons may misinterpret sensory inputs, it is because of *cognitive* disturbances, not sensory malfunction. To the remaining three nonsocial reaction systems, we shall add a fourth class of behavior: *social* or interpersonal behavior. All abnormal behavior may be encompassed under these four classes.

Instrumental

Instrumental behavior involves interaction with the environment, usually through chains of responses made sequentially and often with considerable skill. With normality associated with moderation, it should come as no surprise that abnormality involves either *too much* or *too little* instrumental behavior.

EXCESSIVE BEHAVIOR. The varieties of excessive behavior may be aligned along a continuum of abnormality (see Figure 26.3). The mildest form consists of the muscular twitches and facial grimaces called *tics,* the most common example of

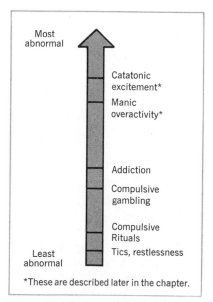

Figure 26.3 *A continuum of excessive instrumental behavior.*

which is rapid eyeblinking. *Restlessness,* the spilling over of "nervous tension" into behavior, is also but a short step from normality. Further up the continuum are compulsive rituals, which are superstitious responses that hold the person in a tight grip. Many normal persons will "knock on wood" just to take no chances that ill fortune will befall them, but they do not become so upset if they fail to make the responses. The compulsive person becomes so tense and uncomfortable if he is unable to run through his ritual that he is driven to go back and complete it. Many compulsions involve an exaggerated attention to details, such as lining up books in a bookcase. Some have symbolic significance such as Lady Macbeth's attempt to rid herself of guilt by compulsively washing her hands of "blood."

Compulsive gambling is somewhat more abnormal in that it usually affects a broader range of the individual's life. There are ample opportunities in our society to indulge this passion, from bingo at church socials to the clubs of Las Vagas, Nevada. Gambling, as we noted in Chapter 14, fits neatly into the model of schedules of reinforcement: the payoff comes on a variable interval schedule, which guarantees persistent responding. Superstition, especially of the individualistic, abnormal sort, may also be explained by schedules of reinforcement. Interestingly enough, most inveterate gamblers are extremely superstitious, their beliefs being attempts to impose some sort of rationale on the random schedule of reinforcement to which they are bound. Many gamblers have a "system," which represents an attempt to make comprehensible the incomprehensible payoffs of the variable interval schedule (see Chapter 14).

The various addictions to alcohol and other drugs constitute even more abnormal behavior in that they seriously affect the health and efficiency of the addicted persons. In extreme cases it is easy to see the abnormality of addiction: chronically drunk persons who may eventually develop brain damage, and heroin addicts who require larger and larger doses to assuage the extreme physiological discomfort called *withdrawal symptoms.* The problems are caused primarily by the drugs, which induce physiological abnormality in addition to the psychological abnormality of ad-

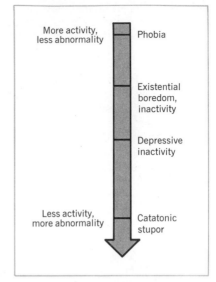

Figure 26.4 A continuum of insufficient instrumental behavior.

diction. In milder cases, such as cigarette or marijuana smoking, it is questionable whether the addiction should be called abnormal. Here we run into two problems. First, so many persons smoke tobacco and marijuana that statistically such activity cannot be called abnormal; second, the activity causes so little harm in the short run (cigarettes are bad for health only over a period of decades) that it may well be within normal limits. After all, we cannot label all strong habits as addictions and therefore abnormal, or we would have to include avid sports fans, excessive television watchers, and overeaters. In brief, addictions pose serious problems in terms of deciding whether they are normal or abnormal.[2] This is simply another aspect of the continuous nature of the normal-abnormal dimension: there is no single point at which we can unequivocally state that a particular behavior is abnormal, as contrasted with a similar behavior we wish to call normal.

Finally, at the most abnormal end of the con-

[2] *We shall discuss this point further at the end of the chapter.*

tinuum are manic overactivity and catatonic excitement. They both involve fantastic bursts of energy in a tumultuous output of physical activity. Manics are typically better organized and may offer a rationale for their energetic behavior ("my plan for achieving world peace"). Schizophrenics are usually disorganized and docile, but occasionally they have outbursts of aggression or destruction that have helped to generate a stereotype of the disturbed person as a "crazy, wild man."

INSUFFICIENT BEHAVIOR. The inability to respond appropriately may also be aligned along a continuum of abnormality, with less activity being associated with more abnormality (see Figure 26.4). The mildest form is the phobia, which consists of abnormal fear and avoidance of objects or events. Our emphasis here is on the avoidance response; the person refrains from dealing with the object of his fear. Thus some persons refuse to travel on airplanes, others will not remain in an enclosed space, and still others have strong enough stage fright to avoid all public performances. There are probably as many phobias as there are objects and events in the environment, and the only difference between an ordinary fear and a phobia is that the latter is unreasonable. In this context unreasonable means that the probability of danger is sufficiently small as to make fearing the event unwarranted. Thus the same person who fears that the airplane may crash will gladly make trips in an automobile, which, in terms of probability of harm, is more dangerous than the airplane. Thus a phobia is a fear or an avoidance of innocuous objects and events; as such, it is only a little different from a normal fear (or avoidance) based on a higher probability of harm.

Existential boredom and inactivity are a little more serious; the person does not initiate activities because he thinks, "What's the use?" Presumably, if such a person were to acquire appropriate goals and values, he would bestir himself. This potential for action makes his behavior less abnormal than the inactivity of the depressive, who is bogged down in a morass of melancholia. When everything is black, the future hopeless, and all prospects gloomy (as in depression), then no activity is entirely worthwhile. With appropriate

therapy, usually chemical or electrical, the depression often lifts and activity resumes. The outcome is less favorable in the most severe abnormality, *catatonic stupor;* the patient, usually hospitalized, typically does not move, talk, eat, or initiate *any* activities. He must be fed, cared for, and led around. Again, such profound inactivity does not persist, but the catatonic rarely moves to a normal level of instrumental behavior, whereas the depressive may.

Affective

Most of the misery of abnormality may be found in the affective sphere, in either anxiety or depression. The *anxious* person may be acutely or chronically fearful; we shall use *anxiety* and *fear* as synonymous. The autonomic components have been described earlier (see Chapter 21), and we need not repeat them here. The discomfort, though private, is so prevalent that it needs no special description.

Miserable as the state of anxiety is, its discomfort is exceeded by that of *depression.* The depressed patient is so beset with melancholy, pessimism and self-depreciation that he may be driven to attempt suicide. This is one of the most serious problems, for the depression usually lifts eventually, but the danger of self-harm warrants extreme caution while the depression lasts.

A third kind of affective excess consists of the extreme elation found in *mania.* The manic patient feels on top of the world, and there may be no limit to his grandiose schemes. Actually, it is not his buoyant mood that is the real problem but the overactivity and unrealistic behavior that accompany it.

So far we have considered only an excess of affect, but insufficiency of affect may be found in both existential neurosis and schizophrenia. In both kinds of cases there is an inability to *feel,* especially to experience joy. Reports of the inner experience vary—a feeling of flatness, of being hollow, of being empty, and so on—but they all share the common problem of a lack of affective involvement, which is merely another aspect of the boredom and apathy that characterize existential neurosis and schizophrenia.

Cognitive

The cognitive aspects of abnormality range from mild symptoms that are difficult to distinguish from normal behavior to bizarre symptoms that are present only in seriously disturbed persons. The mildest cognitive symptom is *worry*. The anxious person is usually apprehensive about one or more objects and events. Some of these worries are minor, such as the fear of dogs; others are major and may seriously affect basic adjustment, such as a fear of airplanes in a man who must travel extensively as part of his job. Several years ago a major league baseball player was forced to retire prematurely because he could not overcome his fear of flying and therefore could not keep up with his team's schedule. Fears have been surveyed in clinical practice and have been divided into two kinds (Dixon et al., 1957). The first is fear of *separation* and the second is fear of *harm* (see Table 26.2). The former is more childish and therefore unrealistic when it occurs in adults. Fear of harm is certainly realistic, and normal adults have good reason to be afraid of the aversive contingencies of the dentist's office or the hospital. Thus the mere presence of worry is not necessarily a sign of abnormality. Only childish fears, when they appear in adults, should be regarded as abnormal. This tells us something about abnormal persons: their behavior often appears to be immature.

Somewhat more serious are *obsessions:* preoccupations with certain topics to the exclusion of all others. This is the other side of the coin of compulsions. If the compulsive person must repeat his actions over and over again because he cannot be sure, then the obsessive person must continually rethink the same thoughts because he doubts. Often the thoughts are repulsive to the individual: murder, rape, incest, and so on. He is at a loss to know where they come from and cannot believe that he wishes to act on them, but they persist. One of the most frightening obsessions occurs in some new mothers: they wish to kill the infant. Fortunately, obsessions are rarely acted on, and their abnormality consists mainly of the discomfort they cause in the obsessed person.

The most serious cognitive abnormalities concern breaks with reality. All of us have occasional wild, incomprehensible, and seriously mistaken

Table 26.2
*Two Kinds of Fears** (*Dixon et al., 1957*)

FEAR OF SEPARATION	FEAR OF HARM
Being left alone	Surgery
Crossing a bridge	Hospitals
Open spaces	Being hurt
Water, drowning	Bearing pain
Train journey	Dentist
Dark	

* These are the predominant fears observed in clinical practice, but there are other classes of fears seen in everyday life—fear of failure or of being rejected, for example.

impressions and thoughts, but most of us have learned to test these against the consensus of others. Reality is basically a question of consensus, and if no one in the house heard that sound very late at night, one concludes that it must have been part of a dream. To insist otherwise is to fly in the face of reality, whose only criterion must ultimately be the shared opinion of the group.

Among the most serious cognitive abnormalities are *hallucinations,* which are responses to sensory inputs that occur when the sensory inputs simply are not there. These are not *illusions,* which are the ordinary and common mistakes that are part of everyday perception. Hallucinations are based on a confusion between fantasy and reality. Thus most persons know that the voice of conscience is really "inside the head" and actually not spoken at all. If a patient reports that he hears someone admonishing him for past sins and there is no one speaking, then his hallucinations consist in externalizing what is essentially an "inner voice." It is easy to see how such a confusion might arise, but children learn early to distinguish inner from outer, and self from nonself. An inability to make this distinction, as in hallucinations, indicates serious behavior problems.

Equally serious breaks with reality are *delusions,* which are unshakable personal beliefs, obviously mistaken or unreal, that direct significant aspects of the individual's behavior. A delusion usually is an incorrect explanation of events that are very important to the person, and the explanation inevitably fits the deluded person's view of himself and others. Thus when someone believes that he has considerable artistic talent that is unappreciated by everyone else, he may come to believe that it is all a plot to deprive him of his just fame. Such themes are more common than might be supposed, but most persons have learned to check their beliefs against the consensus of others and tend not to let their behavior be guided by false explanations. Seriously disturbed persons, on the other hand, tend to act on their false beliefs, escaping from fantasied pursuers or organizing grandiose schemes.

Finally, among cognitive problems there are disturbances of language and thought. Language is learned so early and is so fundamental to adjustment that its abnormalities show up very quickly. Coherent speech involves sequences of words arranged more or less grammatically and in a way that makes sense associatively. Plays on words, for example, are attempted in humor but not when the object is serious communication. When the speaker's usual language sequences reveal loose associations or plays on words, he has clearly lost his ability to communicate. Language is acquired so easily and so universally that its disturbance therefore must suggest very serious abnormality. For example, a disturbed person might confuse the meanings of words that sound alike because he cannot keep within one associative train: "I refuse to eat chicken (fowl) because it is a *foul* thing to kill these animals."

Case Report

The expression of thoughts in speech or writing offers an excellent opportunity to observe cognitive abnormality. The following letter was sent by a man who had been institutionalized as a schizophrenic.[3] Note the difficulty the writer has in staying with a thought sequence and how easily his associations wander. The real names have been replaced with fictitious ones; mistakes have not been corrected.

Sales Manager
Jones & Jones Drug Company

My family represents the top in the medical field and I want to compliment your company tell Bob hello.

My family is bringing out a coagulation program that will put medicine back where it started.

They say our family is to be awarded for I and my brothers efforts.

We pass our achievements down to the Smiths and Youngs. Our products gain us the patents and it is now time our grandfathers told the truth and put the blame on those under us. We don't participate in insurance programs and Coca Cola and Sunkist products. My family including the women also have fat fingers and my or I should say

[3] *Schizophrenia, representing an extreme of abnormality, will be discussed shortly.*

our familys contribution to Smithville has been a worry and we donated a similar plot to land for others to match our achievements in the Highland Hills. We have a large family and ink and paper along with law has gained us worldwide popularity. My name is Mr. John Doe and my brother is none other than Father Flanagan of Boys Town, Nebr. We sponsor charity also. Although the women as well as Herbert claim your bandaids at one time were to small, I want to thank the Jones for bigger band Aids it is a reward to our family for inventing the childrens nap thus enabling Michael to look into cavietys without noise. He's a dentist.

Sincerely Johnnie

We gave our Winchester & Smith & Wesson stock to the Jones family. Back in Paris we would point and they would hit the target.

My grandfather invented the finger table and we get calls from the husbands of the Smith girls when they see a contact removed by Lawrences wisdom, and a head we can't control.

Respectfully,
Art

As Michael used to say keep the dry eye around you and you've got low security. He got his experience from high security.

Social

We live out our lives in a predominantly social environment in which we are expected to play appropriate roles in relation to those around us. The developing child is expected to discard earlier roles for more mature ones. Some individuals have difficulty in doing this, with the result that as adults they are still clinging to childish ways of relating to others. Children tend to adjust to difficult problems by appealing to adults.

A much more serious problem is the avoidance of all social relationships, most often motivated by strong fear of rejection or harm. Any social attachment has positive and negative features. For most of us the balance is tipped toward the positive side, and the feeling of belonging and the affection outweighing the possibilities of rejection or even harm. For the seriously disturbed person the balance tips the other way: little or no affection, no feeling of affiliation, and strong fear of rejection, or worse. He tends to avoid close social contacts and becomes a social isolate. A solitary existence makes it difficult to test one's perception against the group censensus, and thus one consequence may be a marked deficiency in reality-testing. Close social interaction is a fundamental aspect of human adjustment, and the person who shuts himself away from others is denying part of his humanity. This miserable state of affairs occurs only in the most severe abnormality.

Traditional Categories

Psychiatrists and psychologists have been trying to understand abnormal behavior for a very long time, and they have developed traditional ways of classifying symptoms. Though there are serious problems with all previous attempts to classify abnormal behavior (see Buss, 1966), there is sufficient information in the traditional categories to make their study worthwhile. We shall discuss three major categories: neurosis, psychosis, and conduct disorders.

Table 26.3
Three Kinds of Neurotic Symptoms

CLASSIFICATION	SYMPTOMS
Indicants of excessive fears	Worry, tension, restlessness tremors and distractibility
Self-defeating attempts to cope with fear situation	Excessive forgetting, obsessive thoughts, and compulsive rituals
Psychological residuals of prolonged tension	Depression, tiredness, boredom, and bodily complaints

Neurosis

The mildest forms of abnormality are called neuroses. They include symptoms seen in most persons but manifested in neurotics with greater *frequency, intensity,* or *duration.* All neurotic symptoms may be regarded as expressions of anxiety, unsuccessful attempts to deal with fear situations (see Table 26.3).

The person who is tense, apprehensive, and generally fearful is called an *anxiety neurotic.* He may have specific, unrealistic fears (phobias) or a generalized anxiety that is so pervasive as to paralyze attempts at instrumental behavior. Such symptoms occur more frequently in women, who are allowed in our culture to be fearful and dependent on men to rescue them from dangerous situations. Such dependency hinders the development of responses that would deal with fearful situations rather than giving in to the fear.

When confronted with difficult situations, especially those involving possible harm or rejection, many persons make responses that fail to deal with the source of the problem. Under this heading are *obsessions,* which are cognitive attempts to solve a problem or an inability to stop thinking about the problem; and *compulsions,* which are superstitious responses that fail to attack the source of the trouble. These two symptoms are commonly grouped together under the heading of *obsessive-compulsive neurosis.* Much less frequent are symptoms involving excessive forgetting, a temporary inability to see or hear, or a temporary paralysis; these are grouped under the heading of *hysteria,* a neurosis that presently occurs mainly in persons who have little education and who have been reared in isolated and backward areas. The common thread running through these disparate symptoms is that they represent desperate and unsuccessful attempts to deal with intolerable situations. Consider what would happen if a neurotic heard an air raid siren signal an impending attack from the skies. He might well reach for his rifle and shoot down the air raid siren! It is the essence of self-defeating behavior to eliminate the *signal* while completely failing to deal with the real danger itself.

The third kind of neurotic symptom includes those representing the unsuccessful outcome of prolonged fear and tension. Depending on factors that are still not understood, the neurotic may become *depressed,* chronically *tired,* or bored and apathetic (presumably the existential neurosis). Or he may develop one of a variety of bodily complaints called psychosomatic: high blood pressure, ulcer, headache, allergies, and so on. Those with bodily complaints are usually seen by physicians, who are more and more conceding the important role of psychological factors in what previously appeared to be strictly medical problems.

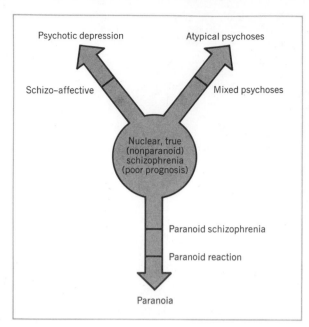

Figure 26.5 *Schizophrenia in relation to other psychoses.* (BUSS AND BUSS, 1969.)

Psychosis

Psychotics are considerably more disturbed than neurotics, and they more or less fit the common notion of an insane person. The legal definition of insanity roughly coincides with psychosis, the implication being that the individual is so disturbed that he cannot be held responsible for his actions. Nevertheless, there are degrees of psychosis, some of which are little different from normality, and we should not forget that every normal person now and then has a crazy thought or impulse at some time or other.

The most common and important psychosis is schizophrenia, which is estimated to occur in one percent of the world's population. The classical symptoms of schizophrenia are

1. Hallucinations.
2. Delusions.
3. Disturbances of language and thought.
4. Gross inefficiency.
5. Isolation from others.

Not all these "textbook symptoms" are seen in all schizophrenics, and they rarely appear together in one person. But, taken together, they constitute the entity called schizophrenia. As might be expected from the foregoing, the diagnosis of schizophrenia is not always reliable. Compounding the problem is the course of schizophrenia over time: it may develop slowly over a period of years, during which the person may show one or another of the symptoms listed above.

Of greater immediate interest is the relationship of schizophrenia to other psychoses. It is often difficult to distinguish schizophrenia from psychotic depression and paranoid reactions (which will be described shortly), and one solution is to consider schizophrenia as an endpoint of these dimensions of psychosis (Buss & Buss, 1969, Chapter 1). The scheme is outlined in Figure 26.5. The *basic, nuclear,* or *true* schizophrenia is defined by the classical, textbook symptoms: severe thought and language disorder, retreat from reality to fantasy, and isolation from others. The prognosis for recovery is usually very poor, and the patient may be expected to remain schizophrenic the rest of his life. Relating to this core psychosis are the other psychoses, each with a better prognosis; the mixed forms of these psychoses have some schizophrenic-like symptoms which cause considerable confusion for diagnosticians.

PSYCHOTIC DEPRESSION. At the end of one dimension is psychotic depression,[4] the major features of which are melancholy and inactivity. It has been clearly established that depressives eventually do recover, the process being hastened by electric shock therapy. True schizophrenics lack affect, manifesting no sorrow or joy, and their prognosis is poor. This has led to the conclusion that the presence of affect is a good prognostic sign, and the facts bear this out. Complicating the diagnostician's tasks are persons with *both* schizophrenic symptoms (thought disorder) and depressive affect. They are called *schizo-affective* psychotics, and their prognosis is better than that of schizophrenics, worse than that of psychotic depressives.

---

[4] *This scheme omits mania, which is often grouped with depression and called manic-depressive psychosis. For present purposes mania may be regarded as equivalent to depression, for presumably mania is the affective component that is responsible for the better prognosis.*

Table 26.4

Differences Between Atypical Psychoses and Schizophrenia

	ATYPICAL PSYCHOSES	TRUE SCHIZOPHRENIA
Onset	Usually sudden	Usually slow
Symptoms	Acute; confusion and disorientation	Chronic; no confusion
Intellectual function	Mildly disturbed	Severely disturbed
Prognosis	Good	Poor

ATYPICAL PSYCHOSIS. At the end of another dimension lies a group of psychoses variously called *cyclic* (Leonhard, 1961), nonprocess (Stephens & Astrup, 1963), or *pseudo-neurotic* (Hock & Polatin, 1949). Here they are called *atypical* because they differ from nuclear, true schizophrenia in the ways described in Table 26.4. Note that the prognosis is good in the atypical psychoses, poor in true schizophrenia. Presumably there are also mixed forms, having features of both schizophrenia and atypical psychoses and having a prognosis between the two.

PARANOIA. Paranoids generally have delusions, and the most salient characteristic of paranoia is a serious *misinterpretation* of reality. The long-standing controversy over whether to include them with schizophrenics has never really been resolved. In the present scheme *paranoia* is represented as the end of the third dimension of psychosis, with *paranoid reactions* and *paranoid schizophrenia* being mixed forms (see Figure 26.5). Paranoids have been described by Foulds and Owen (1963) in terms of five characteristics:

1. Massive, well-ingrained delusions of persecution or grandiosity, which are usually put together in a systematic fashion.

2. Long-standing traits of suspiciousness and placing blame on others.
3. Late onset of symptoms, much later than in schizophrenia.
4. Relative absence of thought disorder, disturbance of intellectual functions, or deterioration over time.
5. Greater resistance to change but a better prognosis for at least a marginal adjustment outside an institution.

This scheme of relating schizophrenia to three other psychoses is best regarded as an attempt to impose some order on the chaos of a variety of psychotic symptoms. It is in approximate agreement with the facts, and its emphasis on prognosis is entirely appropriate. Nevertheless, it bears repeating that there are few "textbook cases" in everyday life and a patient's symptoms may change over time.

Conduct Disorders

Several of the conduct disorders have already been mentioned: compulsive gambling, addiction to alcohol or other drugs, and sexual deviancy.

These are essentially social problems in that their deviance consists of their being an affront to the formal rules of society. Ours is basically a puritanical culture, if not in practice then in the myths we perpetrate and many of the laws we sometimes enforce. Thus gambling is regarded by many as sinful, and most states have laws prohibiting or restricting it. The drinking of alcohol, prohibited by national law for a dozen years in this century, is strictly regulated by all states and proscribed by most religious groups. And alcohol is the most accepted of the various drugs: witness the fanaticism with which many law officers pursue those who smoke marijuana, which is a less dangerous drug than alcohol. All states forbid homosexuality and various other acts that are labeled perversions (best defined as "what the other fellow does"), and some even forbid heterosexual intercourse out of wedlock. In brief, these conduct disorders are probably more sociological problems than they are psychological problems.

The remaining conduct disorder is *psychopathy,* which includes the following characteristics:

1. Thrill-seeking and disregard of conventions.
2. Inability to control impulses or delay gratification.
3. Rejection of authority and discipline.
4. Failure to alter punished behavior.
5. Pathological lying.
6. Asocial or antisocial (criminal) behavior.

In past decades it was a simple matter to list these features and then discuss the background of such abnormal behavior. In light of the changes in the behavior of young persons during the past generation, however, it has become difficult to distinguish between psychopaths (abnormal) and rather large numbers of normal persons who smoke pot, deceive authority as they have been deceived, refuse to comply with rules they disagree with, and disobey laws they believe are unfair. In previous times there was greater conformity to authority and an easier acceptance of the discrepancy between our myths and our daily real-

ity, between pious promises and their realization, between the sermons preached on Sunday and the often dog-eat-dog competition of the remaining days of the week, and finally between the laws guaranteeing democracy and the actual treatment of minority ethnic and religious groups. If a young black man resists racist laws enforced by racist officials, should we brand him abnormal? If he lies to authority, disregards (white) conventions, and fails to alter his behavior when punished, shall we call him a psychopath? The answer is no, both in psychological terms and (increasingly) in statistical terms. As we have mentioned several times, if the behavior is sufficiently widespread, it cannot be called abnormal. Thus the category *psychopath* is becoming sufficiently blurred that its continued use is being seriously questioned.[5] This is consistent with increasing pressure to eliminate the entire range of conduct disorders from the classification of abnormal behavior. As with sexual deviance, gambling and addiction, so with rebellion against authority: what might have been called abnormal a generation ago may well belong in the normal range today.

*   *   *

This chapter has omitted abnormal behavior in children, behavior related to abnormal brain functioning as in a brain injury, and mental retardation. Each of these involves specialized study and background knowledge that go far beyond the present context. In general, they belong more in applied areas of medicine and education than they do in psychology. This does not lessen their importance, only their relevance to our exposition.

[5] *Elimination of minority rebels and political activists from this category solves part of the problem. There are clear cut instances of psychopathy that are unrelated to ethnic or other social issues. As with any abnormal behavior, the severe cases offer no diagnostic or theoretical problem but the borderline cases do. Psychopathy and the conduct disorders are of special importance because they involve nonconformity to authority.*

abnormal behavior: causes and cures

Biological approach — nervous system — heredity — chemical therapy — Freudian theory — defenses — psychoanalysis — interpersonal theory — psychodrama — T-groups — self theory — existential theory — nondirective therapy — encounter groups — learning approach — anxiety and avoidance — maladaptive responses — absence of responses — behavior modification — general issues in therapy

There are three broad approaches to understanding abnormal behavior: biological, dynamic, and learning.[1] The biological approach derives from medicine and uses a *disease model,* hence the popular term *mental illness*. Historically, it was a huge step forward to regard abnormal behavior as an illness rather than as the result of demons, for it meant that patients could receive treatment rather than punishment. But the useful political tactic of calling disturbed persons *sick* does not necessarily add to our understanding of their behavior. Thus some psychologists suggest that the disease model is never appropriate in the study of behavior problems; others insist that it is always appropriate. The truth, not surprisingly, appears to lie between the extremes: the medical model is useful in understanding psychosis but not other kinds of disturbed behavior.

The dynamic approach starts with psychoanalytic theory, especially the orthodox psychoanalytic theory called Freudian. There are two other dynamic theories, one concerning *interpersonal* aspects of behavior and the other con-

[1] *We omit the sociological approach because it is beyond the bounds of an introductory psychology text.*

cerning self and existential aspects. All three dynamic theories share a common assumption: that the behaviors called symptoms are caused by hidden, underlying conflicts.

The learning approach assumes that the observable symptoms can be explained without recourse to such notions as underlying conflicts. All problems are regarded as learned: too much or too little learning, learning of the wrong kind, failure to extinguish, and so on. Needless to say, learning theorists and dynamic theorists find much to disagree about, and they are united only in their common rejection of the disease model that is part of the biological approach.

Each of the three approaches not only suggests the causes of abnormal behavior but also offers a cure. Nevertheless, there is not necessarily a connection between knowing what *causes* abnormal behavior and what might cure it. An example from medicine may help make this point. The cause of appendicitis is (in nonmedical terms) food that has somehow gotten into this blind alley, followed by infection. The cure for appendicitis is surgery: removing the infected part. Surgery will cure the problem no matter how it originates. Similarly, therapy can alleviate psychological problems even when the basic cause is unknown. For example, electric shock will often help to lift a psychotic depression; no one really knows why electric shock helps, and it does so even when the cause of the depression is not understood at all.

On the other hand, it is possible to understand the cause of a malady without being able to cure it. Thus the general cause of colds is well known: it is one of several viruses. Yet as everyone knows, a cold takes a week to disappear when treated and seven days when untreated.

A final point on the relationship between cause and cure concerns *time*. Abnormal behavior rarely develops in a matter of days or weeks; it takes months or years. Once it occurs, it may last for many years. It is entirely possible that the conditions that *produce* the abnormal behavior are not necessarily the ones that *maintain* it. An individual might develop a phobia because of a sudden, painful experience and then maintain the phobia for years because of the special treatment received thereafter, such as relief from onerous tasks. Insofar as this is true, it means that therapy will have to deal with the factors that are *main-*

taining the abnormal behavior, not the original *causes,* which are no longer operating.

The Biological Approach

The biological approach focuses on the more severe abnormalities, mainly the psychoses. Seen biologically, a psychosis is like a systemic disease such as arthritis. The organism is failing in some way to function normally, and the outcome is a pattern of symptoms. It is assumed that just as *physiological* malfunction underlies medical abnormalities, so *neural* malfunction underlies behavioral abnormalities. Moreover, the defect in the nervous system is likely to be inherited. Thus there are two main thrusts in the biological approach, one emphasizing the biochemical activity of the nervous system and the other emphasizing the inheritance of abnormal behavior.

The Nervous System

Gross defects of the nervous system fall under the heading of *organic brain damage* and will not be further discussed. Our concern is with the possibility of defects of neural *function* in a nervous system that is anatomically intact. The notion that chemical substances might be causing psychoses dates back many years. It was strengthened when *general paresis,* a disease with psychotic symptoms, was found to be caused by the syphilis spirochete, which attacks the central nervous system. Obviously, a person with a damaged nervous system may develop serious behavioral abnormalities, but there are few psychoses like paresis and the most common psychological abnormalities clearly are not caused by infection.

The search for a neural cause of psychosis has been narrowed to the substances underlying neural transmission, the *neurohumors.* These may exist in insufficient quantities, persist too long, or be metabolized to form chemicals that interfere with normal functioning of the nervous system.

Two lines of evidence furnish indirect evidence for biochemical theories of psychosis. First, it is well known that certain drugs cause bizarre cognitive symptoms that appear to be similar to those seen in psychoses. Thus *mescaline,* in the form of

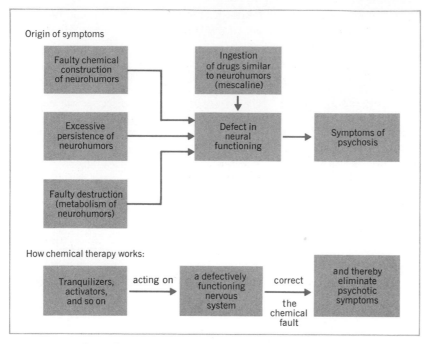

Origin of symptoms

Faulty chemical construction of neurohumors

Ingestion of drugs similar to neurohumors (mescaline)

Excessive persistence of neurohumors

Defect in neural functioning

Symptoms of psychosis

Faulty destruction (metabolism of neurohumors)

How chemical therapy works:

Tranquilizers, activators, and so on

acting on

a defectively functioning nervous system

correct the chemical fault

and thereby eliminate psychotic symptoms

Figure 27.1 *Speculation about the biochemistry of abnormal behavior.*

peyote, has been taken by Indians for hundreds of years to induce hallucinations, and *lysergic acid diethylamide* (LSD) is a laboratory product that has been used by young persons to "turn on." Both drugs are similar to the chemicals underlying neural transmission, but they differ enough to cause the weird experiences reported by the users. The assumption is that either faulty construction of the neurohumors produces chemicals like mescaline naturally, or when the normal neurohumors are destroyed (metabolized), the products are abnormal and cause symptoms.

The second line of evidence comes from the use of drugs in therapy. There are substances called tranquilizers that reduce anxiety and calm excited patients; other substances help lift depression by activating patients; and still others help reduce the patients' confusion and get them in better contact with reality. These various drugs are related chemically to the neurohumors. The relationships are complex and much is still not understood, but the evidence for a biochemical basis for psychosis is strong, if indirect. The two

lines of evidence may be linked speculatively to abnormal functioning of the nervous system (see Figure 27.1).

Heredity

Whatever the nature of the biochemical defects that cause psychoses, presumably they are based on inherited predispositions. It is not a psychosis that is inherited but the *tendency* to become psychotic. One appropriate medical model is *allergy.* The allergic person inherits a tendency to overact to certain foreign substances—ragweed for example. Though the tendency is there, it may never be potentiated into symptoms so long as the individual remains clear of ragweed. Contact with ragweed, however, trips the mechanism, and the result is a runny nose, itchy eyes, breathing difficulty, skin rash, or other symptoms of an overactive rejection mechanism. Similarly, an inherited tendency to become psychotic might not manifest itself under unusually benign kinds of socializa-

Table 27.1

Rates of Incidence of Schizophrenia in Blood Relations of Schizophrenics (from Buss, 1966)

General population	1%
Grandparents	4
Grandchildren	4
Nephews and nieces	4
Cousins	3
Parents	4–10
Half-siblings	7
Siblings	5–14

Children
  one schizophrenic parent
  two schizophrenic parents
	16
	39–68

Dizygotic twins	3–17
Monozygotic twins	67–86

tion, whereas other regimes might potentiate the symptoms in full force. In brief, even those who believe strongly in the hereditary basis of abnormal behavior concede that inheritance is a necessary but not a sufficient cause of psychosis.

Evidence of the inheritance of a tendency toward abnormal behavior is obtained in the same ways as evidence for the heritability of intelligence (see Chapter 24). Statistics are compiled on abnormal behavior in persons who are related, with the expectation that the closer the blood relationship, the higher the incidence of the abnormality will be. The best evidence comes from research on schizophrenia, and Table 27.1 summarizes a number of studies. Three facts in this table stand out. First, the overall rate of schizophrenia in the population is roughly 1%, and this holds for every country for which statistics are available (mainly Western societies). The relatively small variations from one country to the next (0.7 to 2.86) suggests that schizophrenia has a genetic

Table 27.2
Comparison of the Children of Schizophrenic Versus Normal Mothers (from Heston & Denny, 1968)

	CHILDREN OF NORMAL MOTHERS	CHILDREN OF SCHIZOPHRENIC MOTHERS
Number	50	47
Mean Age	36	36
Number adopted	19	22
Schizophrenia	0	5
Mental deficiency (IQ less than 70)	0	4
Psychopathy	7	13

component, but this is of course only indirect evidence.[2]

Second, the incidence of schizophrenia goes up as the blood relationship becomes closer. Thus the incidence is lowest among the most distant relatives of schizophrenics (grandparents, cousins, and so on), and it climbs steadily through parents, siblings, and children of schizophrenics.

The third fact concerns the difference in incidence between monozygotic (identical) and dizygotic (fraternal) twins. As the table shows, the incidence of schizophrenia in monozygotic twins of schizophrenic patients is several times that of dizygotic twins. It might be argued that these data can be explained in environmental terms as well as genetic. The parents who pass on their genes usually raise the children who receive these genes, which means that schizophrenia in the children might be caused by childrearing rather than by an inherited tendency. As for the higher incidence in monozygotic twins than in dizygotic twins, it can be argued that monozygotic twins are treated more alike.

The best way to answer such arguments is with data that indicate the *separate* contributions of the parents as suppliers of genes, as opposed to childrearing agents. The major technique for separating these two effects is the foster home study: the incidence of abnormal behavior is counted in children raised not by their biological parents but by foster parents. Thus the biological parents who contribute their genes are not the

[2] *The evidence is indirect in the sense that it indicates only something about environment: differences in environments from one country to the next appear to make no difference in the incidence of schizophrenia. It may be inferred that if environment is a weaker factor, heredity must be stronger. There is other indirect evidence for a hereditary component in schizophrenia: the admission rates to mental health hospitals were essentially the same in the late nineteenth century and the early 1950s (Goldhamer & Marshall, 1953).*

Table 27.3
Comparison of Children Raised in Institutions Versus Foster Families (from Heston & Denny, 1968)

	INSTITUTIONS	FOSTER FAMILIES
Number	47	50
Age	34	38
Schizophrenic mother	25	22
Schizophrenia	3	2
Mental deficiency	2	2
Psychopathy	5	6
Neurosis	9	11

ones who provide the familial environment for the children.

One of the earliest and best-controlled studies compared the children of schizophrenic mothers with those of normal mothers (Heston, 1966; Heston & Denny, 1968). All the children were permanently separated from their mothers at the age of two weeks and subsequently raised in either foundling or foster homes. Some were eventually adopted; others were not. These various factors were essentially the same for the children of schizophrenic mothers as for the children of normal mothers. The children were subsequently traced after having reached adulthood, and the incidence of abnormality was tabulated. The results are shown in Tables 27.2 and 27.3. Table 27.2 compares children of normal mothers with those of schizophrenic mothers, with roughly equal numbers in each group having been raised in foundling homes and foster homes. The incidence of abnormality is significantly higher in the children of schizophrenic mothers in every category

in the table: schizophrenia, mental deficiency, psychopathy, and neurosis. The fact that only small numbers of the children of schizophrenic mothers later become schizophrenic themselves reinforces the earlier suggestion that heredity is a necessary but not a sufficient condition for psychosis. On the other hand, the contribution of heredity, not only to schizophrenia, but also to other abnormalities, is clearly established by these data.

An important aspect of the environment is the presence of a single set of parents who are the major agents of socialization and the most important purveyors of love during the child's development. Foster parents may or may not be as loving as biological parents, but no one would deny that their presence offers a huge advantage over growing up without a single set of stable parents. The data in Table 27.3 bear on this issue. When abnormal behavior is compared in institution-reared versus foster-reared children, there are essentially no differences. This finding is surprising in that the combination of institutional life and absence of parents would seem to comprise one of the worst environments in which to raise a child. If such a negative environment does not yield more abnormality, all theories emphasizing environmental variables as determinants of abnormality are weakened. Of course there are many other environmental factors, and it may be that some kind of parents contribute more toward the abnormality of their children than no parents at all.

Thus a genetic basis for schizophrenia is clearly established, and there are also supporting, if fewer, data sustaining a genetic approach to mania and psychotic depression. There is no comparable evidence for the inheritance of other abnormalities, though many geneticists believe that it will be found. The same situation prevails for the substances under lying neural transmission. In brief, the biological approach appears to be fruitful in understanding psychoses but perhaps of less value in understanding other abnormalities. The disease model appears to be appropriate only for psychotic behavior.

Therapy

The *genetic* approach cannot suggest any therapy for abnormal behavior, but it does have something to say about prevention. If the basic predisposition toward abnormality is inherited, it follows that the only way to eliminate, or at least reduce, the occurrence of psychosis is through selective mating. If those with a family background of psychosis did not have children, the incidence of psychosis would eventually drop. This of course is unlikely to happen, because no society is presently ready to institute such a preventive program.

Actually, there are reasonable grounds for *not* wanting such a program. Schizophrenia, for example, occurs in 1% of the population, and there must be an adaptive reason for its persistence or it would have vanished long ago. Perhaps those who come from family backgrounds that include schizophrenia have other traits that are desirable or important. A hint that this speculation is correct may be found in the foster home study cited earlier. Among the children of schizophrenic mothers (called Experimental subjects) were many who are making above-average adjustments:

The 21 Experimental subjects who exhibited no significant psychosocial impairment were not only successful adults but in comparison to the Control group were more spontaneous when interviewed and have more colorful life histories. They held the more creative jobs: musician, teacher, home-designer; and followed more imaginative hobbies: oil painting, music, antique aircraft. (HESTON & DENNY, 1968, P. 371.)

Thus persons with a possible hereditary taint in one area may have a superior hereditary potential in other areas. This explains why a tendency toward psychosis can remain in the gene pool in spite of its negative effects on adjustment; any attempt to breed selectively might eliminate or decrease tendencies that society very much values.[3]

The *biochemical* approach does suggest a cure: correcting the ostensible chemical abnormality by adding appropriate drugs. Chemical therapy has been fairly successful in helping to lift some kinds of depression and in bringing many patients closer to reality. Drugs have been especially helpful in controlling the behavior of psychotic patients, thereby eliminating most of the physical restraints that were once needed. But we do not yet know why the chemicals succeed in some instances and fail in others. Nor do we know the precise relationship between the chemicals used in therapy and those that are presumably causing disturbed neural functioning. In brief, it will be some time before chemicals can be prescribed for psychosis the way penicillin is prescribed for an infection.

Freudian Theory

Orthodox psychoanalytic theory starts with the assumption that basic urges, originating primarily in the id, continually strive for discharge, that is, strive to be expressed in behavior. The ego, representing reality, delays or prohibits the discharge of impulses or allows them to be expressed in altered form. The presence of unexpressed impulses cause tension, and it is the task of the ego

[3] *The inheritance of schizophrenia may well be polygenic (multiple minor genes), and this mode of inheritance would also account for the existence of maladaptive traits. The rationale is too complex to discuss here.*

to balance allowable tension against the demands of society.

The Basic Conflict

Society enforces its demands by punishing forbidden behavior. After the expression of an impulse has resulted in punishment, the mere occurrence of the impulse leads to *anxiety*. Fear is a realistic or objective apprehension concerning a clear threat from the environment; the noxious event is presumably inevitable, and the person can avoid the anxiety by inhibiting the impulse. Impulses are inhibited by the ego through mechanisms that are called *defenses* against anxiety. These defenses, like the impulses themselves, are unconscious; in fact, one major purpose of defenses is to prevent awareness of the threatening impulses.

The conflict between acting out and inhibiting impulses is assumed to be fundamental to all abnormal behavior. There are four basic outcomes of the conflict, each involving a different kind of abnormality (see Figure 27.2). First, the anxiety may be expressed directly, as in a panic reaction or in diffuse anxiety. The person is not sure what he fears and is aware only of a nameless dread. Presumably, the ego defenses are effective in preventing the forbidden impulses from being expressed, but they cannot deal with the associated anxiety.

Second, a compromise is effected between the forbidden impulses and the defending forces, the outcome being an expression of the impulses in disguised form. For example, an individual might develop a fear of open places because of the possibility of sexual adventure; he is not aware of the sexual nature of his impulses, only that he has a phobia about open spaces. Thus the defenses are only partially successful: they keep the impulses from being discharged directly and they prevent awareness, but they do not prevent the occurrence of anxiety. Other kinds of defenses, such as compulsions, may be more successful in avoiding anxiety but only by burdening the person with a crippling adjustment (absurd ritual, attention to trivial details, and so on).

Third, the conflict may remain unresolved and become chronic. This causes a continual drain on

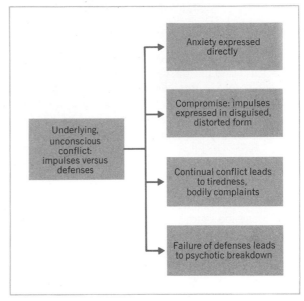

Figure 27.2 *Basic Freudian model of abnormal behavior.*

the ego, resulting in tiredness and even bodily complaints.

Finally, the defenses may fail to stem the impulses or the anxiety or both, and a breakdown ensues. The underlying unconscious material pours forth with all of its distortions and bizarreness, as the individual moves from the defensiveness of neurosis to the surrender of psychosis.

Fixation, Regression, and Repression

Psychoanalytic theory uses a developmental model with a fixed sequence of stages: oral, anal, phallic, and genital. Normal adults reach the genital stage with residuals of earlier stages having been integrated as mature modes of behavior. Abnormal persons carry around excessive residuals of the pregenital stages. To use psychoanalytic metaphors, if a child is deprived of love during the oral phase, he "hungers" for it; if his toilet training is harsh during the anal period, he will subsequently be "anal"—frugal, orderly, and punctilious. Each stage is assumed to have particular problems associated with it:

oral—dependence and affection
anal—independence and resentment
phallic—aggression and sexuality

Thus if a child has unfortunate experiences during the oral period, he will always be to some extent "stuck" in this period. The conflicts associated with the oral period will dog him throughout development and will eventually cause abnormality during adulthood. The retention of early childhood modes is called *fixation,* a term that expresses metaphorically the individual's being excessively preoccupied with the problems of a particular stage of development.

When a person experiences difficulties at any age, he tends to revert to earlier patterns of behavior. This return to earlier modes in the face of present problems is called *regression.* The more trouble the child has had with early stages, the less successful he will be in adjusting to the problems of later stages. Thus fixation paves the way for later regression.

A child presumably can tolerate only small amounts of tension, and he cannot easily cope with strong aggressive or sexual urges, especially when these are subject to strong punishment. His only solution is to employ the most primitive defense against anxiety—repression. Repression may be defined as a mechanism that rejects impulses from consciousness and keeps them unconscious. It isolates ideas and impulses from consciousness and keeps them unconscious. It isolates ideas and impulses from the rest of the personality, placing them in a "deep freeze." Thus encapsulated, the bothersome thoughts and motivations are prevented from participating in the growth experiences of the developing child. Most of the self continues to mature and acquire the mechanisms and controls needed for adult adjustment, but the smaller part isolated by repression fails to undergo these experiences and remains childlike. Thus part of the personality remains fixated at an earlier stage, while the remainder progresses to maturity. These notions are designed to explain puzzling instances of childishness in otherwise mature adults.

The more severe the repression and the larger the part of the self that is isolated, the more severe is the abnormality that subsequently develops. During childhood—especially during the latency period between early childhood and puberty—conflicts over aggression, sexuality, and dependence may be sealed off from the rest of the personality; but this state of affairs cannot endure. At puberty there is a surge of basic impulses, especially sexual impulses, that destroys the tenuous equilibrium between impulses and childish defenses. At this point the individual either adds new defenses and intensifies the conflict or expresses his anxiety directly in the form of panic. Both outcomes involve abnormality. In brief, the psychoanalytic theory of abnormality involves the following sequential steps:

1. Painful experiences during early childhood →
2. Repression of the impulses that cause anxiety →
3. Isolation of part of the self from maturation (fixation) →
4. Persistence of childish trends to adulthood →
5. Upsurge of basic urges at puberty →
6. Reversion to childish modes of solving problems (regression) →
7. Occurrence of abnormal behavior.

Defenses

A defense is any mechanism that protects against anxiety. Thus one can fail to remember that an event occurred (repression) or revert to childish modes of coping with threats (regression). These two defenses are merely the beginning of a list of psychoanalytic mechanisms implicated in unconscious conflicts. The other major defenses are denial, projection, isolation, displacement, reaction formation, and sublimation.

DENIAL. This defense is closely allied with repression. Whereas repression involves an inhibition of *memory,* denial involves a refusal to acknowledge present events or future certainties. Thus a grief-stricken mother may deny that her child has died and ask bystanders where the child is, or a parachutist may deny that there is really any danger in what he is doing. Like most defenses, denial is also used by well-adjusted persons. Most adolescents, for example, implicitly believe that they will never die, though if pressed, they will admit that death is certain; many also are sure that they will never become old, wrinkled, and gray like their parents—and this too is part of normal denial. It becomes abnormal when the mistaken belief persists and directs behavior in the face of strong evidence to the contrary. One problem many physicians have with diabetics is that some patients deny the seriousness of their illness and continue to eat foods that seriously harm them. A similar problem occurs in elderly cigarette smokers who have heart disease or emphysema.

PROJECTION. It is a short step from avoiding blame to improperly placing it on someone else. One way of justifying aggression against another person is to say, "He started it." Suppose that a young man finds himself attracted to other men, but these feelings cause severe anxiety. He can partially assuage the anxiety by projecting the homosexual impulses, which will lead him to report that men are making advances to him. The problem may become quite complex in that the young man may be acting so as to invite homosexual advances, thus validating his belief. Similarly, the person who projects his hatred to others may act in such a hostile fashion that others do come to dislike him.

ISOLATION. Impulses can be "detoxified" by stripping them of their affective qualities. This is accomplished by the mechanism of isolation, which splits the cognitive components of an urge from its affective components, enabling the individual to think the forbidden impulses in an unemotional detached manner. Thus an obsessive person may have continual thoughts of murder and rape without being aroused at all. The thoughts typically appear alien, as if they had come from someone else. Isolation has its normal counterpart in objective thinking, in which the person attempts to set aside passion and reflect calmly. When the mechanism extends to personal issues that cannot be dealt with objectively, the outcome is abnormal behavior. The neurotic may thus buy some peace of mind by using isolation as a defense against anxiety, but the price is emotional sterility, aloofness, and inability to let go and enjoy any passionate involvement.

DISPLACEMENT. If a forbidden impulse were to become conscious, it would precipitate panic. One way to prevent this is to disguise the unconscious urge so that it cannot be recognized. As we mentioned earlier, a fear of open places may symbolize a fear of sexual provocation. In this way the impulse gains some expression but only as part of a compromise: it is expressed symbolically rather than in its original form. Psychoanalytic theory regards all phobias as instances of displacement, with the conscious fear representing a deep, unconscious conflict over unacceptable urges.

REACTION FORMATION. One way to deal with a forbidden impulse is to replace it with its opposite, or at least attempt to do so. Suppose a strictly trained young woman has strong hostile urges, which she has been taught to believe are evil. She can convince herself and others that she is anything but hostile by engaging in precisely the opposite behavior, by helping others. She can become a nun and dedicate herself to God, or she can become a nurse and help to heal others. Of course most nuns and nurses do not use the mechanism of reaction formation and are genuinely motivated in their life work. How do we distinguish between the good samaritan and the hostile person with reaction formation? The latter is *driven* to help others and will do so whether or not the help is desired, whereas the normal person will not insist on helping if he is not needed. The neurotic *must* be the helper in order to deny his hostility, which often crops up in resentment about not being appreciated.

SUBLIMATION. This is included in the list more as a means of dealing with impulses than as a way of defending against anxiety. To sublimate is to express a basic urge in socially acceptable and useful ways; it is an entirely normal and adjustive way of dealing with the pressures of socialization. It is especially useful in those individuals with strong urges that might cause considerable difficulty if not properly channeled. Thus the man with intense aggressive impulses can direct them into socially useful pursuits and there are many possibilities in our society. He can become a soldier or a bombardier, a middle linebacker on a football team, a member of the riot squad of the police force, or he can direct his energies to destroying property — by operating one of the huge steel balls used to level old buildings (see Figure 27.3).

Therapy

Psychoanalytic theory assumes that the basic cause of abnormal behavior is unconscious con-

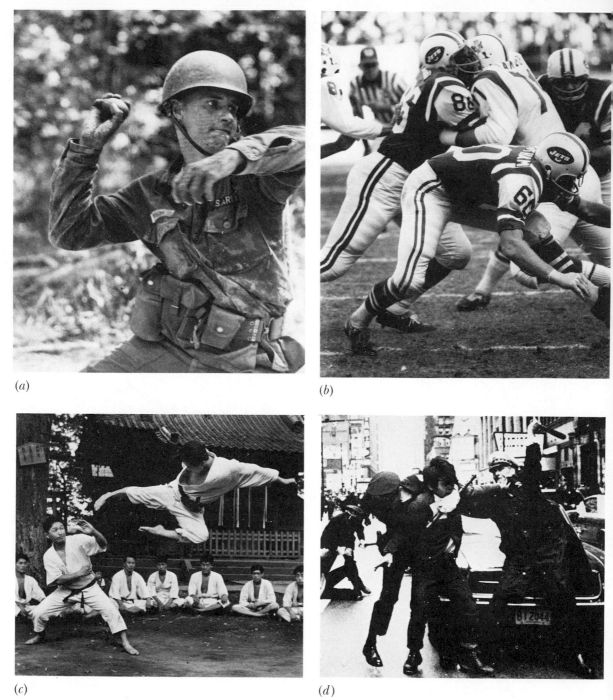

(a)

(b)

(c)

(d)

Figure 27.3 *Sublimation of aggressive urges.* (a) RICHARD DURRANCE/
PHOTO RESEARCHERS: (b) KEN REGAN/CAMERA5: (c) KEN HEYMAN (d) STEVE ROSE/NANCY
PALMER AGENCY)

flicts that have their roots in childhood fixations. If symptoms are merely surface manifestations of underlying problems, then it is these problems that must slowly be brought to the surface. The client must be helped to recognize his early childhood problems, their role in his abnormal behavior, and how he might change.

The client starts out by saying anything that comes to mind. His verbalizations provide hints about the underlying conflicts, and his associations are assumed to symbolize what is really bothering him unconsciously. He also reports his dreams, which ostensibly reflect in symbolic form the basic, unconscious conflicts at the root of the abnormality. The analyst interprets what the client is really saying and how it relates to his past. The analyst also points out the client's various defenses, again linking their origin in childhood to their persistence in adulthood. Though the client begins to learn frightening things about himself, his anxiety is assuaged by the tranquility of the therapy room and the nonjudgmental acceptance of the analyst.

As therapy proceeds and defenses are weakened, the client begins to remember more deeply repressed material. At times he seems to relive an earlier event, experiencing the rage or fear that accompanied the event. This phenomenon, called a *corrective emotional experience,* represents a large step forward in linking isolated childhood experiences with the more mature experiences that have not been repressed. Once the previously repressed experiences are remembered, the conflicts can be *worked through,* the client being shown how the pattern shows up repeatedly in his life.

During therapy the client develops a strong love-hate attachment for the analyst. Presumably he is transferring some of his feelings for important figures in his life (parents, spouse, and so on) to the analyst, hence the name *transference neurosis.* Now the analyst points out discrepancies between the client's view of him as a parental figure and the analyst's real self as a neutral therapist, between feelings of rage and fear carried over from childhood to feelings appropriate to adult situations. The client can increasingly accept these as his ego becomes stronger and more mature. The less his ego is devoted to defending against anxiety, the more it can function at an adult level.

The less the ego must deal with the panic situations of threat, the more it can deal with impulses and affects calmly and adjustively. Psychoanalytic therapy attempts to strengthen these reasonable aspects of the ego by first exposing and then eliminating childish behavior and finally showing the way to mature behavior.

When unconscious conflicts are resolved, there is no need for the defenses that produce symptoms. When the ego is not so defensive, it can better handle threats without resorting to childish modes of behavior. The theory insists that this is the only way to proceed in removing symptoms. Any direct approach might be successful in removing a given symptom, but it would surely be replaced by another: so long as there is unconscious conflict, there will be symptoms. A lasting cure, in this context, requires resolution of all the unconscious conflicts left over from childhood, and the only way to do this is through psychoanalytic therapy.

Interpersonal Theory

Freud's emphasis on the instinctual basis of man's motivation was not accepted by some psychoanalysts. The earliest follower to break with Freud was Adler, who insisted that man is primarily a *social* organism (1939). Adler has been followed by several generations of theorists, who, though dynamically oriented in the same way as Freudian psychoanalysts, insist on the primacy of personal relationships. The theorists include those who have worked mainly with psychotic patients (Sullivan, 1953) and those who have worked mainly with neurotics (Horney, 1945). Whatever the differences among these theorists, they all focused on the interpersonal sphere as the main area of man's problems of adjustment, and therefore we shall discuss them together.

Causes of Abnormality

Interpersonal theory holds that the events that occur during socialization are crucial. Man competes with others and must overcome any feelings of inferiority. He must develop appropriate behaviors in relation to others, especially in the

"Wait for me"

Moving toward

"C'mon get going"

Moving against

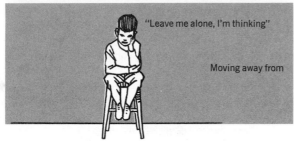

"Leave me alone, I'm thinking"

Moving away from

Figure 27.4 Diagrammatic summary of Horney's theory.

roles required by society. Thus the infant must first relate to his mother, accepting his dependent role but gradually striving for independence. The young child must learn to play with brothers and sisters and other playmates, participating in the give-and-take of peer relationships. Eventually, he must gain sufficient confidence in his own worth as a social being to surrender part of himself in the intimacy of a love relationship.

Abnormality in many cases can be tracked back to problems that occur during socialization. The child may fail to learn appropriate roles and consequently function poorly in the social contexts of adulthood. He may become so closely tied to a parent that he cannot give up his dependent role for the more independent roles demanded of

adults. He may be frightened by domineering and threatening persons, and be too wary of others to develop close personal ties. Or he may come on too strong with domination or aggression, driving others away and thereby destroying all the relationships in which he becomes involved.

Horney (1945) has classified interpersonal situations into three types, depending on how the person responds to others: moving toward, moving against, and moving away from others (see Figure 27.4). The three modes may be regarded as sequential strategies during the individual's life cycle (Bischof, 1964). The helpless infant must move *toward* the parental figures who will offer attention, nurturance, and affection. If his experiences are worthwhile, he will probably continue to reach out to others, seeking affection and close social interaction. If he is ignored or rejected, he will subsequently be wary and suspicious of others, with the likely consequence that he will not seek them out.

The adolescent tends to move *against* others, especially parents, in an attempt to establish his own identity. His rebellion says in effect, "I am not like you; I am my own person." Presumably, if there is too strong a payoff for such behavior, he will continue to move against others and be unable to establish positive social relationships.

The older adult feels that life is passing him by, as he is forced by his waning energies to turn over responsibility to younger persons. His response may be to move *away* from others, becoming more and more isolated. Unfortunately, social withdrawal only worsens the problem by rendering the person less able to cope with new situations.

Each of the three modes of social interaction, if exaggerated, can lead to abnormal behavior. Thus excessive moving toward others sustains a helpless, dependent orientation, which keeps the person childish and clinging. He is unable to become autonomous and sufficiently sure of himself to take chances. Such persons tend to demand much affection from others and yet are continually fearful of rejection. Excessive moving against others can result in chronic rebellion against authority and resistance to being socialized, with one eventual outcome being psychopathy. Excessive moving away from others may become so pronounced as to produce the social isolation typical of schizophrenics.

Therapy

In keeping with the emphasis on interpersonal factors, therapy focuses on the client's role and relationships. In a sense, the transference aspects of the two-person interaction become central, and the therapist plays an active role. In fact, he may play various roles in opposition to the client so that the latter can see relationships more clearly right in the therapy room and can practice role-playing there. The client's life is not always reconstructed, as in orthodox psychoanalytic therapy; but, when it is, the focus is on roles and relationships rather than on defenses and affects. The goal of therapy is of course to improve present relationships. In many ways interpersonal therapy resembles Freudian psychoananlysis, but it is shorter, there is more direct contact between client and therapist (who usually face each other), and the client talks about specific problems rather than saying anything that comes to mind.

The interpersonal approach has spun off several types of *group* therapy, and two major ones being psychodrama and T-groups. Psychodrama, as its name implies, uses a stage and an audience (Moreno, 1946). Its distinguishing feature is that clients *act out* their life situations in the protective "pretend" atmosphere found on the stage:

Psychodrama is a spontaneous drama created and experienced by group members. There is no formal script, only that which is presented through the intimate relationship of the director and protagonist, as representative of the group interest. The psychodramatic structure is in three parts: the warm-up, which involves the entire audience and out of which one person comes forth as protagonist; the drama itself, a presentation of aspects of the person's life; and the sharing, the time in which the audience "share" with the protagonist some of their life experience. In what the protagonist expresses about his life, the individual audience members see parts of themselves reflected and help the protagonist to re-join the group by sharing these. (SIROKA & SIROKA, 1971, P. 110.)

Presumably, clients can express feelings they would otherwise inhibit and see their relationships more clearly when acting them out and receiving feedback from both the other actors and the audience. At times the client may lose himself in the role, coalescing the stage experience with everyday life, and this can lead to both a corrective emotional experience and new behavior.

The *T-group* ("*T*" stands for training) is designed to help participants to observe the ways groups operate and how they as individuals relate to the group (see Figure 27.5). A typical group consists

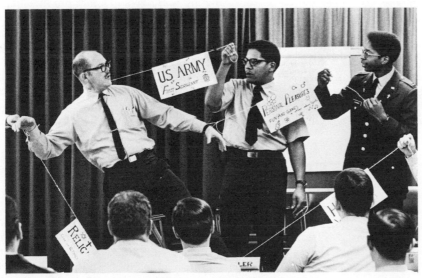

Figure 27.5 *A T-Group session.* (EDITORIAL PHOTOCOLOR ARCHIVES)

of eight to ten persons, with no special topics to discuss and a trainer who refuses to lead the group actively (Bradford et al., 1964). At first members are confused and have no idea what it is all about, but gradually they move toward some structure and a sense of group identity. The trainer helps participants to become aware of the ongoing interpersonal situations that arise, and presumably each person becomes more competent in handling his relationships with others. The goals are (1) to sensitize persons to the way they respond to others and how others reciprocate; and (2) to enhance their ability to relate to other persons, at first within the protective confines of the group and eventually in everyday life. The group interaction is exclusively verbal, and the clients are either normal persons who wish to improve their interpersonal skills or these with only mild abnormality.

Self Theory and Existential Theory

These two approaches are being treated together because they are both in the humanistic tradition. As we saw in Chapter 25, the focus is on the self as an object and on the potential that each person may actualize during his life. Psychologists of this persuasion are interested in man's capacity to create, to love, and to experience. One of the leading exponents of self theory, Carl Rogers, has shifted his orientation during the past two decades to a stance close to existentialism. This orientation emphasizes man as a self-conscious organism who is aware of his state of being (existence) and of the possibility of nonbeing. But whatever the difference between self-theory and existential theory, they share a single view: the best way to approach man is through his own private experience.

Self Theory

We have already discussed the self concept (see Chapter 25) and therefore can move directly to its assumed role in abnormality. Rogers (1942) contrasts the individual's valuation of himself with his ideal self. When there is little discrepancy between self and ideal self, the person is reason-

ably adjusted and content. But when the ideal self is far beyond reach and the person can only devalue himself by comparison, then he is unhappy and maladjusted.

Presumably, abnormality arises from a neglect of one's own experience and a turning away from one's real self. This originates in bad socialization practices that force the child to turn his back on his own natural impulses, disowning them as evil. If his impulses and behavior are branded as bad by others and he is therefore rejected, he tends subsequently to ignore his own immediate experience. He adopts instead the values of others, thereby reducing anxiety over rejection by important figures in his life. Rogers insists that conditional love sets the child on the wrong path, denying himself in order to receive the conditional affection of a parent or related figure. It would be preferable, the theory suggests, for parental love to be unconditional so that the child could develop appropriate self-esteem. But it is difficult to see how a child could be socialized unless parental affection were made conditional on appropriate behavior by the child.

In any event, once the child values affection more than he does his own impulses and direct experience, he has the potential to become abnormal. By denying his real self, he stops self-actualization. Devoted to pleasing others, he does not expand his experience, reach out for intimate relationships, and develop latent creative capacities. Self theory views the traditional symptoms of abnormality as unimportant by-products of the underlying problems about the self. In this respect the approach is dynamic: outer, observable symtoms are caused by inner, underlying conflicts.

Existential Theory

The basic assumption of existential theory is that man's greatest strength is also his greatest weakness: his self-awareness. All animals are of course aware of what is happening around them, but presumably man is the only one with consciousness of self; he knows that he knows. The theory suggests that this awareness allows man to make a *choice* in deciding what he will do (see Chapter 2 for a discussion of free will), and this choice makes him *responsible.* To the extent that man chooses to attend to his own experience as he interacts with others and with stimuli, he will self-actualize. All this is part of normal, adjustive living: not only *being* but also *becoming.*

Self-consciousness is also a weakness in that man can conceive of *nonbeing* which consists of emptiness, isolation, and ultimately, death. Presumably, each person is aware of his basic isolation in that private feelings cannot truly be shared. Nevertheless, through empathy and identification each of us can reach out to others and share some aspects of another's experiences and feelings. But the basic fear of nonbeing always lurks in the background. No one can rid himself of this dread, and it can cause abnormality if the person attempts to avoid dealing with the dread, mainly by cutting down on self-awareness. The person becomes defensive, worries about what little identity he has previously acquired, and devotes his energies to escaping from guilt and anxiety rather than to actualizing his potentials; these characteristics are abnormal.

Like self theory, existential theory emphasizes man's uniqueness and his sense of identity. In these terms, the major cause of maladjustment is *dehumanization:* treating individuals as machines or as animals. It is argued that modern technology has made the machine into a god, and men now serve machines instead of machines serving men. Thus individuals are "programed" and "tabulated" rather than treated as unique individuals. In this context each person loses much of his identity and his feeling of significance, and he begins to believe that he cannot affect what happens to him. To feel that one is merely a pawn of fate is part of the existential neurosis, which also include boredom, apathy, and inactivity.

Therapy

Rogers' self theory was associated with a technique of therapy called *nondirective* to distinguish it from techniques in which the therapist takes charge and directs the client (psychoanalytic therapy, for example). The nondirective therapist attempts to *reflect* the underlying emotional content of what the client verbalizes. Thus if the client spends much time talking about his brother's

achievements, the therapist would probably reflect the (assumed) underlying jealousy and resentment. When the client hears his own wishes and feelings verbalized, this time by another person he can deal with them more openly and see them more clearly. The major thrust is directed toward the client's self-concept, which is usually too low. The first step is to encourage the client to verbalize feelings and emotions of which he may be unaware or only dimly aware. Once this occurs, the therapist can help him to understand them better and above all to accept them. In this second step the therapist's acceptance and warmth assist the client in extinguishing his fear and in realizing that his feelings and impulses are not bad after all. His self-concept improves, and he becomes sufficiently confident to try new behaviors.

Rogers gradually evolved from nondirective therapy toward *encounter groups,* which also encompass several nonconformist approaches to psychotherapy. In the encounter group there is no leader in the sense of an authority who directs the group, and it is different from a T-group which emphasizes the interpersonal situation. Encounter groups focus more on inner experience, and this approach is in keeping with both self and existential theory.

The focus on inner experience may be seen in two of the basic techniques of the encounter group. First, members are encouraged to touch each other, and close their eyes and feel each others' faces or even bodies (see Figure 27.6). This is one answer to dehumanization and isolation: touching one another presumably brings everyone into closer contact and makes each person more aware of immediate sensory experience. Second, each person is encouraged to say what is on his mind, to reveal himself to the group with nothing held back. Each must search within himself for his innermost thoughts and impressions. As the group progresses, individual members become impatient with anyone who attempts to maintain a facade or who merely plays out his normal everyday roles. What is demanded is that each person reveal his "true self," the confused, doubting, scared person who is presumably hiding behind the roles that are assumed in everyday life.

Judging from the events that occur in encounter

Figure 27.6 An encounter group.   (KEN HEYMAN)

groups, such revelations do occur. The group experience is more intense than most interpersonal encounters, and there are several reasons for this. The sessions are inordinately long, lasting from an entire day to a weekend (so-called *marathon* groups). As individuals become fatigued and irritable, their defenses crumble and they reveal themselves more fully. Without an authoritarian leader to assume responsibility for the outcome, the members of the group must assume this responsibility themselves. This fosters a strong group identity and a willingness to "open up." The fact that members will not see each other again in everyday life facilitates openness and candor. The same phenomenon may be seen in a milder form in the intimate conversations that sometimes occur with strangers on a long airplane trip, the reason being that each will probably never see the other again. Finally, there is strong reinforcement for revealing one's forbidden impulses and hidden

thoughts. Other members of the group typically offer solace and sympathy, for they have similar problems. Sympathy and affection facilitate further unburdening and encourage the belief that someone else really does care. Participants learn that they can reach out for help and another human being will respond, which is believed to enhance group identity and support the notion that there is a chance for a decent life after all.

Members emerge from encounter groups with a feeling akin to a religious experience: it has been painful and exhausting but also exalting. They have been able to reveal themselves to others and have received sympathy and affection; others do care. They have come into closer contact with others through touching and shared feelings than they have in years. They have been part of a process group formation and share a warm feeling of identity with other members of the group. How much these feelings carry over into everyday life is a much-debated question, nor is it clear that behavior changes. But those who participate come away with a glow and a feeling that they are more alive, more human, and perhaps even better able to face their problems; to the extent that these outcomes do occur, encounter groups are helpful. In a way the groups seem to be tailormade to handle the existential neurosis: the person is not allowed to be bored and apathetic within the group. If his behaviors in the group carry over into everyday life, he should be able "to experience" better and begin to self-actualize. But it remains for research to demonstrate that such carry-over does indeed occur.

The Learning Approach

There are different kinds of learning and several different theories about how learning occurs, but all learning theorists make a common assumption about abnormality: *the symptom is the disease.* This position denies the need to postulate underlying, unconscious conflict or existential problems as causes of abnormal behavior. Abnormal behavior is regarded as learned in the same way that normal behavior is learned, the only difference being in the *outcome* of the responses. Normal behavior presumably leads to the rewards needed or sought after by the individual; abnormal behavior either fails to lead to the sought after rewards or is associated with excessive anxiety. In these terms, there are three kinds of abnormal behavior:

1. An excess of anxiety or avoidance.
2. Incorrect or unwanted responses (those that fail to lead to reward or that lead to excessive punishment).
3. Absence of appropriate response.

Excessive Anxiety or Avoidance

Most persons have fears, and abnormal anxiety is different only in that it is more frequent and intense. Anxiety can be learned in three different ways; consider a fear of dogs (see Figure 27.7). The fear may be *classically conditioned:* a barking snarling dog (unconditioned stimulus) ordinarily

elicits a fear reaction (unconditioned response). When the unconditioned stimulus is paired with the *sight* of the dog (conditioned stimulus), the fear response comes to be elicited by merely seeing the dog. This is emotional conditioning, and it is the way many childhood fears are learned.

The avoidance aspects of the fear response can easily be *instrumentally conditioned.* The barking dog elicits fear, which is aversive. When the person runs away from the dog, his fear diminishes and the escape response is thereby reinforced. If the escape responses moves ahead in time, it becomes an *avoidance response,* and such avoidance behavior is extremely resistant to extinction (see Chapter 15). Thereafter the person is fearful of dogs and avoids them.

Finally, the fear may be acquired by *imitation.* When a child watches his mother's behavior in the presence of stimuli she fears, he may copy her behavior. There is abundant evidence of such vicarious learning (see Chapter 16), and many common fears are acquired solely by imitation. Once the fear is acquired, it is usually long-lasting. The feared stimulus elicits an avoidance response, which takes the person away from the aversive stimulus. By avoiding it, he need never cope with the feared stimulus and thus cannot discover that it may really be harmless. In brief, the avoidance response prevents the fear response from extinguishing.

Maladaptive or Unwanted Responses

The first appearance of an instrumental response may occur randomly or through imitation, but thereafter it is maintained by reinforcement. Thus maladaptive or unwanted responses arise principally through instrumental conditioning. Incorrect responses result in punishment, by definition; that is, a response is incorrect or maladaptive in that it leads to aversive consequences. Thus, if a person wishes others to like him but behaves in a hostile fashion, then others will dislike him. What maintains the hostile response if it leads to dislike, an aversive consequence? The only logical answer is that the hostile response must be reinforced, perhaps as a justification for the individual's self-concept. For example, the potential

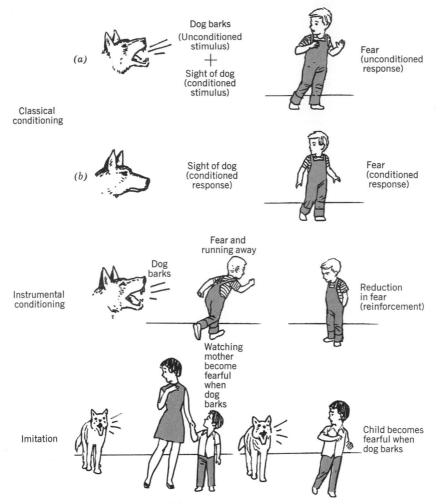

Figure 27.7 *Three ways to learn a fear of dogs.*

paranoid who believes that his talent is not appreciated tends to become angry with those who fail to give him his due; his hostile attitude turns others away from him, and their rejection sustains his belief that they are denying him just rewards. The hostile behavior fails to attain the acclaim originally desired, but it elicits responses expected by the individual and is thereby reinforced.

Most maladaptive or unwanted responses are even more strongly reinforced. Homosexual behavior has as its reward the sexual arousal that

is universally sought after, and it can become as strong a tendency as heterosexual behavior, which is similarly reinforced. The crucial difference is that homosexual responses may be punished severely, either by the social ostracism of others or by the homosexual's own self-condemning behavior. Presumably the sexual reinforcement of engaging in homosexual behavior is more potent than any subsequent punishment, and the behavior continues. This kind of reinforcement probably exists for a variety of socially prohibited responses (including addiction to drugs) and for such "normal" problems as smoking cigarettes and overeating. When the reward is sufficiently powerful, the response tends to persist even in face of severe punishment.

Aside from the strength of the reinforcer, what else will maintain incorrect or unwanted behavior? We know from research on schedules of reinforcement that partial reinforcement leads to resistance to extinction (see Chapter 14). Once a response has been acquired, the rate of reinforcement can be reduced to a fairly low level to maintain the response. This means that the response need be successful only occasionally to be made at a high rate. The principle holds for a wide range of superstitious and compulsive behavior, including gambling and compulsive rituals.

The tendency to make responses that are later punished has been called the *neurotic paradox*. One way to resolve the paradox is to consider the *timing* of the punishment. When an individual is faced with a threatening stimulus, he may make an inappropriate response such as fainting or running away (see Figure 27.8). His anxiety level immediately drops, and this relief of fear is a strong reinforcement. Hours or days later, his cowardly or inappropriate behavior is detected and punished, but the punishment is so remote from the response that it has little effect. Thus some persons tend to panic when taking an examination and respond by leaving the room, only to face the punishment of a failing grade much later in time. If delayed punishment is so ineffective, why are such inappropriate escape responses not more common? There are two reasons. First, most persons learn to tolerate moderate or even high levels of anxiety temporarily, and make instrumental responses even though they are scared. It is common among actors to suffer stage fright at the start of each performance but remain acting on stage until the fear dies down. Second, most persons can link the eventual punishment to an immediate escape response *cognitively* either by imagining the punishment or by telling themselves about it verbally. Such cognitive behavior links the punishment with the response, thereby inhibiting it. Thus the neurotic may suffer from one of two problems: either he has not learned to tolerate anxiety long enough to remain in the situation and make appropriate instrumental responses, or he fails to use his cognitive skills in linking future punishment to present behavior.

Absence of Responses

Most of the learning that is crucial to everyday adjustment takes place outside of school. During socialization young persons must learn a variety of responses that lead to reward, and these responses must be made at the right time, in the right place, in the right way. Thus young persons must learn how to compete, attract the opposite sex, and how to fit into new groups. Some of this learning is easy, some of it difficult. Most normal young persons have ample opportunity to acquire appropriate social responses; some do not. Those who are shy face an especially difficult problem: their social anxiety prevents them from interacting with others and learning the very social responses that would reduce their shyness. Thus there may be an absence of appropriate social responses because the individual has removed himself from situations in which such learning would occur. Responses may also fail to occur merely because there was no prior exposure to the appropriate situations or to the appropriate models.

On the other hand, responses that have already

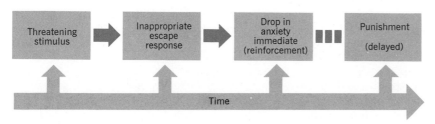

Figure 27.8 Timing of punishment and the neurotic paradox.

been learned may be inhibited when punishment is anticipated. This is likely to occur when there is a conflict between two roles. Consider the case of a law-abiding citizen who is called on to testify against a friend or business associate. As a citizen it is his duty to testify; as a friend it is his duty not to testify. One way to resolve the conflict is to be unable to speak, as in *hysterical aphonia.* The absence of talking is essentially an escape response, and it is reinforced by the avoidance of punishment (either from the friend or from the law). Similarly, a writer who fears that his work will be criticized may develop writer's cramp and be unable to continue his work. These are extreme examples of a common phenomenon that is usually seen in milder forms: playing the sick role. When a person is unable to perform as expected because of illness, he has a socially acceptable excuse. There need be no real faking involved, and the afflicted person is usually unaware of what he is doing. The pain, headache, visual difficulty, or muscular cramp is very real to the person himself, and it can incapacitate him.

Therapy

The therapeutic techniques used when the learning approach is adopted are derivatives of laboratory learning procedures. Undesirable behavior can be eliminated by extinction or by counterconditioning of an incompatible response. If the problem is an absence of behavior, it can be solved by operant shaping techniques. In addition to such direct procedures, the therapist can employ the vicarious techniques involved in imitation learning and vicarious reinforcement. The basic tools have emerged from laboratory research, and psychologists now are building a technology based on their application to clinical situations. The overall therapeutic approach is called *behavior modification.*

EXCESSIVE ANXIETY OR AVOIDANCE. One of the most straightforward ways to eliminate anxiety is to *countercondition* an incompatible response. The procedure consists of substituting an adaptive response for the anxiety response. The usual adaptive response is relaxing; since one cannot be both tense and relaxed at the same time, conditioning a relaxation response must eventually

eliminate the anxiety. The technique originated with Wolpe (1958), who calls it *systematic desensitization.* Therapy starts with a detailed description of the stimuli feared by the client. These are arranged in a hierarchy of intensity, from least to most feared. Then the client is trained to relax; first he tenses various muscles and then relaxes them, and soon he can relax his muscles without tensing them first. Finally the client is asked to imagine a mild fear stimulus; when he envisions it clearly, he is told to relax. As he relaxes in the (imagined) presence of fear stimuli, he becomes less fearful. As the fear diminishes, he is able to imagine previously intense stimuli with less anxiety. As he relaxes to the previously intense stimuli, he gradually dissipates his anxiety.

Wolpe's technique was first used in the laboratory with college students who were afraid of snakes (Lang & Lazovik, 1963), and since then behavior modification research has accelerated considerably (see Bandura, 1969). Fear of snakes is used because it is so common, but systematic desensitization has been found to work with a variety of complaints, and Wolpe (1964) has reported an improvement rate of 89% in neurotics with complex symptoms. Some critics have suggested that behavior modification can succeed only with simple or mild problems, but the evidence suggests the contrary, as we shall see shortly. Moreover, the effects of systematic desensitization are long-lasting (Paul, 1968; Nolan et al., 1970).

An alternative technique is to extinguish the anxiety by presenting the fear stimuli without any accompanying aversive consequences—the threat without the punishment. Presumably, when the conditioned stimuli occur without the aversive, unconditional stimuli, the anxiety response to the conditioned stimuli will collapse or implode. For this reason the technique is called *implosive therapy:*

The basic premise is that anxiety is a learned response to sets of cues based on previous trauma in the patient's life. If these cues elicit the anxiety response in the absence of primary reinforcement, the anxiety response will extinguish after repeated evocations.

(STAMPFL & LEVIS, 1967, P. 500.)

There have been reports of success with implosive therapy (Hogan & Kirschner, 1967;

Levis & Carrera, 1967) but also reports of failure (Fazio, 1970) and even worsening of fears (Eysenck, 1968). Clearly it is too early to evaluate implosive therapy, and the flooding of persons with anxiety obviously needs to be done with care. Implosive therapy does not use the notion of a *hierarchy* of fears; rather it assumes that the person must experience the full intensity of anxiety so that it may extinguish. Some indirect evidence consistent with this notion has come from research on systematic desensitization, showing that it is not necessary to proceed slowly from mild fears to intense ones. Starting with the strongest fears works equally well (Krapfl & Nawas, 1970), and this is precisely what is done in implosive therapy.

The last technique for eliminating excessive fear and avoidance is *modeling,* which is known to be a powerful means of introducing new behavior (see Chapter 16).

Research Report

Modeling has been shown to compare favorably with systematic desensitization as a treatment for phobia (Bandura et al., 1969). The study is a good example of how therapy can be examined in the laboratory under controlled conditions and with precise measurement. The subjects were normal persons, recruited through a newspaper advertisement, who had a strong fear of snakes. They were tested on a graded series of tasks involving how close they would approach a four-foot harmless snake, whether they would pick it up, and so on. Then they were divided into four different treatment groups. The first, call Systematic Desensitization, went through the usual relaxation procedure, with the subject imagining fearful situations involving snakes. The second group, Symbolic Modeling, watched a film of another person handling a snake; they could stop the film when it made them anxious and they, too, had relaxation training. The third, Live Modeling With Participation, watched a snake being handled and were then encouraged to approach, touch, and handle the snake. The fourth, Control, received no treatment, only testing. All subjects were tested before and after with the snake.

The major findings may be seen in Figure 27.9; the approach measure consists of the number of tests passed out of 29. All three treatment groups benefited in comparison to the Control subjects, but Live Modeling With Participation yielded the best results. Subjects in this group were able not only to approach closely and touch the snake but also to pick it up and play with it after merely two hours or so of treatment. There is an obvious reason why this treatment might be superior to the others; only in this treatment did the subjects actually practice approach responses with the snake. A follow-up study (Blanchard, 1970) showed that this was indeed true, but modeling alone (without actual participation) was also found to be an effective treatment.

This research suggests that modeling is a powerful therapeutic tool that should enjoy wider use. Its major limitation is that many activities cannot ethically or practically be modeled. For example, how would a therapist use modeling when the client's problem is sexual or aggressive? In such situations the use of imagined stimuli is obviously more practical, even though the therapy may not be as efficient.

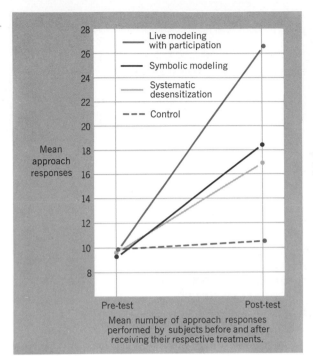

Figure 27.9 *Effectiveness of different behavior modification techniques (Bandura et al, 1969).*

INCORRECT AND UNWANTED RESPONSES. Presumably, unwanted or incorrect behavior is sustained by some sort of reinforcement. One approach to treatment is to oppose the reinforcement by punishment; this is called *aversion therapy.* In one of the earliest attempts, Wolpe (1954) used electric shock to punish a food obsession in a woman who, for medical reasons, was required to maintain a strict diet. Her problem was that she could not stop thinking about the delicious foods that were forbidden to her. She was told to imagine a particular desirable food and raise her hand when she could picture it. She was then given a very strong electric shock, which was kept on until she signaled that it was unbearable. This procedure continued for five sessions at the rate of ten shocks per session. At this point the thought of the forbidden foods filled her with revulsion, and she spent very little time thinking about food in general. Such avoidance conditioning has been used

with some success to treat smoking, excessive drinking, homosexual tendencies, and a variety of other incorrect or unwanted behaviors (see Lazarus, 1968). It does not always work, perhaps because some of the habits are so strong or so heavily reinforced (especially the taking of drugs like heroin) that the unwanted response is maintained inspite of intense punishment.

There are two problems involved in using aversion therapy. First, by the very nature of the treatment, it makes clients anxious; therefore it should be used with care so as not to add anxiety to the client's problems. Of course, once the client refrains from making the proscribed response, he need have no fear of punishment. Second, the avoidance response tends to extinguish, allowing the unwanted response to reappear. The likelihood of recurrence can be reduced by using a schedule of reinforcement in administering shock, which slows down extinction, or by having the client return for booster sessions of avoidance conditioning.

Incorrect or unwanted responses can also be eliminated by having the client practice the unwanted behavior until he is virtually exhausted. A person with a tic, for example, can practice the movement over and over again until he is tired. Yates (1958) had one client with multiple tics make all the various facial twitches voluntarily and succeeded in reducing the frequency of the involuntary tics to a manageable number.

ABSENCE OF RESPONSE. When responses necessary for adjustment have never been learned, it is a relatively simple matter to teach them through modeling. First the therapist makes the response, and then the client copies it. To facilitate social behavior, the therapist can then play an appropriate role opposite to the one that the client is to learn, thus giving the client practice in the give-and-take of social situations.

When the desired response is being inhibited, as in hysterical paralysis or blindness, the problem is more difficult. Here the technique of choice is operant conditioning, especially the early shaping procedure. This must ordinarily be done in a hospital or similar environment in which the client's life can be under the therapist's control. He needs to deprive the client of something he wants, such as canteen privileges or access to candy. Then he can withhold such reinforcers unti

Table 27.4
The Various Learning Therapies

ABNORMALITY	THERAPIES
Excessive anxiety or avoidance	Systematic desensitization Implosive therapy Modeling
Incorrect or unwanted behavior	Aversion therapy Excessive practice
Absence of response	Modeling Operant shaping

the client makes a response that is at least in the right direction. As soon as the appropriate response is made, it is reinforced. Then it is gradually shaped by requiring closer and closer approximations to the response ultimately desired. In this way psychotic children have been taught to eat with the appropriate utensils, depressives have learned to initiate activities rather than remaining inert, and hysterics have regained sight after being "blind" (Brady & Lind, 1961; Ayllon, 1963).

*   *   *

We have been discussing six different learning therapies that have had some measure of success in dealing with abnormal behavior: systematic desensitization (a specific form of counterconditioning), implosive therapy, modeling, aversion therapy, excessive practice, and operant shaping. As the discussion indicated, these are not used on every client that comes in with a problem; rather, each technique is more or less specific to one of the three kinds of abnormality described in learning terms—excessive anxiety, incorrect responses, and absence of responses. The learning therapies preferred in each of the three kinds of abnormality are listed in Table 27.4.

General Issues in Therapy

We have considered three broad approaches to abnormal behavior and the therapies arising out of these approaches, but several general questions remain unanswered. Does treating symptoms work? Is a therapist-client relationship necessary for treatment? Are some therapies better for certain problems than others?

Does Treating Symptoms Work?

The answer obviously depends on the goals of therapy. If the goal is to give the client a deep understanding of his life, a fresh orientation to his problems, and novel means of contending with life situations, then merely treating symptoms will not do the job. To accomplish these goals, it is necessary to go through a systematic reconstruction of the client's life history, dredging up forgotten or half-remembered incidents and attempting to integrate the memories with current events and problems. On the other hand, if the goals are to relieve misery, eliminate bizarreness, and increase efficiency, then treating symptoms can be entirely effective.

Table 27.5
Treatments of Choice for Abnormal Behaviors

ABNORMAL BEHAVIOR	THERAPY
Thought disorder	Chemical therapy
Disturbing memories of childhood, neurotic conflicts	Psychoanalysis
Disturbed roles and relationships	Relationship therapy
Existential neurosis	Encounter group
Anxiety, compulsion, and lack of behavior	Behavior modification

Psychoanalytic and related theories suggest that underlying conflicts lie at the root of symptoms, which means that merely removing symptoms will not suffice. If the unconscious conflicts are not resolved, removing one symptom would surely result in another taking its place. The learning approach makes the opposite assumption: the symptom is the disease. Therefore removing a symptom should not result in the substitution of another one. Behavior modifiers, sensitive to the issue of symptom substitution, have attempted to collect evidence by following up clients who have been helped by the various learning therapies. They report that there is no symptom substitution (Yates, 1958; Rachman, 1963). Evidence collected by behavior modifiers that is consistent with their position may not be entirely objective, but it is the only evidence available. Psychologists of dynamic persuasion have always assumed that there is symptom substitution but have never produced corroborating data.

Thus the evidence supports the learning approach—that there is no symptom substitution. Actually, the disappearance of symptoms often has a salutary effect on the client. Free from anxiety or unwanted responses, he is usually more relaxed and better able to deal with the everyday problems of living.

Is a Client-Therapist Relationship Necessary?

The answer depends on the kind of therapy used. Clearly, such a relationship is an essential aspect of psychoanalysis, relationship therapy, and (in a sense) encounter groups. But chemical therapy and electric shock therapy certainly do not require a close bond between therapist and client. The question becomes tricky when we consider behavior modification, in which the therapist assumes the role of teacher or trainer. Insofar as the learning therapist is reinforcing the client for certain behaviors, a close relationship might facilitate learning, but is such a relationship *necessary* for therapy to be successful? To answer this question, Lang et al. (1970) automated the systematic desensitization procedure so that it could be run through in the absence of a therapist. Then the automated therapy was compared with the usual desensitization procedure in treating snake phobia, and the automated procedure was found to be slightly *superior.* Thus not only is a relationship not necessary, but even the *presence* of a therapist might cause therapy to be *less* effective. Of course, a therapist might be helpful in dealing with the client's questions, but the larger theoretical issue is clear: a therapeutic relationship is not *necessary* for therapy to succeed.

Are Some Therapies Better for Certain Problems?

The answer here is an unequivocal *yes,* and it could hardly be otherwise. Physicians do not prescribe a single treatment for all ailments, and it is difficult to conceive of a magical treatment that would successfully deal with all abnormal behavior. Thus the treatment should be prescribed to fit the problem, and the best bet would be to handle a particular problem with the therapy specifically designed for it. If the client seems tied up in knots, has disturbing but vague childhood memories, and appears to be using several defense mechanisms, the treatment of choice would be psychoanalysis. If the person has bizarre thoughts and a range of cognitive abnormalities, chemical therapy would probably be best. Disturbed relationships might call for relationship therapy, and an existential neurosis might best be handled in an encounter group. Finally, those with anxiety complusions, or absence of behavior would best be treated by behavior modification. These points are summarized in Table 27.5.

section nine
social behavior

chapter 28

communication

*Model of communication — channels (tactile,
chemical, acoustic, and optical) — human
nonverbal communication — feedback —
supplements to language — alternatives to
language — gaze — eyebrow flash — smiling
and language — speech — evolution of human
language — Washoe — uniqueness of human
language — development of verbal communication — egocentric versus social communication
— role-playing — two communication styles*

Men and animals receive information from the world around them, a phenomenon called *perception*. When they receive information from other members of the species (and sometimes from members of other species), it is called *communication*. Actually, this definition is too inclusive, for the mere presence of another person may offer information without being communication. Thus if a mother checks to see if her baby is sleeping, her looking at the child is perception in that she receives information, but the baby is not communicating with her.

Communication involves not only a *target organism* that receives information but also a *signaler* that sends a *message* along a *channel*. Thus a traffic policeman raises his hand and holds it in a vertical position to indicate "Stop" visually to a motorist at an intersection. A signal is not sent unless it is probable that it will be received and understood. In humans and many animals this probability is established through learning. Thus we learn that particular vocal patterns of gestures tend to evoke particular responses in others, for example, holding the hand up vertically to indicate that the approaching person should stop see Figure 28.1. For many lower animals the probability is programed geneti-

Signaler → Target organism
Message along a channel

Holds his hand up,
signaling "STOP"
(visual channel)

Example:

Police officer   Driver of car

Figure 28.1 *Model of communication.*

cally, and they emit signals that are understood without any learning. Thus ants leave chemical trails for other ants to follow, and they emit chemicals that warn of danger; no ant needs to learn these signals, because they are programed in the nervous system.

Messages typically are transmitted directionally from the signaler to a particular target organism, as when one person makes a request of another. But the message may be broadcast with no specific target organism. A bird may chirp and twitter to inform anyone and everyone that it has staked out its territory, or it may vocalize loudly to warn off a particular invader of its territory. A man may use a telephone to call a specific person, or he may go on television to deliver a telecast to anyone who might view it. One aspect of socialization is learning to direct transmission, and it is mastered so well that we become aware of it only when mistakes are made. For instance, a person driving his car may wish to signal a friend he sees standing on the sidewalk. He does so by sounding the car's horn, but this transmission is so general that it may not only deliver a message to the friend but also (mistakenly) to others.

This example illustrates the difference between communication and perception. Communication is *goal-directed:* the signaler *intends* to transmit information to the target. Nontarget organisms may *perceive* information coming from the signaler, but the signaler is not communicating with them.

Certainly the driver who sounds his horn to signal a friend is not trying to communicate with other drivers or pedestrians. Similarly, the boy who bursts into tears when he fails or is disappointed is not trying to communicate his affective state. Communication is instrumental in that the signaler is attempting to transmit information.

Some behavior is *expressive* in that the person is *reacting* but not attempting to communicate. For example, if a wife observed her husband trip and fall with his arms and legs flailing about, she might spontaneously laugh at the sight but would not be trying to tell him that she was happy that he fell. If she wished to *communicate* hostility toward him rather than merely *react* with laughter, she would tell him "I'm glad you fell." Expressive behavior may contain information and therefore be perceived, but it is not communication.

Channels

A message consists of information that has been encoded and transmitted through a physical medium. The words on this page convey a message through the *optical* medium, as the reader perceives patterns of light and then decodes the written message. Light is the *channel* for visual communication; there are three other channels: chemical, tactile, and acoustic. We shall focus first on animal communication because it is less familiar, and then follow with human communication.

Tactile

Tactile communication obviously requires that the sender and receiver be in close contact, and it characterizes the most intimate social contacts, especially sexual, friendly, and aggressive interchanges. Good examples are the cradling behavior of mothers with their infants and the grooming behavior of friendly primates (see Figure 28.2). Human mothers soothe their infants by stroking, patting, holding, and rocking them, all of which communicate positive affect. Tactile communication can be ritualized, as in the handshake that connotes the friendly attitude of both parties.

The tactile channel is a minor one in communication, partly because it requires proximity. Organisms need to communicate most when they are separated in space, and they require channels that can bridge distance. Nevertheless, the tactile mode has the potential for considerable communication when other channels become unavailable. Helen Keller, for example, lost both sight and hearing early in life; through intensive tutoring she was taught a code involving touch, and the communication proved to be so good that she eventually learned to speak. Helen Keller was a special case, but any person can be taught a "skin language" using intensity, duration, and body location as the basic dimensions. Geldard (1966) showed that vibrations on the skin could be used to develop 45 separate signals, which could be learned in just a few hours. These could constitute an "alphabet" on which to base a language suitable for tactile communication.

Figure 28.2 *Tactile communication between primate mother and infant.*

(UNIVERSITY OF WISCONSIN PRIMATE CENTER)

Chemical

The chemical channel is widely used by animals, especially mammals, but less so by primates and humans. We are most familiar with chemical communication in household pets; female cats and dogs in heat emanate odors that attract most of the males in the neighborhood. The odors are caused by chemical substances called *pheromones*. Communication by pheromones can extend over considerable distances (the male gypsy moth can pick up the scent of the female gypsy moth half a mile away), it is not hindered by obstacles (the odor extends around barriers), and

it works equally well by day or night.

Most of the odors emitted by animals remain active for some time, especially when they cling to trees, leaves, and brush. Thus they can bridge time as well as space: the odor delivers a message that is received long after the signaler has departed. Odors therefore are especially useful in marking off a territory, allowing the animal to communicate the boundaries that it will defend.

The relatively long duration of chemical signals also has drawbacks. It is of little use in rapid interchange among animals, such as occurs in courting behavior and the exchanging of information. It is also potentially dangerous in that it may signal the location of the animal to predators. Fire ants have evolved a solution to the latter problem in the way they lay chemical trails to food (see Fig-

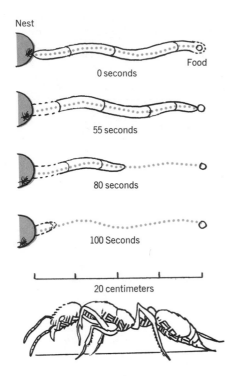

Nest

0 seconds

Food

55 seconds

80 seconds

100 Seconds

20 centimeters

Figure 28.3 *The fire ant,* Solenopsis saevissma *(after Wilson, 1962).*

ure 28.3). The trail lasts for only a few minutes, long enough to be followed by other ants but brief enough to escape detection by predators (Wilson, 1962, 1965).

The chemical channel is widely used to identify fellow members of the species, the group, or the family. Most mammalian mothers can recognize their young by their specific odor, part of which derives from contact with the mother. Honey bees have evolved a means of identification that is analogous to the badge or pass-card system employed in many industrial plants and military bases. When a worker bee leaves the hive, it carries with it the odor of the hive. When it returns, it opens its scent gland to the guards at the entrance to the colony. Bees with the appropriate scent are allowed through, but strangers are attacked.

Acoustic

Sound signals can be made quickly and in rapid succession, as each individual sound fades away immediately. This on-off quality makes sound a valuable channel for rapid interchange from signaler to receiver and back. The speed of emission offers a coding device, with the message varying according to how fast the sounds are emitted. Loud sounds are particularly useful in commanding the attention of the target organism, and sound easily moves around obstacles to fill space completely.

When animals make sounds *vocally,* they need not stop all other activities, which confers advantages in a number of situations. Thus the animal that is attempting to escape from a predator can still sound the alarm as it runs away, or it can even call for help. Predators that hunt in packs (wolves, for example) can easily maintain communication with one another while continuing with the chase.

Sea animals transmit information to one another by vocalizing. Whales emit high-pitched squeaks that tell other whales not only their position but also their affective state. Porpoises emit click sounds that convey information and affect to one another, and it has been speculated that they are capable of communicating in this way with men (Lilly, 1963).

Aside from man, the animals with the most highly developed ability to vocalize are birds:

They use sounds to convey information between the members of a pair or a potential pair, between parent and young, between siblings, between conspecifics [members of the same species] in feeding or migrating or roosting flock, and often between different species within such a flock. Moreover, their vocalizations are incomparably more complex and more precisely modulated and controlled than are those of other animals. . . . (THORPE, 1972, P. 153.)

Some species of birds have a vocal imitative ability comparable to that of man. Parrots, for example, can be taught the *sounds* of human speech. They are not communicating, for the sounds have no meaning to them; the situation is analogous to a man learning to make bird calls without knowing what information is being transmitted to the birds.

Optical

Messages along the optical channel can be turned on and off quickly, as in the eyeblink; or they can be graded along various dimensions of intensity, color, and size, as in a display of feathers, in variations in the size of the mouth opening, and in the sexual skin of baboons in heat. Of course at least some light is required, and visual communication is reduced at night. Moreover, light is easily obstructed by such barriers as trees, bushes, and hills, which means that visual communication at a distance is difficult except in flat, open terrain. On the other hand, the optical channel is superb for locating the source of the communication, being the most precise channel for this purpose. In man, as in many animals, hearing is used to locate the source approximately and vision is used to locate it precisely.

Light contains more potential information than any of the other modes of communication, and for this reason the message may be lost or ignored. Thus it is essential to capture the attention of the target organism, and *movement* is the best kind of signal for this purpose. As we discovered in studying perception, eyes are very well adapted to capturing movement, and it is no accident that most

visual communication involves movement by the signaler. Many species engage in ritual movements that have been derived from everyday activities but which have been altered for communication. The best examples occur in courtship displays, in which the male and female may proceed through a sequence of elaborate rituals reminiscent of seventeenth-century court dances (see Figure 28.4). Courtship is a somewhat complex form of reproductive behavior, requiring high-level communication by each member to match its actions to the other. The communication involved in the sex acts of most animals is usually simpler and more one-sided: the female signals the male of her availability and interest, and the male usually accepts the invitation. Thus in many species, it is the female who does the communicating about sexual interest, though it is not entirely clear whether this is also true of humans.

Nonverbal Human Communication

Most human communication occurs through the acoustic and optical channels. Humans sweat and exude distinctive body and mouth odors, but these convey virtually no information. There is tactile communication, but it is restricted to friendly or sexual contacts and to aggressive, antagonistic contacts. Messages delivered along the acoustic channel are almost exclusively *vocal*. The only natural exceptions are clapping the hands and stamping the feet. When the hands are clapped sharply once or twice, it is a signal for attention in our culture. *Repeated* clapping is usually a sign of approval, as when an audience claps at the end of a performance, whereas *rhythmic* clapping by an audience indicates impatience at delay. Children and some adults occasionally clap their hands together when they are elated. Rhythmic stamping of feet by an audience indicates the same thing as rhythmic hand clapping: impatience at delay. When a person stamps his foot, it indicates stubbornness, and this negativistic message is usually delivered by children.

As vision is the dominant sense, it is not surprising that much information is exchanged along the optical channel. The face is the prime signaling area, especially the eyes and mouth, but the hands are also important in signaling. Bodily

(a)

(b)

(c)

Figure 28.4 *Courtship in the great crested grebe (Etkin, 1967, p. 59).*

movements and postures contribute, but their role is minor.

Functions of Nonverbal Communication

The term *nonverbal* is used here as a synonym for nonlanguage: all the vocal, facial, and gestural responses exclusive of the *content* of speech (words and sentences). Thus a rising inflection, which usually accompanies a question, is nonverbal — in contrast to the words in the question.

Nonverbal communication has three functions, First, it is used to sustain and control conversation. While the speaker is talking, he needs *feedback* about the flow of information, whether his listener is attending, and so on.

Second, the speaker often *supplements* the verbal message with responses that enhance or negate the message. For example, the question, "How are you, you old horse thief" — when accompanied by a broad smile — is a friendly greeting, not a hostile accusation. The smile reverses the meaning of the words.

Third, gestures and facial expressions can serve as alternatives to language. In Western societies, for example, everyone knows the meanings of nodding the head and shaking the head.

Feedback

The listener is free to use the vocal channel, and sometimes he does — saying "Yes, I see" or "What?" or "umhm." But the listener's vocalizations interrupt the speaker's, and therefore most

Table 28.1
Feedback from the Listener (Ekman & Friesen, 1969)

EXPRESSION	MESSAGE TO SPEAKER
Head nod, once or twice	Continue
Questioning look	Repeat or elaborate
Glancing away	Get to the point or become more interesting
Expression of disgust	Stop talking about an unpleasant topic
Taking a breath, opening the mouth	Let the listener talk

feedback occurs in the *visual* channel. The listener may nod to keep the conversation going, look puzzled, appear bored, and so on (see Table 28.1). Most of this feedback is facial because the speaker and the listener are usually looking at one another.

The speaker may respond to the nonverbal communication of the listener with his own feedback. If the listener tends to glance away, the speaker may frown; if the listener attends closely, the speaker may nod or smile. Thus communication may be occurring at two levels: the more overt level of speech and the more subtle level of nonverbal feedback.

Supplements to Language

Language can be supplemented vocally[1] or visually. The vocal supplements concern the *delivery* of speech, which varies along several dimensions. The same sentence may mean different things when shouted than when whispered.

[1] *We are omitting the* prosodic *features of speech (such as stress and intonation) because most linguists consider them as part of grammar and therefore* verbal *(Lyons, 1972).*

Speech may be delivered in a clipped, teeth-clenched manner that suggests precision and formality, or it may be slurred in a manner that suggests casual communication and informality. The tempo may be rapid (indicating urgency) or slow and measured (indicating great pith and substance).

The visual supplements to language are more discernible because the channel of communication is different. Their function is to illustrate what is being said (see Figure 28.5). They can intensify the meaning of speech by being sharp or rapid (as in banging the fist) or diminish intensity by implying a lack of importance (as in waving the hand in a dismissing motion). Most of the supplements are gestures of the arms or body rather than facial expressions.

Alternatives to Language

When noise or distance make speech impractical or when custom decrees, specific signs are used to communicate. Thus two friends might wave to one another when the distance between them is great. In our culture the thumb is used extensively in signals that communicate how well things are

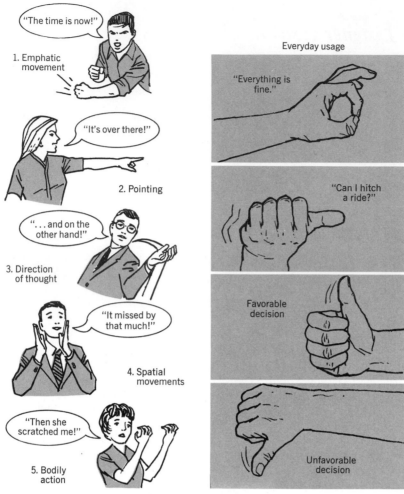

Figure 28.5 *Movements supplementing speech (Ehman and Frieser, 1969).*

Figure 28.6 *Emblems—signs substituting for speech.*

going or that some one wants a lift in a car (see Figure 28.6).

Some gestures are coded for highly specific situations. Traffic policemen tend to develop sets of movements that are sufficiently complex to stop one line of traffic while encouraging another line to move. Orchestra conductors must develop a repertoire of hand and arm movements to indicate loudness, tempo, and emphasis. And in sports, referees and empires signal their decisions almost exclusively by gestures (the "out" and "safe" gestures in baseball are familiar to everyone).

GAZE. The eyes are the most mobile part of the face, and the face sends more messages than any other part of the body. Direct eye contact between two persons involves at least some social interaction, and most strangers avoid looking at one another except for brief glances. In crowded close quarters—as in an elevator or waiting room, strangers usually focus on something else than each others' eyes.

A direct stare at another person may connote a challenge, this is its usual meaning for animals (Kendon, 1967). Being stared at is annoying for

Figure 28.7 *Eyebrow flash in two ethnic groups: (a, b) Papuan; (c, d) Balinese.*
(EIBL-EIBESFELDT, 1972.)

humans (Ellsworth et al., 1972). When the context is clearly noncompetitive, a direct stare is often a sexual invitation, either heterosexual or homosexual. Downcast eyes can connote one of three attitudes or moods, depending on the rest of the expressive pattern: submission to a dominant person, embarrassment, or melancholy. Anxiety and tension are often signaled by rapid blinking, and darting, sidelong glances tend to communicate insecurity or suspiciousness.

It is an American stereotype to look someone directly in the eye when telling him the truth, and liars are presumably "shifty-eyed." Anyone who has been socialized in this culture knows this ste-reotype and therefore when one tells a lie, he tends to look directly at his listener; in fact, salesmen are encouraged to do this. Thus whatever the original basis for the belief, it cannot be relied on now.

EYEBROW FLASH. A universal social response, which most persons are unaware of, is the *eyebrow flash* (Eibl-Eibesfeldt, 1972). In this friendly expression, the eyebrows are rapidly raised to the maximum and held there for roughly one-sixth of a second (see Figure 28.7). Eibl-Eibesfeldt photographed different people around the world, and this response was absent only in Japan—where it is considered indecent.

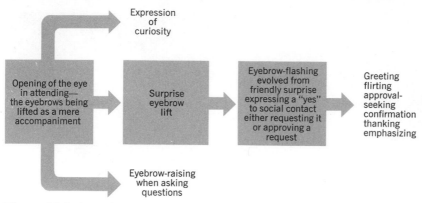

Figure 28.8 *Hypothetical evolution of the eyebrow flash (Eibl-Eibesfeldt, 1972).*

The occasions that elicit an eyebrow flash vary from one culture to the next. The same stereotyped response occurs in greeting, flirting, approving, thanking, and in general in communicating that there is a positive social bond.[2]

How did the eyebrow flash evolve? Eibl-Eibesfeldt suggests that its origin resides in directing one's attention to another person (see Figure 28.8):

As a hypothesis I would propose that the eyebrow lift of surprise—originally part of the opening of the eye—was the starting point for ritualization of several "attention" signals. Some of these can be grouped together as the friendly attention signals, as represented by the eyebrow flash, and are mostly given in combination with nodding and smiling. Further evidence that the starting point for the evolution of these friendly attention signals is the fact that surprise is often involved in meeting somebody; the utterance "Ah, it's you" when meeting in Central Europe is regularly accompanied by an eyebrow flash. (1972, p. 301.)

SMILING AND LAUGHING. Human smiling and laughing are usually regarded as being on the same continuum: both express relaxed, friendly social interaction—with smiling being a milder or

[2] *In some contexts, lifting of the eyebrows can be a threat—for example, when accompanied by a prolonged stare—but the most common meaning is that of* positive *affect.*

less intense expression than laughing. But there are good reasons for believing that their evolutionary origin—and perhaps what they communicate—are somewhat different (van Hooff, 1972).

Laughing and smiling differ along two dimensions—how wide the mouth is opened and how much the teeth are bared. The two extremes of these dimensions are the broad smile and the open-mouth laugh (see Figure 28.9). The laugh occurs in primates, and the smile (bared teeth display) may be traced back to lower mammals. There is a startling resemblance between smiling and laughing in humans and similar expressions in chimpanzees (see Figure 28.10).

What do smiling and laughing communicate? Smiling is believed to have started earlier in evolution as teeth-baring—a defensive response (van Hooff, 1972). It evolved to become a signal for submission or at least nonaggression. From there it was a short evolutionary step to smiling as a signal for friendship and reassurance.

Laughter derives from the open-mouth display, which in lower mammals and primates is associated with play fighting. Kittens, puppies, and the young of primates all engage in mock fighting, and the open-mouth display prevents any serious biting. From there it was only a short evolutionary step to the open-mouth laugh as a signal that ongoing behavior is not to be taken seriously. Thus in van Hooff's words:

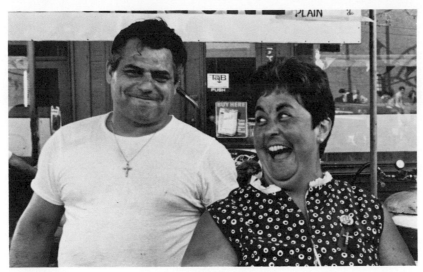

Figure 28.9 *Wide smile versus open-mouth laugh.*
(JOEL LAST EDITORIAL PHOTOCOLOR ARCHIVES)

Laughter then fits neatly in the phylogenetic developmental range of the relaxed open-mouth *display . . . signaling the behavior with which it is associated as mock-aggression or play. Smiling fits well as the final stage of the development of the* silent bared-teeth *display. Originally reflecting an attitude of submission, this display has come to represent nonhostility and finally has become emancipated to an expression of social attachment or friendliness. . . .*

(1972, P. 235.)

Verbal Communication (Speech)

Human *non*verbal communication has much in common with animal communication. Some of the facial expressions and gestures are similar to those of primates; the human smile and laugh *look* the same in humans and chimpanzees (see Figures 28.9 and 28.10). Other human nonverbal communication—though superficially different from that of animals—is similar in *what* is communicated: *aspects of self* or *the immediate environment.*

Two aspects of self are readily communicated nonverbally: affects and desires: Thus smiling suggests friendliness and sociability, whereas frowning and scowling suggest rejection of hostility. And desires or wants are easily indicated: beckoning with the fingers or hands to indicate "come closer," or placing the forefinger vertically over the mouth to indicate silence. Concerning the immedi-

Bared-teeth display   Relaxed open-mouth display

Figure 28.10 *Responses analogous to smiling and laughing in the chimpanzee (Van Hooff, 1972 p. 219).*

ate environment, objects can be located by pointing, size can be signaled by the distance between the hands, speed can be indicated by the tempo of hand movements, and so on.

In brief, nonverbal communication can crudely but adequately transmit to others information about affects, needs, wants, and features in the immediate surroundings. Note that the messages are closely related to the stimuli that elicit them. Stirred by an affective state or a need, the communicator signals this state to others; stimulated by an object or event he has just perceived, the communicator signals its presence to others.

Human language can do all these things, but it is different from nonverbal communication in that it is more detached from immediate stimuli and affective states.[3] Words and sentences can do more than signify the presence of objects and events; human language can describe the objects and events in neutral terms—disengaged from the positive or negative reactions of the speaker. Sentences can also refer to events that happened previously or that will happen later—that is, human language can be disengaged from the here-and-now. Human language is also different from nonverbal communication in the construction of sentences—an issue that will be discussed below.

Evolution of Human Language

Human gestures and facial expression communicate information in essentially the same ways that higher animals do. What is different and uniquely human is *verbal* communication. How did language evolve from the primate line that led to man? Five sequential steps have been suggested as a logical sequence:

(1) a delay between the arrival of the stimulus and the utterance of the message that it has provoked or between receipt of the incoming signal and the sending onto of a signal;
(2) the separation of affect or emotional charge from the content of instruction which a message carries;
(3) the prolongation of reference, namely the ability to refer backward and forward in time and to ex-

change messages which propose action in the future;
(4) the internalization of language, so that it ceases to be only a means of social communication and becomes also an instrument of reflection and exploration with which the speaker constructs hypothetical messages before he chooses one to utter; and
(5) the structural activity of reconstruction, which consists of two linked procedures—namely a procedure of analysis, by which messages are not treated as inviolate wholes but are broken down into smaller parts, and a procedure of synthesis by which the parts are rearranged to form other messages.

(BRONOWSKI & BELLUGI, 1970, P. 670.)

This sequence is only one of several reconstructions of the evolution of human language, but it does offer several advantages. First, it presents the logical steps that might have led from nonverbal communication to language. Second, it offers a characterization of language: the five features that distinguish it from other communication. And third, it suggests that some modern primates would have the cognitive ability required for at least the first few steps in the five-step sequence.

The last point is especially relevant to recent research with chimpanzees. One chimpanzee, Sarah, was taught a "vocabulary" consisting of plastic pieces of different color, size, shape, and texture (Premack, 1971). Sarah has learned to combine these "words" in a fashion that superficially resembles sentences. However, no linguist regards a sentence as merely a combination of words, and there is some controversy over whether Sarah has learned a "language."

The other chimpanzee, a female named Washoe, has been taught the American version of sign language—the hand communication used by deaf persons (Gardner & Gardner, 1969). Her mastery of sign learning has been so far beyound expectations that it has challenged traditional notions about the uniqueness of human language.

Washoe

Washoe was caught in the wild as an infant and arrived at the Gardner's laboratory at the age of roughly one year. From the beginning the Gardners used only sign language in her pres-

---

[3] *The following discussion leans heavily on a paper by Bronowski and Bellugi (1970).*

ence; the only vocalizations were laughing, whistling, and similar nonverbal sounds. Sign language was chosen because chimpanzees do not have the vocal capabilities needed for speech, but they can manipulate their hands precisely enough to make signs. Chimpanzees are well known imitators, and imitation learning was used extensively. Basically, the learning consisted of exposing Washoe to a variety of objects and events, and showing her the appropriate signs:

Routine activities — feeding, dressing, bathing, and so on — have been highly ritualized, with appropriate signs figuring prominently in the rituals. Many games have been invented which can be accompanied by appropriate signs. Objects and events have been named as often as possible, especially when Washoe seemed to be paying particular attention to them. New objects and new examples of familiar objects, including pictures, have been continually brought to her attention, together with the appropriate signs.

(GARDNER & GARDNER, 1969, P. 667.)

After almost two years of training, Washoe had learned more than 30 signs, and she continued to add to her vocabulary subsequently. Table 28.2 lists several of the signs, from those learned early in training to those learned late.

After learning eight or ten signals, Washoe started combining them; with time her usage of combinations increased. Many of the combinations were imitated, for the Gardners used combinations in communicating with Washoe. Nevertheless, Washoe did invent several combinations herself — "gimme tickle" for example.

We are limited to discussing only a few of this chimpanzee's remarkable achievements. She clearly can name objects — an ability once believed to be restricted to humans. She can combine words, and she can refer to events or objects in the immediate past. Thus her communications are at least partially detached from the immediate context of her own affective state and the local environment. Surely these facts challenge the notion that human language is unique.

The Uniqueness of Human Language

Washoe's combination of signs are roughly at the level of the language of a two-year-old human child. But a two-year-old child is just starting to acquire language, and his verbal communications are primitive compared to those of older children and adults. A two-year-old child is in transition between the sensory-motor and concrete operations stages of cognitive development (see Chapter 17). Presumably, no animal progresses cognitively much beyond the sensory-motor stage. Thus in the context of human cognitive development:

. . . the earliest stages of language development, but not the later stages, are under the control of sensory-motor intelligence; and that as a consequence, we might expect certain species of animals to reach, but not go beyond, these earliest stages. In view of the structural and functional parallels that have been drawn between human nonverbal communication (including the non-verbal component in language) and animal signalling systems, one might perhaps go on to hypothesize that non-verbal communication, in general, is under the control of "sensory-motor intelligence, whereas language in its fully developed form . . . requires the higher modes of cognitive ability.

(LYONS, 1972, P. 91.)

In this view, Washoe has come only a little way in cognitive development; what she and all other animals lack is the necessary level of cognition, not a specific language ability.

Consider the five steps in the evolution of language (Bronowski & Bellugi, 1970).

1. Delay between stimulus and utterance. Like most higher animals and all primates, Washoe can easily delay responding (see Chapter 16).
2. Separation of affect from content. Washoe can go beyond her own desires and name objects and events. But Washoe cannot understand neutral descriptive statements; unlike young children, she cannot distinguish between current motivation ("I want" or "Gimme food") and objective statements ("She washes him.").
3. Prolongation of reference. Washoe can make statements about the immediate past (something is gone) or desires for rewards that are not present ("more food"). But young children can refer to a more distant past and can make statements about future intentions ("Going to the circus next week.").
4. Internalization. Washoe has been observed to

Table 28.2
Hand Signs Learned by Washoe (Gardner & Gardner, 1969)

SIGNS	DESCRIPTION	CONTEXT
More	Fingertips are brought together, usually overhead. (Correct ASL* form: tips of the tapered hand touch repeatedly.)	When asking for continuation or repetition of activities such as swinging or tickling, for second helpings of food, etc. Also used to ask for repetition of some performance, such as a somersault.
Up	Arm extends upward, and index finger may also point up.	Wants a lift to reach objects such as grapes on vine, or leaves; or wants to be placed on someone's shoulders; or wants to leave potty-chair.
Sweet	Index or index and second fingers touch tip of wagging tongue. (Correct ASL form: index and second fingers extended side by side.)	For dessert; used spontaneously at end of meal. Also, when asking for candy.
Hear-listen	Index finger touches ear.	For loud or strange sounds: bells, car horns, sonic booms, etc. Also, for asking someone to hold a watch to her ear.
Sorry	Fisted hand clasps and unclasps at shoulder. (Correct ASL form: fisted hand is rubbed over heart with circular motion.)	After biting someone, or when someone has been hurt in another way (not necessarily by Washoe). When told to apologize for mischief.
Flower	Tip of index finger touches one or both nostrils. (Correct ASL form: tips of tapered hand touch first one nostril, then the other.)	For flowers.
I-me	Index finger points at, or touches, chest.	Indicates Washoe's turn, when she and a companion share food, drink, etc. Also used in phrases, such as "I drink," and in reply to questions such "Who tickle?" (Washoe: "you"); "Who I tickle?" (Washoe: "Me.")
Shoes	The fisted hands are held side by side and strike down on shoes or floor. (Correct ASL form: the sides of the fisted hands strike against each other.)	For shoes and boots.
Baby	One forearm is placed in the crook of the other, as if cradling a baby.	For dolls, including animal dolls such as a toy horse and duck.

* ASL stands for American Sign Language

make hand signs to herself or in front of a mirror, but, according to the Gardners, these are idle chatter. Young children talk to themselves and try out various word arrangements. Later in development, language is used as a cognitive tool in thinking and planning; no animal is capable of such self-stimulation with its own communicative acts.

5. Reconstruction. Washoe does combine words, but she can neither analyze nor synthesize sentences. As we saw in Chapter 17, children extract rules from the speech they hear, and they use these rules in making up their own sentences. The best examples are found in errors: "two mans," "I goed," "he falled," and so on.

These five steps presumably constitute the sequence that led to human language. Note that with each successive step, Washoe falls further behind young children. Washoe can delay her "utterances," and her naming of objects suggest some separation of affect from content. But her communications refer largely to the here-and-now, and she shows no real capacity for internalization (communication as a cognitive tool). Finally, she completely lacks the cognitive ability that underlies the reconstitution of language. It is this underlying cognitive ability that makes human language unique:

What the example of Washoe shows in a profound way is that it is the process of total reconstitution which is the evolutionary hallmark of the human mind, and for which so far we have no evidence in the mind of the nonhuman primate, even when he is given the vocabulary ready made."

(BRONOWSKI & BELLUGI, 1970, P. 673.)

This conclusion seems a fair statement of the facts now available. Of course, if researchers were to train a chimpanzee to arrange hand signs into something like "sentences," the above conclusion would be knocked flat. Until then, however, it is safe to say that human language is unique.

Development of Verbal Communication

Verbal communication consists of a signaler sending a message through speech along the

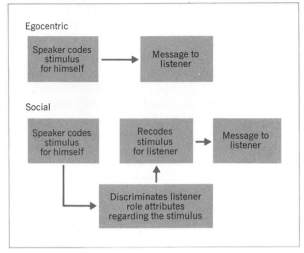

Figure 28.11 Egocentric versus social communication (after Flavell, et al., 1968).

acoustic channel to a receiver. The speaker encodes information that the listener must be able to decode. This exchange is so common in everyday life that we take it for granted, and it is likely to become a problem mainly for travelers to other countries. The American who tries to communicate with a French citizen in France has no trouble in coding the information into his native tongue, but his listener will not be able to decode the message. We say that his speech is *egocentric* in that he can code only for himself and cannot place himself in the role of the other.

As Piaget and others have pointed out, the young child is extremely egocentric (see Chapter 17). He assumes that his perspective is the only one and that his *concrete operations* are the only ones possible. This means that his verbal communication consists of a two-stage process (see Figure 28.11). First he codes stimuli for himself and then he delivers the message to his listener. He is not aware of the listener's different perspective, vocabulary, or informational needs. In contrast, the speech of the older child and adult is *social* in that it allows for the listener's needs. It is a four-stage process involving coding, discriminating the listener's attributes, *recoding* the information, and then sending the message (Flavell, 1968). The process is probably more complicated than the diagram, for the speaker's initial coding for himself may compete with the cognitions involving listener attributes. This is especially true in older children, who sometimes regress to egocentric tendencies in the middle of otherwise social communication.

Research Report

The way to study egocentric and social communication is to examine the speech of a subject who must communicate to a listener who has an obviously different perspective. This is precisely what was done by Krauss and Glucksberg (1970) in a series of experiments. The basic task is to communicate about a set of graphic stimuli that are so novel that they cannot be named easily (see Figure 28.12). The designs are located on the facets of wooden blocks each of which has a hole drilled in it. Both the speaker and the listener have a set of the blocks and a vertical pole. The speaker's blocks emerge from a dispenser, the listener's are spread out in front of her, and the speaker and listener are visually separated by a barrier (see Figure 28.13). The subject's task is to instruct the listener about the order in which the blocks are to be stacked on the pole.

Children four years of age and younger cannot master this task, as their verbalizations are too egocentric to communicate adequately. Five- and six-year-old children do master the task with varying degrees of success, for they are better listeners than speakers. There are clear developmental trends, with older children making fewer errors than younger children. Krauss and Glucksberg believed that the basic problem was in the *encoding* of the message by the speaker, not the decoding of it by the listener. To test this notion, they tried the messages spoken by grade school children on college students as listeners, the independent variable being the grade of the young speakers. The results are shown in Figure 28.14. Clearly, the listeners' accuracy improved with increasing age (grade placement) of the speaker, a fact that suggests that it is mainly the *encoding* process that hinders communication in children. Presumably, the ability to decode develops earlier than the ability to encode, which is not surprising in light of the more active, role-taking requirements of the encoding process.

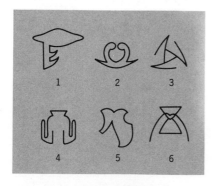

Figure 28.12 Designs of low codability (Krauss and Glucksberg, 1970).

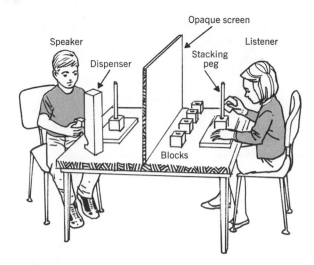

Figure 28.13 *Studying verbal communication (after Krauss and Glucksberg, 1970).*

The *associative* aspects of encoding have been studied in a task involving only words (Cohen & Klein, 1968). Again one subject acts as speaker, the other as listener. They face away from each other, and each has a card on which are printed the same two words, say RIVER-OCEAN. On the speaker's card one of these words is underlined, and his task is to say one word that will enable the listener to guess the correct (underlined) word. The two stimulus words are somewhat similar, and the speaker must select a word that is associatively linked with one but not the other. Thus for RIVER he might say STREAM, whereas for OCEAN he might say SEA or BAY. In this task seventh graders were clearly more proficient than third graders, and the difference lay mainly in the clue words supplied by the speakers. Evidently, younger speakers simply do not have the vocabulary to allow them to communicate slight differences among words (or even objects). Thus the research to date has established two reasons for the poor communication for children: their relative inability to take the role of the listener and their limited vocabulary.

Communication and Role-Playing

As we have seen, social communication requires that the speaker be able to assume the role of his listener so that he may send unequivocal messages. We should therefore not be surprised that both role-playing and communication can be analyzed in the same way. Flavell (1968) has done just that, specifying five steps common to both processes.[4]

[4] *Though we are using his concepts, the names have been changed in the hope of achieving greater descriptive clarity.*

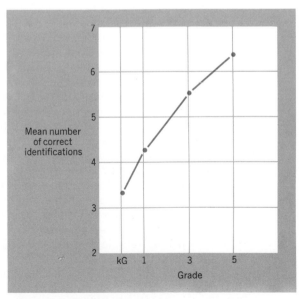

Figure 28.14 *Accuracy as a function of speaker's grade (after Krauss and Glucksberg, 1969).*

1. *Perspective.* This is merely recognition that there is another perspective, different from one's own; this has been discussed earlier.
2. *Awareness.* It is possible to be aware that differences in perspective exist but fail to realize that these differences are important in a given situation; the speaker must know that *in this particular context* he must allow for the viewpoint of the listener. Thus a speaker may continue for some time to talk softly before he discovers that his listener is either deaf or hard of hearing, or a person giving directions to a stranger might use local names in his description, failing to understand the listener's ignorance of such locales. It is a common fault of new PhDs that their vocabulary level and expectations of students are both too high, largely because their listeners for several previous years have been fellow graduate students and faculty — whose technical vocabulary and mastery of specific concepts are far beyond that of the undergraduate student.
3. *Knowledge of others.* This category includes both knowing facts about the listener and possessing the ability to make good guesses about him. Ignorance of the listener's attributes may lead not only to failure to communicate but also to downright hostility. Consider the reaction of an American Indian who is told that Columbus "discovered" America or the reaction of a black high school student who is told that his school's flag is the same as the Confederate flag. Evaluating the other's role can avoid embarrassment. For example, a guest must accurately gauge whether his hostess can be kidded about food she has prepared, and a raconteur must be a shrewd judge of whether his audience will enjoy a risqué story.
4. *Social primacy.* It may be assumed that there is continual competition between egocentric and social communication. Even when the speaker is aware of the need for perspective and has accurately gauged his listener's attributes, he may still slip back into self-centered communication. For example, when talking to a blind person, he may temporarily forget this fact and say, "Look over there"; or when talking to a black, he may inadvertently blurt out, "That's damn white of you" (meaning that the other has been a real gentleman). Thus failing to maintain the role-taking approach when encoding speech may lead to embarrassment and hostility.
5. *Repertoire.* As indicated earlier, the listener must have the appropriate responses available to him. He needs to know the correct words or the responses that go with the role he is attempting to play. For example, when a young man is attempting to impress others with his intellect by using big words, he had better be correct in his usage or he will show up as a pompous fool. The American traveler in a foreign country may clearly recognize that his listener will not understand English, but in the absence of the appropriate vocabulary he will be unable to communicate.

Two Communication Styles

During the era when the child is learning first language and then social communication, one of the most crucial roles is that played by the mother. Her verbal responses to the child teach him how to communicate by imitation and also show the child what he can expect from others. The child learns not only how to communicate verbally (imitation) but also the way others will typically react to him (knowledge of the other's role).

Two divergent maternal styles of communication have been demonstrated in a study of mothers and their children (Hess & Shipman, 1965). The mothers were shown a simple task and asked to teach it to their four-year-old children. One task was to sort toys by either their function or color, and the mother's instructions are especially revealing:

"All right, Susan, this board is the place where we put the little toys; first of all you're supposed to learn how to place them according to color. Can you do that? The things that are all the same color you put in one section; in the second section you put another group of colors, and in the third section you put the last group of colors. Can you do that? Or would you like to see me do it first?"
"I want to do it." (p. 881)
Contrast these logical, complete instructions which

Table 28.3
Restricted Versus Elaborated Styles of Communication (Bernstein, 1962)

	RESTRICTED	ELABORATED
DESCRIPTION	Stereotyped Undifferentiated, imprecise Implicit meaning More connotative	Individualized Differentiated, precise Explicit meaning More denotative
CONTROL	Appeal to status or prescribed norms	Appeal to feelings and preferences
OUTCOME	Passive learning Compliance to authority	Assertive learning Compliance to rational, logical considerations

offer the child a rationale, with the following terse interrogation:

"I've got some chairs and cars, do you want to play the game?"

(No response)

"O.K. What's this?"

"A wagon?"

"HM?"

"A wagon?"

"This is not a wagon. What's this?" (P. 882.)

These two extremes of maternal communication are typical of two opposed styles of communicating, *restricted* and *elaborated,* as outlined by Bernstein (1962). In general, the restricted style is egocentric in that it fails to take account of the listener's perspective and needs, whereas the elaborated style is social in that it makes contact with the listener's perspective and needs (see Table 28.3). The restricted style is stereotyped, imprecise, and undifferentiated in its message. It tends to be connotative and relies on nonverbal aspects of the interaction to get its meaning across. The elaborated style is more tailored to the individual listener, and it is explicit in getting its message across by verbal means only.

Bernstein has linked the restricted style with the kind of parental control that uses authority and appeals to status or norms. For example, if a child is playing noisily and the telephone rings, the mother might say, "Shut up!" or "Be quiet." If the mother makes a demand that the child questions, she tends to reply that she is the mother and knows best—"Do it because I say so." In contrast, the elaborated style is linked with control that rests on appeals to logic or to the preferences and feelings of others. Thus the noisy child might be told, "Would you keep quiet for a minute. I want to talk on the phone." If the child questioned a maternal demand, he would be told the underlying reason for the demand: cleanliness, health, avoidance of danger, the feelings of others, and so on.

The two styles differ sharply in their outcomes. The restricted style produces passive learning of the sort obtained by teachers who have their pupils recite merely by repeating the teacher's own words. Accompanying this passivity is compliance to authority: "Teacher (mother, big brother) knows best." The communication, the learning, and the control all converge to produce the obedience fostered by military training ("You are not paid to think, just to obey orders"). Moreover, such training makes it difficult for the child later to communicate with others in any other way. The elaborated style, in contrast, leads to the child taking the initiative in exploring on his own and bids him comply with demands because they make sense rather than because they originate from a higher authority. Thus a child learns to trust and obey his parents (authority in general) because they have knowledge and skills and are interested in helping rather than because they have power and control over the child.

Hess and Shipman (1965) found class difference in style roughly equivalent to the above distinction, lower class style being more restricted and middle class style more elaborated. Some corroboration has come from subsequent research (see Alvy, 1971; Baldwin et al., 1971; Brooks et al., 1969; & Heider, 1971), and it may be that disadvantaged children (largely lower-class) suffer severe educational deficits because of inability to communicate with middle-class teachers or to answer questions by middle-class testers.

chapter 29
attitudes

Opinions, beliefs, and attitudes — attitudes and behavior — attitude change — credibility of source — attractiveness and similarity — mass media — face-to-face contacts — affect and fear arousal — sequence of presentation — role playing — intelligence and self-esteem of target person — cognitive dissonance — commitment and choice — self-perception theory — prejudice — group norms — Robber's Cave study — dissimilar beliefs — prejudice pays

Most persons have *opinions* about where to live, where to take a vacation, who would make a good president, and which movie stars are good actors. They also have *beliefs* about democracy, God, science, astrology, and natural foods. Most opinions are essentially personal preferences and beliefs are essentially *inferences* and *generalizations,* but both are related to *attitudes:*

"Attitudes refer to the stands the individual holds and cherishes about objects, issues, persons, groups, or institutions" (Sherif et al., 1965, p. 4). Many attitudes are abstract (a stand on communism) or impersonal (the "evils" of smoking pot), but the most important ones concern other persons. Thus there is much turmoil in this country over racial and ethnic issues — involving attitudes toward blacks, Chicanos, Puerto Ricans, Indians, and other minority groups — and the tremors of a forthcoming eruption over men's attitudes toward a *majority* group, women. Such attitudes involve *prejudice,* which warrants separate treatment in the chapter.

Three Aspects of Attitudes

Attitudes have three aspects — cognitive, affective, and instrumental — corresponding to three of the

Table 29.1
Cognitive, Affective, and Instrumental Aspects of an Attitude*

Cognitive (belief)	"Those gals in Women's Lib are simply frustrated women who are too unattractive to get a man."
Affective (feeling)	"They are really beginning to get on my nerves."
Instrumental (overt behavior)	"Today I told one off and broke up her picket sign."

* This particular attitude is obviously a prejudice—and it will be discussed later in the chapter.

four reaction systems (the fourth is *sensory*). Beliefs and opinions are of course *cognitions* about objects, events, and persons. But not all beliefs are attitudes. We believe that the earth is round and that there is a force called gravity, but these cognitions are not considered attitudes. The difference involves the presence or absence of an *affective* component. The age of the universe is believed to be 10 billion years, but for most persons this belief (estimate) is not accompanied by any positive or negative evaluation. If the estimate were revised tomorrow to 29 billion years, there would be considerable surprise but virtually no joy, melancholy, or anger. But consider another scientific belief: the value of fluoridating the water supply. Scientists have proved that fluorides in the water supply sharply reduce dental decay, with no important negative side effects. Yet millions of persons believe that fluoridation is harmful, and they have in many instances prevented it. They *evaluate* fluoridation negatively, revealing an affective component that is absent from their belief about gravity, the roundness of the earth, or the age of the universe.

Note that many antifluoridation persons actively seek to prevent fluoridation. They not only possess cognitions and affects about fluorides but also engage in relevant *instrumental* behavior. Attitudes imply a *readiness to act,* but often the oc-

casion does not arise. Thus an individual may hate a political candidate, believing him to be a poor man for the job, but refrain from voting against him because of laziness or inability to vote. Most of us have attitudes that are never expressed in overt behavior, either because the opportunity does not arise or because other factors intervene (fear, laziness, inability, and so on).[1] But the *disposition* to act in accordance with the cognitive and affective aspects of the attitude is usually present, and it may reveal itself in action. In brief, attitudes encompass the three reaction systems involving beliefs, feelings, and overt behavior (see Table 29.1).

Attitudes and Behavior

The instrumental aspect of attitude is dispositional in that it refers to a *readiness* to act. As has been noted, the occasion for action may or may not arise. Remember, also, that attitudes include beliefs and feelings, as well as dispositions toward action. Therefore, it is appropriate to ask about the relationship between attitudes and behavior.

[1] *Some attitudes do not call for any action—as, for example, one's attitude toward Buddhism or toward modern art.*

Table 29.2
Attitudes Toward Birth Control (Kothandapani, 1971)

Feeling Component

I am *happy* to learn about the benefits of birth control.
The very thought of birth control *disgusts* me.

Belief Component

Birth control *will help* me postpone childbirth as long as I want.
I believe that birth control *causes* many birth defects.

Intention to Act Component

I would volunteer to *speak* about the merits of birth control.
I would *walk* a mile to get my birth control supplies.

Knowing a person's beliefs or feelings, can we predict his actual behavior? Thus if a person believes that fluoridation is harmful and therefore bad for the community, will he join a protest against fluoridation or go the polls to vote against it?

The answer is that psychologists can do better than chance in predicting behavior from beliefs and feelings, but not enough better to make accurate predictions. The reason for poor prediction is not hard to find: neither the affective component (feelings) nor the cognitive component (beliefs) is necessarily closely related to the instrumental component (behavior). This explanation assumes that the three components are distinct and that they need not be consistent with one another.[2] Furthermore, it follows that the best way to predict behavior is to assess the instrumental component—that is, by determining the individual's *intention to act.*

[2] *For an advanced but interesting theoretical account of relationships among the three components, see Insko and Schopler (1967). For a review of attitudes versus actions, see Wicker (1969). A novel and intriguing approach is Abelson's (1968) notion of opinion molecules: encapsulated units made up of a belief, an attribute, and social support.*

These points have been confirmed in laboratory research on attitudes toward the church (Ostrom, 1969) and the controversial issue of birth control (Kothandapani, 1971). Kothandapani started by constructing items involving feelings, beliefs, and intentions to act—in relation to birth control (see Table 29.2). A number of such items were given to black women, who also reported on their actual use of birth control methods. There were two salient findings: (1) the three components—cognitive, affective, and instrumental—were clearly differentiated from one another, which means there was little consistency among them for most persons; and (2) though beliefs and feelings did predict actual use of birth control, the best predictions came from intentions to act. The explanation for the second finding may be couched in stimulus-response terms:

Performance of an act may be considered a function of learned intentions, beliefs, and feelings in combination with current stimulus conditions. The feeling component stimulates or inhibits performance. The belief component aids in building up stimulus-response-reinforcer relationships. The intention component functions as an organizer, coordinating the feeling and belief input with the behavioral output.

(KOTHANDAPANI, 1971, P. 332.)

Table 29.3
Major Variables That Determine Attitude Change

Source	1. Credibility 2. Attractiveness and similarity
Channel	1. Modality—visual versus acoustic 2. Directness—face-to-face versus mass media
Message	1. Affect—factual versus emotional 2. Sequence of presentation
Target person	1. Activity—role-playing versus passivity 2. Individual differences

Inconsistency of attitudes was neatly demonstrated in a field study in the 1930s (LaPiere, 1934). At that time there was a strong prejudice against Orientals. An American man and a Chinese couple tried to obtain rooms at a large number of hotels, and in most instances they succeeded. Later a letter was sent to the proprietors, asking if they would accept Chinese or Japanese as guests. Of those managers who answered the letter, most said they would not. This finding emphasizes the differences between attitudes and behavior: a person with a prejudice against Chinese (attitude) would find it hard to turn away a well-dressed Chinese couple accompanied by an American (behavior).

Attitude Change

Attitudes are acquired throughout the life of a person in the same way as anything else that is learned: through classical conditioning, instrumental conditioning, imitation, and rule-learning. No one is ever really free from attempts to change his attitudes. The influences start in childhood and continue through adolescence into adulthood.

To understand the details of how attitudes are acquired, psychologists have studied *change,* usually in adults. Attitudes can be altered only when persons *communicate,* which means that the basic communication model is appropriate (see Figure 28.1). The model specifies four aspects: signaler (source), channel, message, and receiving organism. Each has been studied intensively for many years, and—as in any area of science—the more that is known, the more complex are the findings. Our discussion will be brief,[3] limited to two variables for each part of the model (see Table 29.3).

Source

CREDIBILITY. The opinions of some persons are inevitably valued more than those of others. We are more likely to be persuaded by someone who has special knowledge, talent, or experience relevant to the issue at hand. Consider the effect of smoking on health, an issue that is largely re-

[3] *Details may be found in Zimbardo and Ebbesen (1969) and especially in McGuire (1969). Table 29.3 contains only the major determinants of attitude change.*

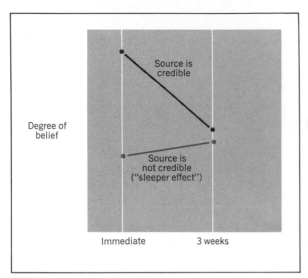

Degree of
belief

Source is
credible

Source is
not credible
("sleeper effect")

Immediate   3 weeks

Figure 29.1 *Effect of source credibility over time*
(*Kelman and Hovland, 1953*).

solved—though there are a few die-hards who
deny the evidence. Most of us would be persuaded
by the reports of physicians, public health officials, or unbiased scientists who study smoking;
they are credible sources. A less credible source,
such as the man next door, would be less persuasive, and most persons would resist the statements of someone paid by the tobacco industry.

This influence, however, is surprisingly short-
lived. Strong as it is immediately after the message is delivered, the effects of credibility dis-
sipate within only a few weeks; stranger still, a
low-credible source has an *increasing* effect over
time (Hovland & Weiss, 1951). The phenomenon
is called the *sleeper effect* (see Figure 29.1). A
reasonable explanation is that the listeners remember the message but not the person who
delivered it. It follows that reminding them of the
identity of the source should reinstate the effect of
credibility (more agreement with a credible source
than with one who is not credible), and this is
precisely what occurs (Kelman & Hovland, 1953).
ATTRACTIVENESS AND SIMILARITY. Attractive
persons have more influence than unattractive
ones, a fact that has not been lost on politicians or
advertisers. Television sales pitches are usually

delivered by persons of very presentable appearance and grooming. In recent years, advertisers
have discovered another source of influence, similarity. Many of them are having the message delivered by "just folks," persons who are more like the
average man or woman (similarity) rather than
those of outstanding good looks and speech (attractiveness). Both approaches appear to sell
products.

Channel

Most of our information is taken in through the
eyes and ears, and in the area of attitude change
most messages are verbal. Written messages are
easier to understand, but they are impersonal.
Spoken messages involve at least a minimal social
interaction, which means that the attractiveness
and similarity of the source can have an effect.
Therefore, other things being equal, a spoken
message changes attitudes more than a written
one does.
MASS MEDIA. The mass media, especially radio
and television, can rapidly change attitudes. Not
only are products sold but also politicians.[4] Mass
media have also helped stir up popular feeling
about our garbage-filled environment, overpopulation, air and water pollution, and ecology in general.

Two separate commissions, one on pornography
and one on violence, have reported the influence
of television and movies. The findings are complex, but they have been boiled down to these two
(Berkowitz, 1971): (1) both sexual and aggressive
attitudes and behavior are *temporarily* enhanced
by the stimulation offered on television and in
movies; and (2) there are no *enduring* effects on
either sex or aggression. Remember, too, that
most persons selectively attend to the mass
media, listening to what they agree with and
tuning out what they disagree with.
FACE-TO-FACE. Is face-to-face contact more persuasive than movies, television, and other media?

[4] *The public relations efforts to elect Richard Nixon i*
1968 were merely a prelude to massive advertising cam
paigns in subsequent state and local elections—all designed
to sell the product (a candidate for office).

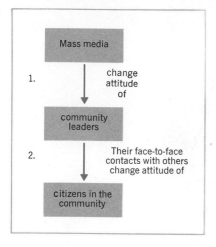

Figure 29.2 *Two steps in widespread attitude change.*

Unfortunately, most of the research bearing on this issue was conducted before television was as pervasive as it is today, but the findings are still instructive.

In a city about to vote on a revision of its charter, citizens were selected who were opposed or undecided (Eldersveld & Dodge, 1954). They either were visited once or received four mailings — in attempts to persuade them to vote *for* the revision. A control group was left alone. The measure of change was their actual votes: personal contact — 75%, mail — 45%, and control — 19% for the charter revision.

These findings fit nicely with those of a large-scale study, which showed that most *attempts* at influence and most *successes* occurred within the family (Katz & Lazarsfeld, 1955). The effects of mass media were filtered through a *two-step* sequence of information flow (see Figure 29.2). First, opinions were acquired by the opinion-leaders of the community, who then passed them on the the others in the community. The leaders may have been influenced by newspapers, books, radio, and television, but most of the community were influenced by the face-to-face contacts with the opinion-leaders. The same two-step process also occurs in getting physicians to adopt a new drug: first it is tried by a leader, and then by the other physicians (Menzel & Katz, 1956). In brief, face-to-face communication is the most effective way to change attitudes for the majority of people.

Message

AFFECT. Emotional appeals do have a strong influence. In 1951 Richard Nixon, then a vice-presidential candidate, was discovered to be the beneficiary of an $18,000 slush fund set up by businessmen. He went on television to defend himself, delivering a sentimental speech about his wife's cloth coat and the poverty of his childhood. He displayed his family and his dog, Checkers. This emotional appeal, subsequently called the Checkers Speech, so strongly swayed public opinion in his favor that Nixon was retained as a candidate and subsequently served two terms as Eisenhower's vice-president. Television audiences are more sophisticated now, and such an affect-laden speech would probably be less effective.

Nixon is also known for his use of fear in swaying opinion. He was one of the outstanding politicians of the witch-hunting era of the 1950s, when the specter of communism was routinely invoked to obtain votes. Opposing candidates were branded as "soft on communism" or "dupes of subversives," and this tactic was successful in changing both attitudes and votes.

Arousing fear is often used today in attempting to affect attitudes about pollution, overpopulation, drunken driving, venereal disease, and smoking (see Figure 29.3). In general, fear tends to sway attitudes, but there are exceptions (see Freedman et al., 1970, p. 326). If the message arouses exces-

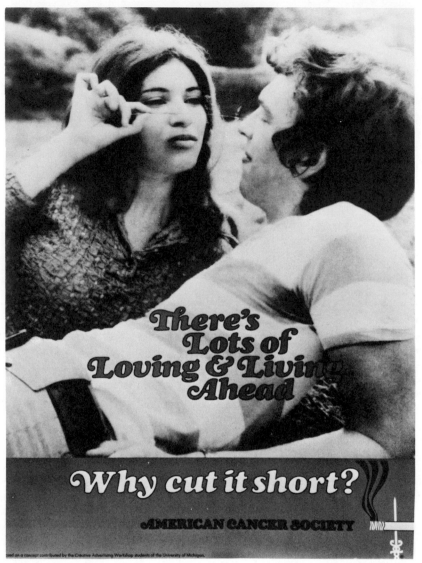

Figure 29.3 A fear-arousing communication.   (AMERICAN CANCER SOCIETY)

sive fear, the target person will find ways to avoid the communication and it will have no effect. Millions of cigarette smokers simply do not read the warning, present on every pack of cigarettes, that they are harmful to health. On the other hand, if the danger is clearly at hand or imminent, the message explicit, and a response easily available, then appeals to fear are attended to and do have a strong impact.

Whether fear arousal changes attitudes also depends on the content of the attitude—that is, what it refers to. When the fear of tetanus is made salient, subjects strengthen their resolve to take tetanus shots (Leventhal et al., 1965). But when the attitude concerns smoking and its relation to lung cancer, fear arousal causes no change in attitude or the desirability of obtaining chest X rays (Leventhal & Watts, 1966). Evidently, fear arousal—or any other manipulation designed to change attitudes—is relatively ineffective in altering strongly held attitudes that concern personal issues and relate to deeply ingrained habits (such as smoking).

SEQUENCE. What is the first thing to do when trying to change the attitudes of an audience? Do *not* forewarn them that the attempt will be made, for this makes them resistant. The best approach is to start by agreeing with opinions already held by the audience. This is the Marc Antony technique: his audience, initially hostile to Julius Caesar, was told that Marc Antony was there "to bury Caesar, not to praise him." As for other aspects of sequence, research has supported these propositions:

1. Present one side of the argument when the audience is generally friendly, or when your position is the only one that will be presented, or when you want immediate, though temporary, opinion change.
2. Present both sides of the argument when the audience starts out disagreeing with you, or when it is probable that the audience will hear the other side from someone else.
3. When opposite views are presented one after another, the one presented last will probably be more effective.[5]

(ZIMBARDO & EBBESEN, 1969, P. 21.)

Target Person

ROLE-PLAYING. In the usual communication context, the target person passively watches or listens to a message. Will his attitude change more if he becomes active and plays the role of "devil's advocate"? There are good reasons for believing that role-playing works. A target person is asked to argue for a position different from his own. In doing so, he must try to understand the other position and at least temporarily marshal arguments for it. The increased understanding and empathy should make him susceptible to attitude change. Laboratory research has shown that advocating a position, even when play-acting, does lead to a more favorable attitude. This fact was first demon-

[5] *For this reason a trial attorney who knows that his opponent will have the last word, prepares the jury for counter-arguments and builds in resistance to him through fore-warning.*

strated for neutral topics (Janis & King, 1954) and subsequently for the emotionally loaded topic of race relations (Culbertson, 1957). How well the role is played in terms of spontaneity or improvisation is unimportant, for the attitude change occurs mainly because the person attends closely to opposing arguments (Zimbardo, 1965).

INDIVIDUAL DIFFERENCES. Some persons are so susceptible to persuasion that their attitudes change like a ping pong ball being batted back and forth. Others take a position and stick to it, refusing to budge even in the face of overwhelming refutation. Most of us belong in a middle ground of persuasibility. What determines these individual differences? We shall cite two variables.

1. *Intelligence.* Less intelligent persons can be influenced more easily than more intelligent persons. This simple relationship is complicated by the tendency of brighter persons to take in more information and attend better to communications. Thus brighter persons may *yield* less but they probably receive more messages aimed at changing their attitudes.
2. *Esteem.* Persons of low self-esteem are easier to influence than those of high self-esteem. The low-esteem person has little confidence in his own values and judgments. If another's views are more trustworthy, they are more easily adopted. High-esteem persons possess the confidence that enables them to resist the arguments of others.

Cognitive Dissonance

Consistency theories all assume that everyone strives to be self-consistent and attempts to eliminate inconsistency from cognitions and behavior. The most controversial and perhaps important consistency theory is that of Festinger (1957, 1964). It is called *cognitive dissonance:* a conflict between two attitudes, between attitudes and behavior, or between attitudes and facts. Consider someone who believed that our Vietnam policy was justified and that the United States Army was fighting to help the Vietnamese people to achieve democracy. Along comes an event like the My Lai massacre, in which American soldiers slaughtered dozens of South Vietnamese old men, women, and children in cold blood. This fact clearly conflicts

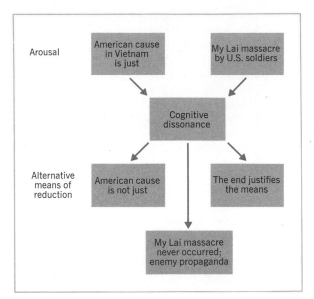

Figure 29.4 *Cognitive dissonance: arousal and means of reduction.*

with the person's belief that the American cause is right and just. Two cognitions are now dissonant (see Figure 29.4). How might the conflict be resolved (the dissonance reduced)? He could alter his belief that our participation in the war was just. Or he could deny that the massacre ever really occurred or that it was justified because the civilians were really helping the enemy. Or he could take refuge in such attitudes as "the end justifies the means," and "you can't make an omelet without breaking a few eggs." This last approach was probably the one most "hawks" adopted to reduce the dissonance caused by My Lai.

At a more personal level, the smoker who is informed that cigarettes cause cancer is also in a bind: that smoking is dangerous is inconsistent with the fact that he smokes. He can reduce his cognitive dissonance by challenging the link between smoking and health hazards ("it's only statistical evidence," and so on), or he can admit that he is living dangerously but simply cannot help himself. The first tactic would lead to a search for inconsistencies in the cigarettes-cancer argument or evidence to the contrary. The second tactic would lead to avoidance of the entire topic. Presumably, one's attempt to reduce dissonance leads to a change in attitude or behavior.

Adherents of the cognitive dissonance theory claim that it specifies clearly the conditions under which cognitive dissonance occurs and how it will be reduced. Critics of the theory dispute this, but both adherents and critics agree that the theory has spawned some ingenious experiments and some surprising findings.[6]

Most persons place a high value on things for which they have struggled or worked hard. Cognitive dissonance theory accounts for this fact by assuming that the overvaluation reduces dissonance. To test this notion, an early dissonance experiment varied the severity of initiation into a group (Aronson & Mills, 1959). The initiation consisted of a discussion of sex. In the Severe condition the girls were embarrassed by having to read aloud twelve obscene words; in the Mild condition they read aloud five words that were related to sex but not at all obscene. The girls in the Severe condition rated the group as more attractive than the girls in the Mild condition. Presumably, placing an excessively high value on the group justified the severity of the initiation. These findings were confirmed when electric shock (severe and mild) was substituted for embarrassment (Gerard & Mathewson, 1966).

The theory also accounts for the unexpected fact that receiving only a little money for talking about a boring task as pleasant results in liking the task more than receiving a lot of money for doing the same task (Festinger & Carlsmith, 1959). Presumably, receiving a large amount of money would lead to no dissonance; there is no dissonance in being well paid to do a mildly unpleasant task. Receiving only a little money would lead to dissonance, because there would be insufficient justification to perform the task. The dissonance could be reduced by evaluating the activity more positively.

As the theory now stands, it includes the variables of *commitment* and *choice* (Brehm & Cohen, 1962). Commitment involves a public act that cannot be easily denied or retracted. Choice involves the person's own volition in engaging in the discrepant behavior, thereby making him *responsible*. The following experiments illustrate these issues.

[6] *The outpouring of research, which is barely sampled here, has been reviewed several times (Brehm & Cohen, 1962, Festinger, 1964; Chapanis & Chapanis, 1964; and Bem 1967).*

Research Report

A worthwhile theory should be verifiable not only in the laboratory but in everyday life. The racetrack is an everyday place where commitment occurs in the form of bets on the races. Once a decision is made, the favorable features of the rejected alternatives (horses) cause doubt that the decision was correct; the favorable features of the alternatives conflict with the decision already made (cognitive dissonance). One way of reducing the dissonance would be to evaluate the chosen horse more favorably, as reflected in greater confidence in the bet already placed. This hypothesis was tested by Knox and Inkster (1968) at a racetrack in Canada. They selected persons who were *about to bet* at the $2 window and compared them with those who had *just made* a $2 bet. The measure was a scale that ranged from *slight* through *fair* and *good* to *excellent,* referring to the horse's chance of winning the race. Before commitment (betting) the average chance was rated *fair*; after commitment (betting) the average chance was rated *good*. Prior to the bet there is no dissonance and therefore no need to inflate one's chance of winning. Evidently, it feels more comfortable (a state of low dissonance) to believe that one's chance of winning is better once the bet has been made.

The second experiment (Brock & Buss, 1962) deals with *choice.* The subjects were college men and women who were opposed to the use of electric shock on humans in scientific research. Each subject was assigned the role of "experimenter" in the *aggression machine* (see Figure 22.6), which requires that he deliver shock to another person. The subject ("experimenter") was routinely given shock from buttons 1, 2, 3, and 5 so that he would know how much he was delivering to the other person. Then he rated these shocks on a scale that ranged from "can't feel a thing" to "extremely painful."

Half the subjects were then given the option of leaving (Choice), and 3 out of 43 actually did leave. The overwhelming majority chose to engage in discrepant behavior: use electric shock when they were opposed to its use. The other half of the subjects were given no option (No Choice); as they were simply following instructions, there should have been no dissonance. After all subjects delivered the electric shock they were given shock from buttons 1, 2, 3, and 5, and the dependent variable was the change in the shock ratings from before and after delivering it to another person.

The results are shown in Figure 29.5. In the No Choice condition men and, to the lesser extent, women perceived the shock as more painful after they had used it on another person. Presumably, they disliked giving electric shock, and this negative feeling made them evaluate the shock even more negatively after they used it: "What you made me do was even worse than I thought it was." The Choice subjects reacted in the *opposite* direction, rating the shock as considerably less painful after they used it on another. Presumably, when they chose to give shock, this behavior was dissonant with their previously expressed opposition to the use of shock. One way to reduce the dissonance would be to deny that the shock was really painful, and this is precisely what they did.

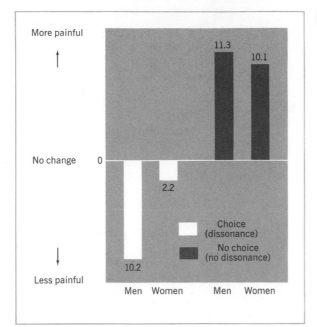

Figure 29.5 *Changes in perceived pain of electric shock in relation to cognitive dissonance (Brock and Buss, 1962).*

Self-Perception Theory

No one seriously denies that the theory of cognitive dissonance has generated a flood of research in attitude change and related areas. Nevertheless, its deductions are not always clearly stated, and not all research has confirmed it.[7] The theory has had its share of critics, some of whom have suggested alternatives to it. Cognitive dissonance, as its name implies, is a *cognitive* theory. As we have noted repeatedly, one strong alternative to the cognitive approach is the stimulus-response approach offered by behaviorists. In the area of attitude change, the major behavioristic alternative to cognitive dissonance is the self-perception theory of Daryl Bem (1967, 1970).

Bem assumes that self-perception is based more on observation of *behavior* than it is on ob-

servation of internal states. Moreover, we infer others' inner states from their behavior:

When we want to know how a person feels, we look to see how he acts. Accordingly, my theory about the origins of an individual's self-knowledge predicts that he might also infer his own internal states by observing his own behavior. (1970, P. 57.

Consider a typical cognitive dissonance experiment (Brehm & Cohen, 1962, pp. 73–77). After police intervention at Yale University, most students reacted unfavorably toward the police actions. Students were asked to write essays giving the police side of the issue, and they were paid 50c, $1, $5, or $10; a control group wrote no essays. Afterward, those who were given $5 or $10 were as unfavorable toward the police as were Control subjects. But those given $1 were more favorable, and those given only 50¢ for the essay were the most favorable toward the police. This can be neatly explained by cognitive dissonance theory: behavior discrepant with the attitude leads to a change in the attitude.

Bem's analysis is entirely different:

If we, as observers, use the payoff to a communicator to help us judge whether or not the individual really believes what he is communicating, then it may also be that the communicator himself, as a self-observer, uses the payoff as a signal to tell himself whether or not his communication represents his true beliefs. (1970, P. 59)

Thus the Yale student who wrote the pro-police essay for almost no money would *infer from his own behavior*[8] that he could not be doing it for the money and must therefore be somewhat more favorable toward the police than he had believed.

Presumably, others could make the same inference about the student as he did himself. To test his notion, Bem (1965) gave subjects *descriptions* of the Brehm and Cohen (1962) experiment on Yale students. Some descriptions noted that the students had been paid 50¢, others that the students had been paid $1. The subjects' task was to judge the attitude of the students after they wrote

[7] *For example, in the Brock and Buss (1962) experiment just mentioned, the main effects were confirmatory but some of the details that were not reported here were not confirmatory.*

[8] *He would not necessarily be* aware *of making the inference.*

the essay. This they did very well. Their judgments showed the same inverse relationship between attitude and amount of money: a more favorable attitude by those paid 50¢ than those paid $1. Bem suggests that the observers (subjects) merely asked themselves what the student's attitude must have been if he had been willing to write a favorable essay for very little money (50¢). Presumably, the student in the original study asked himself the same question about his own behavior, and therefore there was agreement between the student's actual attitude and the observers' judgments of it.

Bem (1967) has used the same procedure in following up several other cognitive dissonance experiments, each time confirming self-perception theory. Experiments by independent researchers (Kiesler et al., 1969) have also supported the theory. Nevertheless, self-perception theory has not accounted for *all* the research findings. Bem may be correct in asserting that attitudes follow behavior, but even he admits that changing beliefs can alter behavior. Evidently, the facts about cognitive dissonance require both a cognitive theory (attitudes drive behavior) and a behavioral theory (attitudes follow behavior).

Prejudice

Prejudice might mean any attitude — positive or negative — toward any object, event, or person (a *pre*judgment made with insufficient information). In *practice,* the term refers to a *negative* attitude toward *groups* of persons, a *generalization* that holds for all members of the group. As an attitude, prejudice includes affective, cognitive, and instrumental aspects. The affective component is always negative, varying from mild dislike to implacable hatred. The cognitive component consists of a set of beliefs that brand the disliked persons as stupid, lazy, cowardly, overemotional, childlike, or even essentially "nonhuman."[9] The instrumental component often involves withdrawal from the disliked persons; when there is contact, either it occurs as part of exploitation of the "infe-

[9] *Some Nazis really believed that non-Aryans were essentially not human, and some slave-owners in this country felt the same way about their black slaves.*

rior persons" or it may lead to aggression against them.

The varieties of prejudice are too numerous to list. The major kinds are racial, ethnic, national, and religious, and the American heritage includes all four. Blacks have been an oppressed minority here for more than three centuries, and the depredations against Indians constitute another shameful chapter in our history. Our bigotry extends to Mexicans, especially those who have settled here (Chicanos). Prejudice against Jews and Catholics is well known. Minority group members are no more egalitarian than anyone else, and they tend to be prejudiced against majority group members. Finally, there is one belief that supersedes nationality, religion, and race, and binds men together everywhere; it is a belief in the inferiority of women.

Of the various theories of prejudice, we shall consider only the psychological ones and concentrate on three: group norms, dissimilarity, and reinforcement.

Group Norms

All groups press their members to conform (see Chapter 30). Acceptance by the group requires adoption of its beliefs and attitudes, and to identify as a member of the group requires that each individual make a sharp "we-they" distinction. The in-group is usually endowed with superior attributes ("America is the best country in the world, and its people are the best"); the out-group is usually labeled as inferior or evil ("Mexicans are lazy, Italians are cowardly, Japanese are sly," and so on). In the process of becoming a full member of the group, and especially during socialization, each person acquires a set of prejudices about members of the out-group. An examination of the textbooks used in public schools drives home this point: the "discovery" of America, the savagery of Indians, the cowardice of Mexicans, the inferiority of blacks, and so on.

Clearly, indoctrination in the beliefs of the group is a major determinant of prejudice: it is acquired as merely one aspect of group norms (Sherif & Sherif, 1953). But this leaves unanswered the question of the *origin* of prejudice. How does one group come to dislike another and establish beliefs that characterize the out-group? Group norm theory suggests that dislike of the out-group is merely the other side of the coin of attraction to the in-group. One prefers members of one's own group because they are smarter, better looking, more talented, more democratic, loyal, steadfast, or any of a large list of desirable traits. If one accepts these as attributes of the in-group, then it follows that the out-group either possesses the traits to a lesser degree or displays opposite, negative traits. If the theory is correct, it follows that as soon as a group is formed, it should show dislike and antagonism toward members of the out-group.

THE ROBBER'S CAVE STUDY. In the early 1950s Muzafer Sherif and his colleagues studied the group behavior of 11- and 12-year-old boys at a summer camp called Robber's Cave (Sherif et al., 1965). Prior to that summer most of the boys were unknown to each other. They were brought to camp in two separate buses, and thereafter the two groups lived separately.

To produce conflict, the two groups were encouraged to play competitive games: baseball, football, tug-of-war, and so on. Gradually, ill feeling developed between the two groups, and they started to call each other "sneaks" and "cheaters." There were raids on one another's bunkhouses, name-calling, and a few fights between members of the opposing groups. This dislike of the out-group was accompanied by increased in-group solidarity and morale—the other side of the coin.

This study demonstrated how easy it is to establish prejudice, which is a rather sad state of affairs. Nevertheless, there was a happy ending. Subsequently, competition between the two groups was halted, and they were called on to cooperate in solving common problems. Thus they worked together in discovering a break in a water pipe and started a truck by pulling it with a rope (the same one used for tug-of-war). These joint efforts reversed the earlier dislike, and the intergroup hostility virtually disappeared. Note two aspects of this "group therapy": (1) the projects avoided competition and instead emphasized cooperation, and (2) the boys could enlarge their group identity to include the camp. All men might heed the lesson to be learned from this study.

SUBSEQUENT RESEARCH. A more recent experiment has frightening implications.[10] Volunteer college students at Stanford were highly paid to participate in research on the effect of being placed in prison. They were *randomly* divided into a group of prisoners and a group of guards. After only a few days the guards became so cruel and abusive that the experiment had to be canceled to protect the prisoners.

How quickly does the "we-they" distinction develop? Almost immediately. The limiting condition is *competition*.[11] If only one group can win and the other must lose, discrimination inevitably develops against the out-group. It does not matter whether the groups are constituted on the basis of a bogus judgment task involving paintings (Tajfel, 1970) or merely on the basis of the flip of a coin (Rabbie & Horwitz, 1969). The results are the same: members of the in-group are rewarded and members of the out-group deprived (and disliked). This outcome is a chilling commentary on man's group behavior.

What is striking in the present experiment is how little it evidently takes to move two randomly formed groups of strangers into mutual antipathy. Flipping a coin to decide the allocation of a scarce resource is commonly used in everyday social life in the effort to be fair. Yet this simple act triggered processes within the two groups of strangers that were far-reaching enough to affect the perception of personal traits. Although subjects had no prior experience with anyone in the room, the flip of a coin was sufficient to shape their views of outgroup members as less friendly, less familiar, less considerate, and less desirable as associates than ingroup members.

(RABBIE & HORWITZ, 1969, P. 276)

Dissimilar Beliefs

It is an established fact that similarity is a major determinant of liking, and this works both ways: not only are similar persons liked but more dissimilar persons are often disliked. Rokeach (1960, 1968) carried this point to its logical conclusion

[10] *This research, by Phillip Zimbardo, was reported on television in 1971.*

[11] *Another limiting condition may be* gender*; all research to date has used males as subjects.*

and reasoned that prejudice is caused by *dissimilar beliefs*. It is not necessary for an individual to know the beliefs of the out-group; he simply assumes that they are different from his own and therefore adopts a negative attitude toward the out-group.

Rokeach does not claim that dissimilarity of belief is the sole cause of prejudice, only that it is a major cause. For example, he believes that in prejudice against blacks, knowing the other's beliefs is more important than knowing his race. There has been considerable research support for this theory (see Sears & Abeles, 1969, for a review), but it has also been criticized. Thus it has been noted that blacks are excluded from white neighborhoods, not because of dissimilar beliefs, but because they are black (Triandis, 1961).

This criticism raises a larger issue: it is possible that belief is important in some kinds of interactions and race in others. Specifically, beliefs might influence how one behaves in impersonal situations, whereas race might determine how one behaves in closer interactions. This notion was tested with Southern white adolescents (Insko & Robinson, 1967). They evaluated four hypothetical persons who differed in race or similarity of beliefs: a similar black, a dissimilar black, a similar white, and a dissimilar white. With both race and similarity of beliefs being varied, it was possible to compute a score for each. Belief was more important than race mainly for *general issues* (fairness, cleanliness, and value), whereas race was much more important than beliefs for close personal relationships (intimate friend, chum, and marriage). These findings suggest that Rokeach's theory holds only for superficial social situations. However, as most contacts among members of different races are superficial, the theory has broad application. It applies less to personal contacts, in which a difference of race, not beliefs, is the prime basis of attitudes. A complete explanation of racial prejudice undoubtedly will have to include both race and belief (Dienstbier, 1972).

Prejudice Pays

One reason for the prevalence of prejudice is that it is strongly reinforced. Our own history with slavery is an excellent example. Slave-trading was a lucrative occupation, and the entire cotton economy of the South in the eighteenth and nineteenth centuries depended on the cheap labor extracted from blacks. The myth of black inferiority was tacked on as justification for treating blacks as property rather than as human beings.

Presently, women are protesting their relegation to the menial chores of life, especially around the home. Housekeeping, which consists of caretaking of children and cleaning and general care of the home, is considered appropriate for women but not for men. Men have a vocation, but their wives are often "just housewives." Thus masculine prejudice nicely maintains the superior status of men. Racial prejudice is most virulent when there is competition for jobs. White laborers and factory workers are believed to be the most racially bigoted segment of the population, and it is they who are being treatened by competition from blacks for their jobs.

So long as there is a payoff for prejudice, it will persist.[12] It has been argued that "legislation cannot change the hearts and minds of men" (Allport, 1954). This is untrue. Starting with the Supreme Court decision of 1954 and continuing with civil rights legislation, American attitudes have moved more and more in the direction of integration (Ostrom & Upshaw, 1970). No one argues that our progress toward equality for blacks is fast enough, but legal compliance has affected attitudes. This makes sense in terms of what was discussed earlier in the chapter: attitudes follow behavior. When prejudice is allowed to pay off, it becomes entrenched. When tolerance pays off, prejudice tends to disappear or at least is sharply reduced.

In brief, legislation can change the conditions of life, which in turn can change the hearts and minds of men. Thus racial prejudice has been reduced in the armed services by changing regulations—thereby creating the conditions for more equality.

---

[12] *There is a small segment of the population whose prejudice may be linked to their personalities (Adorno et al., 1950). Presumably, they would be prejudiced even in the absence of a payoff.*

affiliation, attraction, and conformity

Affiliation — reasons for affiliating — social comparison — ingratiation — similarity — conformity — pressures for conformity — independence and anticonformity — Asch technique — group size and unanimity — birth order — gender — ethnic group — obedience

Individual members of any given species are both attracted to and repelled by one another, and the outcome of these opposing forces determines how they relate to each other. This chapter starts with affiliation: the reasons people seek each other out and why they like each other. If there are advantages in associating with others, these rewards can be withheld by the group, which can thereby put pressure on any individual member. Thus the processes of affiliation, attraction, and conformity are linked by the social rewards and punishments that groups can bestow on individuals.

Affiliation

As we noted in previous chapters, there are compelling reasons for any individual to seek the presence of others. A group can better defend itself against attack than any single person can, and close association guarantees a synchrony of activities that helps in feeding, mating, and nurturing the young. In addition, the close mother-infant bond strengthens affiliative tendencies by teaching the young to seek others for nurturance, affection, and help. Thus men and many animals seek the company of others for protection, help,

Table 30.1
Reasons for Affiliating with Others

1. Help	Obtaining cooperation: group problem-solving Obtaining rewards: money, status, and so on
2. Esteem	Being liked: smiling, gestures of affection Being admired: compliments on appearance or performance
3. Information	About the situation: reality-testing About self: social comparison

affection, and cooperation in the pursuit of common goals. There are also reasons for affiliating that are uniquely human, and not surprisingly they tend to be essentially cognitive.

Reasons for Affiliating

Men affiliate with others because they can obtain help, enhance their self-esteem, and obtain information about the environment and themselves (see Table 30.1). Like many social animals, men cooperate in getting a job done that is best accomplished by a group or by several individuals. In this respect man is perhaps more like social insects than mammals or primates. The extent of human cooperation in solving problems is considerably greater than that of man's closest animal relatives and is approached only by ants, wasps, and other insects that perform social activities *instinctively.* Human teamwork requires *training:* it requires years to train the various members of a highly skilled surgical team consisting of physicians, nurses, and technicians. Like any human activity, group problem-solving can become ridiculous, as when committees are assigned creative work that can be done only by individuals. No committee ever painted a decent picture or wrote a satisfactory novel.

Help may come from others more directly in the form of direct disbursement of rewards — usually in attachment situations, with the dominant person distributing rewards to the subordinate person. If an individual is willing to accept a subordinate status in the group and act submissively, he will often be rewarded. One example is the way political parties reward the faithful hacks when the spoils are being divided after a successful election.

The need to have one's self-esteem elevated is of course peculiarly human. This can occur when others deliver affection by verbal and nonverbal communication. There is perhaps no more powerful force that moves one person toward another than to know that he is liked and will receive affection. Self-esteem thrives not only on love but also on admiration. A person may be liked for the qualities that make him *attractive,* or respected and admired for the qualities that make him *competent.* Thus an extremely aggressive football player like Dick Butkus is esteemed because he is an excellent athlete, but the admiration is not accompanied by affection; it is asking too much of us to like someone who, by his own admission, delights in hurting others.

The third generic reason to affiliate is to obtain information. All developing children quickly learn that older persons contribute much to their knowledge, and all technologically advanced societies have institutionalized this relationship in the form of schools. But there is a kind of information that is more basic than school learning: that which contributes to the person's knowledge of *reality.* Our senses can deceive us; with much of perception consisting of implicit inferences based on environmental cues, we need others to correct our own subjectivity. To know the world objectively in general terms is as crucial to the adapting individual as to know it objectively in precise terms is to the scientist. Was that creaking sound caused by a prowler outside, or was it merely the wind? Did the telephone really ring, or was it the doorbell or some event occurring on television? To resolve these and similar questions about what really happened, we need to obtain information from others to correct for the egocentricity of our perceptions.

Finally, we need information about our own reactions: "Did I do well? Am I angry, fearful, or just generally upset?" These and related questions require *social comparison:* we can evaluate ourselves by comparing our own reactions to those of others, and we can establish our place in the scheme of things only by knowing where others belong. When a student receives a numerical grade on an examination, he cannot possibly know how well he did unless he can compare his score with those of others (unless there is an absolute scale, which is rare nowadays). Thus after every examination, students cluster together not only to compare answers and obtain information about the material but also to discover their relative positions in the group and even to learn how they should react. If one student raises the issue of unfairness in grading, those who are uncertain about how they stand in this issue are likely to be swayed in his direction. Here reality-testing merges into social comparison: if a student becomes convinced that there is unfair grading or even cheating, his reaction changes in the direction of anger. This change harks back to the cognitive determinants of emotion and affect, which we discussed in Chapter 21. In general, when a person either does not know how to act or is uncertain of his "inner feelings," he attempts to affiliate with others in order to obtain information that will resolve the uncertainty.[1]

---

[1] *This is the basic assumption of social comparison theory (Festinger, 1954), which attempts to account for both affiliation (this chapter) and attitude change (last chapter).*

Anxiety and Affiliation

One of the most prevalent childhood fears is that of being left alone, and children who cry when left alone quickly regain their composure when joined by an adult. If isolation increases fear, affiliation should decrease it. Schachter (1959) examined this proposition in his pioneering laboratory research. College women were introduced to an ostensible professor of neurology and psychiatry, who told them that they would receive electric shocks. The High Fear group was told that the shocks would be severe and would hurt but were necessary if anything were to be learned. The Low Fear group was told that the shocks were so mild that they would only tingle. The results were as predicted (see Figure 30.1): most of the High Fear subjects, when given the option of waiting alone or with others, chose to wait with others; most of the Low Fear subjects preferred to wait alone.

Schachter did turn up an unexpected finding: first-born children tended to affiliate much more than later-born children. Subsequent research has corroborated these findings, but no one has unequivocally explained them. The speculation adopted by most psychologists assumes that the first-born child receives considerably more attention than his later siblings. Parents are often more anxious about rearing the first child, and they also tend to spend more time with him. When the child is hurt or fearful, he is quickly attended to and helped—more so than later children. Thus the first-born learns that he can expect succorance from parents and other adults, and eventually from persons in general. When he is scared, his first impulse is to seek others. The tendency also exists in later-born children, but it is somewhat weaker. This account neatly explains Schachter's

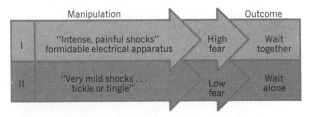

Figure 30.1 *Effect of fear on affiliation (Schachter, 1959).*

findings but only after-the-fact; what we need now is research demonstrating stronger affiliation in first-born children when they are still quite young—say, of nursery school age.

UNCERTAINTY. As we indicated earlier, one reason for affiliating is *social comparison,* which enables a person to obtain information about his own reactions to situations. This social comparison hypothesis suggests that the more uncertain a person is about his reactions, the stronger should be his desire to be with others. In testing this hypothesis, Gerard and Rabbie (1961) repeated the Schachter experiment, with one difference. The subjects were told that their emotionality was being measured and would be reflected in a meter that they could see. One group of subjects was given information about themselves (the meter readings) and a second group information about themselves and the persons they could choose to wait with. Virtually all subjects chose to wait with others after being frightened, but the two groups differed in the intensity of their affiliative urge (as measured by a rating). Subjects who had information only about themselves had a stronger desire to affiliate than those who knew about themselves and others. Presumably, the uncertainty of not knowing others' reactions enhanced the tendency to affiliate; this finding is consistent with the notion of social comparison.

Another way of manipulating uncertainty is to provide unclear information to the subject—for instance, by having the meter fluctuate wildly when indicating the subject's emotional level. When the subject cannot be sure of his own emotional level, his urge to affiliate is intensified (Gerard, 1963).

SIMILARITY. If social comparison theory is correct, a fearful person wishes to affiliate with someone who is like him, for in this way he would obtain the most information. For example, if a student is worried about the results of a test he has already taken, he cannot learn much from someone who is not in the class and is therefore not in the same bind. This expectation has been confirmed in several experiments. Schachter (1959) gave frightened subjects the option of waiting alone or with other subjects about to be shocked; another group of subjects had the option of waiting alone or waiting with students who were about to be advised. The fearful subjects generally chose to wait with those who were similar (appre-

hensive) but *not* with those who were very different (not fearful). Schachter's comment was that, "Misery doesn't love just any company, it loves only miserable company." This conclusion is strengthened by the finding that subjects prefer to wait with others who are about to be shocked rather than with others who have completed the onerous task (Zimbardo & Formica, 1963).

Does a frightened person prefer to be with an equally frightened person or with a calmer person who might have a soothing effect? Social comparison theory suggests that similarity should predominate, the choice being to wait with a person of similar emotional arousal. This is precisely what occurs (Gerard, 1963; Darley & Aronson, 1966).

REDUCTION OF FEAR. Presumably, if frightened persons can talk among themselves, they will be reassured and therefore less fearful; the possibility of being reassured is a strong reason for affiliating. If this is true, preventing people from talking about their fears should weaken their desire to affiliate. In one of Schachter's experiments (1959) he told frightened subjects that if they did wait with others, they could not talk at all or could talk only about unrelated topics. These subjects still preferred to wait with others, but the preference was considerably weaker than the affiliative tendency of those for whom there was no restriction about talking.

In a more direct test of fear reduction, Wrightsman (1960) took measures of fear before and after waiting. Waiting together reduced fear more than waiting alone, especially in first-born children. Why should merely waiting together decrease the level of fear? Perhaps when persons can exchange information about their reactions to aversive and uncertain events, they are somehow comforted to discover that others share their own feelings.

Affiliation and Attraction

In research on affiliation the basic question asked of the subject is "Do you want to be alone or with others?" As we noted, the answer depends in part on who the others are. If the others can offer no help or are in some way aversive, the person usually prefers to be alone. This raises the issue of *preference* for being with some persons rather

Table 30.2
Differences Between Affiliation and Attraction

	AFFILIATION	ATTRACTION
Choice	Being alone versus with others	One person versus another
Basic issues	Sociability	Preference, liking
Implied reference group	Many others (kinship, membership)	One person (friendship, romance)
Demands by others	Conformity	Affection
Value of others	Reality-testing	Self-esteem

than with others, which has been investigated under the heading of *attraction.* Another way of viewing this behavior is to consider it as a two-stage process. First, does the person wish to be alone or with others (affiliation)? Second, if he wishes to be with others, which others (attraction)? Clearly, the two issues are related, and some of the same factors that lead an individual to wish to be with others will surely lead him to prefer some persons to other persons. Other things being equal, we tend to affiliate with those to whom we are attracted, and we are often attracted to those with whom we affiliate.[2] If affiliation and attraction are so closely related, why treat them as separate issues?

It is a matter of emphasis. In affiliation the focus is on the tendency to seek out others (sociability); in attraction the focus is on which persons are liked (preference). Affiliation concerns reference groups of many persons, sometimes unorganized but usually organized. Thus we usually affiliate with a club, a vocational group, a state, or a

country, and there is a feeling of *identification* with something larger than ourselves. More often than not we are born into or placed in the groups with which we affiliate, and these groups usually demand loyalty and conformity to group standards and goals.

In contrast, attraction usually involves only one other person, typically in the more intimate personal relationships of friends or lovers. There is considerably more choice here, and the demands are not so much for conformity as for affection. A person is attracted to friends but affiliates with kin. No one can choose his own family, but he can select his friends. The family makes demands and expects obedience or conformity; friends make few demands (or they do not remain friends) and they expect affection.

Finally, though affiliation and attraction share similar determinants, there are some reasons for affiliation that do not carry over to attraction and vice versa. As attraction involves closer personal relationships, it is not surprising that esteem and affection are salient; reality-testing is less important. Again, these are matters of emphasis rather than all-or-none; this should be borne in mind when the summary in Table 30.2 is read.

[2] *The latter part of this statement is probably not as true as the former. Familiarity may (proverbially) breed contempt and in many instances, boredom and apathy.*

Attraction

Liking someone involves making judgments along such dimensions as good-bad, better-worse, and approach-withdrawal, and these dimensions define *affective* reactions (see Chapter 21). Why are we attracted more to some persons than to others? Some of the reasons are so obvious and straightforward that they can be discovered merely by casual observation of everyday life. Those who are better looking, brighter, more competent, and pleasant in behavior to be liked, as are those who offer help and rewards. Of course there are exceptions that arise because of jealousy of another's admired attributes or resentment at being helped, but the general tendency is to be attracted to persons held in esteem. Other reasons for attraction—by no means obvious or straightforward—have emerged from research in the area. We shall discuss them under the headings of *optimism, reciprocity,* and *similarity.*

Optimism

When meeting for the first time, most persons anticipate the event with mild trepidation but also with optimism. They tend to believe that the interaction will be pleasant and the other person will be worthwhile. This attitude occurs in the absence of information about the other person, but what happens when there is advance information? There is selective attention and even enhancement of the other's positive attributes and a tendency to minimize his negative features (Mirels & Mills, 1964; Darley & Berscheid, 1967). In this research the subjects were college students, and it is entirely possible that college students, being young and predominantly middle-class, may be somewhat more optimistic than either older or lower-class persons.

On meeting new persons, we usually present ourselves in the best possible light, setting up an interesting sequence: we expect them to be pleasant, and therefore we behave pleasantly, and our own friendly behavior may predispose us to like them. The assumption is that we attempt to make our behavior and our attitudes and beliefs consistent with one another, the basic assumption of balance theory (Heider, 1958). Thus in the interest of

consistency, we square our liking with our behavior: if we behave pleasantly toward someone, it follows that we must like him. A direct test of the hypothesis was made by inducing subjects to be kind or harsh toward other "subjects" (in reality, confederates), and discovering the effect on their liking (Schopler & Compere, 1971). As expected, when subjects were induced to act kindly toward a person, they liked him better than when they were induced to act harshly.[3]

Reciprocity

We generally like those who like us. This may be so evident that we need no research to substantiate the point, but the fact has been established in the laboratory (Newcomb, 1956, 1961). There are some minor exceptions—an extremely hostile man may be disliked by someone he likes—but liking is generally reciprocated. This is nothing more than common sense.

But common sense has nothing to say about *changes* in liking: what are the effects of positive feelings changing to negative feelings or vice versa? Aronson (1969) has suggested answers in the context of his *gain-loss* theory:

Increases in rewarding behavior from another person (P) have more impact on an individual than constant, invariant reward from P. Thus a person whose esteem for us increases over time will be liked better than one who has always liked us. This would be true even if the number of rewards were greater in the latter case. Similarly, losses in rewarding behavior have more impact than constant punitive behavior on P's part. Thus a person whose esteem for us decreases over time will be more disliked than someone who has always disliked us. . . . (P. 150.)

These hypotheses were tested in an experiment with college women (Aronson & Linder, 1965). Confederates, playing the role of subjects, gave their impressions of the real subjects, who overheard the impressions. There were four experimental conditions: (1) the confederate made all

[3] *This is an example of cognitions (judgment about liking) following behavior (doing a favor), which was discussed in Chapter 29.*

positive remarks; (2) the confederate made all negative remarks; (3) the confederate started with positive evaluations and then switched to negative; and (4) the confederate started with negative evaluations and switched to positive. The findings are presented in Figure 30.2. The greatest difference was between the two conditions in which the confederates' evaluations changed: the switch from positive to negative eliciting relative dislike by the real subjects, and the switch from negative to positive eliciting strong liking. In the consistently negative condition there were more negative evaluations than in the positive-to-negative condition, but the latter led to stronger dislike. Similarly, though the negative-to-positive condition contained fewer positive evaluations than the consistently positive condition, it led to greater liking. All these findings tend to confirm the theory, which suggests that a *gain* leads to more liking than consistently good events, and a *loss* leads to greater dislike than consistently bad events.

Like most laboratory research, this experiment may appear to be far removed from everyday activities, but Aronson and Linder (1965) suggest that it is relevant to some of our most intimate relationships:

One of the implications of the gain-loss notion is that "you always hurt the one you love." i.e., once we have grown certain of the good will (rewarding behavior) of a person (e.g., a mother, a spouse, a close friend), that person may become less potent as a source of reward than a stranger. If we are correct in our assumption that a gain in esteem is a more potent reward than the absolute level of the esteem itself, then it follows that a close friend (by definition) is operating near ceiling level and, therefore, cannot provide us with a gain. To put it another way, since we have learned to expect love, favors, praise, etc. from a friend, such behavior cannot possibly represent a gain in his esteem for us. On the other hand, the constant friend and rewarder has great potential as a punisher. The closer the friend, the greater the past history of invariant esteem and reward, the more devastating is its withdrawal. Such withdrawal, by definition, constitutes a loss of esteem. (P. 168.)

One implication is that a loving husband's compliments mean little to his wife, who has become accustomed to them. A compliment from a

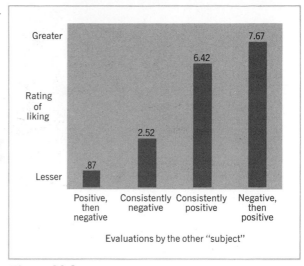

Figure 30.2 *Liking in relation to the sequence of comments heard about oneself (Aronson and Linder, 1965).*

stranger represents a clear gain and will therefore increase the attractiveness of the stranger. Though there is no direct evidence on this point, there are findings that indirectly support it. Being positively evaluated by a dissimilar person leads to more liking than being positively evaluated by a similar person (Jones et al., 1971). If we assume that a husband and wife are likely to be similar and strangers are likely to be dissimilar, this finding is related to the notion that a wife will respond better to a stranger's compliments than to her husband's. Jones et al. (1971) also found that being disliked by a similar person led to more dislike than a negative evaluation from a dissimilar person. If we equate similarity with a close relationship, this fact is consistent with the hypothesis that *we can be hurt more by those we love.*

INGRATIATION. As the gain-loss theory and its associated research have demonstrated, the effect of being liked on attraction is not the simple matter that it might appear to be at first glance. Another complication is the motivation of the person who delivers compliments. Consider the "apple-polishing" behavior of some students, who effusively praise the teacher's lecture, exclaiming at its clarity, humor, scholarship, and meaningfulness. Other things being equal, the teacher will

"There's something about you I like, but I can't put my finger on it."

Figure 30.3 Similarity leads to liking.

dergoing training to observe accurately and objectively. In the other, the observer was ostensibly a graduate student who hoped to use the subjects later in an experiment of her own (selfish motive). Later the subjects rated how much they liked the observers. Regardless of the observer's evaluations, she was liked less if she had a selfish motive. The most striking differences occurred when the observer evaluated the subject positively; then her compliments were dismissed as being attributable to the selfish motive of wishing to use the subject in a later experiment.

Similarity

Balance theory (Heider, 1958) suggests that persons who are similar will tend not only to affiliate but also to like one another (see Figure 30.3). This hypothesis has been confirmed many times over, but one of the best studies was also one of the earliest. Newcomb (1961) investigated the behavior of college men in a house where they were observed over a period of many months. When the men first moved into the house, there was only a weak relationship between similarity of attitudes and liking, but as the months passed, this relationship grew in strength. Evidently, it took time for the men to discover who shared their attitudes and who did not. By the end of the study there was a strong relationship between similarity and liking, and knowledge of a student's attitudes *before* he entered the dormitory was sufficient to predict who his friends would eventually be.

Laboratory research on similarity and liking was initiated in a series of experiments by Byrne, summarized in a recent book (1972). The subject fills out a questionnaire concerning his attitudes and interests, and then he is shown a questionnaire ostensibly filled out by a stranger, another student. Actually, the "stranger's" questionnaire is rigged so that it is either more or less similar to that of the real subject, who is then asked to evaluate the stranger along several dimensions, including attraction. A number of studies by Byrne and others have converged on the same finding: the more similar the attitudes, the greater the degree of liking (see Figure 30.4). This is true even in real-life computer dating (Byrne et al., 1970).

like such a student better than one who does not compliment him or one who criticizes him. Nevertheless, the teacher will take the student's remarks with the proverbial grain of salt, knowing that the student wishes to ingratiate himself and thereby obtain a good grade. When someone has rewards to dispense, he must be careful in evaluating the compliments of those who might receive the rewards. The problem lies in distinguishing between an honest compliment and flattery that has an ulterior motive.

Ingratiation has been investigated in the laboratory by Jones and his students (1964). In one experiment, college girls were interviewed and asked about their opinions on a variety of subjects. They were told that they were being observed behind a one-way-vision mirror. Subsequently, the observers evaluated the subjects either neutrally or positively. There were two experimental conditions. In one, the subjects were told that the observer was a graduate student un-

Though we are usually attracted to those who are like us, there are exceptions. Persons who are confident that they are liked often seek out those who are dissimilar, perhaps because they are curious; those who are insecure about being liked are likely to play it safe and associate only with persons similar to themselves. This notion was tested in a study (Berscheid & Walster, 1969) in which college women were given the option of associating with persons similar to themselves (other students in introductory psychology) or persons dissimilar to themselves (factory workers, psychologists, and so on). Some of the subjects were told that they would probably be liked; others were told that they probably would not be liked; control subjects were told nothing. The results were in line with expectations:

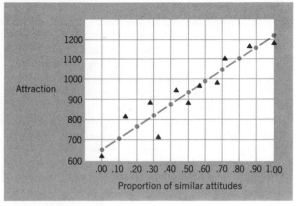

Figure 30.4 *Attraction is a function of similarity (Byrne and Nelson, 1965).*

Those students who had been assured that everyone would find them likable, were much more willing to associate with dissimilar people than were subjects in the other conditions. In fact, they vastly preferred dissimilar groups to similar ones. Those students who were instructed that they would not be liked by any group members were more anxious to talk with similar people than were control subjects. It appears then that the more concerned one is about whether others will like him, the more anxious he will be to associate with similar others. Presumably, one has more hope of winning over similar strangers than dissimilar ones.

(BERSCHEID & WALSTER, 1969, P. 74.)

Persons can be similar or dissimilar in ways that carry no evaluative component; the person who prefers fishing is no better or worse than one who prefers hiking. But some persons are pleasant and others unpleasant, and here we do evaluate one as preferable and better than the other. What is the effect of similarity when the similar person acts pleasantly or obnoxiously? Taylor and Mettee (1971) answered this question in a study called "When Similarity Breeds Contempt." College women were told that the other "subject" (really an experimental confederate) was either very similar or very dissimilar, presumably on the basis of personality tests taken earlier. In one group the confederate proceeded to behave pleasantly, and in the other group, obnoxiously (acting in a conceited, derogatory manner). When the partner was pleasant, the usual similarity effect prevailed: the

similar partner was liked better than the dissimilar partner. But when the partner acted obnoxiously, similarity led to greater *dislike*. The explanation by Taylor and Mettee (1971) appears reasonable: similarity makes the other person's characteristics more salient. Once we find that we are like someone else, we pay closer attention to that person's behavior. Thus if he is pleasant, we tend to like him more; if he is unpleasant, we *dislike* him more — simply because we are focusing more sharply on what he does and it therefore has a greater impact.

That the characteristics of the other person determine whether he is liked comes as no surprise — in some circumstances they are clearly more important than similarity. Thus extraverts are liked better than introverts by both introverts and extraverts (Hendrick & Brown, 1971). That extraverts should like other extraverts follows from the similarity hypothesis, but why should introverts like extraverts better? The answer comes from the study itself. Extraverts were not only liked better but also considered to be more interesting at parties, more ideal in personality, and preferable as leaders — by both introverted and extraverted subjects. But introverted subjects preferred fellow introverts as reliable friends and ethical persons. Thus the fact that extraverts are liked better by both extraverts and introverts may be explained by the greater friendliness and pleasantness to be expected from extraverts in social situations. We like those with whom we can easily interact, though we may fall back on those similar to ourselves when other issues (reliability, for example) become more important. Clearly, we like persons with attractive features better than those with unattractive features (Sigall & Aronson, 1969), and likability is different from similarity though it has the same effect on attraction (McLaughlin, 1971).

Finally, the individual's own personality or state of being affects his liking for others. Thus when a person's self-esteem has been lowered, he likes an accepting person more than does an individual whose self-esteem has been raised (Walster, 1965; Jacobs et al., 1971). A man who has been sexually aroused (with reading material) tends to find women more attractive, and this holds whether or not they are accessible to him (Stephan et al., 1971). In brief, though similarity is a powerful determinant of attraction, other factors can alter or even reverse its effects. This conclusion should give pause to anyone who contemplates using computer-dating, which depends solely on similarity in matching partners and neglects as powerful a factor as attractiveness (Byrne et al., 1970).

Conformity

Every group has its own *norms:* expectations about the appearance, behavior, attitudes, and beliefs of its members. Every group exerts pressure, whether weak or strong, on its members to conform to its norms—in the name of group solidarity, patriotism, science, or even God. Demands for conformity that come from authority have been associated with some of the most murderous and bigoted practices in the history of Western man, notably in relation to political and religious tyranny. Our concern is not with the political, religious, and economic aspects of conformity but with the underlying psychological aspects, which may be subsumed under a single question: What makes people conform?

Pressures for Conformity

Conformity is the counterpart of affiliation. If a person affiliates with a group in order to attain certain rewards, the group can demand conformity by

threatening to withhold these rewards. There are three classes of rewards (see Table 30.1): help, esteem, and information. If a member of the group refuses to go along with the others, they can immediately stop giving him direct rewards or stop cooperating in solving problems; they can stop liking him and start disliking him, stop admiring him and start criticizing him; or they can stop giving him information about either the situation or his place in the scheme of things. In brief, they can turn off all the good things that would cause someone to affiliate in the first place.

A group can do worse things to a nonconformist. It can punish him by rejecting him from its society and branding him as different, as the Nazis did in Germany when they required Jews to wear yellow armbands and forbade them to participate in most of the activities of the society. It can torture nonconformists to extract confessions from them, as was done during the Inquisition in Spain several centuries ago. And it can lock them behind bars, as many states do today to those who smoke marihuana in defiance of the laws that mistakenly brand it a narcotic.

The mere fact that a person is deviant, regardless of the content of his nonconformity, is sufficient for him to receive ill treatment. This has been documented by Freedman and Doob (1968), who manipulated deviancy per se without specifying the dimensions of the differences among people:

The basic procedure was to give the subjects very complex, impressive "personality" tests. Then, some of them were told that they were quite different from most people while others were told that they were quite similar to most people. Throughout this procedure the nonevaluative nature of the tests was stressed—we were simply trying to find out about the subjects, there were no right or wrong answers, and so on. (P. 16.)

Thus some subjects were made to feel deviant, others nondeviant. In one experiment a group of subjects was told to choose which person would receive a painful electric shock, a deviant or a nondeviant person. Another group chose which person to reward, and the nondeviant subjects tended to choose the nondeviant person. By extrapolation, the average (nondeviant) member of a group tends to select deviants for punishment and nondeviants for reward. Deviant subjects acted in essentially the same way, choosing to punish nondeviants and rewarding deviants. Evidently, similarity is a powerful determinant not only of attraction but also of how rewards and punishments are administered.

Options

If conformity is *moving toward agreement with the group,* then nonconformity should be its opposite.[4] But nonconformity may take either of two forms: anticonformity, which is *moving away from agreement with the group,* or *independence,* which is *remaining different from the group* (Willis, 1963). Despite some disagreement among psychologists about how to conceptualize the three kinds of behavior (conformity, anticonformity, and independence), recent research (Stricker et al., 1970), has shown that they are best regarded as falling along two dimensions (see Figure 30.5). In response to group pressure, one can either give in (conformity) or counterattack (anticonformity); or the choice can be giving in (conformity) versus resisting (independence). Virtually all research in this area has considered only one of these two dimensions — conformity versus independence — though there are exceptions (Willis & Hollander, 1964; Stricker et al., 1970).

Why should anyone risk group displeasure by deviating? One answer is that most persons find it necessary to assert their individual identity at some time or other. To resist group pressure and stand one's own ground is an act of self-assertion that cannot help but sustain a feeling of identity and self-esteem. Moreover, part of American ideology is the notion of independence, which requires at least an occasional stubborn resistance to the pressures of the group. Other things being equal, we should expect resistance from persons who are low on the temperament of sociability, and therefore less susceptible to social rewards and punishment.

Why does anyone anticonform? There are several possible reasons. First, every person belongs

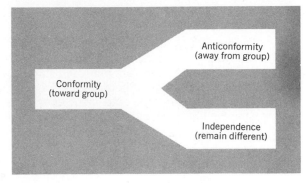

Figure 30.5 *Two dimensions of responses to group pressure.*

to many different groups, and there are times when their multiple demands tend to conflict: the pressures of one group may require behavior opposite to that demanded by another group. Consider draft resisters. As male citizens of this country, they were expected to conform to their country's call to arms, but as members of the peace movement they were expected to oppose any aspect of the war effort.[5] Their response was anticonformity to the laws of the land — as manifested in burning draft cards and raiding draft offices and destroying records.

A second reason for anticonformity is the desire to seize power, which can be accomplished by opposing the aims of the group in power. This is the classical stance of the revolutionary, who hopes to overthrow the prevailing power structure and take over the group himself. Interestingly enough, the histories of virtually all successful revolutions reveal that they have instituted pressures for conformity that exceeded those they rebelled against.

Finally, anticonformity can originate in *negativism:* a petulant, rebellious person opposes the group merely to assert his own independence, but his opposition is so strong that he not only resists but fights against the group. Such persons tend to be immature and are still attempting to break away from all authority to establish their own adult identities.

---

[4] *A related phenomenon is* reactance: *the attempt to restore freedom of choice when it is abridged* (Brehm, 1966). *Reactance theory and research are too advanced for this text.*

[5] *Some men resisted the draft for personal or religious reasons — not as members of the peace movement.*

Conformity in the Laboratory

The first major laboratory research on conformity was done in the dark. In such an experiment subjects are seated in a dark room and stare at a stationary point of light (Sherif, 1936). Soon the light appears to move—the autokinetic effect (see Chapter 11). When subjects call out the amount of movement they see, there is at first considerable divergence. But over time, a group consensus develops—presumably because of pressures to conform.

The study of conformity spurred suddenly with the development of a new technique for its investigation. This was the Asch technique (1952), which showed how the effects of group pressure could be measured in the laboratory.

Research Report

The Asch technique requires that a group of persons assemble in an experimental room, ostensibly to participate in an experiment on visual perception (see Figure 30.6). They are shown two cards, one with a standard line and one with three other lines, one of which matches the standard. The task is to determine which of the three lines is the same length as the standard. The subjects announce their choices in the order in which they are seated. The task is so easy as to be boring. On the first two trials (the cards change from one trial to the next) the choices are unanimous. On the third trial one person chooses differently from everyone else. This occurs again on the next trial and on many of the succeeding trials. This person is of course amazed. What he does not know is that he is the only real subject and

Figure 30.6 Pressure for conformity by a majority. "Subjects" called out their judgments starting from the left. They are all confederates except for #6, who is the real subject.

(SCIENTIFIC AMERICAN, NOVEMBER 1955; PHOTOS WILLIAM VAN DIVERT)

that all the others are confederates of the experimenter. On two-thirds of the trials the confederates comprise a majority that consistently makes an obviously wrong choice, thereby putting considerable pressure on the subject. Should he trust his own perceptions or those of the group? We have all learned to trust our senses, but we have also learned to check our perceptions against a consensus to correct for any subjectivity. In the Asch technique these two tendencies are pitted against one another, the choice being conformity versus independence.

As might be expected, there were marked individual differences in reactions to group pressure. Roughly one-fourth of the real subjects staunchly resisted it and never agreed with the incorrect choices of the majority. A small proportion of persons completely agreed with the majority. Most subjects conformed part of the time and remained independent part of the time. In the original research roughly one third of all the judgments were conformity choices.

The Asch technique has proved to be extremely valuable, but it does require a large number of confederates, and the subject must make his choices in a face-to-face situation. Crutchfield (1955) improved the technique by eliminating actual confederates and allowing the subject to make his choices unseen. Each (real) subject sits in a cubicle, hidden from the other subjects. All are shown stimuli such as lines of different lengths, and they make their choices by closing numbered switches in front of them. They do this in a predetermined order, and their choices are presumably shown in the lighted panels in front of each of the others. Actually, the experimenter manipulates all of the lighted panels, and what each subject sees as the choices of the others are actually the choices programed by the experimenter. In this way the experimenter can make it appear that all the other subjects agreed on a single incorrect choice, thus bringing group pressure to bear on each subject as he is about to make his choice. This innovation not only eliminates the need for confederates but also allows the subject to make choices in a less public situation — at least he is not facing the other "subjects."

Characteristics of the Group

Certain kinds of groups can induce more conformity than others, depending on how the group is constituted and how its members make their decisions. We shall consider three such characteristics of groups: size, unanimity, and anonymity.[6]

SIZE. The original Asch experiments used a group of from seven to nine men. Would there be more conformity if the group were larger? Would there be less if the group were smaller? In Asch's original studies (1951) there was virtually no conformity when there was only one other person, but the amounts of conformity rose with increased size of the group, reaching a peak at four and leveling off (see Figure 30.7). Later research has shown that increasing group size beyond four *does* enhance conformity (Gerard et al., 1968), and it is a reasonable guess that extending group size to hundreds or thousands of persons would probably yield at least some increase in conformity.

UNANIMITY. So long as only one person is holding out against the group, there is very strong pressure on him to conform. This was illustrated in a movie called *Twelve Angry Men,* in which one man (played by Henry Fonda) held out for more discussion before finding an adolescent guilty of murder; the other 11 jurors were for a verdict of *guilty*. He said that if no one else would agree with him on a secret ballot, he would conform, his rationale being that it would be unfair to hold up proceedings by being stubborn if he were the only dissenter. One other juror did go along with him, and the ensuing discussion eventually led to a verdict of *not guilty.*

Asch further found that if only one other member of the group agreed with the dissenter, then his tendency to conform dropped sharply (see Figure 30.8). This held true regardless of the size of the group. It should not be forgotten that in these experiments the subject's task is easy, and he will not alter his choice unless there is strong pressure to do so. Once the majority is no longer unanimous, he is free to question its choices and fall back on his own sensory abilities. Moreover, an insistent *minority* can, if it hangs together, at least partially alter the perceptions of the majority (Moscovici et al., 1969).

ANONYMITY. As groups tend to punish deviancy, it should be easier to nonconform if it can be done anonymously. In fact, there is more conformity in a face-to-face situation than when choices are made in a private booth (Deutch & Gerard, 1955), and there is more conformity when the identity of the subject is revealed than when it is not (see various studies reviewed in Nord, 1969).

[6] *For a complete list, see Allen, (1965).*

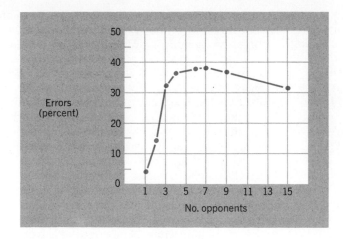

Figure 30.7 Effect of group size on conformity (Asch, 1951).

Individual Differences

Why do some persons conform and others refuse to go along? One possibility is self-esteem: the person who is confident of himself and his abilities will generally trust his own perceptions over those of others. The person with low self-esteem knows that his abilities may well be less than those of others and will therefore depend more on their judgment than on his own. Beyond self-esteem there are several characteristics of individ-

uals that render them more or less susceptible to group pressures: birth order, gender, and ethnic group.

BIRTH ORDER. There is abundant evidence that first-born children tend to be more affiliative and dependent on others than later-born children (Schachter, 1959). It follows that first-borns should conform more in the Asch situation, and research has borne out this expectation (Becker & Carroll, 1962). Presumably, first-borns are very susceptible to group pressure in comparison to later-

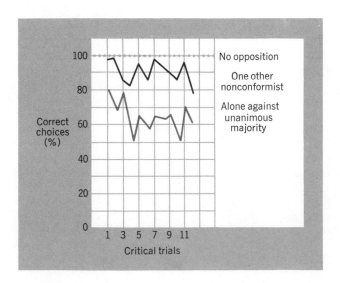

Figure 30.8 Effects of unanimous versus nonunanimous group pressure (Asch, 1951).

borns. But what happens when there is a payoff (money) for making correct judgments? Under these conditions, a subject should be more willing to trust the judgments of others (the majority) who are presumably just as eager to win as he is. Indeed, later-borns do conform more when there is a payoff, but first-borns do not yield any more when there is a payoff than when there is none (Becker et al., 1964). When there is no payoff, subjects yield presumably because they have stronger affiliative needs; when there is a payoff, they yield because the judgments of others constitute important information. Most of us would be reluctant to defy others in situations where a group consensus usually offers the best information, and this is the way later-borns react. But first-borns are so dependent on others that they yield to group pressure without any extrinsic rewards such as money.

GENDER. It is commonplace to observe that women tend to conform more than men, and there is abundant evidence supporting this contention in research on a wide variety of judgments (Nord, 1969). However, this straightforward gender difference may be more apparent than real, and it has been subjected to a strong attack by Sistrunk and McDavid (1971). They contend first, that there is evidence that men and women do not differ in conformity and second, that conformity depends on the nature of the task. Most early research used judgments involving geometric designs and arithmetic problems or questions about political and economic issues. Rarely have there been items of more real interest to women: fashion, clothes, design, or family affairs. To test their hypothesis, these researchers devised items that were rated as being predominantly masculine or predominantly feminine:

On masculine items females conformed more than males 3 out of 4 times, with no differences on the fourth time. On feminine items, males conformed more than females 2 out of 4 times, with no differences the other times. On neutral items, there was no difference 3 out of 4 times, with males conforming more on the exception. Neither sex ever conformed significantly more on items of interest and sophistication to its sex, and only once was there a difference on items of equal sophistication.

(SISTRUNK & MCDAVID, 1971, P. 206.)

Thus there is no basis for saying that women are more conforming than men. Each gender tends to conform when dealing with unfamiliar material, a fact that should surprise no one. Previous research has established what common sense suggests: when a subject is dealing with areas in which he has some competence, he is less likely to yield than when dealing with areas in which he has little competence. As far as can be determined by laboratory research, women are no more conforming than men.

ETHNIC GROUP. Differences in conformity between blacks and whites have been studied mainly in children. As blacks have inferior status in our society, it might seem that they would conform more than whites. The opposite is true. Whites conform more than blacks, but the difference is due largely to white girls conforming more than black girls; there is no difference between white and black boys in conformity (Iscoe et al., 1964; Schneider, 1970). One aspect of Schneider's research is of interest. White children conformed more to a white majority than to a black majority, whereas for black children the ethnicity of the majority made no difference.

These findings with children may be more revealing than research with college students, who often do what is expected of them or what they think is right—rather than doing what they wanted to do, as children are likely to do. The greater autonomy of black girls is especially interesting, for it suggests that they are socialized in the direction of less conformity than white girls. Again, white girls conform more than boys only when making judgments on masculine-related topics. In the two experiments with children the topics were essentially masculine-related, yet black girls were no more conforming than either white or black boys. There are two possible explanations: black girls may be trained in the direction of greater autonomy or black girls simply make no distinction between masculine- and feminine-related topics when they are being pressured by a group.

Obedience

The demands made by a group on its members are indirect and diffuse; the demands made by authority figures (boss, parents, teachers, and so on) are direct and focused. How far will a person go in obeying the demands of a superior? Would he harm innocent victims if ordered to do so? Yes, when the orders are given in the name of an authoritarian regime. Many thousands of Germans participated in the killing of six million Jews during World War II. The Jews had to be rounded up, transported to camps, housed, gassed, and finally, disposed of. The numerous German workers who participated in this genocide were merely "following orders." This was the excuse offered by Adolph Eichmann, who supervised the mass extermination.

Americans properly reacted with horror when the facts of the German concentration camps became known. But surely this was an aberration of the German people—or perhaps only of the Nazis. Americans would never kill innocent men, women, and children. However, American soldiers did kill innocent civilians in Vietnam—at My Lai and probably at other places not so well documented.

The soldiers at My Lai and the Germans in World War II existed in an authoritarian social order, and the penalty for disobedience might be severe. Would a person obey an order to harm an innocent victim even when disobedience would not be punished? Laboratory research has supplied the answer. Milgram (1963) devised a laboratory task similar to the aggression machine (see Chapter 22). Instead of 10 shock buttons, there were 30 switches with voltage levels marked from 15 to 450 volts. There were appropriate labels that ranged from "Slight Shock" to "Danger—Severe Shock." The unseen victim was actually a confederate who received no shock but made sounds as if he were being shocked. The subject was instructed to raise the shock level one step each time an error was made. If the subject was unwilling to continue, the experimenter used this sequence of "prods":

1. Please go on.
2. The experiment requires that you continue.
3. It is absolutely essential that you continue.
4. You have no other choice, you *must* go on.

Milgram (1963) was surprised and horrified at the results:

Of the 40 subjects, 26 obeyed the orders of the experi-

menter to the end, proceeding to punish the victim until they reached the most potent shock available on the shock generator. At this point, the experimenter called a halt to the session. (The maximum shock is labeled 450 volts, and it is two steps beyond the designation Danger: Severe Shock.) Although obedient subjects continued to administer shocks, they often did so under extreme stress. Some expressed reluctance to administer shocks beyond the 300-volt level, and displayed fears similar to those who defied the experimenter; yet they obeyed. (P. 376.)

Thus normal persons will obey orders to punish an innocent victim severely, even when there is no penalty for disobedience. It is important however, to specify the conditions under which such obedience occurs. First, all those involved were men. The experimenter (authority) was a man, and both the subject and the victim were men. It has been demonstrated elsewhere (Buss, 1966b) that men have little compunction about harming other men, but they do not punish women so easily; women will lower the intensity of punishment as soon as they discover that they are causing harm, whether the victim is a man or a woman.

Second, In Milgram's original experiment, the victim was out of sight. It is easier to aggress against a victim when the latter is not face-to-face with the aggressor. It is easier to drop a bomb from thousands of feet in the air than to shoot an enemy soldier; and it is easier to shoot someone than to bayonet him. Milgram (1965) found that bringing the victim into the room decreased the subject's obedience; as the distance between the two decreased, obedience diminished.

Third, the subjects were prodded by the experimenter, who implied by his directions that the experiment was very important. Without prodding, there would have been less obedience. Moreover, when the status of the authority was reduced from Yale University to "Bridgeport Research Associates," fewer subjects complied with the experimenter.

Fourth, the subjects moved in small steps from giving mild punishment to giving severe punishment. Apparently, they habituated to each small increment. There are clear parallels between the experiment and the escalation of brutality against Jews in Germany and Asians in Vietnam.

Milgram's research and the atrocities of everyday life drive home an important point: we should not be surprised at the potential of man for good or evil. Thus it is meaningless to say that no one can be made to perform acts — say, under hypnosis — that he would normally be incapable of doing. The key word is *normally;* it refers to the usual or average behavior observed in the person. But if the appropriate conditions prevailed, the person would engage in "abnormal" behavior. Thus the honest man may cheat, the crook may turn honest, the selfish person may turn altruistic, and the peaceable citizen may murder — under appropriate circumstances. It is the task of psychologists to specify the conditions that elicit or influence behavior. Man is the most adaptable of all animals; this means that he is more influenced by environmental determinants of behavior. The result is that — in terms of morality — man has the widest range of behavior: from the depths of bestiality to the heights of altruism.

reference list

Abelson, R. P. Computers, polls, and public opinions — some puzzles and paradoxes, *Transaction,* 1968, *5,* 20–27.

Adler, A. Social interest. New York: Putnam, 1939.

Adorno, T. W., E. Frenkel-Brunswick, D. J. Levinson, and R. N. Sanford. The authoritarian personality. New York: Harper, 1950.

Ainsworth, M. D. S. The development of infant-mother interaction among the Ganda. In B. M. Foss (ed.) *Determinants of infant behavior.* Vol. 2. New York: Wiley, 1963, 67–104.

_____. *Infancy in Uganda.* Baltimore: Johns Hopkins Press, 1967.

_____. Object relations, dependency, and attachment: A theoretical review of the infant-mother relationship. *Child Development,* 1969, *40,* 969–1026.

Ainsworth, M. D. S., and S. M. Bell. Attachment, exploration, and separation: Illustrated by the behavior of one-year-olds in a strange situation. *Child Development,* 1970, *41,* 49–67.

Alker, H. A. Is personality situationally specific or intrapsychically consistent? *Journal of Personality,* 1972, *40,* 1–16.

Allen, V. L. Situational factors in conformity. In L. Berkowitz (ed.) *Ad-*

vances in experimental social psychology. Vol. 2, New York: Academic Press, 1965.

Allport, G. W. The nature of prejudice. Reading, Mass.: Addison-Wesley, 1954.

————. *Pattern and growth in personality.* New York: Holt, Rinehart & Winston, 1961.

Altman, J. Organic foundations of animal behavior. New York: Holt, Rinehart & Winston, 1966.

Alvy, K. T. The development of listener-adapted communications in grade school children from different social class backgrounds. *Dissertation Abstracts,* 1971, *32,* 2375–B.

Amadeo, M., and E. Gomez. Eye movements, attention and dreaming in subjects with lifelong blindness. *Canadian Psychiatric Association Journal,* 1966, *2,* 501–508.

Ammons, C. H., P. Worchel, and K. M. Dallenbach. "Facial vision," the perception of obstacles out-of-doors by blindfolded and blindfolded-deafened subjects. *American Journal of Psychology,* 1953, *66,* 519–553.

Amoore, J. E., J. W. Johnson, and M. Rubin. The stereochemical theory of odor. *Scientific American,* 1964, *210,* 42–49.

Amsel, A. Partial reinforcement effects on vigor and persistance: advances in frustration theory derived from a variety of within-subjects experiments. In K. W. Spence and J. T. Spence (eds.) *The psychology of learning and motivation.* New York: Academic Press, 1967, 1–65.

Anand, B. D., and J. R. Brobeck. Hypothalamic control of food intake. *Yale Journal of Biological Medicine,* 1951, *24,* 123–140.

Anrep, G. V. Pitch discrimination in the dog. *Journal of Physiology,* 1920, *53,* 367–385.

Armstrong, H. The relationship between a dimension of body image and two dimensions of conditioning. Unpublished doctoral dissertation, Syracuse University, 1964.

Arnold, M. B. Emotion and personality. Vols. 1 and 2, New York: Columbia University Press, 1960.

————. (ed.) *Feelings and emotions.* New York: Academic Press, 1970.

Aronfreed, J. The internalization of social control through punishment: Experimental studies of the role of conditioning and the second signal system in the development of conscience. *Proceedings of the Eighteenth International Congress of Psychology,* Moscow, 1966.

————. *Conduct and conscience.* New York: Academic Press, 1968.

————. The problem of imitation. In L. P. Lipsitt and H. W. Reese, (eds.) *Advances in Child Development and Behavior.* New York: Academic press, 1969.

Aronfreed, J., and R. Leff. The effects of intensity of punishment and complexity of discrimination upon the learning of internalized suppression. Unpublished manuscript, University of Pennsylvania, 1963.

Aronfreed, J., and A. Reber. Internalized behavior suppression and the timing of social punishment. *Journal of Personality and Social Psychology,* 1965, *1,* 3–16.

Aronson, E. Some antecedents of interpersonal attraction. *Nebraska Symposium on Motivation,* 1969, *17,* 143–173.

Aronson, E., and D. Linder. Gain and loss of esteem as determinants of interpersonal attractiveness. *Journal of Experimental Social Psychology,* 1965, *1,* 156–171.

Aronson, E., and J. Mills. The effect of severity of initiation on liking for a group. *Journal of Abnormal and Social Psychology,* 1959, *59,* 177–181.

Asch, S. E. Effects of group pressure upon the modification and distortion of judgments. In H. Guetzkow (ed.) *Groups, leadership and man.* Pittsburgh, Pa.: Carnegie Press, 1951, 177–190.

———. *Social psychology.* Englewood Cliffs, N. J.: Prentice-Hall, 1952.

Aschoff, J. (ed.) *Circadian clocks.* Amsterdam: North-Holland, 1965.

Aschoff, J., M. Fatranska, and H. Giedke. Human circadian rhythms in continuous darkness: Entrainment by social cues. *Science,* 1971, *171,* 213–215.

Aserinsky, E., and N. Kleitman. Regularly occurring periods of eye motility, and concomitant phenomena, during sleep. *Science,* 1953, *118,* 273–274.

———. A motility cycle in sleeping infants as manifested by ocular and gross bodily activity. *Journal of Applied Physiology,* 1955, *8,* 11–18.

Atkinson, J. W. An introduction to motivation. Princeton, N.J.: Van Nostrand, 1964.

Averbach, E., and A. S. Coriell. Short-term memory in vision. *Bell System Technical Journal,* 1961, *40,* 309–328.

Averill, J. R. Autonomic response patterns during sadness and mirth. *Psychophysiology,* 1969, *5,* 399–419.

Ax, A. F. The physiological differentiation between fear and anger in humans. *Psychosomatic Medicine,* 1953, *15,* 433–442.

Ayllon, T. Intensive treatment of psychotic behavior by stimulus satiation and food reinforcement. *Behavior Research and Therapy,* 1963, *1,* 53–61.

Azrin, N. H., and W. C. Holz. Punishment. In W. K. Honig (ed.) *Operant behavior: Areas of research and application.* New York: Appleton-Century-Crofts, 1966.

Badia, P., S. Suter, and P. Lewis. Preference for warned shock: Information and/or preparation. *Psychological Reports,* 1967, *20,* 271–274.

Baldwin, J. M. Genetic theory of reality. New York: Putnam, 1915.

Baldwin, T. L., P. T. McFarlane, and C. J. Garvey. Children's communication accuracy related to race and socioeconomic status. *Child Development,* 1971, *42,* 345–358.

Bandura, A. Influence of models' reinforcement contingencies on the acquisition of imitative responses. *Journal of Personality and Social Psychology,* 1965a, *1,* 589–595.

————. Vicarious processes: A case of no-trial learning. In L. Berkowitz (ed.), *Advances in experimental social psychology,* Vol. 2. New York: Academic Press, 1965b, 1–55.

————. *Principles of behavior modification.* New York: Holt, Rinehart & Winston, 1969a.

————. Social learning theory of identificatory processes. In D. A. Goslin (ed.) *Handbook of socialization in theory and research.* Chicago: Rand McNally, 1969b, 213–262.

Bandura, A., E. B. Blanchard, and B. Ritter. Relative efficacy of desensitization and modeling approaches for inducing behavioral, affective, and attitudinal changes. *Journal of Personality and Social Psychology,* 1969, *13,* 173–199.

Bandura, A., J. E. Grusec, and F. L. Menlove. Observational learning as a function of symbolization and incentive set. *Child Development,* 1966, *37,* 499–506.

Bandura, A., and F. J. McDonald. The influence of social reinforcement and the behavior of models in shaping children's moral judgments. *Journal of Abnormal and Social Psychology,* 1963, *67,* 274–281.

Bandura, A., D. Ross, and S. A. Ross. Transmission of aggression through imitation of aggressive models. *Journal of Abnormal and Social Psychology,* 1961, *63,* 311–318.

————. Vicarious reinforcement and imitative learning. *Journal of Abnormal and Social Psychology,* 1963a, *67,* 601–607.

————. A comparative test of the status envy, social power, and secondary reinforcement theories of identificatory learning. *Journal of Abnormal and Social Psychology,* 1963b, *67,* 523–534.

Barber, T. X., and D. S. Calverley. Experimental studies in "hypnotic" behavior: Suggested deafness evaluated by delayed auditory feedback. *British Journal of Psychology,* 1964, *55,* 439–446.

Barber, T. X., and K. W. Hahn. Physiological and subjective responses to pain-producing stimulation under hypnotically suggested and waking-imagined "analgesia." *Journal of Abnormal and Social Psychology,* 1962, *65,* 411–418.

Bardwick, J. M. Psychology of women. New York: Harper & Row, 1971.

Barlow, J. D. Pupillary size as an index of preference in political candidates. *Perceptual and Motor Skills,* 1969, *28,* 587–590.

Bartlett, F. C. Remembering. Cambridge, England: Cambridge University Press, 1932.

Bartley, S. H. Principles of perception. 2nd ed. New York: Harper & Row, 1969.

Basser, L. S. Hemiplegia of early onset and the faculty of speech with special reference to the effects of hemispherectomy. *Brain*, 1962, *85*, 427–460.

Beach, F. A. The descent of instinct. *Psychological Review*, 1955, *62*, 401–410.

Becker, S. W., and J. Carroll. Ordinal position and conformity. *Journal of Abnormal and Social Psychology*, 1962, *65*, 129–131.

Becker, S. W., M. J. Lerner, and J. Carroll. Conformity as a function of birth order, payoff, and type of group pressure. *Journal of Abnormal and Social Psychology*, 1964, *69*, 318–323.

Bell, R. Q. A reinterpretation of the direction of effects in studies of socialization. *Psychological Review*, 1968, *75*, 81–95.

Bem, D. J. An experimental analysis of self-persuasion. *Journal of Experimental Social Psychology*, 1965, *1*, 199–218.

————. Self-perception: An alternative interpretation of cognitive dissonance phenomena. *Psychological Review*, 1967, *74*, 183–200.

————. *Beliefs, attitudes, and human affairs.* Belmont, Cal.: Brooks-Cole, 1970.

————. Constructing cross-situational consistencies in behavior: Some thoughts on Alker's critique of Mischel. *Journal of Personality*, 1972, *40*, 17–26.

Berger, R. J. Oculomotor control: A possible function of REM sleep. *Psychological Review*, 1969, *76*, 144–164.

Berger, S. M. Incidental learning through vicarious reinforcement. *Psychological Reports*, 1961, *9*, 477–491.

————. Observer practice and learning during exposure to a model. *Journal of Personality and Social Psychology*, 1966, *3*, 696–701.

Berko, J. The child's learning of English morphology. *Word*, 1958, *14*, 150–177.

Berkowitz, L. Aggressive cues in aggressive behavior and hostility catharsis. *Psychological Review*, 1964, *71*, 104–122.

————. Some aspects of observed aggression. *Journal of Personality and Social Psychology*, 1965, *2*, No. 3, 359–369.

————. Experimental investigations of hostility catharsis. *Journal of Consulting and Clinical Psychology*, 1970, *35*, 1–7.

————. Sex and violence: We can't have it both ways. *Psychology Today*, 1971, *5*, 14–23.

Berkowitz, L., and R. G. Geen. Film violence and the cue properties of available targets. *Journal of Personality and Social Psychology*, 1966, *3*, 525–530.

Bernstein, B. Social class linguistic codes and grammatical elements. *Language and Speech*, 1962, *5*, 221–240.

Bersh, P. J., J. M. Notterman, and W. N. Schoenfeld. Generalization to varying tone frequencies as a function of intensity of unconditioned stimulus. School of Aviation Medicine, U.S.A.F., Randolph Air Force Base, Tex. 1956. Cited in Kimble, 1961.

Berscheid, E., and E. H. Walster. When does a harm-doer compensate a victim? *Journal of Personality and Social Psychology,* 1967, *6,* 435–441.

――――. *Interpersonal attraction.* Reading, Mass.: Addison-Wesley, 1969.

Bever, T., J. A. Fodor, and W. Weksel. On the acquisition of syntax: A critique of "contextual generalization." *Psychological Review,* 1965, *72,* 467–482.

Bexton, W. H., W. Heron, and T. H. Scott. Effects of decreased variation in the sensory environment. *Canadian Journal of Psychology,* 1954, *8,* 70–76.

Biddle, B. S., and E. J. Thomas. (eds.) *Role theory: Concepts and research.* New York: Wiley, 1966.

Biller, H. B. Father, child and sex role. Lexington, Mass.: Heath, 1971.

Bindra, D. Neuropsychological interpretation of the effects of drive and incentive-motivation on general activity and instrumental behavior. *Psychological Review,* 1968, *75,* 1–22.

Birch, H. G. Sources of order in the maternal behavior of animals. *American Journal of Orthopsychiatry,* 1956, *26,* 279–284.

Bischof, L. J. Interpreting personality theories. New York: Harper & Row, 1964.

Bisese, V. S. Imitation behavior as a function of direct and vicarious reinforcement. *Dissertation Abstracts,* 1966, *26,* 6155.

Blanchard, E. B. Relative contributions of modeling, informational influences, and physical contact in extinction of phobic behavior. *Journal of Abnormal Psychology,* 1970, *76,* 55–61.

Bodmer, W. F. and L. L. Cavalli-Sforza. Intelligence and race. *Scientific American,* 1970, *223,* 19–29.

Bolles, R. C. Species-specific defense reactions and avoidance learning. *Psychological Review,* 1970, *77,* 32–48.

Bolles, R. C., and S. A. Moot. Derived motives. In P. H. Mussen and M. R. Rosenzweig (eds.) *Annual Review of Psychology.* Vol. 23. Palo Alto, Cal.: Annual Reviews, 1972, 51–72.

Bossom, J., and C. R. Hamilton. Interocular transfer of prism-altered coordinations in split-brain monkeys. *Journal of Comparative and Physiological Psychology,* 1963, *56,* 769–774.

Bourne, L. E., Jr. Knowing and using concepts. *Psychological Review,* 1970, *77,* 546–556.

Bourne, L. E., Jr., and K. O'Banion, Conceptual rule learning and chronological age. *Developmental Psychology,* 1971, *5,* 525–534.

Bourque, L. B. Social correlates of transcendental experiences. *Sociological Analysis,* 1969, *30,* 151–163.

Bower, G. H., and L. S. Bolton. Why are rhymes easier to learn? *Journal of Experimental Psychology,* 1969, *82,* 453–461.

Bower, G. H., M. C. Clark, A. M. Lesgold, and D. Winzenz. Hierarchical retrieval schemes in recall of categorized word lists. *Journal of Verbal Learning and Verbal Behavior,* 1969, *8,* 323–343.

Bower, T. G. R. The visual world of infants. *Scientific American,* 1966, *215,* 80–92.

―――. The object in the world of the infant. *Scientific American,* 1971, *225,* 30–38.

Bowlby, J. Foreword in M. D. S. Ainsworth, *Infancy in Uganda.* Baltimore: Johns Hopkins Press, 1967.

―――. *Attachment and loss. Vol. 1. Attachment.* London: Hogarth, 1969.

Bradford, L. P., J. R. Gibb, and K. D. Benne. (eds.) T-group theory and laboratory method. New York: Wiley, 1964.

Bradshaw, J. L., N. C. Nettleton, and G. Geffen. Ear differences and delayed auditory feedback: Effects on a speech and on a music task. *Journal of Experimental Psychology,* 1971, *91,* 85–92.

Brady, J. V. Emotion: Some conceptual problems and psychological experiments in M. B. Arnold (ed.) *Feelings and Emotions.* New York: Academic Press, 1970, 69–100.

Brady, J. P., and D. L. Lind. Experimental analysis of hysterical blindness. *Archives of General Psychiatry,* 1961, *4,* 331–339.

Brainerd, C. J., and T. W. Allen. Experimental inductions of the conservation of "first order" quantitative invariants. *Psychological Bulletin,* 1971, *75,* 128–144.

Brehm, J. W. A theory of psychological reactance. New York: Academic Press, 1966.

Brehm, J. W., and A. R. Cohen. Explorations in cognitive dissonance. New York: Wiley, 1962.

Breland, K., and M. Breland. The misbehavior of organisms. *American Psychologist,* 1961, *16,* 681–684.

Brim, O. G., Jr. Socialization through the life cycle. In O. G. Brim, Jr. and S. Wheeler (eds.) *Socialization after childhood: Two essays.* New York: Wiley, 1966. 1–49.

Broadbent, D. E. Perception and communication. New York: Pergamon, 1958.

Broadbent, D. E., and M. Gregory. Stimulus set and response set: The alternation of attention. *Quarterly Journal of Experimental Psychology,* 1964, *16,* 309–312.

Brobeck, J. R. Food and temperature. *Recent Progress in Hormones Research,* 1960, *16,* 439–446.

Brock, T. C. and A. L. Becker. "Debriefing" and susceptibility to subsequent experimental manipulations. *Journal of Experimental Social Psychology,* 1966, *2,* 314–323.

Brock, T. C., and A. H. Buss. Dissonance, aggression, and evaluation of pain. *Journal of Abnormal and Social Psychology,* 1962, *65,* 197–202.

Brogden, W. J. Sensory pre-conditioning. *Journal of Experimental Psychology,* 1939, *25,* 323–332.

Bronowski, J., and U. Bellugi. Language, name, and concept. *Science,* 1970, *168,* 669–673.

Bronson, G. The hierarchical organization of the central nervous system: Implications for learning processes and critical periods in early development. *Behavioral Science,* 1965, *10,* 7–25.

Brooks, R., L. Brandt, and M. Wiener. Differential response to two communication channels: Socioeconomic class differences in response to verbal reinforcers communicated with and without tonal inflection. *Child Development,* 1969, *40,* 453–470.

Broverman, D., E. L. Klaiber, Y. Kobayashi, and W. Vogel. Roles of activation and inhibition in sex differences in cognitive abilities. *Psychological Review,* 1968, *75,* 23–50.

Brown, R. W., and D. McNeill. The "tip of the tongue" phenomenon. *Journal of Verbal Learning and Verbal Behavior,* 1966, *5,* 325–337.

Bruner, J. S. The course of cognitive growth. *American Psychologist,* 1964, *19,* 1–15.

———. Eye, hand, and mind. In D. E. Elkind and J. H. Flavell (eds.) *Studies in cognitive development.* New York: Oxford University Press, 1969, 223–235.

Bruner, J. S., J. J. Goodnow, and G. A. Austin. A study of thinking. New York: Wiley, 1956.

Bruner, J. S., R. R. Olver, and P. Greenfield. (eds.) *Studies in cognitive growth.* New York: Wiley, 1966.

Bugelski, R. Extinction with and without subgoal reinforcement. *Journal of Comparative Psychology,* 1938, *26,* 121–134.

Burt, C. The structure of the mind: A review of the results of factor analysis. *British Journal of Educational Psychology,* 1949, *19,* 100–111, 176–199.

———. The genetic determination of differences in intelligence: A study of monozygotic twins reared together and apart. *British Journal of Psychology,* 1966, *57,* 137–153.

———. Inheritance of general intelligence. *American Psychologist,* 1972, *27,* 175–190.

Buss, A. H. Rigidity as a function of reversal and nonreversal shifts in the learning of successive discriminations. *Journal of Experimental Psychology,* 1953, *45,* 75–81.

———. *The psychology of aggression.* New York: Wiley, 1961.

———. Physical aggression in relation to different frustrations. *Journal of Abnormal and Social Psychology,* 1963, *67,* 1–7.

———. Instrumentality of aggression, feedback, and frustration as determinants of physical aggression. *Journal of Personality and Social Psychology,* 1966a, *2,* 153–162.

———. The effect of harm on subsequent aggression. *Journal of Experimental Research in Personality,* 1966b, *1,* 249–255.

———. *Psychopathology.* New York: Wiley, 1966c.

———. Stimulus generalization and the matching principle. *Psychological Review,* 1967, *74,* 40–50.

Buss, A. H., W. Braden, A. R. Orgel, and E. H. Buss. Acquisition and extinction with different reinforcement combinations. *Journal of Experimental Psychology,* 1956, *52,* 288–295.

Buss, A. H., and E. H. Buss. *Theories of schizophrenia.* New York: Atherton, 1969.

Buss, E., A. H. Buss, and A. Booker. Firing a weapon and aggression. *Journal of Personality and Social Psychology,* 1972, *22,* 296–302.

Buss, A. H., and H. Gerjuoy. The scaling terms used to describe personality. *Journal of Consulting Psychology,* 1957, *21,* 361–369.

Buss, A. H., and N. W. Portnoy. Pain tolerance and group identification. *Journal of Personality and Social Psychology, 1967,* 6, 106–108.

Butler, R. A. The effect of deprivation of visual incentives on visual exploration in monkeys. *Journal of Comparative and Physiological Psychology,* 1957, *50,* 177–179.

Byrne, D. *The attraction paradigm.* New York: Academic Press, 1972.

Byrne, D., C. R. Ervin, and J. Lamberth. Continuity between the experimental study of attraction and real-life computer dating. *Journal of Personality and Social Psychology,* 1970, *16,* 157–165.

Byrne, D., and D. Neison. Attraction as a linear function of proportion of positive reinforcement. *Journal of Personality and Social Psychology,* 1965, *1,* 659–663.

Cairns, R. B. Attachment behavior of mammals. *Psychological Review,* 1966, *73,* 409–426.

Campbell, D. T. Variation and selective retention in sociocultural evolution. In H. R. Barringer, G. I. Blanksten, and R. W. Mack (eds.) *Social change in developing areas: A reinterpretation of evolutionary theory.* Cambridge, Mass.: Schenkman, 1966.

Cannon, W. B. *Bodily changes in pain, hunger, fear and rage.* New York: Appleton, 1929.

Cannon, W. B., and A. L. Washburn. An explanation of hunger. *American Journal of Physiology,* 1912, *29,* 441–454.

Capaldi, E. J., and D. Lynch. Repeated shifts in reward magnitude: Evidence in favor of an associational and absolute (noncontextual) interpretation. *Journal of Experimental Psychology,* 1967, *75,* 226–235.

Carlsmith, J. M., and A. E. Gross. Some effects of guilt on compliance. *Journal of Personality and Social Psychology,* 1969, *11,* 232–239.

Carlson, A. J. *The control of hunger in health and disease.* Chicago: University of Chicago Press, 1916.

Carlson, R. Stability and change in the adolescent's self image. *Child Development,* 1965, *36,* 659–666.

Carthy, J. D., and F. J. Ebling. (eds.) *The natural history of aggression.* New York: Academic Press, 1964.

Cattell, R. B. *Personality and motivation structure and measurement.* New York: World Book, 1957.

Chapanis, N. P., and A. Chapanis. Cognitive dissonance: Five years later. *Psychological Bulletin,* 1964, *61,* 1–22.

Chapman, L. J., J. P. Chapman, and T. Brelje. Influence of the experimenter on pupillary dilation to sexually provocative pictures. *Journal of Abnormal Psychology,* 1969, *74,* 396–400.

Cherry, E. C. Some experiments on the recognition of speech, with one and with two ears. *Journal of the Acoustical Society of America,* 1953, *25,* 975–979.

Chomsky, N. A. Aspects of the theory of syntax. Cambridge, Mass.: MIT Press, 1965.

————. The formal nature of language. In E. H. Lenneberg, *Biological foundations of language.* New York: Wiley, 1967, 397–442.

Clark, G., and H. G. Birch. Hormonal modification of social behavior. *Psychosomatic Medicine,* 1945, *7,* 321–329.

Cleveland, E. E., and S. Fisher. A comparison of psychological characteristics and physical reactivity in ulcer and rheumatoid arthritic groups: I. Psychological measures. *Psychosomatic Medicine,* 1960, *22,* 283–289.

Cohen, B. D., and J. F. Klein. Referent communication in school age children. *Child Development,* 1968, *39,* 597–609.

Cohen, B. D., C. D. Noblin, and A. J. Silverman. Functional asymmetry of the human brain. *Science,* 1968, *162,* 475–477.

Colbert, E. H. Morphology and behavior. In A. Roe and G. G. Simpson (eds.) *Behavior and evolution.* New Haven, Conn.: Yale University Press, 1958, 26–47.

Coopersmith, J. The antecedents of self-esteem. San Francisco: Freeman, 1967.

Cornsweet, T. Visual perception. New York: Academic Press, 1970.

Cotzin, M., and K. M. Dallenbach. "Facial vision": The role of pitch and loudness in the perception of obstacles by the blind. *American Journal of Psychology,* 1950, *63,* 485–515.

Cowles, J. T. Food tokens as incentives for learning by chimpanzees. *Comparative Psychology Monographs,* 1937, *14* (Whole No. 71).

Creel, W., P. C. Boomsliter, and S. R. Power, Jr. Sensations of tone as perceptual forms. *Psychological Review,* 1970, *77,* 534–545.

Crespi, L. P. Quantitative variations of incentive and performance in the white rat. *American Journal of Psychology,* 1942, *55,* 467–517.

Cronbach, L. J. Essentials of psychological testing. 3rd ed. New York: Harper & Row, 1970.

Crutchfield, R. S. Conformity and character. *American Psychologist,* 1955, *10,* 191–198.

Culbertson, F. M. Modification of an emotionally held attitude through role playing. *Journal of Abnormal and Social Psychology,* 1957, *54,* 230–233.

Dallenbach, K. M. Pain: History and present status. *American Journal of Psychology,* 1939, *52,* 331–347.

Dalton, K. The premenstrual syndrome. Springfield, Ill.: Charles Thomas, 1964.

D'Amato, M. R., J. Fazzaro, and M. Etkin. Discriminated bar-press avoidance maintenance and extinction as a function of shock intensity. *Journal of Comparative and Physiological Psychology,* 1967, *63,* 351–354.

D'Amato, M. R., and W. E. Gumenik. Some effects of immediate versus randomly delayed shock on an instrumental response and cognitive processes. *Journal of Abnormal and Social Psychology,* 1960, *60,* 64–67.

Darley, J. M., and E. Aronson. Self-evaluation vs. direct anxiety reduction as determinants of the fear-affiliation relationship. In B. Latane (ed.) *Studies in social comparison.* New York: Academic Press, 1966.

Darley, J. M. and E. Berscheid. Increased liking caused by the anticipation of personal contact. *Human Relations,* 1967, *20,* 28–40.

Darwin, C. The origin of species by means of natural selection. London: Murray, 1859.

Davis, C. M. Self-selection of diet by newly-weaned infants. *American Journal of Diseases of Children,* 1928, *36,* 651–679.

Davis, J. D., R. L. Gallagher, and R. Ladove. Food intake controlled by a blood factor. *Science,* 1967, *156,* 1247–1248.

Delgado, J. M. R. Physical control of the mind. New York: Harper & Row, 1969.

Dember, W. N. Response by the rat to environmental change. *Journal of Comparative and Physiological Psychology,* 1956, *49,* 93–95.

Dement, W. C. An essay on dreams: The role of physiology in understanding their nature. In F. Barron, et al. *New directions in psychology.* Vol. 2. New York: Holt, Rinehart & Winston, 1965, 135–258.

Dement, W., and N. Kleitman. The relation of eye movements during sleep to dream activity: An objective method for the study of dreaming. *Journal of Experimental Psychology,* 1957, *53,* 339–346.

Dethier, V. G., and E. Stellar. Animal behavior: Its evolutionary and neurological basis. 2nd ed. Englewood Cliffs, N.J.: Prentice-Hall, 1964.

Deutch, J. A., and D. Deutch. Attention: Some theoretical considerations. *Psychological Review,* 1963, *7,* 80–90.

Deutch, M., and H. A. Gerard. A study of normative and informational social influences upon individual judgment. *Journal of Abnormal and Social Psychology,* 1955, *51,* 629–636.

DeValois, R. L. Behavioral and electrophysiological studies of primate vision. In W. D. Neff (ed.) *Contributions to sensory physiology,* Vol. 1, New York: Academic Press, 1965, 137–178.

DeValois, R. L., and G. H. Jacobs. Primate color vision. *Science,* 1968, *162,* 533–540.

Devenport, L. D., and S. Balagura. Lateral hypothalamus: Reevaluation of function in motivated feeding behavior. *Science,* 1971, *172,* 744–746.

DeVore, I. Mother-infant relations in free-ranging baboons. In H. L. Rheingold (ed.) *Maternal behavior in mammals.* New York: Wiley, 1963, 305–335.

Diamond, S. *Personality and temperament.* New York: Harper & Row, 1957.

DiCara, L. V. Learning in the autonomic nervous system. *Scientific American,* 1970, *222,* 30–39.

DiCara, L. V., and N. E. Miller. Instrumental learning of vasomotor responses by rats: Learning to respond differentially in the two ears. *Science,* 1968, *159,* 1485–1486.

Dienstbier, R. A. A modified belief theory of prejudice emphasizing the mutual causality of racial prejudice and anticipated belief differences. *Psychological Review,* 1972, *79,* 146–160.

Dixon, J. J., C. de Monchaux, and J. Sandler. Patterns of anxiety: The phobias. *British Journal of Medical Psychology,* 1957, *30,* 34–40.

Dollard, J., L. W. Doob, N. E. Miller, O. H. Mowrer, and R. R. Sears, *Frustration and aggression.* New Haven, Conn.: Yale University Press, 1939.

Driscoll, R. H. and K. E. Davis. Sexual restraints: A comparison of perceived and self-reported reasons for college students. *The Journal of Sex Research,* 1971, *7,* 253–262.

Duke-Elder, S. *The eye in evolution.* London: Henry Kimpton, 1958.

Eckhardt, R. B. Population genetics and human origins. *Scientific American.* 1972, *226,* 94–103.

Edwards, D. A. Early androgen stimulation and aggressive behavior in male and female mice. *Physiology and Behavior,* 1969, *4,* 333–338.

Egeth, H. Selective attention. *Psychological Bulletin,* 1967, *67,* 41–57.

Ehrlich, A. Neural control of feeding behavior. *Psychological Bulletin,* 1964, *61,* 100–114.

Eibl-Eibesfeldt, I. Similarities and differences between cultures in expressive movements. In R. A. Hinde (ed.) *Non-verbal communication.* London: Cambridge University Press, 1972, 297–312.

Ekman, P., and W. V. Friesen. The repertoire of nonverbal behavior — categories, origins, usage, and coding. *Semiotica,* 1969, *1,* 49–98.

Eldersveld, S. J., and R. W. Dodge. Personal contact or mail propaganda? An experiment in voting turnout and attitude change. In D. Katz, D. Cartwright, S. Eldersveld, and A. McC. Lee (eds.) *Public opinion and propaganda.* New York: Dryden Press, 1954. 532–542.

Elkind, D., and J. H. Flavell (eds.) *Studies in cognitive development: Essays in honor of Jean Piaget.* New York: Oxford University Press, 1969.

Elkind, D., and A. Sameroff. Developmental psychology. In P. H. Mussen and M. R. Rosenzweig (eds.) *Annual Review of Psychology.* Vol. 21, Palo Alto, Cal.: Annual Reviews, 1970, 191–238.

Ellsworth, P. C., J. M. Carlsmith, and A. Henson. The stare as a stimulus to flight in human subjects. *Journal of Personality and Social Psychology,* 1972, *21,* 302–311.

Epstein, A. N., and P. Teitelbaum. Regulation of food intake in the absence of taste, smell and other oro-pharyngeal sensations. *Journal of Comparative and Physiological Psychology,* 1962, *55,* 753–759.

Epstein, S., and W. D. Fenz. Theory and experiment on the measurement of approach-avoidance conflict. *Journal of Abnormal and Social Psychology,* 1962, *64,* 97–112.

Erikson, E. Childhood and society. 2nd ed. New York: Norton, 1963.

Erlenmeyer-Kimling, L. and L. F. Jarvik. Genetics and intelligence: A review. *Science,* 1963, *142,* 1477–1479.

Eron, L. D., L. R. Huesmann, N. M. Lefkowitz, and L. O. Walder. Does television violence cause aggression? *American Psychologist,* 1972, *27,* 253–263.

Ervin, S. Imitation and structural change in children's language. In E. H. Lenneberg (ed.). *New directions in the study of language.* Cambridge, Mass.: MIT Press, 1964, 163–190.

Escalona, S. K. and G. Heider. Prediction and outcome. New York: Basic Books, 1959.

Estes, W. K. An experimental study of punishment. *Psychological Monographs,* 1944, *57* (Whole No. 263).

———. Toward a statistical theory of learning. *Psychological Review,* 1950, *62,* 369–377.

Etkin, W. Social behavior from fish to man. Chicago: University of Chicago Press, 1970.

Eysenck, H. J. Dimensions of personality. London: Routledge, Kegan Paul, 1947.

———. A theory of incubation of anxiety/fear responses. *Behavior Research and Therapy,* 1968, *6,* 309–321.

Eysenck, H. J. and S. B. G. Eysenck. On the dual nature of extraversion. *British Journal of Social and Clinical Psychology,* 1963, *2,* 46–55.

Fantz, R. L. Visual perception and experience in early infancy: A look at the hidden side of behavior development. In H. W. Stevenson, E. H. Hess, and H. L. Rheingold (eds.) *Early behavior: Comparative and developmental approaches.* New York: Wiley, 1967, 181–224.

Farley, F. H. Further investigation of the two personae of extraversion. *British Journal of Social and Clinical Psychology,* 1970, *9,* 377–379.

Fazio, A. I. Treatment components in implosive therapy. *Journal of Abnormal Psychology,* 1970, *76,* 211–219.

Federman, D. D. Abnormal sexual development: a genetic and endocrine approach to differential diagnosis. Philadelphia: Saunders, 1967.

Fehr, F. S. and J. A. Stern. Peripheral physiological variables and emotion: The James-Lange theory revisited. *Psychological Bulletin,* 1970, *74,* 411–424.

Ferster, C. B., and C. E. Hammer, Jr. Synthesizing the components of behavior. In W. K. Honig (ed.) *Operant behavior: Areas of research* and application. New York: Appleton-Century-Crofts, 1966, 634–676.

Ferster, C. B., and B. F. Skinner. Schedules of reinforcement. New York: Appleton-Century-Crofts, 1957.

Festinger, L. A theory of social comparison processes. *Human Relations,* 1954, *7,* 117–140.

————. *A theory of cognitive dissonance.* Stanford, Cal.: Stanford University Press, 1957.

————. *Conflict, decision and dissonance.* Stanford, Cal.: Stanford University Press, 1964.

Festinger, L., and J. M. Carlsmith. Cognitive consequences of forced compliance. *Journal of Abnormal and Social Psychology,* 1959, *58,* 203–210.

Festinger, L., H. W. Riecken, and S. Schachter. When prophecy fails. Minneapolis Minn.: University of Minnesota Press, 1956.

Fincher, C. A preface to psychology. New York: Harper & Row, 1964.

Fisher, A. E. Effects of stimulus variation on sexual satiation in the male rat. *Journal of Comparative and Physiological Psychology,* 1962, *55,* 614–620.

Fisher, S. A. Body image and personality. Princeton, N.J.: Van Nostrand, 1958.

————. A further appraisal of the body boundary concept. *Journal of Consulting Psychology,* 1963, *27,* 62–74.

————. Sex differences in body perception. *Psychological Monographs,* 1964, *78,* No. 14 (Whole No. 591).

————. *Body image and personality.* 2nd rev. ed. New York: Dover, 1968.

Fisher, S., and S. E. Cleveland. The role of body image in psychosomatic symptoms. *Psychological Monographs,* 1955, *69,* No. 17 (Whole No. 402).

Fisher, S., and Fisher, R. Body image boundaries and patterns of body perception. *Journal of Abnormal and Social Psychology,* 1964, *68,* 255–262.

Flanders, J. P. A review of research on imitative behavior. *Psychological Bulletin,* 1968, *69,* 316–337.

Flavell, J. H. Developmental psychology of Jean Piaget. Princeton, N.J.: Van Nostrand, 1963.

————. *The development of role-taking and communication skills in children.* New York: Wiley, 1968.

Fodor, J. A., and T. G. Bever. The psychological reality of linguistic segments. *Journal of Verbal Learning and Verbal Behavior,* 1965, *4,* 414–420.

Ford, C. S. and F. A. Beach. Patterns of sexual behavior. New York: Harper & Row, 1951.

Forgus, R. H. Perception: The basic process in cognitive development. New York: McGraw-Hill, 1966.

Foulkes, D. Dream reports from different states of sleep. *Journal of Abnormal and Social Psychology,* 1962, *65,* 14–25.

Frankenhaeuser, M. Behavior and circulating catecholamines. *Brain Research,* 1971, *31,* 241–262.

Frankenhaeuser, M., B. Nordheden, A. L. Myrsten, and B. Post. Psychophysiological reactions to understimulation and overstimulation. *Acta Psychologica,* 1971, *35,* 298–308.

Fraser, C., U. Bellugi, and R. Brown. Control of grammar in imitation, comprehension and production. *Journal of Verbal Learning and Verbal Behavior,* 1963, *2,* 121–135.

Freedman, J. L., and A. N. Doob. Deviancy. The psychology of being different. New York: Academic Press, 1968.

Freedman, J. L., J. M. Carlsmith, and D. O. Sears. Social psychology. Englewood Cliffs, N.J.: Prentice-Hall, 1970.

Freedman, J. L., S. A. Wallington, and E. Bless. Compliance without pressure: The effect of guilt. *Journal of Personality and Social Psychology,* 1967, *7,* 117–124.

Freud, S. Beyond the pleasure principle. New York: Boni and Liverright, 1927.

Fries, M. E. and P. J. Woolf. Some hypotheses on the role of congenital activity types in personality development. *Psychoanalytical Study of the Child,* 1953, *8,* 48–62.

Funkenstein, D. H. Nor-epinephrine-like and epinephrine-like substances in relation to human behavior. *Journal of Nervous and Mental Disease,* 1956, *124,* 58–68.

Furth, H. G. Piaget's theory of knowledge: The nature of representation and interiorization. *Psychological Review,* 1968, *75,* 143–154.

Gagné, R. M. Contributions of learning to human development. *Psychological Review,* 1968, *75,* 177–191.

Galanter, E. Contemporary psychophysics. In R. Brown. *New directions in psychology.* Vol. 1. New York: Holt, Rinehart & Winston, 1965, 87–156.

Garai, J. E., and A. Scheinfeld. Sex differences in mental and behavioral traits. *Genetic Psychology Monographs,* 1968, *77,* 169–299.

Garattini, S., and E. B. Sigg. Aggressive behavior. New York: Wiley, 1969.

Gardner, R. A., and B. T. Gardner. Teaching sign language to a chimpanzee. *Science,* 1969, *165,* 664–672.

Gardner, W. J., J. C. R. Licklider, and A. Z. Weisz. Suppression of pain by sound. *Science,* 1960, *132,* 31–32.

Garrett, M., T. G. Bever, and J. A. Fodor. The active uses of grammar in speech perception. *Perception and Psychophysics,* 1966, *1,* 30–32.

Gazzaniga, M. S. The split brain in man. *Scientific American,* 1967, *217,* 24–29.

Geen, R. G. Effects of frustration, attack, and prior training in aggressiveness upon aggressive behavior. *Journal of Personality and Social Psychology,* 1968, *9,* 316–321.

Geen, R. G., and L. Berkowitz. Some conditions facilitating the occurrence of aggression after the observation of violence; *Journal of Personality,* 1967, *35,* 666–676.

Geldard, F. A. The human senses. New York: Wiley, 1953.

_____. Cutaneous coding of optical signals: The Optohapt. *Perception and Psychophysics,* 1966, *1,* 377–381.

Gelfand, S., L. P. Ullman, and L. Krasner. The placebo response: An experimental approach. *Journal of Nervous and Mental Disorder,* 1963, *136,* 379–387.

Gentry, W. D. Effects of frustration, attack, and prior aggressive training on overt aggression and vascular processes. *Journal of Personality and Social Psychology,* 1970, *16,* 718–725.

Gerard, H. B. Emotional uncertainty and social comparison. *Journal of Abnormal and Social Psychology,* 1963, 66, 568–573.

Gerard, H. B., and G. L. Mathewson. The effects of severity of initiation on liking for a group: A replication. *Journal of Experimental Social Psychology,* 1966, *2,* 278–287.

Gerard, H. B., and J. M. Rabbie. Fear and social comparison. *Journal of Abnormal and Social Psychology,* 1961, *62,* 582–592.

Gerard, H. B., R. A. Wilhelmy, and E. S. Connolley. Conformity and group size. *Journal of Personality and Social Psychology,* 1968, 8, 79–82.

Gergen, K. J. The concept of self. New York: Holt, Rinehart & Winston, 1972.

Gerst, M. S. Symbolic coding processes in observational learning. *Journal of Personality and Social Psychology,* 1971, *19,* 7–17.

Gerwitz, J. L. Mechanisms of social learning: Some roles of stimulation and behavior in early human development. In D. A. Goslin (ed.) *Handbook of socialization theory and research.* Chicago: Rand McNally, 1968, 57–212.

Gerwitz, J. L. and K. G. Stingle. The learning of generalized imitation as the basis for identification. *Psychological Review,* 1968, *75,* 374–396.

Geschwind, N. The organization of language and the brain. *Science,* 1970, 940–944.

_____. Language and the brain. *Scientific American,* 1972, *226,* No. 4, 76–83.

Geschwind, N., and W. Levitsky. Human brain: Left-right asymmetries in temporal speech region. *Science,* 1968, *161,* 186–187.

Gibson, E. J. Principles of perceptual learning and development. New York: Appleton-Century-Crofts, 1969.

Gibson, J. J. Perception of the visual world. Boston: Houghton Mifflin, 1950.

_____. Observations on active touch. *Psychological Review,* 1962, *69,* 477–491.

_____. *The senses considered as perceptual systems.* Boston: Houghton Mifflin, 1966.

Gillespie, J. Aggression in relation to frustration, attack, and inhibition. Unpublished doctoral dissertation, University of Pittsburgh, 1961.

Glaser, R. (ed.) Teaching machines and programed learning, II: Data and directions. Washington, D.C.: National Education Association, 1965.

Gleason, K. K. and J. H. Reynierse. The behavioral significance of pheromones in vertebrates. *Psychological Bulletin,* 1969, *71,* 58–73.

Goldfarb, W. Infant rearing and problem behavior. *American Journal of Orthopsychiatry,* 1934, *13,* 249–266.

———. Effects of psychological deprivation in infancy and subsequent stimulation. *American Journal of Psychiatry,* 1945, *102,* 18–33.

Goldman, R., M. Jaffa, and S. Schachter. Yom Kippur, Air France, dormitory food, and the eating behavior of obese and normal persons. *Journal of Personality and Social Psychology,* 1968, *10,* 117–123.

Goldstein, D., D. Fink, and D. R. Mettee. Cognition of arousal and actual arousal as determinants of emotion. *Journal of Personality and Social Psychology,* 1972, *21,* 41–51.

Goldstein, M. L. Physiological theories of emotion: A critical historical review from the standpoint of behavior theory. *Psychological Bulletin,* 1968, *69,* 23–40.

Gollin, E. S. and E. J. Shirk. A developmental study of oddity-problem learning in young children. *Child Development,* 1966, *37,* 214–217.

Gray, J. A. and A. A. I. Wedderburn. Graphing strategies with simultaneous stimuli. *Quarterly Journal of Experimental Psychology,* 1960, *12,* 180–184.

Green, D. M., and G. B. Hemming. Audition. In P. H. Mussen and M. R. Rosenzweig (eds.) *Annual Review of Psychology,* 1969, *20,* 105–128.

Gregory, R. L. Visual illusions. *Scientific American,* 1968, *217,* 66–76.

———. The evolution of eyes and brains—a hen-and-egg problem. In S. J. Freedman (ed.) *The neuropsychology of spatially oriented behavior.* Homewood, Ill.: Dorsey, 1968, 1–6.

Grether, W. F. Pseudo-conditioning without paired stimulation encountered in attempted backward conditioning. *Journal of Comparative Psychology,* 1938, *25,* 91–96.

Grier, J. B., S. A. Counter, and W. M. Shearer. Prenatal auditory imprinting in chickens. *Science,* 1967, *155,* 1692–1693.

Griffard, C. D., and J. T. Peirce. Conditioned discrimination in the planarian. *Science,* 1964, *144,* 1472–1473.

Griffen, D. R. Echoes of bats and men. Garden City, N.Y.: Doubleday & Co., 1959.

Grosser, G. G., and A. W. Siegal. Emergence of a tonic-phasic model for sleep and dreaming: Behavioral and physiological observations. *Psychological Bulletin,* 1971, *75,* 60–72.

Grossman, M. I., G. M. Cummings, and A. C. Ivy. The effect of insulin on food intake after vagotomy and sympathectomy. *American Journal of Physiology*, 1947, *149*, 100–102.

Grossman, M. I., and I. F. Stein. The effect of vagotomy on the hunger-producing action of insulin in man. *Journal of Applied Physiology*, 1948, *1*, 263–266.

Grossman, S. P. A textbook of physiological psychology. New York: Wiley, 1967.

Groves, P. M. and R. F. Thompson. Habituation: A dual-process theory, *Psychological Review*, 1970, *77*, 419–450.

Grundfest, H. Evolution of conduction in the nervous system. In A. D. Bass (ed.) *Evolution of nervous control from primitive organisms to man.* Washington, D.C.: American Association for the Advancement of Science, 1959.

Guilford, J. P. Personality. New York: McGraw-Hill, 1959.

————. *The nature of human intelligence.* New York: McGraw-Hill, 1967.

Guilford, J. P. and W. S. Zimmerman. Fourteen dimensions of temperament. *Psychological Monographs*, 1956, *70*, No. 10.

Gummerman, K., and C. R. Gray. Age, iconic storage, and visual information processes. *Journal of Experimental Child Psychology*, 1972, *13*, 165–170.

Guthrie, E. R., and G. P. Horton. Cats in a puzzle box. New York: Holt, Rinehart & Winston, 1946.

Guttman, N. Equal-Reinforcement values for sucrose and glucose solutions compared with equal-sweetness values. *Journal of Comparative and Physiological Psychology*, 1954, *47*, 358–361.

Guttman, N., and H. I. Kalish. Experiments in discrimination. *Scientific American*, January 1958, 77–82.

Haan, N., M. B. Smith, and J. Block. Moral reasoning of young adults: Political-social behavior, family background, and personality correlates. *Journal of Personality and Social Psychology*, 1968, *10*, 183–201.

Haber, R. N., and R. B. Haber. Eidetic imagery: I. Frequency. *Perceptual and Motor Skills*, 1964, *19*, 131–138.

Haber, R. N. (ed). *Information-processing approaches to visual perception.* New York: Holt, Rinehart & Winston, 1969.

Hampson, J. L. Determinants of psychosexual orientation. In F. A. Beach (ed.) *Sex and behavior.* New York: Wiley, 1965, 108–132.

Hardt, M. E., R. Held, and M. J. Steinbach. Adaptation to displaced vision: A change in the central control of sensorimotor coordination. *Journal of Experimental Psychology*, 1971, *89*, 229–239.

Harlow, H. F. The formation of learning sets. *Psychological Review*, 1949, *56*, 51–65.

————. Primate learning. In C. P. Stone (ed.) *Comparative Psychology.* 3rd ed. New York: Prentice-Hall, 1951.

————. The development of affectional patterns in infant monkeys. In B. M. Foss (ed.) *Determinants of infant behavior.* Vol. 1. New York: Wiley, 1961, 75–88.

Harlow, H. F., and M. K. Harlow. Social deprivation in monkeys. *Scientific American,* 1962, *207,* No. 5, 136–146.

_____. The affectional systems. In A. M. Schrier, H. F. Harlow, and F. Stollnitz. (eds.) *Behavior of nonhuman primates.* Vol. 2. New York: Academic Press, 1965, 287–334.

Harlow, H. F., M. K. Harlow, and E. W. Hansen. The maternal affectional system of monkeys. In H. L. Rheingold (ed.) *Maternal behavior in mammals,* New York: Wiley, 1963, 254–281.

Harlow, H. F., and S. J. Suomi. Nature of love—simplified. *American Psychologist,* 1970, *25,* 161–168.

Harlow, H. F., and R. R. Zimmerman. Affectional responses in the infant monkey. *Science,* 1959, *130.* 421–422.

Harris, C. S. Perceptual adaptation to inverted, reversed, and displaced vision. *Psychological Review,* 1965, *72,* 419–444.

Harris, J. D. Forward conditioning, backward conditioning, and pseudo-conditioning, and adaptation to the conditioned stimulus. *Journal of Experimental Psychology,* 1941, *28,* 491–502.

Harter, S. Mental age, IQ, and motivational factors in the discrimination learning set performance of normal and retarded children. *Journal of Experimental Child Psychology,* 1967, *5,* 123–141.

Hartmann, D. P. Influence of symbolically modeled instrumental aggression and pain cues on aggressive behavior. *Journal of Personality and Social Psychology,* 1969, *11,* 280–288.

Hartmann, E. The 90-minute sleep-dream cycle. *Archives of General Psychiatry,* 1968, *18,* 280–286.

_____. Functions of sleep. Unpublished paper delivered at the Wurzburg Symposium: The Nature of Sleep. September, 1971.

Hayes, K. J., and C. Hayes. Imitation in a home-raised chimpanzee. *Journal of Comparative and Physiological Psychology,* 1952, *45,* 450–459.

Haygood, R. C., and L. E. Bourne, Jr. Attribute- and rule-learning aspects of conceptual behavior. *Psychological Review,* 1965, *72,* 175–195.

Hebb, D. O. A textbook of psychology 2nd ed. Philadelphia: Saunders, 1966.

Heckhausen, H. The anatomy of achievement motivation. New York: Academic Press, 1967.

Heider, E. R. Style and accuracy of verbal communications within and between social classes. *Journal of Personality and Social Psychology,* 1971, *18,* 33–47.

Heider, F. The psychology of interpersonal relations. New York: Wiley, 1958.

Held, R. Plasticity in sensory-motor systems. *Scientific American,* 1965, *213,* 84–94.

Held, R., and A. Hein. Movement-produced stimulation in the development of visual guided behavior. *Journal of Comparative and Physiological Psychology,* 1963, *56,* 872–876.

Hendrick, C., and S. R. Brown. Introversion, extraversion, interpersonal attraction. *Journal of Personality and Social Psychology,* 1971, *20,* 31–36.

Herrnstein, R. J. Method and theory in the study of avoidance. *Psychological Review,* 1969, *76,* 59–69.

Herrnstein, R. J., and P. N. Hineline. Negative reinforcement as shock-frequency reduction. *Journal of the Experimental Analysis of Behavior,* 1966, *9,* 421–430.

Hess, E. H. Space perception in the chick. *Scientific American,* 1956, *195,* 71–80.

————. Imprinting. *Science,* 1959, *130,* 133–141.

————. Ethology. In R. Brown, et al. *New directions in psychology, II* New York: Holt, Rinehart & Winston, 1962, 157–266.

————. Attitude and pupil size. *Scientific American,* 1965, *212,* 46–54.

Hess, E. H., and J. M. Polt. Pupil size in relation to mental activity during simple problem-solving. *Science,* 1964, *143,* 1190–1192.

Hess, E. H., A. L. Seltzer, and J. M. Schlien. Pupil response of hetero- and homosexual males to pictures of men and women: A pilot study. *Journal of Abnormal Psychology,* 1965, *70,* 165–168.

Hess, R. D. and V. C. Shipman. Early experience and the socialization of cognitive modes in children. *Child Development,* 1965, *36,* 869–886.

Heston, L. L. Psychiatric disorders in foster-home-reared children of schizophrenic mothers. *British Journal of Psychiatry,* 1966, *112,* 819–825.

Heston, L. L., and D. Denney. Interactions between early life experience and biological factors in schizophrenia. In D. Rosenthal and S. S. Kety (eds.) *The transmission of schizophrenia.* New York: Pergamon, 1968. 363–376.

Higgins, J. D., B. Tursky, and G. E. Schwartz. Shock-elicited pain and its reduction by concurrent tactile stimulation. *Science,* 1971, *172,* 866–867.

Hilgard, E. R., and G. Bower. *Theories of learning.* 3rd ed. New York: Appleton-Century-Crofts, 1966.

Hill, S. D. The performance of young children on three discrimination-learning tasks. *Child Development, 1965, 36,* 425–435.

Hill, W. F. Learning theory and the acquisition of values. *Psychological Review,* 1960, *67,* 317–331.

Hinde, R. A., and N. Tinbergen. The comparative study of species-specific behavior. In A. Roe and G. G. Simpson (eds.) *Behavior and evolution.* New Haven: Yale University Press, 1958, 251–268.

Hirsch, J., R. H. Lindley, and E. C. Tolman. An experimental test of an alleged innate sign stimulus. *Journal of Comparative and Physiological Psychology,* 1955, *48,* 278–280.

Hoch, P., and P. Polatin. Pseudoneurotic forms of schizophrenia: Implications for interpreting heterogeneity in schizophrenia. *Journal of Nervous and Mental Disease,* 1959, *129,* 450–466.

Hodos, W., and C. B. G. Campbell. Scala Naturae: Why there is no theory in comparative psychology. *Psychological Review,* 1969, 76, 337–350.

Hoffman, M. L. Moral development. In P. H. Mussen (ed.) *Carmichael's manual of child psychology.* New York: Wiley, 1970, 261–359.

Hogan, R. A dimension of moral judgment. *Journal of Consulting and Clinical Psychology,* 1970, 35, 205–212.

Hogan, R. A., and J. H. Kirschner, Preliminary report of the extinction of learned fears via short-term implosive therapy. *Journal of Abnormal Psychology,* 1967, 72, 106–109.

Hokanson, J. E., M. Burgess, and M. F. Cohen. Effect of displaced aggression on systolic blood pressure. *Journal of Abnormal and Social Psychology,* 1963, 67, 214–218.

Hokanson, J. E., and R. Edelman. Effects of three social responses on vascular processes. *Journal of Personality and Social Psychology,* 1966, 3, 442–447.

Hokanson, J. E., K. R. Willers, and E. Koropsak. The modification of autonomic responses during aggressive interchange. *Journal of Personality,* 1968, 36, 386–404.

Holz, W. C., and N. H. Azrin. A comparison of several procedures for eliminating behavior. *Journal of the Experimental Analysis of Behavior,* 1963, 6, 399–406.

Hooker, E. The homosexual community. In *Proceedings of the XIV International Congress of Applied Psychology. Volume 2. Personality Research.* Copenhagen: Munksgaard, 1962.

Horney, K. Our inner conflicts. New York: Norton, 1945.

Hovland, C. I., and W. Weiss. The influence of source credibility on communication effectiveness. *Public Opinion Quarterly,* 1951, 15, 635–650.

Hunt, J. McV. Intelligence and experience. New York: Ronald, 1961.

———. Intrinsic motivation and its role in psychological development. In D. Levine (ed.) *Nebraska symposium on motivation.* Vol. 13. Lincoln, Neb.: University of Nebraska Press, 1965, 189–282.

Hunter, W. S. The delayed reaction in animals and children. *Behavior Monographs,* 1913, 2, 24.

Hurvich, L. M., and D. Jameson. An opponent-process theory of color vision. *Psychological Review,* 1957, 64, 384–404.

Hutt, P. J. Rate of bar pressing as a function of quality and quantity of food reward. *Journal of Comparative and Physiological Psychology,* 1954, 47, 235–239.

Hyman, R. The nature of psychological inquiry. Englewood Cliffs, N.J.: Prentice-Hall, 1964.

Insko, C. A., and J. E. Robinson. Belief similarity versus race as determinants of reactions to Negroes by Southern white adolescents: A further test of Rokeach's theory. *Journal of Personality and Social Psychology,* 1967, 7, 216–221.

Insko, C. A., and J. Schopler. Triadic consistency: A statement of affective-cognitive-conative consistency. *Psychological Review,* 1967, *74,* 361–375.

Iscoe, I., M. Williams, and J. Harvey. Age, intelligence, and sex as variables in the conformity of behavior of Negro and white children. *Child Development,* 1964, *35,* 451–460.

Jacobs, L., E. Berscheid, and E. Walster. Self-esteem and attraction *Journal of Personality and Social Psychology,* 1971, *17,* 84–91.

James, W. The principles of psychology. New York: Holt, 1890.

Janis, I. L. Psychological stress. New York: Wiley, 1958.

Janis, I. L., and B. T. King. The influence of role-playing on opinion change. *Journal of Abnormal and Social Psychology,* 1954, *49,* 211–218.

Jay, P. Mother-infant relations in langurs. In H. L. Rheingold (ed.) *Maternal behavior in mammals.* New York: Wiley, 1963, 282–304.

Jenkin, N., and K. Vroegh. Contemporary concepts of masculinity and femininity. *Psychological Reports,* 1969, *25,* 679–697.

Jenkins, J. G., and K. M. Dallenbach. Oblivescence during sleep and waking. *American Journal of Psychology,* 1924, *35,* 605–612.

Jensen, G. D. Preference for bar pressing over "free-loading" as a function of number of rewarded presses. *Journal of Experimental Psychology,* 1963, *65,* 451–454.

Jones, E. E., L. Bell, and E. Aronson. The reciprocation of attraction from similar and dissimilar others. In C. C. McClintock (ed.) *Experimental social psychology.* New York: Holt, Rinehart & Winston, 1971.

Jourard, S. M., and P. F. Secord. Body cathexis and the ideal female figure. *Journal of Abnormal and Social Psychology,* 1955, *50,* 243–246.

Jouvet, M. The states of sleep. *Scientific American,* 1967, *216,* 62–72.

Jouvet, M. Paradoxical sleep — A study of its nature and mechanisms. In K. Akert, C. Bally, and J. P. Schade (eds.) *Sleep mechanisms,* Vol. 18. Amsterdam: Elsevier, 1965.

Julesz, B. Binocular depth perception without familiarity cues. *Science,* 1964, *145,* 356–362.

Kagan, J. and H. A. Moss. Birth to maturity. New York: Wiley, 1962.

Kagan, J., L. Pearson, and L. Welch. The modifiability of an impulsive tempo. *Journal of Educational Psychology,* 1966, *57,* 359–365.

Kagan, J., and W. Phillips. The measurement of identification. *Journal of Abnormal and Social Psychology,* 1964, *69,* 442–443.

Kahneman, D., B. Tursky, D. Shapiro, and A. Crider. Pupillary, heart rate, and skin resistance changes during a mental task. *Journal of Experimental Psychology,* 1969, *79,* 164–167.

Kamen, L. J. The gradient of delay of secondary reward in avoidance conditioning. *Journal of Comparative and Physiological Psychology,* 1957, *50,* 445–449.

Kamisaruk, B. R., and J. Olds. Neuronal correlates of behavior in freely moving rats. *Science,* 1968, *161,* 810–813.

Kamiya, J. Operant control of the EEG alpha rhythm and some of its reported effects on consciousness. In C. T. Tart (ed.) *Altered states of consciousness.* New York: Wiley, 1969, 507–517.

Kanfer, F. H., and A. R. Marston. Human reinforcement: vicarious and direct. *Journal of Experimental Psychology,* 1963, *65,* 292–296.

Kaplan, H. B. Social class and self-derogation: A conditional relationship. *Sociometry,* 1971, *34,* 41–64.

Katkin, E. S., and E. N. Murray. Instrumental conditioning of autonomically mediated behavior: Theoretical and methodological issues. *Psychological Bulletin,* 1968, *70,* 52–68.

Katz, E., and P. Lazarsfeld. Personal influence. Glencoe, Ill.: The Free Press, 1955.

Katz, R. C. Interactions between the facilitative and inhibitory effects of a punishing stimulus in the control of children's hitting behavior. *Child Development,* 1971, *42,* 1433–1446.

Kaufman, I. C., and L. A. Rosenblum. Depression in infant monkeys separated from their mothers. *Science,* 1967, *155,* 1030–1031.

Kaufman, I. C., and Rosenblum, L. A. Effects of separation from mother on the emotional behavior of infant monkeys. *Annals of the New York Academy of Sciences,* 1969, *159,* 681–695.

Kaufmann, L., and I. Rock. The moon illusion. *Scientific American,* 1962, *207,* No. 1, 120–131.

Kelley, H. H. Moral evaluation. American Psychologist, 1971, *26,* 283–300.

Kelman, H. L., and C. I. Hovland. "Reinstatement" of the communicator in delayed measurement of opinion change. *Journal of Abnormal and Social Psychology,* 1953, *48,* 327–335.

Kendler, H. H. Enviromental and cognitive control of behavior. *American Psychologist,* 1971, *26,* 962–973.

Kendler, H. H. and T. S. Kendler. Vertical and horizontal processes in problem solving. *Psychological Review,* 1962, *69,* 1–16.

_____. An ontogeny of optional shift behavior. *Child Development,* 1970, *41,* 1–27.

Kendon, A. Some functions of gaze-direction in social interaction. *Acta Psychologica,* 1967, *26,* 22–63.

Kesner, R. P., and H. S. Conner. Independence of short- and long-term memory: A neural system analysis. *Science,* 1972, *176,* 432–434.

Kiesler, C. A., and S. B. Kiesler. Conformity. Reading, Mass.: Addison-Wesley, 1969.

Kiesler, C. A., R. E. Nisbett, and M. P. Zanna. On inferring one's beliefs from one's behavior. *Journal of Personality and Social Psychology,* 1969, *11,* 321–327.

Kimble, G. A. Hilgard and Marquis' conditioning and learning. 2nd ed. New York: Appleton-Century-Crofts, 1961.

Kimmel, H. D. Instrumental conditioning of autonomically mediated behavior. *Psychological Bulletin,* 1967, *67,* 337–345.

Kimmel, H. D., and F. A. Hill. Operant conditioning of the GSR. *Psychological Reports,* 1960, *7,* 555–562.

Kimura, D. Cerebral dominance and the perception of verbal stimuli. *Canadian Journal of Psychology,* 1961, *15,* 166–171.

————. Speech lateralization in young children as determined by an auditory test. *Journal of Comparative and Physiological Psychology,* 1963, *56,* 899–902.

Kimura, D., and S. Folb. Neural processing of backwards-speech sounds. *Science,* 1968, *161,* 395–396.

Kinsey, A. C., W. B. Pomeroy, and C. E. Martin. Sexual behavior in the human male. Philadelphia: Saunders, 1948.

Kinsey, A. C., W. B. Pomeroy, C. E. Martin, and D. H. Gebhard. Sexual behavior in the human female. Philadelphia: Saunders, 1953.

Kintch, W. Learning, memory, and conceptual processes. New York: Wiley, 1970.

Kirk, R., J. Lackner, and J. A. Bever. An experiment on the effect of syntactic structures in speech perception. Unpublished paper, MIT, Cambridge, Mass., 1965.

Kish, G. B. Learning when the onset of illumination is used as reinforcing stimulus. *Journal of Comparative and Physiological Psychology,* 1955, *48,* 261–264.

Kleitman, N. Sleep and wakefulness. Chicago: University of Chicago Press, 1963.

Knox, R. E., and J. A. Inkster. Postdecision dissonance at post time. *Journal of Personality and Social Psychology,* 1968, *8,* 319–323.

Kohlberg, L. Development of moral character and moral ideology. In M. L. Hoffman and L. W. Hoffman (eds.) *Review of child development research.* Vol. 1. New York: Russell Sage Foundation, 1964, 383–342.

————. A cognitive-developmental analysis of children's sex role concepts and attitudes. In E. E. Maccoby (ed.) *The development of sex differences.* Stanford, Cal.: Stanford University Press, 1966, 82–172.

————. Stage and sequence: The cognitive-developmental approach to socialization. In D. A. Goslin (ed.) *Handbook of socialization theory and research.* Chicago: Rand McNally, 1969, 347–480.

Kohlberg, L., and R. Kramer. Continuities and discontinuities in childhood and adult moral development. *Human Development,* 1969, *12,* 93–120.

Kohler, W. The mentality of apes. New York: Harcourt, 1925.

Kolodny, R. C., W. H. Masters, J. Hendryx, and G. Toro. Plasma testosterone and semen analysis in male homosexuals. *New England Journal of Medicine,* 1971, 1170–1174.

Korner, A. F., and R. Grobstein. Visual alertness as related to soothing in neonates: Implications for maternal stimulation and early deprivation. *Child Development,* 1966, *37,* 867–876.

Kothandapani, V. Validation of feeling, belief, and intention to act as three components of attitude and their contribution to prediction of contraceptive behavior. *Journal of Personality and Social Psychology,* 1971, *19,* 321–333.

Krapfl, J. E., and M. M. Nawas. Differential ordering of stimulus presentation in systematic desensitization. *Journal of Abnormal Psychology,* 1970, *75,* 333–337.

Krauss, R. M., and S. Glucksberg. The development of communication: Competence as a function of age. *Child Development,* 1969, *40,* 255–266.

———. Socialization of communication skills. In R. A. Hoppe, G. A. Milton, and E. C. Simmel (eds.) *Early experiences and the process of socialization.* New York: Academic Press, 1970, 145–166.

Krogman, W. M. The scars of human evolution. *Scientific American,* 1951, *185,* 54–57.

Lacey, J. I. The evaluation of autonomic responses: Toward a general solution. *Annals of the New York Academy of Sciences,* 1956, *67,* 123–164.

———. Psychophysiological approaches to the evaluation of psychotherapeutic process and outcome. In E. A. Rubenstein and M. B. Parloff (eds.) *Research in psychotherapy.* Washington, D.C.: American Psychological Association, 1959.

Lacey, J. I., J. Kagan, B. C. Lacey, and H. A. Moss. The visceral level: Situational determinants and behavioral correlates of autonomic response patterns. In P. H. Knapp (ed.) *Expression of the emotions in man.* New York: International Universities Press, 1963.

Ladefoged, P., and D. Broadbent. Perception of sequence in auditory events. *Quarterly Journal of Experimental Psychology,* 1960, *12,* 162–170.

Lambert, W. E., E. Libman, and E. G. Poser. The effect of increased salience of a membership on pain tolerance. *Journal of Personality,* 1960, *28,* 350–357.

Lang, P. J., J. Geer, and M. Hnatiow. Semantic generalization of conditioned autonomic responses. *Journal of Experimental Psychology,* 1963, *65,* 552–558.

Lang, P. J., and A. D. Lazovik. Experimental desensitization of a phobia. *Journal of Abnormal and Social Psychology,* 1963, *66,* 519–525.

Lang, P. J., B. G. Melamed, and J. Hart. A psychophysiological analysis of fear modification using an automated desensitization procedure. *Journal of Abnormal Psychology,* 1970, *76,* 220–234.

Lange, D. L., R. K. Baker, and S. J. Ball. Mass media and violence. Vol. 11. Washington, D.C.: U.S. Government Printing Office, 1969.

Langer, J. Theories of development. New York: Holt, Rinehart & Winston, 1969.

LaPiere, R. T. Attitudes versus actions. *Social Forces,* 1934, *13,* 230–237.

Lashley, K. S. The mechanism of vision: I. A method for rapid analysis of pattern vision in the rat. *Journal of Genetic Psychology,* 1930, *37,* 453–460.

Lazarus, A. A. Aversion therapy and sensory modalities: Clinical impressions. *Perceptual and Motor Skills,* 1968, *27,* 178.

Leask, J., R. N. Haber, and R. B. Haber. Eidetic imagery in children: II. Longitudinal and experimental results. *Psychonomic Monograph Supplements,* 1969, *3,* 25–48.

Lee, B. S. Effects of delayed speech feedback. *Journal of the Acoustical Society of America,* 1950, *22,* 824–826.

Leonhard, K. Cycloid psychoses — endogenous psychoses which are neither schizophrenic nor manic-depressive. *Journal of Mental Science,* 1961, *107,* 633–648.

Lenneberg, E. H. Biological foundations of language. New York: Wiley, 1966.

———. On explaining language. *Science,* 1969, *164,* 635–643.

Lerner, M. J., and C. H. Simmons. Observer's reaction to the "innocent victim": compassion or rejection. *Journal of Personality and Social Psychology,* 1966, *4,* 203–210.

Lettvin, J. Y., H. R. Maturana, W. S. McCullough, and W. H. Pitts. What the frog's eye tells the frog's brain. *Proceedings of the Institute of Radio Engineers,* 1959, *47,* 1940–1951.

Leventhal, H., and R. P. Singer. Affect arousal and positioning of recommendations in persuasive communication. *Journal of Personality and Social Psychology,* 1966, *4,* 137–146.

Leventhal, H., R. P. Singer, and S. Jones. Effects of fear and specificity of recommendation upon attitudes and behavior. *Journal of Personality and Social Psychology,* 1965, *2,* 20–29.

Levis, D. J., and R. N. Carrera. Effects of ten hours of implosive therapy in the treatment of outpatients: A preliminary report. *Journal of Abnormal Psychology,* 1967, *72,* 504–508.

Lewis, D. J., and C. P. Duncan. Effect of different percentages of money reward on extinction of a lever pulling response. *Journal of Experimental Psychology,* 1956, *52,* 23–27.

———. Expectation and resistence to extinction of a lever-pulling response as a function of percentage of reinforcement and number of acquisition trials. *Journal of Experimental Psychology,* 1958, *55,* 121–128.

Lewis, J. L. Semantic processing of unattended messages using dichotic listening. *Journal of Experimental Psychology,* 1970, *85,* 225–228.

Liberman, A. M., F. S. Cooper, D. P. Shankweiler, and M. Studdert-Kennedy. Perception of the speech code. *Psychological Review,* 1967, *74,* 431–461.

Liebert, R. M., and J. M. Neale. TV violence and child aggression. *Psychology Today,* 1972, *5,* 38–40.

Lilly, J. C. Productive and creative research with man and dolphin. *Archives of General Psychiatry,* 1963, *8,* 111–116.

Lindsley, D. B. Psychophysiology and motivation. In M. R. Jones (ed.) *Nebraska symposium on motivation.* Lincoln, Neb.: University of Nebraska Press, 1957, 44–105.

Lindsley, D. B., L. H. Schreiner, and W. B. Knowles. Behavioral and EEG changes following chronic brain stem lesions in the cat. *EEG and Clinical Neurophysiology,* 1950, *2,* 483–498.

Linner, B. Sex and society in Sweden. New York: Random House, 1967.

Lindzey, G. Some remarks concerning incest, the incest taboo, and psychoanalytic theory. *American Psychologist,* 1967, *22,* 1051–1059.

Lipsitt, L. P. and S. A. Serunian. Oddity problem learning in young children. *Child Development,* 1963, *34,* 201–206.

Lorenz, K. Evolution and modification of behavior. Chicago: University of Chicago Press, 1965.

_____. Ritualized fighting. In J. D. Carthy and F. J. Ebling (eds.) *The natural history of aggression.* New York: Academic Press, 1966*a*, 39–50.

_____. *On aggression.* New York: Harcourt, Brace and World, 1966*b*.

Lowell, E. L. The effect of need for achievement on learning and speed of performance. *Journal of Psychology,* 1952, *33,* 31–40.

Luria, A. R. The functional organization of the brain. *Scientific American,* 1970, *222* (No. 3), 66–78.

Luschen, M. E., and D. M. Pierce. Effect of the menstrual cycle on mood and sexual arousability. *The Journal of Sex Research,* 1972, *68,* 41–47.

Lyons, J. Human language in R. A. Hinde (ed.) *Non-verbal communication.* London: Cambridge University Press, 1972, 49–95.

McAdam, D. W., and H. A. Whitaker. Language production: Electroencephalographic localization in the normal human brain. *Science,* 1971, *172,* 499–502.

McClelland, D. C., J. W. Atkinson, R. A. Clark, and E. L. Lowell. The achievement motive. New York: Appleton-Century-Crofts, 1953.

_____. *The achieving society.* Princeton, N.J.: Van Nostrand, 1961.

McCutcheon, N. B., and J. Saunders. Human taste papilla stimulation: Stability of quality judgments over time. *Science,* 1972, *175,* 214–216.

McGraw, M. B. Growth: A study of Johnny and Jimmy. New York: Appleton-Century-Crofts, 1935.

_____. Later development of children specially trained in infancy. *Child Development,* 1939, *10,* 1–19.

McGregor, D. The human side of enterprise. New York: McGraw-Hill, 1960.

McGuire, W. J. The nature of attitudes and attitude change. In G.

Lindzey and E. Aronson (eds.) *The handbook of social psychology.* 2nd ed. Vol. 3. Reading, Mass.: Addison-Wesley, 1969.

McLaughlin, B. Effects of similarity and likableness on attraction and recall. *Journal of Personal and Social Psychology,* 1971, *20,* 65–69.

McNeill, D. Developmental psycholinguistics. In F. Smith and G. A. Miller (eds.). *The genesis of language: A psycholinguistic approach.* Cambridge, Mass.: MIT Press, 1966, 15–91.

Maccoby, E., and J. C. Masters. Attachment and dependency. In P. H. Mussen (ed.) *Carmichael's manual of child psychology.* 3rd ed. New York: Wiley 1970, 159–259.

Mack, A. An investigation of the relationship between eye and retinal image movement in the perception of movement. *Perception and Psychophysics,* 1970, *8,* 291–298.

Mackworth, J. F. Vigilance, arousal, and habituation. *Psychological Review,* 1968, *75,* 308–322.

Macnamara, J. Cognitive basis of language learning in infants. *Psychological Review,* 1972, *79,* 1–13.

MacNichol, E. F. Three-pigment color vision. *Scientific American,* 1964, *211,* 48–56.

Maddi, S. R. The existential neurosis. *Journal of Abnormal Psychology,* 1967, *72,* 311–325.

Magee, K. R., S. F. Schneider, and N. Rosenzweig. Congenital indifference to pain. *Journal of Nervous and Mental Disease,* 1961, *132,* 249–259.

Magoun, H. W. The waking brain. 2nd ed. Springfield, Ill.: Charles Thomas, 1963.

Mandler, G. Emotion. In R. Brown, et al. *New directions in psychology.* Vol. 1. New York: Holt, Rinehart & Winston, 1962, 267–343.

———. Verbal learning. In T. M. Newcomb (ed.) *New directions in psychology.* Vol. 3. New York: Holt, Rinehart & Winston, 1967*a,* 1–50.

———. Organization and memory. In K. W. Spence and J. T. Spence (eds.) *The psychology of learning and motivation.* New York: Academic Press, 1967*b,* 327–372.

———. Association and organization: Facts, figures, and theories. In T. R. Dixon and D. L. Horton (eds.) *Verbal behavior and general behavior theory.* Englewood Cliffs, N.J.: Prentice-Hall, 1968, 109–119.

Manosevitz, M. Early sexual behavior in adult male homosexuals. *Journal of Abnormal Psychology,* 1970, *76,* 396–402.

———. The development of male homosexuality. *The Journal of Sex Research,* 1972, *8,* 31–40.

Marler, P. R., and W. J. Hamilton, III. Mechanisms of animal behavior. New York: Wiley, 1966.

Maslow, A. H. A dynamic theory of human motivation. *Psychological Review,* 1943, *50,* 370–396.

Mason, W. A. Determinants of social behavior in young chimpanzees. In A. M. Schrier, H. F. Harlow, and F. Stollnitz (eds.) *Behavior in nonhuman primates.* Vol. 2. New York: Academic Press, 1965*a,* 335–364.

_____. The social development of monkeys and apes. In I. DeVore (ed.) *Primate behavior: Field studies of monkeys and apes.* New York: Holt, Rinehart & Winston, 1965*b*, 514–543.

_____. Motivational aspects of social responsiveness in young children. In H. W. Stevenson, E. H. Hess, and H. L. Rheingold (eds.) *Early behavior: Comparative and developmental approaches.* New York: Wiley, 1967, 103–126.

_____. Early social deprivation in nonhuman primates: Implications for human behavior. In D. C. Glass (ed.) *Biology and behavior: Environmental influences.* New York: Rockefeller University Press, 1968, 70–101.

_____. Motivational factors in psychosocial development. In U. J. Arnold and N. M. Page (eds.) *Nebraska symposium on motivation.* Lincoln, Neb.: University of Nebraska Press, 1970, 35–62.

Massaro, D. W. Preperceptual auditory images. *Journal of Experimental Psychology,* 1970*a*, *85*, 411–417.

_____. Perceptual processes and forgetting in memory tasks. *Psychological Review,* 1970*b*, *77*, 557–567.

_____. Preperceptual images, processing time, and perceptual units in auditory perception. *Psychological Review,* 1972, *79*, 124–145.

Masserman, J. H. Principles of dynamic psychiatry. Philadelphia: Saunders, 1946.

Mast, S. O., and L. C. Pusch. Modification of response in amoeba. *Biological Bulletin,* 1924, *46*, 55–59.

Masters, W. H. and V. E. Johnson. The sexual response cycles of the human male and female: Comparative anatomy and physiology. In F. A. Beach (ed.) *Sex and behavior.* New York: Wiley, 1965, 512–527.

_____. *Human sexual response.* Boston: Little, Brown, 1966.

Mathews, L. H. Overt fighting in mammals. In J. D. Carthy and F. J. Ebling (eds.) *The natural history of aggression.* New York: Academic Press, 1964, 23–32.

Mayer, J. Regulation of energy intake and the body weight: The glucostatic theory and the lipostatic hypothesis. *Annals of the New York Academy of Science,* 1955, *63*, 15–43.

Mayer, J., and D. W. Thomas. Regulation of food intake and obesity. *Science,* 1967, *156*, 328–337.

Meehl, P. E. Clinical versus statistical prediction. Minneapolis, Minn.: University of Minnesota Press, 1954.

Melzack, R., and T. H. Scott. The effects of early experience on the response to pain. *Journal of Comparative and Physiological Psychology,* 1957, *50*, 155–161.

Melzack, R., and P. D. Wall. Pain mechanisms: A new theory. *Science,* 1965, *150*, 971–979.

_____. Interaction of fast- and slow-conducting fiber systems involved in pain and analgesia. *Pharmacology of Pain,* 1968, *9*, 231–242. New York: Pergamon.

Meneghini, K. A., and H. W. Leibowitz. The effect of stimulus distance and age on shape constancy. *Journal of Experimental Psychology,* 1967, *74,* 241–248.

Menzel, H., and E. Katz. Social relations and innovations in the medical profession: The epidemiology of a new drug. *Public Opinion Quarterly,* 1956, *19,* 337–352.

Mermelstein, E., and E. Meyer. Conservation techniques and their effects on different populations. *Child Development,* 1969, *40,* 471–490.

Michael, C. R. Retinal processing of visual images. *Scientific American,* 1969, *220,* 104–114.

Milgram, S. Behavioral study of obedience. *Journal of Abnormal and Social Psychology,* 1963, *67,* 371–378.

————. Some conditions of obedience and disobedience to authority. *Human Relations,* 1965, *18,* 57–76.

Miller, G. A. The magic number seven, plus or minus two: Some limits on our capacity for processing information. *Psychological Review,* 1956, *63,* 81–97.

————. Some preliminaries to psycholinguistics. *American Psychologist,* 1965, *20,* 15–20.

Miller, N. E. The frustration-aggression hypothesis. *Psychological Review,* 1941, *48,* 337–342.

————. Central stimulation and other new approaches to motivation and reward. *American Psychologist,* 1958, *13,* 100–108.

————. Learning of visceral and glandular responses. *Science,* 1969, *163,* 434–445.

Miller, N. E., and L. V. DiCara. Instrumental learning of heart-rate changes in curarized rats: Shaping and specificity to discriminate stimulus. *Journal of Comparative and Physiological Psychology,* 1967, *63,* 12–19.

Miller, N. E. and J. Dollard. Social learning and imitation. New Haven, Conn.: Yale University Press, 1941.

Mills, A. W. On the minimum audible angle. *Journal of the Acoustical Society of America,* 1958, *30,* 237–246.

Milne, L. J., and M. Milne. The senses of animals and men. New York: Atheneum, 1962.

Milner, B. The memory defect in bilateral hippocampal lesions. *Psychiatric Research Reports,* 1959, *11,* 43–52.

Milner, B., C. Branch, and T. Rasmussen. Observations on cerebral dominance. In A. V. S. DeRueck and M. O. O'Conner (eds.) *Disorders of language: A CIBA foundation symposium.* Churchill: 1964, 200–214.

Milner, B., L. Taylor, and R. W. Sperry. Lateralized suppression of dichotically presented digits after commissural section in man. *Science,* 1968, *161,* 184–186.

Mirels, H., and J. Mills. Perception of the pleasantness and competence of a partner. *Journal of Abnormal and Social Psychology,* 1964, *68,* 456–460.

Mischel, W. Personality and assessment. New York: Wiley, 1968.

Missakian, E. A. Effects of adult social experience on patterns of reproductive activity of socially deprived male rhesus monkeys (*Macaca Mulatta*). *Journal of Personality and Social Psychology,* 1972, *21,* 131–134.

Moncrieff, R. W. The chemical senses. London: Hill, 1951.

Money, J. Sexual dimorphism and homosexual gender identity. *Psychological Bulletin,* 1970, *74,* 425–440.

Montagu, M. F. A. Time, morphology, and neoteny. In M. F. A. Montagu (ed.) *Culture and the evolution of man.* New York: Oxford University Press, 1962, 324–342.

_____. *The human revolution.* Cleveland: World Publishing Company, 1965.

Moos, R. H. Fluctuations in symptoms and moods during the menstrual cycle. *Journal of Psychosomatic Research,* 1969, *13,* 32–44.

Moray, N. Attention in dichotic listening: Affective cues and the influence of instructions. *Quarterly Journal of Experimental Psychology,* 1959, *11,* 56–60.

_____. *Attention. Selective processes in vision and hearing.* New York: Academic Press, 1970.

Moreno, J. L. Psychodrama, Vol. 1. Beacon, N.Y.: Beacon House, 1946.

Morgan, C. T., and R. A. King. Introduction to psychology, 3rd ed. New York: McGraw-Hill, 1966.

Morgan, C. T., and J. D. Morgan. Studies in hunger. II. The relation of gastric denervation and dietary sugar to the effect of insulin upon food intake in the rat. *Journal of General Psychology,* 1940, *57,* 153–156.

Morrell, L. K., and Salamy, J. G. Hemispheric asymmetry of electrocortical responses to speech stimuli. *Science,* 1971, *174,* 164–166.

Moruzzi, G., and H. W. Magoun. Brain stem reticular formation and activiation of the EEG. *EEG and Clinical Neurophysiology,* 1949, *1,* 455–473.

Moscovici, S., E. Lage, and M. Naffrechoux. Influence of a consistent minority on the responses of a majority in a color perception task. *Sociometry,* 1969, *32,* 365–380.

Mowrer, O. H. A stimulus-response analysis of anxiety and its role as a reinforcing agent. *Psychological Review,* 1939, *46,* 553–565.

_____. On the dual nature of learning—A reinterpretation of "conditioning" and "problem-solving." *Harvard Education Review,* 1947, *17,* 102–148.

_____. *Learning theory and personality dynamics.* New York: Ronald, 1950.

Mowrer, O. H., and P. Viek. An experimental analogue of fear from a sense of helplessness. *Journal of Abnormal and Social Psychology,* 1948, *43,* 193–200.

Murdock, B. B., Jr. The retention of individual items. *Journal of Experimental Psychology,* 1961, *62,* 618–625.

Munn, N. L. The evolution and growth of human behavior. 2nd ed. Boston: Houghton Mifflin, 1965.

Mussen, P. H., J. J. Conger, and J. Kagan. Child development and personality. 2nd ed. New York: Harper and Row, 1963.

Nagel, E. Determinism and development. In D. B. Harris (ed.) The concept of development. Minneapolis, Minn: University of Minnesota Press, 1957, 15–24.

Natsoulas, T. Concerning introspective "knowledge." Psychological Bulletin, 1970, 73, 89–111.

Needham, J. G. About ourselves. Lancaster, Pa.: Jacques Cattell Press, 1941.

Neisser, U. Cognitive psychology. New York: Appleton-Century-Crofts, 1967.

Neisser, V., and P. Weene. Hierarchies in concept attainment. Journal of Experimental Psychology, 1962, 64, 640–645.

Neuringer, A. L. Animals respond for food in the presence of free food. Science, 1969, 166, 399–401.

Newcomb, T. M. The prediction of interpersonal attraction: American Psychologist, 1956, 11, 575–586.

———. The acquaintance process. New York: Holt, Rinehart and Winston, 1961.

Nichols, D. C., and B. Tursky. Body image, anxiety, and tolerance for experimental pain. Psychosomatic Medicine, 1967, 29, 103–110.

Nisbet, R. A. The social bond: An introduction to the study of society. New York: Knopf, 1970.

Nisbett, R. E. Taste, deprivation, and weight determinants of eating behavior. Journal of Personality and Social Psychology, 1968, 10, 107–116.

Nisbett, R. E. and S. B. Gurowitz. Weight, sex, and the eating behavior of human newborns. Journal of Comparative and Physiological Psychology, 1970, 73, 245–253.

Nisbett, R. E., and D. E. Kanouse. Obesity, food deprivation, and supermarket shopping behavior. Journal of Personality and Social Psychology, 1969, 12, 289–294.

Nissen, H. W., K. L. Chow, and J. Semmes. Effects of restricted opportunity for tactual, kinesthetic, and manipulative experience on the behavior of the chimpanzee. American Journal of Psychology, 1951, 64, 485–507.

Nolan, J. D., P. R. Mattis, and W. C. Holliday. Long-term effects of behavior therapy: A 12-month follow up. Journal of Abnormal Psychology, 1970, 76, 88–92.

Nord, W. R. Social exchange theory: An integrative approach to social conformity. Psychological Bulletin, 1969, 71, 174–208.

Norman, D. A. Toward a theory of memory and attention. Psychological Review, 1968, 75, 522–536.

Norman, D. A. Memory and attention: An introduction to human information processing. New York: Wiley, 1969.

Nowlis, D. P., and J. Kamiya. The control of electroencephalographic alpha rhythms through auditory feedback and the associated mental activity. *Psychophysiology,* 1970, *6,* 476–484.

Olds, J. The central nervous system and the reinforcement of behavior. *American Psychologist,* 1969, *24,* 114–132.

Olds, J., and P. Milner. Positive reinforcement produced by electrical stimulation of septal area and other regions of rat brain. *Journal of Comparative and Physiological Psychology,* 1954, *47,* 419–427.

Olds, J., and M. Olds. Drives, rewards, and the brain. In F. Barron, et al. *New directions in psychology.* Vol. 2. New York: Holt, Rinehart & Winston, 1965, 329–410.

Olson, D. R. Language and thought: Aspects of a cognitive theory of semantics. *Psychological Review,* 1970, *77,* 257–273.

Orbach, J., A. C. Traub, and R. Olsen. Psychophysical studies of body image II. Normative data on the adjustable body-distorting mirror. *Archives of General Psychiatry,* 1965, *12,* 126–135.

Osgood, C. E. Method and theory in experimental psychology. New York: Oxford University Press, 1953.

Ostrom, T. M. The relationship between the affective, behavioral, and cognitive components of attitudes. *Journal of Experimental Social Psychology,* 1969, *5,* 12–30.

Ostrom, T. M., and H. S. Upshaw. Race differences in the judgment of attitude statements over a thirty-five year period. *Journal of Personality,* 1970, *38,* 235–248.

Oswald, I. Sleeping and waking. New York: Elsevier, 1962.
——. *Sleep.* Baltimore: Penguin, 1966.

Oswald, I., A. M. Taylor, and M. Treisman. Discriminative responses to stimulation during human sleep. *Brain,* 1960, *83,* 440–453.

Oswald, I., and V. R. Thacore. Amphetamine and phenmetrazine addiction: Physiological abnormalities in the abstinence syndrome. *British Medical Journal,* 1963, *2,* 427–431.

Overmier, J. B., and M. E. P. Seligman. Effects of inescapable shock upon subsequent escape and avoidance responding. *Journal of Comparative and Physiological Psychology,* 1967, *63,* 28–33.

Paivio, A. Mental imagery in associative learning and memory. *Psychological Review,* 1969, *76,* 241–263.

Palmer, R. D. Cerebral dominance and audio asymmetry. *Journal of Psychology,* 1964, *58,* 157–167.

Parke, R. D. Effectiveness of punishment as an interaction of intensity, timing, agent nurturance, and cognitive structuring. *Child Development,* 1969, *40,* 213–236.

Parke, R. D., and R. H. Walters. Some factors influencing the efficacy of punishment training for inducing response inhibition. *Monographs of the Society for Research in Child Development,* 1967, *32,* No. 1, (Serial No. 109).

Paul, G. L. Two-year follow-up of systematic desensitization in therapy groups. *Journal of Abnormal Psychology,* 1968, *73,* 119–130.

Penard, E. Habituation. *Journal of the Royal Microscopical Society,* 1948, *67,* 43–45.

Penfield, W., and L. Roberts. Speech and brain mechanisms. Princeton, N.J.: Princeton University Press, 1959.

Perin, C. T. A quantitative investigation of the delay-of-reinforcement gradient. *Journal of Experimental Psychology,* 1943, *32,* 37–51.

Perkins, C. C., Jr. The relation of secondary reward to gradients of reinforcement. *Journal of Experimental Psychology,* 1947, *37,* 377–392.

————. The stimulus conditions which follow learned responses. *Psychological Review,* 1955, *62,* 341–348.

————. The concept of reinforcement. *Psychological Review,* 1968, *75,* 155–172.

Perrott, D. R., and L. F. Elfner. Monaural localization. *The Journal of Auditory Research,* 1968, *8,* 185–193.

Persky, H., K. D. Smith, and G. K. Basu. Relation of psychologic measures of aggression and hostility to testosterone production in man. *Psychosomatic Medicine,* 1971, *33,* 265–277.

Peterson, L. R. Concurrent verbal activity. *Psychological Review,* 1969, *76,* 376–386.

Peterson, L. R., and M. J. Peterson. Short-term retention of individual verbal items. *Journal of Experimental Psychology,* 1959, *58,* 193–198.

Pfaffman, C. De Gustibus. *American Psychologist,* 1965, *20,* 21–33.

Phillips, J. L., Jr. The origins of intellect: Piaget's theory. San Francisco: Freeman, 1969.

Piaget, J. The language and thought of the child. New York: Meridian Books, 1926.

————. *The moral judgment of the child.* Glencoe, Illinois: The Free Press, 1948.

————. *The origins of intelligence in children.* New York: International University Press, 1952.

————. *The construction of reality in the child.* New York: Basic Books, 1954.

————. Piaget's theory. In P. H. Mussen (ed.) *Carmichael's manual of child psychology.* New York: Wiley, 1970, 703–732.

Pierrel, R., and Sherman, J. G. Barnabus, the rat with a college education. *Brown Alumni Monthly,* 1963, February, 8–12.

Porges, S. W. Heart rate variability and deceleration as indexes of reaction time. *Journal of Experimental Psychology,* 1972, *92,* 103–110.

Posner, M. I., and S. J. Boies. Components of attention. *Psychological Review,* 1971, *78,* 391–408.

Posner, M. I., and S. W. Keele. Decay of visual information from a single letter. *Science,* 1967, *158,* 137–139.

Premack, D. Toward empirical behavior laws: I. Positive reinforcement. *Psychological Review,* 1959, *66,* 219–233.

_____. Language in chimpanzee? *Science,* 1971, *172,* 808–822.

Pribram, K. H. A review of theory in physiological psychology. *Annual Review of Psychology,* 1960, *11,* 1–40.

Provence, S., and R. Lipton. Infants in institutions. New York: International Universities Press, 1962.

Putterman, A. H., A. L. Robert, and A. S. Bregman. Adaptation of the wrist to displacing prisms. *Psychonomic Science,* 1969, *16,* 79–80.

Quinlan, D. Effects of sight of the body and active locomotion in perceptual adaptation. *Journal of Experimental Psychology,* 1970, *86,* 91–96.

Rabbie, J. M., and M. Horwitz. Arousal of ingroup-outgroup bias by a chance win or loss. *Journal of Personality and Social Psychology,* 1969, *13,* 269–277.

Rachman, S. Introduction to behavior therapy. *Behavior Research and Therapy,* 1963, *1,* 127–132.

Ratliff, F., and H. K. Hartline. The response of *Limulus* optic nerve fibers to patterns of illumination on the retinal mosaic. *Journal of General Physiology,* 1959, *42,* 1241–1255.

Ratliff, F., H. K. Hartline, and W. H. Miller. Spatial and temporal aspects of retinal inhibitory interaction. *Journal of the Optical Society of America,* 1963, *53,* 110–120.

Ratner, S. C. and M. R. Denny. Comparative psychology. Homewood, Ill.: Dorsey, 1964.

Raven, J. C. Progressive Matrices. London: H. K. Lewis, 1938.

Razran, G. The conditioned evocation of attitudes. *Journal of Experimental Psychology,* 1954, *48,* 278–282.

_____. The observable unconscious and the inferable conscious in current Soviet psychophysiology: Interoceptive conditioning, semantic conditioning, and the orienting reflex. *Psychological Review,* 1961, *68,* 81–147.

Reese, H. W. Discrimination learning set and perceptual set in young children. *Child Development,* 1965, *36,* 153–161.

Regan, J. W. Guilt, perceived injustice, and altruistic behavior. *Journal of Personality and Social Psychology,* 1971, *18,* 124–132.

Reynoles, G. S. A primer of operant conditioning. Glenview, Ill.: Scott, Foresman, 1968.

Rheingold, H. L., and C. O. Eckerman. The infant separates himself from his mother. *Science,* 1970, *168,* 78–83.

Richards, W., and J. F. Miller, Jr. Convergence as a cue to depth. *Perception and Psychophysics,* 1969, *5,* 317–320.

Richardson, A. Mental imagery. New York: Springer, 1969.

Richter, C. P. Salt taste thresholds of normal and adrenolectomized rats. *Endocrinology,* 1939, *24,* 367–371.

Richter, C. P., and J. F. Eckert. Mineral metabolism of adrenalectomized rats studied by the appetite method. *Endocrinology,* 1938, *22,* 214–224.

Richter, C. P., L. E. Holt, and B. Barelare. Nutritional requirements for normal growth and reproduction in rats studied by the self-selection method. *American Journal of Physiology,* 1938, *122,* 734–744.

Riess, B. F. The effect of altered environment and of age on mother-young relationships among animals. *Annals of the New York Academy of Science,* 1954, *57,* 606–610.

Rock, I. The nature of perceptual adaptation. New York: Basic Books, 1966.

————. When the world is tilt. *Psychology Today,* 1968, *2,* 24–31.

Rock, I., and C. S. Harris. Vision and touch. *Scientific American,* 1967, *216* (No. 5), 96–104.

Roffwarg, H. P., J. N. Muzio, and W. C. Dement. Ontogenetic development of the human sleep-dream cycle. *Science,* 1966, *152,* 604–619.

Roffwarg, H. P., W. C. Dement, J. N. Muzio, and C. Fisher. Dream imagery: relationship to rapid eye movements of sleep. *Archives of General Psychiatry,* 1962, *7,* 235–258.

Rogers, C. R. Counseling and psychotherapy. Boston: Houghton Mifflin, 1942.

————. A theory of therapy, personality, and interpersonal relationships as developed in the client-centered framework. In S. Koch (ed.) *Psychology: A study of a science.* Vol. 3. New York: McGraw-Hill, 1959, 184–256.

————. *On becoming a person.* Boston: Houghton Mifflin, 1961.

Rohwer, W. D., Jr. Images and pictures in children's learning. *Psychological Bulletin,* 1970, *73,* 393–403.

Rokeach, M. (ed.) The open and closed mind. New York: Basic Books, 1960.

————. *Beliefs, attitudes, and values.* San Francisco: Jossey-Bass, 1968.

Rosenbaum, M. E. and S. J. Arenson. Observational learning: Some theory, some variables, some findings. In E. C. Simmel and G. A. Milton (eds.) *Social facilitation and imitative behavior.* Boston: Allyn & Bacon, 1968, 111–134.

Rosenberg, B. G., and B. Sutton-Smith. Sex and identity. New York: Holt, Rinehart & Winston, 1972.

Rotter, J. B. Generalized expectancies for internal vs. external control of reinforcement. *Psychological Monographs,* 1966, *80,* No. 1 (Whole No. 609).

————. External control and internal control. *Psychology Today,* 1971, *5,* 37–42, 58–59.

Ryan, E. D., and R. Foster. Athletic participation and perceptual augmentation and reduction. *Journal of Personality and Social Psychology,* 1967, *6,* 472–476.

Savage, J. M. Evolution. New York: Holt, Rinehart & Winston, 1963.

Scarr, S. Genetic factors in activity motivation. *Child Development,* 1966, *37,* 663–673.

————. Social introversion-extroversion as a heritable response. *Child Development,* 1969, *40,* 823–832.

Scarr-Salapatek, S. Book review: Unknowns in the IQ equation. *Science,* 1971a, *174,* 1223–1228.

———. Race, social class, and IQ. *Science,* 1971b, *174,* 1285–1295.

Schachter, J. Pain, fear, and anger in hypertensives and normotensives. *Psychosomatic Medicine,* 1957, *19,* 17–29.

Schachter, S. The psychology of affiliation. Stanford, Cal.: Stanford University Press, 1959.

———. Obesity and eating. *Science,* 1968, *161,* 751–756.

———. Some extraordinary facts about obese humans and rats. *American Psychologist,* 1971, *26,* 129–144.

———. *Emotion, obesity, and crime.* New York: Academic Press, 1971.

Schachter, S. and J. E. Singer. Cognitive, social, and physiological determinants of emotional state. *Psychological Review,* 1962, *69,* 379–399.

Schaffer, H. R., and P. E. Emerson. The development of social attachment in infancy. *Society for Research in Child Development Monographs,* 1964, *29,* (No. 3).

Schiff, W. The perception of an impending collision: A study of visually directed avoidant behavior. *Psychological Monographs,* 1965, *79,* (Whole No. 604).

Schiff, W., J. A. Caviness, and J. J. Gibson. Persistent fear responses in rhesus monkeys to the optical stimulus of "looming." *Science,* 1962, *136,* 982–983.

Schiffrin, R. M., and R. C. Atkinson. Storage and retrieval processes in long-term memory. *Psychological Review,* 1969, *76,* 179–193.

Schilder, P. The image and appearance of the human body. New York: International Universities Press, 1950, (Originally published 1935).

Schleidt, W. Über die Auslösung der Flucht vor Raubvogeln bei Truthahn. Naturwissenschaften, 1961, 48, 141–142. Cited in Marler, P., & Hamilton, W. J., III. *Mechanisms of animal behavior.* New York: Wiley, 1966.

Schneider, F. W. Conforming behavior of black and white children. *Journal of Personality and Social Psychology,* 1970, *20,* 155–159.

Schneider, G. E. Two visual systems. *Science,* 1969, *163,* (No. 3870), 895–902.

Schneiderman, L. The estimation of one's own bodily traits. *Journal of Social Psychology,* 1956, *44,* 89–99.

Schneirla, T. C. An evolutionary and developmental theory of biphasic processes underlying approach and withdrawal. In M. R. Jones (ed.) *Nebraska symposium on motivation.* Lincoln: University of Nebraska Press, 1959, 1–42.

Schneirla, T. C., J. S. Rosenblatt, and E. Tobach. Maternal behavior in the cat. In H. L. Rheingold (ed.) *Maternal behavior in mammals,* New York: Wiley, 1963, 122–168.

Schonbuch, S. S., and R. E. Schell. Judgments of body appearance by fat and skinny male college students. *Perceptual and Motor Skills,* 1967, *24,* 999–1002.

Schopler, J., and J. S. Compere. Effects of being kind or harsh to another on liking. *Journal of Personality and Social Psychology,* 1971, *20,* 155–159.

Schwartz, G. E. Voluntary control of human cardiovascular integration and differentiation through feedback and reward. *Science,* 1972, *175,* 90–93.

Scott, E. M. Self selection of diet: I. Selection of purified components. *Journal of Nutrition,* 1946, *31,* 397–406.

Scott, J. P. Aggression. Chicago: University of Chicago Press, 1958.

———. Critical periods in behavior development. *Science,* 1962, *138,* 949–958.

Sears, D. O., and R. P. Abeles. Attitudes and opinions. In P. H. Mussen and M. R. Rosenzeig (eds.) *Annual Review of Psychology,* 1969, *20,* Palo Alto, Calif.: Annual Reviews, 1969, 253–288.

Secord, P. F., and S. M. Jourard. The appraisal of body-cathexis: body-cathexis and the self. *Journal of Consulting Psychology,* 1953, *17,* 342–347.

Segall, M. H., D. I. Campbell, and M. J. Herskovits. The influence of culture on visual perception. Indianapolis: Bobbs-Merrill, 1966.

Seidman, D., S. B. Bensen, I. Miller, and T. Meeland. Influence of a partner on tolerance for self-administered shock. *Journal of Abnormal and Social Psychology,* 1957, *54,* 210–212.

Seligman, M. E. P. On the generality of the laws of learning. *Psychological Review,* 1970, *77,* 406–418.

Seligman, M. E. P., and S. F. Maier. Failure to escape traumatic shock. *Journal of Experimental Psychology,* 1967, *74,* 1–9.

Seligman, M. E. P., S. F. Maier, and J. H. Geer. Alleviation of learned helplessness in the dog. *Journal of Abnormal Psychology,* 1968, *73,* 256–262.

Shankweiler, D., and M. Studdert-Kennedy. Identification of consonants and vowels presented to left and right ears. *Quarterly Journal of Experimental Psychology,* 1967, *19,* 59–63.

Sherif, M. The psychology of social norms. New York: Harper & Row, 1936.

Sherif, M., and C. Sherif. Groups in harmony and tension. New York: Harper & Row, 1953.

Sherif, M., O. J. Harvey, B. J. White, W. R. Hood, and C. W. Sherif. Intergroup conflict and cooperation: The Robber's Cave experiment. Norman, Okla.: University Book Exchange, 1965.

Shontz, F. C. Perceptual and cognitive aspects of body experience. New York: Academic Press, 1969.

Sidman, M. Time out from avoidance as a reinforcer: A study of response interaction. *Journal of the Experimental Analysis of Behavior,* 1962, *5,* 423–434.

Siegel, P. V., S. J. Gerathewohl, and S. R. Mohler. Time-zone effects. *Science,* 1969, *164,* 1249–1255.

Sigall, H., and E. Aronson. Liking for an evaluator as a function of her physical attractiveness and nature of the evaluations. *Journal of Experimental Social Psychology,* 1969, *5,* 93–100.

Siguish, V., G. Schmidt, A. Reinfeld, and I. Wiedemann-Sutor. Psychosexual stimulation: Sex differences. *Journal of Sex Research,* 1970, *6,* 10–24.

Silverman, I. W. The incidence of guilt reactions in children. *Journal of Personality and Social Psychology,* 1967, *7,* 338–340.

Simon, C. W., and W. H. Emmons. Responses to material presented during various levels of sleep. *Journal of Experimental Psychology,* 1956, *51,* 89–97.

Simpson, G. G. The study of evolution: Methods and present status of theory. In A. Roe and G. G. Simpson (eds.) *Behavior and evolution.* New Haven, Conn: Yale University Press, 1958, 7–26.

Simpson, G. G., and W. S. Beck. Life. An introduction to biology. 2nd ed. New York: Harcourt, Brace & World, 1965.

Singh, D. Preference for bar pressing to obtain reward over free-loading in rats and children. *Journal of Comparative and Physiological Psychology,* 1970, *73,* 320–327.

———. The pied piper vs. the Protestant ethic. *Psychology Today,* 1972, *5,* 53–56.

———. Role of response habits and cognitive factors in determination of behavior in obese humans. *Journal of Personality and Social Psychology,* in press.

Siroka, E. K., and R. W. Siroka. The psychodramatic approach to sensitivity training. In R. W. Siroka, E. K. Siroka, and G. A. Schloss (eds.) *Sensitivity training and group encounter.* New York: Grosset and Dunlap, 1971, 109–118.

Sistrunk, F., and J. W. McDavid. Sex variable in conforming behavior. *Journal of Personality and Social Psychology,* 1971, *17,* 200–207.

Skinner, B. F. The behavior of organisms. New York: Appleton-Century-Crofts, 1938.

———. "Superstition" in the pigeon. *Journal of Experimental Psychology,* 1948, *38,* 168–172.

———. The science of learning and the art of teaching. *Harvard Educational Review,* 1954, *24,* 86–97.

Skolnick, P. Reactions to personal evaluations: A failure to replicate. *Journal of Personality and Social Psychology,* 1971, *18,* 62–67.

Sluckin, W. Imprinting and early learning. Chicago: Aldine, 1965.

Socarides, C. W. Homosexuality and medicine. *Journal of the American Medical Association,* 1970, *212,* 1199–1202.

Sokolov, E. N. Perception and the conditioned reflex. New York: Macmillan, 1963.

Solomon, R. L., L. J. Kamen, and L. C. Wynne. Traumatic avoidance learning: The outcomes of several extinction procedures with dogs. *Journal of Abnormal and Social Psychology,* 1953, *48,* 291–302.

Solomon, R. L., and L. C. Wynne. Traumatic avoidance learning: The principles of anxiety conservation and partial irreversibility. *Psychological Review,* 1954, *61,* 353–385.

Spear, N. E. Retention of reinforcer magnitude. *Psychological Bulletin,* 1967, *74,* 216–234.

Spearman, C. *The abilities of man.* London: MacMillan, 1927.

Sperling, G. The information available in brief visual presentation. *Psychological Monographs,* 1960, *74,* No. 11.

Sperling, H. G., and R. S. Harwerth. Red-green cone interactions and the increment-threshold spectral sensitivity of primates. *Science,* 1971, *172,* 180–184.

Sperry, R. W. Hemisphere deconnection and unity in conscious awareness. *American Psychologist,* 1968, *23,* 723–733.

Spitz, R., and K. M. Wolf. Anaclitic depression: An inquiry into the genesis of psychiatric conditions in early childhood. In A. Freud, et al (eds.) *The psychoanalytic study of the child.* Vol. 2. New York: International Universities press, 1946, 313–342.

Stampfl, T. G., and D. J. Levis. Essentials of implosive therapy: A learning-theory-based psychodynamic behavioral therapy. *Journal of Abnormal Psychology,* 1967, *72,* 496–503.

Stellar, E. Hunger in man: Comparative and physiological studies. *American Psychologist,* 1967, *22,* 105–117.

Stephan, W., E. Berscheid, and E. Walster. Sexual arousal and heterosexual perception. *Journal of Personality and Social Psychology,* 1971, *20,* 93–101.

Stephens, J. H., and C. Astrup. Prognosis in "process" and "non-process" schizophrenia. *American Journal of Psychiatry,* 1963, *119,* 945–953.

Stettner, L. J., and K. A. Matyniak. The brain of birds. *Scientific American,* 1968, *218,* 64–72.

Stevens, S. S., and J. R. Harris. The scaling of subjective roughness and smoothness. *Journal of Experimental Psychology,* 1962, *64,* 489–494.

Stevenson, H. W. Learning in children. In P. H. Mussen (ed.) *Carmichael's manual of child psychology,* Vol. 1., 3rd ed. New York: Wiley, 1970, 849–938.

Stratton, G. M. Vision without inversion of the retinal image. *Psychological Review,* 1897, *4,* 341–360, 463–481.

Stricker, L. J., S. Messick, and D. N. Jackson. Conformity, anticonformity, and independence: Their dimensionality and generality. *Journal of Personality and Social Psychology,* 1970, *16,* 494–507.

Stromeyer, C. F., III. Eidetikers. *Psychology Today,* 1970, *4,* No. 6, 76–80.

Stromeyer, C. F., III., and J. Psotka. The detailed texture of eidetic images. *Nature,* 1970, *225,* 346–349.

Strong, P. N., and M. Hedges. Comparative studies in simple oddity learning: cats, raccoons, monkeys, and chimpanzees. *Psychonomic Science,* 1966, *5,* 13–14.

Stunkard, A. J., and S. Fox. The relationship of gastric motility and hunger: A summary of the evidence. *Psychosomatic Medicine,* 1971, *33,* 123–134.

Sullivan, H. S. *Conceptions of modern psychiatry.* New York: Norton, 1953.

Suls, J. M., and R. W. Weisberg. Processing syntactically ambiguous sentences. *Journal of Experimental Psychology,* 1970, *86,* 112–114.

Suomi, S. J., F. H. Harlow, and C. J. Domek. Effect of repetitive infant-infant separation of young monkeys. *Journal of Abnormal Psychology,* 1970, *76,* 161–172.

Supa, M., M. Cotzin, and K. M. Dallenbach. "Facial vision" The perception of obstacles by the blind. *American Journal of Psychology,* 1944, *57,* 133–183.

Swets, J. A., and A. B. Kristofferson. Attention. *Annual Review of Psychology,* 1970, *21,* 339–366.

Tajfel, H. Experiments in intergroup discrimination. *Scientific American,* 1970, *223,* 96–102.

Tanner, W. P., Jr., and J. A. Swets. A decision-making theory of visual detection. *Psychological Review,* 1954, *61,* 401–409.

Taylor, S. E., and D. R. Mattee. When similarity breeds contempt. *Journal of Personality and Social Psychology,* 1971, *20,* 75–81.

Teitelbaum, P., and A. N. Epstein. The lateral hypothalamic syndrome: Recovery of feeding and drinking after lateral hypothalamic lesions. *Psychological Review,* 1962, *69,* 74–90.

Thomas, A., S. Chess, and H. G. Birch. *Temperament and behavior disorders in children.* New York: New York University Press, 1968.

_____. The origin of personality. *Scientific American,* 1970, *223,* No. 2, 102–109.

Thomas, H. Visual-fixation responses of infants to stimuli of varying complexity. *Child Development,* 1965, *36,* 629–638.

Thompson, W. R. Development and the biophysical bases of personality. In E. F. Borgatta and W. W. Lambert (eds.) *Handbook of personality theory and research,* Chicago: Rand McNally, 1968, 149–214.

Thorndike, E. L. Animal intelligence: An experimental study of the associative processes in animals. *Psychological Monographs,* 1898, *2,* No. 8.

Thornton, J. W., and P. D. Jacobs. Learned helplessness in human subjects. *Journal of Experimental Psychology,* 1971, *87,* 367–372.

Thorpe, W. H. *Learning and instinct in animals.* Cambridge, Mass. Harvard University Press, 1956.

_____. The comparison of vocal communication in animals and man. in R. A. Hinde (ed.) *Non-verbal communication.* London: Cambridge University Press, 1972, 27–47.

Thouless, R. H. Phenomenal regression to the real object. *British Journal of Psychology,* 1931, *21,* 338–359.

Thurstone, L. L. Primary mental abilities. *Psychometric Monographs,* 1938, No. 1.

Tinbergen, N. *The study of instinct.* London: Oxford University Press, 1951.

Tolman, E. C. Cognitive maps in rats and men. *Psychological Review,* 1948, *55,* 189–208.

Traub, A. C., and J. Orbach. Psychological studies of the body image: Vol. 1. The adjustable body distorting mirror. *Archives of General Psychiatry,* 1964, *11,* 53–66.

Treisman, A. M. Contextual cues in selective listening. *Quarterly Journal of Experimental Psychology,* 1960, *12,* 242–248.

————. Monitoring and storage of irrelevant messages in selective attention. *Journal of Verbal Learning and Verbal Behavior,* 1964, *3,* 449–459.

————. Strategies and models of selective attention. *Psychological Review,* 1969, *76,* 282–**299.**

Treisman, A. M., and G. Geffen. Selective attention: Perception or response? *Quarterly Journal of Experimental Psychology,* 1967, *19,* 1–17.

Triandis, H. A note of Rokeach's theory of prejudice. *Journal of Abnormal and Social Psychology,* 1961, *62,* 184–186.

Tulving, E. and S. A. Madigan. Memory and verbal learning. In P. H. Mussen and M. R. Rosenzeig (eds.) *Annual Review of Psychology.* Vol. 21. Palo Alto, Cal.: Annual Reviews, 1970, 437–484.

Turiel, E. An experimental test of the sequentiality of developmental stages in the child's moral judgments. *Journal of Personality and Social Psychology,* 1966, *3,* 611–618.

Turner, E. R. A. Social feeding in birds. *Behavior,* 1964, *24,* 1–46.

Valenstein, E. S. Problems of measurement and interpretation with reinforcing brain stimulation. *Psychological Review,* 1964, *71,* 415–438.

————. The anatomical locus of reinforcement. In E. Stellar and J. M. Sprague (eds.) *Process in physiological psychology.* Vol. 1. New York: Academic Press, 1966, Pp. 149–190.

Valins, S. Cognitive effects of false heart-rate feedback. *Journal of Personality and Social Psychology,* 1966, *4,* 400–408.

————. Emotionality and information concerning internal reactions. *Journal of Personality and Social Psychology,* 1967, 456–463.

van Hooff, J. A. R. A. M. A comparative approach to the phylogeny of laughter and smiling. In R. A. Hinde (ed.) *Non-verbal communication.* London: Cambridge University Press, 1972, 209–238.

Vernon, P. E. The structure of human abilities. New York: Wiley, 1950.

von Békésy, G. *Experiments in hearing.* New York: McGraw-Hill, 1960.

von Holst, E. Relations between the central nervous system and the peripheral organs. *British Journal of Animal Behavior,* 1954, *2,* 89–94.

Wall, P. D., and W. H. Sweet. Temporary abolition of pain in man. *Science,* 1967, *155,* 108–109.

Wallace, J., and E. Sadalla. Behavioral consequences of transgressions: The effects of social recognition. *Journal of Experimental Research in Personality,* 1966, *1,* 187–194.

Wallach, H. The role of head movements and vestibular and visual cues in sound localization. *Journal of Experimental Psychology,* 1940, *27,* 339–368.

Walk, R. D., and E. J. Gibson. A comparative and analytical study of visual depth perception. *Psychological Monographs,* 1961, *75,* Whole No. 519.

Walk, R. D., E. J. Gibson, and T. J. Tighe. Behavior of light- and dark-reared rats on a visual cliff. *Science,* 1957, *126,* 80–81.

Walster, E. The effect on self-esteem on romatic liking. *Journal of Experimental Social Psychology,* 1965, *1,* 184–197.

Walters, R. H., and R. D. Parke. The influence of punishment and related disciplinary techniques on the social behavior of children: Theory and empirical findings. In B. A. Maher (ed.) *Progress in Experimental Personality Research.* Vol. 4. New York: Academic Press, 1967, 179–228.

Wapner, S., and H. Werner. (eds.) The body percept. New York: Random House, 1965.

Warren, J. M. Primate learning in comparative perspective. In A. M. Schrier, H. F. Harlow and F. Stollnitz (eds.) *Behavior in nonhuman primates.* Vol. 1. New York: Academic Press, 1965, 249–291.

Warrington, E., and L. Weiskrantz. Amnesic syndrome: Consolidation or retrieval? *Nature,* 1970, *228,* 628–630.

Watson, J. B. Psychology as the behaviorist views it. *Psychological Review,* 1913, *20,* 158–177.

Watson, J. B., and R. Rayner. Conditioned emotional reactions. *Journal of Experimental Psychology,* 1920, *3,* 1–4.

Webb, W. B. Sleep. An experimental approach. New York: Macmillan, 1968.

Wechsler, D. The measurement of adult intelligence. Baltimore: Williams & Wilkins, 1939.

Weinstein, B. The evolution of intelligent behavior in rhesus monkeys. *Genetic Psychology Monographs,* 1945, *31,* 3–48.

Welch, R. B. Prism adaptation: The "target-pointing effect" as a function of exposure trials. *Perception and Psychophysics,* 1971, *9,* 192–104.

Welker, W. L. Effects of age and experience on play and exploration on young chimpanzees. *Journal of Comparative and Physiological Psychology,* 1956, *49,* 223–226.

Wenger, M. A., J. R. Averill, and D. D. Smith. Autonomic activity during sexual arousal. *Psychophysiology,* 1968, *4,* 468–478.

Wenger, M. A., T. L. Clemens, M. L. Darsie, B. T. Engel, F. M. Esters, and R. R. Sonnenschein. Autonomic response patterns during intravenous infusion of epinephrine and nor-epinephrine. *Psychosomatic Medicine,* 1960, *22,* 294–307.

Werboff, J., D. Duane, and B. D. Cohen. Extinction of conditioned avoidance and heart rate responses in rats. *Journal of Psychosomatic Research,* 1964, *8,* 29–33.

Werner, H. Comparative psychology of mental development. Chicago: Follett, 1948.

Wever, E. G. Theory of hearing. New York: Wiley, 1949.

Wever, E. G., and C. W. Bray. Present possibilities for auditory theory. *Psychological Review,* 1930, *37,* 3, 101–114.

White, R. W. Motivation reconsidered: The concept of competence. *Psychological Review,* 1959, *66,* 297–333.

White, S. H. Evidence for a hierarchial arrangement of learning processes. In L. P. Lipsitt and C. C. Spiker (eds.). *Advances in child behavior and development.* Vol. 2. New York: Academic Press, 1965.

Wickens, D. D. Encoding categories of words: An empirical approach to meaning. *Psychological Review,* 1970, *77,* 1–15.

Wicker, A. W. Attitudes versus actions: The relationship of verbal and overt behavioral responses to attitude objects. *Journal of Social Issues,* 1969, *25,* 41–78.

Wiegal, D. B., and A. S. Rodwan. A test of the preparatory response theory by measurement of increased stimulus attractiveness following a signal. *Journal of Experimental Psychology,* 1970, *86,* 225–229.

Winslow, C. E. A., L. P. Herrington, and A. P. Gagge. Relations between atmospheric conditions, physiologic reaction, and sensations of pleasantness. *American Journal of Hygiene,* 1937, *26,* 103–115.

Williams, H. L., H. C. Morlock, Jr., and J. V. Morlock. Instrumental behavior during sleep. *Psychophysiology,* 1966, *2,* 208–216.

Williams, R. L., and A. G. Krasnoff. Body image and physiological patterns in patients with peptic ulcer and rheumatoid arthritis. *Psychosomatic Medicine,* 1964, *26,* 701–709.

Willis, R. H. Two dimensions of conformity-nonconformity. *Sociometry,* 1963, *26,* 499–513.

———. Conformity, independence, and anticonformity. *Human Relations,* 1965, *18,* 373–388.

Willis, R. H., and E. P. Hollander. An experimental study of three response modes in racial influence situations. *Journal of Abnormal and Social Psychology,* 1964, *69,* 150–156.

Wilson, E. O. Chemical communication among workers of the fire ant, *Solenopsia Saeirssima* (Fr. Smith). *Animal Behavior,* 1962, *10,* 134–164.

———. Pheromones. *Scientific American,* 1963, *208,* No. 5, 100–114.

———. Chemical communication among social insects. *Science,* 1965, *149,* 1064–1071.

Wodinsky, J. and M. B. Bitterman. Solution of oddity problems by the rat. *American Journal of Psychology,* 1953, *66,* 137–140.

Wohlwill, J. F. From perception to inference: A dimension of cognitive development. In W. Kessen and C. Kuhlman (eds.) *Thought in the young child. Monographs of the Society for Research in Child Development,* 1962, *27,* No. 2.

Wolf, S. and H. G. Wolff. Human gastric functions. 2nd ed. New York: Oxford University Press, 1947.

Wolfe, J. B. The effect of delayed reward upon learning in the white rat. *Journal of Comparative Psychology,* 1934, *17,* 1–21.

_____. Effectiveness of token-rewards for chimpanzees. *Comparative Psychology Monographs,* 1936, *12,* Whole No. 60.

Wolff, J. L. Concept shift and discrimination-reversal learning in humans. *Psychological Bulletin,* 1967, *67,* 369–408.

Wolpe, J. Reciprocal inhibition as the main basis of psychotherapeutic effects. *Archives of Neurology and Psychiatry,* 1954, *72,* 205–226.

_____. *Psychotherapy by reciprocal inhibition.* Stanford, Cal.: Stanford University Press, 1958.

_____. Behavior therapy in complex neurotic states. *British Journal of Psychiatry,* 1964, *110,* 28–34.

Wood, C. C., W. R. Goff, and R. S. Day. Auditory evoked potentials during speech perception. *Science,* 1971, *173,* 1248–1251.

Woodworth, R. S., and H. Schlosberg. Experimental psychology. New York: Holt, Rinehart & Winston, 1954.

Worchel, S., and J. W. Brehm. Direct and implied social restoration of freedom, *Journal of Personality and Social Psychology,* 1971, *18,* 294–304.

Wrightsman, L. S., Jr. Effect of waiting on others on changes in level of felt anxiety. *Journal of Abnormal and Social Psychology,* 1960, *61,* 216–222.

Wynne, L. C., and R. L. Solomon. Traumatic avoidance learning: acquisition and extinction in dogs deprived of normal peripheral autonomic functioning. *Genetic Psychology Monographs,* 1955, *52,* 241–284.

Wyrwicka, W., and C. Dabrzecka. Relationship between feeding and satiation centers of the hypothalamus. *Science,* 1960, *123,* 805–806.

Yarrow, L. Separation from parents during early childhood. In M. L. Hoffman and L. W. Hoffman (eds.) *Review of child development research.* Vol. 1. New York: Russell Sage Foundation, 1964, 89–136.

Yates, A. J. The application of learning theory to the treatment of tics. *Journal of Abnormal and Social Psychology,* 1958, *56,* 175–182.

Yates, F. A. The art of memory. Chicago: University of Chicago Press, 1966.

Yerkes, R. M., and J. H. Elder. Oestrus, receptivity and mating in the chimpanzee. *Comparative Psychology Monographs,* 1936, *13,* 1–39.

Zeaman, D. Response latency as a function of the amount of reinforcement. *Journal of Experimental Psychology,* 1949, *39,* 446–483.

Zeaman, D. and B. J. House. The role of attention in retardate discrimination learning. In N. R. Ellis (ed.) *Handbook of mental deficiency.* New York: McGraw-Hill, 1963, 159–223.

Zimbardo, P. G. The effect of effort and improvisation on self-persuasion produced by role-playing. *Journal of Experimental Social Psychology,* 1965, *1,* 103–120.

Zimbardo, P. G., and E. B. Ebbessen. Influencing attitudes and changing behavior. Reading, Mass.: Addison-Wesley, 1969.

Zimbardo, P. G., and R. Formica. Emotional comparisons and self-esteem as determinants of affiliation. *Journal of Personality,* 1963, *31,* 141–162.

Zotterman, Y. Studies in the neural mechanism of taste. In W. A. Rosenblith (ed.), *Sensory Communication.* New York: Wiley, 1961, 205–216.

Zuckerman, M. Physiological measures of sexual arousal in the human. *Psychological Bulletin,* 1971a, 75, 297–329.

_____. Dimensions of sensation seeking. *Journal of Consulting Psychology,* 1971b, *36,* 45–52.

author index

subject index